HARVARD ECONOMIC STUDIES

Volume 155

The studies in this series are published under
the direction of the Department of Economics
of Harvard University. The department does not
assume responsibility for the views expressed.

Growth, Distribution, and Prices

Stephen A. Marglin

HARVARD UNIVERSITY PRESS

Cambridge, Massachusetts, and London, England   1984

Library of Congress Cataloging in Publication Data

Marglin, Stephen A.
    Growth, distribution, and prices.

    (Harvard economic studies; v. 155)
    Bibliography: p.
    Includes index.
    1. Capitalism.   2. Economic development.   3. Distribution
(Economic theory).   4. Prices.   5. Neoclassical
school of economics.   6. Marxian economics.   7. Keynesian
economics.   I. Title.   II. Series.
HB501.M317 1984   330.12′2   83-18569
ISBN 0-674-36415-5 (alk. paper)

For Marc, David, and Elizabeth

Acknowledgments

I have incurred many debts along the way to writing these words, which although appearing first in the text are the last act of a long drama. Masahiko Aoki and Tsuneo Ishikawa collaborated in early teaching ventures from which this book grew. I am especially indebted to them, as well as to successive generations of students at Harvard University over the past decade and a group of students at Concordia University during 1976–77. Among the Harvard students, J. Mohan Rao and Klaus Nehring made particularly important observations.

In addition to forming the basis for a course in economic theory, central ideas of this book were presented in seminars and lectures from which I received crucial feedback. Even though many years have passed, the strategic comments and questions interjected by Kenneth Arrow, Galen Burkhardt, Tjalling Koopmans, and Assar Lindbeck remain fresh in my mind. Robert Dorfman, Herb Gintis, David Gordon, Zvi Griliches, Frank Hahn, Edwin Kuh, William Lazonick, Michael Mandel, Andreu Mas-Colell, Alfredo Medio, Luigi Pasinetti, Hashim Pesaran, Joan Robinson, Bertram Scheffold, Robert Solow, Lance Taylor, and two anonymous referees read parts of the book in draft. The final product has benefited from their observations.

My biggest debt was incurred in connection with the econometrics of Chapter 18. Mark Watson provided instruction and initiation into the mysteries of statistics and econometrics, and Daniel O'Reilly gave invaluable help in putting the theory into practice. I could not have carried out the tests described in the appendix to Chapter 18 without their help, which went well beyond the norms of collegiality and professional courtesy. I should add that Chapter 18 utilized data that Charles Steindel kindly made available from his thesis.

I have been extremely fortunate in the assistance I have received in preparing the book for publication. Andrew Newman was exemplary in correcting both galleys and page proofs, as well as in preparing the index. He was ably assisted in both these endeavors by Rebecca Ramsay. In addition, Mr. Newman read through the entire book in search of technical and mathematical mishaps and confusions. His painstaking effort saved me from certain embarrassment and you from certain aggravation. Many people contributed over the years to translating various versions of the manuscript into typescript. If I single out Beverly Petersen, it is not because I am unappreciative of the contributions of many others. William Minty did the figures, and in many cases redid them to correct errors in my original specifications or to accommodate changes in the text. The clarity of his drawings has added immeasurably to the exposition. Thomas Brush assisted in the early stages of the regression analysis described in Chapter 18.

Various delays in delivering copy and last-minute changes in the text complicated the lives of my editors. I regret that Michael Aronson, Maria Ascher, and Mary Ellen Geer had to pay for my propensity to gild what may or may not be a lily.

The National Science Foundation supported my research in 1979, 1980, and 1981 and again in 1983. The Harvard Institute for Economic Research provided support for secretarial and computational assistance in 1981, 1982, and 1983. I am grateful to both organizations.

Frederique Apffel Marglin provided *inter alia* an anthropological perspective that has helped me understand the limits of economic analysis. Having twice celebrated the completion of this book prematurely, she was the second most happy person in the world when it was finally done.

Contents

From the terms of the endowment of the Hollis Professorship of Mathematicks and Natural Philosophy at Harvard College, 1726:

"That his Province be to instruct the students in a Sistem of Natural Philosophy . . . in which [is] to be comprehended . . . the motions of the Heavenly Bodys according to the different Hypotheses of Ptolemy, Tycho Brahe, and Copernicus."

1 Introduction

There is a fundamental paradox in the Western world that escapes our attention only because of the inconvenience and discomfort of observing it. A visitor from Mars, however, could hardly fail to notice the disjunction between the high degree of egalitarianism that characterizes both our religious and political beliefs and the inequality that reigns in the economic sphere. All may be equal before God (Romans 2:11) and the United States Constitution, but those who do the dirtiest, least pleasant, and most exhausting work in general receive the lowest incomes, while those at the opposite end of the income distribution do the most pleasant work — work involving mental rather than physical exertion, often as not the work of organizing and directing other people's work. Indeed, at the upper limit one need not work at all: in the United States the top one percent of wealth holders receive corporate dividends, not to mention other forms of property income, that are adequate to support a standard of living far in excess of that enjoyed by most of the population.

Economists, along with theologians, have struggled with the paradoxical relation between exertion and reward, although much of the effort of both groups is more accurately described as an attempt to explain the paradox away than as an attempt to understand it. This book has elements of both explanation and apology, although it is probably fair to say that readers will differ as to which is which: it presents neoclassical, neo-Marxian, and neo-Keynesian approaches to the problem of how distribution is determined under capitalism.

A second focus of this book, indeed a focus of economics since the days of Adam Smith, is the causes of growth. How have capitalist countries as different as Japan, Italy, Germany, and France managed to

1

grow rapidly over the post – World War II period, while Great Britain and the United States have not?

Finally, this book analyzes alternative views of the determination of relative prices. Elementary texts conventionally devote considerable space to the "paradox of value," the question of why the price of a necessity like water is low relative to the price of a luxury like diamonds. There is considerable agreement in the textbooks as to the answer, but this agreement is more the product of the dominance of a particular theory than a reflection of unanimity across theories. In fact, different theoretical approaches attach very different roles to the consumer, the sovereign of the neoclassical realm; the business investor, who dominates the neo-Keynesian world; and the balance of class power, on which neo-Marxian theory turns.

These, then, are the concerns of this book: What determines the distribution of the economic pie between property income and wage income? How is distribution related to economic growth? What relationship does the structure of commodity prices have to growth and distribution? To what extent does consumer demand influence growth, distribution, and prices? Behind these questions lies a problem that has engaged economists as well as moral philosophers for centuries: Why does property income exist as an economic category, and is it ethically justified? The ethical issue, I should make clear at once, will not be directly addressed. The intent of this book is to examine growth, distribution, and prices from a descriptive rather than a normative viewpoint: it will be left to the reader to draw such moral inferences as the analysis suggests.

I should probably deal with a terminological point before getting any further into the discussion. Property income is conventionally separated into rent, interest, and profit. But throughout this book I abstract from land as an input to production and hence abstract from rent. So we are left with interest and profit. In the business world profit is customarily identified with the return to equity capital and interest with the return to debt capital, but business usage is far from the meaning these terms have in economic theory. Neoclassical discourse, at least in the United States, identifies interest with a competitive return to capital and treats the return to the capitalist as organizer of production, innovator, and risk bearer as a wage, explicit or implicit. Profit is regarded as the consequence of market imperfections, a somewhat odd terminological twist in view of the importance from Adam Smith to Alfred Marshall of the idea of "natural" or "normal" profit as the competitive reward of capitalists that includes a return to the active participation of the capitalist as well as interest on capital. In neoclassical terms, a competitive equilibrium under constant returns to scale is characterized by a positive interest rate and zero profits. Neo-Marxian and neo-Keynesian usage, paradoxically, is truer to the spirit of Smith and Marshall: profit is identified with capitalists' income; interest is simply one component of profit. Under competitive conditions, the neo-Marxian and neo-Keynesian rate of profit includes both the competitive interest rate and the capitalist's "wage"; the neoclassical notion of zero profits corresponds to zero supernormal profits in neo-Marxian and neo-Keynesian terminology.

This book uses nonneoclassical language: distribution is characterized as a problem of determining profits and wages. Since product markets are generally treated as competitive, the neoclassically inclined may be tempted to substitute the word "interest" whenever they see "profit," and for the most part this is a harmless substitution. But some care must be exercised in working through both the neo-Marxian model, where the organization of production is the outcome of class struggle rather than of a competitive market process, and the neo-Keynesian model, where the difference between profit as a return to capitalists and interest as a cost of capital plays an important role. The problem becomes more serious in models in which workers are assumed to own a significant portion of the capital stock.

Basic Differences between the Three Approaches

The basic differences between the three theories lie in the way they approach capital accumulation and the labor market. In the neoclassical model desired accumulation of capital is determined by the lifetime utility maximization of households, whose number grows at an exogenously given rate. Employment is determined by the interplay of demand — determined by accumulation and technology — and supply — determined in the first instance by population and secondarily by households' tastes with respect to leisure and goods: the real wage adjusts demand and supply to each other and guarantees full employment, or at least a job for every willing worker. In equilibrium, profit and wage rates must make the growth rate of capital desired by households equal to the exogenously given rate of population growth. Thus, in the neoclassical view, an exogenously given rate of growth combines with household psychology and production technology to determine the distribution of income. Distribution in the neoclassical theory is a special application of price theory: equilibrium wage and profit rates are those that clear labor and capital markets. This basic neoclassical idea extends easily to a model in which there are many commodities; the additional complexity is that now there is an entire price structure, not just profit and wage rates, that must adjust to growth, tastes, and technology. In the multicommodity version of the neoclassical model, distribution cannot be separated from the problem of determining the whole array of equilibrium prices.

The neo-Marxian model starts at a fundamentally different place, with classes — capitalists and workers — rather than with households. Class division is central both to the determination of the real wage and to the determination of accumulation. Class power, along with technology and custom, determines the real wage rate, and hence — given the institutional structure that Marxians call the "social relations of production" — the profit rate. Class also affects saving: capitalists have a higher saving propensity than do workers. Together, the profit rate and capitalists' saving propensity normally determine the rate of growth. In the multiple-good version of the model, there is, as in the neoclassical model, an entire price structure to be reckoned with, but, unlike the neoclassical model, consumption preferences do not shape the price structure. In the neo-Marxian model, consumption preferences determine only the composition of output.

Thus, in the neo-Marxian view, causality runs from distribution to growth and is sharply counterintuitive to the neoclassically trained mind, accustomed to an exogenous, "natural" rate of growth to which the distribution of income responds. A key assumption that allows the rate of growth to be determined within the model is that the labor supply is endogenous: the "reserve army" adjusts the supply of labor to demand.

The neo-Keynesian model introduces a feature lacking in both neoclassical and neo-Marxian models: investment demand. Investment demand, assumed to be a positive function of the profitability of investment, combines with capitalists' saving propensity to determine equilibrium rates of profit and growth. The rate of profit, along with technology, determines the real wage. With multiple goods, the profit rate also determines relative prices, but, like the neo-Marxian model and unlike the neoclassical model, consumer preferences shape the composition of output, not the rate of profit and the structure of prices. In the neo-Keynesian model, the rate of growth and the distribution of income are simultaneously determined: what affects one must affect the other.

At least up to a point. In fact, the neo-Keynesian theory of the labor market is an uneasy amalgam of neo-Marxian and neoclassical theories, implicitly sharing the neo-Marxian conception of a reserve army but, borrowing a leaf from the neoclassical book, implicitly imposing a ceiling on the reserve army. The consequence is that the natural rate of growth does not determine the rate of growth, but rather places an upper limit on feasible growth rates. It is fair to observe that neo-Keynesian theory has in this respect never transcended its origins in the Great Depression, when growth, not to mention growth in excess of natural increase, was hardly an issue.

Roots

The origins of this book lie in a series of attempts to persuade graduate students in microeconomics to see neoclassical theory as *one*, rather than the *only*, approach to the determination of growth, distribution, and prices. My first attempt consisted of an announcement to this effect at the end of a semester that had intensively initiated students into the mysteries of neoclassical general-equilibrium theory, welfare economics, and the like, a semester preceded by an equally intense study of the neoclassical theory of consumption, production, and partial equilibrium. Needless to say, students did not happily receive the message that utility maximization, marginal productivity, marginal rates of substitution and transformation, competitive equilibrium, and Pareto optimality, as well as the associated agonies of Jacobians, Lagrangians, and bordered Hessians, provided only one of many ways of looking at the economic world. Indeed, it is more accurate to say that they did not receive the message at all. Though over a decade has passed, the incomprehension etched on their faces remains a vivid memory.

Recognizing the wisdom of the old adage that you can't fight something with nothing, I resolved that in the future I would present my students with at least the sketch of an alternative to neoclassical orthodoxy. This book is the end result of that resolution.

It soon became apparent that there were two distinct lines along which alternative models could be developed, one deriving from Karl Marx and the classical economists, another from John Maynard Keynes and Michal Kalecki. It turned out that these theories are as different from one another as they are from the mainstream neoclassical theory, and the exploration of these differences is a basic theme of this book.

A first summary of these alternatives (Marglin and Aoki 1973) appeared as a short paper in a Japanese volume on radical economics edited by Masahiko Aoki, a collaborator in one of these early teaching ventures. A second attempt (Marglin 1976a) took the form of a working paper in the Harvard Institute of Economic Research series. The HIER paper has served as the basis for the present book.

A more critical purpose is perhaps implicit in any effort to acquaint students with the possibility of seeing the world through nonneoclassical lenses. I would not be so concerned with providing alternatives were it not that I find the neoclassical approach so limiting and, ultimately, unpromising. Let me be quite clear on this point. I do not claim either that neoclassical theory is lacking in logical completeness or consistency or that nonneoclassical theories are at this point in time demonstrably better at the level of prediction.

On the contrary. This book goes to great lengths to establish that all three theories are roughly equivalent with respect to issues of completeness and consistency. Indeed a principal purpose is to shift the grounds of the debate from the domain of logic to the domain of empirical relevance.

With respect to prediction, we economists — all of us — are roughly in the position of astronomers in the days of Nicholaus Copernicus, *before* Tycho Brahe and Johannes Kepler, not to mention Isaac Newton: neither the geocentric nor the heliocentric model was very effective from a predictive point of view; both required the addition of epicyles to predict the future course of the planets.

Nevertheless, there is more to empirical relevance than prediction. At the end of this book I will present a model that combines elements of both the neo-Marxian and the neo-Keynesian theories; its attractiveness, I will suggest, lies in its capacity for making sense of the reality we experience. In this respect it offers a sharp contrast to the neoclassical model, which is ultimately inadequate because its constructs are so out of touch with that reality. My synthesis of Marx and Keynes may be no better at this point as a basis of prediction. Nor would I argue superiority from a logical point of view. But the proposed model at least has the sun at its center, so to speak, not the earth.

Up to now, the account of this book's origins has stressed the demand side. On the supply side, this book, like so much of contemporary critical theory, owes a great debt to Piero Sraffa's attack on neoclassical orthodoxy (1960). After twenty years, the precise thrust of Sraffa's criticism remains obscure. Some (for example, Joan Robinson 1961) have interpreted Sraffa's project as the construction of a price and distribution theory in which demand plays no role. Others (Maurice Dobb 1970) have taken the main point to be an attack on the aggregation of capital, a subject to which Chapter 12 of this book adverts. Still others (Sen 1978; Velupillai 1980, 1982) contend that the intention was to purify economics of the reliance on counterfactuals implicit in the use of marginal analysis, an interpretation for which Sraffa's preface (pp. v–vii) provides support.

The lesson I myself drew from Sraffa was less subtle, perhaps because

I had been schooled in a relatively simple-minded version of neoclassical theory in which the distribution of income is determined by factor marginal productivities at full employment. With this background, I took Sraffa's point as being the incompleteness of a theory based on production relationships alone, and more specifically, the inadequacy of a theory that relies on continuously varying margins to determine factor returns. In effect, I understood — or misunderstood — Sraffa's challenge to the orthodox to be this: "If you have a general theory of distribution, it should hold in the special case of fixed proportions; but with fixed proportions, marginalism is irrelevant. So what is your theory?"

This challenge, whether or not it was Sraffa's, I have come to believe to be misdirected. Neoclassical theory is not fundamentally marginalist. Chapter 2 presents a complete and consistent neoclassical model in the context of fixed production coefficients. Chapter 11 extends that model to the multiple-good case. There are difficulties with the existence and stability of equilibrium in this model, but these difficulties do not disappear merely by virtue of the introduction of continuous substitution. As Chapter 9 demonstrates, the elasticity of substitution plays a key role. Moreover, whatever the elasticity of substitution, marginal productivity equations do not in themselves determine the distribution of income even in the short run: a theory of employment is required whatever might be assumed about production coefficients. And in the long run, even that is not enough: a theory of saving is necessary too. In short, marginal-productivity relationships do not constitute a theory of distribution; these relationships are neither necessary (in the fixed-proportions case) nor sufficient (in the variable-proportions case).

But if a challenge to neoclassical theory based on its association with marginalism is, as I now believe, off target, it nevertheless serves an important clarificatory purpose. Drawing attention to the limits of technological relationships as a theory of distribution leads naturally to asking what the neoclassical theory of distribution is, and how its technological and nontechnological components relate to one another. One is led, as it were by an Invisible Hand, to consider alternative theories.

Sraffa himself was quite reticent, not to say Delphic, about his own views on the determinants of equilibrium in a capitalist economy. The closest he came to a definite opinion was the suggestion that the rate of profit might be "determined from outside the system of production, in particular by the level of the money rates of interest" (1960, p. 33). Sraffa was careful to subtitle his book *Prelude to a Critique of Economic*

Theory. But now, two decades later, it is certainly high time to move beyond the prelude.

A Few Words on Methodology

This book, then, is an attempt to carry out a program inspired to a great extent by *Production of Commodities*. I lay out neoclassical, neo-Marxian, and neo-Keynesian theories of capitalism as alternative ways of closing a basically indeterminate production model that forms the common core of all the theories. Let me add that, since my concern is with the central features of the three approaches, I shall not hesitate to simplify drastically in the interest of emphasizing and clarifying the essential differences between them. "Essence," of course, has a subjective component, and will do so until there is agreement on what is fundamental to each approach. But the models analyzed in this book are hardly idiosyncratic. If they were, I should not have made the effort to attach labels customarily identified with particular schools of thought. Nevertheless, I fully anticipate that readers of various persuasions will amicably join hands on one point: each will allow that I have got the *other* theories down all right, but that, having failed totally to comprehend his own brand of truth, I have presented a caricature in its place!

The production models analyzed in this book become progressively more complicated as we go along, for the expositional strategy is to introduce complexity only incrementally, as the capacity of simpler models for further insights is exhausted. Nevertheless, even at its most complex, the production side of the model remains highly simplified. Such features of the real world as natural resources, joint production, fixed capital, technological change, and nonconvexities are eschewed, in the belief that the important differences in the three approaches with respect to the questions at issue — the determination of growth, distribution, and prices in a capitalist economy — can be set out in models from which these complexities are absent.

Moreover, government is conspicuously absent, as are foreign trade and investment. I do not pretend that capitalism can be understood in abstraction from government and international economic relations, but rather that these features of the real world are appropriately omitted from models whose purpose is to clarify the differences between alternative approaches to the study of capitalism.

For a similar reason, product markets are — except in Chapter 14 — assumed to be perfectly competitive. Were the purpose to describe contemporary capitalism faithfully, I should doubtless introduce a large dose of oligopoly at the outset. But for the purpose of distinguishing neoclassical, neo-Marxian, and neo-Keynesian theories, the much simpler competitive model suffices. In the first place, the differences between the theories emerge clearly in the context of competitive product markets, and, in the second, the degree of competitiveness is not in my judgment an issue that divides the theories.

Thus the principle of model building at work in this book is one of minimalism. The models are the minimally complex ones in which pertinent differences between the theories can be examined. Given my purpose and perspective, it will not be difficult to understand why there is no echo here of rationing, which recent research, notably by Robert Barro and Herschel Grossman (1976) and Edmond Malinvaud (1977, 1980), has placed at the heart of differences between Keynesian and neoclassical (classical, in their terminology) theories. On the one hand, as rationing theorists themselves recognize (Barro and Grossman 1976, p. 89n; Malinvaud 1977, p. 32n), rationing in the goods market is neither faithful to Keynes nor necessary to the distinction between Keynes and the neoclassicals. On the other hand, if realism is the goal, rationing seems to me a cumbersome and misleading way of characterizing goods markets under contemporary, largely oligopolistic, conditions; under oligopoly it is not even clear what meaning should be attached to the notion of a supply curve.

I am more sympathetic to the notion of rationing in the labor market, but even here it seems to me to add little to our understanding. It seems to me clearer, simpler, and more to the point to do away with the idea of a labor-supply curve altogether for the short run and, over the longer run of a generation, to accept (on the basis of a reserve army) the endogeneity of the labor supply, or, what amounts to the same thing in more familiar language, to assume an infinitely elastic labor supply at the "subsistence" wage.

One final methodological point. It has been, and will doubtless again be, objected that I give away too much to neoclassical economics in the very framework of analysis. Many will find the ahistorical emphasis on steady growth particularly offensive, especially in analyzing capitalism from a neo-Marxian or neo-Keynesian point of view.

The focus on steady growth may require explanation, but it does not, I think, require apology. The long-run equilibrium of steady growth may be regarded by neoclassicals as a state that will, in the absence of exogenous shocks, endure forever; I regard it as simply a device for abstracting from the business cycle.

Other assumptions are more frankly concessions to the neoclassical majority. These concessions will doubtless appear dubious on that ground alone to those who believe that economic theory is a form of warfare best fought on one's own terrain. There are of course some issues on which it would be self-defeating to attempt theoretical comparisons within a neoclassical or any other common framework: Different theories ask different questions, and theories cannot be compared at all if one or the other of them fails to speak to a given issue. In this set are such issues as the secular evolution of an economy's institutional structure, for instance, the transformation of the medieval economy based on serfdom into the modern economy based on capitalism. Equally in this set is the relationship between economic structure, on the one hand, and political, social, and cultural structures, on the other. Marx, for better or worse, offers a theory. Indeed Marx's overarching purpose lay in explaining such relationships as these. Keynesian and neoclassical economics, by contrast, are largely silent here. Someone far more bold or more reckless than I might attempt to articulate a Keynesian or neoclassical counterpart to the materialist conception of history, but the sole (neoclassical) attempt with which I am familiar hardly gives ground for encouragement. On these issues there seems little point in forcing Marxian concepts into neoclassical categories. Effectively, there are no neoclassical categories.

By the same token, it makes little sense to search for a specifically Marxian or Keynesian analysis of, say, the effect of a frost at apple-blossom time on the supply of apples or the demand for pears or the equilibrium prices of the two fruits the following autumn. On this and a variety of similar questions, nonneoclassical theory has nothing to say, at least nothing different from the neoclassical view.

But there is a second set of issues on which alternative theories overlap, with each offering a different explanation for the same phenomenon. The subject matter of the present book — the determination of growth, distribution, and prices under capitalism — falls into this second set. On these issues the choice of theoretical terrain must depend on one's purposes. Let me therefore be clear as to mine. I regard myself neither as preaching to the converted nor as waging polemical warfare. Rather I see this book as speaking to readers whose minds are not yet made up. But in the nature of things, most English-speaking students of economics, at least those who have gotten this far, will approach the subject from an essentially neoclassical perspective. In theoretical exegesis, as in politics, it behooves one who would persuade to start where one's audience is, not where one might be oneself.

Plan of the Book

The first task of this book is to outline the structure of the three approaches in the simplest possible terms. To this end, Chapter 2 examines the steady-growth properties of a neoclassical model of a one-good economy in which production takes place on the basis of a fixed-coefficient, constant-returns-to-scale technology.[1] Chapters 3 and 4 do the same thing for the neo-Marxian and neo-Keynesian models, and Chapter 5 draws out differences between the neo-Marxian and neo-Keynesian notions of equilibrium that turn on conceptual differences with respect to the labor market.

The central result of these chapters has already been summarized: given the technology, neoclassical equilibrium is determined by (1) an exogenously given labor force and (2) utility maximization by households with respect to lifetime consumption; neo-Marxian equilibrium by (1) a "subsistence" wage and (2) the saving propensity of capitalists; and neo-Keynesian equilibrium by (1) capitalists' investment demand and (2) their saving propensities. In the neoclassical model growth determines distribution, whereas in the neo-Marxian model it is the other way around. In the neo-Keynesian model, growth and distribution are simultaneously determined; both are endogenous variables.

The next two chapters, 6 and 7, deal with shortcomings of the classical saving function that assumes all profits are saved and all wages consumed. Chapter 6 examines the "Cambridge" modifications—allowing workers to save and capitalists to consume. On balance, the results are favorable to the contention of Luigi Pasinetti (1962) that in long-run equilibrium workers' saving affects only their share of capital and income, not the rate of profit and growth. But this result has to be qualified when it comes to the stability of neo-Keynesian equilibrium.

Chapter 7 provides microeconomic foundations of the Cambridge saving function. Separate saving propensities are derived for capitalists and workers on the assumption that capitalists adjust consumption to income more slowly than do workers. The point is to show the existence of an alternative to the neoclassical view that saving propensities are grounded in lifetime utility maximization.

---

1. It is to be anticipated that the assumption of constant returns to scale casts doubt upon the legitimacy of my claim of Sraffa as an intellectual ancestor. Despite Sraffa's prominent statements to the contrary (1960, preface), constant returns to scale is, I believe, tacitly assumed: else how justify the assumption of uniform profit rates across industries?

Models combining elements from different theories are discussed in Chapter 8. Models based on contributions of Robert Solow (1956), Nicholas Kaldor (1956, 1957, 1961), Pasinetti (1962), and others are analyzed as "hybrids" that marry the neoclassical assumption of full employment (that is, a natural rate of growth) to one or another neo-Keynesian assumption.

Variable proportions are analyzed in Chapters 9 and 10. Contrary to the stance of many critics of neoclassical economics, I take the position that even the most extreme form of variable proportions—continuous substitution—is not inherently neoclassical. Thus continuous-substitution versions of all three models are elaborated in which the conventional marginal-productivity conditions hold. It is suggested that there are in fact two "marginal-productivity theories." First, there is a general theory valid in neo-Marxian and neo-Keynesian, as well as in neoclassical, models; this marginal-productivity theory assumes nothing but constant returns to scale and profit maximization in competitive product markets. Second, there is a special theory, valid only in the neoclassical model, that adds full employment to the assumption of competitive profit maximization and constant returns to scale. It is only in the domain of the special theory that the capital stock and the labor force can be said to determine the distribution of income between wages and profits, and even this limited statement requires qualification.

Continuous substitution, if the common property of all theories, nevertheless has substantially different effects on each. In the fixed-coefficient case, neoclassical equilibrium is at worst nonexistent and at best unstable for that most regular of utility functions, the Cobb-Douglas. A sufficient elasticity of substitution in production, however, guarantees not only existence, but stability as well. Thus continuous substitution has obvious appeal for the neoclassically inclined. By contrast, with a high elasticity of substitution, the rate of surplus value ceases to be an innocuous if superfluous basis for the real wage rate in the neo-Marxian model, and becomes instead a glaringly inconsistent element of the model. It is equally no wonder that continuous substitution models lack appeal for those inclined to follow Marx, at least for those inclined to follow him rather strictly.

Chapters 11, 12, and 13 examine the models in the context of many goods. The point of these chapters is basically to argue that the claims made in the one-good case are generally (though by no means invariably) valid regardless of the number of commodities. The experience of the capital controversy of the 1960s has made economists rightly skeptical of results derived in the context of one-good models, and the specialist will presumably therefore forgive the relatively heavy demands made on his patience. Even the generalist may find something of interest in these chapters. A multiplicity of goods, for instance, makes it possible to clarify the differences in the role of demand and consumer sovereignty between neoclassical and nonneoclassical models: consumer demands based on utility maximization are defined only over current goods in the two nonneoclassical models, but over future as well as current goods in the neoclassical model. The result is that household demand enters into the determination of the distribution of income and relative prices in the neoclassical model but only into the composition of output in the nonneoclassical models.

The consequences of assuming a noncompetitive market structure are examined in Chapter 14. The motivation for this chapter is not so much to substitute a more realistic market structure for a less realistic one as it is to examine the contention that Kalecki's degree-of-monopoly theory (1938, 1943) provides a distinct alternative to the three theories on which the book focuses. My conclusion on this point is negative: Kalecki's theory is to be understood not as a separate and distinct theory, but as a supplementary argument that can be grafted onto any of the other theories—neoclassical, neo-Marxian, or neo-Keynesian. It deals not with the overall rate of profit but with the division of the profit pie among industries. This problem arises only because in the monopoly context we are obliged to abandon the assumption of uniform profit rates, an assumption that makes no sense outside the context of perfect competition.

Chapter 15 provides a relatively full summary of the entire argument up to that point, purified of equations and graphs. Some readers may wish to begin with this chapter in order to get a more complete overview before immersing themselves in the particulars.

Chapter 16 broaches the problem of using empirical data to evaluate the three theories. This chapter focuses on the comparative statics of an energy shock as a means of distinguishing the theories in terms of their empirical predictions. It also treats briefly the possibility of discovering empirically observable differences from the differences in labor-market theories. On the whole the results are negative. Neither an energy shock nor labor markets are likely to produce data that permit a clear choice among the theories.

The difficulty of resolving intertheoretical disputes by means of real-world data is developed in Chapters 17 and 18, in which neoclassical and nonneoclassical theories of household saving behavior are pitted against each other. Although the results of these tests are relatively favorable to the nonneoclassical view, they are hardly conclusive.

Devotees of Irving Fisher or his latter-day disciples, Milton Friedman and Franco Modigliani, will not feel compelled to abandon the neoclassical faith.

My own evaluations and criticisms of the three approaches are set out in Chapter 19. Chapter 20, which effectively concludes the book, synthesizes the neo-Marxian theory of wage determination with the neo-Keynesian theory of investment and the "Cambridge" theory of saving common to the two models. In combining the strong points of each, this synthesis of Marxian and Keynesian elements repairs the weaknesses of the two theories taken separately. Keynesian theory is simplistic in the extreme in its theory of the real wage: only in the very short run is it plausible to argue for a demand-determined real wage on the grounds that the wage bargain is generally formulated in money terms. For its part, the neo-Marxian model appears to me decidedly anachronistic in its lack of an investment-demand function.

One aspect of this model that might have reasonably wide appeal is the framework it provides for sorting out demand-pull and cost-push inflation. As a by-product, it offers a way of making sense of the debate over the Phillips curve and related phenomena. In addition to providing a nonneoclassical basis for the Phillips curve, the model suggests a reason why output and price movements are sometimes positively correlated and sometimes negatively correlated: the crucial issue is whether equilibrium is disturbed by a change in investment demand, in the propensity to save, or in the conventional wage or other elements of cost.

For all its virtues, the proposed synthesis of Chapter 20 is not unproblematic. A consequence of simultaneously imposing an investment-demand function and a real-wage constraint as well as a saving function is to overdetermine the model. Accordingly, we are required to revise substantially what we mean by equilibrium. Rationing à la Barro and Grossman or Malinvaud is not the issue. Rather, demand and supply in the goods market are temporarily equated by the price mechanism in every period, but still diverge over the long run. Nevertheless, equilibrium of a kind still can exist: steady growth can take place when the investment intentions of capitalists and the attempts of workers to maintain a conventional level of real wages are frustrated in equal measure.

The Production Model

In its simplest form production is characterized by a one-commodity model in which "corn" is produced by means of a fixed-coefficient technology in which the only inputs are seed corn and labor. (Land ready for the plow is assumed to be available in superabundance, and need not be considered further. The same goes for plows and plow teams.) The production relationship is thus

$$X = C + a_1 X_{+1},   \tag{1.1}$$

where X represents current corn output, C consumption from this year's harvest, X_{+1} output in the following year, and a_1 the requirements of seed corn per unit of corn harvest. The only other technological datum with which we must concern ourselves is a_0, which represents the labor requirement (in man-years) per bushel of corn output.

Our price formation equation is

$$P = Wa_0 + (1 + r)Pa_1.   \tag{1.2}$$

Equation (1.2) says, à la Sraffa (1960), that the price of this year's corn P is the sum of (1) the labor cost Wa_0 (in which W is the current wage), (2) the cost of seed corn Pa_1, and (3) the profit—interest in neoclassical terminology—earned on seed corn rPa_1, all valued in terms of this year's price. Note that, following Sraffa, it has implicitly been assumed that wages are paid at harvest time and that no profit accrues on this portion of costs. This assumption is by no means essential to anything that follows.[2]

The year's consumption will be assumed to take place all at once, in a grand feast that immediately follows the harvest. Seed corn will be assumed to be indestructible—for a limited period. In our models seed corn does not deteriorate in quantity or quality between harvest and the subsequent planting, but it cannot be stored beyond that time. Such a limitation on storage removes the usual objection to negative profit rates. Thus, in principle the lower bound to r is -1.

As Eqs. (1.1) and (1.2) stand, they together contain six unknowns for each time period, but we can quickly reduce the number of unknowns to four by normalizing both the production and price equations and concentrating our attention on "steady states" in which (1) the rate of growth of output is constant (and in multicommodity versions of the model, equal for all outputs), as is the level (and composition) of

---

2. It serves rather to facilitate the resolution of a Ricardian problem never far from Sraffa's heart, namely the search for a measure of value invariant to the distribution of income. However, the alternative of including wages advanced before the harvest as an element of an economy's stock of capital goods appears to me more in harmony with Ricardo (not to mention Marx) than Sraffa's own assumption that wages are paid at harvest time. Nonetheless, in order to highlight my intellectual debt, I shall adopt the Sraffian convention.

consumption per worker, and (2) prices, wage rates, and profit rates are constant over time. In general we have $X_{+1} = (1 + g)X$ where g is the rate of growth of corn output from this year to next, as well as the rate of growth of seed corn between last year and this. Substituting into Eq. (1.1), we have

$$X = C + a_1(1 + g)X. \qquad (1.3)$$

But the scale of output in any single year is for our purposes arbitrary: we can endow the world with any amount of seed corn we like. So we can do all our calculations on the basis of a single bushel by dividing Eq. (1.3) through by X,

$$1 = \frac{C}{X} + a_1(1 + g). \qquad (1.4)$$

Treating C as consumption per worker rather than consumption in the aggregate, and denoting employment by L, we have $a_0 = L/X$ and

$$1 = a_0 C + a_1(1 + g). \qquad (1.5)$$

(Equivalently, we can simply fix

$$a_0 X = 1 \qquad (1.6)$$

and C becomes consumption per worker as well as consumption in the aggregate. Equation (1.6), it should be observed, is a normalization, not an equilibrium condition. It fixes the level of employment in one year and says nothing about the path of employment.)

Similarly, the price equation can be simplified by making corn the unit of account, or numéraire. With $P = 1$, W becomes the real wage, and we have

$$1 = Wa_0 + (1 + r)a_1. \qquad (1.7)$$

In one sense, this completes the description of production and price formation in the corn model. But as Sraffa himself (1960, pp. 3–33) and others following his lead (Dobb 1973, note to chap. 9; Robinson 1965) have recognized, the corn model is incomplete as it now stands. The production equation (1.5) still contains two unknowns, C and g. Similarly, the price equation (1.7) contains two unknowns, W and r. Both equations, conveniently, can be illustrated in a single diagram (Figure 1.1). This figure can be interpreted as representing a "growth-consumption frontier" or as a "factor-price frontier," the first showing the boundary of feasible combinations of growth and consumption, the second the boundary of feasible combinations of wage and profit rates. To each point on this locus corresponds a distribution of corn income

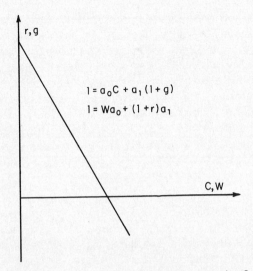

$$1 = a_0 C + a_1 (1 + g)$$
$$1 = W a_0 + (1 + r) a_1$$

Figure 1.1 Growth-consumption and factor-price frontiers

between wages and profits and an allocation of corn resources between consumption and investment. Both the distribution of income and the allocation of resources depend, as Eqs. (1.5) and (1.7) show, on the particular technology summarized in the coefficients a_0 and a_1. The share of wages per unit of corn output is $W a_0$, the share of (gross) profit $(1 + r) a_1$. Similarly, the shares of consumption and (gross) investment are, respectively, $a_0 C$ and $a_1 (1 + g)$.

It should be noted that at this point there is no implication that wages and consumption or profit rates and growth rates are equal. As matters stand, (1.5) and (1.7) are independent relationships, and no more can be inferred from Figure 1.1 than that (1) C and W are measured in a common unit — corn per worker per year; (2) g and r are measured in a common unit — both are annual rates; (3) the maximum consumption per worker that the technology is capable of delivering (when $g = -1$) is equal to the maximum wage rate it is capable of supporting (when $r = -1$); (4) the maximum growth rate that can be sustained (when $C = 0$) is equal to the maximum profit rate the system can support (when $W = 0$); and (5) the trade-offs between growth and consumption dg/dC and between profits and wages dr/dW take place at a constant and equal rate, namely $-a_0/a_1$.[3]

3. The linearity of the factor-price frontier is central to Sraffa's solution to the problem of defining an invariant standard of value. The assumption that wages are paid

The price equation deserves closer scrutiny, since it plays a fundamental role in our analysis. It is, as we have seen, an accounting relationship pure and simple, which says no more than that what is not wages must be (gross) profit. Given that the only two categories of income in our model are wages and profit, and given that profit is made only on seed corn, a bushel of corn can be distributed between wages and profits only in accordance with Eq. (1.7) and Figure 1.1. Indeed, with the rate of profit fixed, Eq. (1.7) can be taken to define the wage rate as a residual. Directly from Eq. (1.7) we have

$$W(r) = \frac{1 - a_1}{a_0} - r \frac{a_1}{a_0}, \qquad (1.8)$$

in which the first term on the right-hand side represents net output of corn per worker after provision for seed corn and the second term represents profit per worker. Similarly, Eq. (1.7) can be interpreted as defining a rate of profit, given the wage rate. We have

$$r(W) = \frac{1 - a_1}{a_1} - W \frac{a_0}{a_1},$$

with the first term on the right representing the net output of corn per bushel of seed corn and the next term labor cost per unit of seed corn.

Just as Eq. (1.7) says only that what is not paid out as wages is profit, so Eq. (1.5) is an accounting relationship which says no more than that the portion of output not invested in corn growing must be consumed. We may interpret C as a function of g:

$$C(g) = \frac{1 - a_1}{a_0} - g \frac{a_1}{a_0}, \qquad (1.9)$$

or g as a function of C:

$$g(C) = \frac{1 - a_1}{a_1} - C \frac{a_0}{a_1}.$$

In each case one of the two unknowns — profit or wage rate and consumption or growth rate — must be determined from outside the production model, which is why it is emphasized that Eqs. (1.5) and (1.7) provide accounting relationships rather than *theories* of distribution and growth.

---

at the end of the production period is necessary for linearity but sufficient only in the one-good case. In the multiple-good case, additional assumptions are required (see the introduction to Chapter 11).

Thus, as has already been indicated, two independent relationships must be added to complete our model, that is, to solve the model for r, W, C, and g. At the risk of some oversimplification, it is fair to say that (1) the neoclassical approach is to complete the model by specifying additional relationships that first determine g and C, and then r and W; (2) the neo-Marxian approach is to provide additional relationships to determine W and C, then to determine r and g as residuals; (3) the neo-Keynesian approach is to determine r and g, then to determine W and C residually.[4] It is to the mechanics of these alternative ways of closing the model that we now turn.

4. "First" does not indicate a temporal but a logical priority. Growth and consumption are logically prior in the neoclassical case, for instance, because a change in the natural rate of growth will change the equilibrium values of all the variables — r and W as well as g and C. By contrast, in the fixed-coefficient case at least, a change in the parameters of households' utility functions will change the equilibrium values only of r and W; the equilibrium values of g and C are unaffected. More formally, the solution to the general-equilibrium problem is decomposable by virtue of a triangular structure.

PART ONE

Growth and Distribution with Homogeneous Capital and Output

2 The Neoclassical Approach

Neoclassical theory argues that growth and distribution are determined by preferences, biology, and technology—all given exogenously—interacting in a regime of markets in which the price mechanism holds universal sway, clearing the labor and capital markets as it does markets for fish, horses, and shoes. It is this essence that the model described in the next few pages seeks to capture.

The fundamental social unit of the neoclassical model is the household. In our model we assume each household lives for two periods, a year of work and a year of retirement. That is, we assume each generation comes into the economic world as adults, works for a year, spends a year in retirement, and then passes from the scene. But in keeping with the assumption that consumption takes the form of post-harvest feasts, a working household consumes—out of its own assets at least—only *after* it produces. It consumes a second time, after a period of retirement, just before its final leave-taking.

Further, we assume for the time being that each household comes naked into the world and leaves the same way. In other words, there are no bequests in this model, so each household has to support itself for two periods out of its wage earnings from one. (It is immaterial whether we assume that households support their offspring until maturity or whether we assume that workers enter the scene full grown.) Finally, we assume overlapping generations, so there is always one generation working and one generation living in retirement, as illustrated in Table 2.1.

It is assumed that all households are identical in composition and preferences, and that each allocates its corn wage ($P = 1$) between consumption in the two periods of its economic life (C^1 and C^2) accord-

Table 2.1. Overlapping generations

	$t = 1$	$t = 2$	$t = 3$	$t = 4$	. . .
generation 1	working	retired	†		
generation 2		working	retired	†	
generation 3			working	retired	

ing to maximization of a "life-cycle" utility function of the form

$$U(C^1, C^2), \tag{2.1}$$

subject to the life-cycle budget constraint[1]

$$C^1 + \frac{C^2}{1 + r} = W. \tag{2.2}$$

The assumption that households maximize utility subject to their budget constraints allows us to define a typical household's demand for consumption of corn as a function of the real wage W and the profit rate r. We can go a step further by utilizing the information embodied in the price equation. In the form of Eq. (1.8) the accounting relationship between r and W determines W as a function of r, to wit $W(r)$. Thus we may write the budget constraint as

$$C^1 + \frac{C^2}{1 + r} = W(r) \tag{2.5}$$

and define the household's demands as a function of r alone, $\langle C^1(r), C^2(r) \rangle$.

But consumption demand in any one year is the sum of demands of overlapping generations of working households and retired house-

---

1. Equation (2.2) implicitly fixes the work effort at one man-year per household. We might instead incorporate a leisure : goods choice into the model by means of a utility function of the form

$$U(C^1, C^2, z) \tag{2.3}$$

and a budget constraint of the form

$$C^1 + \frac{C^2}{1 + r} = zW. \tag{2.4}$$

It would not be difficult to work with (2.3) and (2.4) rather than (2.1) and (2.2), but on the other hand, it would hardly enrich the model either. Thus for the time being we stick with (2.1) and (2.2) and will return to the leisure : goods choice only when the rest of the story is complete (see the appendix to this chapter).

holds. If there is at present one worker, and if production is growing at the rate g, then there must have been $1/(1+g)$ workers in the last period, and there must, therefore, be $1/(1+g)$ retired households today. Hence, aggregate consumption demand is

$$C(r, g) = C^1(r) + \frac{C^2(r)}{1+g}. \tag{2.6}$$

Observe that the functional form of $C(r, g)$ depends on intertemporal preferences with respect to consumption, that is to say, on the utility function U—even though the notation does not reflect this dependence.

Demand and Supply

Equilibrium requires that consumption demand $C(r, g)$ equal $C(g)$, the supply of corn per worker that remains after provision for replacement of this year's seed as well as for growth at the rate g. From the production equation we have

$$C(g) = \frac{1 - a_1}{a_0} - g \frac{a_1}{a_0}, \tag{1.9}$$

so equality of consumption demand and supply

$$C(r, g) = C(g)$$

is equivalent to

$$C^1(r) + \frac{C^2(r)}{1+g} = \frac{1 - a_1}{a_0} - g \frac{a_1}{a_0}. \tag{2.7}$$

But the budget constraint (2.5) gives us

$$C^1(r) = W(r) - \frac{C^2(r)}{1+r},$$

and the price equation (1.7) gives us

$$W(r) = \frac{1 - a_1}{a_0} - r \frac{a_1}{a_0}. \tag{1.8}$$

Substituting from these two equations into Eq. (2.7) and collecting terms, we have the condition

$$(r - g) \frac{C^2(r)}{(1+r)(1+g)} = (r - g) \frac{a_1}{a_0}. \tag{2.8}$$

Look closely at Eq. (2.8). It appears to provide us with *two* equilibrium conditions: *either*

$$r = g \qquad (2.9)$$

or

$$\frac{C^2(r)}{1+r} = (1+g)\frac{a_1}{a_0} \qquad (2.10)$$

equalizes demand for food-grain consumption with the available supply of corn. In fact, however, only one of these two conditions — Eq. (2.10) — survives scrutiny as a characterization of equilibrium, for besides a balance between food-grain demand and food-grain supply, equilibrium supposes a balance between effective demand for seed corn and the requirements for replacement and growth. In other words, gross desired saving $S(r, g)$ must be equal to gross investment requirements $I(g)$.

But whatever happened to Walras' Law? Doesn't this "law" guarantee that if consumption demand and supply balance, then saving and investment must balance too? Unfortunately the writ of Walras does not run here. It *is* true that desired gross saving $S(r, g)$ is the difference between perceived income Y and desired consumption $C(r, g)$:

$$S(r, g) = Y - C(r, g).$$

And gross investment is by definition the difference between gross output and consumption:

$$I(g) \equiv X - C(g).$$

Thus $C(r, g) = C(g)$ and $Y = X$ together imply

$$S(r, g) = I(g). \qquad (2.11)$$

The problem is that Y and X are not necessarily equal. Y, the income on which $C(r, g)$ and $S(r, g)$ are based, is not the actual output $X = 1/a_0$, but the revenue perceived by workers and retired folks, on the basis of given r and g. Perceived wages are given by r alone,

$$\text{wages} = W(r) = \frac{1-a_1}{a_0} - r\frac{a_1}{a_0},$$

and perceived profits are given by r and g,

$$\text{gross profits} = (1+r)\frac{[W(r) - C^1(r)]}{1+g} = \frac{C^2(r)}{1+g}.$$

So perceived income is

$$Y = \frac{1 - a_1}{a_0} - r\frac{a_1}{a_0} + \frac{C^2(r)}{1 + g}. \qquad (2.12)$$

It becomes clear from Eq. (2.12) that for Y and X to be equal, we must have

$$\frac{1}{a_0} - (1 + r)\frac{a_1}{a_0} + \frac{C^2(r)}{1 + g} = \frac{1}{a_0}. \qquad (2.13)$$

Thus

$$Y = X \quad \Leftrightarrow \quad \frac{C^2(r)}{1 + r} = (1 + g)\frac{a_1}{a_0},$$

which leads us directly back to Eq. (2.10) but not to (2.9). In other words, a food-grain equilibrium characterized by

$$r = g \qquad (2.9)$$

is not in general compatible with a saving = investment equlibrium, whereas a food-grain equilibrium characterized by

$$\frac{C^2(r)}{1 + r} = (1 + g)\frac{a_1}{a_0} \qquad (2.10)$$

is simultaneously a saving = investment equilibrium for which Walras' Law holds.

The meaning of Eq. (2.10) becomes clearer if we examine the source of gross saving in the present model. Present retirees, who will fade from the scene with the coming winter's snows, have no reason to save. Indeed, retirees are *dissavers,* who consume not only their income but their capital as well. (Bequests change this story in detail, but not in its general conclusions; see the appendix to this chapter.) Neither are next year's workers a source of saving: they may have a motive, but they will not have the wherewithal to buy corn until after next year's harvest. This leaves the current generation of workers, who alone have both reason (to provide for their retirement) and means (their wages) to buy and hold corn. Equilibrium thus requires that an *ownership condition* be satisfied. The present generation of workers must be willing to become owners of the seed corn required for replacement and growth. The model thus embodies the Great American Dream, in which workers, by dint of abstinence, become capitalists who live off their wealth during retirement.

Gross saving per worker is given by the equation

$$S(r, g) = W(r) - C^1(r) = \frac{C^2(r)}{1 + r}. \tag{2.14}$$

Since gross saving is a function of the profit rate alone, we can rewrite Eq. (2.14) as

$$S(r) = \frac{C^2(r)}{1 + r}$$

and the saving = investment equilibrium condition as

$$S(r) = I(g). \tag{2.15}$$

Gross investment per worker is the sum of replacement seed a_1/a_0 and the net addition ga_1/a_0:

$$I(g) = (1 + g)\frac{a_1}{a_0}.$$

Hence desired saving is equal to investment requirements, that is, Eq. (2.15) holds, when Eq. (2.10) holds:

$$\frac{C^2(r)}{1 + r} = (1 + g)\frac{a_1}{a_0}. \tag{2.10}$$

It is in fact easier to work with Eq. (2.10) in terms of capital rather than labor, and to express saving in net rather than gross terms. To transform the units from a per-worker basis to a per-bushel basis, we multiply through by the labor : capital ratio a_0/a_1 to obtain

$$\frac{C^2(r)}{1 + r}\frac{a_0}{a_1} = 1 + g.$$

To put saving and investment on a net basis, we subtract unity from both sides of the equation: net saving per bushel of seed corn is

$$s(r) = \frac{C^2(r)}{1 + r}\frac{a_0}{a_1} - 1,$$

and net investment per bushel of seed corn is

$$i(g) = g.$$

Thus the ownership condition becomes

$$s(r) = i(g),$$

or

$$\frac{C^2(r)}{1+r} \frac{a_0}{a_1} - 1 = g. \tag{2.16}$$

Observe that for any $r \in (-1, r_{\max}]$, there is a corresponding g. In other words, for any rate of profit (except possibly $r = -1$), there is a corresponding rate of growth at which the present generation of workers are just willing to hold the requisite seed corn. But the converse does not in general hold. For arbitrarily given g, there may be no r at which the requisite saving is willingly forthcoming. To see this, one need only consider the extreme case in which workers assume they will live on air during their retirement (or, like Indian *senyasis*, on the offerings of the faithful). In this case the only growth rate that becomes feasible in terms of the ownership condition is $g = -1$. That is, if each household maximizes a utility function of the form

$$U(C^1, C^2) = C^1,$$

then for $r \in (-1, r_{\max}]$,

$$\frac{C^2(r)}{1+r} = 0$$

and

$$s(r) \equiv -1.$$

But we do not need to go to such extremes to make the point. Even with the most conventional of utility functions the range of the saving function need not contain the set of growth rates defined by the production equation (1.5), not to mention an arbitrarily given growth rate. Consider the case of a Cobb-Douglas utility function

$$U(C^1, C^2) = (C^1)^{\alpha}(C^2)^{\beta}, \qquad \alpha + \beta = 1$$

for which the saving function has the form

$$s(r) = \beta W(r) \frac{a_0}{a_1} - 1 = \beta \left[\frac{1}{a_1} - (1+r) \right] - 1.$$

If saving and investment are to be equal, we must have

$$g = s(r) = \beta \left[\frac{1}{a_1} - (1+r) \right] - 1. \tag{2.17}$$

Now observe the representation of Eq. (2.17) in Figure 2.1. If a rate of growth like g is specified exogenously, there is no equilibrium in the sense of a balance between desired saving and investment requirements.

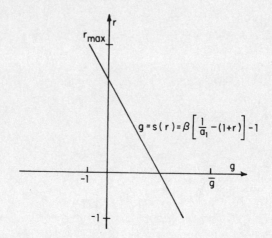

Figure 2.1 Net saving as a function of the rate of profit

On the other hand, equilibrium cannot be determined by Eq. (2.17) alone. Here the problem is an embarrassment of riches: *any* point on the straight line representing the saving function is a possible equilibrium in terms of balancing both saving with investment and food-grain demand with food-grain supply.

Full Employment

Both these problems arise from a common source: the ownership condition linking saving = investment equilibrium to rates of profit and growth provides only one of the two relationships required to close the model. The other relationship is provided by the neoclassical theory of employment. According to neoclassical theory, competitive labor markets guarantee full employment. But what does "full employment" mean in the present context? It *cannot* mean simply full utilization of artibrarily given quantities of labor and seed corn at a moment of time: for although the ratio of seed corn to labor is technologically fixed at a_1/a_0, we can set the scale of operation at any desired level for any *one* moment of time t merely by endowing the economy with the appropriate quantity of seed corn at time t. In the present context, in which the focus is on an equilibrium *path*, full employment requires that the rate of growth of output and employment g be equal to the rate of expansion of the labor force, which in neoclassical theory is an *exogenously* given population growth rate n.

Thus it is consistent with a variety of models to assume full employment at any one time, but it requires an additional, peculiarly neoclassical, assumption to guarantee full employment in a steady state. Specifically, it must be argued that under competitive conditions a persistent tendency of g to exceed n must over the long haul put pressure on the supply of labor that will increase the real wage; conversely, if g is persistently below n, growing unemployment will drive the real wage down. Since a constant real wage is one of the attributes of a steady state (in the absence of technological progress), we may conclude that the only rate of investment consistent with a neoclassical steady state is

$$g = n. \tag{2.18}$$

In other words, the equilibrium growth rate is Roy Harrod's "natural rate" (Harrod 1948).

Existence of Equilibrium

Neoclassical theory, in the form of Eqs. (2.17) and (2.18), closes the model, but only for a subset of possible technologies and utility functions. Look again at the graph of saving = investment equilibrium in Figure 2.1, which is reproduced in Figure 2.2(a) and (b) along with the graphs of full-employment investment corresponding to two different rates of population growth, n_1 and n_2.

In Figure 2.2(a), desired seed corn equals the investment required by population growth for $r = r^*$, and the corresponding levels of real

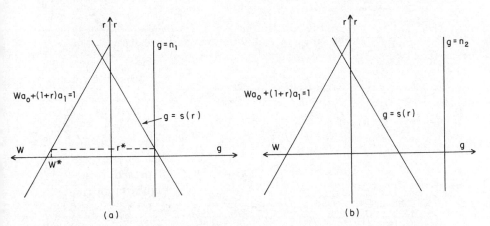

Figure 2.2 Net saving as a function of the rate of profit with two different rates of growth of population

wages and consumption, $W*$ and $C*$, can be found by solving Eqs. (1.7) and (1.5):

$$W* = \frac{1 - (1 + r*)a_1}{a_0},$$

$$C* = \frac{1 - (1 + g*)a_1}{a_0}.$$

In Figure 2.2(b), by contrast, there is *no* equilibrium since n_2 lies outside the range of the saving function.

There is no way to guarantee the existence of an equilibrium other than to assume it. Evidently the elasticity of utility with respect to future consumption β plays a critical role in determining whether or not an equilibrium exists. As we saw in the extreme case of zero elasticity,

$$U(C^1, C^2) = C^1,$$

in which desired seed-corn holdings are identically zero for each generation, steady-state equilibrium is impossible for any rate of population growth except $g = -1$.

To ensure the existence of equilibrium, the utility function must be restricted so that the excess-saving function, defined as desired seed-corn holdings less population-determined investment,

$$\frac{C^2(r)}{1 + r} \frac{a_0}{a_1} - 1 - n,$$

vanishes somewhere in the interval $[-1, r_{max}]$. Whatever the utility function might be, W and hence $C^2(r)$ vanish at r_{max}, so excess saving is negative for $r = r_{max}$. Thus it suffices to assume that excess saving is nonnegative at the lower end of the interval. In other words, a sufficient condition for the existence of neoclassical equilibrium is

$$\lim_{r \to -1} \left[\frac{C^2(r)}{1 + r} \frac{a_0}{a_1} - 1 \right] \geq n,$$

or equivalently,

$$\lim_{r \to -1} \frac{C^2(r)}{1 + r} \geq (1 + n) \frac{a^1}{a_0}. \tag{2.19}$$

In the Cobb-Douglas case, these conditions reduce to

$$\frac{\beta}{a_1} - 1 \geq n.$$

The Geometry of Equilibrium

A geometric examination of this sufficiency condition has the merit of clarifying the relationship between the true equilibrium and the "pseudo-equilibrum" $r = n$, defined by Eqs. (2.9) and (2.18). Figure 2.3 graphs the function $\langle C^1(r), C^2(r)\rangle$, defined by varying r—and $W(r)$—parametrically over the domain $(-1, r_{max}]$ while holding the preference map fixed. Two features of this function, which I shall refer to as the "consumption-demand function," should be noted, for each plays an important role in the geometry of inequality (2.19). First, its graph necessarily intersects the n-budget—the budget line corresponding to $W(n)$—where the n-budget is tangent to an indifference curve. This point, $\langle C^1(n), C^2(n)\rangle$ in Figure 2.3, corresponds to the pseudo-equilibrium $r = n$. Second, the graph of this function passes through the origin since $W(r_{max}) = 0$ implies $\langle C^1(r_{max}), C^2(r_{max})\rangle = \langle 0, 0\rangle$.

For the inequality (2.19) to be sufficient for the existence of equilibrium, it must be demonstrated that if this condition is satisfied, the graph of the consumption-demand function intersects the n-budget at

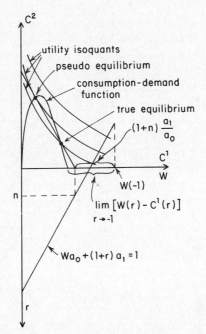

Figure 2.3   Consumption demand as a function of the rate of profit

some point $\langle C^1(r), C^2(r) \rangle$ other than $\langle C^1(n), C^2(n) \rangle$, that is, at a point where $r \neq n$. For at such an intersection the two equations

$$C^1(r) + \frac{C^2(r)}{1 + r} = W(r) \tag{2.20}$$

and

$$C^1(r) + \frac{C^2(r)}{1 + n} = W(n) \tag{2.21}$$

are simultaneously satisfied, the first by definition of the consumption-demand function, the second by definition of the n-budget. By subtracting Eq. (2.21) from Eq. (2.20) and using Eq. (1.8), we have directly

$$(n - r) \frac{C^2(r)}{(1 + r)(1 + n)} = (n - r) \frac{a_1}{a_0}.$$

So when $n \neq r$, we have

$$\frac{C^2(r)}{1 + r} = (1 + n) \frac{a_1}{a_0},$$

which characterizes a true equilibrium.

The geometrical significance of the sufficiency condition embodied in inequality (2.19) is precisely that it guarantees this second intersection. To see this requires only that we examine the geometry of the various terms of this expression. The right-hand intercept of $\langle C^1(r), C^2(r) \rangle$ on the C^1-axis represents the limit of this function as r approaches -1. The point labeled $W(-1)$ represents the projection on the W-axis of the wage rate that corresponds to $r = -1$ in the price equation

$$1 = Wa_0 + (1 + r)a_1. \tag{1.7}$$

Since wages and consumption are both measured in terms of corn, the distance between these two points corresponds to the difference

$$\lim_{r \to -1} [W(r) - C^1(r)] = \lim_{r \to -1} \frac{C^2(r)}{1 + r},$$

which is the left-hand side of (2.19).

Now consider the distance between the projections of $W(-1)$ and $W(n)$ on the W-axis:

$$W(-1) = \frac{1}{a_0}, \qquad W(n) = \frac{1}{a_0} - (1 + n) \frac{a_1}{a_0}$$

so that

$$W(-1) - W(n) = (1 + n) \frac{a_1}{a_0},$$

which is the right-hand side of (2.19).

Thus in terms of Figure 2.3, the inequality expressed in (2.19),

$$\lim_{r \to -1} \frac{C^2(r)}{1 + r} \geq (1 + n) \frac{a_1}{a_0}, \tag{2.19}$$

amounts to the requirement that the intersection of the consumption-demand function with the horizontal axis take place to the *left* of the intersection of the n-budget with the horizontal axis.

Suppose this condition is fulfilled. There are two possibilities. We know that consumption-demand function intersects the n-budget at $\langle C^1(n), C^2(n) \rangle$, but we do not know in general whether it cuts the n-budget from above or below, that is, whether or not its slope is smaller (in algebraic value) or greater than the slope of the n-budget. As Figure 2.3 is drawn, and this is the hard case, the consumption-demand function cuts the n-budget from below at the pseudo-equilibrium. Now follow the consumption-demand function down to the C^1-axis. If, as inequality (2.19) requires, the limit of the consumption-demand function as r approaches -1 is to the left of the n-budget, the consumption-demand function must once again intersect the n-budget between $\langle C^1(n), C^2(n) \rangle$ and the horizontal intercept. That is to say, an equilibrium must exist.

Now take the easy case, alternative to the picture in Figure 2.3, in which the consumption-demand function cuts the n-budget from above at $\langle C^1(n), C^2(n) \rangle$. In this case, forget about the right-hand intercept and follow the consumption-demand function in the opposite direction, that is, in the direction that leads from $\langle C^1(r), C^2(n) \rangle$ to the origin. It is easy to visualize that to get to the origin the consumption-demand function must again cross the n-budget between $\langle C^1(n), C^2(n) \rangle$ and the vertical intercept, and such an intersection too constitutes an equilibrium.

Thus, whichever way the consumption-demand function and the n-budget intersect at $\langle C^1(n), C^2(n) \rangle$, a second intersection must exist, provided the inequality embodied in formula (2.19) is satisfied. That is, at least one true equilibrium must exist alongside the pseudo-equilibrium $\langle C^1(n), C^2(n) \rangle$. (The foregoing is of course only the sketch of a proof rather than a formal proof itself. However, we may forego this luxury since the geometrical argument is supposed only to clarify; the

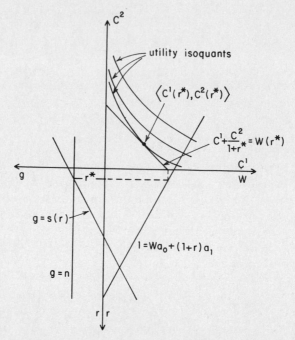

Figure 2.4 Neoclassical equilibrium

sufficiency of formula (2.19) for the existence of equilibrium has already been established by examining the behavior of the excess-saving function.)

To summarize, then, if the utility function is restricted to make the ratio of saving to wage income suitably large, the neoclassical model is closed by assuming (1) that a competitive labor market guarantees full employment over time and (2) that households allocate income between saving and consumption to maximize the utility of lifetime consumption. At least one combination of wage rate W^* and profit rate r^* exists for which desired seed-corn holding is equal to the investment necessary to sustain full employment. The precise value of the pair $\langle r^*, W^* \rangle$ depends on the shape of the utility function $U(C^1, C^2)$ and the natural rate of growth n. Geometrically, the determination of equilibrium is pictured in Figure 2.4.

Equilibrium and Efficiency

Before we finish with Figure 2.4 we might return for a moment to the pseudo-equilibrium associated with $r = n$. If we superimpose the n-

budget on this diagram, as in Figure 2.5, we can see that the pseudo-equilibrium affords a higher level of utility than the true equilibrium r^*. The reason is obvious: $\langle C^1(r^*), C^2(r^*)\rangle$ lies on the n-budget, and therefore must be inferior to the best point on the n-budget, namely $\langle C^1(n), C^2(n)\rangle$. But so long as it is required that workers' saving be adequate to purchase the stock of seed corn, $\langle C^1(n), C^2(n)\rangle$ remains — except by accident — unobtainable.

The constraint that the seed-corn market clear could, however, be removed by socializing production and investment. If we insert into the model a government that owns all the seed corn, it could fix the rate of profit at n by legislative fiat, and use gross profits $(1 + n)a_1/a_0$ for seed corn, thus ensuring that the expansion of seed corn matches the expansion of the labor force. Households would still save according to the dictates of contrained utility maximization, but private capital would take the form of interest-bearing government paper; the bonds sold to the present generation would just cover the payments of interest and principal to retired folk. On the one hand, government borrowing

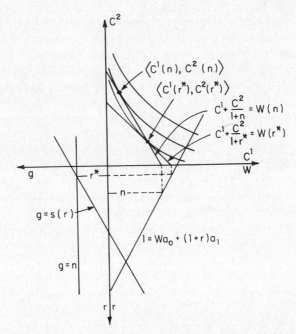

Figure 2.5 Utility maximization on the n-budget gives the highest sustainable utility

from workers would be equal to

$$S(n) = W(n) - C^1(n) = \frac{C^2(n)}{1 + n}.$$

On the other hand, payments of interest and principal per retiree would be

$$n \, \frac{C^2(n)}{1 + n} \; + \; \frac{C^2(n)}{1 + n} = C^2(n),$$

$$\underset{\substack{\text{interest} \\ \text{per} \\ \text{retiree}}}{} \quad \underset{\substack{\text{principal} \\ \text{per} \\ \text{retiree}}}{}$$

but since there are $1/(1 + n)$ retirees for each worker, new borrowings would just equal the sum of debt service and debt retirement.

Thus aggregate consumption would equal aggregate wages, as on a "golden-rule" growth path (Phelps 1961), but this is not the same thing as saying that all wages are consumed; workers save — unless perchance $C^2(n) = 0$ — but their savings are just offset by the consumption of retirees. The government, as the owner of seed corn, assures the investment of profits.

This result has much in common with the "optimum" configuration in Paul Samuelson's consumption-loan model (1958). In both, the laissez-faire equilibrium is inefficient in the sense that it is not "Pareto optimal." In both models, however, it is not steady-state *consumption* that the "biological rate of interest" $r = n$ maximizes. For consumption in our model is determined solely by technology and population growth and in Samuelson's by a gift of the gods. It is rather steady-state *utility* that is maximized, and this result, it should be noted, does not require restrictions on the utility function of the kind required to ensure the existence of equilibrium in our original model. On the other hand, the introduction of a Visible Hand in the form of the government, essential to implement the utility optimum, hardly squares with pure neoclassical theory, in which the government is supposed to play a part only when externalities, nonconvexities, and the like rear their ugly heads.

It should be observed that public *ownership*, as distinct from public *intervention*, is necessary only when desired saving at the $r = n$ "equilibrium" is less than the full-employment investment requirement. If $S(n)$ exceeds $I(n)$, then the government can intervene *à la* Peter Diamond (1965) to sell bonds in amounts sufficient only to take up the slack,

$$S(n) - I(n),$$

redeeming them the following period, with redemptions plus interest,

$$(1 + n) \, [S(n) - I(n)]$$

just offsetting the debt issued to absorb the excess saving of the new generation of workers. But note these points: first, there is no analogous mechanism that can be employed in the case of insufficient saving. The issuance of debt unaccompanied by public ownership of seed corn only works to achieve the golden-rule allocation $\langle C^1(n), C^2(n)\rangle$ when the problem is one of *excess* desired saving. Second, the optimum allocation that is achieved through the debt mechanism is, as in the case of public ownership, a reallocation of a given level of aggregate consumption between workers and retirees. This contrasts with Diamond's own model, in which the proportions of labor and capital are allowed to vary so that public debt affects the steady-state consumption level as well as its composition.[2]

A Preliminary Summary

To summarize this discussion of the neoclassical model, we might spotlight the central aspects of the original, laissez-faire equilibrium. First in importance is the logical primacy of resource allocation over income distribution under neoclassical assumptions. Resource allocation is determined solely by technology and population growth; to find $C*$, the equilibrium consumption level, all we need know is $g*$, the equilibrium growth level, plus the input-output structure. The assumption of full employment, from which it follows that $g* = n$, determines investment, and therefore—given the input-output structure—the amount of corn left over to consume. Thus neither household preferences nor wage-profit relationships enter into the determination of aggregate consumption and investment. Preferences enter only at the stage of determining the life-cycle distribution of consumption, which

2. Finally, observe that the optimum allocation of resources does not necessarily require the present generation to "rob" the next generation, and each succeeding generation to compensate itself at the expense of the next. If the laissez-faire equilibrium rate of interest exceeds the biological rate (that is, if $r* > n$), then the reallocation of consumption required to move from $r*$ to n will imply *less* postponement of consumption by each generation. This result, it should be noted, is at odds with the usual interpretation of the Pareto inoptimality of neoclassical competitive equilibrium in the context of a world without end. If, moreover, the population is growing at a negative rate, an infinite quantity of corn is not necessary for laissez-faire equilibrium to be inefficient: with $n < 0$, the aggregate population from the present (taken as $t = 0$) forward is $1/(-n)$, evidently a finite number, and the aggregate amount of corn is a finite multiple of $1/(-n)$. There remain, to be sure, an infinite number of generations, for it is the weight of successive generations that declines, not the number of generations. By contrast, in the customary interpretation, which Karl Shell (1971) puts with eminent clarity, compensated robbery is at the heart of the matter, and an infinite amount of corn appears as necessary to the argument as an infinity of traders.

Table 2.2. Causality in the neoclassical model

Exogenous	Endogenous
$\left. \begin{array}{l} a_1, a_0 \\ n \end{array} \right\} \rightarrow$	C^*
$\left. \begin{array}{l} a_1, a_0 \\ n \\ U(C^1, C^2) \end{array} \right\} \rightarrow$	$W^*, r^*, \langle C^1(r^*), C^2(r^*) \rangle$

takes places simultaneously with the determination of the distribution of income. These causal relationships are summarized in Table 2.2.

Observe that wages and profits depend on the three factors — technology (the labor and capital coefficients a_0 and a_1); biology (the rate of growth n); and tastes (the utility function U) — that are normally invoked by neoclassical theorists to explain distribution.

Instability of Equilibrium

It is natural to inquire about the behavior of the system out of long-run equilibrium, that is, to pose the question of stability. The important features of the simple neoclassical model analyzed in the preceding section can be pointed out in short order. The principal result is that the equilibrium pictured in Figures 2.2 and 2.4 is unstable — assuming equilibrium exists at all — at least for the simple adjustment mechanism that naturally suggests itself in the context of this model. That is to say, an arbitrarily small displacement from equilibrium will result in the economy moving further away from, rather than back to, the path of steady-state growth with $g = n$ and $r = r^*$.

Look once again at Figure 2.2(a), reproduced on the next page as Figure 2.6. Assume that wages adjust according to the relationship between actual employment L and full employment N:

$$W - W_{-1} = \Delta W = \theta\left(\frac{L_{-1}}{N_{-1}} - 1\right),$$

or, denoting seed corn per member of the labor force by V and the capital : labor ratio a_1/a_0 by k,

$$W = \theta\left(\frac{V_{-1}}{k} - 1\right) + W_{-1}. \tag{2.22}$$

This assumption about wage adjustment, along with the accumulation

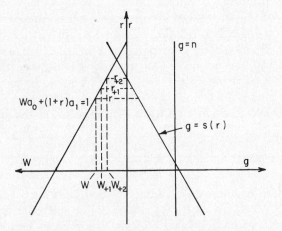

Figure 2.6 Instability of equilibrium

equation

$$V = (1 + g_{-1}) \frac{V_{-1}}{1 + n},\tag{2.23}$$

maps out a determinate path of short-run equilibrium once the initial configuration $\langle W_{-1}, V_{-1} \rangle$ is given and a procedure for determining g_{-1} in Eq. (2.23) is specified.

It might appear natural to determine g_{-1} from Eq. (2.17):

$$g_{-1} = \beta \left[\frac{1}{a_1} - (1 + r_{-1}) \right] - 1,$$

with r_{-1} given by the short-run price equation

$$1 = W_{-1}a_0 + (1 + r_{-1})a_1.\tag{2.24}$$

But in general this procedure will not work. The reason is that, special cases apart, there are in fact *two* rates of profit in the saving equation. We start from a generalization of Eq. (2.17),

$$g = \beta(r)W(r)k^{-1} - 1 = \beta(r) \left[\frac{1}{a_1} - (1 + r) \right] - 1,\tag{2.25}$$

relating growth to desired net saving per bushel of seed corn. In this equation, however, the parameter β, generalizing the Cobb-Douglas case, depends on the rate of profit, the precise form of the functional dependence being determined by how the utility function balances substitution and income effects of changes in r.

Equation (2.25) shows the two roles of the profit rate clearly: r enters the equation both through the general-equilibrium relationship between W and r and through the partial-equlibrium dependence of β, the fraction of wages saved, on r. The two roles are in general distinct: the relevant rate of profit in the first relationship is the *current* rate r, whereas in the second it is an *expected* rate of profit r_{+1}^e, the rate of profit households use to discount future consumption in the budget constraint

$$C^1 + \frac{C^2}{1 + r_{+1}^e} = W.$$

In the analysis of long-run, steady-growth equilibrium, it is natural to identify the expected rate of profit with the current rate of profit because this expectation is continually validated by experience. But such an argument obviously lacks force in the short run. So in the context of the short run, the equilibrium relationship between growth and profit takes the form

$$g = \beta(r_{+1}^e)W\,k^{-1} - 1 = \beta(r_{+1}^e)\left[\frac{1}{a_1} - (1 + r)\right] - 1. \qquad (2.26)$$

Two simple expectational hypotheses suggest themselves for the short run. One is the "rational expectations" hypothesis of perfect foresight (up to a stochastic term that plays no role in the present model). In this case the expected rate of profit is the actual rate r_{+1}; Eq. (2.26) becomes

$$g = \beta(r_{+1})\left[\frac{1}{a_1} - (1 + r)\right] - 1,$$

r_{+1} being determined simultaneously with V and W from the wage-adjustment equation (2.22), the capital-stock adjustment equation (2.23), and the price equation, given V and W.

Alternatively, we can posit the naive expectation that the future will resemble the present, in which case

$$g = \beta(r)\left[\frac{1}{a_1} - (1 + r)\right] - 1.$$

Evidently, more complicated expectations hypotheses could be formulated (for example, the expected rate of profit might be a distributed lag of past r's), but it is difficult to imagine a hypothesis that would lead to results qualitatively different from those obtained with rational or naive expectations unless r^e_{+1} is highly volatile with respect to changes in r.

Observe that the Cobb-Douglas utility function presents a special case in which the complexities of expectations can be ignored. For in the Cobb-Douglas case, desired saving is totally independent of the expected rate of profit! In this case Eq. (2.26) becomes

$$g = \beta \left[\frac{1}{a_1} - (1 + r) \right] - 1, \qquad (2.27)$$

and the results are independent of which particular expectations model we might use. The profit rate enters the determination of accumulation in Eq. (2.27) *only* through its (general-equilibrium) relationship to the wage rate, not through the income and substitution effects whose resultant is measured by β.

Suppose then we begin at time -1 with $W = W_{-1}$ in Figure 2.6 and $V_{-1} = k$. (For definiteness let $N_{-1} = 1$, but the precise value of N_{-1} does not really matter; only the ratio V_{-1} is relevant.) Does the path $\langle r_t, g_t \rangle$ converge to a neighborhood of $\langle r^*, n \rangle$?

The answer is no. According to (2.22) we have $\Delta W = 0$, and therefore $\Delta r = 0$. According to (2.23) we have $\Delta V < 0$. Hence in the next period, we have $\Delta W_{+1} < 0$ and $\Delta r_{+1} > 0$. But because of the negative slope of the saving equation in Figure 2.6, this means $\Delta V_{+1} < 0$. So once again, we have $\Delta W_{+2} < 0$, and $\Delta r_{+2} > 0$. Evidently, the successive short-run equilibria are further and further away from $\langle r^*, n \rangle$. (Observe that the process does eventually converge to a steady state at which economic activity ceases: $g = -1$, $r = r_{\max}$, $W = 0$. But only in a formal sense might this be called a steady-growth path.)

The root source of the instability is the *negative* slope of the saving function. If we form the matrix of partial derivatives of the equation system

$$G(W, V) = \theta \left(\frac{V}{k} - 1 \right) + W, \qquad H(W, V) = (1 + g) \frac{V}{1 + n},$$

we have, at an equilibrium characterized by $G(W, V) = W$ and $H(W, V) = V$,

$$\mathbf{J} = \begin{bmatrix} \dfrac{\partial G}{\partial W} & \dfrac{\partial G}{\partial V} \\[2ex] \dfrac{\partial H}{\partial r} \dfrac{dr}{dW} & \dfrac{\partial H}{\partial V} \end{bmatrix} = \begin{bmatrix} 1 & \dfrac{\theta}{k} \\[2ex] \dfrac{-s'(r)}{1 + n} & 1 \end{bmatrix}.$$

The equilibrium is unstable if any of the characteristic values of this matrix are greater than unity in absolute value. This will be the case if either of the Routh-Hurwitz inequalities

$$|\text{tr } \mathbf{J}| < |1 + \det \mathbf{J}| \tag{2.28}$$

or

$$|\det \mathbf{J}| < 1 \tag{2.29}$$

fails to hold (Kalman and Bertram 1960).

In the present case, one or the other of these two conditions *must* be violated. We have

$$\det \mathbf{J} = 1 + \frac{\theta}{k} \frac{s'(r)}{(1+n)},$$

so that condition (2.29) makes $s'(r) < 0$ a necessary condition for stability. However, we have $\text{tr } \mathbf{J} = 2$, so that condition (2.28) makes $s'(r) > 0$ equally necessary. Obviously both conditions cannot hold simultaneously

The difference-equation formulation of the stability question is misleading, however, in suggesting that the two cases $s'(r) < 0$ and $s'(r) > 0$ are symmetrical. In fact, in the case $s'(r) > 0$, instability is the result of the discrete characterization of time: the problem is one of overshooting and disappears in a continuous-time version of the model. By contrast, the instability of the case $s'(r) < 0$ is independent of how time is characterized and carries over into the continuous-time model. To see this, examine the continuous-time analog of Eqs. (2.22) and (2.23),

$$\dot{W} = \theta\left(\frac{V}{k} - 1\right), \qquad \dot{V} = (g - n)V.$$

In this case, stability hinges on the roots of the matrix

$$\mathbf{M} = \begin{bmatrix} 0 & \dfrac{\theta}{k} \\ -s'(r) & 0 \end{bmatrix}.$$

When $s'(r) > 0$, we have what is called "neutral stability." With $s'(r) > 0$, there is no guarantee of full employment even asymptotically, but neither is there a tendency for the economy to move ever further from equilibrium, as in the unstable case. With $s'(r) > 0$, the economy will oscillate around equilibrium characterized by $g = n$ and $g = s(r)$, and the *average* rate of unemployment will be zero.

By contrast, $\det \mathbf{M} < 0$ is sufficient to guarantee true instability, as in the discrete version of the model. Thus even with continuous adjustment, a downward-sloping saving function — $s'(r) < 0$ — would imply an unstable neoclassical equilibrium.

But how can the saving function slope downward? Typically, neo-classical supply functions are drawn to reflect positive, or at least nonnegative, price elasticities. In particular, a Cobb-Douglas utility function is customarily reflected in a saving function whose interest elasticity is zero. Why then does the saving function represented in Figure 2.6 show a negative elasticity with respect to r?

Neither ours nor the typical representation is incorrect. The difference is that the standard derivation of a completely inelastic saving function from a Cobb-Douglas utility function takes place in a partial-equilibrium setting, in which household resources (W in our case) are held constant as r is varied. By contrast, our saving function is derived in a general-equilibrium framework that reflects the interdependence of r and W embodied in Eq. (1.7). Thus in our case, the derivative of g with respect to r is a total derivative that includes the indirect effect of r on g through W along with the direct income and substitution effect of r in the denominator of $C^2(r)$. In the Cobb-Douglas case, direct effects just cancel out; β is constant and the general-equilibrium effect is all there is to reckon with.

Now it should be easy to see why desired saving falls as the profit rate rises: an increase in the profit rate lowers the wage rate, and (in the Cobb-Douglas case) desired saving is exactly proportional to wages. A moment's thought establishes that the "perverse" negative elasticity of the saving function must hold for *any* utility function for which overall income effects (including the indirect effects of changes in r on W) outweigh substitution effects. In any case $\beta(r)$ is confined to the unit-interval $[0, 1]$, and since $W(r) \rightarrow 0$ as $r \rightarrow r_{max}$, Eqs. (2.25) and (2.26) will have nonpositive derivatives in the neighborhood of r_{max}.

Even if the present models are all much too simple to permit more than an exposition of approaches to the study of capitalism, the possible perversity of the neoclassical saving function ought to give pause to defenders of the hypothesis of life-cycle maximization. For as we shall see as this book unfolds, it requires strong medicine to rid the saving function of its negative slope entirely. One way out is to assume a high degree of substitution between future and present consumption, but this is an assumption that even the most die-hard of the neoclassical faith would be hard put to defend. This possibility apart, we have two choices. First, we can abandon the fixed-coefficient model in favor of models with substitution between labor and seed corn. In Chapter 9 I shall show that technical substitution saves the day, at least partially: a high degree of technical substitution virtually guarantees the existence of a stable equilibrium.

Alternatively, we can modify the neoclassical saving function by dropping the assumption that all households are alike. In place of a homogeneous population, we might assume class divisions, with one class depending on profits for its income over its entire life, not just during retirement. In this case the saving function will once again have a "normal" (that is to say, positive) elasticity with respect to the rate of profit. We may continue to believe, if we must, that people allocate lifetime resources according to the dictates of a utility function. But neoclassical utility maximization would at best play a minor role in the explanation of the workings of a capitalist economy; the primary determinant would now be the division of the population into permanent classes of capitalists and workers. Such a division is central to the neo-Marxian and neo-Keynesian models expounded in the next two chapters.

Appendix: Two Complications to the Neoclassical Model

Leisure: Goods Choice

This section demonstrates that the leisure : goods choice plays no essential role in the determination of neoclassical equilibrium. If we replace the utility function and budget constraint by one that allows the household to determine its work effort, we have, with z the fraction of the year worked,

$$U(C^1, C^2, z) \tag{2.3}$$

and

$$C^1 + \frac{C^2}{1+r} = zW. \tag{2.4}$$

Fixing the scale of the model at z, we have

$$a_0 X = z$$

in place of

$$a_0 X = 1, \tag{1.6}$$

and

$$z = a_0 C + (1+g)a_1 z \tag{2.30}$$

in place of

$$1 = a_0 C + a_1(1+g). \tag{1.5}$$

Consequently, equilibrium in the seed-corn market requires

$$\frac{C^2(r)}{1+r} = z(1+g)\frac{a_1}{a_0} \tag{2.31}$$

rather than

$$\frac{C^2(r)}{1+r} = (1+g)\frac{a_1}{a_0}, \tag{2.10}$$

or in terms of corn per unit of corn,

$$g = \frac{1}{z}\frac{C^2(r)}{1+r}\frac{a_0}{a_1} - 1$$

in place of

$$g = \frac{C^2(r)}{1+r}\frac{a_0}{a_1} - 1.$$

Now z is a function of r in general; the functional relationship is determined by maximization of the utilty function (2.3) subject to the budget constraint (2.4). Thus, taking the full employment condition into acount, the existence of equilibrium depends on the existence of r such that

$$\frac{1}{z(r)}\frac{C^2(r)}{1+r}\frac{a_0}{a_1} - 1 = n. \tag{2.32}$$

The essence of the characterization of equilibrium is unchanged from the characterization in the main body of this chapter, which is why the role of choice between goods and leisure is judged an inessential complication.

Observe that although introducing a leisure : goods choice does not enrich the model, it is nevertheless the case that in general equilibrium wage and profit rates depend on leisure : goods preferences. Indeed W^* and r^* are independent of leisure : goods preferences only if the ratio of workers' desired saving to wage income is independent of the labor effort. That is, if we define $C^1(r, \bar{z})$ and $C^2(r, \bar{z})$ as the consumption pair that maximizes the utility function $U(C^1, C^2, \bar{z})$ subject to the budget constraint

$$C^1 + \frac{C^2}{1+r} = \bar{z}W$$

for fixed $\bar{z}$, a sufficient condition for independence of r^* and W^* from the equilibrium level of work effort z^* is that the equation

$$\frac{\dfrac{C^2(r, \bar{z})}{1+r}}{\bar{z}W} = \frac{\dfrac{C^2(r, 1)}{1+r}}{W} \tag{2.33}$$

hold for all $\bar{z}$ in the interval $[0, 1]$.

The sufficiency of Eq. (2.33) is easily established. Consider the expression for desired saving found on the left-hand side of Eq. (2.32). We have

$$s(r) = \frac{1}{z(r)} \frac{C^2(r)}{1+r} \frac{a_0}{a_1} - 1.$$

But from Eq. (2.33),

$$C^2(r, \bar{z}) = \bar{z} C^2(r, 1)$$

for all $\bar{z}$. Hence for all r,

$$C^2(r) = z(r) C^2(r, 1).$$

So for all r we have

$$s(r) = \frac{C^2(r, 1)}{1+r} \frac{a_0}{a_1} - 1, \qquad (2.34)$$

so that, if equilibrium exists, r^* and hence W^* are independent of $z(r)$.

A sufficient condition, by the way, for the desired saving rate to be independent of z is that the utility function be representable in the separable form

$$U(C^1, C^2, z) = u(C^1, C^2) h(z) + j(z).$$

Thus if $u(C^1, C^2)$ continues to be Cobb-Douglas, then the desired saving function represented in Eq. (2.34) will continue to have the form

$$s(r) = \beta \left[\frac{1}{a_1} - (1+r) \right] - 1, \qquad (2.35)$$

where β is, as before, the elasticity of utility with respect to future consumption. Since the essence of the problem of equilibrium is captured in the saving function represented in Eq. (2.35), it hardly seems worthwhile to complicate matters by taking account of leisure: goods choice.

Bequests

A second way in which the model might be elaborated is by introducing bequests. Like leisure, bequests complicate but do not enrich the model: the existence of equilibrium requires much the same restriction on the utility function as under a strict life-cycle model of saving behavior. Consider: equilibrium is still defined in terms of a combination of profit and growth rates for which the seed-corn market clears. Only now saving is tied up with bequest behavior. That is, the relevant utility function is

$$U(C^1, C^2, b^2),$$

and the budget constraint becomes

$$C^1 + \frac{C^2}{1+r} + \frac{b^2}{1+r} = W + b^1,$$

where b^2 represents the bequest to the subsequent generation and b^1 the inheritance from the previous generation. Thus, workers' effective demand for seed corn is no longer their net saving defined as the difference between income and consumption

$$S(r) = W(r) - C^1(r),$$

but the sum of saving and inheritance

$$S(r, b^1) + b^1,$$

with

$$S(r, b^1) = W(r) - C^1(r, b^1).$$

The seed market clears if

$$S(r, b^1) + b^1 = (1 + n)\frac{a_1}{a_0}. \tag{2.36}$$

Thus a new independent variable b^1 appears to enter into the determination of equilibrium—until we recognize that b^1 is not really exogenous. For in the steady state, each generation must leave to its successor an endowment per worker equal to what it received from its forebears. Hence for any r, the only values of b^1 we need consider are those for which the equation

$$b^2(r, b^1) = (1 + n)b^1 \tag{2.37}$$

holds. Figure 2.7 represents one solution, for a given r, to Eq. (2.37), assuming utility to be represented by the Cobb-Douglas utility function

$$U = (C^1)^\alpha (C^2)^\beta (b^2)^\gamma, \qquad \alpha + \beta + \gamma = 1.$$

Maximization of this utility function subject to the budget constraint implies

$$b^2(r, b^1) = \gamma(1 + r)[W(r) + b^1], \tag{2.38}$$

which along with (2.37) provides a unique solution for b^1 and b^2.

Note that the existence and uniqueness of the pair $\langle b^1(r), b^2(r) \rangle$ is the result of

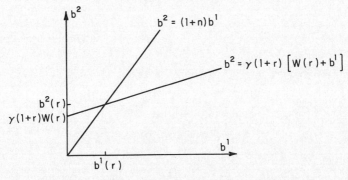

Figure 2.7 Endogenous determination of bequests

assuming a Cobb-Douglas utility function and restricting r by the inequality

$$\gamma(1 + r) < 1 + n,$$

which is to say,

$$r < \frac{1 + n - \gamma}{\gamma}.$$

For larger r, the steady-state bequest would have to be negative, which would require somewhat different property laws than those generally associated with capitalism. For non-Cobb-Douglas utility functions the possibility exists that the corresponding generalization of the system (2.37) and (2.38) has multiple solutions. If, for example, the elasticity of utility with respect to bequests changes monotonically with the size of one's inheritance, the bequest function that replaces Eq. (2.38) might intersect the ray defined by the equation $b^2 = (1 + r)b^1$ at two points. More complicated utility functions would lead to more complicated solutions $\langle b^1(r), b^2(r) \rangle$.

We may nevertheless assume a unique positive solution $\langle b^1(r), b^2(r) \rangle$ for each r, either by sticking with the Cobb-Douglas utility function and suitably restricting r, or by positing an increasing elasticity of utility with respect to bequests along with a positive intercept of the bequest function (2.38) on the b^1-axis (which says roughly that bequests are a luxury good). In either case, we can define not only bequests but also demand for food and seed corn as functions of r alone. Thus consumption demand becomes

$$C(r, n) = C^1(r) + \frac{C^2(r)}{1 + g},$$

where

$$C^i(r) = C^i(r, b^1(r)), \qquad i = 1, 2.$$

After taking account of Eq. (2.37), Eq. (2.36) becomes

$$S(r) + b^1(r) = (1 + n) \frac{a_1}{a_0}, \tag{2.39}$$

where

$$S(r) = W(r) - C^1(r, b^1(r)).$$

For the Cobb-Douglas utility function, we have

$$S(r) + b^1(r) = (\beta + \gamma)[W(r) + b^1(r)] \tag{2.40}$$

and, taking Eqs. (2.37) and (2.38) together,

$$(1 + n)b^1(r) = \gamma(1 + r)[W(r) + b^1(r)]$$

or

$$b^1(r) = \frac{\gamma(1 + r)W(r)}{1 + n - \gamma(1 + r)}. \tag{2.41}$$

Substituting from Eq. (2.41) into Eq. (2.40) and then back into Eq. (2.39), we have

$$(\beta + \gamma)\left[W(r) + \frac{\gamma(1 + r)W(r)}{1 + n - \gamma(1 + r)}\right] = (1 + n)\frac{a_1}{a_0}. \tag{2.42}$$

Upon simplifying Eq. (2.42), we find

$$(\beta + \gamma)\, W(r)\frac{a_0}{a_1} + \gamma(1 + r) - 1 = n,$$

which, after substituting from the price equation

$$W(r) = \frac{1 - a_1}{a_0} - r\frac{a_1}{a_0}, \tag{1.8}$$

gives

$$n = (\beta + \gamma)\left[\frac{1}{a_1} - (1 + r)\right] + \gamma(1 + r) - 1$$

or

$$n = \beta\left[\frac{1}{a_1} - (1 + r)\right] + \gamma\frac{1}{a_1} - 1.$$

If we compare this last expression with the corresponding equation for seed-corn market equilibrium in the simple life-cycle case,

$$n = \beta\left[\frac{1}{a_1} - (1 + r)\right] - 1,$$

it is clear that in the Cobb-Douglas case bequests only affect the equation for seed-corn market equilibrium by the addition of the constant term γ/a_1 to the right-hand side. It should be clear, therefore, that the introduction of bequests, like the introduction of leisure:goods choice, may embellish the neoclassical model but does not enrich it.

3 The Neo-Marxian Approach

It should be recognized at the outset that it is potentially misleading to cast Karl Marx in the mold of a steady-growth model, however necessary this might be to accomplish the comparative purposes of this book. Marx's primary concern lay elsewhere — with how modes of production develop, and, more important, with how old modes of production give way to new ones once they have exhausted their potential for growth. Moreover, in explaining both the development and breakdown of the capitalist mode of production, Marx placed particular emphasis on the role of crisis (what orthodox economists generally today refer to as recession), which is hardly compatible with a steady-state model. Nevertheless, one can formalize Marx's views on the determination of growth, distribution, and prices in a capitalist system in terms of a steady-state model without doing substantial violence to the approach, provided it is understood as a subset of Marxian theory and not as an attempt to represent the whole.

With this warning, let us turn to the model. The basic social units for Marx are not households, but classes defined in terms of the relations of production. Capitalists, small in number relative to the total population, own the seed corn and reap the net profits of corn growing, defined as the surplus remaining when wage payments are made and last year's seed corn is replaced. Most of the people own no seed corn whatsoever and earn a living by selling their labor power to capitalist planters.

For Marx, as for his classical forebears, labor is a "produced" commodity whose cost of production is defined by the material goods required to sustain the worker and his family. The family, it should be noted, enters the picture not out of sentiment but because the production of a labor force entails not only its availability from one day to the next, but also its availability from one generation to the next. Thus, production of a worker inevitably involves reproduction, and we might think of making the rate of growth of population dependent on real wages. There is some textual justification for this line of argument, but ultimately this approach seems to me more Malthusian than Marxian; as we shall see, in the Marxian model growth can come from outside as well as inside the present labor force.

The Marxian "subsistence" is not a biological subsistence bordering on starvation or even malnutrition. Adam Smith and David Ricardo had already attached considerable importance to cultural and institutional determinants of real wages. Marx went to even greater lengths to emphasize the historical, social, and moral elements (Marx 1865, p. 57 and 1867, p. 171) that enter into wage determination. Of these, class struggle is perhaps the most important single element in the Marxian view. But along with the organization and militance of the working class relative to capitalists, the subsistence wage reflects the average standard of living of potential wage workers as capitalist production is getting established.

Such a framework might lead one to expect the real wage to rise or fall according to shifts in the relative power of contending classes. How then are we to interpret the general historical tendency of wages to increase over the past century and a half throughout western Europe, North America, and Japan? Does this general upward trend in real wages imply a steady growth in working-class power? Not necessarily, for the present model omits technological change, which has increased dramatically the size of the pie whose division is at stake. In a world with technological change, the real wage rate can increase so as to maintain for workers a roughly constant share of the national product without a fundamental shift in the balance of class power. With technological change, it is more reasonable to focus on the wage *share* than on the wage *rate* as the reflection of relative power of workers and capitalists. It is only in a bare-bones model such as ours, with a given technology, that the wage rate becomes the relevant variable.

Indeed, the essence of the Marxian approach lies neither in a constant wage rate nor in a constant wage share, but — in stark contrast to both the neoclassical model of Chapter 2 and the neo-Keynesian model of Chapter 4 — in an exogenous role for wages in the determination of equilibrium. Exogeneity translates into a constant real wage rate only in the context of steady-growth equilibrium in the simplest model possible.

For the present, it will be assumed that all wages are consumed. This point receives further attention down the line, but for now we make the simplest assumption that captures the essence of a Marxian analysis of the *capitalist* mode of production, namely a sharp division between workers and capitalists as classes. Individual workers may save and become capitalists. And individual capitalists may fail and become workers. It is not castes but classes that are at issue, and individual mobility affects the argument only insofar as it undermines class consciousness and weakens class power.

The point of the present assumption is that whatever may happen to individuals, workers do not *as a class* acquire meaningful quantities of the means of production. To a first approximation, such saving as the working *class* might do (for example, saving that takes the form of owner-occupied housing) can be lumped with consumption, and the analytically neat assumption that all wages are consumed can be adopted — at least for the steady state. Later, as I have indicated, this assumption will be relaxed to allow for positive accumulation on the part of workers.

Capitalists, by contrast, will for the present be assumed to consume nothing. The drive to accumulation implicit in this assumption is not, it should be emphasized, primarily psychological. No explanation could be further from the Marxian method than one that relies on how people's heads are screwed on. The psychological element enters only in assuming that initially there is at least *one* capitalist who regularly plows back his profits into expanding the means of production. After sufficient time has elasped, the leading capitalist necessarily becomes the normal capitalist.

The essence of the accumulation drive for Marx lies in translating the relatively weak assumption that one accumulation-minded capitalist exists into a law of capitalist survival *à la* Darwin. To do so, Marx made use of a microeconomic model of production that appears to assume both increasing returns to scale and the embodiment of technological progress in new capital goods. Those who accumulate capital goods more rapidly, therefore, can take advantage of lower-cost production methods and get an edge on more sluggish competitors. Indeed, capitalists who dissipate more profits in consumption than those who lead the accumulation race will ultimately find not only their share of the total stock of capital goods becoming progressively smaller, but the unit value of their capital goods dwindling in relation to the more productive capital goods acquired by the leaders. This makes it reasonable for Marx to take the accumulation rate of the leading capitalists as the norm, for the others can be assumed to have fallen by the wayside in the process of reaching the steady state.

An upper limit on capitalists' propensity to save can be fixed by abstracting from debt financing, that is, by assuming self-financing for all capitalists. Then, provided there are initially *any* capitalists who regularly reinvest all profits, it is this subset who will eventually dominate, regardless of the initial distribution of saving propensities.

Actually, for purposes of analyzing the steady state, Marx's emphasis on increasing returns to scale and "embodied" technological progress is frosting on the cake, and can be easily dispensed with. It suffices to assume that capitalists' investment is self-financing, and that the initial distribution of capitalists over saving propensities includes a nonempty subset of capitalists who plow back all profits into expanding the means of production. This subset of capitalists will eventually dominate with or without increasing returns to scale. By assigning the winnowing process to prehistory, we can analyze the steady state on the basis of the assumption that all profits are saved.

In any case, it is not necessary to assume that *all* profits are saved; it is only analytically simpler to do so. At a latter stage in the argument I shall allow for capitalists' consumption along with workers' saving.

It should be noted that I consistently abstract from the problem of translating saving into investment. As near as I can tell, the importance of this problem for Marx lay in its role in the analysis of economic fluctuations, an area beyond the scope of the present inquiry. Apart from this problem (the so-called "realization" problem), net investment and profit as well are determined residually, as the amount of surplus remaining after wages are paid and the previous stock of seed corn is replenished. Expressed as a ratio to the stock of seed corn, the quantity of surplus corn becomes a profit and growth rate.

What happens to the natural rate of growth n, the exogenously given rate of growth of the labor force? At this point in the story it is, in a word, irrelevant. Insofar as Marx can be cast in a steady-state framework at all, it is in a steady state of the *capitalist sector*, not a steady state for the economy as a whole. Accordingly, the capitalist sector is assumed to coexist, indeed to compete, with other modes of production. A growth rate g in excess of n means only that the capitalist sector grows at the expense of other modes; g less than n means that the capitalist sector is declining relatively.

But does this not vitiate the idea of a steady state? Isn't a steady state properly *defined* in terms of a "long run" in which $g = n$ is a binding constraint? The answer to both questions, I think, is no. In the context of this book, the steady state is an analytic device whose sole purpose is to permit us to abstract from economic fluctuations, and for this purpose the "long run" need only be of the order of a generation.

There is nothing inherent in the concept of a steady state that makes it essential to assume the maintenance of a rate of growth of employment equal to the rate of growth of the labor force.

Neither is it, on a finite planet, inherently more realistic to define the steady state in terms of full employment of an exogenously given labor force, as the neoclassical model does. In short, to characterize the steady state by full employment as the neoclassical model does is to make a particular assumption about competition in the labor market—namely, that the real wage equilibrates the supply of labor with its demand—rather than to offer a neutral and natural definition. The absence of this assumption in the Marxian model involves only a shift in focus from the economy as a whole (in which differences in the mode of production are ignored) to the capitalist mode of production itself and a shift in the interpretation of the long run over which the steady state is defined. This last shift does not, I hasten to add, absolve us from the requirement to analyze the significance of departure of g from n. It rather allows us to posit an alternative mechanism for adjusting labor demand and supply, one that hinges on quantity adjustments between the capitalist sector and the rest of the economy. We shall come back to this question after the mechanics of analyzing the steady state have been worked through.

The Classical Saving Equation

Now for these mechanics. To begin, recall the equations relating growth to consumption per worker, and profits to real wages per worker:

$$1 = a_0 C + a_1(1 + g), \tag{1.5}$$

$$1 = W a_0 + (1 + r)a_1. \tag{1.7}$$

Subtracting one from another of these two equations leads directly to the following relationship between wages and consumption, on the one hand, and profits and growth, on the other:

$$(W - C) = (g - r)\frac{a_1}{a_0}. \tag{3.1}$$

If all wages are consumed and all profits are saved, then

$$W = C, \tag{3.2}$$

and the left-hand side of Eq. (3.1) vanishes. It follows directly that profits per worker, ra_1/a_0, equal net investment per worker, ga_1/a_0, or in other words that

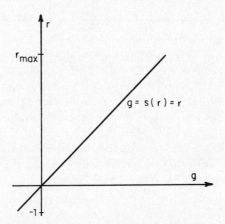

Figure 3.1 The classical saving function

$$g = s(r) = r. \tag{3.3}$$

Equation (3.3) is represented in Figure 3.1. Note that the domain of this functional relationship between r and g is $[-1, r_{max}]$, where r_{max} is defined, as in the neoclassical case, by setting $W = 0$ in Eq. (1.7).

No particular stress should be laid on the precise form of Eq. (3.3). For one thing, it is not peculiarly Marxian, stemming as it does from the classical saving assumption alone: if wages and consumption are assumed equal, then profits and saving are bound to be equal, and profit and growth *rates* are simply profit and saving expressed as ratios to the capital stock. In any case, as we shall see, the precise equality of formula (3.3) no longer holds once capitalists are assumed to consume part of their income, and workers to save part of theirs. It *is* of importance that the classical saving function in Figure 3.1, in contrast with the neoclassical, slopes upward. As we shall see in Chapter 6, this property is preserved even when the stringent assumptions of Eq. (3.3) are relaxed.

The Labor Theory of Value

What makes the model Marxian is the union of a saving assumption like that reflected in Eq. (3.3) with a distinctive explanation of what determines the rate of profit: a rate of exploitation that emerges from the labor theory of value. In my view, the underlying idea is best captured by a definition that says that *exploitation* occurs whenever (1) a worker's annual production of corn exceeds the quantity of corn required for the replenishment of seed and his own subsistence, and (2) workers do not exercise control over the disposition of surplus production. Since by assumption capitalists own and control the means of production, the capitalist mode of production obviously meets both criteria, but in general the existence of exploitation is as much a political question as it is an economic one: the mere existence of surplus is not determining. For example, in a surplus-producing society in which the means of production are collectively owned, the existence of exploitation hinges on whether the exercise of political power is broadly shared by citizens or monopolized by a particular class, group, or party. By this test, many societies in which the dominant mode of production is generally reckoned to be "socialist" are as exploitative as societies in which capitalism predominates.

The *rate of exploitation* depends on the conditions of production and the subsistence wage. In principle the relationship is straightforward: the labor theory of value assigns to every commodity a value defined by its "cost," as measured by the labor time embodied in its production. It defines *surplus value* as the difference between the value of a bushel of corn (the labor time required to produce one bushel) and the value of the embodied labor power. Under capitalism, the rate of exploitation is the *rate of surplus value*, defined as the ratio of surplus value per worker to the value of labor power.

To quantify this theory requires us to be more explicit about the concept of "embodied labor power." Clearly the labor power represented by a bushel of corn includes its direct (living) labor content: the time spent planting, weeding, and harvesting. But it includes as well the time spent producing the seed for this year's crop. And what about two years ago? Indeed, the indirect (dead) labor of previous seasons is an infinite sum stretching backward to the very beginning of time: the labor time required last year for this year's seed, the labor time required two years back to grow the seed for last year's seed, and so forth—even to the tiniest grain of seed from which present corn production putatively springs. Table 3.1 summarizes past labor-time requirements for this year's crop. The sum of direct and indirect labor time is thus

$$a_0 + a_0 a_1 + a_0 a_1^2 + \cdots + a_0 a_1^i + \cdots,$$

which equals

$$\frac{a_0}{1 - a_1} \tag{3.4}$$

provided the system is "productive," which is to say, provided

$$a_1 < 1.$$

Table 3.1. Labor-time requirements for the current crop

Time	Labor requirement (man-years per bushel)
This year	a_0
Last year	$a_0 a_1$
Two years back	$a_0 a_1^2$
.	.
.	.
.	.
t years back	$a_0 a_1^t$
.	.
.	.

The value of one man-year of labor power is measured by the amount of labor time required directly and indirectly to provide a single worker (and his family) with the corn that makes up the subsistence wage W: the product of the value of a single bushel $a_0(1 - a_1)$, multiplied by the number of bushels W. Denoting the value of labor power by v, we have

$$v = \frac{a_0}{1 - a_1} W. \tag{3.5}$$

Finally, we may calculate the labor-time value of seed corn by the same principles; a_1 bushels embody

$$\frac{a_0}{1 - a_1} a_1 \tag{3.6}$$

man-years of labor time.

With the help of expressions (3.4), (3.5), and (3.6), we can easily show that the value of a worker's maintenance and the seed he uses during one year do not necessarily exhaust the value of the corn he produces. The difference

$$s = \frac{a_0}{1 - a_1} \times \frac{1}{a_0} - \frac{a_0}{1 - a_1} W - \frac{a_0}{1 - a_1} \times \frac{a_1}{a_0}$$

$$s = \begin{bmatrix} \text{labor time} \\ \text{per bu.} \\ \text{of corn} \\ \text{output} \end{bmatrix} \times \begin{bmatrix} \text{gross} \\ \text{output} \\ \text{per worker} \\ \text{per year} \end{bmatrix} - \begin{bmatrix} \text{labor time} \\ \text{per man-} \\ \text{year of} \\ \text{subsistence} \end{bmatrix} - \begin{bmatrix} \text{labor} \\ \text{time} \\ \text{per bu.} \\ \text{of corn} \end{bmatrix} \times \begin{bmatrix} \text{seed} \\ \text{corn} \\ \text{per} \\ \text{man-year} \end{bmatrix}$$

represents surplus value per worker:

$$s = \frac{1}{1 - a_1} (1 - a_0 W - a_1). \tag{3.7}$$

Now substitute from the price equation, (1.7), to obtain

$$s = \frac{a_1}{1 - a_1} r. \tag{3.8}$$

Thus positive surplus value and a positive profit rate go together, a result that is as easy to prove as it is intuitive in the one-good model.[1] Surplus value per worker is equal to the capital : output ratio multiplied by the rate of profit, which is to say the share of net profit in net output.

We can now combine Eqs. (3.5) and (3.8) into an expression for the rate of exploitation (ε) or the rate of surplus value (s/v):

$$\varepsilon = \frac{s}{v} = \frac{ra_1}{Wa_0}, \tag{3.9}$$

which is to say that the rate of exploitation is equal to the ratio of (net) profit to wages.[2]

For Marx, a given rate of exploitation is the starting point from which the price equation is solved. That is, for a given level of subsistence W^*, we can determine s^* and v^* directly from Eqs. (3.7) and (3.5); with $(s/v)^* = \varepsilon^*$ given, we can solve for r by substituting from (3.9) into (1.7). We have

$$\frac{r^* a_1}{1 - a_1} = \frac{\varepsilon^*}{1 + \varepsilon^*}. \tag{3.10}$$

With this interpretation, the labor theory of value becomes a theory of the profit share. Given the saving function $g = r$, it is a theory of growth too.

Equilibrium

It is a separate question—one to which we shall return—whether or not it is a *useful* theory. This much is clear: we could go *directly* from a subsistence wage W^* to the equilibrium profit rate r^*, as in Figure 3.2.

1. In its multiple-good version, this result is the basis of what Michio Morishima (1973) calls the Fundamental Marxian Theorem, originally proved by Nobuo Okishio (1963).

2. Note that with "constant capital" per unit of output defined by $c = a_1/(1 - a_1)$, we have $s/c = r$, a departure from the standard Marxian formula $s/(v + c) = r$. This departure from the usual equation is occasioned by the assumption that wages are paid at harvest time and hence do not form part of "capital."

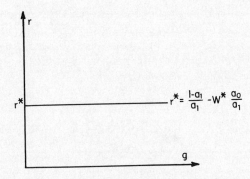

Figure 3.2 Subsistence wage and equilibrium profit

With the addition of the saving function (3.3), the entire equilibrium is determinate, as Figure 3.3 shows. Starting from W^* on the horizontal axis separating the second and third quadrants, we determine the equilibrium rate of profit r^* by means of the price equation (1.7). We move then to the first quadrant to determine the equilibrium growth

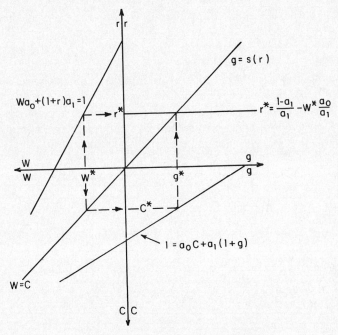

Figure 3.3 Neo-Marxian equilbrium

GROWTH AND DISTRIBUTION

rate g^* by combining the profit-rate equation with the saving function (3.3), and finally to the fourth quadrant to determine C^*.

In this construction, the labor theory of value is bypassed altogether. Equilibrium $\langle r^*, g^* \rangle$ is determined from W^* and the classical saving equation alone. The complete system is

$$W = W^* \tag{3.11}$$

$$g = s(r) = r \tag{3.3}$$

$$1 = a_0 C + a_1(1 + g) \tag{1.5}$$

$$1 = W a_0 + (1 + r) a_1. \tag{1.7}$$

What about causality? Early on we said that Eq. (1.5) defines a mapping that associates growth rates and levels of consumption to one another without any causal implications. In the neoclassical model this equation became a causal relationship by virtue of the assumption that the rate of growth is determined exogenously and the level of consumption is determined residually. Here causality runs the other way: according to the neo-Marxian model, the wage rate is determined by an exogenously given standard, and this along with the saving function determines the rate of growth, as well as the rate of profit, residually. In contrast with the neoclassical model, in which resource allocation determines income distribution, causality here runs from distribution to growth. Table 3.2 summarizes causal relationships in the neo-Marxian model.

It would be misleading, however, to impute a role to the subsistence wage symmetric to the role of the natural rate of growth in the neoclassical model. For the production coefficients, particularly a_0, are not purely technological parameters in the neo-Marxian model; the Marxian view stresses the dependence of these coefficients on the cultural and institutional structure in which production takes place, what Marx called the social relations of production. I shall return to this point at the end of the chapter.

Observe that the rate of profit is conceptually distinct from the

Table 3.2. Causality in the neo-Marxian model

Exogenous	Endogenous
a_1, a_0 W^* $g = r$ $\Big\} \rightarrow$	g^*, r^*, C^*

neoclassical idea of profit as interest, as a return to waiting, the level of which is determined by the trinity of technology, biology, and utility. Of these three factors, only one, technology, continues to play a role in the neo-Marxian characterization of the profit rate. Of course, technology is not the sole determinant. Indeed, the distinguishing feature of the present model is the role accorded cultural and institutional factors, such as class power, in the determination of the profit rate. It is a uniquely Marxian notion that the profit rate varies directly with the power of capitalists and inversely with the power of workers.

We have yet to deal with the issue of stability, but this is quickly done. Having abstracted from technological progress and economic fluctuations, the only factor that might change the subsistence wage permanently is a change in the balance of power between classes. If we take class power as stable, however, then any transitory shocks that move the wage away from the equilibrium should be self-correcting. Thus we have

$$W = -\theta(W_{-1} - W^*) + W_{-1}, \tag{3.12}$$

which — provided $0 < \theta < 2$ — makes any equilibrium stable.

This result is noteworthy, especially in comparison with the corresponding neoclassical result: it is, to say the least, paradoxical that a model designed to discover the internal contradictions of capitalism produces a stable equilibrium under very general assumptions about adjustment speeds, whereas the equilibrium in a model designed to illustrate the inherent harmony of capitalism leads readily to instability. The neo-Marxian result is, however, an artifact of the constraints I have imposed on this book in order to facilitate its comparative purposes; the main culprit is the omission of any consideration of economic fluctuations. The neo-Marxian stability result tells us more about the limitations of this enterprise than it does about the neo-Marxian model.

$g^* \neq n$: The Reserve Army

Nevertheless, the model captures important Marxian insights. But the most interesting of them have only been hinted at. The point of departure for further analysis lies in the definition of a Marxian equilibrium in terms of steady growth of a specific — capitalist — sector rather than in terms of growth of an economy as a whole. The implication of this definition is, as we have seen, that it is only by accident that the steady-state rate of growth of employment is equal to the rate of growth of the labor force. That is, if the natural rate of reproduction expands the labor force at the annual rate n, then only by chance would n be equal to g^*. What are the consequences of a divergence between g^* and n? The insight into the nature of capitalism afforded by the Marxian answer to this question is perhaps the most powerful argument for forcing Marx into a steady-state model.

Suppose $g^* > n$. We may assume, if we wish, that initially employment within the capitalist mode of production is small relative to the total labor force of the unit—whether conceived politically, socially, or geographically—in which the capitalist sector is embedded. Thus the capitalist sector can grow for a time by drawing on labor resources of other sectors, causing them to shrink, first relatively, then absolutely.

Other sectors of production thus constitute a "reserve army" of workers for the capitalist sector when g^* exceeds n. Various modes of production can be distinguished both from the capitalist mode and from each other. And the historical norm over the last two centuries, in the West at least, has been for the capitalist mode to grow at their expense. One such mode is the "petty commodity" mode of production composed of small proprietors and tenants in agriculture and crafts. Petty-commodity production resembles capitalism in that production is for the market rather than for the direct use of the producer, but differs in that those who control the (nonhuman) means of production also supply much if not all of the labor power, with wage labor playing a secondary role. The petty-commodity mode can be subdivided into a "petty tenant" mode and a "petty proprietor" mode, distinguished by whether land and capital goods are leased or owned.

Not all modes of production center on commodities, that is, on markets. A noncommodity mode of production is the "subsistence" mode in which production takes place primarily for the direct use of the producer. The archetypical example of a subsistence mode is the self-sufficient agricultural or hunting-gathering household, but the provision of such services as cooking, cleaning, and child rearing within the household in contemporary society also constitutes a separate and distinct "subsistence" mode of production that has been an important source of labor power to modern capitalism. The progressive incorporation of women into the capitalist mode of production is at once the cause and the consequence of the breakdown of this form of subsistence production.

No matter how small the capitalist mode of production might be as we first observe its operation, it cannot persist in growing in excess of the natural rate of growth n without absorbing the entire population of any given geographical, social, or political unit. At this point, according to the neo-Marxian argument, one of two things can happen. Either the pressure of demand for labor on supply will increase the steady-state real wage W^* sufficiently to bring the rate of profit and growth into line with the natural rate of growth (Marx 1867, pp. 619–621), or the "given" geographical, social, or political unit must be expanded.

As for the first argument, it is appropriate to observe that Marx apparently understood demand and supply conditions as much in terms of how they might affect systematic (if not necessarily organized) struggle between bosses and workers as in terms of their impact through the Invisible Hand of atomistic competition, the only way supply and demand are understood in neoclassical theory. Neither is the Marxian adjustment of g^* to n the smooth approach characteristic of neoclassical theory.

In any case, the adjustment of the real wage as a means of bringing g^* into line with n is—again in contrast with the neoclassical model— only one of the mechanisms that might operate in the neo-Marxian model, and a second line of argument is without doubt more distinctively Marxian. Extending the geographical, political, or social unit in response to pressures of demand for workers can take one of two forms: either the mountain can be brought to Mahomet, or Mahomet can be brought to the mountain. Either capital goods can be exported to make use of labor resources beyond the original unit, or labor resources can be imported. Historically, both forms of adjusting g^* and n have been utilized. Capitalist production has been progressively if unevenly extended geographically, politically, and socially; and immigration has played an important historical role in the development of capitalism, above all in North America.

Nor are these methods of coping with an excess of g^* over n relics of the past. The export of capital goods and of the capitalist mode of production continues to be a feature of contemporary capitalism, and the reliance of the center of European capitalism in the north and the west of the continent on the importation of labor power from its periphery to the south and the east is one of the most striking features of the post–World War II period. Indeed, of the economically powerful nations in which the capitalist mode is dominant, only the United States and Japan have had large enough untapped domestic reserve armies to escape recourse to external ones.[3]

It is important to bear in mind that reserve armies are not spontaneously integrated into the capitalist mode of production. Marx rightly insisted on a process of *creation* and *re-creation* of reserve armies, and the deliberation behind this process becomes especially clear in the context

3. This statement may pay insufficient attention to aliens who live and work illegally in the United States, whose numbers are intrinsically difficult to measure.

of the politics of immigration. This is not to argue for a conspiracy theory of capitalist development; it is rather to point out the limitations of the Invisible Hand. (It should be noted for completeness that Marx laid great stress on labor-displacing technological progress as a means of recruiting people into the reserve army, an aspect of reality from which our highly simplified production model abstracts.)

The situation is not symmetric when $g*$ is less than n. In the first place (and this certainly distinguishes the neo-Marxian from the neoclassical argument) there is no necessity for $g*$ or n to adjust at all in this case! Nothing prevents the capitalist mode of production from declining relative to other modes in the same social, political, or geographical unit, and such decline is after all the sole implication of equilibrium in which $g*$ happens to be below n.

Some will find in this configuration echoes of the reality of advanced capitalism, especially if technological progress is allowed for, so that an increasing real wage can mask the tendency of employment to grow at less than the natural rate. (More on this in Chapter 5, under *Secular Stagnation: $g* < n$.*) Personally I am more impressed by the tendency of the capitalist mode of production to grow at the expense of other modes than by its putative tendency to stagnate, masked or unmasked. Whatever one's opinion on this issue, however, the power of the neo-Marxian model to encompass both possibilities must be counted an analytic strength.

The Social Element in the Determination of a_0 and a_1

One final point. In the neoclassical model we took the coefficients a_0 and a_1 to be technologically given. By contrast, the neo-Marxian model, as we have observed, stresses the social element in the determination of input-output relationships. Even with only one technology available for growing corn, the number of man-years that it takes for planting, weeding, and harvesting will depend on the intensity of the work effort and on the organization of work.

The neoclassical model, abstracting from conflict born of differences in the way people relate to the production process, resolves these issues in terms of atomistic exchange between households each pursuing its own utility. Thus the intensity of work becomes, like the length of the working day, a question of leisure:goods choices. In the Marxian model, however, the extent and intensity of work are assumed to be determined by struggle between workers and capitalists.

At the core of the Marxian emphasis on class struggle as a determinant of what are otherwise held to be technological parameters is a distinction between labor and nonhuman commodities. On the one hand, as we have seen, labor is, like other commodities, perceived to have a cost of production based on a subsistence wage. There is, however, an important difference. What the worker sells is not so many bushels of corn delivered to the capitalist's barn, but so many days of work, or in Marxist terminology, so much labor power. Nor is that the end of the matter, with the capitalist free to convert labor power to other commodities as best he can, in other words free to make the most productive use possible of the time he has purchased. Rather the length of the working day, its intensity, the very organization of the production process, remain objects of struggle. Indeed, outside the neoclassical camp, the struggle over the extent and intensity of work becomes an important element in the explanation of changes or inertia in the organization of work. For example, the dramatic shift from dispersed production characteristic of the putting-out system to the centralized workplace, the manufactory, in the early decades of the nineteenth century in England can be understood largely in terms of this struggle (Marglin 1974).

As in the determination of the real wage rate, moral elements enter along with naked power. The question of what constitutes a fair day's work—the length and intensity of the working day—is indeed the other side of the coin to what constitutes a fair day's pay.

It is not only the labor coefficient a_0 that is affected; a similar argument can be made about the capital:output ratio a_1. Even with only one basic technology available, workers and capitalists might struggle over the amount of ancillary capital introduced for reasons of safety or comfort. It might be objected that such an argument undermines the assumption of a single technology more fundamentally than the parallel argument with respect to a_0. In a strict sense it probably does, but no matter. The real issue is not a semantic one, which in any case disappears in Chapter 9 when we consider the variable-proportions case. Once variable proportions are admitted, the question becomes one of whether input proportions are determined by the interaction of nature with utility-maximizing exchange among atomistic households or by the interaction of nature and class struggle.

The important point for present purposes is that in the neo-Marxian model the resolution of the struggle over the conditions of work, and hence over a_0 and a_1, is inseparable from the determination of equilibrium growth and distribution. For with the subsistence wage given, the coefficients a_0 and a_1 determine the rates of surplus value, profit, and growth.

Moreover, the struggle over the determination of a_0 and a_1 feeds back upon the determination of the subsistence wage. Not only does class power affect the choice of technique, but the technique affects the degree to which workers rather than capitalists control the work process, and accordingly the relative power of the two groups in bargaining over wages. It is for these reasons that Marxism and other nonneoclassical approaches emphasize the production process and particularly the social relations of production in economic analysis. By contrast, the neoclassical approach tends to dismiss these considerations as "noneconomic," as if that terminology decided anything.

Nonetheless, the comparative purposes of this book preclude me from developing this aspect of the neo-Marxian model. As I said at the outset of this chapter, I do not pretend to a complete exposition of the neo-Marxian approach to economics, but only of those areas or questions that intersect with neoclassical and neo-Keynesian concerns.

4 The Neo-Keynesian Approach

It might be well to sketch the Keynesian background that justifies the label "neo-Keynesian" on what follows. Indeed, it is not universally recognized that Keynes, at least the Keynes of the *General Theory* (1936), had a theory of distribution. And no wonder: neither Keynes nor his American followers stressed this aspect of his pathbreaking work. (The title modestly limits its scope to *Employment, Interest, and Money.*) Nevertheless there *is* a Keynesian theory of distribution, and the neo-Keynesian theory is best understood as an extension of this theory to the longrun.

The Keynesian Background

Let me start from what should be safe common ground. In the Keynesian model investment demand, represented by the "marginal efficiency of capital" schedule, is exogenous. Though couched in formal language, the marginal efficiency of capital is essentially a subjective parameter, since "prospective yields," the streams of quasi-rents that are discounted to determine marginal efficiencies, are for Keynes more the product of the state of confidence — of the strength of "animal spirits" that "urge to action rather than inaction" — than of objective calculation (Keynes 1936, chap. 12, especially pp. 148–150, 161–163).

The quantity of investment demanded at any point in time depends not only on the marginal efficiency of capital schedule, but on the (long-term) rate of interest determined by the interaction of the quantity of money and the asset preferences of individuals and firms. The

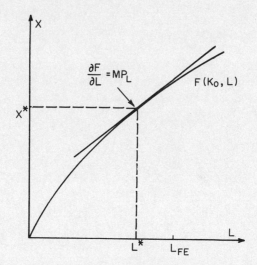

Figure 4.1 The relationship between output and employment

precise details of this interaction, though essential to Keynes's argument, need not detain us here.

In a manner that has long since become the stuff of introductory economics courses, the quantity of investment demand and the propensity to consume combine through the "multiplier" to determine an equilibrium level of output. The equilibrium level of output determines the level of employment according to a variable-proportions production function relating output (X) to employment (L) and capital (K_0).[1] This relationship is shown in Figure 4.1.

The most significant implication of the *General Theory* is of course that an equilibrium level of output such as $X*$ might lead to an equilibrium level of employment $L*$ well below full employment, L_{FE}. But for our purposes the relevance of this diagram lies elsewhere, specifically in its implications for the distribution of income between wages and profits. Keynes saw no reason to disown the notion that in equilibrium the real wage must be equal to the marginal productivity of labor, so that the real wage corresponding to the equilibrium $\langle X*, L* \rangle$ is given by the slope of the production function at this point in Figure 4.1. (This is but a logical consequence of competitive profit maximization under conditions of variable proportions and by no means the same thing as marginal-productivity *theory* of distribution—more on

---

1. In the Keynesian context of the short run, variable proportions should offend not even the severest critics of this concept since capital can be expressed in physical terms.

the difference between the two in Chapter 10.) The essential reason for Keynes to be concerned with distribution is that each producer must be in equilibrium if $\langle X^*, L^* \rangle$ is to be an equilibrium for the economy as a whole. But this can only be true if profits are at a maximum, which in turn requires, under competitive conditions, the marginal productivity of labor to equal the real wage.

But how does this equality come about? We seem to have used up all degrees of freedom in determining equilibrium. Not quite: enter here the idea that the wage bargain is made in money rather than in real terms; this allows macroeconomic equilibrium to be translated into microeconomic equilibrium — in other words, it allows the equilibrium for the economy as a whole to be translated into an equilibrium for each producer. Letting W represent the money wage and P the price level, the assumption that wage bargains are made in money terms allows P to adjust the real wage (W/P) to the equilibrium level of the marginal productivity of labor (MP_L).

Note that the price level *can* adjust. I think it is fair to charge Keynes with at the very least an amazing lack of attention to the *mechanism* by which the price level adjusts the real wage to marginal productivity. With output determined by aggregate demand, one can appeal to a Walrasian adjustment process, by which the price level adjusts the supply of goods to the given level of demand, at the same time adjusting the real wage to the marginal productivity of labor: competitive supply is determined by marginal cost (MC), so that at equilibrium $P = MC$ and — since $MC \equiv W/MP_L$ — we also have $MP_L = W/P$. The only problem with this argument is its decidedly un-Keynesian flavor. In the Keynesian model outputs rather than prices generally do the adjusting, so an appeal to price adjustment seems at least a bit contrived — Walras *ex machina,* as it were.

In any case, the lines of causality in the Keynesian model, if not all the mechanisms, are clear: investment demand is the volatile variable that drives the system, determining (along with the stock of money, asset preferences, and the propensity to consume) equilibrium output, which in turn determines employment; together output and employment, given the production function, determine the marginal productivity of labor, which, through adjustments in the price level, sets the real wage. Schematically,

$$I \rightarrow X \rightarrow L \rightarrow MP_L \rightarrow \frac{W}{P}.$$

A similar causality characterizes the neo-Keynesian approach to growth and distribution, albeit in a different time frame. Indeed it seems reasonable to describe neo-Keynesian growth and distribution theory as the transposition of the basic ideas of the Keynesian model, designed to respond to short-run problems, to the long run. The question of whether or not this transposition is justified I shall postpone until the basic task of exposition is completed.

Harrod: A Bridge to Neo-Keynesianism

Roy Harrod's deservedly famous growth model (1948) serves as a bridge between Keynes and the neo-Keynesians. Harrod's "warranted" rate of growth, the equivalent of our steady-state $g*$, is determined by two functional relationships, one relating the output : capital ratio to the rate of growth of output, the other relating growth in capital to growth in output. The first is based on a tautology. Denoting the incremental output : capital ratio by $\Delta X / \Delta K$, we may write

$$\frac{\Delta X}{\Delta K} = \frac{X_{-1}}{\Delta K} \frac{\Delta X}{X_{-1}}. \tag{4.1}$$

Now $X_{-1} / \Delta K$ is the inverse of the realized saving ratio, ΔK representing additions made *last year* to the capital stock available this year for production, and $\Delta X / X_{-1}$ the rate of growth of output. If we require that fulfillment of desired saving intentions be a condition of equilibrium, Eq. (4.1) ceases to be a mere identity with $\Delta K / X_{-1}$ equal to the ex post, realized saving ratio; it becomes an equilibrum relationship, with $\Delta K / X_{-1}$ equal to the ex ante, desired saving ratio. Letting s stand for the desired ratio of saving to income, we may write this relationship as

$$\frac{\Delta X}{\Delta K} = \frac{1}{s} \frac{\Delta X}{X_{-1}}. \tag{4.2}$$

Observe that Eq. (4.2) implicitly ignores depreciation and suppresses the difference between gross and net income: the symbol s conventionally denotes a net rather than a gross saving rate, but X is used in this book to denote gross output. Nothing is lost thereby: depreciation plays no crucial role in Harrod's model. If we assume further that desired saving is a constant fraction of income whatever its level—hardly necessary to the argument but a useful expository simplification—Eq. (4.2) becomes a linear relationship between the two variables $\Delta X / \Delta K$ and $\Delta X / X_{-1}$, as illustrated in Figure 4.2.

The second equilibrium relationship connects the rate of growth of output with the desired rate of investment expressed as a ratio to the capital stock. It is a dynamic counterpart of the Keynesian investment

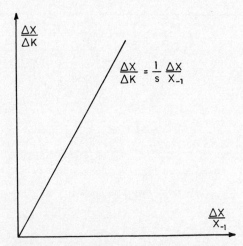

Figure 4.2 Output growth and the incremental capital:output ratio: The saving equation

function, with a shift in emphasis from the rate of interest to the rate of expansion of production as the explicit determinant of desired investment. In essence, Harrod's argument (1948, chap. 3, especially pp. 81–87) is that desired investment responds positively to the rate of growth of output. The greater the rate of expansion of production, that is, the greater is $\Delta X/X_{-1}$, the greater is the rate of desired investment, or growth of the capital stock, $\Delta K/K_{-1}$.[2]

Figure 4.3 illustrates the Harrodian investment function,

$$\frac{\Delta K}{K_{-1}} = i\left(\frac{\Delta X}{X_{-1}}\right) \tag{4.3}$$

where, to reiterate,

$$\Delta K = K - K_{-1}$$

represents the current addition to the available capital stock (representing last year's investment), and

$$\Delta X = X - X_{-1}$$

represents this year's increase in production.

In contrast with Evsey Domar's approach to the long run (1946), in which the relationship between capital and output is purely technologi-

2. There is of course a simultaneity problem, but this problem disappears in a steady-growth equilibrium and need not detain us.

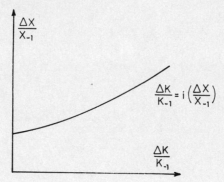

Figure 4.3 Output growth and capital growth: The investment-demand function

cal, the precise form of Harrod's functional relationship depends, *à la* Keynes, on capitalists' "animal spirits": equilibrium requires that the various players — investors as well as savers — be satisfied. Equilibrium indeed is defined as a steady growth path that makes capitalists content to carry on the existing rate of growth (Harrod 1948, p. 82).

As Figure 4.4 shows, the two relationships between output and capital together determine g^*, the equilibrium growth rate (Harrod's G_w), and $(\Delta X/\Delta K)^*$, the equilibrium incremental output:capital ratio (the inverse of Harrod's C_r). The fourth quadrant contains the investment function, along with a 45° ray reflecting the requirement of steady growth, namely, $\Delta K/K_{-1} = \Delta X/X_{-1}$. The intersection of the investment function with the 45° ray determines the equilibrium ("warranted") rate of growth. The required incremental output:capital ratio is determined by the projection of the equilibrium growth rate in the figure's first quadrant.

At the risk of taking some liberty with Harrod's own presentation, the basic ideas of the Harrodian model can be laid out more simply in terms of a two-way relationship between the *average* output:capital ratio and the rate of growth of the capital stock. We have first the tautological relationship

$$\Delta K = \frac{\Delta K}{X_{-1}} X_{-1},$$

which becomes

$$\frac{\Delta K}{K_{-1}} = s\frac{X_{-1}}{K_{-1}} \tag{4.4}$$

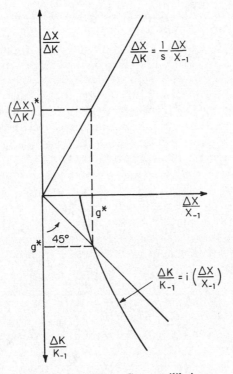

Figure 4.4 Harrodian equilibrium

when the relationship is interpreted as an equilibrium condition reflecting a linear saving function. For a given amount of investment ΔK
and a given capital stock K_{-1} in period -1, Eq. (4.4) determines
equilibrium output X_{-1} and the equilibrium capital:output ratio
X_{-1}/K_{-1}:

$$\frac{X_{-1}}{K_{-1}} = \frac{1}{s}\frac{\Delta K}{K_{-1}}.$$

The ratio $1/s$ is the Keynesian multiplier. Next we have, in place of Eq.
(4.3), an investment function that relates desired growth in the capital
stock $\Delta K/K_{-1}$ in period -1 to the rate of capital-stock utilization in
period -2, as reflected in X_{-2}/K_{-2}:

$$\frac{\Delta K}{K_{-1}} = i\left(\frac{X_{-2}}{K_{-2}}\right). \tag{4.5}$$

The idea behind Eq. (4.5) is the same as the idea behind (4.3)—that greater output stimulates greater investment. Only now, "greater output" is expressed in terms of capacity utilization, X_{-2}/K_{-2}, rather than in terms of growth, $\Delta X/X_{-1}$. The argument remains faithful to Harrod (and Keynes) in the crucial respect: animal spirits still underlie the functional relationship and determine its form.

The point of formulating the model in terms of X_{-2}/K_{-2} and $\Delta K/K_{-1}$ is to permit us to represent the two relationships in a single diagram, as in Figure 4.5. Equilibrium takes place at the point $\langle (X/K)^*,$ $g^* \rangle$, where both Eq. (4.4) and Eq. (4.5) are satisfied simultaneously. The equilibrium rate of growth of output $(\Delta X/X_{-1})$ is also g^*, since the output:capital ratio $(X/K)^*$ remains constant in the steady state.

Three features of this equilibrium should be noted. First, as Harrod notes (1948, pp. 85–87), the steady-growth equilibrium is unstable. If the economy were to begin with an output:capital ratio in excess of $(X/K)^*$, for example $(X/K)_1$, capitalists would respond with so much investment that the rate of growth would be g_1, which in turn would increase income and capacity utilization to the point represented by $(X/K)_2$. Investment would respond still more, so that the capital stock would grow at the higher rate g_2—and so on, output and capital increasing without bound. Similarly, if the initial output:capital ratio lay below $(X/K)^*$, the economy would spiral downward, in the direction of the origin.

It should be observed, however, that the instability of the steady-growth path is purely a consequence of the shape imputed to the saving

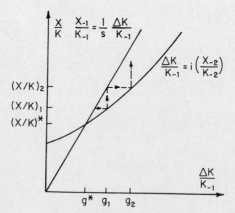

Figure 4.5 A reformulation of Harrodian equilibrium

and investment functions. The investment function could be redrawn to cut the saving function from below rather than from above, in which case the adjustment mechanism sketched in the preceding paragraph would lead to stability rather than instability. Indeed, there is no reason to rule out the possibility of multiple equilibria, alternating between stable and unstable.

The second point to be made about the Harrodian equilibrium is that, except by accident, it diverges from the rate of growth of the labor force. In Harrod's terminology, and my notation, there is no reason for the "warranted" (g^*) and "natural" (n) rates of growth to coincide.

One might expect that (as in the neo-Marxian formulation) the case $g^* > n$ would produce boom conditions, with continual pressure on the labor resources available to the economy. The opposite case, $g^* < n$, might similarly be expected to lead to stagnation. And these are indeed reasonable conclusions if the growth rate conforms consistently to g^*. But for Harrod, g^* is only a measure of central tendency. In fact, investment demand will fluctuate in response to haphazard shocks, including temporary changes in animal spirits. Thus even if the economy once settles down to a g^* equilibrium it will soon find itself out of equilibrium. Consequently, the appropriate context for a Harrodian analysis of divergence between g^* and n is the behavior of the economy out of equilibrium, rather than a direct comparison of the magnitudes of g^* and n. And, paradoxically, the conclusions drawn from analyzing the divergence of g^* and n in the context of a disequilibrium economy are almost the opposite of those that an intuition based on the Marxian analysis suggests! In short, $g^* > n$ implies chronic depression, $g^* < n$ frequent booms (Harrod 1948, pp. 87–90). Let us see why.

Harrod's economy has no institutionalized "reserve army," certainly not as a permanent feature, and so is unable to sustain growth at a rate in excess of n in the long run. Hence in Figure 4.6(a) and (b) the feasible region lies to the left of $g = n$. But if g^* exceeds n, as in Figure 4.6(a), then any time the growth rate is less than n, it will, barring a favorable shock, tend to fall further — because of the instability of the equilibrium. Hence, paradoxically, $g^* > n$ implies chronic depression, with growing unemployment, not secular exhilaration. In other words, the line $g = n$ truncates the distribution of growth rates, leaving only those to its left as feasible short-run equilibria. But with $g^* > n$, any time we start to the left of $g = n$, we move further to the left!

The converse situation, in which n exceeds g^*, is shown in Figure 4.6(b). Here too there is no cure for a downward departure of g from g^* save a favorable shock that temporarily improves animal spirits. But the

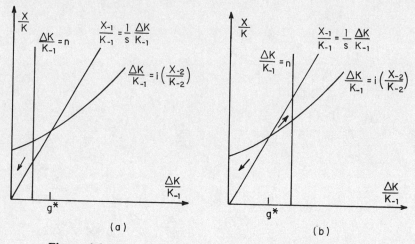

Figure 4.6 Divergence of $g*$ and n in the Harrodian model

situation is not symmetrical to the right of $g*$. If g temporarily exceeds $g*$, the growth rate will continue to increase (barring now a *dampening* of animal spirits) until full employment is reached and the economy runs out of workers. Thus $g* < n$ is compatible with frequent booms, certainly an unexpected result.

Evidently Harrod's paradoxical results derive from the shapes imputed to the saving and investment functions and are intimately related to the instability of equilibrium. If the investment function were redrawn to cut the saving function from below, not only would $g*$ be stable, but the implications of divergence between $g*$ and n would conform to intuition based on the neo-Marxian model: $g* > n$ would inevitably produce a "permanent" strain on the economy's labor resources, and $g* < n$ would lead to stagnation. Hence there is the possibility, but not the necessity, of opposition between the neo-Marxian and the Harrodian frameworks.

Finally, the distributional consequences of the Harrodian equilibrium deserve some discussion. The key to a Harrodian distribution theory lies in relaxing one of the restrictive assumptions Harrod made, namely that the rate of profit (or interest in Harrod's terminology) is fixed. Once the rate of profit is allowed to vary, we can drop the assumption of a constant long-run capital:output ratio. And if, along with a continuously variable capital:output ratio, we assume constant returns to scale, the capital:output ratio alone suffices to determine competitive wage and profit rates.[3] Thus equilibrium growth determines equilibrium distribution.

In any case all this is by way of preliminary—a bridge, as has been said before, between Keynes and the neo-Keynesians. Now that the bridge has been crossed, which road do we take? That is, which neo-Keynesian do we follow? Joan Robinson? Nicholas Kaldor? Michal Kalecki? (Though to call Kalecki, whose work was contemporary with Keynes's, a "neo-Keynesian" may be an anachronism reflecting nothing but Anglo-Saxon ethnocentrism!) It seems to me that the neo-Keynesian model I sketch here is more faithful to Kalecki (1933, 1934, 1935) and to Robinson (1956, especially chap. 7, and 1962, chap. 2) than to Kaldor, but I should be surprised if, in the development of these ideas, each of them did not learn from the others—as I have learned from all of them.

The Investment-Demand Function

The neo-Keynesian model, like Harrod's, is closed by an investment function interacting with a saving function. But both functions differ in important respects from their Harrodian counterparts.

In the first place, in the neo-Keynsian model the independent variable on which investment demand explicitly depends is neither a rate of interest representing a "cost of capital" (as for Keynes) nor the intensity of capital utilization (as for Harrod). It is rather the expected rate of profit, the prospective "quasi-rent" per unit of capital that forms the numerator of each of the terms of the present value sums which determine Keynes's "marginal efficiency of capital." Each point on the neo-Keynesian investment-demand schedule corresponds to a point on a different marginal-efficiency-of-capital schedule; each point reflects different expectations with respect to quasi-rents but a constant cost of capital.

I shall for the most part ignore the influence of the cost of capital on investment demand, assuming implicitly either that the cost of capital is

---

3. I shall deal with the variable-proportions case in Chapter 9. But, in passing, we may observe that the investment-demand functions (4.3) and (4.5) already assume implicitly that the capital:output ratio can vary. Harrod is ambiguous on whether he means to assume that the capital:output ratio is fixed, which is to assume away capital-labor substitution, or only that it is constant in equilibrium. Suffice it to say that in contrast with Robert Solow (1956), I do not find fixed proportions at the heart of Harrod's message. Neither the instability of the equilibrium rate of growth g^*, nor the divergence of g^* from n—Harrod's two key results—depends essentially on fixed coefficients in production. See the section headed *Solow Again: A Short Digression* in Chapter 9.

constant, or alternatively that within the range of potential variation, it exercises no influence on demand. With this assumption, it is reasonable to posit that a higher expected rate of profit stimulates a greater amount of desired investment; in other words, the higher must be the prospective rate of profit in order that businessmen be content with higher rates of investment.

Of course, at any given rate of profit, investment demand will vary directly with prevailing attitudes in the business community. The expected rate of profit is to be understood as the first moment of a probability distribution of outcomes. The certainty equivalent of this parameter depends on the degree of risk aversion of the business community. The more risk averse are businessmen, the lower is the certainty equivalent of a given expected rate of profit, and the less investment will be forthcoming. By the same token, the rate of profit necessary to "justify" a given rate of investment will vary directly with the prevailing degree of risk aversion. Thus in the neo-Keynesian model, as in the Keynesian and Harrodian models from which it derives, central importance attaches to the psychology of the business community, its state of confidence or "animal spirits." But this central force is always behind the scenes, implicitly determining the shape of investment demand as a function of the profit rate rather than appearing as an explicit argument of the function.

Neo-Keynesian investment demand, defined as a function of the prospective profit rate, becomes a function of the present rate of profit only if we assume that the expected rate of profit is the current rate. But however controversial this idea might be when applied to the short run, it is surely reasonable in the context of steady growth since equilibrium continually validates the static expectation that the future will resemble the past. If we add the assumption that the functional relationship between investment demand and the rate of profit is stable over time when demand for additional capital is defined in terms of investment per unit of capital, the dependent variable becomes the rate of growth of the capital stock $\Delta K_{+1}/K$. Since with fixed production coefficients, output and employment grow at the same rate as the capital stock (even without fixed coefficients, all magnitudes grow at the same rate in the steady state!), this transformation permits us to represent neo-Keynesian investment demand as a function relating *the* rate of growth to the rate of profit:

$$g = i(r). \tag{4.6}$$

The graph of this function is shown in Figure 4.7.

Of course the investment demand function does not determine the

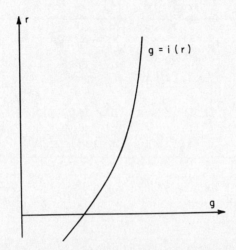

Figure 4.7 Neo-Keynesian investment demand

rate of growth by itself: *any* point satisfying Eq. (4.6) is an equilibrium in terms of the investment propensities of the business community.

The Saving Function

Evidently what is lacking is a saving function. Were we to follow Harrod's lead and assume saving to be a constant fraction of aggregate output, the saving function in the context of the corn model would become independent of the rate of profit. On a per worker basis saving would be equal to

$$s\frac{1-a_1}{a_0},$$

where s is the fraction of income saved and $(1 - a_1)/a_0$ is net output per worker. If savings intentions are realized, we should have to have

$$g\frac{a_1}{a_0} = s\frac{1-a_1}{a_0},$$

or, per unit of capital,

$$g = s\frac{1-a_1}{a_1}. \tag{4.7}$$

As Figure 4.8 indicates, a steady-growth equilibrium exists provided

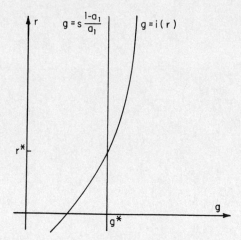

Figure 4.8   Steady growth equilibrium with a Harrodian saving function

the right-hand side of Eq. (4.7) lies within the range of the investment function (4.6). Observe that if the rate of profit responds positively to an excess of investment demand over desired saving and negatively to an excess of desired saving, the equilibrium represented in Figure 4.8 is unstable, as in the original Harrod model.

However, the neo-Keynesian model draws on the classical assumption about saving behavior rather than on Harrod's, namely, that all wages are consumed and all profits are saved. Formally, as in the neo-Marxian model,

$$g = s(r) = r \tag{3.3}$$

—provided that saving intentions are realized. The domain of this function continues to be the interval $[-1, r_{max}]$ with r_{max} defined as the rate of profit corresponding to a zero wage:

$$r_{max} = \frac{1 - a_1}{a_1}$$

In Figure 4.9 we superimpose the saving function defined by Eq. (3.3) on Figure 4.7.

The Existence of Equilibrium

The equilibrium labeled $\langle r^*, g^* \rangle$ in Figure 4.9 is defined by the solution to the equation pair

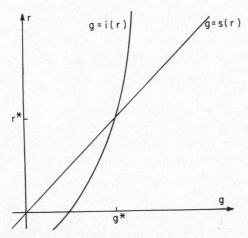

Figure 4.9 Neo-Keynesian investment and saving functions

$$g = i(r) \tag{4.6}$$

$$g = s(r) = r. \tag{3.3}$$

Substituting $g*$ and $r*$ into the price and production equations determines consumption per worker $C*$ and the real wage $W*$ residually:

$$C* = \frac{1 - a_1}{a_0} - g* \frac{a_1}{a_0} \tag{4.8}$$

$$W* = \frac{1 - a_1}{a_0} - r* \frac{a_1}{a_0}. \tag{4.9}$$

Causality is summarized in Table 4.1. This schema is represented graphically in Figure 4.10. Equilibrium is here presented as unique, but we are probably far along enough in the story by now that it need hardly be said that uniqueness is a consequence of the draftsman's pen, not a result of the structure of the theory. It would be a simple enough matter to redraw the investment function to intersect the saving func-

Table 4.1. Causality in the neo-Keynesian model

Exogenous	Endogenous
$\left.\begin{array}{l} a_1, a_0 \\ g = i(r) \\ g = r \end{array}\right\}$ $\rightarrow$	$g*, r*, W*, C*$

GROWTH AND DISTRIBUTION

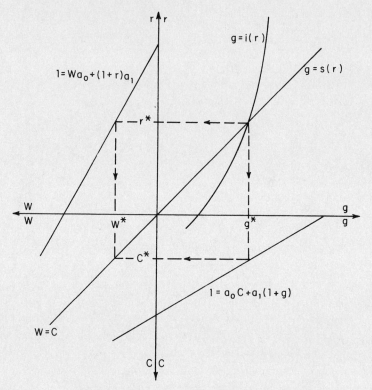

Figure 4.10   Neo-Keynesian equilibrium

tion any number of times—without sacrificing the (implicit) assumptions of continuity and smoothness.[4]

Growth, in the neoclassical model, was observed to be "prior" to distribution: an "other-things-equal" change in the utility function will change the distribution of income but not the rate of growth. In a similar sense, distribution "precedes" growth in the neo-Marxian

4. For the existence of equilibrium, it is sufficient to assume $i(-1) > -1$. It is not necessary to assume that investment demand is bounded from above if we are willing to countenance the possibility of a boundary solution at $r = r_{max}$ for which $i(r)$ exceeds r, that is, an "equilibrium" at which investment demand exceeds saving. Observe that the failure to satisfy investment demand does not prevent the configuration $r = g = r_{max}$, $W = C = 0$ from being realized indefinitely. In this respect the neo-Keynesian boundary solution has no counterpart in the neoclassical or neo-Marxian models, for in both these cases equilibrium requires the relationships that close the model to be satisfied exactly. (Some will object to the notion of an equilibrium with a zero real wage; this issue will be addressed in Chapter 5.)

model: once we relax the assumption that capitalists save all profits, the growth rate will turn out to be sensitive to capitalists' saving propensities, but the profit rate does not. In the neo-Keynesian model, by contrast, growth and distribution are simultaneously determined: anything that affects one must affect the other.

The determination of the profit rate in the neo-Keynesian model also differs from both the neoclassical and the neo-Marxian. It will hardly be surprising that like neo-Marxian theory, neo-Keynesian theory rejects the specifically neoclassical idea that biology and utility play important roles in determining the rate of profit. More surprisingly, neo-Keynesian theory also rejects the common element in the neoclassical and neo-Marxian stories—namely, technology. In the neo-Keynesian view, the rate of profit is independent of technology as well as of biology and utility. It depends only on investment demand and—in a more general version of the model considered in Chapter 6—on the saving propensity of capitalists.[5]

Stability

Assume that profits are determined before investment plans are laid and that saving intentions are always realized, in or out of equilibrium. Add the conventional assumption that the rate of profit rises in response to a positive excess investment demand and declines in response to positive excess savings, and stability follows immediately: an initial position like $\langle r_1, g_1 \rangle$ in Figure 4.11 sets the rate of profit, and hence the rate of growth, moving in the direction of the arrow, towards the equilibrium $\langle r^*, g^* \rangle$. Similarly, if we start at $\langle r_2, g_2 \rangle$ the rate of profit falls until the economy comes to rest at equilibrium.

There is a problem with this story, however: why should the profit rate rise when investment demand exceeds desired saving? One can appeal to a quite conventional line of reasoning to establish that the *interest* rate will respond positively to excess investment demand (if one is willing to assume that the interest rate clears the saving-investment market), but to apply the conventional argument to the rate of *profit*, one must argue that as the interest rate rises, the price of capital goods falls. In this case the rate of profit will rise in pace with the interest rate. However, such an argument cannot possibly work in the present model, because there is only one asset—corn—and the relative price of seed corn to food corn is technologically fixed at unity.

5. Observe that class power, the other determinant of profits in the neo-Marxian model, plays no role either. At least not until, as in Chapter 20, class power is argued to be a determinant of capitalists' "animal spirits."

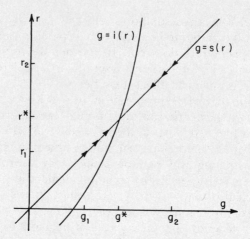

Figure 4.11 Stability of neo-Keynesian equilibrium: Investment plans laid after profit rate is determined

The Crucial Role of Investment Demand

We must conclude that we are without a story to motivate an adjustment process based on the realization of saving intentions and the planning of investment on the basis of the current rate of profit. No wonder, therefore, that the adjustment mechanism implicit in the neo-Keynesian literature is one in which, in part at least, *investment* intentions are realized: out of long-run equilibrium, saving adapts to investment. In the extreme, in which investment plans are completely realized, the current profit rate is determined *by* the current rate of growth, in consequence of investment plans. Formally the equation

$$g = r \tag{4.10}$$

continues to govern the relationship between saving and investment, but the causality in Eq. (4.10) runs from g to r rather than from r to g.

Suppose that the expected profit rate is equal to *last* year's profit rate. That is, investment demand this year is a function of profit last year:

$$g = i(r_{-1}). \tag{4.11}$$

With this assumption coupled to Eq. (4.10), the adjustment process is qualitatively similar to the case in which current profit rates are determined before investment plans are laid. If we begin with $r = r_1$, the economy follows the path indicated in Figure 4.12. For year 2, investment demand is given by

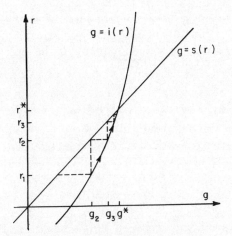

Figure 4.12 Stability of neo-Keynesian equilibrium: Investment plans laid before profit rate is known

$$g_2 = i(r_1).$$

If saving adjusts completely to investment intentions, the realized rate of profit in year 2 must be r_2. But as the rate of profit climbs, so does investment demand per unit of capital. Thus investment demand in year 3 is

$$g_3 = i(r_2).$$

Once again the profit rate must increase if saving is to adjust to investment. And the process continues until the rate of profit and the rate of growth are compatible, which is to say, until long-run equilibrium is reached at $\langle r^*, g^* \rangle$. An analogous story obtains if we begin with r in excess of r^*; the only difference is that the adjustment involves a decline in the rate of profit and growth.

Observe that investment demand is both changing and fixed: changing over time in response to changes in the rate of profit, but fixed in each period on the basis of last period's rate of profit. At every step of the way the economy is in short-run, temporary equilibrium, but only at $\langle r^*, g^* \rangle$ is the economy in long-run equilibrium on a path of steady growth.

The "short run" and the "long run" are not just different periods of time; the mechanisms of equilibrium are quite different. Short-run equilibrium is shaped by investment propensities: investment and growth, exogenous in the short run (being determined from last period's profit rate), determine current rates of saving and profit. By contrast, the determination of long-run equilibrium is more symmetric: investment and saving are both endogenous in the long run, both being functions of the rate of profit.

The Determination of Wages

At each stage of the adjustment process the wage rate is determined residually, as a consequence of the interaction between investment and saving propensities:

$$W^* = \frac{1 - a_1}{a_0} - r^* \frac{a_1}{a_0}.$$

But here the resemblance between the neo-Keynesian model and its Keynesian and Harrodian antecedents ends. Marginal productivity and the dovetailing of micro-equilibrium with macro-equilibrium play no role — the assumption of fixed coefficients guarantees that! Rather the real wage adjusts to clear the market for food corn; that is, W settles at a level at which workers' consumption demand just equals the supply of corn available after investment plans are carried out.

The simplest story that one might tell to describe the behavior of wages goes something like this. After each harvest, the entire stock of corn is heaped together at a central place, the "Corn Exchange Bank." The bank then opens for a half day, *before* wages and profits for the current crop are determined. Capitalists now borrow seed corn for the next crop, on the basis of expectations formed by last year's realized profit rate. In the present context to assume that investment intentions are realized is tantamount to assuming that capitalists are always accommodated by their bankers, and for our purposes we lose nothing by abstracting from the influence of the rate of interest or other credit-market factors on investment demand. Each capitalist is debited for the amount of corn he actually borrows, and since it is is the capitalist corn growers (not the bankers) who own the corn, each is *credited* with a fraction of the total borrowing equal to the fraction of corn production he accounted for during the past season. (Thus the Corn Exchange Bank is more a clearing house than a bank.) After loan arrangements are complete, the remaining corn is distributed to the workers, each worker's share representing his real wage.

What happens to profits? Each individual capitalist will calculate his (gross) profit as the difference between his output and the wages he pays out. For some capitalists profit will exceed investment, whereas for others investment will exceed profits. But for capitalists as a whole, profits will just equal aggregate investment—profits represent the difference between output and wages, investment represents the difference between output and consumption, and wages and consumption are equal. And since the share of profits accruing to each capitalist is proportionate to the share of output he controls, his individual profit will just equal the amount of outstanding loans credited to his account by the bank. The net balance of each capitalist with the bank of course reflects the amount by which his investment and profit differ. Moreover, all these transactions take place only on paper; profits never take a form more tangible than a ledger entry.

Suggestive as this story might be, it remains more a "just-so" story than a serious attempt to mirror the processes of any actual capitalist economy. For it fails to provide a plausible explanation of how it is that capitalists come to have first claim on output for investment purposes, leaving wages to be determined by the residual output available—obviously an essential ingredient of the Corn Exchange story as it stands.

Money

A more faithful picture of capitalist reality, according to the neo-Keynesians, requires us to drop the assumption that money is a mere unit of account.

For the neo-Keynesians it is of the essence that wages are fixed in money terms, and real wages are determined by adjustments in the price level. Formally the money wage is set once and for all at $\overline{W}$, and the price equation becomes

$$P = \overline{W}a_0 + (1 + r)Pa_1, \tag{4.12}$$

with P (the price of corn) and $\overline{W}/P$ (the real wage) unknowns to be determined. Given the rate of profit r (which ex post must equal the rate of growth of output), we can solve for the price level

$$P = \frac{\overline{W}a_0}{1 - (1 + r)a_1},$$

with the numerator representing money wages, and the denominator the supply of corn available for consumption (namely, output less gross investment)—both on a per-bushel basis.

But how is the rate of profit determined with the price level a variable? Enter the Corn Exchange Bank, which now really functions like a bank rather than a clearinghouse. As before, the entire harvest is heaped up in a grand pile in front of the bank, but now only the seed requirements for maintaining production at its previous level are set aside as a first claim on output. At the same time, workers are paid money wages at the rate $\overline{W}a_0$ per bushel of corn output and capitalists borrow money from the bank to finance current investment plans, before this year's price and profit rate are known. In money terms, net investment demand per bushel of corn is

$$P_{-1}i(r_{-1})a_1$$

if last year's price forms the basis of capitalists' calculations.[6]

Aggregate expenditure per bushel of corn output is

$$\overline{W}a_0 + P_{-1}i(r_{-1})a_1, \qquad (4.13)$$

with the first term representing wage earners' consumption expenditure, the second term net investment in money terms. Demand in physical terms (the units are corn per bushel of corn output) is equal to aggregate expenditure (4.13) divided by the (as yet unknown) price of corn:

$$X^d = \frac{\overline{W}a_0 + P_{-1}i(r_{-1})a_1}{P}. \qquad (4.14)$$

The demand function is thus a rectangular hyperbola, as illustrated in Figure 4.13. The available supply of corn per bushel of corn, X^s, is equal to the corn remaining after seed-replacement requirements are met,

$$X^s = 1 - a_1.$$

If the corn market is to clear, we must have $X^s = X^d$, which is to say

$$P(1 - a_1) = \overline{W}a_0 + P_{-1}i(r_{-1})a_1 \qquad (4.15)$$

or

$$Pr = P_{-1}i(r_{-1}). \qquad (4.16)$$

We can solve for the rate of profit in terms of the predetermined variables P_{-1} and $i(r_{-1})$,

$$r = \frac{P_{-1}i(r_{-1})(1 - a_1)}{\overline{W}a_0 + P_{-1}i(r_{-1})a_1}. \qquad (4.17)$$

6. It may be objected that the "irrationality" of expectations implied in this formulation of investment demand is inconsistent with one of the assumptions underlying Figure 4.7, namely that the expected profit rate is realized in equilibrium. There is, however, no contradiction. $P_{-1}i(r_{-1})a_1$ refers explicitly to *disequilibrium* conditions; in the limit r_{-1} and r jointly approach r^*, and so does the anticipated rate of profit. By the same token, as P_{-1} and P approach P^*, the expected price approaches the actual. The problem of expectations recurs in Chapter 20, but there the solution is more complex. (See the section of Chapter 20 headed *Expectations, Naive and Rational* and the appendix to that chapter.)

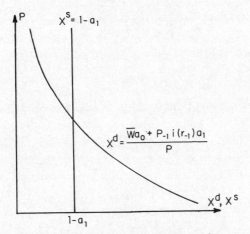

Figure 4.13 Demand and supply

But since P_{-1} is determined through the price equation by the rate of profit r_{-1},

$$P_{-1} = \frac{\overline{W}a_0}{1 - (1 + r_{-1})a_1},$$

Eq. (4.17) in effect describes the adjustment process in terms of r alone. Starting from r_{-1}, we can use this equation recursively to generate the rate of profit in each subsequent period.

We have yet to verify that the process described by Eq. (4.17) converges to a long-run equilibrium, in other words, that the long-run equilibrium is stable. But this is easily shown, at least if the investment and saving functions have the general shape of Figure 4.9, so that

$$i(r) \gtrless r \quad \Leftrightarrow \quad r^* \gtrless r, \tag{4.18}$$

which in turn implies

$$i'(r) < 1 \equiv s'(r).$$

From Eqs. (4.17) and (4.12), we have

$$r = \frac{\overline{W}a_0[i(r_{-1}) - r_{-1}]}{\overline{W}a_0 + P_{-1}i(r_{-1})a_1} + r_{-1}, \tag{4.19}$$

so that Δr is positive whenever desired investment exceeds desired saving and negative whenever saving exceeds investment. Convergence of $\{r_{-1}, r, r_{+1}, \ldots\}$ to r^*, which is to say stability of equilibrium, depends on the derivative of the right-hand side of Eq. (4.19). Forming

$$G(r_{-1}) = \frac{\overline{W}a_0[i(r_{-1}) - r_{-1}]}{\overline{W}a_0 + P_{-1}i(r_{-1})a_1} + r_{-1},$$

the stability condition is

$$|G'(r^*)| < 1.$$

Now, if we take note of the equality of desired saving and investment at r^*,

$$i(r^*) = r^*,$$

we may write

$$G'(r^*) = \frac{\overline{W}a_0[i'(r^*) - 1]}{\overline{W}a_0 + P^*i(r^*)a_1} + 1. \qquad (4.20)$$

A necessary condition for stability is

$$i'(r^*) < 1.$$

This condition is also sufficient since $i'(r^*) \geq 0$, so that the expression in brackets is less than unity in absolute value, as is $\overline{W}a_0 / [\overline{W}a_0 + P^*i(r^*)a_1]$. Thus, as the previous paragraph suggested, stability requires that at equilibrium investment demand be less responsive to the profit rate than is desired saving, as pictured in Figure 4.9. The adjustment process described by Eq. (4.17) or (4.19) is represented in Figure 4.14.

Observe that the real wage $\overline{W}/P$ continues to be residually determined, as in the simpler story without money. In the neo-Keynesian phrase, workers "spend what they get," namely $\overline{W}a_0$, but the amount of corn they receive depends on the price level P which varies positively (given the technology and last year's profit rate) with the amount of investment demand that capitalists add to workers' consumption demand. This is not to say that capitalists completely realize their investment intentions. Quite the contrary: in the present model, investment demand is completely realized only in equilibrium. With $r < r^*$, capitalists are frustrated by rising prices that reduce real investment below its intended level. Similarly with $r > r^*$, a falling price level means that actual investment exceeds the amount calculated in terms of the price level of the previous period. It is important to the short-run dynamics, if not to long-run equilibrium, that investment is committed in money terms before the current price level is determined.

But the effect of price changes on capitalists is nevertheless not the

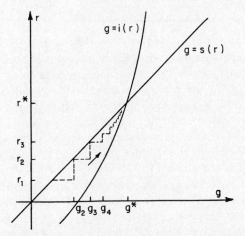

Figure 4.14 Adjustment to neo-Keynesian equilibrium with fixed money wages

same as the effect on workers. Price increases that lower real wages raise the rate of profit. Formally we have

$$r = \frac{P_{-1}(1 - a_1)i(r_{-1})}{\overline{W}a_0 + P_{-1}i(r_{-1})a_1},$$

$$\frac{\overline{W}}{P} = \frac{(1 - a_1)\overline{W}}{\overline{W}a_0 + P_{-1}i(r_{-1})a_1}.$$

So if we for the moment treat $i(r_{-1})$ as a parameter, and examine the effect of variations in investment demand on profits and wages, we find

$$\frac{\partial r}{\partial i} = \frac{P_{-1}(1 - a_1)\overline{W}a_0}{[\overline{W}a_0 + P_{-1}i(r_{-1})a_1]^2},$$

$$\frac{\partial(\overline{W}/P)}{\partial i} = -\frac{(1 - a_1)\overline{W}P_{-1}a_1}{[\overline{W}a_0 + P_{-1}i(r_{-1})a_1]^2}.$$

That is, investment expenditure has a positive effect on profits and a negative effect on wages. In fact, whereas workers "spend what they get," capitalists "get what they spend," with excess investment demand translating itself into higher saving by means of a shift in income from workers to capitalists, a shift accomplished through an increase in the price level relative to a fixed money wage.

The Secret of the Widow's Cruse

Thus the metaphor of the "widow's cruse"[7] that magically refills as it is emptied. As a class, if not individually, capitalists' pockets refill with profit as they are emptied by investment expenditure.

But the magic in the process, if any, is the result of the priority implicitly attached to capitalists' claims on output. In the simplest story in which money played no role, this priority was absolute: capitalists' investment demand was a first charge on the corn harvest; only after this charge was met was the residual distributed to workers in the form of wages. In the present story, in which wages are fixed in money terms and investment is financed with borrowed money rather than borrowed corn, capitalists' priority is not so transparent: by assumption, capitalists and workers bid in the same market for the total net output of corn, and the price that is established by Eq. (4.16) is the price that clears this unified market. Nevertheless, transparent or not, capitalists' priority is built into the model—*in the assumption that capitalists have a monopoly of bank credit.* Capitalists borrow to finance investment; workers do not borrow to finance consumption.

The assumption that capitalists have priority is certainly more realistic when formulated as a monopoly of the credit market than formulated as an absolute prior claim on output. Even so, the argument may seem to be overstated. Workers do borrow to finance expenditures, and, in the United States at least, the average annual addition to household debt has been of the same order of magnitude as the addition to business debt—with as much volatility over the business cycle (Board of Governors of the Federal Reserve System 1976, pp. 4–6).

The quantitative magnitudes notwithstanding, there are important differences between household and business debt which give support to the idea that capitalists at least have privileged access to bank credit, if not an absolute monopoly. First, business debt is orders of magnitude larger than household debt relative to the appropriate income base, business income (profits) on the one hand and household income on the other. This higher debt ratio is in some part the consequence of capitalists' disproportionate control of assets suitable for collateral. Whatever the merits of regarding a worker's skills as "human capital," it has been a long time since individuals could pledge their bodies as security for loans. Workers' borrowing is for the most part limited to

7. The terminology is Keynes's (1930, p. 139), but the idea appears in Kalecki (1933, p. 13) as well.

residential mortgages to finance housing purchases and installment loans to finance automobiles and other consumer durables.

There is a second difference between workers and capitalists that transcends the issue of concentration of assets suitable for collateral. Whereas workes can borrow *only* on their assets, capitalists borrow on their prospects as well as on their assets. Capitalists' collateral frequently falls short of their liabilities. In practice if not in theory, the availability of credit reflects the same psychological variables that determine capitalists' investment demand. Thus, on both quantitative and qualitative grounds, ignoring consumer borrowing altogether and attributing to capitalists a monopoly of banking and credit can be defended as a plausible abstraction from actual credit-market institutions that are the historical product of the needs of capitalists rather than consumers.

In any case, plausible or not, the crucial role of the assumption that capitalists have priority in the division of output between themselves and workers is very clear in the fixed-coefficient version of the neo-Keynesian model. In this respect the present model differs crucially from its Keynesian antecedent. In Keynes's model, the focus is on the short run, and production coefficients are variable. To assume that saving adjusts to investment demand is to assume nothing more than the existence of excess capacity, that is to say, to assume variable proportions in the manner of Figure 4.1. In that model, profits rise or fall in accordance with investment demand by means of a multiplier process that works itself out in real terms, that is, at least in part through adjustments in aggregate output. In the present context, in which production coefficients are fixed, excess capacity plays no role either in the short run or the long; the adjustment of saving to investment demand cannot depend on variations in capacity utilization rates. Since the pie is fixed (on a per-worker basis), the entire burden of adjusting saving to investment demand necessarily involves assigning a priority to capitalists in the competition for output.

5 Neo-Marxian and Neo-Keynesian Conceptions of the Labor Market

The neo-Keynesian model has two points of contact with the neo-Marxian model. First, the neo-Keynesians concede that there might be a floor to real wages, akin to the Marxian subsistence wage. In one of Nicholas Kaldor's early models (1957), the capitalist mode of production is typically expected to go through a "Marxian" phase in which the wage floor is an operative constraint before entering a "Keynesian" phase in which this constraint is no longer binding.

But Kaldor's argument does not justify the assumption of a fixed subsistence wage. The passage from the Marxian to the Keynesian phase in his model is the result of technological progress, a factor absent from the present discussion. But to fix a real-wage floor once and for all in a model that incorporates technical progress seems to me to miss the essence of the neo-Marxian argument, which is not that wages are independent of productivity but that productivity is one of the background parameters against which the class struggle takes place. Hence in a model with technological progress, a neo-Marxian approach requires a rising "subsistence" wage, not a fixed one: the appropriate assumption is perhaps one of a fixed wage *share* rather than a fixed wage *rate*. There is certainly no reason to suppose the automatic passage from the Marxian to the Keynesian phase simply by virtue of rising productivity.

The Inflation Barrier

For this reason, perhaps, Joan Robinson's model includes a "subsistence" wage but reflects no temporal dichotomy in its application. Robinson's wage floor is argued both in terms of biological subsistence and in terms of what happens when "organized labor has the power to oppose any fall in the real wage rate" (1962, pp. 58–59). Labeled poetically a "bastard golden age" by Robinson, the steady-growth configuration corresponding to a binding wage constraint is shown in Figure 5.1. Evidently the effect of a wage floor is to impose a ceiling on the rate of profit. With the real wage rate fixed at $(W/P)_{min}$, the equilibrium $\langle r^*, g^* \rangle$ becomes unobtainable, and growth and profit rates settle at $\bar{r}$.

A bastard golden age perpetuates itself by means of inflation. Observe that investment demand exceeds desired saving at $\bar{r}$. Ordinarily this would increase prices and shift income from workers to capitalists. But if $\bar{r}$ reflects a floor on *real* wages, then workers must be able to resist erosion of real wages below $(W/P)_{min}$ by successfully demanding higher money wages as prices rise. The Marxian subsistence wage becomes the Robinsonian "inflation barrier" (1962, p. 59)—wage inflation becomes the weapon by which the working class defends its standard of living, and a barrier to expansion of investment and growth. As a result, excess investment demand does not increase profits, and the system never arrives at an equilibrium at which desired investment and desired saving are equal. When the inflation barrier operates, the neo-Keynesian model becomes effectively neo-Marxian, at least in its real elements. The only role left for Keynesian investment demand, ironically, is to influence the monetary side of the model, chronic inflation reflecting the chronic frustration of capitalists' investment plans.

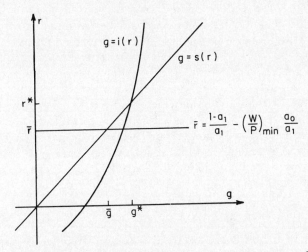

Figure 5.1 A "bastard golden age," the result of a floor on real wages

The Absence of Full Employment

The second point of contact between the neo-Keynesian and neo-Marxian models is the absence of a built-in assumption of full employment. In the neo-Marxian model, the equilibrium g^* may be higher or lower than the natural rate of growth n. The neo-Keynesian treatment of the case $g^* < n$ is similar to the neo-Marxian, but the neo-Keynesian treatment of the problems that arise when g^* exceeds n is sufficiently different from the neo-Marxian to merit special attention.

Beforehand, however, it might be useful to comment briefly on the basic Kaldor model (1957) as well as a slightly earlier (1956) and a slightly later (1961) model. Kaldor resolutely describes his models as "Keynesian," but goes on to assume full employment! The first model (1956) omits the investment function altogether. The second and third models (1957 and 1961), translated into the present context of a fixed-coefficient model from which technological progress is absent, implicitly assume an investment-demand function that makes equilibrium investment demand per unit of capital just equal to the rate of growth of the labor force; this is in effect to *assume* $g = n$. In all three models, the price level is assumed to fix profits and desired saving at levels that make the equilibrium rate of growth of capital (and output) equal to the rate of growth of the labor force. (In fact, Kaldor assumes that production techniques adjust to permit investment demand to equal desired saving at equilibrium, a way out that is not only inadmissible in a fixed-coefficient model of the present kind, but—more damaging—violates the logic of competitive profit maximization in a variable-coefficient model. This, however, gets ahead of the story.)

It should be noted in this context that whereas Luigi Pasinetti (1962) modified the Kaldorian saving function, he retained the assumption of full employment. For this reason Pasinetti's contribution, like Kaldor's, will be treated later, in Chapter 8, under a separate category of "hybrid" models.

If we do not build full employment into the model, steady growth at the rate n can emerge only as a fortuitous coincidence—a pure, as distinct from bastard, "golden age" whose very name, according to Robinson, is intended "to indicate its mythical nature" (1962, p. 52). Barring this fortuitous (and felicitous) coincidence, there are two possibilities: either $g^* > n$, or $g^* < n$.

Secular Exhilaration: $g^* > n$

Consider first the case where steady-state growth exceeds the natural rate $g^* > n$. This situation is pictured in Figure 5.2. Robinson describes

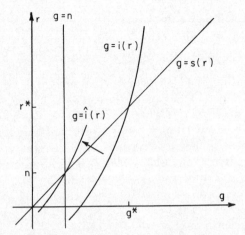

Figure 5.2 A "restrained golden age": Equilibrium initially in excess of population growth

this configuration as a "restrained golden age" (1962, pp. 54–56): either the fellow-feeling of capitalists or changes in the availability of credit and the cost of capital can restrain investment demand to the saving available at $r = n$. Whatever the mechanism, the end is the same: in Figure 5.2 the investment-demand function is shifted inward, from $i(r)$ to $\hat{\imath}(r)$.

If we imagine an initial backlog of unemployment, the capitalist sector could settle down at $\langle r^*, g^* \rangle$ until this backlog is absorbed by expanding capitalist production. At this point capitalist class interest would shift the equilibrium from $\langle r^*, g^* \rangle$ to $\langle n, n \rangle$. Observe that in the process the real wage would rise, as it does in one solution to the problem of secular exhilaration in the neo-Marxian model, and in one of Kaldor's models (1961, p. 186). But, in contrast with the neo-Marxian model, the real wage rises because of capitalists' restraint, imposed either from within or without, not because of competition among capitalists for workers or because workers are able to drive a better bargain as demand for labor presses on the available supply. There is nothing of the bastard in the restrained golden age!

Two other differences between the neo-Keynesian and neo-Marxian analyses of secular exhilaration should be noted. First, whereas the neo-Keynesian model requires a mechanism for bringing the growth rate into line with the natural rate, this outcome is only one possibility in the neo-Marxian model; it is not necessary or even likely. The reserve army provides an elastic, endogenous labor supply for which the neo-Keynesian model has no counterpart. Thus, secular exhilaration can be only a temporary condition in the neo-Keynesian model but can exist "permanently" in the neo-Marxian model—as permanently as capitalism in any case.

The second difference between the two models lies in the causes of secular exhilaration. In the neo-Keynesian model, it is either too much investment demand or (in a generalization of the model in which capitalists consume a portion of profit) too little saving, that is, too low a saving propensity. In the neo-Marxian model investment demand plays no role, and while capitalists' saving propensity may cause secular exhilaration, it is too much saving, too *high* a saving propensity, that is at fault.[1] The other possible source of secular exhilaration in the neo-Marxian model lies in the subsistence wage: the lower the subsistence wage, the higher will be the rate of growth.

Secular Stagnation: $g^* < n$

The converse situation, $g^* < n$, becomes in Robinsonian parlance a "leaden age." At one point Robinson is careful to note the asymmetry between this and the overfull employment case we have been considering up to now: when g^* is less than n, there is no reliable mechanism for increasing g^* (1956, p. 81). In another place, however, "Malthusian misery" is suggested as an adjustment mechanism—not to increase g^* to n, but to reduce n to g^* (1962, p. 54). If the ghost of Malthus is not invoked, a growing surplus of labor is the inevitable concomitant of a leaden age. Figure 5.3 illustrates the leaden-age equilibrium.

The Robinsonian leaden age is the long-run, steady-growth counterpart of the stagnationist argument put forward by left-wing critics of economic orthodoxy a generation ago. In both its liberal form, as articulated by Alvin Hansen (1938, 1941, 1951), and its radical form, as articulated by Paul Baran and Paul Sweezy (1966), the stagnationist view emphasized a putative inability of the capitalist mode of production to generate sufficient demand to absorb productively a growing population. Cast in short-run terms, the central stagnationist proposition was that private investment demand would fall short of full-employment saving. However, "full employment" changes its meaning when we move to a steady-growth model: the long-run equivalent of short-run stagnation is $n > i(n)$, which is to say that the level of saving required to sustain employment *growth* equal to labor-force *growth*

1. See Figure 6.1 and the accompanying discussion at the beginning of the next chapter for amplification of the difference between the two models with respect to the role of capitalists' saving propensity.

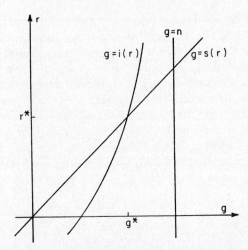

Figure 5.3 A "leaden age": Equilibrium growth rate less than the population growth rate

exceeds the level of investment demand. A glance at Figure 5.3 will verify that with a concave investment function, a stable equilibrium with $g^* < n$ produces the stagnationist condition $i(n) < n$.

Observe that both the liberal and the radical arguments on the causes of stagnation derive from a Keynesian world view rather than a Marxian one: both emphasize the insufficiency of investment demand, a concept which, when present at all, is hardly central to the Marxian analysis. As with secular exhilaration, the neo-Marxian view is distinct from the neo-Keynesian view: whereas the neo-Keynesian model identifies the saving-investment nexus as the source of the problem, the neo-Marxian model finds the difficulty in the saving rate or in the subsistence wage. Correspondingly, the two models suggest different solutions to the problem of stagnation. The neo-Keynesian analysis leads to policies designed to stimulate investment demand or to reduce capitalists' propensity to save; the neo-Marxian model leads (in the more general case in which capitalists consume as well as save) to policies that will stimulate saving, or to policies that will reduce the subsistence wage. The first of these neo-Marxian policies is the opposite of the corresponding neo-Keynesian policy, and the second has no counterpart in neo-Keynesian theory. In the neo-Keynesian model the real wage is a thermometer of economic conditions, not a thermostat.

Initially, stagnation may in any case appear theoretically as well as empirically implausible. If wage rates in the capitalist sector are higher than productivity in the sectors that absorb the surplus workers, a relative decline in the fraction of the labor force employed in the capitalist sector implies a decline in the average standard of living of the working population, not much in evidence in the long-run perform-ance of economies in which capitalism plays a prominent role.

To reconcile stagnation with the absence of a general decline in standards of living requires us, momentarily at least, to admit techno-logical change, in order to break the link between the growth rate of output and the growth rate of employment. Suppose technological change is "labor augmenting," so that the labor coefficient declines at the rate μ:

$$a_{0t} = a_0(1 + \mu)^{-t}.$$

Consequently, employment at time t is given by

$$L_t = a_{0t}X_t = a_0(1 + \mu)^{-t}X_t.$$

If output grows at the rate g,

$$X_t = (1 + g)^t X_0,$$

we have

$$L_t = a_0(1 + \mu)^{-t}(1 + g)^t X_0.$$

Now

$$(1 + \mu)^{-t}(1 + g)^t \simeq (1 + g - \mu)^t,$$

at least for small g and μ, which is to say that employment grows approximately at the rate $g - \mu$:

$$L_t \simeq (1 + g - \mu)^t L_0.$$

Evidently employment in the capitalist sector grows less rapidly than output, and it is certainly conceivable that employment would grow less rapidly than population. That is, the inequality

$$g > n > g - \mu$$

is a possible configuration if hardly a necessary one. In this case, technological change might permit growth in capitalist production to mask stagnation in capitalist employment. The population as a whole —unemployed as well as employed—might enjoy a rising standard of living thanks to the increasing output of the ever-shrinking proportion of the labor force productively engaged in the capitalist sector.

It seems to me impossible to rule this story out of court as a descrip-tion of advanced capitalism. Nevertheless, my own intuition, already suggested in the discussion of the neo-Marxian model, is that, despite the experience of the last decade, the more prevalent tendency is for the capitalist mode of production to exhibit a rate of growth g^* in excess of n, to grow therefore at the expense of other modes of production, as well as by means of migration of men and machines.

Two Conceptions of the Reserve Army

The emphasis by Robinson on capitalists' fellow-feeling and changes in the cost and availability of credit as the processes by which g^* is brought down to n and the real wage adjusted to the supply of labor reflects a significant difference from Marx, who emphasized the power of *workers* to increase the real wage when labor demand presses on the available supply. But even more fundamental is the implicit rejection in Robinson's model of the Marxian insight into a totally different mechanism for resolving the differences between g^* and n: the adjustment of n to g^* by means of a continual re-creation of the reserve army. Robinson, along with other neo-Keynesians, appears to treat the reserve army as a fixed resource rather than one that is continually reconstituted according to the needs of capitalist production. Neither assault on competing modes of production nor importation of foreign workers is considered. Nor, for that matter, is the possibility of reducing g^* to n by exporting capital, a possibility that would obviate the necessity of increasing the real wage, be it through restraint from above or pressure from below.

The contrast between the neo-Marxian and neo-Keynesian conceptions of labor supply seems clearly related to the origins of the two theories. For Marx, witness to the tremendous expansion of nineteenth-century capitalism, it was natural to formulate the reserve army in dynamic terms. For Keynes, witness to the calamity of the Great Depression, it was equally natural to formulate the reserve army in static terms suitable for the analysis of the short run. In the short run, if not in the long, it makes sense to consider the labor force as given exogenously.

Viewed from a neoclassical perspective, however, there is a serious problem with the Keynesian equilibrium sketched at the beginning of Chapter 4: how, with a fixed supply of labor N_0, could a point like L^* in Figure 5.4 be an equilibrium? How is it that the unemployed workers $(N_0 - L^*)$ do not undercut the going wage? What prevents capitalists from taking advantage of the pressure of unemployed workers milling about the factory gates to cut wages? What, in short, prevents the neoclassical wage-adjustment equation

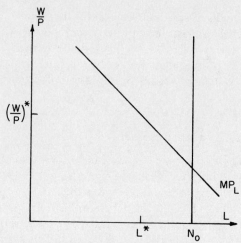

Figure 5.4 Keynesian short-run labor-market equilibrium: L^* is the assumed equilibrium level of employment; $(W/P)^*$ is the corresponding real wage

$$W = \theta\left(\frac{V_{-1}}{k} - 1\right) + W_{-1} \qquad (2.22)$$

from functioning — either in money or in real terms?

The explanation of Keynesian short-run equilibrium can take place in terms of rationing the given supply of labor, in the manner of Robert Barro and Herschel Grossman (1976) or Edmond Malinvaud (1977, 1980), but this approach seems to me to obscure the essential Keynesian insight rather than to elucidate it. It seems to me much more Keynesian simply to do away altogether with the notion of a short-run labor-supply *function* like the vertical line at N_0 in Figure 5.4. In the short run, *any* amount of labor (up to full employment of the labor force N_0) is available at *any* real wage, in the manner of Figure 5.5. To the Keynesian, the difficulties of immediately securing a livelihood outside the capitalist sector suggest that in the short run at least there need be no absolute reservation wage, at least not for the working class as a whole. Or rather, in the absence of unemployment benefits and accumulated household wealth, the *class* reservation wage may fairly be taken to be zero: workers and their families must eat, and any wage is better than none.

Nevertheless, Friedrich Engels and Bertolt Brecht notwithstanding, feeding one's face need not come before morality. Whatever the privation involved, workers may refuse to accept work at less than the

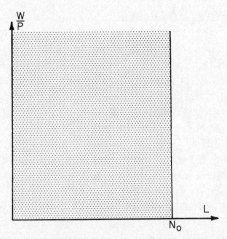

Figure 5.5   Keynesian labor supply (represented by shaded area)

going wage, so that *any* wage level can persist despite the absence of a positive class reservation wage. In other words, the going wage, whatever it might be, may become the *individual* reservation wage, which prevents wage cutting by workers.

Arthur Pigou made a similar point in emphasizing the importance of perceptions of fairness in wage determination, both in his pre-Keynesian (1933) and post-Keynesian (1945) incarnations. John Hicks (1974) and Robert Solow (1980) have recently reiterated the point: standards of fairness — Marxists would say *class* standards of fairness — may make an unemployed individual loath to underbid his more fortunate fellows in order to secure a job. Ultimately, Solow suggests, these standards may rest on social pressure for their enforcement, but social pressure is perhaps a tame terminology for a repertoire of mechanisms that run the gamut from ostracism to violence, a repertoire as much political as social in nature.[2]

There is probably another mechanism at work. In societies like ours, one's work and pay play an important role in the very definition of self. To offer to work for less than the going wage is necessarily to lower one's self-image. It is not surprising that the unemployed resist a

2. The example Solow uses to drive home his point is less than compelling. He invites us to recognize the implausibility of a colleague "of roughly [equal] status in the profession, but teaching in a less desirable department . . . offering to teach [in one's own department] for less money" (1980, p. 5). Implausible, to be sure, but as much — if not more — because of George Akerlof's "lemons principle" (1970) than because of behavioral standards.

wage-cutting strategy, whatever the community's tolerance for such behavior.

These supply-side arguments are reinforced by demand-side considerations: employers' wage strategies may be as insensitive to the prevailing degree of unemployment as workers'. Andrew Ure,[3] struck by the failure of the wage rate to clear the labor market in the textile industry a century and a half ago, asked "how with . . . surplus hands the wages of fine spinners can be maintained at their present high pitch" (1835, p. 336).

The answer lay in what was to become the Marxian distinction between labor power and labor, between labor time purchased or piece rates agreed to and product delivered to the capitalists' storeroom. In the capitalists' best of all possible worlds, workers internalize notions of duty and obligation, which obviates the necessity for supervision and discipline to bridge the gap between labor power and labor. But operating a newly established mode of production, capitalists in Ure's time could hardly appeal to usage sanctified by custom, and even in traditional modes of production the power of internalized norms is limited. Relatively heavy-handed supervision and discipline are the obvious substitutes for internalized standards of performance; indeed, I argued in an earlier article (Marglin 1974) that supervision and discipline, rather than new sources of energy — water and steam power — were the key to the emergence of the factory system. Whether or not one ranks supervision and discipline as highly as I do in the list of reasons for the transition from the putting-out system to the factory, it is difficult to read the history of the industrial revolution without acquiring a healthy respect for the magnitude of the organizational problem. And supervision and discipline were as expensive as they were necessary. It is no wonder, therefore, that right from the outset capitalists sought alternatives to direct oversight of the production process.

Here is where the wage rate came in; high and stable wages, wages in excess of what the traffic might bear at any given moment, were a means of purchasing the loyalty and commitment of workers. Listen once again to Ure: "To this question [of why wages remain high in the face of unemployment] one of the best informed manufacturers made me this reply: 'We find a moderate saving in the wages to be of little consequence in comparison of contentment and we therefore keep them as high as we can possibly afford, in order to be entitled to the best quality of work. A spinner reckons the charge of a pair of mules in our

3. An early enthusiast of the industrial revolution, Ure is better known to history as the *bête noire* of Karl Marx.

factory a fortune for life, he will therefore do his utmost to retain his situation, and to uphold the high character of our yarn'" (p. 336). This argument would seem to have lost little of its force in the intervening century and a half. Thus, capitalists as well as workers may be loath to engage in wage cutting as a response to unemployment, for the attempt to be penny-wise in terms of short-run labor costs may be pound-foolish when reckoned in terms of the role of the wage rate in bridging the gap between labor power and labor.

Such is a conception of the labor market appropriate to Keynesian theory. Of course, these demand- and supply-side arguments, singly or together, can explain no more than the *persistence* of "high" wages in the face of unemployment — why, in other words, the wage rate fails to equilibrate labor-market demand and supply in the face of even massive unemployment. Neither fairness and fellow-feeling on the workers' side nor the purchase of commitment and loyalty on the capitalists' explains *how* the wage rate is determined. This is where, in the Keynesian story, aggregate demand comes in. Aggregate demand determines output, employment, and the marginal productivity of labor. The price level adjusts the real wage to the marginal productivity of labor.[4]

The neo-Keynesian conception of the labor market is essentially an extension of the short-run Keynesian conception to a longer period. In the neo-Keynesian formulation, short-run labor supply is implicitly conceptualized as a set bounded by the size of the labor force, as in Figure 5.5. In the long run, natural increase continually moves the boundary of this set outward, as in the neoclassical model; but, in sharp contrast with the neoclassical model, any point in the interior of the set, as well as on the boundary, is feasible in long-run equilibrium as well as out of equilibrium. Thus the asymmetry in the neo-Keynesian results: in the long run, the natural growth rate n puts a ceiling on feasible growth rates, but not a floor (Robinson 1962, p. 87).

This extension of the short-run Keynesian conception of the labor market to the long run is problematic. To begin with, the argument against a positive absolute reservation wage loses much of its force in the context of the long run. Hence so do the arguments that emphasize the persistence of any given wage, whatever its level might be. Even if the costs of shifting to and from the capitalist sector are sufficiently high that these options can be ignored in calculating a short-run labor-supply

4. In the standard Keynesian analysis, it is the *level* of aggregate demand that determines the real wage, as outlined at the beginning of Chapter 4. In the neo-Keynesian analysis, at least in the bare-bones version of Chapter 4, it is the *composition* of aggregate demand that is crucial. In Chapter 9, which relaxes the assumption of fixed proportions, the neo-Keynesian model comes to resemble the Keynesian more closely.

set, movement of workers between sectors—and even across national borders—is a realistic alternative over the long run. Fellow-feeling and fairness may play a role, but in the long run the availability of employment outside the capitalist sector cannot be ignored in calculating the opportunity cost of labor or the reservation wage. This would seem to be the logic, or at least a logic, behind the introduction of a real-wage floor, the Robinsonian inflation barrier, into a model in which the wage is otherwise completely determined by demand and supply in the goods market.

Neither is the argument *à la* Ure for the independence of the wage rate from labor-market conditions as plausible in the long run as in the short. To be sure, capitalists may be equally inclined to purchase the loyalty of workers, but in the long run this is a sufficient reason only for the wage to contain an element of rent, for the wage to exceed the worker's opportunity cost. It is not in itself a reason for the wage to be invariant with respect to the rate of unemployment. Ure effects, indeed, need hardly prevent the wage from clearing the labor market in the long run, at least in the sense of adjusting demand and supply to an equilibrium rate of unemployment, and this would be enough to restore the long-run equilibrium condition $g = n$.

For both these reasons, the neo-Marxian conception of the labor market relies neither on fairness and fellow-feeling nor on the purchase of loyalty to explain the absence of $g = n$ as an equilibrium condition. The neo-Marxian assumption of a variety of alternative sources of supply of labor to the capitalist sector is essentially a generalization of W. Arthur Lewis's notion of unlimited supplies of labor (1954). The effect is to make the labor force an endogenous variable determined solely by demand. Population growth is neither a ceiling nor a floor in the neo-Marxian model; in the long run, the supply of labor is infinitely elastic at the subsistence wage, in the manner of Figure 5.6.

The labor force available to the capitalist sector expands (or contracts) according to demand. In the neo-Marxian view, a buoyant capitalism will meet its labor requirements much as the countries of northern and western Europe did in the quarter century of expansion that followed World War II, first by drawing on the labor resources of family agriculture and other noncapitalist modes of production, then by drawing on the labor resources of an ever-widening geographical periphery that ultimately included the entire Mediterranean basin and beyond.

By the same token, a stagnant capitalism will simply fail to attract labor. In the extreme case of declining demand for labor, the labor force available to the capitalist sector will decline absolutely. In the

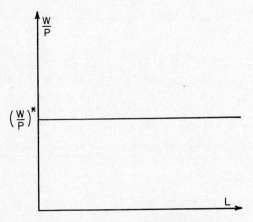

Figure 5.6   Neo-Marxian labor supply

place of the overt unemployment that characterizes stagnation in the neo-Keynesian view, neo-Marxian unemployment is characteristically "disguised unemployment." As the capitalist mode of production declines relatively if not absolutely, a growing percentage of the population may be absorbed in various petty modes of production as well as in the government sector. And some may emigrate. Relatively few of the unemployed need be on the bread line.

I shall come back to the differences between the neo-Marxian and neo-Keynesian conceptions of the labor supply towards the end of this book, in Chapter 16. But these differences should not be allowed to obscure a fundamental similarity between the two theories, at least relative to the neoclassical view. Absent from both neo-Marxian and neo-Keynesian approaches to the labor market is the reliance on the price mechanism, the Invisible Hand, that in neoclassical theory equates the demand for labor with the exogenously given supply.

6 Generalizing the Classics: The Cambridge Saving Equation

It is at the very least premature to attempt to make the models behaviorally, institutionally, and technologically realistic. Even so, some of the assumptions must be relaxed simply to satisfy doubts that the bare-bones models presented so far really do capture a fundamental essence of neoclassical, neo-Marxian, and neo-Keynesian theories.

A first step in this direction is to generalize the classical saving function to reflect the possibility that capitalists might not save their entire incomes. If the fraction s_C of profits is saved, and the remainder $(1 - s_C)$ consumed, saving per worker becomes

$$s_C r \frac{a_1}{a_0},$$

and saving per unit of seed corn becomes

$$g = s(r) = s_C r.$$

Evidently this modification hardly changes either the neo-Marxian or the neo-Keynesian analysis. With $s_C < 1$, the saving function merely makes a sharper angle with the vertical axis, as Figure 6.1(a) and (b) shows. Of course in both cases the result $g^* = r^*$ goes by the board, but this result never had anything more than symmetry to recommend it anyway.

More interesting is the difference between neo-Marxian and neo-Keynesian comparative statics, shown in Figure 6.1. Differentiating the equilibrium condition

$$g^* = s_C r^*$$

with respect to s_C, we obtain

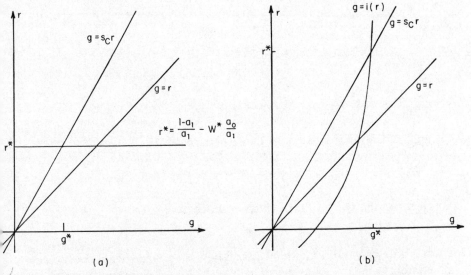

Figure 6.1 Equilibrium with $s_C < 1$. (a) neo-Marxian equilibrium; (b) neo-Keynesian equilibrium

$$\frac{dg^*}{ds_C} = r^* + s_C \frac{dr^*}{ds_C}. \tag{6.1}$$

In the neo-Marxian case we have

$$r^* = \frac{1 - a_1}{a_1} - W^* \frac{a_0}{a_1}$$

as the second equilibrium condition, so

$$\frac{dr^*}{ds_C} = 0.$$

Thus we have

$$\frac{dg^*}{ds_C} = r^*,$$

with the result that an increase in s_C implies an increase in g^*. The logic is straightforward: a higher propensity to save means that more surplus is available for accumulation.

In the neo-Keynesian case an increase in s_C leads to a *decrease* in g^*: a lower profit rate is needed to finance the given rate of investment, but the lower profit rate induces a lower rate of investment and growth. Formally, the second equilibrium condition is

$$g^* = i(r^*),$$

so

$$\frac{dr^*}{ds_C} = \frac{r^*}{i'(r^*) - s_C},$$

and, substituting into Eq. (6.1), we obtain

$$\frac{dg^*}{ds_C} = r^* \frac{i'(r^*)}{i'(r^*) - s_C}.$$

Generalizing the results of Chapter 4, we have

$$i'(r^*) - s_C < 0$$

as a stability condition, which establishes that at a stable neo-Keynesian equilibrium, dg^*/ds_C is negative. We shall have occasion to return to this asymmetry in Chapters 16 and 20.

If capitalists need not save all their income, workers need hardly consume all theirs. Nicholas Kaldor (1956) posits that workers save the fraction s_W of wages,

$$0 \le s_W < s_C \le 1.$$

On a per-worker basis, aggregate saving becomes

$$s_C r \frac{a_1}{a_0} + s_W W,$$

W denoting the real wage. Saving per unit of seed corn becomes

$$g = s(r) = s_C r + s_W W \frac{a_0}{a_1}.$$

Or, since

$$1 = W a_0 + (1 + r)a_1, \tag{1.7}$$

the rate of saving per unit of capital can be written

$$g = s(r) = s_W \frac{1 - a_1}{a_1} + (s_C - s_W)r. \tag{6.2}$$

With a Kaldorian saving function, the basic neo-Marxian and neo-Keynesian diagrams take the form shown in Figure 6.2(a) and (b). Once again the analysis does not change very much, provided workers save a

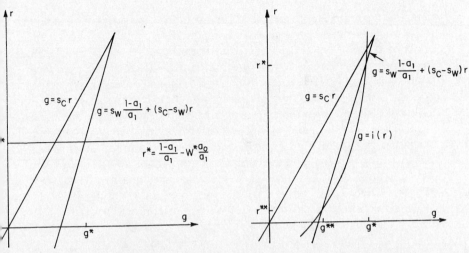

Figure 6.2 Equilibrium with a Kaldorian saving function. (a) neo-Marxian equilibrium; (b) neo-Keynesian equilibrium

smaller fraction of their incomes than do capitalists.[1] The proportionality of profit and growth rates disappears, and the neo-Keynesian equilibrium $\langle r^*, g^* \rangle$ becomes dependent on the capital:output ratio $(1 - a_1)/a_1$ and consequently on technology. (By contrast, the neo-Marxian equilibrium is *always* technology-dependent. Even with the simplest version of the Cambridge equation, the classical saving function $g = r$, the equilibrium profit rate depends on technology—specifically, on the labor:capital ratio a_0/a_1—as well as on the subsistence wage.)

The only other novelty introduced by the Kaldorian saving function is that multiple equilibria become more plausible in the neo-Keynesian case. A strictly concave investment function with a positive intercept is no longer sufficient to ensure the uniqueness of equilibrium.

There is a real problem with the Kaldorian saving function represented by Eq. (6.2). In a celebrated article Luigi Pasinetti (1962) objected to this formulation on the ground that workers, if they save,

---

1. On the other hand, the analysis changes radically if $s_W > s_C$. In this case the saving function defined by Eq. (6.2) has a negative slope, and we are essentially back to the neoclassical case. Indeed the case $s_W = \beta$, $s_C = -1/r$ is exactly the life-cycle saving function under the assumption of Cobb-Douglas utility. In this case, Eq. (6.2) becomes

$$g = s(r) = \beta \frac{1 - a_1}{a_1} + \left(-\frac{1}{r} - \beta\right) r = \beta \left[\frac{1}{a_1} - (1 + r)\right] - 1. \qquad (2.17)$$

must own part of the stock of seed corn and that *their* propensity to save (s_W), not the higher propensity (s_C) of capitalists, rightly applies to the portion of total *profits* accruing to workers. Kaldor's response (1966) also had considerable merit: the appropriate distinction, he maintained, is not between categories of *savers* but between categories of saving. The propensity to save profits is higher than the propensity to save wages, not because capitalists have higher incomes or are more avaricious, but because of differences in saving behavior between organizations (like the corporation, which accounts for most of the saving out of profits) and individuals, be they wage earners or *rentiers*. This, I confess, is a view with which I have great sympathy, having tried my own hand at developing it independently of Kaldor (Marglin 1975). Pasinetti in effect associates himself with an extreme neoclassical position in seeing the corporation as a mere veil for the interest of its owners, in whose hands the real decisions lie.

But it won't do as an answer to Pasinetti simply to emphasize the distinctive nature and independent role of the corporation, for even if we accept this point, we must recognize that there may be differences in the saving behavior of wage earners and *rentiers* with respect to the share of profits that *is* distributed to the legal owners of capitalist enterprise (roughly half of after-tax profits in the United States). Indeed the full force of Pasinetti's argument can be best appreciated by starting with a simple model in which *all* profits are distributed as dividends, adding in corporate retentions only after the basic model is worked out.

A Simple Pasinetti Saving Function

Let capitalists save the fraction s_C of their income (profits), and let workers save the fraction s_W of their income (wages *plus* profits on the share of seed corn they own). Then, assuming the profit rate on all seed corn is the same, aggregate saving per worker is

$$S = s_W W + s_W r \frac{K_W}{L} + s_C r \frac{K_C}{L},$$

where K_W and K_C represent the seed corn owned by workers and capitalists respectively. This can be translated into saving per unit of seed corn by multiplying through by the labor : capital ratio, L/K:

$$g = S \frac{L}{K} = s_W W \frac{L}{K} + s_W r \frac{K_W}{K} + s_C r \frac{K_C}{K}.$$

If we denote the shares of seed corn owned by workers and capitalists by $(1 - \delta)$ and δ, which is to say

$$1 - \delta = \frac{K_W}{K}, \qquad \delta = \frac{K_C}{K},$$

and we rewrite L/K as a_0/a_1, we have

$$g = s(r, \delta) = s_W W \frac{a_0}{a_1} + (1 - \delta)s_W r + \delta s_C r. \qquad (6.3)$$

By virtue of the price equation

$$1 = W a_0 + (1 + r)a_1, \qquad (1.7)$$

we obtain

$$g = s(r, \delta) = s_W \frac{1 - a_1}{a_1} + (s_C - s_W)\delta r \qquad (6.4)$$

from Eq. (6.3).

At first blush, the quasi-Kaldorian equation (6.4) would hardly seem to differ from the pure Kaldorian equation (6.2). The only difference is the coefficient δ in the second term. For any given δ we can draw a saving function, and Figure 6.3 illustrates three such, for $\delta = 0$, 0.5, and 1.0.

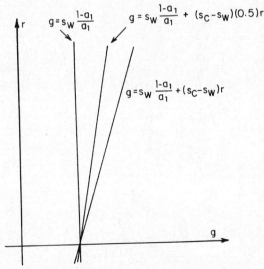

Figure 6.3 Quasi-Kaldorian saving functions for different values of δ

But Figure 6.3 is misleading as a description of long-run equilibrium, for in the long run δ is not a given parameter but an endogenous variable: $\delta = \hat{\delta}(r)$, or more simply $\delta = \hat{\delta}$ where this shorthand is not misleading. It is easy to see that the relationship defined by $\hat{\delta}(r)$ is generally positive: when $r = 0$, all saving takes place out of wages, so $\hat{\delta}(0) = 0$. At the other extreme, when $r = r_{max}$, $W = 0$, so—assuming $s_C > s_W$—$\hat{\delta}(r_{max}) = 1$.

An immediate consequence of Pasinetti's reformulation of the saving function is the addition of a new dimension to the determination of the "long run." A substantially longer period may be required for ownership shares δ and $(1 - \delta)$ to adjust to steady-growth proportions $\hat{\delta}$ and $(1 - \hat{\delta})$ than is required simply to average out economic fluctuations.

More important, the shape of the long-run Pasinetti saving function differs substantially from the quasi-Kaldorian function pictured in Figure 6.3. According to Figure 6.4, there is a corner in the saving function: with $r < s_W(1 - a_1)/s_C a_1$,

$$s(r) = s_W(1 - a_1)/a_1;$$

with $r > s_W(1 - a_1)/s_C a_1$,

$$s(r) = s_C r.$$

Moreover, above the corner the classical form of the saving function is

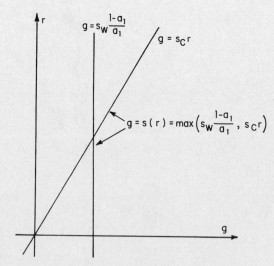

Figure 6.4 Long-run saving function *à la* Pasinetti

restored: growth and profit rates are proportional. In short, with δ defined endogenously by $\hat{\delta}(r)$ to reflect long-run, steady-growth proportions, the Pasinetti saving function is given by

$$s(r) = \max\left(s_W \frac{1-a_1}{a_1}, s_C r\right). \tag{6.5}$$

The shortest proof that the quasi-Kaldorian saving function (6.4) tends to Eq. (6.5) in the long run—that is, as $\delta \to \hat{\delta}(r)$—is provided by an examination of the behavior of δ over time. Taking first differences on both sides of the definitional equation

$$\delta = \frac{K_C}{K}$$

and noting that

$$\frac{(\Delta K_C)_{+1}}{K_C} = s_C r,$$

we have

$$\delta = \delta_{-1} \frac{1 + s_C r_{-1}}{1 + s(r_{-1}, \delta_{-1})}. \tag{6.6}$$

Equation (6.6) defines $\hat{\delta}(r)$ by virtue of its implicit steady-growth condition: given r, the requirement of long-run equilibrium is $\delta = \delta_{-1}$, which requires either

$$\left.\begin{array}{c} \delta_{-1} = 0 \\ \\ s_C r_{-1} = s(r_{-1}, \delta_{-1}). \end{array}\right\} \tag{6.7}$$

or

Now couple Eqs. (6.7) with (1) the continuity of $\hat{\delta}(r)$; (2) the boundary condition $\hat{\delta}(0) = 0$—which is to say that with a zero profit rate capitalists' share of seed corn eventually vanishes; and (3) the boundary condition $\hat{\delta}(r_{\max}) = 1$—which says that with a zero wage capitalists come eventually to own all but a vanishing share of the capital stock (provided their initial endowment is positive). The result is the Pasinetti saving function represented by Eq. (6.5) and illustrated in Figure 6.4.

This demonstration has the virtue of succinctness, but its intuitive appeal leaves much to be desired. A longer discussion is required to reach the economic relationships underlying Pasinetti's results. We start from the steady-growth condition

$$\frac{(\Delta K_W)_{+1}}{K_W} = \frac{(\Delta K_C)_{+1}}{K_C}, \tag{6.8}$$

which holds whenever the equilibrium shares of workers and capitalists are both positive. When $\hat{\delta}$ lies at one of the end points of the interval $[0, 1]$, the corresponding conditions are

$$\frac{(\Delta K_W)_{+1}}{K_W} > \frac{(\Delta K_C)_{+1}}{K_C} \tag{6.9}$$

with $\hat{\delta} = 0$, and

$$\frac{(\Delta K_C)_{+1}}{K_C} > \frac{(\Delta K_W)_{+1}}{K_W} \tag{6.10}$$

with $\hat{\delta} = 1$. The end points are relevant, it should be noted, because $\hat{\delta}$ represents a *share* of a stock, a stock whose size increases without bound with the passage of time. We cannot rule out the possibility that the steady state is achieved only as the share of one class or the other goes to zero.

Evidently, if workers' and capitalists' shares of seed corn are growing at the same rate, the overall stock of corn must also grow at this rate. So in the long run we may amend (6.8) to read

$$g = \frac{(\Delta K_W)_{+1}}{K_W} = \frac{(\Delta K_C)_{+1}}{K_C}, \qquad 0 < \hat{\delta} < 1.$$

Similarly, if workers or capitalists own all but a vanishing fraction of the stock of corn, the long-run rate of growth of seed corn is the same as the rate of growth of the corn owned by the one class. Conditions (6.9) and (6.10) become

$$g = \frac{(\Delta K_W)_{+1}}{K_W} > \frac{(\Delta K_C)_{+1}}{K_C}, \qquad \hat{\delta} = 0,$$

and

$$g = \frac{(\Delta K_C)_{+1}}{K_C} > \frac{(\Delta K_W)_{+1}}{K_W}, \qquad \hat{\delta} = 1.$$

But that is not all. The growth of capitalists' seed corn obeys the rule

$$(\Delta K_C)_{+1} = s_C r K_C.$$

Moreover, in the long run we have from Eq. (6.4)

$$g \begin{Bmatrix} > \\ = \end{Bmatrix} s_W \frac{1 - a_1}{a_1}, \qquad \text{as } \hat{\delta} \begin{Bmatrix} > \\ = \end{Bmatrix} 0.$$

Combining these relationships gives the following long-run results:

$$g = \frac{(\Delta K_W)_{+1}}{K_W} = \frac{(\Delta K_C)_{+1}}{K_C} = s_C r > s_W \frac{1 - a_1}{a_1}, \qquad 0 < \hat{\delta} < 1, \qquad (6.11)$$

$$g = \frac{(\Delta K_W)_{+1}}{K_W} = s_W \frac{1 - a_1}{a_1} > \frac{(\Delta K_C)_{+1}}{K_C} = s_C r, \qquad \hat{\delta} = 0, \qquad (6.12)$$

$$g = \frac{(\Delta K_C)_{+1}}{K_C} = s_C r > s_W \frac{1 - a_1}{a_1}, \qquad \hat{\delta} = 1. \qquad (6.13)$$

Taking conditions (6.11), (6.12), and (6.13) together gives the long-run saving function the shape pictured in Figure 6.4. Geometrically, the long-run saving function is constructed from the short-run function described in Eq. (6.4) by varying $\hat{\delta}$ parametrically. The vertical segment corresponding to $\hat{\delta} = 0$ defines the long-run saving function from the horizontal axis up to the point at which $g = s_C r$. The short-run saving function corresponding to each positive value of $\hat{\delta}$ contributes exactly one point to the long-run function, namely the point at which, for the given value of $\hat{\delta}$, $g = s_C r$.

Observe that a positive wage rate is a necessary *and* sufficient condition for workers' seed corn to grow at least as rapidly as capitalists'. That is to say, workers asymptotically own a positive share of the capital stock, $\hat{\delta} < 1$, for all $r < r_{max}$.

The necessity of $W > 0$ for $\hat{\delta} < 1$ is obvious. For with $W = 0$ workers' accumulation is governed by the relationship

$$(\Delta K_W)_{+1} = s_W r K_W$$

so that

$$\frac{(\Delta K_W)_{+1}}{K_W} = s_W r < s_C r = \frac{(\Delta K_C)_{+1}}{K_C},$$

and $\delta \to 1$ in the long run.

It may not be quite as obvious that a positive wage is a *sufficient* condition for workers' corn to accumulate at least as rapidly as capitalists'. In fact, however, if $W > 0$, then, whatever the growth rate of seed corn as a whole, workers' corn must ultimately grow at this rate. So workers always own a nonvanishing share of total corn; this is to say that in the steady state, $\hat{\delta} < 1$. Formally,

$$W > 0 \Rightarrow \lim_{t \to \infty} \frac{(\Delta K_W)_{+1}}{K_W} = g. \qquad (6.14)$$

To prove (6.14) we must solve the difference equation for worker's accumulation:

$$(\Delta K_W)_{+1} = s_W W L + s_W r K_W.$$

With L growing at the rate g and $L_0 = 1$, we have

$$L_t = (1 + g)^t,$$

and, for $t \geq 1$,

$$K_{Wt} = (1 + s_W r)^t K_{W0} + s_W \sum_{\tau=0}^{t-1} (1 + s_W r)^{t-1-\tau}(1 + g)^\tau W. \qquad (6.15)$$

On simplifying, Eq. (6.15) becomes

$$K_{Wt} = (1 + s_W r)^t K_{W0} + \frac{s_W W}{g - s_W r}\left[1 - \left(\frac{1 + s_W r}{1 + g}\right)^t \right][1 + g]^t,$$

provided $g \neq s_W r$, an inequality guaranteed by Eq. (6.3). Now the rate of growth of workers' seed corn is

$$\frac{(\Delta K_W)_{t+1}}{K_{Wt}} = \frac{s_W (1 + g)^t W}{K_{Wt}} + s_W r$$

$$= \frac{s_W W}{\left(\dfrac{1 + s_W r}{1 + g}\right)^t K_{W0} + \dfrac{s_W W}{g - s_W r}\left[1 - \left(\dfrac{1 + s_W r}{1 + g}\right)^t \right]} + s_W r.$$

However, not only is $g \neq s_W r$, but $g > s_W r$; by virtue of Eq. (6.3), g is at least as big as any weighted average of $s_W r$ and $s_C r$, and $s_C r$ is greater than $s_W r$. So $[(1 + s_W r)/(1 + g)]^t$ goes to zero as t increases without bound. Thus

$$\lim_{t \to \infty} \frac{(\Delta K_W)_{t+1}}{K_{Wt}} = \frac{1}{\dfrac{1}{g - s_W r}} + s_W r = g. \qquad (6.16)$$

The logic of Eq. (6.16) is that workers' seed corn must ultimately grow at the same rate as total wages, since a constant fraction of wages is added to the stock in every period, and the growth of total wages (g) is necessarily more rapid than the growth that results from the reinvestment of profits on previously accumulated corn ($s_W r$). It is the periodic "injection" from wages that ensures that workers' ultimate share of seed corn is positive whenever the wage rate is positive. By contrast, for capitalists' ultimate share of seed corn to be positive requires that the rate of profit be high enough that $s_C r$ is equal to the overall rate of growth.

Evidently, this is the crucial difference between Pasinetti's formulation and Kaldor's. In Kaldor's original formulation, the seed corn owned by workers grows as rapidly as capitalists' seed corn even without the periodic injection of a positive fraction of wages. Whenever the wage rate is positive, therefore, workers' corn must grow at a *faster* rate than capitalists' corn. Thus in Kaldor's formulation, the fraction of seed corn held by capitalists necessarily vanishes in the steady state *except* in the limiting case when the wage rate is zero. This logical consequence of the Kaldor model is obscured by the fact that the division of the stock of corn plays no role in the model. It might indeed go totally unnoticed were it not for Pasinetti's reformulation.

Neo-Keynesian Equilibrium

A seemingly minor change in the assumptions — lowering the propensity to save on the proportion of profits that accrues to workers from s_C to s_W — makes a big difference. If we superimpose the Keynesian investment function on Figure 6.4, as in Figure 6.5, we restore the simple and neat equilibrium condition

$$g = s(r) = s_C r, \tag{6.17}$$

a hallmark of nonneoclassical theory by virtue of the emphasis it gives

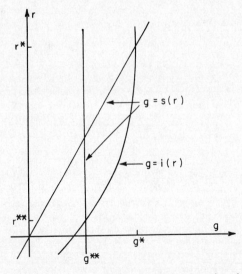

Figure 6.5 Neo-Keynesian equilibria with a Pasinetti saving function

to a particular relationship between growth and distribution: the growth rate is independent of technology and workers' propensity to save, and so is the distribution of income between wages and profits.

But a word of warning may be in order: the restoration of Eq. (6.17) as an equilibrium condition is a result of limited significance for three reasons. First, although the functional distribution of income is independent of workers' saving as well as of technology, the personal distribution of income between *workers* and *capitalists* is not: $\hat{\delta}$ is a function of both s_W and a_1.[2]

Second, Eq. (6.17) necessarily obtains only if we rule out the possibility of an equilibrium in the $\hat{\delta} = 0$ region of "people's capitalism," what Paul Samuelson and Franco Modigliani (1966) have called the "anti-Pasinetti" region. A people's capitalism equilibrium can be challenged either on theoretical or on empirical grounds. But the theoretical argument, based on the instability of a people's capitalism equilibrium, relies essentially on fixed coefficients and the absence of corporate retentions.[3] And the empirical argument is equivocal, as the discussion at the end of this chapter shows.

Third, Pasinetti's restoration of the classical verities is limited to the characterization of equilibrium. An important change in stability conditions accompanies the introduction of δ as a variable exogenous in the short run but endogenous in the long.

Stability

In Chapter 4, successive short-run equilibria were characterized by a fixed money wage $\overline{W}$ and a variable price level P. The adjustment equation

2. The relative importance of property income to capitalists and workers does not depend on $\hat{\delta}$ alone. For capitalists property income is everything regardless of $\hat{\delta}$; for workers the importance of property income is determined by the ratio $[(1 - \hat{\delta})rK]/[WL + (1 - \hat{\delta})rK]$, hence by rK and WL as well as by $\hat{\delta}$. Thus property income may be of modest importance to workers even if $\hat{\delta}$ is reasonably large. If, for instance, $\hat{\delta} = 0.5$, $r = 0.1$, $K/L = 3$, and $W = 1$, then

$$\frac{(1 - \hat{\delta})rK}{WL + (1 - \hat{\delta})rK} = 0.13,$$

so that returns from capital constitute little more than one-eighth of a worker's income. Thus even with workers owning a relatively large share of the capital stock, we can reasonably differentiate them from capitalists on the basis of the differences in the principal source of income. In any case, the source of income is by no means the only basis for distinguishing capitalists from workers. It will be argued presently that the essence of the matter is *control* over the production process; historically, control and ownership have been correlated only imperfectly.

3. With $\hat{\delta} = 0$, it is of course the workers who own the corporations!

$$Pr = P_{-1}i(r_{-1}), \tag{4.16}$$

generalizes directly to

$$Ps(r, \delta) = P_{-1}i(r_{-1}) \tag{6.18}$$

in the context of the Pasinetti saving function. Together Eq. (6.18) and Eq. (6.6),

$$\delta = \delta_{-1} \frac{1 + s_C r_{-1}}{1 + s(r_{-1}, \delta_{-1})}, \tag{6.6}$$

implicitly define two functions,

$$r = G(r_{-1}, \delta_{-1}) \tag{6.19}$$

and

$$\delta = H(r_{-1}, \delta_{-1}), \tag{6.20}$$

that jointly describe the movement of the neo-Keynesian system from one short-run equilibrium to another.

A long-run equilibrium $\langle r^*, \delta^* \rangle$, as a stationary point of this system, is characterized by

$$r^* = G(r^*, \delta^*), \qquad \delta^* = H(r^*, \delta^*)$$

or

$$s(r^*, \delta^*) = i(r^*), \qquad \delta^*[s_C r^* - s(r^*, \delta^*)] = 0.$$

Stability of this equilibrium depends on the characteristic roots of the matrix of first derivatives of the functions G and H evaluated at $\langle r^*, \delta^* \rangle$. For stability it is necessary and sufficient that the real parts of the characteristic roots of the matrix

$$\mathbf{J} = \begin{bmatrix} \dfrac{\partial G}{\partial r_{-1}} & \dfrac{\partial G}{\partial \delta_{-1}} \\ \dfrac{\partial H}{\partial r_{-1}} & \dfrac{\partial H}{\partial \delta_{-1}} \end{bmatrix}$$

be less than unity in absolute value at $\langle r_{-1}, \delta_{-1} \rangle = \langle r^*, \delta^* \rangle$, a requirement equivalent to the Routh-Hurwitz conditions

$$|\text{tr } \mathbf{J}| < |1 + \det \mathbf{J}| \tag{6.21}$$

and

$$|\det \mathbf{J}| < 1. \tag{6.22}$$

From Eq. (6.18) we have the two equations

$$\frac{dP}{dr}\frac{\partial G}{\partial r_{-1}}s(r,\delta) + P\frac{\partial s}{\partial r}\frac{\partial G}{\partial r_{-1}} + P\frac{\partial s}{\partial \delta}\frac{\partial H}{\partial r_{-1}} = \frac{dP_{-1}}{dr_{-1}}i(r_{-1}) + P_{-1}i'(r_{-1}),$$

$$\frac{dP}{dr}\frac{\partial G}{\partial \delta_{-1}}s(r,\delta) + P\frac{\partial s}{\partial r}\frac{\partial G}{\partial \delta_{-1}} + P\frac{\partial s}{\partial \delta}\frac{\partial H}{\partial \delta_{-1}} = 0,$$

where $\partial s/\partial r \equiv (s_C - s_W)\delta$. From Eq. (6.6) we have

$$\frac{\partial H}{\partial r_{-1}} = \delta_{-1}\frac{s_C - (s_C - s_W)\delta_{-1}\left(\dfrac{1 + s_C r_{-1}}{1 + s(r_{-1}, \delta_{-1})}\right)}{1 + s(r_{-1}, \delta_{-1})},$$

$$\frac{\partial H}{\partial \delta_{-1}} = \frac{1 + s_C r_{-1}}{1 + s(r_{-1}, \delta_{-1})}\frac{1 + s_W\dfrac{1 - a_1}{a_1}}{1 + s(r_{-1}, \delta_{-1})}.$$

Differentiating the price equation

$$P = \overline{W}a_0 + (1 + r)Pa_1 \tag{4.12}$$

gives

$$\frac{dP}{dr} = \frac{P^2}{\overline{W}}\frac{a_1}{a_0},$$

so that

$$\frac{\partial G}{\partial r_{-1}} = \frac{\dfrac{P_{-1}^2}{\overline{W}}\dfrac{a_1}{a_0}i(r_{-1}) + P_{-1}i'(r_{-1}) - P(s_C - s_W)r\dfrac{\partial H}{\partial r_{-1}}}{\dfrac{P^2}{\overline{W}}\dfrac{a_1}{a_0}s(r,\delta) + P\dfrac{\partial s}{\partial r}},$$

$$\frac{\partial G}{\partial \delta_{-1}} = -\frac{P(s_C - s_W)r\dfrac{\partial H}{\partial \delta_{-1}}}{\dfrac{P^2}{\overline{W}}\dfrac{a_1}{a_0}s(r,\delta) + P\dfrac{\partial s}{\partial r}}.$$

At $r_{-1} = r^*$ we thus have

$$\det \mathbf{J} = \frac{[1 + s_C r^*]\left[1 + s_W\dfrac{1 - a_1}{a_1}\right]\left[\dfrac{P^*}{\overline{W}}\dfrac{a_1}{a_0}i(r^*) + i'(r^*)\right]}{[1 + s(r^*, \delta^*)]^2\left[\dfrac{P^*}{\overline{W}}\dfrac{a_1}{a_0}s(r^*, \delta^*) + \dfrac{\partial s}{\partial r}\right]}.$$

As long as the saving and investment functions are nondecreasing, both

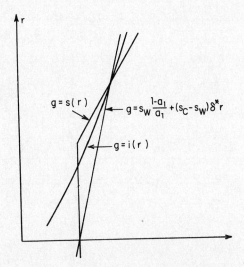

Figure 6.6 Short-run stability condition violated: $i'(r^*) > \partial s / \partial r$

$i'(r^*)$ and $\partial s / \partial r$ are nonnegative, so $\det \mathbf{J}$ is necessarily positive. Hence a sufficient condition for the second of the Routh-Hurwitz inequalities is

$$i'(r^*) < \frac{\partial s}{\partial r}, \tag{6.23}$$

according to which investment demand is less responsive in the *short run* to changes in the rate of profit than is saving. That is, in order to guarantee stability, the investment-demand function must be steeper (relative to the g-axis) than the short-run, quasi-Kaldorian saving function. In Figure 6.6 this condition is not satisfied, even though the investment-demand function is steeper than the *long-run* saving function. So the equilibrium may or may not be stable.

It remains to verify the conditions under which the first of the Routh-Hurwitz inequalities,

$$|\text{tr } \mathbf{J}| < |1 + \det \mathbf{J}|, \tag{6.21}$$

holds. With $\delta^* > 0$ we have

$$\text{tr } \mathbf{J} = \frac{[1 + s(r^*, \delta^*)]\left[\dfrac{P^*}{\overline{W}} \dfrac{a_1}{a_0} i(r^*) + i'(r^*)\right]}{[1 + s(r^*, \delta^*)]\left[\dfrac{P^*}{\overline{W}} \dfrac{a_1}{a_0} s(r^*, \delta^*) + \dfrac{\partial s}{\partial r}\right]}$$

$$-\frac{(s_C - s_W)\delta^* r^*[(1-\delta^*)s_C + \delta^* s_W]}{[1 + s(r^*, \delta^*)]\left[\dfrac{P^*}{\overline{W}}\dfrac{a_1}{a_0}s(r^*, \delta^*) + \dfrac{\partial s}{\partial r}\right]}$$

$$+\frac{\left[1 + s_W\dfrac{1-a_1}{a_1}\right]\left[\dfrac{P^*}{\overline{W}}\dfrac{a_1}{a_0}s(r^*, \delta^*) + \dfrac{\partial s}{\partial r}\right]}{[1 + s(r^*, \delta^*)]\left[\dfrac{P^*}{\overline{W}}\dfrac{a_1}{a_0}s(r^*, \delta^*) + \dfrac{\partial s}{\partial r}\right]}$$

$$= 1 + \det \mathbf{J} - \frac{(s_C - s_W)\delta^* r^*[s_C - i'(r^*)]}{[1 + s(r^*, \delta^*)]\left[\dfrac{P^*}{\overline{W}}\dfrac{a_1}{a_0}s(r^*, \delta^*) + \dfrac{\partial s}{\partial r}\right]}.$$

And with $\delta^* = 0$, we have

$$\mathrm{tr}\,\mathbf{J} = \frac{\left[1 + s_W\dfrac{1-a_1}{a_1}\right]\left[\dfrac{P^*}{\overline{W}}\dfrac{a_1}{a_0}i(r^*) + i'(r^*)\right]}{\left[1 + s_W\dfrac{1-a_1}{a_1}\right]\left[\dfrac{P^*}{\overline{W}}\dfrac{a_1}{a_0}s_W\dfrac{1-a_1}{a_1}\right]}$$

$$+\frac{[1 + s_C r^*]\left[\dfrac{P^*}{\overline{W}}\dfrac{a_1}{a_0}s_W\dfrac{1-a_1}{a_1}\right]}{\left[1 + s_W\dfrac{1-a_1}{a_1}\right]\left[\dfrac{P^*}{\overline{W}}\dfrac{a_1}{a_0}s_W\dfrac{1-a_1}{a_1}\right]}$$

$$= 1 + \det \mathbf{J} + \frac{\left[s_W\dfrac{1-a_1}{a_1} - s_C r^*\right]i'(r^*)}{\left[1 + s_W\dfrac{1-a_1}{a_1}\right]\left[\dfrac{P^*}{\overline{W}}\dfrac{a_1}{a_0}s_W\dfrac{1-a_1}{a_1}\right]}.$$

Thus in either case $\mathrm{tr}\,\mathbf{J}$ is positive, and (6.21) becomes equivalent to

$$\mathrm{tr}\,\mathbf{J} < 1 + \det \mathbf{J}, \tag{6.24}$$

which is satisfied if and only if

$$i'(r^*) < s'(r^*), \tag{6.25}$$

where $s'(r^*)$ is the slope of the long-run saving function

$$s'(r^*) = \begin{cases} 0, & \delta^* = 0, \\ s_C, & \delta^* > 0. \end{cases}$$

In short, inequality (6.24) is satisfied if saving is more responsive to the rate of profit than is investment in the *long run*.

But this adds little to the story: (6.25) is automatically satisfied whenever (6.23) holds. This is because with fixed coefficients a_0 and a_1, saving is always more responsive to the profit rate in the long run than in the short whenever $\delta^* > 0$; and the long-run and short-run functions coincide with $\delta^* = 0$.

The Routh-Hurwitz inequalities permit us to rule out the possibility of a stable neo-Keynesian equilibrium in the $\delta^* = 0$ region. Unfortunately, however, the significance of this result is rather limited. It hinges on a property of the Pasinetti saving function — its vertical slope in the $\hat{\delta} = 0$ region — that disappears once we abandon the simplifying assumptions that production coefficients are fixed and all corporate profits are paid out as dividends.

Neo-Marxian Equilibrium

The neo-Marxian equilibrium fares differently as we pass from Kaldor's to Pasinetti's assumption with respect to saving, as Figure 6.7 indicates. First off, in contrast with the neo-Keynesian model, in which — outside the $\hat{\delta} = 0$ region at least — $\langle r^*, g^* \rangle$ is independent of technological parameters, the equilibrium in Figure 6.7 is *not* independent

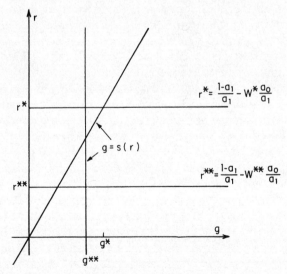

$$r^* = \frac{1-a_1}{a_1} - W^* \frac{a_0}{a_1}$$

$$r^{**} = \frac{1-a_1}{a_1} - W^{**} \frac{a_0}{a_1}$$

$$g = s(r)$$

Figure 6.7 Neo-Marxian equilibria with a Pasinetti saving function

of technology. As we observed in connection with the Kaldorian saving function, the equilibrium profit rate r^* always depends on the labor and seed-corn coefficients, a_0 and a_1, as well as on the real wage rate W^* defined by subsistence:

$$r^* = \frac{1 - a_1}{a_1} - W^* \frac{a_0}{a_1}.$$

Thus, even if at the equilibrium $\langle r^*, g^* \rangle$ the saving relationship

$$g^* = s_C r^*$$

is independent of technology, the equilibrium itself is not. It is misleading to characterize the role of technology in a model by its role in one of *two* equilibrium conditions, namely by its absence in the saving equation.

A second contrast with the neo-Keynesian case is that stability considerations do not rule out the $\hat{\delta} = 0$ equilibrium $\langle r^{**}, g^{**} \rangle$. In principle at least, a sufficiently powerful working class might succeed in imposing a wage high enough that with the passage of time capitalists would come to own a vanishing share of the seed corn in the economy.

A Short Digression on People's Capitalism: Claims on Profit, Ownership, and Control

How should we characterize an economy in which capital is no longer the exclusive property of capitalists? The answer must be equivocal. Workers may have claims on capital (such as bonds) but not own it. Furthermore, whoever owns capital, it may not be the owners who control the production process, and control is the decisive factor in characterizing a mode of production.

Let me amplify. Thus far the difference between direct ownership and claims on profits has been elided, but in characterizing a $\hat{\delta} = 0$ economy the difference becomes crucial. Obviously if all capital takes the form of seed corn, then the concepts of ownership and claims on profit merge into one. But if we allow for a variety of financial assets, then concentration of equity capital in the hands of a relatively small class is quite compatible with a long-run equilibrium in which $\hat{\delta}$ vanishes. It is necessary only to assume that workers' saving takes the form of cash, bank deposits, life insurance, corporate bonds, and other financial claims that do not constitute direct ownership of seed corn.

Moreover, even in the absence of financial intermediation, owners need not control the production process; and it seems fair to say that it is the distribution of control rather than ownership that distinguishes the operation of one mode of production from another. Concentration of control of the production process into a relatively few hands, along with the parceling of control into distinct segments (individual companies), is the distinguishing characteristic of capitalism, not the distribution of ownership. Only as long as ownership conveys meaningful control is the identification of the dominant class with the class of owners-in-severalty unexceptionable. Certainly this identification was reasonable in the early years of British and American capitalism, perhaps right through the nineteenth century, but once it becomes plausible that ownership no longer implies control, then a correct characterization of the mode of production no longer revolves about dispersion or concentration of ownership.

The existence of nonequity capital may itself lead to a separation of ownership and control: creditors may exert effective control, especially when profits are too small to cover fixed obligations. But this is unlikely to redound to the interest of the workers, even if they account ultimately for 100 percent of the claims on profits. In view of the widespread financial intermediation that characterizes present-day capitalism, it is undoubtedly banks, life insurance companies, pension funds, and the like that will exercise whatever control attaches to nonequity profit claims.

But the existence of nonequity capital is not the only basis for separating ownership and control. If the ownership of the corporations that comprise the individual parcels of capitalism becomes sufficiently dispersed, no single ownership interest may be large enough to exercise effective control. Control may devolve to, or be usurped by, the upper-echelon managers, as Adolph Berle and Gardiner Means (1932) suggested, or by a much broader group of technocrats who together monopolize the knowledge of production and distribution, John Kenneth Galbraith's technostructure (1967). Observe that Berle and Means wrote half a century ago and Galbraith more than a decade: if the separation of control from ownership is plausible in the context of an economy in which ownership is so concentrated that roughly one-half of the means of production is owned by one percent of the population, it is all the more reasonable a conjecture looking to a world in which workers own all the capital.

Thus both the separation of claims on profit from ownership and the separation of ownership from control provide reasons for continuing to speak of a $\hat{\delta} = 0$ steady state as "capitalist."

The separation of ownership and control would favor Kaldor's original conjecture that the saving out of profits that is carried on by corporations cannot be treated simply as the indirect extension of the owners. But this does not, as I have indicated, resolve the problem with Kaldor's saving equation. In the first place, if *all* profits are retained by the corporation, workers necessarily end up owning all the capital, and—directly or indirectly—we are back to an "anti-Pasinetti" regime of $\hat{\delta} = 0$. Alternatively, if part of profits are paid out as dividends, the Pasinetti model continues to hold with very little amendment. For one thing, it can be argued that capitalists and workers both adjust their direct saving to take account of corporate retentions so that ultimately it is household saving propensities that count. But even if households ignore corporate saving in reaching their own saving decisions—an assumption much more in keeping with nonneoclassical theory—corporations make an important difference to the story.

What If Corporations Save?

The last point becomes clear if we let s_π represent the retention:profit ratio, so that saving per unit of seed corn becomes

$$g = s(r, \delta) = s_W W \frac{a_0}{a_1} + s_W(1 - \delta)(1 - s_\pi)r + s_C \delta(1 - s_\pi)r + s_\pi r \quad (6.26)$$

or

$$g = s(r, \delta) = s_W \frac{1 - a_1}{a_1} + (1 - s_W)s_\pi r + (s_C - s_W)(1 - s_\pi)\delta r. \quad (6.27)$$

Evidently the hybrid saving function represented by Eqs. (6.26) and (6.27) has elements of both the original Kaldor saving equation represented by Eq. (6.2) and the Pasinetti equations (6.3) and (6.4). By an argument parallel to the argument that leads to the Pasinetti saving function, Eq. (6.27) leads to the long-run "Kaldor-Pasinetti" saving function

$$g = s(r) = \max \left\{ s_W \frac{1 - a_1}{a_1} + (1 - s_W)s_\pi r, [s_C(1 - s_\pi) + s_\pi]r \right\} \quad (6.28)$$

in which $\delta = \hat{\delta}(r)$. As Figure 6.8 illustrates, the qualitative difference between the Kaldor-Pasinetti saving function and Pasinetti's own formulation of the model is that in the hybrid model saving shows a positive response to the rate of profit even with $\hat{\delta} = 0$; saving responds to the profit rate even when workers own all the capital because the profit rate affects the distribution of income between workers and corporations. As a result, a stable neo-Keynesian equilibrium becomes possible in the anti-Pasinetti range.

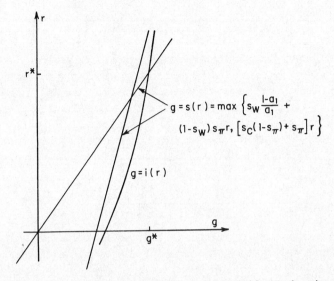

$$g = s(r) = \max \left\{ s_W \frac{1-a_1}{a_1} + (1-s_W)s_\pi r, \ [s_C(1-s_\pi) + s_\pi]r \right\}$$

$$g = i(r)$$

Figure 6.8   Neo-Keynesian equilibrium with a Kaldor-Pasinetti saving function

Another Digression: Are We Moving to People's Capitalism?

Putting aside questions of interpretation, what can we say about the *likelihood* of a steady-growth equilibrium in the $\hat{\delta} = 0$ range? According to Samuelson and Modigliani (1966a, p. 274), the parameters of advanced capitalism make this outcome quite likely. Pasinetti (1966, p. 304) and Kaldor (1966, pp. 312ff.) argue the contrary. It would take us too far afield to assess the claims and counterclaims advanced by the various parties to the debate, but it might be worthwhile to interrupt the theoretical narrative long enough to give an independent answer to this question.

If $\hat{\delta} = 0$, then according to Eq. (6.28) we have

$$s_W \frac{1-a_1}{a_1} + (1-s_W)s_\pi r \geq [s_C(1-s_\pi) + s_\pi]r$$

or, with W representing the real wage,

$$s_W W \frac{a_0}{a_1} \geq (s_C - s_W)(1 - s_\pi)r,$$

which is to say

$$\frac{s_W W a_0}{(s_C - s_W)(1 - s_\pi)ra_1} \geq 1. \tag{6.29}$$

Now to the numbers. If we suppose the capitalist mode of production to be coincident with the corporate sector under contemporary conditions, we can use readily available national-income data for the parameters and variables on the left-hand side of (6.29). We identify the share of wages in net output with the ratio of compensation of employees to net corporate product, and the share of profits paid out to nominal owners of capital with the ratio of the sum of dividends and interest to net corporate product. We thus have

$$\frac{W a_0}{(1 - s_\pi)ra_1} = \frac{\text{EMPLOYEES' COMPENSATION}}{\text{DIVIDENDS} + \text{INTEREST}}.$$

So the relevant test of whether or not current parameter values are compatible with a steady-state "people's capitalism" characterized by $\hat{\delta} = 0$ is whether or not the inequality

$$\frac{s_W}{s_C - s_W} \times \frac{\text{EMP COMP}}{\text{DIV} + \text{INT}} \geq 1 \tag{6.30}$$

holds. In the postwar period,

$$\frac{\text{EMP COMP}}{\text{DIV} + \text{INT}} \approx 15.$$

Hence $\hat{\delta} = 0$ requires the parameters s_W and s_C to satisfy the inequality

$$\frac{s_W}{s_C - s_W} \geq \frac{1}{15} \quad \text{or} \quad 16\, s_W \geq s_C.$$

That is, the existence of a $\hat{\delta} = 0$ steady state requires only that s_C be less than sixteen times as large as s_W!

At this point it must be admitted that it is very difficult to arrive at any good idea of the relative magnitudes of s_C and s_W. It *is* possible to estimate the average saving propensity of the population in the aggregate: if we limit personal saving to the net acquisition of financial assets (including increases in the assets of pension funds)—presumably the most relevant measure for present purposes—an overall saving propensity of approximately 0.05 of (before-tax) income seems appropriate for the household sector as a whole in the United States. But it is more difficult to break this overall propensity into separate propensities for capitalists and workers. In truth very little is known about the saving behavior of the very rich, the subset that presumably includes much of the capitalist class, and it is necessarily as difficult to generalize about the complement of this subset, which presumably includes the working class. But it can hardly be ruled out that s_C is less than sixteen times the magnitude of s_W. In short, the Samuelson-Modigliani vision of a steady state in which capitalist ownership has shrunk to a vanishing percentage of the total seems at least plausible.

There are, however, serious difficulties with this interpretation of the direction of the American economy. In the first place, it is the steady-growth values of the parameters that are relevant, and to use observed values of s_W and s_C to represent steady-growth values is either to assume that a steady-growth equilibrium obtains, or that s_W and s_C are independent of observed growth rates. The first assumption is at least debatable, whereas the second runs counter to Modigliani's life-cycle hypothesis as well as to a nonneoclassical alternative developed in the next chapter.

Second, whether or not the inequality $16s_W \geq s_C$ is likely to be satisfied may depend critically on what is included in saving, particularly on the treatment of pension-fund saving and consumer durables (including housing). I return to this issue in Chapters 17 and 18, but the reader should be forewarned that the results are unsatisfactory in this respect, in part because the national income accounts which the analysis in Chapter 18 utilizes follow Kaldor rather than Pasinetti in distinguishing between wages and profits rather than between workers and capitalists. To identify the propensity to save out of wages with workers' propensity to save and the propensity to save out of profits with capitalists' propensity to save may introduce an important downward bias to the estimate of the differences in saving propensities.

The problem goes beyond Pasinetti's observation that workers must be reckoned to own capital if they save. Not only do workers own capital, but capitalists receive wages: a portion of what the national income accounts include under employee compensation is the "wages" of senior executives. Certainly some part of executive compensation is more reasonably allocated to profits than to wages.

In principle, the capitalist is an active participant in the production process—a boss, organizer, and entrepreneur—not a passive recipient of dividends and interest. Indeed, in an earlier day the capitalist as owner and the capitalist as manager were one and the same person. The rise of "professional management," however, makes it arguable that managers' compensation is in fact capitalists' income whether the professional manager is regarded as the agent of owners or whether he is regarded as the real controller of the enterprise. In either case the salaries and bonuses of the presidents, vice presidents, and divisional managers of General Motors can hardly be regarded as part of the workers' share of income. With, for instance, one-tenth of employees' compensation shifted to the denominator of the ratio $Wa_0/(1 - s_\pi)ra_1$, we should find

$$\frac{(0.9)(\text{EMP COMP})}{\text{DIV} + \text{INT} + (0.1)(\text{EMP COMP})} \simeq 5$$

instead of 15. But here we come square up against our empirical ignorance: we simply do not know whether 5, 10, or 20 percent of employees' compensation is the appropriate amount to shift to the denominator.

We must conclude that $\hat{\delta} = 0$ is only a possible outcome of the growth process, hardly a compelling probability. In any case, "people's capitalism," à la Samuelson-Modigliani, must be recognized as providing at best an opportunity for working people to develop institutional structures that might permit them to control the production process. It hardly guarantees such control.

Appendix: Pension Funds in the Cambridge Saving Equation

A reasonable modification in the model presented in this chapter makes "people's capitalism" in one form or another a virtual certainty, at least in the long run. The modification is to assume that pension funds accumulate capital and to treat this accumulation explicitly.

Let us assume for simplicity that all workers are enrolled in a pension program and that each works for N years and lives in retirement for R years thereafter. If each worker pays in a fixed fraction z of his (constant) real wage W every year, and we normalize so there is one worker in the oldest vintage, then employment is given by the equation

$$L = \sum_{t=0}^{N-1} (1 + g)^t = \frac{(1 + g)^N - 1}{g},$$

and total contributions (CON) are

$$CON = \frac{(1 + g)^N - 1}{g} zW.$$

Suppose now that retired pensioners draw annuities (ANN) over the R years of their retirement, the present value of which (discounted at the rate r) is equal to the value of contributions over the working life (accumulated at the rate r). Thus for each retired person, the present value of benefits equals the present value of contributions,

$$\left[\frac{1-(1+r)^{-R}}{r}\right]ANN = \frac{(1+r)^N-1}{r}zW$$

or

$$ANN = \frac{(1+r)^N-1}{1-(1+r)^{-R}}zW.$$

At any one time, however, there are R different vintages of pensioners drawing benefits, with progressively smaller numbers in each successive vintage. Thus the total benefits (BEN) paid out in the reference year (in which there is one person in the oldest working vintage) are

$$BEN = \sum_{t=1}^{R}(1+g)^{-t}ANN = \left[\frac{1-(1+g)^{-R}}{g}\right]\left[\frac{(1+r)^N-1}{1-(1+r)^{-R}}\right]zW.$$

Setting contributions and benefits equal to each other, we have

$$\frac{(1+g)^N-1}{g}zW = \frac{1-(1+g)^{-R}}{g}\frac{(1+r)^N-1}{1-(1+r)^{-R}}zW.$$

Evidently, the necessary and sufficient condition for this equality is $g = r$, a condition that can hardly be guaranteed to hold. We shall explore two ways of bridging the gap between benefits and contributions, a "pay-as-you-go" scheme and a funded scheme.

A Pay-As-You-Go Scheme

Write

$$\gamma = \frac{1-(1+g)^{-R}}{(1+g)^N-1}\frac{(1+r)^N-1}{1-(1+r)^{-R}}$$

and

$$v = \frac{(1+g)^N-1}{g}z$$

and observe that

$$BEN - CON = (\gamma - 1)vW.$$

Assume the difference $BEN - CON$ is made up by a tax on wage income:

$$TAX = (\gamma - 1)vW$$

and that the same propensity to save, s_W, applies to pensions as to wage income. Then saving out of wages is no longer s_WW, but

$$s_WW - s_W\,TAX = s_WW - s_W(\gamma-1)vW = s_W[1-(\gamma-1)v]W.$$

The Kaldor-Pasinetti saving function becomes

$$s(r) = \max \left\{ s_W[1 - (\gamma - 1)v] \frac{1 - a_1}{a_1} \right.$$

$$\left. + [s_\pi(1 - s_W) + s_W(\gamma - 1)v]r, [s_C(1 - s_\pi) + s_\pi]r \right\}, \quad (6.31)$$

which differs from Eq. (6.28) only by the presence of the terms in $(\gamma - 1)v$ in the coefficients of $(1 - a_1)/a_1$ and r.

The effect on saving of treating shortfalls or surpluses in the pension account on a pay-as-you-go basis depends on the rate of profit. At low rates of profit, with $\hat{\delta} = 0$, saving increases; at higher rates, still with $\hat{\delta} = 0$, saving responds negatively. At still higher rates, once $\hat{\delta} > 0$, the balance of contributions and benefits has no effect whatsoever on saving.

The results for the $\hat{\delta} = 0$ branch follow from the definition of γ. We have not only

$$\gamma = 1 \quad \Leftrightarrow \quad g = r \qquad (6.32)$$

but also

$$\gamma < 1 \quad \Leftrightarrow \quad g > r \qquad (6.33)$$

$$\gamma > 1 \quad \Leftrightarrow \quad g < r, \qquad (6.34)$$

the last two results following from the fact that γ is a decreasing function of g

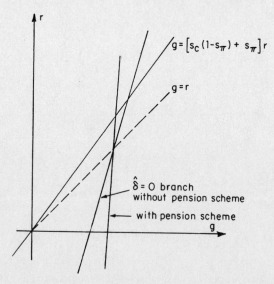

Figure 6.9 Kaldor-Pasinetti saving function with and without pension schemes: Pension-account deficits and surpluses treated on a pay-as-you-go basis

and an increasing function of r.[4] Now from (6.32), Eqs. (6.31) and (6.28) are identical for $g = r$. By (6.33), the $\hat{\delta} = 0$ branch of Eq. (6.31) lies to the right of the corresponding branch of Eq. (6.28) for $g > r$, and by (6.34), the positions of the $\hat{\delta} = 0$ branches are reversed for $g < r$. These results are summarized in Figure 6.9, which shows the two $\hat{\delta} = 0$ branches along with the common $\hat{\delta} > 0$ branch.

A Funded Scheme

The logic of a pension scheme is significantly different when the difference between contributions and benefits is accommodated by the income of a pension fund which itself owns a portion of the economy's seed corn. The pension fund may be assumed to derive originally from the time when the scheme is first instituted, and contributions are positive while benefits are nil. Once the pension scheme is fully operative, in the sense that all retired workers receive full benefits, the growth of the fund follows the equation

$$(\Delta PF)_{+1} = (1 - \gamma)vW + (1 - s_\pi)rPF + s_\pi rPF, \qquad (6.35)$$

where PF measures the size of the pension fund. The first term on the right represents the difference between contributions and benefits, the second direct saving out of pension-fund income, and the third indirect saving through corporate retention of earnings. Equation (6.35) simplifies to

$$(\Delta PF)_{+1} = (1 - \gamma)vW + rPF. \qquad (6.36)$$

Observe that Eqs. (6.35) and (6.36) assume that all net income is plowed back.

Now, instead of the two-way division of capital between workers and capitalists in the proportions $(1 - \delta):\delta$, we require a three-way division of the capital stock to reflect the composition of claims on capital and profits: δ_W, δ_C, and δ_{PF} indicate the respective shares of workers, capitalists, and the pension fund, and we have

$$\delta_W + \delta_C + \delta_{PF} = 1. \qquad (6.37)$$

The short-run saving function becomes

$$s(r, \delta_W, \delta_C, \delta_{PF}) = s_W[1 - (\gamma - 1)v]W\frac{a_0}{a_1} + s_W(1 - s_\pi)\delta_W r$$

$$+ s_C(1 - s_\pi)\delta_C r + (1 - s_\pi)\delta_{PF} r + s_\pi r$$

or, eliminating Wa_0 by means of the price equation and δ_W by means of Eq. (6.37),

4. To see this, write

$$\phi(h) = \frac{(1 + h)^N - 1}{1 - (1 + h)^{-R}} = (1 + h)^R \frac{(1 + h)^N - 1}{(1 + h)^R - 1},$$

from which it follows that ϕ is a monotonically increasing function of h for $N \geq R$.

$$s(r, \delta_C, \delta_{PF}) = s_W \left[1 - (\gamma - 1)v\right] \frac{1 - a_1}{a_1} + [s_\pi(1 - s_W) + s_W(\gamma - 1)v]r$$

$$+ (s_C - s_W)(1 - s_\pi)\delta_C r + (1 - s_W)(1 - s_\pi)\delta_{PF} r. \tag{6.38}$$

Asymptotically, the growth rate of the capital stock as a whole is equal to the growth rate of its most rapidly growing component:

$$g = \max \left[\frac{(\Delta K_W)_{+1}}{K_W}, \frac{(\Delta K_C)_{+1}}{K_C}, \frac{(\Delta PF)_{+1}}{PF}\right]. \tag{6.39}$$

Now

$$(\Delta K_C)_{+1} = [s_C(1 - s_\pi) + s_\pi]rK_C$$

and

$$(\Delta K_W)_{+1} = s_W[1 - (\gamma - 1)v]WL + [s_W(1 - s_\pi) + s_\pi]rK_W,$$

so that the growth of capital belonging to capitalists is still governed by the equation

$$\frac{(\Delta K_C)_{+1}}{K_C} = [s_C(1 - s_\pi) + s_\pi]r, \tag{6.40}$$

and the growth of workers' capital, at least in the long run, follows the rule

$$\frac{(\Delta K_W)_{+1}}{K_W} = \max \left\{\frac{(\Delta L)_{+1}}{L}, [s_W(1 - s_\pi) + s_\pi]r\right\}. \tag{6.41}$$

But

$$\frac{(\Delta L)_{+1}}{L} = g \geq \max \left[\frac{(\Delta K_C)_{+1}}{K_C}, \frac{(\Delta K_W)_{+1}}{K_W}\right]$$

$$\geq [s_C(1 - s_\pi) + s_\pi]r$$

$$> [s_W(1 - s_\pi) + s_\pi]r. \tag{6.42}$$

The first inequality holds in the long run because the capital stock as a whole asymptotically grows as fast as its fastest-growing component; the second inequality holds by virtue of (6.40) and (6.41); and the last because s_C exceeds s_W. But from the chain (6.42), we also have

$$\frac{(\Delta K_W)_{+1}}{K_W} = g.$$

None of this is new; it is the basis on which the original Pasinetti saving function was shown to have a corner where it moves from the $\hat{\delta} = 0$ range to the $\hat{\delta} > 0$ range.

But now we have the pension fund to reckon with, and its growth asymptotically obeys the rule[5]

$$\frac{(\Delta PF)_{+1}}{PF} = \max\left[\frac{(\Delta L)_{+1}}{L}, r\right] = \max(g, r). \tag{6.43}$$

Thus whenever r exceeds g, the pension fund grows asymptotically at the rate r. In this case, however, according to (6.39) the asymptotic growth rate must equal g! In other words, r cannot exceed g in the long run, because whenever r exceeds g, the growth rate of the capital stock as a whole climbs toward r as the share of the pension fund increases.

Now comes the shocker: whenever s_C and s_π are both less than one, the rate of growth of capital belonging to capitalists invariably is less than r, that is,

$$[s_C(1 - s_\pi) + s_\pi]r < r. \tag{6.44}$$

So r must exceed g for capitalists to own a nonvanishing share of capital. But this, as we have just seen, is impossible. Conclusion: in the long run, the existence of a funded pension scheme precludes capitalists from maintaining a positive share of the capital stock! Since a pension fund plows back its profits at a faster rate than capitalists, it eventually crowds out a capitalist class that has no source other than profits from which to augment its capital; the pension fund's rate of compound growth must inevitably be higher than the rate of growth of the stock belonging to capitalists. Workers, by contrast, periodically augment their capital by saving out of wages, which allows them to maintain a nonvanishing share of capital even though their capital does not grow sufficiently rapidly by the compound-interest route to achieve this end. The pension fund is like workers' capital in this regard, with the result that in the long run, Eq. (6.38) reduces to

$$s(r, \delta_{PF}) = s_W[1 - (\gamma - 1)v]\frac{1 - a_1}{a_1} + [s_\pi(1 - s_W) + s_W(\gamma - 1)v]r$$

$$+ (1 - s_W)(1 - s_\pi)\delta_{PF}r$$

or

$$s(r) = \max\left\{s_W[1 - (\gamma - 1)v]\frac{1 - a_1}{a_1} + [s_\pi(1 - s_W)\right.$$

$$\left. + s_W(\gamma - 1)v]r + (1 - s_W)(1 - s_\pi)\delta_{PF}^{MIN}r, r\right\}.$$

Observe that the range of $\delta_{PF} = \delta_{PF}(r)$ is

$$\delta_{PF}^{MIN} \leqq \hat{\delta}_{PF} \lesseqgtr 1,$$

5. Strictly speaking, Eq. (6.43) is valid only on the condition $\gamma \leqq 1$; otherwise employment and wage-bill growth *deplete* the pension fund at the rate g. But since $\gamma > 1$ if and only if $g < r$, the argument still holds.

with the parameter δ_{PF}^{MIN} defined by the historical ratio PF/K at the time when the scheme matures to the point that all retired workers receive full pensions. The Kaldor-Pasinetti saving function in the presence of a long-run funded pension scheme is illustrated in Figure 6.10.

We have in a sense come full circle. Having abandoned the simplest version of a classical saving function in which all profits are saved and all wages consumed, and with it the neat corollary that in equilibrium the rate of growth equals the rate of profit, we have restored the corollary through the round-about route of a funded pension scheme—at least for the very long run and over a portion of the range of equilibrium pairs $\langle r, g \rangle$.

In the process, the capitalist class might seem to have disappeared altogether from the capitalist mode of production. At least that is the case if we judge from the long-run value of $\hat{\delta}_C$, which is zero. However, such an inference must be strongly resisted, even at the risk of repetition. In the first place, ownership cannot necessarily be identified with control of an enterprise, and it is control that counts.

Second, the shares of capital on which our analysis focused represent claims on profit rather than ownership—unless we assume away financial intermediation. This point is particularly relevant in the light of the turn the analysis took at the last: since workers obviously do not directly mark the proxies of the equity shares that "their" pension funds vote, it must be asked who controls the pension funds, and in whose interests. To the extent that pension-fund interests are conceived in terms of profit maximization—whether this be by law (Taft-Hartley and the ERISA legislation of 1974, for instance), custom, or the

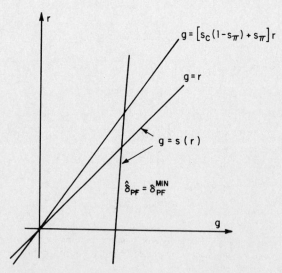

Figure 6.10 Kaldor-Pasinetti saving function with a funded pension scheme

incapacity of working-class leadership to develop alternative strategies of fund management—it hardly matters that Sears, Roebuck and Company might become the property of the Sears, Roebuck Pension Fund rather than the Sears and Roebuck families.

Finally, it might be reiterated that the appropriate concept of profit includes the share of income that accrues to management, as well as dividends, retained earnings, and interest. In effect, therefore, active capitalists receive a higher profit rate than do passive owners, be they workers, *rentiers,* or pension funds. It is certainly possible that the extra profits that derive from active participation are high enough to offset the higher rate of saving by pension funds. If overall profits are divided between passive owners (pension funds and *rentiers*) and managers in the proportions $\mu:(1-\mu)$, then various claimants will plow back profits at the following rates:

$$[s_W(1-s_\pi)+s_\pi]\mu r \qquad \text{(workers)}$$
$$\mu r \qquad \text{(pension funds)}$$
$$[s_C(1-s_\pi)+s_\pi]\mu r \qquad \textit{(rentiers)}$$
$$[s_C(1-s_\pi)+s_\pi]\mu r + s_C(1-\mu)r \qquad \text{(active capitalists)}$$

In contrast with Eq. (6.44), the relevant inequality when all profit rates are identical, the relationship between the growth rate of the capital belonging to active capitalists and the growth rate of pension-fund capital is indeterminate. For sufficiently low values of μ, we shall find

$$[s_C(1-s_\pi)+s_\pi]\mu r + s_C(1-\mu)r > \mu r,$$

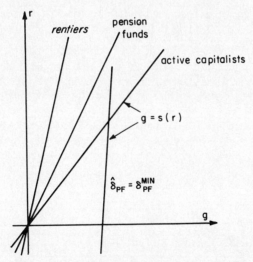

Figure 6.11 Generalized Kaldor-Pasinetti saving function with different profit rates

so that pension funds rather than capitalists are crowded out in the course of accumulation, or at least prevented from ever accumulating a larger share of the capital stock than the ratio δ_{PF}^{MIN} achieved at the time all pensioners first receive pensions that are built up over a lifetime of contributions. The Kaldor-Pasinetti saving function now becomes

$$s(r) = \max \left\{ [s_W[1 - (1 - \gamma)v] \frac{1 - a_1}{a_1} + [s_\pi(1 - s_W) + s_W(1 - \gamma)v]r \right.$$
$$\left. + (1 - s_W)(1 - s_\pi)\delta_{PF}^{MIN}r, \, [s_C(1 - s_\pi) + s_\pi]\mu r + (1 - \mu)r \right\}$$

as shown in Figure 6.11. Thus the conflict between capitalists and workers can scarcely be finessed on the grounds that time and compound interest will do the capitalist class in. No doubt an indefinite increase in the relative share of workers' and pension funds' claims on profits is a possibility. But it is at best a possibility, not the inevitability pictured by Peter Drucker (1976). Even then, pension funds represent only an opportunity for workers to take control of the capitalist mode of production. Nothing guarantees that the opportunity will be seized.

7 Foundations for the Cambridge Saving Equation

Outside the neoclassical camp, economists have had surprisingly little to say about the determination of saving propensities. John Maynard Keynes was himself content to do hardly more than state "that men are disposed, as a rule and on the average, to increase their consumption as their income increases, but not by as much as the increase in their income" (1936, p. 96). For Keynes this propensity was a "fundamental and psychological law" — presumably one sufficiently self-evident that it needed no justification. To be sure, Keynes qualified this "law" to limit it to a short period relevant to the study of economic fluctuations, "during which habits . . . are not given time enough to adapt themselves to changed objective circumstances" (1936, p. 96). This Keynesian insight has been developed in theoretical and practical application in the work of Tillman Brown (1952) and Hendrik Houthakker and Lester Taylor (1966), who have modeled consumption behavior on the basis of habit persistence. A related idea was the basis for the disequilibrium hypothesis set forth in "What Do Bosses Do? Part II" (Marglin 1975).

"Bosses" had in fact several goals, incidental to which was an attempt to square observed savings data with the Keynesian view quoted in the previous paragraph. (This attempt is elaborated in Chapters 17 and 18 of this book.) According to "Bosses," deliberately planned accumulation of the means of production is limited to *organizations*. The corporation is the archetype of the accumulation-oriented organization in a capitalist mode of production, but it is not the only one: unions have pension funds, governments promote accumulation, and religious establishments occasionally amass large amounts of productive capital. Individuals and households, by contrast, are hypothesized to accumulate neither productive capital nor the financial assets that are its counterpart, except by accident. The pressures to spend are supposed to be too great for the typical household to resist. In short, household saving is hypothesized to be a disequilibrium phenomenon (whence the name "disequilibrium" hypothesis) that occurs only when income is increasing at a faster rate than households can learn to spend it.

This theory does not claim to account for the observed saving behavior of the corporation. Corporate saving propensities are presented simply as a historical compromise between the interests of two groups within the capitalist class: the professional managers, who favor high retention rates, and the *rentier*-owners, who favor high dividend payouts. But there is no theoretical justification for the specific retention ratio s_π at which the conflict of interests is resolved.

But if the disequilibrium hypothesis has nothing very cogent to say about corporate saving, it does do a reasonable job of explaining the observed saving behavior of households, as Chapter 18 will show. To be sure, household saving figures appear at first sight to be much too high to be consistent with the notion that households tend at equilibrium to spend all available income: in the United States over the period 1952 to 1979, personal saving, defined as the sum of net investment in owner-occupied housing and net acquisition of financial assets by households, averaged just over 7.5 percent of disposable income according to Flow of Funds data.[1] But a close look at the figures suggests results more compatible with the disequilibrium view.

In the first place, investment in owner-occupied housing has claimed almost half of personal saving, on average 3.5 percent of disposable income. For the study of accumulation of the means of production in the *capitalist* sector of the economy, however, this portion of saving is, in a word, irrelevant. For present purposes it is appropriate to limit our attention to *financial* saving, which measures the resources that households make available to the rest of the economy. The financial saving rate is 4.0 percent of disposable income — still a sizable figure, espe-

1. According to national income accounts published by the Department of Commerce, the personal saving rate over this period averaged just under 7 percent. The discrepancy between Flow of Funds and national income data results primarily from differences in measurement technique rather than from conceptual differences: in the national income accounts, household saving is a residual category, the difference between disposable income and consumption expenditures. Flow of Funds saving data, by contrast, are based on direct estimation of saving, a more useful approach for present purposes in view of the importance of the composition of household saving. There is also a minor conceptual difference between the two figures: the 7.5 percent figure excludes investment in plant and equipment by nonprofit organizations, which NIA personal saving includes. Tables 17.5 and 17.6 provide a statistical breakdown of private saving.

cially in comparison with the other principal source of net private saving, the retained earnings of corporations. But more than one-third of this saving is "personal" in name only: in the Flow of Funds accounts, contributions to pension funds, equal on average to 1.5 percent of disposable income, are lumped in with the direct saving of households, even though these contributions are better conceptualized as organizational rather than personal in nature, more like corporate retentions than like deposits to a savings account.

Subtracting pension-fund contributions as well as investment in housing from personal saving reduces the saving rate to about 2.5 percent of disposable income. This residual, I shall argue in Chapter 18, can be explained by growth in personal income: spending, under the disequilibrium hypothesis, lags behind income as long as income is rising. Thus saving, or at any rate household saving, emerges in this view as the consequence rather than the cause of growth.

A Formal Model of the Disequilibrium Hypothesis

Household saving, in the disequilibrium hypothesis, is a residual. Positive saving occurs when income rises faster than households can adapt their spending habits; dissaving occurs when income falls faster than households can rein in their spending. This conception of the household can be modeled by a difference equation that relates the change in household consumption ΔC to $Y - C_{-1}$ and ΔY:

$$\Delta C = \theta(Y - C_{-1}) + \zeta \Delta Y. \tag{7.1}$$

$Y - C_{-1}$ is the rate of saving that would take place if last period's consumption C_{-1} were to persist at the current level of income Y. This hypothetical saving rate serves as a proxy for the household's ignorance, or if you will, inexperience, in spending matters; it measures the amount of learning that remains to be done with the new level of income and the old level of consumption. The parameter θ thus measures the rate of learning over the period until spending catches up to income. The second term $\zeta \Delta Y$ reflects the presence of unmet wants for which no learning is necessary. The parameter ζ represents the immediate adjustment of spending to income. The sum, $\theta + \zeta$, is the short-run marginal propensity to consume in the sense of the passage from the *General Theory* cited at the beginning of this chapter; accordingly, $1 - \theta - \zeta$ is the short-run marginal propensity to save (*MPS*).

In terms of saving, Eq. (7.1) is

$$S = (1 - \theta)S_{-1} + (1 - \theta - \zeta)\,\Delta Y, \tag{7.2}$$

where $S = Y - C$. In the steady state we have $\Delta Y/Y_{-1} = g$ and $S/Y = S_{-1}/Y_{-1} = s$. Thus

$$s(1 + g) = (1 - \theta)s + (1 - \theta - \zeta)g \tag{7.3}$$

and

$$s = \frac{(1 - \theta - \zeta)g}{\theta + g}, \tag{7.4}$$

where s is the *average* propensity to save under conditions of steady growth.

Observe that the saving propensity defined by Eq. (7.4) makes no distinction between workers and capitalists: thus far all households are assumed to behave similarly with respect to disposable income. The spirit of classical saving theory, however, requires us to distinguish between the two classes of households — notwithstanding the fact that the available data hardly facilitate separate estimation of capitalists' and workers' saving functions.[2] If $\zeta_W > \zeta_C$, then $MPS_W < MPS_C$, and we have $s_W < s_C$ in the long run, with

$$s_W = \frac{(1 - \theta_W - \zeta_W)g_W}{\theta_W + g_W} = \frac{MPS_W g_W}{\theta_W + g_W} \tag{7.5}$$

and

$$s_C = \frac{(1 - \theta_C - \zeta_C)g_C}{\theta_C + g_C} = \frac{MPS_C g_C}{\theta_C + g_C}, \tag{7.6}$$

where subscripts on the right-hand sides distinguish the income-growth rates, marginal propensities to save, and adjustment speeds of capitalists and workers.

If we substitute from (7.5) and (7.6) into the long-run Pasinetti saving function

$$g = s(r) = \max\left(s_W \frac{1 - a_1}{a_1}, s_C r\right), \tag{6.5}$$

the relationship between growth and profit rates becomes

2. Indeed, the data analyzed in Chapter 18 do not permit separate estimation of θ_W and θ_C. But they do allow, in principle, the possibility of testing whether ζ_W exceeds ζ_C and consequently whether MPS_W is less than MPS_C. The tests are, to say the least, disappointing. Although consistent with the hypothesis $MPS_W < MPS_C$, the data hardly offer strong support to this view: the results of Chapter 18 are also consistent with the hypothesis $MPS_W = MPS_C$.

$$g = \max\left(\frac{MPS_w g_w}{\theta_w + g_w}\frac{1 - a_1}{a_1}, \frac{MPS_c g_c}{\theta_c + g_c}r\right). \qquad (7.7)$$

Consider the $\hat{\delta} = 0$ branch of the saving function: with $g = g_w$, we may write

$$g = \frac{MPS_w g}{\theta_w + g}\frac{1 - a_1}{a_1}. \qquad (7.8)$$

Evidently there are two solutions:

$$g = 0 \quad \text{and} \quad g = -\theta_w + MPS_w \frac{1 - a_1}{a_1}.$$

Which one is relevant? It is straightforward to show that for $\hat{\delta} = 0$, the larger of the two is the one that counts:

$$g = \max\left(0, -\theta_w + MPS_w \frac{1 - a_1}{a_1}\right).$$

This result hinges on the fact that the maximal root of (7.8) is the only stable solution. Consider the following two diagrams. In each the overall saving-to-income ratio s is linked to the growth rate g by two equations. On the one hand, when $\hat{\delta} = 0$ we have

$$s = s_w = \frac{MPS_w g}{\theta_w + g}. \qquad (7.9)$$

On the other hand, we have the tautological relationship,

$$\frac{\Delta K}{K_{-1}} = \frac{\Delta K}{Y_{-1}}\frac{Y_{-1}}{K_{-1}}$$

which can be rewritten

$$g = s\frac{1 - a_1}{a_1}. \qquad (7.10)$$

Now look at Figure 7.1(a). The equilibrium at

$$g = -\theta_w + MPS_w \frac{1 - a_1}{a_1}$$

could never be attained unless the economy happened by chance to start there. If, for example, the saving ratio happened to be s_1, then the growth rate, according to Eq. (7.10), would be g_1. But with a growth rate g_1, saving would, by virtue of Eq. (7.9), tend to s_2. But $s = s_2$ leads to the higher growth rate of g_2 — and so on, until the process converges at $g = 0$.

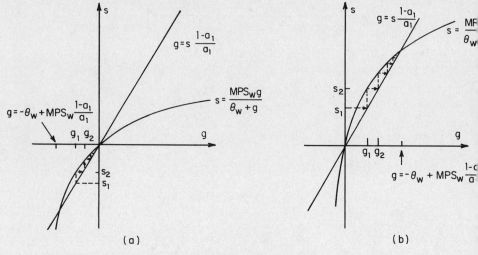

Figure 7.1 Simultaneous relationships between s and g determine equilibrium. (a) $g = 0$; (b) $g > 0$

Compare Figure 7.1(b). If initially $s = s_1$, the corresponding growth rate is g_1. But $g = g_1$ implies $s = s_2$. The limiting point of this process, however, is not $g = 0$, but

$$g = -\theta_W + MPS_W \frac{1 - a_1}{a_1}.$$

These asymmetrical results are illustrated in Figure 7.2. In Figure

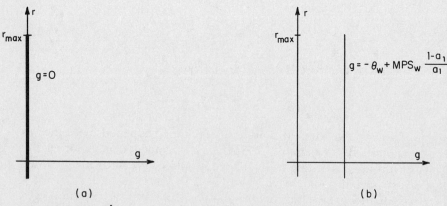

Figure 7.2 $\hat{\delta} = 0$ range of Pasinetti saving function. (a) $g = 0$; (b) $g > 0$

7.2(a) the $\hat{\delta} = 0$ range of the Pasinetti saving function corresponds to the r-axis; in Figure 7.2(b), which assumes $(1 - a_1)/a_1 > \theta_W$, the positive root of Eq. (7.8) is the relevant solution.

The $\hat{\delta} > 0$ range is characterized by a similar problem. With

$$g = g_C,$$

we have

$$g = \frac{MPS_C g}{\theta_C + g} r, \tag{7.11}$$

which leads to two solutions:

$$g = 0 \quad \text{and} \quad g = -\theta_C + MPS_C r.$$

An argument analogous to the one that accompanied Figure 7.1 establishes that the maximal root of Eq. (7.11) is the relevant one. So we end up with

$$g = \max (0, -\theta_C + MPS_C r).$$

The Pasinetti saving function as a whole can be represented by the relationship

$$g = s(\theta_W, \theta_C, r) = \max \left(0, -\theta_W + MPS_W \frac{1 - a_1}{a_1}, -\theta_C + MPS_C r \right), \tag{7.12}$$

which is illustrated in Figure 7.3. It will be observed that the "Pasin-

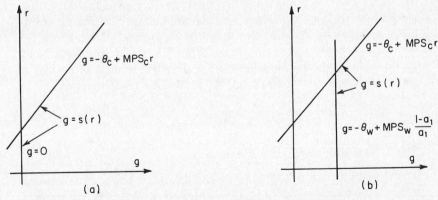

Figure 7.3 Pasinetti saving function under the disequilibrium hypothesis. (a) $g = 0$ on $\hat{\delta} = 0$ branch; (b) $g > 0$ on $\hat{\delta} = 0$ branch

etti" saving function of Figure 7.3 no longer exhibits one of Pasinetti's key results: the proportionality of the profit rate and growth rate over the portion of its range that corresponds to $\hat{\delta} > 0$. In a more general sense the spirit of Pasinetti's results does survive, however: in the $\hat{\delta} > 0$ range in Figure 7.3, as in the pure Pasinetti case of Chapter 6, r and g are positively related to one another.

It will also be noted that the similarity of the saving function in Figure 7.3 to the Pasinetti saving function relies implicitly on the assumption that capitalists adjust consumption to changes in income more slowly than do workers ($\theta_C < \theta_W$, $\zeta_C < \zeta_W$). But surely this is a reasonable assumption within the disequilibrium framework: capitalists have larger assets with which to cushion falls in income, and consumption desires press less urgently on increases in income.

Moreover, the internal logic of the disequilibrium hypothesis, as summarized in Eq. (7.12), requires

$$MPS_W \frac{1 - a_1}{a_1} > \theta_W \quad \text{and} \quad MPS_C r > \theta_C \qquad (7.13)$$

for long-run household saving to be positive, as in Figure 7.3(b). This means that although the disequilibrium hypothesis continues to be formally consistent with the Pasinetti model, a substantive difficulty appears as soon as we examine the likely range of parameter values. If the two inequalities of (7.13) are to hold for the estimates of $1 - \theta$ and $1 - \theta - \zeta$ derived in Chapter 18, both $(1 - a_1)/a_1$ and r will have to be higher than the output : capital ratios and rates of profit generally reckoned to obtain in contemporary capitalist economies. The results of Chapter 18 are not compelling, and we need not accept them. But if we do, we have two choices: either we scrap the disequilibrium framework altogether, or we retain it as an explanation not of why households save, but of the *failure* of households to save. The second tack seems more promising: I am inclined to look outside the household, particularly to the corporation, as the principal vehicle of saving, at least with respect to the saving that fuels the capitalist sector of the economy.

The Model with Corporate Retentions

The disequilibrium hypothesis can be integrated into a more general model, along Kaldor-Pasinetti lines, in which corporate retentions and similar organizational saving (for example, pension funds) are the principal institutional arrangements for accumulation. We have in the long run

$$g = s(r) = \max \left\{ s_W \frac{1 - a_1}{a_1} + (1 - s_W)s_\pi r, \ [s_C(1 - s_\pi) + s_\pi]r \right\},$$

$$(6.28)$$

with

$$s_W = \frac{MPS_W g_W}{\theta_W + g_W} \quad \text{and} \quad s_C = \frac{MPS_C g_C}{\theta_C + g_C}.$$

Again we have two ranges in the saving function. In the $\hat{\delta} = 0$ range,

$$g = \frac{MPS_W g}{\theta_W + g} \frac{1 - a_1}{a_1} + \frac{\theta_W + (1 - MPS_W)g}{\theta_W + g} s_\pi r, \qquad (7.14)$$

and in the $\hat{\delta} > 0$ range,

$$g = \frac{MPS_C g}{\theta_C + g} (1 - s_\pi)r + s_\pi r. \qquad (7.15)$$

As in the pure Pasinetti case, the disequilibrium hypothesis introduces an extraneous solution into (7.14) and (7.15). Rejecting the minimal root of the solution, we have

$$g = g_W = \frac{\beta_1 + \sqrt{\beta_1^2 + 4\theta_W s_\pi r}}{2}, \qquad \hat{\delta} = 0, \qquad (7.16)$$

$$g = g_C = \frac{\beta_2 + \sqrt{\beta_2^2 + 4\theta_C s_\pi r}}{2}, \qquad \hat{\delta} > 0, \qquad (7.17)$$

where

$$\beta_1 = MPS_W \frac{1 - a_1}{a_1} + (1 - MPS_W)s_\pi r - \theta_W,$$

$$\beta_2 = MPS_C(1 - s_\pi)r + s_\pi r - \theta_C.$$

Equation (6.28) becomes

$$g = \max (g_W, g_C), \qquad (7.18)$$

which is represented graphically in Figure 7.4.

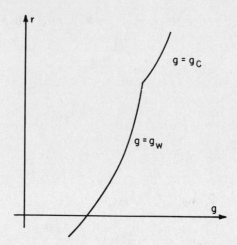

Figure 7.4 Kaldor-Pasinetti saving function incorporating corporate retentions

Saving and the Distribution of Income

The disequilibrium model has been introduced in order to illustrate an alternative foundation for saving propensities to the usual neoclassical one based on life-cycle utility maximization. But the existence of this alternative should not obscure other essential differences between neoclassical and classical saving hypotheses, differences that have nothing to do with the rationality of households.

Whether deliberate choice or habit determines saving propensities is largely independent of the life-cycle claim that the bulk of saving takes place to provide for retirement. The corollary of the central role that provision for retirement plays in the life-cycle saving hypothesis is a peculiar role for the distribution of income: the distribution of income is determined by the need for profit to provide retirees (who account for the bulk of capital in this view) with an even flow of consumption beyond their working life. Thus, the higher the level of per capita wages, the greater is the corresponding level of profits. But in a general-equilibrium framework with a single technology, the higher the level of wages, the lower is the *rate* of profit. So the higher must be the capital stock to provide an adequate flow of profits, and therefore the higher must be the requisite rate of saving. For this reason, life-cycle-determined saving in a single-technology world varies positively with wages and negatively with the rate of profit. In short, neoclassical theory leads to the conclusion $s_W > s_C$.[3] Hence the downward slope of the neoclassical saving function in Chapter 2.[4]

By contrast, in the classical view the rate of saving tends to vary positively with the share of income going to profits, that is to say, directly with the profit rate. Implicit in this view is the notion that saving does not take place primarily to satisfy life-cycle needs. The majority of *savers* may or may not be motivated by life-cycle considerations: the essence of the matter is that most *saving* is done by a small minority of savers who own most of the capital, for whom life-cycle considerations are at best a small part of the story and for whom the propensity to save is higher than for those for whom profits constitute an insignificant portion of income.

In this way of looking at alternative hypotheses, the textbook Keynesian notion of a linear saving function, which in our notation takes the form

$$g = s \frac{1 - a_1}{a_1},$$

is intermediate to the classical and neoclassical views. The saving rate is in this case completely independent of the distribution of income. Thus the vertical shape of the saving function in Figure 4.8.

In short, there are two important distinctions between classical and neoclassical saving functions. One lies in the foundations of the two theories, in the distinction between utility maximization and disequilibrium as the basis of saving. We shall come back to the foundations of saving behavior in Chapters 17 and 18. Until then this issue will be more or less suppressed, and in the chapters that follow the second major distinction between the theories will be emphasized, namely, the relationship of the saving function to the distribution of income. In fact we shall formalize the classical saving function in terms of the simplest expression that reflects a positive relationship between profits and saving while allowing workers as well as capitalists to save.

3. In fact, the pure life-cycle model leads to the stronger result $s_C < 0$: capitalists are retirees who consume principal as well as interest. However, the crucial result is not the negativity of s_C, but the inequality $s_W > s_C$, which follows from more general premises than those of the pure life-cycle model.

4. This argument ignores the income and substitution effects of a change in the rate of profit. These changes normally work to offset one another and, as we have seen, they wash out altogether in the case of a Cobb-Douglas utility function. In any case, these effects have been empirically unobservable in studies of household saving behavior and are in fact generally ignored in practical application.

Subsequent chapters thus ignore corporate retentions. This omission is not, needless to say, justified on the grounds that this form of saving is theoretically or quantitatively unimportant. Evidently the logic of this chapter points in quite the opposite direction. Rather, corporate retentions are excluded because this simplification does not alter the basic shape of the saving function. It is for similar reasons that we shall treat the parameters s_W and s_C as fixed, despite the arguments of this chapter that they in fact depend on r. In short, we shall continue to represent the classical saving hypothesis by the quasi-Kaldorian function

$$s(r, \delta) = s_W \frac{1 - a_1}{a_1} + (s_C - s_W)\delta r$$

in the short run and the Pasinetti function

$$s(r) = \max \left(s_W \frac{1 - a_1}{a_1}, s_C r \right)$$

in the long.

8 Some Hybrid Models

An assumption about the determinants of saving together with an assumption about employment, wages, or investment defined the models we have labeled as "neoclassical," "neo-Marxian," and "neo-Keynesian." More precisely, these assumptions close a common production model to capture the distinctive elements of the three approaches. Schematically we can write

Neoclassical = Life-Cycle Saving + Full Employment

Neo-Marxian = Cambridge Saving + Subsistence Wage

Neo-Keynesian = Cambridge Saving + Animal-Spirits Investment

Nothing, however, prevents us from mixing the constituent assumptions in other combinations. In principle there are three alternatives we might consider:

Hybrid I   = Cambridge Saving + Full Employment

Hybrid II = Life-Cycle Saving + Subsistence Wage

Hybrid III = Life-Cycle Saving + Animal-Spirits Investment

These hybrids are not of equal interest, however. For the first, unlike the other two, has received considerable theoretical attention as a model of capitalist growth and distribution.

Kaldor's Model

In the context of fixed coefficients, Hybrid I is the model proposed by Nicholas Kaldor in a series of articles published between 1956 and

1961. In Kaldor's first version (1956), the model is stripped to its bare bones:

$$g = s(r) = s_W \frac{1 - a_1}{a_1} + (s_C - s_W)r \qquad (6.2)$$

and

$$g = n. \qquad (2.18)$$

Together these assumptions determine equilibrium, as shown in Figure 8.1.

Observe that the equilibrium is stable. Indeed, Kaldor's hybrid and the neo-Keynesian model share not only a common assumption about the determination of saving, but a common mechanism to bring profit and wage shares into line with steady-state values. If investment is determined by full-employment growth requirements, $r < r^*$ implies investment in excess of desired saving, which in turn puts upward pressure on prices and downward pressure on real wages (remember that *money* wages are fixed). This increases the rate of profit, a process that continues until the equilibrium r^* is reached. Similarly, $r > r^*$ implies desired saving in excess of investment and downward pressure on prices and profits, a process that likewise comes to rest at r^*.

Kaldor qualifies the role of the natural rate of growth, n, in two ways. First, as observed in Chapter 5, a real-wage floor — Karl Marx's subsis-

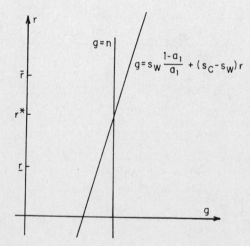

Figure 8.1   Hybrid I equilibrium: Kaldorian saving function + full employment

tence wage or Joan Robinson's inflation barrier—puts a ceiling on the rate of profit, $\bar{r}$. Second, capitalists' animal spirits put a floor on the rate of profit, $\underline{r}$: $\underline{r}$ is assumed to be the minimum rate of profit at which capitalists will invest at a rate sufficient to maintain full-employment growth. So the characterization of equilibrium in terms of Eqs. (6.2) and (2.15) is subject to the condition $\underline{r} \leq r^* \leq \bar{r}$.[1]

In subsequent models (1957, 1961) Kaldor introduced an explicit investment-demand function, along with technological progress and variable factor proportions. However, Kaldor's investment-demand function does not accord a central role to the psychology of businessmen in determining equilibrium growth and profit *rates*, a fact obscured by the admixture of variable proportions. As we shall see in Chapter 10, the role of investment demand is limited to determining the equilibrium capital: output ratio as well as the speed of adjustment to the equilibrium. In the fixed-coefficient version of Kaldor's model, "animal spirits" disappear altogether, and the role of the investment-demand function is completely taken over by the assumption of full employment.

Pasinetti's Model

Luigi Pasinetti (1962), as we have seen, modified the Kaldorian version of the classical saving function by assuming that the saving propensity of workers s_W, rather than propensity of capitalists s_C, applies to the portion of capital owned by workers. But he did not tamper with Kaldor's full-employment assumption. Thus the Pasinetti model, described by the equations

$$g = s(r) = \max\left(s_W \frac{1 - a_1}{a_1}, s_C r \right) \tag{6.5}$$

and

$$g = n, \tag{2.18}$$

also falls into the Hybrid I classification. It is represented graphically in Figure 8.2.

Examination of Figure 8.2 suggests a noteworthy feature of the Pasinetti version of the Hybrid I model. Although the figure is drawn to make equilibrium occur within the $\hat{\delta} > 0$ ("Pasinetti") range of the

1. Kaldor suggests that the "degree of monopoly" will impose another floor, r°, on the rate of profit, which will be relevant only if $r^\circ > \underline{r}$. The degree of monopoly is considered in Chapters 10 and 14.

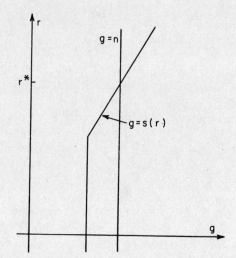

Figure 8.2 Hybrid I equilibrium: Pasinetti saving function + full employment with interior solution

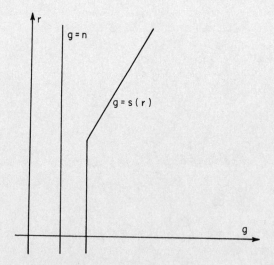

Figure 8.3 Hybrid I equilibrium: Pasinetti saving function + full employment with excess saving

saving function—characterized by the simple relationship between growth and profit rates $g = s_c r$—this result is an arbitrary consequence of the draftsman's pen. Suppose the full-employment condition $g = n$ were graphed to the left of the $\hat{\delta} = 0$ region of the saving function $g = s_W(1 - a_1)/a_1$. With

$$ n \leq s_W \frac{1 - a_1}{a_1}, $$

as in Figure 8.3, the equilibrium rate of profit would ultimately settle at -1, and if saving intentions are realized, equilibrium would involve a superfluous addition to seed corn equal in each period to

$$ s_W \frac{1 - a_1}{a_1} - n $$

bushels of corn per worker.

Solow's Model

This is perhaps the place to introduce Robert Solow's model of economic growth (1956), despite the emphasis in Solow's own presentation on variable proportions. For in terms of the logic of the present classification, it too is a hybrid: its basic constituents are first a Keynesian saving function which in our notation takes the form

$$ g = s \frac{1 - a_1}{a_1}, $$

where s is a propensity to save that is independent of distribution as well as growth. In addition we have the full employment condition

$$ g = n. \tag{2.18} $$

Observe that with fixed proportions the Solow hybrid admits only of extreme solutions. As Figure 8.4 is drawn, the full employment condition cannot be met at all if saving intentions are realized. By contrast, it is easy to see—look again at Figure 8.3—that reversing the relative positions of the saving function and the full employment condition shifts the steady-growth equilibrium to one characterized by growing stocks of useless seed corn.

The Euclidean geometry of parallel lines is relentless, but variable proportions change Solow's model in important ways. I shall come back to it in the next chapter.

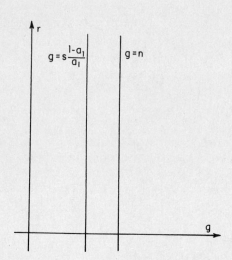

Figure 8.4 Solow hybrid: Keynesian saving function + full employment

Money in a Neoclassical Model

The hybrid models we have examined so far share a common feature, both with each other and with the parent models from which they derive: each adds two independent equations to the production and price equations to permit exact determination of the four unknowns — wage and consumption levels and profit and growth rates. Another line of hybridization would be to superimpose an equation from one model onto another complete model, making in all five equations. For instance, a *long-run* model constructed in the spirit of the short-run models of Robert Barro and Herschel Grossman (1976) and Edmond Malinvaud (1977, 1980) might include an investment-demand equation along with a life-cycle saving function and a full-employment condition.[2]

---

2. Though the term "neo-Keynesian" is widely used to describe models in the Barro-Grossman-Malinvaud mold, the stance of these models toward the longer period reflects important assumptions that are distinctly neoclassical in flavor. The Barro-Grossman model is explicit with respect to the role of full employment in characterizing long-run equilibrium, and in fact the investment-demand function is allowed to determine only the speed of adjustment to the equilibrium capital stock. (In this respect Barro and Grossman resemble the Kaldor model discussed earlier in this chapter and developed more fully in Chapter 10.) Malinvaud is closer in spirit to the neo-Keynesian approach as that term is used in this book. In particular, his idea of the investment-demand function (1980) is similar to Joan Robinson's. Indeed, the principle neoclassical element in Malinvaud's approach is the assumption that the economy is always in the neighborhood

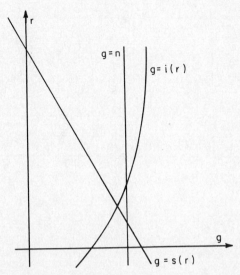

Figure 8.5 Equilibrium overdetermined by saving, investment, and full employment

We run into an obvious difficulty following this approach, at least if we continue to define long-run equilibrium in terms of equality between supply and demand—a conception I shall not challenge until very nearly the end of this book. We now have too many equations for the number of unknowns, as Figure 8.5 makes clear.

There would appear to be an easy solution to the problem illustrated in Figure 8.5: increase the number of unknowns by introducing a new variable. One possibility was already proposed in a slightly different context in Chapter 5: there the cost and availability of credit as well as capitalists' fellow-feeling were suggested as variables that might eliminate excessive investment demand relative to full-employment saving. The situation represented in Figure 8.5 calls for the opposite medicine, measures to increase the attractiveness of investment, in other words measures that move the investment-demand curve outward, as in Figure 8.6.

Alternatively, we might seek to solve the problem of overdetermination by explicitly introducing money as a new variable in the household

---

of a "Walrasian" (neoclassical, in our terminology) equilibrium in the short and intermediate periods. All told, it appears reasonable to classify Malinvaud with Barro-Grossman, as hybrids of neoclassical and neo-Keynesian strains.

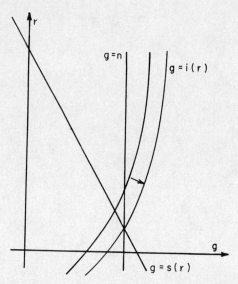

Figure 8.6 Overdetermination eliminated by shifting investment demand outward

budget equation. The household's endowment of money—which yields a return equal to r through a steady decrease in the price of corn and labor—might then be adjusted to equate desired saving with investment demand exactly where the saving function intersects the full-employment equation, as in Figure 8.7.

The solution is not, however, as straightforward as it looks; and the problem is worth exploring because it suggests a generic difficulty with introducing financial assets into growth models based on life-cycle theories of saving. Recall the model of Chapter 2, in which saving and consumption were determined by household maximization of a utility function of the form

$$U(C^1, C^2) \tag{2.1}$$

subject to a budget constraint normalized by $P = 1$,

$$C^1 + \frac{C^2}{1 + r} = W. \tag{2.2}$$

Taking into account the price equation in the form

$$W(r) = \frac{1 - a_1}{a_1} - r \frac{a_1}{a_0}, \tag{1.8}$$

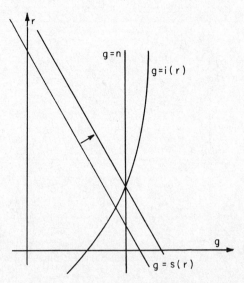

Figure 8.7 Overdetermination eliminated by shifting saving function upward

we could, for a given utility function, write C^1 and C^2 as functions of r alone, $C^1 = C^1(r)$ and $C^2 = C^2(r)$. By virtue of the budget constraint and the price equation, aggregate consumption demand

$$C(r, g) = C^1(r) + \frac{C^2(r)}{1 + g} \qquad (2.6)$$

and aggregate supply

$$C(g) = \frac{1 - a_1}{a_0} - g \frac{a_1}{a_0} \qquad (1.9)$$

turned out to be equal when

$$(r - g) \frac{C^2(r)}{(1 + r)(1 + g)} = (r - g) \frac{a_1}{a_0}. \qquad (2.8)$$

Equation (2.8) is graphed for the special case of a Cobb-Douglas utility function in Figure 8.8. Further analysis eliminated the $r = g$ branch of the diagram; unlike the branch characterized by

$$\frac{C^2(r)}{1 + r} = (1 + g) \frac{a_1}{a_0}, \qquad (2.10)$$

the $r = g$ branch failed to satisfy the ownership condition: with $r = g$,

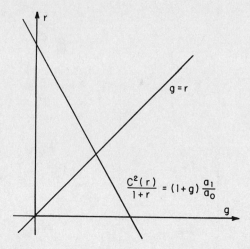

Figure 8.8 Locus of $\langle r, g \rangle$ equating consumption demand and supply

there is no reason for workers' desired saving to equal the investment necessary for a given rate of growth, and in a life-cycle model, only the present generation of workers is in a position effectively to save.

For Eq. (2.10) simultaneously to satisfy both the ownership condition and the food-grain equilibrium condition $C(r, g) = C(g)$ turns out to depend critically on the absence of money from the model. More accurately, the crucial point is the absence of fiat wealth, a monetary asset whose level in terms of corn can be set independently of the real flows in the economy.

To see this, put fiat money into the model. The household's budget equation becomes

$$C^1 + \frac{C^2}{1 + r} = W + M, \qquad (8.1)$$

in which W is the corn wage and M the endowment of money measured in terms of corn. In place of $C^1 = C^1(r)$ and $C^2 = C^2(r)$, we have $C^1 = C^1(r, M)$ and $C^2 = C^2(r, M)$. The level of money with which the household is endowed is constrained only to be nonnegative. The food-grain equilibrium condition, Eq. (2.8), generalizes to

$$Q(r, g, M) \equiv (1 + g)M + (r - g)\left[\frac{C^2(r, M)}{1 + r} - (1 + g)\frac{a_1}{a_0}\right] = 0. \quad (8.2)$$

For definiteness, suppose the utility function is Cobb-Douglas and let M be greater than zero. Then Eq. (8.2) has the shape illustrated in Figure

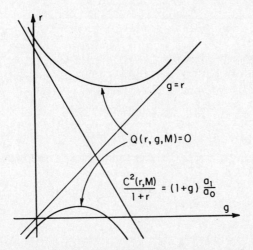

Figure 8.9 $Q(r, g, M) = 0$ equates consumption demand and supply, $M > 0$

8.9. Now superimpose the ownership condition onto the diagram, as in Figure 8.10. Workers' real saving, measured by their abstinence from consumption, continues to be reflected in the difference between corn wages and first-period consumption, $W - C^1(r, M)$. The ownership condition now becomes an inequality:

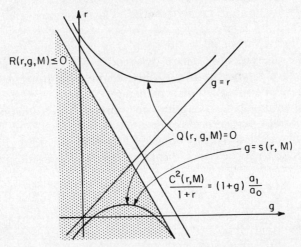

Figure 8.10 Locus of $\langle r, g \rangle$ equating consumption demand and supply and satisfying ownership condition is given by $g = s(r, M)$

$$W - C^1(r, M) \geq (1 + g) \frac{a_1}{a_0}. \tag{8.3}$$

Workers' excess real saving, the difference between the left- and right-hand sides of (8.3), is transferred to the retired generation in exchange for their financial assets. Thus, we have

$$W - C^1 - (1 + g) \frac{a_1}{a_0} = \frac{1 + r}{1 + g} \left[M + W - C^1 - (1 + g) \frac{a_1}{a_0} \right], \tag{8.4}$$

a relation equivalent to the food-grain equilibrium condition $Q(r, g, M) = 0$.

If we substitute from the budget constraint (8.1) into (8.3), we can write the ownership condition as

$$R(r, g, M) \equiv M - \left[\frac{C^2(r, M)}{1 + r} - (1 + g) \frac{a_1}{a_0} \right] \leq 0. \tag{8.5}$$

The shaded area of Figure 8.10 represents the set of points that satisfy the ownership condition. Evidently (8.2) and (8.5) are satisfied simultaneously only by the *lower* branch of $Q(r, g, M) = 0$, which becomes the saving function $g = s(r, M)$ for $M > 0$.

The general point is that, in a private-ownership neoclassical model, money cannot displace the saving function arbitrarily, in the manner of Figure 8.7, to insure that the equation system $s(r, M) = i(r) = n$ holds simultaneously. Only if the problem is one of excess saving, $s(r) > i(r) = n$, with $r < n$, can it be resolved by introducing a financial asset at an appropriate level. (This asymmetry is essentially the same one that was observed in Chapter 2, pp. 36–39.)

Observe that this problem does not arise outside the life-cycle context of the overlapping generations model. Models with a classical, Cambridge, or Keynesian saving function implicitly view the capitalist class as permanent rather than as being recreated each generation. Hence the ownership condition, the source of the difficulty in the life-cycle model, plays no role in these models. Monetary intervention to manipulate real variables, *à la* James Tobin (1955, 1965), thus makes more sense outside the neoclassical framework than inside.

9 Variable Proportions

It is widely but incorrectly maintained that, by introducing variable proportions into the argument, Robert Solow long ago (1956) proved the existence of a full-employment equilibrium in a neoclassical model. The confusion is twofold. First of all, Solow's model is, as we have seen, only half neoclassical: the saving function is basically "Keynesian" in nature.[1] Second, Solow hardly *proves* the existence of full employment. He rather assumes it, either baldly (1956, p. 67) or in the barely disguised form of a labor market that immediately adjusts demand to supply at every moment of time (1956, p. 86).

I do not mean to labor Solow unduly. The confusion about Solow's results is symptomatic of a broader question: to what extent do any of the results we have reached up to now in this book depend on the assumptions of fixed coefficients? This question can be answered only by dealing with the variable-proportions case directly.

Discrete Technologies

As a preliminary to the case of continuous substitution between the quantity of seed corn sown and the amount of time spent pulling weeds, let us examine the intermediate case of discrete technologies. Suppose,

1. In an extension of the model (1956, pp. 87–88), Solow introduces a saving function compatible with neoclassical theory. However, his explanation of this function is cryptic in the extreme, so that it is possible to impute to it a nonneoclassical as well as a neoclassical flavor: all Solow says is that the rate of saving might be sensitive to the rate of profit. The problem with this formulation is that it is precisely the nature of the dependence between the profit rate and the saving rate that is at issue between neoclassicals and nonneoclassicals!

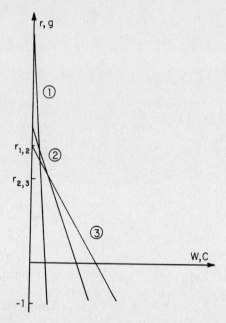

Figure 9.1 Growth-consumption and factor-price frontiers with multiple technologies

for definiteness, three corn-growing techniques are available, as represented in Figure 9.1. The straight lines corresponding to the circled numbers 1, 2, and 3 represent the production and price equations corresponding to the three technologies. For each, there is a separate equation:

$$1 = a_0^i C + a_1^i (1 + g), \qquad i = 1, 2, 3, \tag{9.1}$$

$$1 = W a_0^i + (1 + r) a_1^i, \qquad i = 1, 2, 3. \tag{9.2}$$

Profit maximization ensures that at any given wage the most profitable technique will be chosen, so that the outer envelope defines the overall growth-consumption and wage-profit frontiers. "Switch points," defined by profit rates at which two techniques are equally profitable, are denoted $r_{1,2}$ and $r_{2,3}$. Observe that in the one-good model, the difficulties associated with the "reswitching controversy" (about which more will be said in Chapter 12) cannot arise. The mapping between a_1 and intervals of the profit axis is one-to-one: higher profit rates map to lower capital intensities.

The Neoclassical Model

The effect of multiple technologies on the neoclassical model is illustrated in Figure 9.2. The saving function

$$
\left.
\begin{aligned}
g = s(r) = \beta \left[\frac{1}{a_1^1} - (1 + r) \right] - 1 \qquad & \frac{1}{a_1^1} - 1 \geq r \geq r_{1,2} \\
g = s(r) = \beta \left[\frac{1}{a_1^2} - (1 + r) \right] - 1 \qquad & r_{1,2} \geq r \geq r_{2,3} \\
g = s(r) = \beta \left[\frac{1}{a_1^3} - (1 + r) \right] - 1 \qquad & r_{2,3} \geq r \geq -1
\end{aligned}
\right\} \qquad (9.3)
$$

is drawn on the assumption of a Cobb-Douglas utility function for which the elasticity of utility with respect to future consumption is β. Its zigzag shape follows directly from the fact that its three branches, corresponding to the three different techniques, fall on parallel straight lines with a common slope $-\beta$. Indeed the only difference between the three lines is the constant term equal to the product of the output : capi-

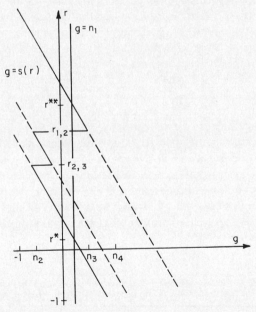

Figure 9.2 Neoclassical equilibria with multiple technologies

tal ratio $(1 - a_1^i)/a_1^i$ and the elasticity β. The shift from one to another portion of the saving function takes place at the switch points $r_{1,2}$ and $r_{2,3}$. Note the horizontal segments connecting the separate branches of the saving function; points on these segments are attainable by operating separate techniques in tandem—feasible at switch points alone because there and only there are two techniques equally profitable.

The existence of a multiplicity of techniques creates the possibility of multiple equilibria. If the full-employment rate of growth is $n = n_1$, then r^* and r^{**}, as well as $r_{1,2}$, are equilibrium rates of profit: saving is just adequate to sustain full employment growth at all three of these profit rates.

Three observations are in order: first, techniques 1 and 2 must both be utilized in order to provide full-employment growth at $r = r_{1,2}$. Now, there is no reason why the two techniques might not be operated in the requisite intensity, but neither is there any reason inherent in the logic of capitalist profit maximization why corn growers should settle on the appropriate combination of techniques rather than some other. As is generally the case in linear models, the most that can be said is that the equilibrium $\langle r_{1,2}, n_1 \rangle$ is equally desirable from the private perspective as are neighboring nonequilibrium points.

Second, of the three equilibria, only the middle one is stable, and then only in the profit dimension. The stability argument of Chapter 2 applies directly: no matter how close an initial profit rate might be to r^* or r^{**}, neoclassical wage dynamics would propel the economy away from these equilibria. But the same logic means that an initial profit rate in the interval (r^*, r^{**}) would lead to a sequence of profit rates which—overshooting apart—converges towards $r_{1,2}$. Observe, however, that with or without overshooting, the growth rate need not converge to n_1. Because of the equiprofitability of techniques 1 and 2 at the equilibrium $r_{1,2}$, the growth rate can oscillate within the interval $[n_2, n_3]$ while the profit rate converges to $r_{1,2}$. The most we can expect is that the *average* rate of growth will tend to n_1.[2]

Finally, it should be emphasized that the existence of multiple techniques creates the possibility but not the certainty of multiple equilibria. For $n \in [n_3, n_4]$, a single (unstable) equilibrium exists. For $n > n_4$, no equilibrium exists at all!

2. The possibility that the growth rate will oscillate about n_1 differs in kind from the possibility that the profit rate will oscillate about $r_{1,2}$. The oscillation of g is not the consequence of the discreteness of time, but of the shape of the mapping $s(r)$. It does not disappear as the length of the time period goes to zero.

The Neo-Marxian Model

The existence of a multiplicity of techniques introduces changes in the neo-Marxian and the neo-Keynesian stories too, but it is fair to say that the changes are hardly as dramatic as in the neoclassical case, for the Cambridge saving equation is much less affected than the neoclassical. Indeed, the version that assumes workers save nothing,

$$g = s(r) = s_C r,$$

makes saving per unit of seed corn totally independent of technology, hence completely unaffected by the introduction of variable proportions.

But as soon as workers are assumed to save a positive fraction of wages, technology enters into the saving equation as well as into the price equation. In particular, in the presence of the multiplicity of techniques, the Pasinetti saving function has the shape represented in Figure 9.3. The vertical segments of the saving function represent the $\hat{\delta} = 0$ range, in which workers own all but a vanishing share of the capital stock. Each of the three vertical branches corresponds to a

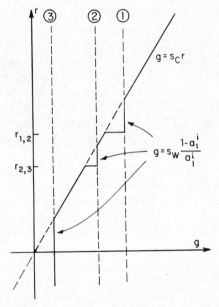

Figure 9.3 Pasinetti saving function with multiple technologies

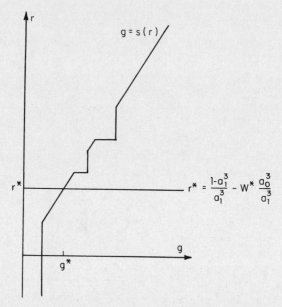

Figure 9.4 Neo-Marxian equilibrium with a Pasinetti saving function

specific technique of production, and the horizontal branches represent combinations of two (equiprofitable) techniques.

Now add the specifically Marxian assumption that the real wage is determined by "subsistence," and it becomes clear that the neo-Marxian story is little affected by the existence of multiple techniques: given the array of production possibilities determined by existing forces and relations of production, the wage rate determines the technology as well as the distribution of income: the propensities to save of workers and capitalists combine with the distribution of income and with productivity to determine the rate of growth. Figure 9.4 shows one possible equilibrium.

Two words of caution are in order. First, in consequence of the endogeneity of the social relations of production, it would be inappropriate to interpret the relationship between wage rate and technology in a neoclassical fashion, which makes profit maximization into a mechanical process of sorting through the physical possibilities. In the neo-Marxian approach, the coefficients a_0 and a_1 depend on social as well as physical relationships so that profit maximization may lead to different technological choices in situations where wage rates and the state of the technological art are similar but the relations of production differ.

Second, while there is nothing that in principle rules out an equilibrium in which workers own the means of production, such a configuration is hardly the reality Marx intended to describe.

The Neo-Keynesian Model

The neo-Keynesian model changes a little more. Multiple equilibria, represented in Figure 9.5, are not new, but the possibility of a *stable* equilibrium in the $\hat{\delta} = 0$ range is a consequence of introducing multiple techniques. Obviously a stable people's capitalism is a possibility, not a certainty: given the saving function, all depends on the shape of the investment function. For example, the $\hat{\delta} = 0$ equilibria at $\langle r^*, g^* \rangle$ and $\langle r^{***}, g^{***} \rangle$ are unstable, as in the single-technique case.

Perhaps the most striking consequence of introducing multiple techniques in the context of Cambridge saving assumptions is the impact on the correspondence between profit rates and the share of capital owned by capitalists. In the single-technique case, increasing the rate of profit increases this share or at least does not diminish it: r and $\hat{\delta}$ are positively related. But this is not necessarily so in the multiple-technique case. In

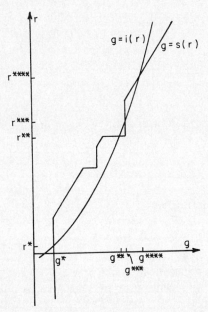

Figure 9.5 Neo-Keynesian equilibria with a Pasinetti saving function

Figures 9.4 and 9.5 increasing the rate of profit leads to a shift from the $\hat{\delta} > 0$ segment corresponding to one technique to the $\hat{\delta} = 0$ segment corresponding to a less capital-intensive technique. Thus in the neo-Keynesian case an equilibrium like $\langle r^{***}, g^{***} \rangle$ is compatible with a lower $\hat{\delta}$ than the equilibrium $\langle r^{**}, g^{**} \rangle$, despite the fact that profit (and growth) rates are higher for the first than for the second of these pairs. We shall encounter this phenomenon again at the end of this chapter.

Continuous Substitution

In short, the changes introduced by a multiplicity of discrete technologies are interesting but hardly profound. One is almost tempted to label them marginal. Not so the case of continuous substitution. In this case — especially in the neoclassical model — substantial substitution makes a substantial difference to the characterization of equilibrium. To see this, we start from the assumption that a_0 and a_1 are determined from a production function of the general form

$$X_{+1} = F(X - C, L_{+1}), \tag{9.4}$$

with $X - C$ representing seed corn, L_{+1} representing employment, and X_{+1} representing gross corn output. By definition we have

$$a_{0,+1} = \frac{L_{+1}}{X_{+1}}, \tag{9.5}$$

$$a_{1,+1} = \frac{X - C}{X_{+1}}. \tag{9.6}$$

If we add to these definitions the assumption of constant returns to scale, we can write Eq. (9.4) in the form

$$\frac{1}{a_{0,+1}} = f\left(\frac{a_{1,+1}}{a_{0,+1}}\right), \tag{9.7}$$

where, again by definition,

$$f\left(\frac{a_{1,+1}}{a_{0,+1}}\right) = F\left(\frac{X - C}{L_{+1}}, 1\right). \tag{9.8}$$

If we do our calculations in terms of a single worker at time 0, with corn as the unit of account $(P = 1)$, the price equation takes the customary form

$$1 = Wa_0 + (1 + r)a_1, \tag{1.7}$$

but the production equation the novel form

$$1 = a_0 C + a_{1,+1}(1 + g^X_{+1}), \tag{9.9}$$

or the form

$$1 = a_0 C + a_1(1 + g^K). \tag{9.10}$$

In Eq. (9.9), g^X represents the growth of *output*, no longer necessarily equal to the growth of capital g^K in Eq. (9.10). In the continuous-substitution case g^X and g^K are defined by the equations

$$1 + g^X_{+1} = \frac{X_{+1}}{X}$$

and

$$1 + g^K = \frac{X - C}{X_{-1} - C_{-1}} = \frac{K_{+1}}{K},$$

where $K_{+1} = X - C$ is the stock of seed corn available for production next year. The two growth rates are related by the equation

$$(1 + g^X_{+1})a_{1,+1} = (1 + g^K)a_1.$$

Under steady-state conditions Eqs. (9.7), (1.7), (9.9), and (9.10) reduce to the timeless form

$$1 \ = Wa_0 + (1 + r)a_1 \tag{1.7}$$

$$1 \ = a_0 C + a_1(1 + g), \qquad g = g^K = g^X \tag{1.5}$$

$$\frac{1}{a_0} = f\left(\frac{a_1}{a_0}\right). \tag{9.11}$$

The basic production and price-formation model is now described by *three* equations—(9.11) as well as (1.5) and (1.7)—but contains *six* unknowns—a_0 and a_1 in addition to C, g, W, and r. Neoclassical, neo-Marxian, and neo-Keynesian models each provide *two* relationships, which apparently gives us five independent relationships to determine six variables: in other words, we are one equation short.

This is where marginal productivity enters the picture. By assuming that the marginal productivity of labor (MP_L) is equal to the wage rate, or formally

$$MP_L \equiv f\left(\frac{a_1}{a_0}\right) - f'\left(\frac{a_1}{a_0}\right)\frac{a_1}{a_0} = W, \tag{9.12}$$

we can close each of the models. Or instead of (9.12), we can specify that the gross marginal productivity of seed corn (MP_K) be equal to the gross profit rate. Formally

$$MP_K \equiv f'\left(\frac{a_1}{a_0}\right) = 1 + r. \tag{9.13}$$

Observe that (9.12) and (9.13) are alternative assumptions. Equations (9.11), (1.7), and (9.12) together imply (9.13). Conversely, Eqs. (9.11), (1.7), and (9.13) imply (9.12). And (1.7), (9.13), and (9.12) jointly imply (9.11). The mutual interdependence of these equations results from the assumption of constant returns to scale.

It might appear from the foregoing that the introduction of variable proportions serves only to complicate the story, by adding two new variables a_0 and a_1 and two new relationships $1/a_0 = f(a_1/a_0)$ and $MP_L = W$. But it changes things qualitatively too.

The Neoclassical Model

As we have indicated, these qualitative changes are most pronounced in the neoclassical model, characterized by full employment

$$g = n \tag{2.18}$$

and a saving-investment relationship determined by utility maximization, which in the case of a Cobb-Douglas utility function has the simple form

$$g = s(r) = \beta \left[\frac{1}{a_1} - (1 + r)\right] - 1. \tag{2.17}$$

Consider the relationship between growth and profit summarized in (2.17). Substitute from (9.11) to obtain

$$g = s(r) = \beta \left[f\left(\frac{a_1}{a_0}\right)\left(\frac{a_1}{a_0}\right)^{-1} - (1 + r)\right] - 1. \tag{9.14}$$

Now set

$$k \equiv \frac{a_1}{a_0} \tag{9.15}$$

and differentiate totally with respect to r:

$$s'(r) = \beta\left\{\left[f'(k)k^{-1} - f(k)k^{-2}\right]\frac{dk}{dr} - 1\right\}. \tag{9.16}$$

The difference between (9.16) and the fixed-proportions case is that in (9.16) the capital : labor ratio is not constant, so dk/dr does not vanish.

But how to calculate this derivative? Again marginal productivity plays a crucial role. If the marginal productivity of capital is to equal the profit rate,

$$f'(k) = 1 + r,$$

then, as we vary the right-hand side, the left-hand side must vary accordingly. Hence,

$$f''(k) \frac{dk}{dr} = 1$$

or

$$\frac{dk}{dr} = [f''(k)]^{-1}. \tag{9.17}$$

Now substitute from (9.17) into (9.16) and collect terms to obtain

$$s'(r) = \beta \left[\frac{\sigma}{(1 + r)a_1} - 1 \right], \tag{9.18}$$

where σ is the elasticity of substitution in production,

$$\sigma = \frac{dk}{d\left(\dfrac{W}{1 + r}\right)} \frac{W/(1 + r)}{k} = -\frac{W(1 + r)}{f(k)kf''(k)}. \tag{9.19}$$

The parameter $\sigma/(1 + r)a_1$, the ratio of the elasticity of substitution to the share of gross profits in output, measures the response of the output : capital ratio to changes in the rate of profit,

$$\frac{d(1/a_1)}{dr} = \frac{\sigma}{(1 + r)a_1}.$$

This parameter plays, as we shall see, a critical role in the analysis of equilibrium: in the neoclassical model, it — along with the utility function — determines the slope of the saving function.

ROLE OF THE ELASTICITY OF SUBSTITUTION A positive elasticity of substitution is guaranteed by the assumption of diminishing marginal productivity of seed corn (or of labor), essentially equivalent to assuming additivity of production processes as well as constant returns. (See the appendix to this chapter for an elaboration of this point.) If, in addition, we are willing for the sake of simplicity to assume that the production function has the general shape

$$f(k) = \gamma[\eta k^{-\rho} + 1 - \eta]^{-1/\rho}, \tag{9.20}$$

with $\gamma > 0$, $0 < \eta < 1$, $\rho \geq -1$, then σ becomes a constant,

$$\sigma = \frac{1}{1 + \rho},$$

and the analysis is thereby considerably simplified.

The constant-elasticity-of-substitution (CES) production function (9.20) behaves differently according to whether ρ is positive or negative, which is to say according to whether σ is smaller or larger than unity. The two possibilities are represented in Figure 9.6, along with the intermediate case of Cobb-Douglas production defined by the limit as ρ goes to 0. (In fact, since our interest focuses on the extreme points of the profit interval, the analysis of CES production functions is more general than it might appear. Provided the elasticity of substitution approaches limiting values as the rate of profit goes to its extreme

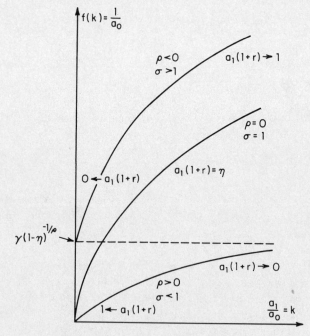

Figure 9.6 CES production functions

values, the limiting behavior of the production functions can be described in terms of σ, which is all we require.)

INELASTIC SUBSTITUTION With relatively inelastic substitution possibilities ($\sigma < 1$), the share of profit $(1 + r)a_1$ approaches zero as the capital:labor ratio increases without bound and the (net) profit rate approaches -1. Hence, according to (9.18), the slope of the saving function becomes infinite at the lower boundary. But as the rate of profit increases, the capital:labor ratio falls. Hence the share of profit increases, and the slope of the saving function *decreases*. When $(1 + r)a_1$ increases to the numerical value of σ, the saving function reaches its maximum in the $r \times g$ plane. Beyond this point, the slope of the saving function is negative, and the saving function goes to -1 as r goes to r_{max} and $(1 + r)a_1$ goes to 1. Figure 9.7 illustrates the saving function for this case.

The crucial result should be clear from Figure 9.7, in which vertical lines representing two population growth rates are superimposed: continuous substitution in production does *not* of itself guarantee the existence of a neoclassical equilibrium. If the labor force is growing at a rate equal to n_2, saving will be inadequate to generate capital to match population growth no matter what the rate of profit!

(Observe that the basic shape of the saving function is the same for all σ between 0 and 1. But, though the fixed-coefficient case can be viewed

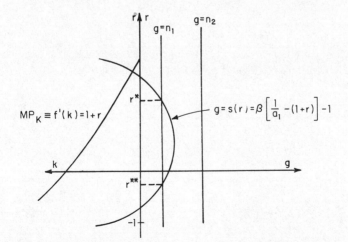

Figure 9.7 Neoclassical saving function for CES production function
with $\sigma < 1$

as the limiting case of a CES production function as $\sigma \rightarrow 0$, the saving function for the fixed-coefficient case — a straight line — is obviously *not* the limiting saving function for CES production as σ goes to 0! The problem is that the convergence of the CES production function to the limiting fixed-coefficient function is not uniform, so that the saving function of the limiting case is not the limiting saving function. The same problem exists, it will become clear, at the upper end, as we pass to the limiting saving function as $\sigma \rightarrow 1$.)

ELASTIC SUBSTITUTION If ρ is negative, that is, if σ exceeds unity, the saving function changes shape dramatically. At $r = r_{\min} = \gamma \eta^{-1/\rho} - 1$, the slope $s'(r)$ is positive (but finite), and with each increase in r, $(1 + r)a_1$ falls, so that $s'(r)$ increases, becoming infinite in the limit as k goes to zero. Moreover, with $\sigma > 1$ there is no upper limit on r: as k approaches zero, r approaches ∞. Taken together, these considerations, which make the range of the saving function equal to $(-1, +\infty)$, guarantee the existence of an equilibrium, as Figure 9.8 illustrates. For any rate of population growth in the interval $(-1, +\infty)$, a rate of profit exists that generates the saving necessary to maintain that growth. Moreover, the equilibrium is unique.

The borderline case, $\sigma = 1$, corresponds, as has been noted, to Cobb-Douglas production:

$$f(k) = \gamma k^\eta.$$

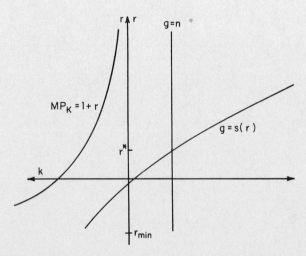

Figure 9.8 Neoclassical saving function for CES production function with $\sigma > 1$

The distinguishing feature of this case is that $(1 + r)a_1$ is constant over the entire domain. Thus the slope $s'(r)$ is constant. (It is obviously positive, since $(1 + r)a_1$ is necessarily less than unity.) Since the domain of r is $(-1, +\infty)$, equilibrium is once again assured. Moreover, equilibrium is again unique. In essence, the Cobb-Douglas case resembles the $\sigma > 1$ CES case, as Figure 9.9 shows.

STABILITY The crux of the stability issue remains the slope of the saving function, as in Chapter 2. Recall the adjustment process described in the section "Instability of Equilibrium" in that chapter, which, allowing for a variable capital : labor ratio, is summarized in the following equations:

$$W_{+1} = \theta \left(\frac{V}{k} - 1 \right) + W \qquad \text{(wage adjustment)} \qquad (9.21)$$

$$V_{+1} = (1 + g^K) \frac{V}{1 + n} \qquad \text{(capital accumulation)} \qquad (9.22)$$

$$f(k) = W + (1 + r)k \qquad \text{(price equation)}$$

$$f(k) - f'(k)k = W \qquad \text{(marginal-productivity equation)}$$

$$g^K = \beta(r^e_{+1}) \left[\frac{f(k)}{k} - (1 + r) \right] - 1 \qquad \text{(saving equation)} \qquad (9.23)$$

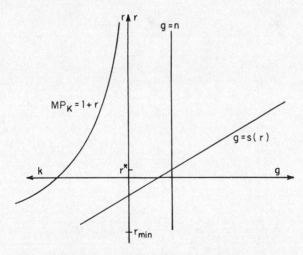

Figure 9.9 Neoclassical saving function for Cobb-Douglas production function ($\sigma = 1$)

The notation in these equations follows the notation of Chapter 2; in particular, V is equal to seed corn per capita,

$$V = \frac{X_{-1} - C_{-1}}{N} = \frac{K}{N}.$$

Figure 9.10 illustrates the process of short-run employment determination: $\hat{L}$ represents a short-run equilibrium at which profits are maximized, given the wage rate W. With the current wage rate and stock of seed corn determined last period, the levels of output and employment, the capital:labor ratio, and the profit rate emerge jointly from the profit-maximization process. The new growth rate is determined by the saving-investment relationship expressed in Eq. (9.23).

Let $\beta(r^e_{+1}) = \beta$ — that is, assume Cobb-Douglas utility — and the dependence of stability on the elasticity of substitution emerges clearly. Form the equation system

$$\left. \begin{array}{l} G(W, V) = \theta \left(\dfrac{V}{k} - 1 \right) + W, \\[2ex] H(W, V) = (1 + g^K) \dfrac{V}{1 + n}. \end{array} \right\} \tag{9.24}$$

Taking note of the relationships implied by the price, marginal-productivity, and saving equations,

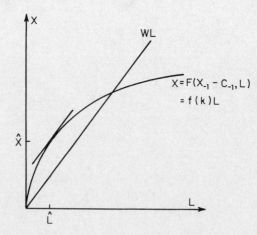

Figure 9.10 Short-run employment determination for given W

$$\frac{dr}{dW} = -\frac{1}{k}, \qquad \frac{dk}{dW} = -\frac{1}{f''(k)k} = \sigma \frac{f(k)}{(1+r)W}, \qquad \frac{dg^K}{dr} = s'(r),$$

$$\frac{\partial H}{\partial W} + \frac{\partial H}{\partial k}\frac{\partial k}{\partial W} = \frac{dg^K}{dr}\frac{dr}{dW}\frac{V}{(1+n)} = -\frac{s'(r)V}{k(1+n)}$$

we have at a stationary point of the system defined by Eqs. (9.24)

$$\mathbf{J} = \begin{bmatrix} \dfrac{\partial G}{\partial W} + \dfrac{\partial G}{\partial k}\dfrac{dk}{dW} & \dfrac{\partial G}{\partial V} \\[2mm] \dfrac{\partial H}{\partial W} + \dfrac{\partial H}{\partial k}\dfrac{dk}{dW} & \dfrac{\partial H}{\partial V} \end{bmatrix} = \begin{bmatrix} -\dfrac{\theta}{k^*}\sigma\dfrac{f(k^*)}{(1+r^*)W^*} + 1 & \dfrac{\theta}{k^*} \\[2mm] -\dfrac{s'(r^*)}{1+n} & 1 \end{bmatrix}.$$

For stability, it is necessary and sufficient that both the Routh-Hurwitz inequalities

$$|\mathrm{tr}\ \mathbf{J}| < |1 + \det \mathbf{J}|$$

and

$$|\det \mathbf{J}| < 1$$

hold. As in Chapter 2, $s'(r) < 0$ guarantees that one of these two inequalities will be violated.

The situation with $s'(r) > 0$ is more complicated. In this case there exists a positive wage-adjustment speed θ_0 such that the first of these inequalities will be satisfied for all lower wage-adjustment speeds $\theta < \theta_0$. Moreover, $\theta < \theta_0$ implies $\det \mathbf{J} > 0$. So the second of these inequalities is also satisfied if β is sufficiently small: we have

$$\det \mathbf{J} = \frac{\theta}{k^*}\left\{\beta\left[\frac{\sigma}{(1+r^*)a_1^*} - 1\right](1+n)^{-1} - \sigma\frac{f(k^*)}{(1+r^*)W^*}\right\} + 1,$$

which requires

$$\beta < \sigma\frac{f(k^*)}{(1+r^*)W^*}\frac{1+n}{\left[\dfrac{\sigma}{(1+r^*)a_1^*} - 1\right]}$$

for $\det \mathbf{J} < 1$.

Evidently $s'(r) > 0$ is necessary but not sufficient for stability: just as an excessively high wage-adjustment speed can lead to instability, so can an excessive response of desired saving to changes in the profit rate. But the problem that arises with high values of β or θ is different in kind from the instability that characterizes the case $s'(r) < 0$. With $s'(r) > 0$, the difficulty is one of "overshooting," a problem peculiar to the discrete formulation of the problem. In the continuous-time analog, Eqs. (9.21) and (9.22) become

$$\dot{W} = \theta \left(\frac{V}{k} - 1 \right),$$

$$\dot{V} = (g^K - n)V.$$

In this case $s'(r) > 0$ is sufficient (as well as necessary) for stability for *any* positive values of β and θ, since the real parts of the characteristic roots of the matrix

$$\mathbf{M} = \begin{bmatrix} -\dfrac{\theta}{k^*} \, \sigma \, \dfrac{f(k^*)}{(1 + r^*)W^*} & \dfrac{\theta}{k^*} \\ -\dfrac{s'(r^*)}{1 + n} & 0 \end{bmatrix}$$

are negative—the stability condition when time is characterized as continuous—if and only if $s'(r) > 0$.

The slope $s'(r)$ in turn depends critically on σ. In the case of inelastic substitution, one of the two equilibria (assuming existence) is necessarily unstable— $\langle r^*, n_1 \rangle$ in Figure 9.7. The other is stable, at least in the continuous-time version of the model.

The similarity with the case of discrete technologies is striking. In neither case is there any assurance of the existence of equilibrium, but in both cases the possibility of a stable equilibrium exists with a Cobb-Douglas utility function, a result that is precluded in the fixed-coefficient model. Indeed, with $\sigma < 1$, continuous substitution modifies the discrete-technology results only marginally: in the present case, stability holds for g as well as for r.

In the elastic case ($\sigma \geq 1$), the slope of the saving function is positive everywhere, and the (unique) equilibrium is consequently stable—at least if we bar the possibility of overshooting the equilibrium. Substitution—provided there is enough of it—is thus the *deus ex machina* of the neoclassical model. In Chapter 2, the possibility that equilibrium would fail to exist or would be unstable was traced to the inverse relationship between wages and profits. In the life-cycle model, desired saving depends directly on wages and therefore inversely on profits, apart from overpowering substitution effects in consumption. But a high elasticity of substitution *in production* increases the labor input per unit of output sufficiently to compensate for the reduction in wage accompanying an increase in the profit rate. (With $\sigma > 1$, the *share* of wages in output actually increases; in the limiting Cobb-Douglas case, with

$\sigma = 1$, the share of wages remains constant.) Thus saving per unit of gross output becomes a nondecreasing function of the rate of profit. And, at the same time, each increase in the rate of profit increases the gross output : capital ratio, so that a given quantity of saving per unit of output means a higher quantity of saving per unit of seed corn. Denoting aggregate saving by S, we have in general

$$1 + g = \frac{S}{WL} \frac{WL}{X} \frac{X}{K}.$$

With $\sigma \geq 1$, WL/X and X/K are nondecreasing functions of r, and the assumption of Cobb-Douglas utility guarantees that S/WL is constant.

The role that substitution effects in the utility function play in the analysis now emerges clearly: presupposing a Cobb-Douglas utility function of the form

$$U = (C^1)^\alpha (C^2)^\beta$$

ensures that substitution effects of changing wages are just offset by income effects, with the result that S/WL is constant over the entire profit interval. But we do not need such a strong assumption: after all in the saving function

$$s(r) = \beta \left(\frac{1 - a_1}{a_1} - r \right) - 1,$$

the parameter β is the ratio of gross saving to total wages with or without Cobb-Douglas utility. Interpreted as a propensity to save that may vary as a function of W and r, the only requirement is that β be bounded away from 0 everywhere. If this restriction is met, then the qualitative results derived by assuming β to be constant survive intact. In particular, $\sigma \geq 1$ is sufficient for the existence of a stable equilibrium, at least in the continuous-time version of the model. Moreover, with $\sigma < 1$, equilibrium may or may not exist. But if it does, it exists in pairs.

A CHICAGO MODEL WITH IMMEDIATE WAGE ADJUSTMENT   Up to now, the analysis of stability has implicitly assumed the same adjustment model that characterized the fixed-coefficient case. In other words, saving intentions are always realized:

$$V_{+1} = (1 + g^K) \frac{V}{1 + n}, \tag{9.22}$$

and the real wage adjusts gradually to excess demand or supply in the labor market, according to the equation

$$W_{+1} = \theta \left(\frac{V}{k} - 1 \right) + W. \qquad (9.21)$$

In the short run, if not in the long, unemployment (or overfull employment) is quite compatible with the neoclassical model.

In the fixed-coefficient case, this was the only feasible adjustment process. But with continuous substitution, an alternative adjustment process can be specified that ensures full employment in the short run as well as the long. Instead of assuming that the wage rate responds partially and gradually to demand and supply conditions, we can assume quick adjustment, so that the labor market clears in each period. Thus in each period, the economy is in a temporary equilibrium *à la* John Hicks (1939). This may not be a particularly compelling notion, even for most neoclassical economists — except at the University of Chicago — but it is of some interest to see what difference immediate labor-market adjustment makes to the neoclassical model.

In the "Chicago Story," the wage rate is assumed to clear the labor market as in Figure 9.11(a) and (b). In Figure 9.11(a) the labor supply is assumed to be fixed at each moment of time. Implicitly the marginal disutility of labor is assumed to be zero. The general formula is

$$L_t' = (1 + n)^t,$$

and at time 0 we have

$$L_0 = 1.$$

In this case we have full employment at every moment of time *by assumption*, and the wage rate is determined by the model endogenously.

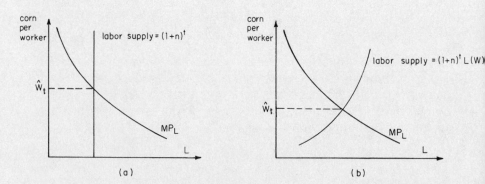

Figure 9.11 Wage determination with period-by-period clearing of labor market. (a) fixed labor supply; (b) labor supply a function of the wage rate

In Figure 9.11(b), the labor supply is once again given exogenously, but as a function of the wage rate,

$$L_t = (1 + n)^t L(W),$$

with the precise functional form $L(W)$ reflecting constrained maximization of a utility function of the kind analyzed in the appendix to Chapter 2, namely $U(C^1, C^2, z)$, in which z represents the fraction of the day allocated to work, and $1 - z$ represents "leisure." In this case the wage rate and employment are determined simultaneously. In both cases the remaining unknowns a_0, a_1, r, and C fall out from the solution to the equations characterizing the neoclassical model.

Observe that with Chicago (period-by-period) market clearing, as with gradual wage adjustment, stability hinges on the sign of $s'(r)$. At a starting point at which the stock of seed corn is growing faster than the labor force, $(g^K - n > 0)$, the capital : labor ratio must increase and the real wage must rise. Hence the rate of profit must fall, whether adjustment is immediate, as in Figure 9.11, or gradual, as in Eqs. (9.21) and (9.22). As long as the growth rate of capital is positively related to the profit rate—$s'(r) > 0$—the growth rate must fall too, until g^K reaches the equilibrium n. Conversely, if $s'(r)$ is negative, as in the upper reaches of Figure 9.7, both adjustment processes move away from equilibrium.

For our purposes there are two important points: first, that steady-state equilibrium values of the variables C, g, r, W, a_0, and a_1 are the same whether we assume the wage clears the labor market in each period or we assume the labor market clears more gradually. In both cases equilibrium is characterized by points of intersection between the full-employment growth function $g = n$ and the saving function $g = s(r)$, as in Figures 9.7–9.9. Second, the stability question is resolved by the slope of the saving function.[3]

Solow Again: A Short Digression

Observe that quick rather than gradual adjustment of the wage rate to labor-market supply and demand conditions characterized Solow's model (1956). As I have said, Solow in effect proved full employment by assuming it! But even if Chicago market clearing is judged to be more neoclassical than a more gradual process (considerations of real-

3. This is not to say that the quicker adjustment process always leads to the same equilibrium as the more gradual one. Since the two processes specify initial conditions differently, the long-run outcomes well might—in the absence of global stability—differ.

ism apart, the gradual process has the expositional virtue of maintaining consistency between fixed-coefficient and continuous-substitution cases), Solow's model can hardly be classified as neoclassical. The "Keynesian" saving function, it has been pointed out, makes the Solow model a hybrid as close to Pasinetti's as to the neoclassical. Indeed, apart from the specifics of the saving function, only the emphasis of Solow on continuous substitution, a matter of secondary importance from our perspective, distinguishes the Solow model from Pasinetti's. With continuous substitution, steady-growth equilibrium *à la* Solow is characterized by the following equations:

$$\frac{1}{a_0} = f\left(\frac{a_1}{a_0}\right) \tag{9.11}$$

$$1 + r = f'\left(\frac{a_1}{a_0}\right) \tag{9.13}$$

$$1 = a_0 C + a_1(1 + g) \tag{1.5}$$

$$1 = W a_0 + (1 + r)a_1 \tag{1.7}$$

$$g = n \tag{2.18}$$

$$g = s(r) = s \frac{1 - a_1}{a_1}. \tag{9.25}$$

Of these six equations, only the last—reflecting saving as a constant fraction of (net) output—differs from the neoclassical model. But this is enough of a difference to change the results in one crucial respect.

Taking account of the interdependence between r and a_1/a_0, the slope of the saving function (9.25) is given by the equation

$$s'(r) = s \frac{\sigma}{(1 + r)a_1}.$$

Thus the slope is everywhere positive for *all* positive values of σ, not just for $\sigma \geq 1$, as in the neoclassical case. This guarantees that, apart from overshooting, any equilibrium will be stable, which is not all Solow claimed he was proving but is by no means an insignificant result nonetheless.

Observe that positivity of $s'(r)$ does not (as Solow recognized) guarantee the existence of equilibrium. Consider Figure 9.12(a), in which the elasticity of substitution is supposed to be less than unity, and Figure 9.12(b), which gives Solow's own representation, adjusted for differences with respect to the treatment of depreciation. For the assumed rate of population growth, no equilibrium exists, not—as in the neo-

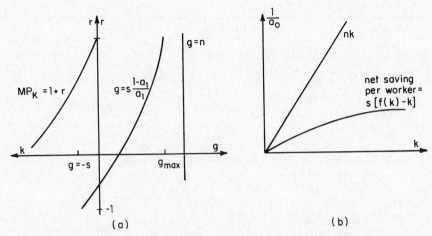

Figure 9.12 Solow model with $\sigma < 1$. (a) in $r \times g$ space; (b) in $k \times 1/a_0$ space

classical model — because of an inverse relationship between profit and saving rates, but because with a low elasticity of substitution, there is an upper limit to the profit rate and hence to the rate of saving and growth. As Figure 9.12(a) and (b) is drawn, the model tends eventually to $\langle r_{max}, g_{max} \rangle$ — but attains this configuration only asymptotically as time approaches infinity and the capital:labor ratio goes to zero. Observe that in the absence of a steady state, quick and gradual wage-adjustment processes lead to different results: quick adjustment ensures full employment at all times, whereas gradual adjustment permits the rate of unemployment to grow without bound!

In the Solow model, unlike the neoclassical model, the existence of equilibrium is not guaranteed by assuming $\sigma > 1$. In this case the difficulty occurs at the lower end of the range of the saving function. The range is $(s(\gamma\eta^{-1/\rho} - 1), \infty)$, which means that too low a population growth rate will make steady-growth equilibrium unobtainable. As Figure 9.13(a) and (b) is drawn, n is less than $g_{min} = s(\gamma\eta^{-1/\rho} - 1)$, and the economy builds up its capital stock indefinitely. Only the borderline Cobb-Douglas case guarantees equilibrium for all positive values of the production-function parameters and the saving rate.[4]

The real problem with Solow's argument is not the failure of equilibrium to exist. Solow was not only aware of this problem, but emphasized it in his exposition (1956, pp. 64–66). Rather, the fundamental

4. The only limitation is that the population cannot be falling at too rapid a rate. For the $\sigma = 1$, the range of the saving function is $(-s, +\infty)$, which necessarily includes the nonnegative half-line. Hence steady-growth equilibrium exists for any $n \geq -s$.

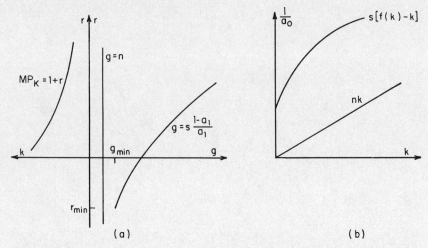

Figure 9.13 Solow model with $\sigma > 1$. (a) in $r \times g$ space; (b) in $k \times 1/a_0$ space

error lies in the claim that the argument has anything to do with Roy Harrod's opposition between warranted and natural rates of growth. In fact Solow's contribution deals solely with the natural rate of growth, for precisely the force of the condition $g = n$ is to define steady-growth equilibrium in terms of the natural rate.

In short, continuous substitution resolves the "knife-edge" problem of Evsey Domar — reflected in Figure 8.4 — by imparting a positive slope to the saving function. But continuous substitution does nothing for Harrod's problem of opposition between warranted and natural growth rates, which exists whether or not the saving function is positively sloped.

It could hardly be otherwise. As Amartya Sen has noted (1965), opposition between warranted and natural rates of growth arises from the existence of an investment-demand function, and Solow steadfastly refused to admit investment demand into the model. If we add an investment-demand function in the $r \times g$ plane, it is natural to identify the warranted rate with the steady-growth equilibrium that results from the intersection of the investment and savings functions. In Figure 9.14 this equilibrium occurs at $\langle r^*, g^* \rangle$. By contrast, the Solow natural-growth equilibrium occurs at $\langle r^{**}, n \rangle$. One can resolve the consequent overdetermination by suppressing the full-employment requirement (as do the neo-Keynesians), or by suppressing the investment-demand function (as do Solow, Pasinetti, the neoclassicals, *and*

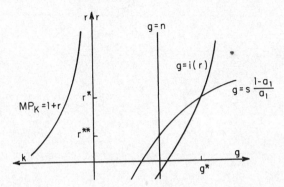

Figure 9.14 Warranted and natural growth equilibria with $\sigma > 1$

the neo-Marxians). But one can hardly pretend that stability of the natural-growth equilibrium itself does the trick!

Nonneoclassical Equilibrium without Workers' Saving

THE NEO-MARXIAN MODEL The avenue by which continuous substitution affects neoclassical equilibrium is the life-cycle saving function. This finds no counterpart in a classical saving function of the form

$$g = s(r) = s_C r,$$

since the capital:labor ratio does not enter into this relationship at all. Nevertheless even in this case, substitution makes a difference because r depends on the production function as well as on W.

In the neo-Marxian model, the "subsistence" wage rate W^* determines the equilibrium capital:labor ratio, *via* the marginal-productivity relationship

$$f(k) - f'(k)k = W^*;$$

the price equation gives us the equilibrium profit rate. Figure 9.15 illustrates the neo-Marxian equilibrium in the continuous substitution case. This construction, it is fair to say, does not differ from the fixed-coefficient case in any essential.

LIMITATIONS OF THE LABOR THEORY OF VALUE In the presence of continuous substitution, it is, however, no longer a matter of indifference whether we proceed directly from W^* to the equilibrium

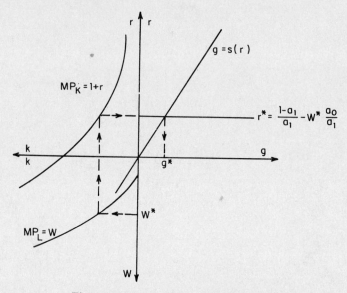

Figure 9.15 Neo-Marxian equilibrium

$\langle W^*, r^*, g^*, C^*, a_0^*, a_1^* \rangle$ or indirectly *via* the labor theory of value. For in contrast with the fixed proportions case, there is not necessarily a one-to-one relationship between the subsistence wage W^* and the rate of exploitation ε^*. Moreover even where the mapping is one-to-one, the range of ε does not necessarily include the positive half-line, as it does in the fixed-proportions case. So one cannot pick an arbitrary rate of exploitation and derive from it an equilibrium configuration.

All this can be demonstrated by making use of the equivalence between the rate of exploitation and the ratio of factor shares,

$$\varepsilon = \frac{ra_1}{Wa_0} = \frac{r}{W} k. \tag{9.26}$$

Assuming that $f''(k)$ is strictly negative everywhere, we can discover the effects of continuous substitution on the adequacy of ε as a determinant of equilibrium by examining the mapping between k and ε which Eq. (9.26) defines; the assumption that $f''(k)$ is negative, along with the assumption that wage and profit rates equal marginal productivities of labor and capital, guarantees that the mapping between k and W will be one-to-one. Thus the mapping $k \rightarrow \varepsilon$ is qualitatively similar to the mapping $W \rightarrow \varepsilon$, and problems of the second will be reflected in the first.

Both ways by which the labor theory might fail—the possibility that the mapping from k to ε lacks an inverse, so that a given rate of exploitation may not determine k (and W) uniquely, and the possibility that the range of ε fails to include the positive half-line—are illustrated by the production function

$$f(k) = k + \gamma k^{\eta}, \tag{9.27}$$

which is the sum of a linear term and a Cobb-Douglas term. We have

$$\varepsilon = \frac{\eta}{1 - \eta} \tag{9.28}$$

for all k between 0 and ∞. So in contrast with the fixed-proportions case shown in Figure 9.16, we have a degenerate situation in which only a single rate of exploitation is possible. Figure 9.17 illustrates the construction of the mapping between the rate of exploitation and the real wage rate, assuming the real wage and the capital:labor ratio are connected by the marginal-productivity equation. We begin in the second quadrant with Eq. (9.28) linking the rate of exploitation to the capital:labor ratio. We then pass, *via* the marginal-productivity equation in the third quadrant and the identity in the fourth, to the first-quadrant mapping between the rate of exploitation and the wage rate. As the illustration shows, only a single rate of exploitation is compatible with the technology hypothesized by Eq. (9.27), and that rate of exploitation, $\eta/(1 - \eta)$, is the image of the whole domain of potential wage rates, $[0, \infty)$. In this case the labor theory of value not

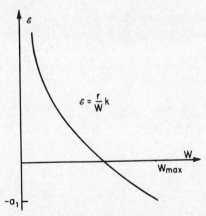

Figure 9.16 Exploitation and real wages with fixed proportions

GROWTH AND DISTRIBUTION

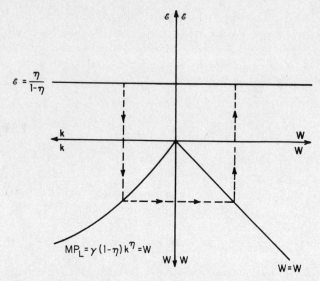

Figure 9.17 Exploitation and real wages with continuous substitution: A special case

only fails to provide a determinate equilibrium configuration, but also does not even narrow down the potential range of equilibria.

The production function (9.27), to be sure, represents a special case, chosen explicitly to illustrate the inadequacy of the labor theory of value in the case of continuous substitution. But the general problem exists in less acute form for a whole class of production functions. Within the set of CES production functions, the critical dividing line is $\sigma = 1$. For $\sigma > 1$, the mapping $W \rightarrow \varepsilon$ may not be one-to-one, nor does its range necessarily include the positive half-line. The problem, as in the degenerate case represented in Figure 9.17, is the mapping linking ε and k.

First recall the limiting behavior of factor shares. With $\sigma > 1$, we have

$$\lim_{k \to 0} W a_0 = 1 \qquad \lim_{k \to 0} (1 + r)a_1 = 0,$$
$$\lim_{k \to \infty} W a_0 = 0 \qquad \lim_{k \to \infty} (1 + r)a_1 = 1.$$

Taking limits in Eq. (9.26), we have

$$\lim_{k \to 0} \varepsilon = 0 \qquad \lim_{k \to \infty} \varepsilon = \frac{\dfrac{r_{min}}{1 + r_{min}}}{0} = \pm\infty.$$

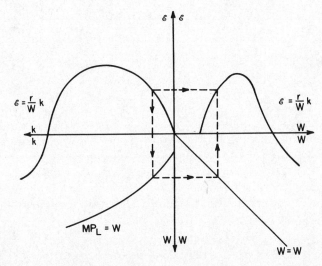

Figure 9.18 Exploitation and real wages with constant elasticity of substitution: $\sigma > 1$, $r_{min} < 0$

Thus, for $r_{min} < 0$, Eq. (9.26), which defines ε as a continuous function of k, must have a finite maximum and cannot include the entire positive half-line.

The other part of the proposition, the lack of isomorphism between W and ε, also follows directly from an examination of factor shares. Since ra_1 is positive for small values of k, so is ε; coupling the positivity of ε near $k = 0$ with the existence of a finite maximum and the continuity of ε precludes isomorphism in the case $r_{min} < 0$.[5] Figure 9.18 illustrates the mapping between W and ε.

The limitations on the labor theory of value implicit in Figure 9.18, it will be seen, are consequences of a high elasticity of substitution. With $\sigma = 1$, for example, we have

5. This result can also be reached by an examination of the derivative of ε with respect to k. Taking account of the marginal-productivity relationships, we have

$$\frac{d\varepsilon}{dk} = \varepsilon' = -\frac{(1+r)}{\sigma W}(1 - a_1) + \frac{r}{W}. \tag{9.29}$$

By virtue of factor-share behavior, we have

$$\lim_{k \to 0} \varepsilon' = +\infty,$$

$$\lim_{k \to \infty} \varepsilon' < 0 \qquad \text{if } r_{min} < 0.$$

Thus at least one intermediate value of k exists at which $\varepsilon' = 0$, and ε has a relative maximum.

$$f(k) = \gamma k^{\eta},$$

in which $(1 + r)a_1 = \eta$ and $Wa_0 = 1 - \eta$. It follows directly from Eq. (9.26) that

$$\varepsilon = \frac{\eta}{1 - \eta} - \frac{a_1}{1 - \eta},$$

which decreases monotonically from $\eta/(1 - \eta)$ to $-\infty$ as k runs from 0 to $+\infty$. So the mapping $W \rightarrow \varepsilon$ is one-to-one. However, the mapping still does not include the entire positive half-line.

If we go further, and restrict ourselves to the case $\sigma < 1$, the results come to resemble the fixed-proportions case: the mapping between W and ε is one-to-one, and the range of ε includes the positive half-line. With $\sigma < 1$, we have

$$\lim_{k \to 0} Wa_0 = 0 \qquad \lim_{k \to 0} (1 + r)a_1 = 1,$$

$$\lim_{k \to \infty} Wa_0 = 1 \qquad \lim_{k \to \infty} (1 + r)a_1 = 0.$$

Moreover,

$$\lim_{k \to \infty} a_1 = \infty,$$

so that ε runs from $+\infty$ to $-\infty$ as k runs from 0 to ∞. To verify that the progress of ε is monotonic requires an examination of the derivative ε' defined by Eq. (9.29) in footnote 5. The salient facts about ε' are first, that ε' goes to $-\infty$ as k approaches 0, and second, that ε' goes to $-1/W_{max}$ as k approaches ∞. Two results follow: (1) starting from $k = 0$, the first relative extremum (if it exists) has to be a relative minimum; (2) there must be an even number of relative extrema. Now if the first extremum is a relative minimum, the second must be a relative maximum, and therefore the value of ε must be higher at the second than at the first. However, $\varepsilon' = 0$ implies

$$\varepsilon = \frac{(1 + r)k}{W\sigma} (1 - a_1),$$

which with $\sigma < 1$ means that ε decreases as k increases. This contradiction proves the impossibility of a relative extremum and establishes the monotonicity of the mapping between k and ε. The picture is given in Figure 9.19.

It is not my intention to dwell disproportionately on the limitations of the labor theory of value as a theory of distribution. There is, after all, an analogous problem in neoclassical theory: the existence of equilib-

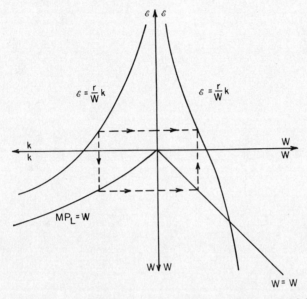

Figure 9.19 Exploitation and real wages with constant elasticity of substitution: $\sigma < 1$

rium is by no means independent of the choice of utility functions. But paradoxically, a sufficiently high substitution elasticity solves the problem for neoclassical theory by virtually guaranteeing the existence of equilibrium, whereas it is precisely a high elasticity of substitution that creates problems for the labor theory of value. In any case, the neo-Marxian approach, at least in its present incarnation, is not wedded to the labor theory of value. We can just as well go directly from the subsistence wage to equilibrium as go *via* the rate of exploitation. The only limitation on the subsistence wage is that it lie within the technological capabilities of the system.

THE NEO-KEYNESIAN MODEL By contrast, equilibrium growth and profit rates are unaffected by substitution in the neo-Keynesian model because the capital : labor ratio enters into the determination of neither the investment function nor the simple classical saving function $g = s_c r$. Rather the equilibrium capital : labor ratio is determined by r^*. But this is not to say that continuous substitution makes no difference, for equilibrium wages and consumption depend on the capital : labor ratio, and hence on the production function. The neo-Keynesian picture is summarized in Figure 9.20, with $W = \overline{W}/P$ representing the real wage.

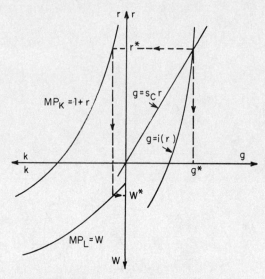

Figure 9.20   Neo-Keynesian equilibrium

Nonneoclassical Models with a Pasinetti Saving Function

THE CHARACTERIZATION OF EQUILIBRIUM   Both the neo-Marxian and the neo-Keynesian stories become more involved as we complicate the saving function. With workers saving the fraction s_W of their incomes, we have in the long run

$$g = s(r) = \max\left(s_W \frac{1 - a_1}{a_1}, s_C r\right)$$

or, more exactly,

$$g = s_W \frac{1 - a_1}{a_1} \qquad s'(r) = s_W \frac{\sigma}{(1 + r)a_1}, \qquad \hat{\delta} = 0,$$

$$g = s_C r, \qquad\qquad s'(r) = s_C, \qquad\qquad \hat{\delta} > 0.$$

With $\sigma < 1$, there are no surprises: the slope of the $\hat{\delta} = 0$ branch of the saving function becomes positive, as Figure 9.21(a) and (b) shows.

With Cobb-Douglas production, a new possibility arises. The $\hat{\delta} = 0$ branch of the saving function now becomes linear, like the $\hat{\delta} > 0$ branch. Moreover, the domain of the saving function is now open-ended at the upper end. And the $\hat{\delta} = 0$ branch lies to the right of the $\hat{\delta} > 0$ branch at the lower end:

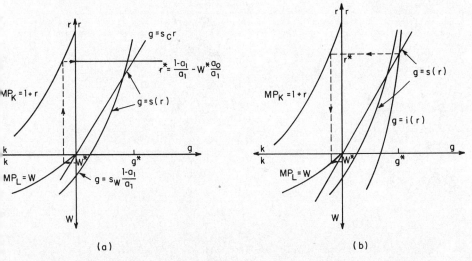

Figure 9.21 Equilibrium with Pasinetti saving function and $\sigma < 1$. (a) neo-Marxian equilibrium; (b) neo-Keynesian equilibrium

$$\lim_{r \to -1} s_W \frac{1 - a_1}{a_1} = -s_W > \lim_{r \to -1} s_C r = -s_C.$$

Hence the existence of an intersection between the two branches — necessary for the existence of a $\hat{\delta} > 0$ equilibrium — requires that the slope of the $\hat{\delta} > 0$ branch,

$$s'(r) = s_C, \qquad \hat{\delta} > 0,$$

exceed the slope of the $\hat{\delta} = 0$ branch,

$$s'(r) = s_W \frac{\sigma}{(1 + r)a_1} = \frac{s_W}{\eta}, \qquad \hat{\delta} = 0,$$

where η is the elasticity of output with respect to seed corn:

$$\frac{1}{a_0} = \gamma \left(\frac{a_1}{a_0}\right)^{\eta}.$$

Figure 9.22 shows the two possibilities. Evidently the critical value for η is s_W/s_C, though a bit of care is necessary with the word "critical." A value of η greater than s_W/s_C does not guarantee the existence of a $\hat{\delta} > 0$ equilibrium, for $\eta > s_W/s_C$ is necessary rather than sufficient for the $\hat{\delta} > 0$ branch to be relevant. By contrast, $\eta < s_W/s_C$ precludes the existence of a $\hat{\delta} > 0$ equilibrium.

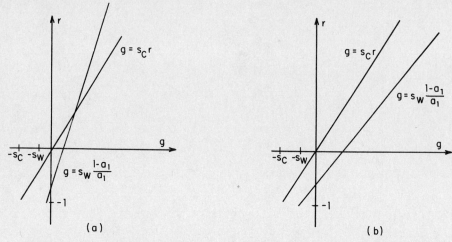

Figure 9.22 Pasinetti saving function with $\sigma = 1$. (a) $s_W/\eta < s_C$; (b) $s_W/\eta > s_C$

The case $\sigma > 1$ introduces still more surprises. Because the share of profits in output $(1 + r)a_1$ is once again variable, the slope of the $\hat{\delta} = 0$ branch varies from $s_W\sigma$ to $+\infty$. Moreover,

$$\lim_{r \to r_{\min}} s_W \frac{1 - a_1}{a_1} = s_W(\gamma\eta^{-1/\rho} - 1) \begin{Bmatrix} > \\ < \end{Bmatrix} \lim_{r \to r_{\min}} s_C r = s_C(\gamma\eta^{-1/\rho} - 1)$$

$$\text{as } (\gamma\eta^{-1/\rho} - 1) \begin{Bmatrix} > \\ < \end{Bmatrix} 0.$$

That is to say, the lower end of the $\hat{\delta} = 0$ branch lies to the left of the $\hat{\delta} > 0$ branch if $r_{\min} > 0$, to the right (as in the Cobb-Douglas case) if $r_{\min} < 0$. Hence in general the two branches of the saving function may or may not intersect, and may even intersect twice. But the slope of the $\hat{\delta} = 0$ branch is increasing in the $\sigma > 1$ case: $(1 + r)a_1$ approaches 0 as r approaches infinity. Thus whatever happens at the lower end, the $\hat{\delta} = 0$ branch dominates at the upper end of the domain, as Figure 9.23 shows.

This reversal is noteworthy. With little or no substitution, lower wage rates not only increase the profit rate, they also increase the share of income in the hands of capitalists. But a substitution elasticity greater than one means that decreases in the wage rate are after a certain point more than offset by reductions in the capital : labor ratio. At sufficiently low wage rates, the increase in employment is so great that the share of wage income, and hence saving and capital ownership on the part of

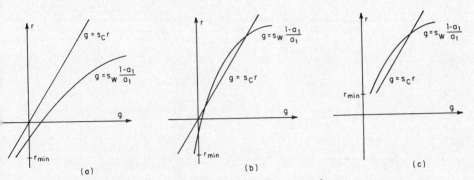

Figure 9.23 Pasinetti saving function with $\sigma > 1$. (a) $\hat{\delta} = 0$ everywhere; (b) $\hat{\delta} > 0$ at intermediate values of r; (c) $\hat{\delta} > 0$ at low values of r

workers, increases. As the rate of profit approaches infinity, wages, as a share of total income, approach unity, and profits approach zero. But long before this limit is reached, the *workers'* share of income (wages plus profits on worker-owned capital), saving, and capital ownership reach unity, and the capitalists' share vanishes.

NEO-KEYNESIAN EQUILIBRIUM   All these twists and turns of the Pasinetti saving function complicate the neo-Keynesian model as well as the neo-Marxian. And there are additional complications, particularly with respect to the stability of equilibrium. As in the fixed-proportions case of Chapter 6, the key to neo-Keynesian stability is the relative responsiveness of investment and saving to the rate of profit. But with $\sigma > 1$, the long-run as well as the short-run responsiveness of saving may be relevant, an important difference from Chapter 6.

We start from the short-run equilibrium condition

$$Ps(r, \delta) = P_{-1}i(r_{-1}) \tag{6.18}$$

and the transition equation for δ

$$\delta = \delta_{-1} \frac{1 + s_C r_{-1}}{1 + s(r_{-1}, \delta_{-1})}, \tag{6.6}$$

which carry over intact from Chapter 6. As in the fixed-coefficient case, these equations define two functions,

$$r = G(r_{-1}, \delta_{-1}),$$

$$\delta = H(r_{-1}, \delta_{-1}),$$

which, along with the price equation

$$Pf(k) = \overline{W} + (1 + r)Pk$$

and the marginal-productivity equation[6]

$$f'(k) = 1 + r$$

describe the evolution from one short-run equilibrium to another. A long-run equilibrium is a stationary point $\langle r^*, \delta^* \rangle$ for which

$$i(r^*) = s(r^*, \delta^*),$$

$$\delta^*[s_C r^* - s(r^*, \delta^*)] = 0.$$

The stability of long-run equilibrium continues to hinge on the characteristic roots of the matrix

$$\mathbf{J} = \begin{bmatrix} \dfrac{\partial G}{\partial r_{-1}} & \dfrac{\partial G}{\partial \delta_{-1}} \\[2mm] \dfrac{\partial H}{\partial r_{-1}} & \dfrac{\partial H}{\partial \delta_{-1}} \end{bmatrix}$$

evaluated at $\langle r^*, \delta^* \rangle$. Specifically, stability requires the Routh-Hurwitz inequalities

$$|\det \mathbf{J}| < 1$$

and

$$|\operatorname{tr} \mathbf{J}| < |1 + \det \mathbf{J}|.$$

Except for the calculation of the long- and short-run responses of saving to r, $s' \equiv s'(r)$ and $\partial s/\partial r$, $\det \mathbf{J}$ and $\operatorname{tr} \mathbf{J}$ are given by the formulas derived in Chapter 6. In present notation these formulas are

6. Or, equivalently, $f(k) - f'(k)k = \overline{W}/P$. The marginal productivity of labor equals the real wage at all times, as in the Keynesian model outlined at the beginning of Chapter 4. With continuous substitution, the price mechanism plays a dual role in the neo-Keynesian model: it simultaneously adjusts investment demand to the supply of saving and adjusts the real wage to the level of employment. Thus, in the neo-Keynesian (and neo-Marxian) as well as in the neoclassical models, labor-market equilibrium is characterized by the marginal-productivity equation $MP_L = \overline{W}/P$. A crucial difference between the two concepts of labor-market equilibrium of course remains: the role of full employment. Nonneoclassical labor-market equilibrium presupposes neither period-by-period full employment *à la* Chicago, nor a more gradual adjustment to full employment based on a responsiveness of the real wage to excess demand or supply in the labor market.

$$\det \mathbf{J} = \frac{[1 + s_C r^*]\left[1 + s_W \dfrac{f(k^*) - k^*}{k^*}\right]\left[\dfrac{P^*}{\overline{W}} k^* i(r^*) + i'\right]}{[1 + s(r^*, \delta^*)]^2 \left[\dfrac{P^*}{\overline{W}} k^* s(r^*, \delta^*) + \dfrac{\partial s}{\partial r}\right]}$$

$$\operatorname{tr} \mathbf{J} = 1 + \det \mathbf{J} - \frac{\left| s_C r^* - s_W \dfrac{f(k^*) - k^*}{k^*} \right| (s' - i')}{[1 + s(r^*, \delta^*)]\left[\dfrac{P^*}{\overline{W}} k^* s(r^*, \delta^*) + \dfrac{\partial s}{\partial r}\right]},$$

where

$$i' \equiv \frac{di(r)}{dr},$$

$$\frac{\partial s}{\partial r} \equiv \frac{\partial s(r, \delta)}{\partial r} = s_W \frac{\sigma}{(1 + r)a_1} + (s_C - s_W)\delta.$$

A sufficient condition for $|\det \mathbf{J}| < 1$ is

$$i' < \frac{\partial s}{\partial r}, \tag{9.32}$$

which is to say that investment must be less responsive in the short run than saving to changes in the rate of profit. Since $\operatorname{tr} \mathbf{J}$ is necessarily positive, the second of the two inequalities,

$$|\operatorname{tr} \mathbf{J}| < |1 + \det \mathbf{J}|,$$

is satisfied whenever

$$i' < s'. \tag{9.33}$$

When $\sigma \leq 1$, these results parallel the fixed-coefficient case. In particular, the condition $i' < s'$ may be superfluous: the slope of the long-run saving function is at least as great as the slope of the short-run saving function, so

$$i' < \frac{\partial s}{\partial r} \implies i' < s'.$$

However, when $\sigma > 1$, long-run saving is more likely to be relevant. And an equilibrium may be unstable, as in Figure 9.24, despite the fact that in the short run, saving is more responsive than investment to

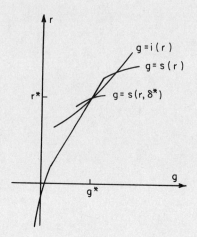

Figure 9.24 Unstable neo-Keynesian equilibrium

changes in the rate of profit. As the figure is drawn, condition (9.32) is satisfied but condition (9.33) is not.

One other change from the fixed-coefficient case is noteworthy: observe that with $\hat{\delta} = 0$, the short-run and long-run saving functions coincide, and conditions (9.32) and (9.33) converge to

$$i' < s_W \frac{\sigma}{(1 + r)a_1}.$$

Unlike the fixed-coefficient case, however, the right-hand side of this equation may be positive, which is to say that continuous substitution makes it possible that a people's capitalism equilibrium be stable.

The Neo-Keynesian Multiplier

Alone among the three models, the neo-Keynesian admits of an independent role for demand in determining equilibrium, and it is natural to investigate the consequences of changes in demand for equilibrium. Up to now, however, the assumption of fixed coefficients has limited this investigation to the properties of long-run growth and distribution: fixed coefficients preclude variations in employment and output per unit of capital. With variable proportions, by contrast, output per unit of capital, output per worker, and capital per worker all vary with the rate of accumulation in both the long and the short run (short-run capital being identified with the total capital stock rather than with the stock actually utilized).

In the long run, the steady-state output : capital ratio X/K responds positively to an increase in the rate of investment, and the output : labor ratio X/L responds negatively. If we write investment demand per unit capital as

$$\frac{I}{k} = i(r) + \Delta,$$

and characterize long-run equilibrium by the solution to the equation

$$i(r) + \Delta = s(r),$$

then we have

$$\frac{d(X/K)}{d(I/K)} = \frac{d[f(k)/k]}{dk} \frac{dk}{dr} \frac{dr^*}{d\Delta} = \frac{\sigma}{(1+r)a_1} \frac{1}{s' - i'}$$

and

$$\frac{d(X/L)}{d(I/K)} = \frac{df(k)}{dk} \frac{dk}{dr} \frac{dr^*}{d\Delta} = -\frac{\sigma k}{(\overline{W}/P)a_0} \frac{1}{s' - i'}.$$

Since $s' - i' > 0$ at a stable equilibrium, output per unit of capital increases while output per worker decreases as the rate of investment increases. The reason for the asymmetry is this. An increase in the rate of investment increases the equilibrium rate of profit $(dr^*/d\Delta > 0)$, which increases employment per unit of capital and thus decreases capital per worker $(dk/dr < 0)$. The decrease in k leads to opposite effects on the output : capital and output : labor ratios since $d[f(k)/k]/dk < 0$ and $df(k)/dk > 0$. (If investment is measured on a per-worker basis, the formulas are slightly different but the results qualitatively similar.)

The short-run consequences of variations in demand are more interesting and sufficiently different from the results emphasized in the conventional multiplier analysis to merit attention. We start from the saving = investment condition

$$Ps(r, \delta) = P_{-1}i(r_{-1}). \tag{6.18}$$

Since desired saving $s(r, \delta)$ is equal to the difference between net output, $[f(k) - k]/k$, and consumption demand, $c(r, \delta)$, Eq. (6.18) is equivalent to

$$P\left[\frac{f(k) - k}{k} - c(r, \delta)\right] = P_{-1}i(r_{-1}), \tag{9.34}$$

where

$$c(r, \delta) = (1 - s_W)\frac{f(k) - k}{k} - (s_C - s_W)\delta r.$$

In Eq. (9.34), output, consumption, and investment are expressed in terms of dollars per bushel of seed corn. To change the units to bushels of seed corn, we multiply through by $K/P = Xk/f(k)P$, and obtain

$$X\left[\frac{f(k) - k}{f(k)} - (1 - s_W)\frac{f(k) - k}{f(k)} + (s_C - s_W)\delta r \frac{k}{f(k)}\right] = K \frac{P_{-1}}{P} i(r_{-1}).$$

Now move depreciation—equal to the entire capital stock $K = Xk/f(k)$ in the corn model, with its annual production cycle—from the left-hand to the right-hand side of the equation, writing gross investment as

$$I^G = K + \frac{P_{-1}}{P} i(r_{-1})K.$$

Do the same thing with consumption, and the equation becomes

$$X = \left[(1 - s_W)\frac{f(k) - k}{f(k)} - (s_C - s_W)\delta r \frac{k}{f(k)}\right]X + I^G. \qquad (9.35)$$

The short-run multiplier treats I^G as a variable and reflects the impact on X of a unit shift in I^G, taking account of the short-run relationship between k and X that assumes labor-market equilibrium based on the marginal-productivity relationship

$$f(k) - f'(k)k = \frac{\overline{W}}{P}.$$

We have

$$X = \frac{f(k)}{k} K$$

so that

$$\frac{dk}{dX} = -\frac{k^2}{\frac{\overline{W}}{P} K}.$$

We also have the marginal-productivity relationship

$$f'(k) = 1 + r.$$

Using these relationships, total differentiation of Eq. (9.35) gives the multiplier as

$$\frac{dX}{dI^G} = \frac{1}{s_W + (s_C - s_W)\delta \frac{(1 + r)a_1}{\sigma}}. \tag{9.36}$$

Equation (9.36) should be compared with the textbook "Keynesian" multiplier

$$\frac{dX}{dI^G} = \frac{1}{s}, \tag{9.37}$$

which assumes that the same marginal propensity to save, s, applies across the board. Both equations can be derived from the common formula

$$\frac{dX}{dI^G} = \frac{1}{\frac{dS}{dX}},$$

where S represents aggregate saving. The conventional analysis posits the simple relationship

$$S = sX$$

so that

$$\frac{dS}{dX} = s.$$

By contrast, in the neo-Keynesian model the relationship between saving and output is more complex: the formula

$$\frac{dS}{dX} = \frac{dS}{ds(r, \delta)} \frac{\partial s(r, \delta)}{\partial r} \frac{dr}{d[f(k)/k]} \frac{d[f(k)/k]}{dX} = K \frac{\partial s}{\partial r} \frac{(1 + r)a_1}{\sigma} \frac{1}{K}$$

leads directly to Eq. (9.36) once we substitute from the equation

$$\frac{\partial s}{\partial r} = s_W \frac{\sigma}{(1 + r)a_1} + (s_C - s_W)\delta.$$

Evidently Eq. (9.36) reduces to (9.37) when $s_C = s_W$, but it is only in this case that the multiplier is insensitive to the elasticity of substitution in production[7] as well as to the distribution of capital ownership and to

7. There is an important conceptual difference between the short-run and the long-run production function, even when both admit of continuous variation in factor proportions. In the short run, the capital stock is fixed, so that the short-run elasticity of "substitution" is likely to be lower than the long-run. "Substitution" is itself a problematic concept in the short-run context, since changes in factor proportions reflect changes

GROWTH AND DISTRIBUTION

the share of profit in national income. In all other cases the parameters σ, δ, and $(1 + r)a_1$, as well as differences in saving propensities s_C and s_W, enter into the determination of the responsiveness of output to changes in investment demand (and, by extension, any other autonomous change in demand). Ignoring the role of distribution in specifying the propensity to save not only obscures the role of the distribution of income and wealth in the multiplier, as might be expected; it also — more surprisingly — obscures the role of the supply side, as reflected in the parameter σ.

In the present model, an expansion of demand increases output until saving rises by enough to offset the added demand, just as in conventional textbook Keynesianism. But here there are two mechanisms that increase saving, not just one. As output increases, so does employment. And overall saving is enhanced by the saving of the newly employed workers. Whence the first term s_W in the denominator on the right-hand side of Eq. (9.36). But at the same time — and this mechanism has no counterpart in the conventional multiplier analysis — overall saving rises because of the distributional shift that accompanies the expansion of output: as output rises, the real wage rate falls, and the profit rate rises. The importance of the distributional shift, reflected in the second term of the multiplier equation, evidently depends on four factors: (1) the degree to which capitalists' propensity to save exceeds workers', $s_C - s_W$; (2) the share of the capital stock owned by capitalists, δ; (3) the share of profits in national income, $(1 + r)a_1$; (4) the elasticity of substitution, σ. Higher values for any but the last of these terms effectively inhibit the expansion of output by increasing the flow of saving accompanying a given change in output.

The elasticity of substitution in production, by contrast, acts on the distribution of income itself: the smaller is σ, the faster the wage rate falls (and the profit rate rises) with a given increase in output. At one extreme, with fixed coefficients, ($\sigma = 0$), a distributional shift occurs without any increase in output, so the entire adjustment of saving to the expansion of demand takes place through the change in factor shares. As σ goes to zero, so does the output multiplier. This is of course the result we observed in the fixed-coefficient model of Chapter 4, a result originally highlighted by Nicholas Kaldor (1956). At the other extreme, with infinite substitution possibilities ($\sigma = \infty$), expansion of pro-

---

in employment and the intensity of capital-stock utilization rather than substitution of one factor for another. In the short-run context, "continuous substitution" and "an elasticity of substitution" are terms whose use can be justified only by long usage.

duction takes place on the basis of labor alone, and is independent of capital: as $\sigma \to \infty$, the production function approaches the limiting form

$$f(k) = \gamma\eta k + \gamma(1 - \eta)$$

or

$$F(K, L) = \gamma\eta K + \gamma(1 - \eta)L.$$

In this case wage and profit rates are totally unaffected by output expansion, and only increased saving out of wages can mop up extra demand. So the multiplier reduces to $1/s_W$.

There is a certain irony in the emergence of a supply side to the multiplier in the context of a neo-Keynesian model, the model distinguished by its emphasis on demand. The supply side has of course been there all the time, obscured on the one hand by exclusion of variable proportions in production in the original Kaldorian formulation, and on the other hand by exclusion of distributional considerations in the conventional formulation of the Keynesian model with a uniform saving propensity.

A Preliminary Assessment of Variable Proportions

In a word, variability in factor proportions—or the lack thereof—hardly seems to be the essential feature that distinguishes one approach to the study of capitalism from another: the same differences exist among the theories whether or not we assume factor proportions to be fixed or variable. The characterization of production has nonetheless been a divisive issue. Nobody who followed the capital controversies of the 1960s would disagree, and we shall return to these debates in Chapter 12.

Even without exploring these debates, however, we can now easily see how the characterization of production might become such a divisive issue. Neoclassical economists generally insist on continuous substitution, whereas neo-Keynesians and neo-Marxians are indifferent if not hostile to this assumption because the neoclassical model needs continuous substitution in ways that the other models do not. No essential point of the neo-Marxian or neo-Keynesian analysis hinges on continuous substitution or even on variable proportions, as do the existence and stability of neoclassical equilibrium.

But the analysis of this chapter reveals that continuous substitution is not itself sufficient to remedy the defects of the fixed-coefficient neoclassical model. It is not the continuity of factor substitution but the elasticity of substitution that is critical. A low elasticity ($\sigma < 1$) guarantees neither existence nor stability of neoclassical equilibrium, whereas $\sigma > 1$ guarantees both.

By contrast, important if not essential aspects of the neo-Marxian and neo-Keynesian models turn out to hinge on a low value of σ. The positive relationship between the rate of profit and the share of the capital stock owned by capitalists, for instance, requires σ to be less than unity. And the labor theory of value suffers in completeness and consistency when σ exceeds unity. Finally, the neo-Keynesian stability conditions are essentially identical in fixed-coefficient and low-elasticity continuous substitution models. But when $\sigma > 1$, it is the long-run responsiveness of saving to changes in the profit rate that matters, not the short-run responsiveness.

In fact, of all the topics examined in this chapter, the only one for which the distinction between fixed coefficients and continuous substitution is crucial is the multiplier analysis of the last section. The output multiplier vanishes, à la Kaldor, in the $\sigma = 0$ case.

In sum, it is not continuous substitution that changes the story, but an elasticity of substitution high enough to create a paradoxical if not perverse relationship between factor *returns* and factor *shares*. The key to the difference between the results with $\sigma < 1$ and $\sigma > 1$ is that in the second case wage and profit shares Wa_0 and $(1 + r)a_1$ move in the opposite direction from wage and profit rates. This in itself ought to be enough to give pause to those of the neoclassical persuasion who might be inclined to take undue comfort from the results obtained by introducing a high degree of substitution into the story.[8]

Appendix: Factor Returns and Scale Returns under Continuous Substitution

Consider a production function

$$X = F(K, L) \tag{9.38}$$

in which K represents capital (seed corn) and for which it is assumed

8. A high elasticity of substitution is difficult to defend on other grounds. With $\sigma > 1$, only one of the two inputs is required for production. But somehow, production of corn with only seed corn *or* labor goes against the grain. Only the borderline Cobb-Douglas production function, for which $\sigma = 1$, simultaneously guarantees stable neoclassical equilibrium, requires both inputs for production, and maintains at least independence if not a positive relationship between factor returns and factor shares. This may explain the popularity of Cobb-Douglas production models, but even the truest believer would be hard pressed in basing the neoclassical case on such a limited foundation as the assumption of Cobb-Douglas production. I shall return to this point in Chapter 13.

$$F_1, F_2 \geq 0, \qquad \text{(nonnegative marginal productivities or free disposability)} \qquad (9.39)$$

$$F(\mu K, \mu L) = \mu F(K, L), \qquad \mu \geq 0. \qquad \text{(linear homogeneity or constant returns to scale)} \qquad (9.40)$$

The point of this appendix is to detail the conditions under which the production function so defined necessarily exhibits diminishing marginal returns, so that the competitive rate of profit, equal to the marginal productivity of capital F_1, is a nonincreasing function of the capital : labor ratio, and F_2 is a nondecreasing function. If we denote the two intensive magnitudes, output per man and capital per man, by $1/a_0$ and k, we have

$$F_1 \equiv f'(k) \geq 0, \qquad \text{(nonnegative}$$
$$F_2 \equiv f(k) - f'(k)k \geq 0, \qquad \text{marginal productivities)}$$
$$\frac{1}{a_0} = f(k) \equiv F\left(\frac{K}{L}, 1\right). \qquad \text{(linear homogeneity)}$$

The question at issue then becomes one of specifying conditions under which $f''(k) \leq 0$.

Before we turn to this question, a word may be in order about motivation. The reswitching debate of the 1960s, which will be examined in Chapter 12, revolved around the nature of the relationship between the profit rate and technology. It was too much to expect that the correspondence between competitive profit rates and technologies would be one-to-one in a discrete-technology, multiple-good model. As was shown earlier in this chapter, an *interval* of the profit rate corresponds to a single technique even in the one-good model. But economists steeped in the neoclassical tradition held that a multiplicity of commodities was an inessential complication: the one-to-one correspondence between particular intervals of the profit rate and particular technologies would hold independently of the number of goods, so that an inverse relationship between capital intensity, suitably measured, and the competitive profit rate would continue to obtain.

We now know, thanks to the work of Luigi Pasinetti (1966b) and others, that a particular technology may correspond to *disjoint* intervals of the profit rate in the multiple-good case. This result not only laid to rest the quest for a suitable measure of capital intensity in the multiple-good case, it has led to a questioning of results once taken quite for granted in the one-good case. What allows us to assume even in the one-good case, with continuous substitution, that a negative relationship exists between capital intensity (as measured by k) and the rate of profit? Do constant returns to scale effectively rule out increasing marginal productivities, so that the conventional picture of the constant-returns-to-scale production function (in intensive form) in Figure 9.25, in which

$$f''(k) \leq 0$$

and

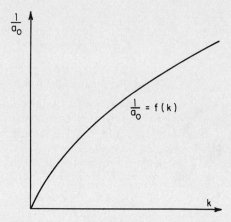

Figure 9.25   Diminishing marginal productivity of capital

$$\frac{dF_1}{dk} \equiv f''(k) \leq 0,$$

$$\frac{dF_2}{dk} \equiv -f''(k)k \geq 0,$$

is anything but arbitrary?

The answer to this question must be equivocal. Literally, linear homogeneity and free disposability are quite consistent with a positive relationship between $f'(k) \equiv F_1$ and k. Consider the production function

$$F(K, L) = \frac{K^2}{L} + 2L, \qquad \frac{K}{L} \leq \sqrt{2}$$

$$f(k) = k^2 + 2, \qquad k \leq \sqrt{2}$$

illustrated in Figure 9.26. It is easy to verify that it exhibits both linear homogeneity and nonnegative marginal productivities when k is restricted to the domain $[0, \sqrt{2}]$. It is equally easy to verify that the marginal productivity of capital, $f'(k)$, *increases* over the entire domain of k. Hence requiring only linear homogeneity and free disposability evidently does not in itself guarantee the "neoclassical" relationship $f''(k) \leq 0$. A further assumption is required.

That assumption is "additivity." It can be shown that if the production function $f(k)$ is assumed to reflect additivity as well as linear homogeneity and free disposability, $f''(k)$ is necessarily nonpositive so that diminishing marginal productivity obtains.

Additivity means that if two points $\langle K_1, L_1, X_1 \rangle$ and $\langle K_2, L_2, X_2 \rangle$ are feasible, then so is $\langle K_1 + K_2, L_1 + L_2, X_1 + X_2 \rangle$. In other words, it must be possible to produce at least $X_1 + X_2$ with the inputs $K_1 + K_2$ and $L_1 + L_2$; thus

$$F(K_1 + K_2, L_1 + L_2) \geq F(K_1, L_1) + F(K_2, L_2). \tag{9.41}$$

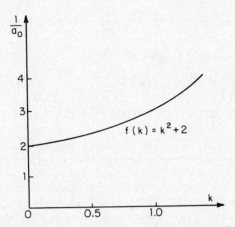

Figure 9.26   Increasing marginal productivity of capital

Defining

$$k_1 = \frac{K_1}{L_1} \quad \text{and} \quad k_2 = \frac{K_2}{L_2},$$

we have in intensive magnitudes

$$(L_1 + L_2)f\left(\frac{L_1 k_1 + L_2 k_2}{L_1 + L_2}\right) \geq L_1 f(k_1) + L_2 f(k_2).$$

Now set

$$\frac{L_1}{L_1 + L_2} = \mu, \qquad \frac{L_2}{L_1 + L_2} = 1 - \mu.$$

Then (9.41) becomes

$$f(\mu k_1 + (1 - \mu)k_2) \geq \mu f(k_1) + (1 - \mu)f(k_2). \tag{9.42}$$

But (9.42) is simply the definition of concavity, and the proof that concavity implies a negative second derivative is straightforward and presumably well known. From the definition of concavity we have

$$\frac{f(\mu k_1 + (1 - \mu)k_2) - f(k_2)}{\mu} \geq f(k_1) - f(k_2).$$

Now, applying L'Hôpital's rule, take the limit of the left-hand side as μ goes to zero; in the limit,

$$f'(k_2)(k_1 - k_2) \geq f(k_1) - f(k_2)$$

or

$$f(k_2) \geq f(k_1) - f'(k_2)(k_1 - k_2). \tag{9.43}$$

A Taylor's series expansion of $f(k)$ around the point k_2 gives at $k = k_1$

$$f(k_1) = f(k_2) + f'(k_2)(k_1 - k_2) + f''(k_2 + \epsilon) \frac{(k_1 - k_2)^2}{2}. \qquad (9.44)$$

Adding (9.43) and (9.44), we obtain

$$0 \geq f''(k_2 + \epsilon) \frac{(k_1 - k_2)^2}{2},$$

which guarantees that $f''(k)$ will be nonpositive.

So much for the mathematics. The economics of the relationship between returns to scale and factor returns is less straightforward. The essential point to be made, I think, is that although in general additivity is by no means an innocuous assumption, it hardly involves much once linear homogeneity is posited. For the basis of both linear homogeneity and additivity is a noninterference principle: if two activities (like $\langle K_1, L_1, X_1 \rangle$ and $\langle K_2, L_2, X_2 \rangle$) can be carried on separately, they can be carried on together without getting in each other's way. Linear homogeneity limits the assumption to the case where the two activities utilize inputs in the same proportion, and in contrast with additivity, rules out the possibility of "synergy," that is, the possibility of increasing returns, at the same time that it rules out mutual interference. Additivity is silent on synergy but extends the principle of noninterference to all input combinations, not just those that lie on the same ray from the origin.

For additivity to fail, the two activities must compete for one or more inputs not explicitly included in the arguments of the production function (clean water, entrepreneurship, or what have you). But if additivity fails in general, it is hard to see why activities on the same ray should be privileged in this regard, as they must be if linear homogeneity is to hold. This suggests that only with great difficulty can one imagine linear homogeneity without additivity when attention is focused on the economic (as distinct from mathematical) content of the two assumptions. I conclude that if linear homogeneity and free disposability fail formally to establish diminishing returns, they do so substantively. In any case, having swallowed linear homogeneity and free disposability, one should hardly choke on additivity.

10 Marginal Productivity and Marginal-Productivity Theory

With continuous substitution, the basic production model is now characterized by four equations with six unknowns. With $P = 1$, the unknowns are W, C, r, g, a_0, and $k = a_1/a_0$, and the equations are

$$\frac{1}{a_0} = f(k),$$

$$f(k) - f'(k)k = W$$
or
$$f'(k) = 1 + r,$$

$$1 = Wa_0 + (1 + r)a_1, \qquad (1.7)$$

$$1 = a_0C + a_1(1 + g). \qquad (1.5)$$

Each of the three approaches—neoclassical, neo-Keynesian, neo-Marxian—adds two independent relationships to close the model, exactly as in the fixed-coefficient case:

Neoclassical	*Neo-Marxian*	*Neo-Keynesian*
$U(C^1, C^2) = \max$		
subject to	$g = \max\left(s_W\dfrac{1 - a_1}{a_1}, s_C r\right)$	
$C^1 + \dfrac{C^2}{1 + r} = W$		
$g = n$	$W = W^*$	$g = i(r)$

Notwithstanding the similarities between the fixed-coefficient and the continuous-substitution cases, there are differences: as we have seen, the elasticity of substitution has an important bearing on the existence, uniqueness, and stability of equilibrium, particularly in the neoclassical case.

But for the present purposes these differences are secondary. The important point is that the shift from fixed coefficients to continuous substitution does nothing to close the model. On the contrary: it changes two parameters into variables and adds two relationships to allow these variables to be determined endogenously — at least in the long run, which is the basic focus of this book.

The Short Run

In the short run, however, the continuous-substitution case differs markedly from the fixed-proportions case: with given capital and employment, wage and profit rates are determined by production conditions alone. For given a_1/a_0, the production function and the price equation, together with one of the marginal-productivity equations, form a determinate subsystem. In the short run at least, marginal productivity would appear to come into its own, providing a theory of distribution independent of the relationships that characterize neoclassical, neo-Marxian, and neo-Keynesian models.

The weakness of this marginal-productivity "theory" of (short-run) distribution is that it assumes that which is to be explained. Marginal productivity may "explain" wage and profit rates for a *given* capital : labor ratio, but what determines the size of the capital stock and the level of employment?

It will hardly do to take the capital stock as "historically" given! But even with a historically given capital stock, short-run marginal-productivity "theory" begs the question of how employment is determined. The results of assuming continual full employment in the Chicago manner or assuming the real wage adjusts gradually in response to excess demand or supply in the labor market will be different *short-run* labor : capital ratios, and hence different *short-run* income distributions, even though both assumptions are neoclassical in conception. The short-run labor : capital ratio that results from neo-Marxian or neo-Keynesian assumptions about employment determination may differ even more. Thus even though all models employ a marginal-productivity relationship, short-run as well as long-run distributional implications of the models differ. Marginal-productivity "theory" obscures these differences by starting at the wrong place in the analysis.

The contrast is strongest between a Chicago model with continual full employment and a neo-Marxian model with a subsistence real wage. In both cases, with $P = 1$ we have $MP_L = W$ in the short run as well as the long, but this marginal-productivity relationship must be interpreted very differently in the two models. With full employment of a temporarily given labor supply, as well as a temporarily given capital stock, the causality runs

$$\frac{K}{L} \equiv k \rightarrow MP_L \rightarrow W.$$

In each period the marginal productivity of labor determines the real wage. By contrast, with W given, the causality runs

$$W \rightarrow MP_L \rightarrow \frac{K}{L}.$$

With a given capital stock, the real wage determines the level of employment. Curiously, the direction of short-run causality between wages and employment in the gradual adjustment characterization of the neoclassical model is identical to the neo-Marxian model. If the wage rate is determined by the history of labor-market excess demand, as in Eq. (9.21), we have, in the short run at least, $W \rightarrow L$! Too high a wage rate will produce unemployment in both models; it is impossible to sort out the differences between the two approaches on the basis of short-run unemployment behavior.[1] It is only when we go beyond a single period that we can distinguish the distributional consequences of the two models — wages respond to excess demand or supply in the labor market in the neoclassical model, while the labor force bears the brunt of the adjustment (*via* the reserve army) in the neo-Marxian model.

A similar contrast exists in the interpretation of the relationship between the rate of profit and the marginal productivity of capital. In Chicago the equation $MP_K = 1 + r$ is read from left to right: the capital:labor ratio determines the marginal productivity of capital, which in turn determines the rate of profit:

$$\frac{K}{L} \rightarrow MP_K \rightarrow 1 + r.$$

In the neo-Keynesian reading, causality runs the other way. The marginal productivity of capital adjusts, along with the level of employment, to the rate of profit:

1. Edmond Malinvaud (1980) labels such unemployment "classical," which — perhaps fittingly — elides the important differences between neoclassical and neo-Marxian approaches.

$$1 + r \rightarrow MP_K \rightarrow \frac{K}{L}.$$

Whether the capital:labor ratio is variable or fixed, it is saving and investment propensities that determine r. The productivity of capital depends on the rate of profit, not the other way around.

A Two-Technique Model

A short digression might drive home the incompleteness of short-run marginal-productivity "theory." Consider the following model with multiple fixed-proportions techniques, in which the marginal productivity of capital is a technologically determined constant. Suppose, for the moment, that corn can be produced by labor alone or by labor in conjunction with tractors—neither seed corn nor tractor fuel nor land is required. Assume that, using an unmechanized technique, two man-years of labor (L) produce a bushel of corn (X). Symbolically,

$$2L \rightarrow 1X.$$

A second, mechanized technique requires a tractor (T) together with a man-year of labor to produce a bushel of corn:

$$(1L,\ 1T) \rightarrow 1X.$$

Furthermore, the tractor never wears out. Finally, ten man-years are required to produce a tractor:

$$10L \rightarrow 1T.$$

Evidently the marginal productivity of capital is 0.10: removing ten workers from the unmechanized technique for one year reduces the labor input per bushel of corn by one worker in perpetuity. What does this imply about the profit rate? And the wage rate?

To answer this question, let us look at the price equations appropriate to the two techniques of production. If wages continue to be paid at harvest time, the use of the unmechanized technique is consistent only with the price of corn being equal to the wages of two men:

$$P_X = 2W. \tag{10.1}$$

The mechanized technique is more complicated: it provides one bushel of corn and one (undepreciated) tractor at the end of the harvest, the market value of which is $P_X + P_T$. This market value must be equal to the wage of one worker, plus the net profit gained from using the machine and the cost of the machine:

$$P_X + P_T = W + (1 + r)P_T. \tag{10.2}$$

Finally, if machines are being produced, we have

$$P_T = 10W. \tag{10.3}$$

We are free, as always, to designate one of the physical elements of the system as the unit of account, and if we assign this role to corn, we have

$$P_X = 1. \tag{10.4}$$

Now Eqs. (10.1), (10.2), (10.3), and (10.4) form a system of four independent equations with four unknowns, the solution of which is

$$P_X = 1, \qquad P_T = 5, \qquad W = 0.5, \qquad r = 0.10.$$

So it would appear that the rate of profit as well as the wage rate is determinate. A multiplicity of techniques seems of itself to close the distribution side of the model.

In fact, no such conclusion is warranted. It is not the existence of a multiplicity of techniques but the assumption that both techniques available for corn production are simultaneously utilized, as well as the assumption that machines are actually being produced, that makes (10.1), (10.2), and (10.3) equalities. Without these assumptions, we have inequalities

$$P_X \le 2W \tag{10.5}$$

$$P_X + P_T \le W + (1 + r)P_T \tag{10.6}$$

$$P_T \le 10W, \tag{10.7}$$

with strict inequality implying that this activity is not utilized. Inequalities (10.5)–(10.7), even augmented by the normalizing equation (10.4), put us right back where we started from: with rates of profit and wages, as well as relative prices, indeterminate.

A neoclassical economist would very likely accept the indeterminacy of the present system in the case where tractors are assumed to be abundant to the point that every potential worker — save those who are producing machines — has a tractor available to him, so that the un-mechanized technique is not utilized. To be sure, if tractors are being produced as well as utilized in corn production, (10.7) as well as (10.6) becomes an equality. In this case, only the price-wage relationship corresponding to the unused technique involving labor alone (10.5) remains an inequality, but this is enough to make the marginal productivity of capital only an upper bound on the profit rate, $r \le 0.10$.

However, in the case where machines are in short supply so that there are not enough to go around for all potential agricultural workers, the neoclassical economist might be tempted to invoke full employment to ensure that the unmechanized technique is utilized, and thus to transform (10.5) into an equality. In this case all three inequalities become equalities, and we are led back to the solution $P_X = 1$, $P_T = 5$, $W = 0.5$, $r = 0.10$.

The hitch in the argument is that full employment must be *assumed* in this case: the superabundance of labor does not guarantee that all workers will find jobs, at least not in the neo-Marxian or neo-Keynesian models — nor for that matter in a short-run neoclassical model in which wages adjust only gradually to excess demand in the labor market! In all these models, a solution like

$$P_X = 1, \qquad P_T = 6, \qquad W = 0.6, \qquad r = 0.067$$

is perfectly compatible with superabundant labor, though the neo-Marxians would attribute the solution to the subsistence wage emerging from class struggle, the neo-Keynesians to the animal spirits of capitalists, and the (non-Chicago) neoclassicals to the lack of an instantaneous adjustment process.

It might be asked why anybody might ever think it important to "explain" short-run income distribution by means of marginal productivities. Historically, an inverse relationship between the capital : labor ratio on the one hand and the marginal productivity of capital and the rate of profit on the other has appealed to defenders of the capitalist faith as an explanation of income distribution that puts the emphasis on past accumulation rather than on capitalists' present power (*à la* Marx) or on capitalists' present investment psychology (*à la* Keynes). If the rate of profit is higher in country A than in country B, it is *because* A has failed to accumulate sufficient capital to drive the marginal productivity of capital to its level in B. Hopefully no one would bother to ask how employment today happens to be what it is or past accumulation turned out to be what it was.[2]

2. In any case, the inverse relationship between the capital : labor ratio and the rate of profit runs into trouble when we leave the one-good model. With a discrete number of fixed-proportions technologies, it is possible that a particular technology will maximize profits on intervals of the profit axis separated by an interval at which some other technology is more profitable. In such a case capital intensity cannot possibly explain profit and wage rates. More on this issue, the so-called "reswitching problem," in Chapter 12.

The Long Run

It is in the long run, in any case, that the limitations of marginal-productivity theory are most in evidence: in the steady state, marginal-productivity "theory" holds, but it explains nothing, except in conjunction with other assumptions—neoclassical, neo-Marxian, neo-Keynesian, or hybrid. In the steady state the capital:labor ratio is necessarily endogenous, so in contrast with the short run, biology and technology cannot possibly be invoked to determine equilibrium. Even continual full employment will not solve the problem for the neoclassical model, because the steady-state stock of capital per worker, on which the wage rate depends, is a consequence of the utility function as well as the rate of growth of population and the production function.

Differences between the models in the role of marginal productivity exist in the long run as well as the short. Whereas in the equation $MP_L = W$ causality runs both ways in the neoclassical model, it continues to be unidirectional, $W \to MP_L$, in the neo-Marxian model. In the neo-Keynesian model, equilibrium with $\hat{\delta} > 0$ implies a unidirectional causality from r to MP_K. Thus the neo-Keynesian model is in a real sense the inverse of the neo-Marxian model, except for the special case of "people's capitalism." (Equilibrium with $\hat{\delta} = 0$ implies two-way causality, as in the neoclassical model.)

These results are summarized in Table 10.1. The arrow indicates the direction of causality between marginal productivity and factor returns. In the neo-Marxian model, the wage rate is independent of the production function and logically prior to the marginal productivity of labor. By the same token, on the $\hat{\delta} > 0$ branch of the saving function in the neo-Keynesian model, the rate of profit logically is prior to the marginal productivity of capital. That is to say, the mathematical structure of the models is "triangular," so that equation systems that are in principle simultaneous can be attacked sequentially, with the marginal-productivity relationships solved last to determine either the

Table 10.1. Causal relationships between marginal productivities and factor returns

Model	$MP_L = W$	$MP_K = 1 + r$
Neoclassical	$\leftrightarrow$	$\leftrightarrow$
Neo-Marxian	$\leftarrow$	$\rightarrow$
Neo-Keynesian	$\rightarrow$	$\leftarrow$

steady-state production technique and profit rate (in the neo-Marxian model) or the technique and wage rate (in the neo-Keynesian model). Thus in the neo-Marxian model, a *ceteris-paribus* shift in technological relationships changes the equilibrium capital:labor ratio and profit rate, but not the equilibrium wage rate.[3] By the same token, a change in technology in the neo-Keynesian model changes k^* and W^*, but not r^*.

In both these cases, marginal-productivity "theory" is nothing more than the logic of competitive profit maximization, which dictates $MP_L = W$ and $MP_K = 1 + r$ as first-order conditions under a regime of continuous substitution. It hardly seems offensive to Marx or Keynes —nor ought it be to Kalecki and Robinson— to assume profit maximization, however inaccurate perfect competition may be as a description of contemporary capitalism. As for the assumption of continuous substitution, a relationship like

$$\frac{1}{a_0} = f(k)$$

must of course be recognized to be a drastic simplification of reality. But it is not in my judgment one that appears a priori inferior to characterizing technology in terms of discrete techniques or other, more complicated representations along the lines of Arrow (1962), Johansen (1959), Kaldor and Mirrlees (1962), Robinson (1956), or Solow (1960, 1962)—at least not for the present purpose of analyzing alternative approaches to the analysis of growth and distribution in a capitalist economy.

The important point is that continuous substitution and the equations $MP_L = W$ or $MP_K = 1 + r$ do not distinguish between theories: continuous substitution is compatible with many theories, and marginal-productivity relationships merely reflect the coupling of competitive profit maximization with continuous substitution.

What distinguishes the models is not the marginal-productivity equations, but the assumptions about (1) how saving and investment are determined and (2) how the labor market functions. Neoclassical theory alone assumes that savings are determined by the utility-maximizing behavior of essentially similar households allocating lifetime resources to life-cycle needs. For neoclassical economists saving behavior is determined by the same process that, in the typical introductory text, determines the allocations of the household's budget between food and cloth or apples and nuts. By the same token, only neoclassical theory formulates labor-market dynamics in terms reminiscent of the

3. Note, however, the qualifying remarks in Chapters 3 and 16.

isolated market of an elementary text. Wage adjustment is supposed to clear the labor market just as price adjustments are supposed to clear Alfred Marshall's fish market or Eugen Böhm-Bawerk's horse market.

By contrast, the neo-Marxian and neo-Keynesian approaches substitute a classical saving function whose shape is determined by the different propensities to save of capitalists and workers, the result of different conditions of life rather than of differences in the life-cycle calculations of these two classes. In addition these two approaches reject the idea that wage adjustments clear the labor market, with the neo-Marxian approach substituting a subsistence wage, the neo-Keynesian an investment-demand function, for the neoclassical conception of full employment as a determinant of equilibrium.

There are, in short, two marginal-productivity theories. There is first of all a *general* theory that assumes nothing more controversial than continuous substitution, constant returns to scale, and competitive profit maximization. This theory, far from being unique to one school of thought, is—or at least ought to be—the common property of all three approaches. The second marginal-productivity theory adds the assumption that sooner or later, in the long run if not in the short, the wage rate clears the labor market and ensures full employment. This version of marginal-productivity theory, the *special* theory, is manifestly the property of the neoclassical model. Neo-Marxians and neo-Keynesians wouldn't touch it with a ten-foot pole!

Dropping Competitive Profit Maximization

This is not to say that we must accept uncritically the assumptions of the general theory, particularly competitive profit maximization. Indeed, there are two theories that reject this assumption, one formulated by Nicholas Kaldor, the other by Michal Kalecki. Kaldor's rejection of competitive profit maximization, to be sure, is more implicit than explicit. It is the concept of a production function relating output per man or output per unit capital to the capital:labor ratio that offends Kaldor; the marginal-productivity relationships characterizing competitive profit maximization are only incidental targets.

Kaldor's problem (1957) is to characterize equilibrium in terms of *both* animal spirits *and* full employment, which clearly is too much to accommodate in the context of a fixed-coefficient model. But continuous substitution allows Kaldor to make the equilibrium capital:output ratio (rather than the rate of growth of capital) a function of the rate of profit, so animal spirits can be accommodated along with full employment. Figure 10.1 illustrates a Kaldorian equilibrium with a Pasinetti

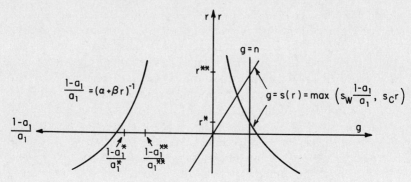

Figure 10.1 Kaldorian equilibria

saving function. In Kaldor (1957) animal spirits are assumed to determine the amount of capital businessmen willingly hold per unit of output as a positive function of the rate of profit. For simplicity Kaldor assumes this function to be linear, and I have added the restriction $\alpha > \beta$ to ensure positivity over the entire range:

$$\frac{a_1}{1 - a_1} = \alpha + \beta r, \qquad 1 > \alpha > \beta \geq 0. \tag{10.8}$$

Observe that the output : capital becomes a hyperbolic function of the rate of profit, as shown in the second quadrant. Observe also that the Kaldor model gives a new twist to the $\hat{\delta} = 0$ branch of the Pasinetti saving function, pictured in the first quadrant. With

$$s(r) = \max \left(s_W \frac{1 - a_1}{a_1}, s_C r \right) \tag{6.5}$$

and

$$\frac{1 - a_1}{a_1} = (\alpha + \beta r)^{-1}$$

we have

$$s'(r) = -s_W \beta (\alpha + \beta r)^{-2}, \qquad \hat{\delta} = 0.$$

Thus, as the rate of profit increases, the output : capital ratio falls and workers' saving per unit of capital falls along with it.

The rate of profit simultaneously determines both the output : capital ratio (in the second quadrant) and the saving rate (in the first quadrant). Equilibrium occurs at the profit rate for which the saving rate sustains full-employment growth.

There is no guarantee of the existence of equilibrium, nor of its uniqueness should it exist. Indeed, as Figure 10.1 is drawn, there are *two* equilibria, r^* in the $\hat{\delta} = 0$ and r^{**} in the $\hat{\delta} > 0$ range. But of the two, only the $\hat{\delta} > 0$ equilibrium can be stable; assuming neoclassical dynamics (what else when long-run full employment is posited?), the negative slope of the saving function at the $\hat{\delta} = 0$ equilibrium guarantees that the r^* equilibrium will be unstable.

A subsequent Kaldor model (1961) differs from the present model in doing away with the investment function altogether, except as a short-run phenomenon. There remains a long-run equilibrium relationship between the capital : output ratio and the rate of profit, but the causality runs in the opposite direction from Kaldor's earlier model. Instead of running from the rate of profit to a desired quantity of capital per unit of output, the relationship runs from the capital : output ratio to the rate of profit: the "risk premium" required to induce capitalists to hold seed corn increases with the capital intensity of production. Otherwise, however, Kaldor's 1961 model is identical in conception to his 1957 model.

In both models, equilibrium growth and profit *rates* are determined by the natural (that is, full-employment) rate of growth and the saving propensities of capitalists. Animal spirits enter into the determination of distributive *shares*, through the effect that capitalists' preferences have on the equilibrium capital : output ratio.

In order to derive the wage *rate*, we could make use of a production-function relationship

$$\frac{1}{a_0} = f(k)$$

and the corresponding relationship between capital : output and capital : labor ratios

$$\frac{1 - a_1}{a_1} = \frac{f(k) - (k)}{k}. \tag{10.9}$$

The production function and Eq. (10.9) enter the picture because the capital : output ratio and the profit rate alone are sufficient to determine only the wage *share*

$$Wa_0 = 1 - (1 + r)a_1.$$

Kaldor is able to ignore the production function and Eq. (10.9) because he is apparently content to stop with the wage share, and does not attempt to decompose it into its constituent elements W and a_0.

However, the resulting wage rate need not be consistent with the marginal-productivity relationships $MP_L = W$ and $MP_K = 1 + r$. For either one of the marginal-productivity relationships overdetermines a model that already contains (1) the animal-spirits relationship

$$\frac{1 - a_1}{a_1} = (\alpha + \beta r)^{-1},$$

(2) the full-employment relationship $g = n$, and (3) a saving function $g = s(r)$.

Kaldor resolved the overdetermination by dismissing the marginal-productivity relationship altogether. But Kaldor's peremptory dismissal derives from the illegitimacy of a production function based on aggregate capital (1956), not from dissatisfaction with the assumption of competitive profit maximization. If the production function and its derivatives are assumed to represent physical relationships, one cannot so easily ignore the implications of profit maximization. Rather, the issue should be faced head-on.

Kalecki's departure from marginal-productivity theory (1938, 1943) does just this. His argument does not substitute capitalists' investment propensities or risk aversion for competitive profit maximization in determining the relationship between the rate of profit and the capital : output ratio, as does Kaldor's, but rather substitutes monopoly for competition in the assumption of profit maximization. Monopolistic profit maximization replaces the marginal-productivity relationships

$$1 + r = f'(k), \qquad W = f(k) - f'(k)k$$

by relationships of the form

$$\mu = f'(k), \qquad \mu W = f(k) - f'(k)k$$

where μ is the "degree of monopoly." By substituting from the first of these marginal conditions into the second, we obtain the mark-up equation

$$1 = \mu(Wa_0 + a_1). \tag{10.10}$$

Now (10.10) is consistent with the price equation

$$1 = Wa_0 + (1 + r)a_1 \tag{1.7}$$

provided we continue to impute all profit to seed corn. But if we put these two equations together we have

$$\frac{\mu - 1}{\mu} = ra_1, \tag{10.11}$$

which allows us to determine the profit *share* from the degree of monopoly alone. Adding (10.11) to the basic neo-Keynesian model determines the equilibrium capital : output ratio along with equilibrium profit, wage, growth, and consumption rates. The equilibrium configuration is determined by the interaction of animal spirits, savings propensities, and the degree of monopoly.

Figure 10.2 summarizes the essential interactions of Kalecki's model. Equilibrium *rates* of profit and growth are determined in the first quadrant by the intersection of an investment-demand function $g = i(r)$ and the Pasinetti saving function

$$s(r) = \max\left(s_W \frac{1 - a_1}{a_1}, s_C r\right). \tag{6.5}$$

Given the rate of profit, the degree of monopoly determines the capital : output ratio as well as the profit share, as pictured in the second quadrant. The production function and the price and production equations

$$\frac{1}{a_0} = f(k),$$

$$1 = W a_0 + (1 + r) a_1, \tag{1.7}$$

and

$$1 = a_0 C + a_1 (1 + g) \tag{1.5}$$

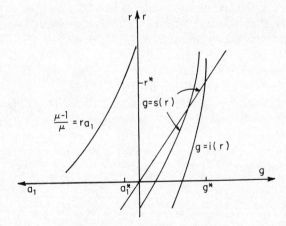

Figure 10.2 Kaleckian equilibrium

complete the story, by allowing us to solve for a_0^*, W^*, and C^*, once g^*, r^*, and a_1^* are known.

This reading of Kalecki, it should be noted, is at variance with the interpretation that takes the degree of monopoly as a substitute for, rather than a complement to, the determination of the rate of profit by means of investment and saving propensities. Evidently, if we take the capital: output ratio a_1 to be fixed, Eq. (10.11) determines the profit *rate* as well as the profit share directly from the degree of monopoly, with no need of animal spirits or saving propensities. But to interpret Kalecki in terms of fixed coefficients strikes me as wrong, for Kalecki's model, it seems to me, not only assumes but requires variable proportions. Not, it is true, in the long-run mold in which the present book is cast—for Kalecki the long run was nothing but a succession of short runs—but in a short-run context in which output and capacity utilization vary. With a fixed capital stock, variations in utilization rates translate directly into variations in capital: labor and capital: output ratios, in other words into variable coefficients!

In the context of long-run equilibrium, capacity utilization is not a variable, but this hardly requires us to assume fixed proportions when we have available the alternative of changing the interpretation from variations in capacity utilization to variations in technique. Unlike the competitive versions of neo-Keynesian and neo-Marxian models, in which it hardly matters whether factor proportions vary or not, Kalecki's emphasis on monopoly requires the extra degree of freedom afforded by continuous substitution, simply to avoid overdetermination.

One final word. In the present interpretation, Kalecki's "degree of monopoly" is neither neo-Keynesian, neo-Marxian, nor neoclassical (although Kalecki's overall approach clearly fits within the first of these camps). If, as I would argue, the issue of competition versus monopoly is separate from the issues that divide these three theories, Kalecki's degree of monopoly can equally well be substituted for competitive marginal-productivity relationships in *any* of them. In Chapter 14, I shall return to this point in the context of multiple goods. In that context degree-of-monopoly theory becomes richer, but the same basic point holds: degree-of-monopoly theory is essentially an alternative to the assumption of perfect competition, not a separate theory of the capitalist economy.

PART TWO

General Equilibrium: The Problems of Heterogeneous Capital and Output

11 The Basic Models in the Multiple-Good Context

Once burned, twice shy. Economists have learned by painful experience not to assume too readily that results of the one-good model carry over to a multiple-commodity world. With the composition of output, capital, and consumption variable, we must go through the models once again to see which results survive from the one-good model and which do not. It is not simply tasting old wine in new bottles, however. Along the way we shall examine important economic questions that do not arise at all until we introduce a multiplicity of commodities.

The object of the theory is now more ambitious: to explain not only the rate of growth and the distribution of income in the aggregate, but relative prices as well. Formally, it is not very difficult to enlarge the model. The scalars a_0 and P now become row vectors,

$$\mathbf{a}_0' = \langle a_{01}, \ldots, a_{0m} \rangle,$$

$$\mathbf{P}' = \langle P_1, \ldots, P_m \rangle,$$

the typical elements of which, a_{0j} and P_j, represent, respectively, the labor requirement per unit of output of good j (in man-years) and the price of good j. Output and consumption become column vectors,

$$\mathbf{X} = \begin{bmatrix} X_1 \\ \cdot \\ \cdot \\ \cdot \\ X_m \end{bmatrix} \qquad \mathbf{C} = \begin{bmatrix} C_1 \\ \cdot \\ \cdot \\ \cdot \\ C_m \end{bmatrix}.$$

The capital coefficient a_1, which in the one-good model represents the requirement of seed corn per bushel of corn output, becomes a Leontief input-output matrix,

$$
\mathbf{A} = \begin{bmatrix} a_{11} & \cdot & \cdot & \cdot & a_{1m} \\ \cdot & & & & \cdot \\ \cdot & & & & \cdot \\ \cdot & & & & \cdot \\ a_{m1} & \cdot & \cdot & \cdot & a_{mm} \end{bmatrix}, \tag{11.1}
$$

whose typical element a_{ij} represents the quantity of good i required per unit of production of good j.

In the new notation, the production equation (1.1) becomes

$$
\mathbf{X} = \mathbf{C} + \mathbf{A}\mathbf{X}_{+1}. \tag{11.2}
$$

Under steady-state conditions, relative growth in the output of each commodity is the same as the relative growth of all others, so that

$$
\mathbf{X}_{+1} = (1 + g)\mathbf{X}, \tag{11.3}
$$

where g remains the growth rate of output, unchanged from the one-good model except that it applies in common to all outputs. The steady-state production equation becomes

$$
\mathbf{X} = \mathbf{C} + (1 + g)\mathbf{A}\mathbf{X}. \tag{11.4}
$$

The price equation (1.2) becomes

$$
\mathbf{P}' = W\mathbf{a}_0' + (1 + r)\mathbf{P}'\mathbf{A}. \tag{11.5}
$$

If perfect competition is assumed to equalize profit rates in the m lines of production, r remains a scalar.

The extension of the model to the many-good case adds not only computational complexity (which in view of the purposes of this book hardly matters), but also a conceptual problem: each additional commodity adds *three* unknowns (C_i, X_i, and P_i) but only two independent equations to the system represented by (11.4) and (11.5). So if we normalize by (1) making all output calculations on the basis of a single worker,

$$
\mathbf{a}_0'\mathbf{X} = 1, \tag{11.6}
$$

and (2) fixing one man-year of labor as the unit of account,

$$
W = 1, \tag{11.7}
$$

we have $3m + 3$ unknowns and $2m + 2$ equations. Thus $m + 1$ equations must be specified by neoclassical, neo-Marxian, or neo-Keynesian models in order to complete the equation system.

There are more problems. The extension of the analysis from one to m goods requires additional assumptions with respect to production.

Specifically, in order to ensure the feasibility of positive growth and the uniformity across commodities of the equilibrium growth rate g, the input-output matrix $\mathbf{A}$ must be assumed to be both "productive" (the direct and indirect requirements of each good for its own production must sum to less than one unit per unit of output) and "indecomposable" (some of each good must be used, directly or indirectly, in the production of every other good). We shall simply assume that the matrix $\mathbf{A}$ possesses these properties; the relevant theorems — and others that we shall need along the way — have been proved in Debreu and Herstein (1953) and from a slightly different point of view mathematically in McKenzie (1960).[1]

Economic Complications

These mathematical assumptions are rather straightforward solutions to purely technical problems. More difficult are the economic problems that arise when there is a multiplicity of goods. In the one-good case we could eliminate output as a variable by an appropriate choice of units, to wit

$$a_0 X = 1,$$

from which followed directly

$$X = \frac{1}{a_0}.$$

In the m-good case, however, the *composition* of output, and hence the required composition of input, depends on the composition of consumption as well as on the rate of growth. Consequently, we cannot eliminate output from the equation system and we cannot analyze the non-steady-state behavior of the system over time without specifying an initial composition of inputs. To do so, however, would dramatically enlarge the scope of the endeavor: in place of a steady-state model, static in nature, we should have to go over to a dynamic analysis in which the steady state (if any) is simply the limit of the period-by-period behavior starting from an arbitrarily given endowment of resources, material and human.

We shall follow an alternative approach, namely, to make the input composition endogenous to the model. That is, rather than working with a historically given bundle of goods, *à la* Walras, we shall let the

---

1. Most advanced texts on growth theory, for example Burmeister and Dobell (1970), provide a summary of the essential matrix algebra.

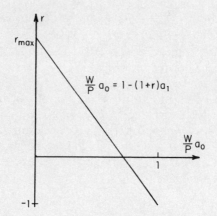

Figure 11.1 Wage share as function of the profit rate with fixed proportions

equilibrium solution determine the composition of inputs and assume that this composition is (and has been) available all along. In return for the simplification this approach affords, we give up the possibility of any meaningful stability analysis. Not to worry: we have enough on our plate as it is.

A second important consequence of a multiplicity of goods is that the fixed-proportions model comes to resemble in some respects the variable-proportions one. In the one-good case, with fixed coefficients a_0 and a_1, factor shares are linear functions of factor prices, as Figure 11.1 shows.[2] By contrast, continuous substitution transforms these relationships into nonlinear relationships, whose shape depends on the elasticity of substitution in production, as in Figure 11.2.

In the multiple-good case, *even with fixed proportions,* wage and profit shares are nonlinear functions of the profit and wage rates. Multiplying (11.5) through by **X**, dividing through by **P′X**, and transposing terms puts the wage share on the left and the profit rate on the right side of the equation:

$$\frac{W\mathbf{a}_0'\mathbf{X}}{\mathbf{P}'\mathbf{X}} = 1 - (1 + r)\frac{\mathbf{P}'\mathbf{A}\mathbf{X}}{\mathbf{P}'\mathbf{X}}$$

or, by virtue of the normalizing equations (11.6) and (11.7),

2. Observe that, even in the simplest case of one good and fixed proportions, the linearity of the wage-share function in Figure 11.1 requires a special assumption—that wages are paid at the end rather than the beginning of the production period. It is presumably for the sake of linearity that Piero Sraffa (1960) makes this peculiar assumption about wages: linearity is important to Sraffa because of his attachment to Ricardo and Ricardian concerns.

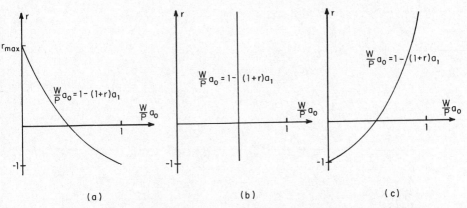

Figure 11.2 Wage share as function of the profit rate with variable
proportions: (a) $\sigma < 1$; (b) $\sigma = 1$; (c) $\sigma > 1$

$$\frac{1}{\mathbf{P'X}} = 1 - (1 + r)\frac{\mathbf{P'AX}}{\mathbf{P'X}}. \tag{11.8}$$

The ratio $\mathbf{P'AX}/\mathbf{P'X}$ is the m-good expression for the capital : output
ratio, which for simplicity of notation we shall denote κ. Observe that
unlike the one-good case κ is not a purely technological parameter,
even apart from Marxian considerations of the relations of production:
unlike a_1, $\mathbf{P'AX}/\mathbf{P'X}$ depends both on prices and on the composition
of output. This fact is of central importance to the analysis that follows.

If we solve the price equation (11.5) for $\mathbf{P}$, we can express the price
vector as a function of the profit rate,

$$\mathbf{P'} = \mathbf{a'_0}[\mathbf{I} - (1 + r)\mathbf{A}]^{-1}, \tag{11.9}$$

and the capital : output ratio therefore becomes a function of the profit
rate and the composition of output:

$$\kappa(r, \mathbf{X}) = \frac{\mathbf{P'AX}}{\mathbf{P'X}} = \frac{\mathbf{a'_0}[\mathbf{I} - (1 + r)\mathbf{A}]^{-1}\mathbf{AX}}{\mathbf{a'_0}[\mathbf{I} - (1 + r)\mathbf{A}]^{-1}\mathbf{X}}. \tag{11.10}$$

Thus (11.8) becomes

$$\frac{1}{\mathbf{P'X}} = 1 - (1 + r)\kappa(r, \mathbf{X}). \tag{11.11}$$

It is clear from (11.11) that nonlinearities in the relationship between
the wage share and the profit rate go hand in hand with nonconstancies
in the capital : output ratio; the one is the necessary and sufficient
condition for the other.

Let us look at (11.11) more closely. It can easily be shown that for any fixed $\mathbf{X}$, $1/\mathbf{P}'\mathbf{X}$ decreases with every increase in r. We have

$$\frac{\partial(1/\mathbf{P}'\mathbf{X})}{\partial r} = -\frac{\dfrac{d\mathbf{P}'}{dr}\mathbf{X}}{(\mathbf{P}'\mathbf{X})^2}, \tag{11.12}$$

and directly from (11.9),

$$\frac{d\mathbf{P}'}{dr} = \mathbf{P}'\mathbf{A}[\mathbf{I} - (1+r)\mathbf{A}]^{-1}. \tag{11.13}$$

Since each of the elements of the right-hand side of (11.13) is positive, the right-hand side of (11.12) is necessarily negative. This rules out the possibility of a "perverse" relationship of the kind that exists in the variable-proportions case when σ exceeds unity, namely, one in which the wage share rises with the profit rate.

However, there is nothing to guarantee that the right-hand side of (11.12) is constant over the interval $(-1, r_{max})$, as it necessarily is in the one-good, fixed-proportions case. Neither is there any guarantee with respect to the curvature of (11.11). Thus for a given technology $\begin{bmatrix} \mathbf{a}_0' \\ \mathbf{A} \end{bmatrix}$, there is no way of ruling out one or the other of the very different functional forms represented for two different commodity bundles in Figure 11.3 — or indeed *any* smooth shape, provided it starts at $\langle r_{max}, 0 \rangle$, slopes downward, and ends at $\langle -1, 1 \rangle$.

So far we have limited our analysis of the capital:output ratio to an

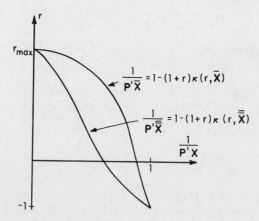

Figure 11.3 Wage share as function of the profit rate for two commodity bundles $\overline{\mathbf{X}}$ and $\overline{\overline{\mathbf{X}}}$.

examination of the effect of changes in the profit rate *via* changes in relative prices. But we have also noted a second difference between the one-good and the m-good models: the possibility that $\kappa(r, \mathbf{X})$ will be sensitive to the composition of output. If final-demand proportions vary with the rate of profit, then, by virtue of Eq. (11.4), so will $\mathbf{X}$, and the wage-profit relationships represented in Eq. (11.11) will be a composite of points on different bundle-specific loci like those pictured in Figure 11.3. The graph of the wage share continues to run from $\langle r_{max}, 0 \rangle$ to $\langle -1, 1 \rangle$ and will continue to be a smooth curve, provided the functional relationship between output composition and profit rate is continuously differentiable.

Equation (11.11) suggests a third complication introduced by extending the commodity basket from one to m goods. Because the capital : output ratio, along with the wage and profit shares, is a function of both r and $\mathbf{X}$, not only distribution but also growth may be sensitive to the composition of output. The m-good analogs of the one-good life-cycle and Cambridge saving equations

$$g = \beta \left[\frac{1}{a_1} - (1 + r) \right] - 1 \quad \text{and} \quad g = \max \left[s_W \frac{1 - a_1}{a_1}, s_C r \right]$$

are

$$g = \beta \left[\frac{1}{\kappa(r, \mathbf{X})} - (1 + r) \right] - 1 \quad \text{and} \quad g = \max \left[s_W \frac{1 - \kappa(r, \mathbf{X})}{\kappa(r, \mathbf{X})}, s_C r \right].$$

And the neo-Marxian profit-rate equation

$$r = \frac{1 - a_1}{a_1} - W* \frac{a_0}{a_1}$$

becomes

$$r = \frac{1 - \kappa(r, \mathbf{X})}{\kappa(r, \mathbf{X})} - \frac{1}{\mathbf{P'X}} \frac{1}{\kappa(r, \mathbf{X})}.$$

Thus variables that are physical constants—a_1 and $W*a_0$—are replaced by variables that depend both on the composition of output and the profit rate—$\kappa(r, \mathbf{X})$ and $1/\mathbf{P'X}$. But the composition of output in turn depends, as has been noted, on both the growth rate and the composition of consumption. Hence g enters on both sides of the life-cycle saving equation, and, in the anti-Pasinetti range, on both sides of the Cambridge saving equation. By the same token, r enters on both sides of the Marxian profit-rate equation. The consequence is that, in general, closed-form solutions in g or r become impossible.

To summarize, the m-good fixed-proportions model differs in critical respects from its one-good counterpart. First, we must either specify the input composition arbitrarily at some historical starting point of the analysis, or determine inputs endogenously as a function of equilibrium output and simply ignore the problem of building up the requisite stock of inputs. Second, for any given output composition, factor shares may vary nonlinearly with factor prices; in addition, distributive shares depend on the composition of output. In other words, the capital : output ratio is a function of r and $\mathbf{X}$.

These problems have different consequences. Making the input composition endogenous to the model, we have observed, rules out any meaningful stability analysis. The dependence of $\kappa(r, \mathbf{X})$ on r and $\mathbf{X}$ has even more serious consequences. Not only does the m-good case in general resemble the continuous-substitution model of Chapter 9 in respect of the variability of $\partial \kappa / \partial r$, but also a new problem arises that has no counterpart in the one-good case: equilibrium growth and distribution become sensitive to output composition.

Technology, Output Composition, and the Capital : Output Ratio

It is natural to examine the structure of production with a view to discovering limitations on the variability of the capital : output ratio. Unfortunately, rather severe restrictions on technology are required; the possible variation of $\kappa(r, \mathbf{X})$ over r and $\mathbf{X}$ turns out to be unbounded as long as the technology $\begin{bmatrix} \mathbf{a}_0' \\ \mathbf{A} \end{bmatrix}$ is restricted only by productivity and indecomposability requirements—a result that can be demonstrated by considering the behavior of the capital : output ratio at the two ends of the profit-rate domain $(-1, r_{\max})$.

At the lower limit of feasible profit rates, $r = -1$, at which

$$\mathbf{P}' = \mathbf{a}_0',$$

we have

$$\kappa(-1, \mathbf{X}) = \frac{\mathbf{a}_0' \mathbf{A} \mathbf{X}}{\mathbf{a}_0' \mathbf{X}}.$$

Let $g = -1$, so that by virtue of the subsystem

$$\mathbf{X} = \mathbf{C} + (1 + g)\mathbf{A}\mathbf{X} \tag{11.4}$$

we have

$$\mathbf{X} = \mathbf{C}.$$

Now consider m different consumption vectors, each defined by

$$\mathbf{C}'_i = \langle 0, \ldots, 0, a_{0i}^{-1}, 0, \ldots, 0 \rangle, \quad i = 1, \ldots, m,$$

for which the corresponding output vector is

$$\mathbf{X}'_i = \langle 0, \ldots, 0, a_{0i}^{-1}, 0, \ldots, 0 \rangle, \quad i = 1, \ldots, m.$$

By virtue of the normalization $\mathbf{a}'_0 \mathbf{X} = 1$, we have

$$\kappa(-1, \mathbf{X}_i) = \frac{\displaystyle\sum_{j=1}^{m} a_{0j} a_{ji}}{a_{0i}} \quad i = 1, \ldots, m.$$

The key point is that productivity and indecomposability put no limits on any individual a_{0i} or a_{ii} other than that they be positive and, in the case of a_{ii}, less than unity. Hence the range of $\kappa(-1, \mathbf{X}_i)$ over the m consumption vectors can lie anywhere on the positive half-line.

At $r = -1$, this variability makes no difference to the wage share:

$$\frac{1}{\mathbf{P}'\mathbf{X}} = 1 - [1 + (-1)]\kappa(-1, \mathbf{X})$$

is equal to unity for any finite value of κ, no matter how large. Hence every wage-profit curve in Figure 11.3 converges to the same point $\langle -1, 1 \rangle$ independently of $\kappa(-1, \mathbf{X})$. However, the *slopes* of the wage-profit curves are not identical at this point:

$$\left[\frac{\partial(1/\mathbf{P}'\mathbf{X})}{\partial r} \right] = -\kappa(-1, \mathbf{X}) \quad \text{at} \quad r = -1.$$

Therefore the effect on the capital : output ratio of the composition of output shows up in the wage-profit curve as soon as we move from $\langle -1, 1 \rangle$. Without further restrictions on technology, the slopes of different wage-profit curves can differ by unlimited amounts at the lower end of the profit interval.

The situation is not noticeably better at the upper end. The maximum profit rate is independent of the composition of output because of the indecomposability of the matrix $\mathbf{A}$, and the productivity assumption guarantees that r_{max} is positive. Indeed, r_{max} is mathematically defined by the so-called Frobenius root of the matrix $\mathbf{A}$. The Frobenius root is the unique nonnegative — by virtue of indecomposability — characteristic root λ of $\mathbf{A}$; it lies in the interval $(0, 1)$ by virtue of the assumption that $\mathbf{A}$ is a productive matrix. Formally, we have the following relationship between λ and r_{max}:

$$1 + r_{max} = \lambda^{-1}.$$

Associated with λ is a characteristic row vector $\mathbf{P}'_\lambda$, for which

$$\lambda \mathbf{P}'_\lambda = \mathbf{P}'_\lambda \mathbf{A}.$$

The characteristic vector $\mathbf{P}'_\lambda$ is unique in its proportions, and as $(1 + r)$ approaches λ^{-1}, $\mathbf{P}'$ approaches $\mathbf{P}'_\lambda$. Thus

$$\kappa(r_{max}, \mathbf{X}) = \frac{\mathbf{P}'_\lambda \mathbf{A} \mathbf{X}}{\mathbf{P}'_\lambda \mathbf{X}} = \lambda = (1 + r_{max})^{-1}$$

independently of $\mathbf{X}$.

Consequently, all wage-profit curves converge to the same point at $r = r_{max}$:

$$\frac{1}{\mathbf{P}'\mathbf{X}} \to 1 - (1 + r_{max})\kappa(r_{max}, \mathbf{X}) = 0.$$

But once again the derivatives do not necessarily converge to a common limit, for in the equation

$$\left[\frac{\partial(1/\mathbf{P}'\mathbf{X})}{\partial r} \right]_{r = r_{max}} = -\kappa(r_{max}, \mathbf{X}) - (1 + r_{max})\frac{\partial \kappa}{\partial r},$$

the second term in general depends on $\mathbf{X}$:

$$\frac{\partial \kappa}{\partial r} = \frac{\dfrac{d\mathbf{P}'}{dr}\mathbf{A}\mathbf{X}}{\mathbf{P}'\mathbf{X}} - \frac{\dfrac{d\mathbf{P}'}{dr}\mathbf{X}}{\mathbf{P}'\mathbf{X}}\kappa(r, \mathbf{X}).$$

These results show that we cannot put meaningful bounds on $\kappa(r, \mathbf{X})$ in the general case. The question remains whether we can find special cases that are economically interesting.

Equal Organic Composition of Capital

If the capital : output ratio

$$\kappa(r, \mathbf{X}) = \frac{\mathbf{P}'\mathbf{A}\mathbf{X}}{\mathbf{P}'\mathbf{X}}$$

is to be constant for all r and $\mathbf{X}$, $\mathbf{P}'\mathbf{A}$ has to be proportional to $\mathbf{P}'$. In other words, $\mathbf{P}'$ must be a characteristic vector of $\mathbf{A}$. But the characteristic vector $\mathbf{P}'_\lambda$ is unique except for scale, which is to say that *relative* prices of all produced commodities must be independent of the profit rate.

We can calculate these relative prices by taking their limiting values as r approaches -1. $\mathbf{P}'(-1)$ must be a characteristic vector of $\mathbf{A}$ if every $\mathbf{P}'$ is to fulfill that role. But since at $r = -1$

$$\mathbf{P}' = \mathbf{a}_0',$$

we have

$$\mathbf{P}_\lambda' = \mu \mathbf{a}_0',$$

which is to say that each commodity's price P_i must be proportional to its direct labor content a_{0i} whatever the rate of profit. Of course the constant of proportionality μ will vary with r, so we may write it as $\mu(r)$.

If $\mathbf{a}_0'$ is a characteristic vector of $\mathbf{A}$ such that

$$\mathbf{P}' = \mu(r)\mathbf{a}_0', \tag{11.14}$$

we have

$$\frac{\mu(r) - 1}{1 + r}\, \mathbf{a}_0' = \mathbf{P}'\mathbf{A}. \tag{11.15}$$

Now Eq. (11.15) says that, whatever the rate of profit, the ratio of the direct labor content of each commodity to the value of material inputs going into that commodity's production must be identical across commodities. This proportionality is the equivalent of "equal organic composition of capital" in the Marxian formulation: denoting the column vector of material inputs to the ith good by $\mathbf{a}_i$,

$$\mathbf{a}_i = \begin{bmatrix} a_{1i} \\ \cdot \\ \cdot \\ \cdot \\ a_{mi} \end{bmatrix},$$

the 2-vector $\langle a_{0i}, \mathbf{P}'\mathbf{a}_i \rangle$ represents the "organic composition of capital" in the ith industry. Equality holds among the several goods if all m of these 2-vectors lie on the same ray, which will be the case if (and only if) Eq. (11.15) is satisfied.

The specifically Marxian terminology "organic composition of capital" might be a bit confusing: in our model, the relevant relationship is between labor and capital rather than in the composition of capital. But the difference is purely semantic; labor inputs are part of capital for Marx because wages are assumed to be paid at the beginning rather than at the end of the production period. The essential assumption, however, has nothing to do with the timing of wage payments. Rather, the role of the equality of the organic composition of capital in assuring constant relative prices and a constant capital:output ratio lies in a structure of production in which each commodity requires direct and indirect labor in the same proportions. We have

$$\mathbf{P}' = \mathbf{a}_0'[\mathbf{I} - (1 + r)\mathbf{A}]^{-1} = \mathbf{a}_0'[\mathbf{I} + (1 + r)\mathbf{A} + (1 + r)^2\mathbf{A}^2 + \cdot \cdot \cdot],$$

which is a weighted sum of terms of the general form $\mathbf{a}_0'\mathbf{A}^n$. So if the direct labor requirement $\mathbf{a}_0'$ is proportional to the indirect requirement $\mathbf{a}_0'\mathbf{A}$ — which it must be if $\mathbf{a}_0'$ is a characteristic vector of $\mathbf{A}$ — then $\mathbf{a}_0'$ and $\mathbf{a}_0'\mathbf{A}$ are each proportional to $\mathbf{a}_0'\mathbf{A}^2 = (\mathbf{a}_0'\mathbf{A})\mathbf{A}$. And so forth. Hence the sum on the right-hand side,

$$\mathbf{a}_0' + (1 + r)\mathbf{a}_0'\mathbf{A} + (1 + r)^2\mathbf{a}_0'\mathbf{A}^2 + \cdot \cdot \cdot ,$$

is a weighted sum of vectors with the same proportions and must itself have the common proportions of its constituents. The point is that if direct and indirect labor requirements are proportional, the same proportionate amount of labor must have gone into each commodity as for the raw materials, and the raw materials for the raw materials — back to the beginning of time. Hence prices, which are weighted sums of these inputs (the weights reflecting "compound interest"), lie in the same proportion to one another whatever the weights.

Solving the problem of variation in $\kappa(r, \mathbf{X})$ by restricting the technology so that $\mathbf{a}_0'$ is a characteristic vector of $\mathbf{A}$ must be recognized as an ingenious solution to the problem of a variable capital:output ratio. But for all its ingenuity, this solution is hardly acceptable: there is no reason why nature should be so obliging as to limit $\mathbf{A}$ and $\mathbf{a}_0'$ in the requisite way.

An Alternative Solution: The "Standard Commodity"

Piero Sraffa's "standard commodity" (1960) is an alternative, and at first glance a more promising, solution. For it requires no restrictions on technology other than productivity and indecomposability. Rather than imposing conditions on $\begin{bmatrix} \mathbf{a}_0' \\ \mathbf{A} \end{bmatrix}$ for which κ is constant for all $\mathbf{X}$ as well as all r, as does the Marxian equal organic composition, the Sraffian standard commodity provides conditions on $\mathbf{X}$ (as a function of $\mathbf{A}$) for which κ is constant for all r.

For $\kappa(r, \mathbf{X})$ to be invariant with respect to r, it must be invariant with respect to $\mathbf{P}$. That is to say, we must have

$$\frac{\mathbf{P}'\mathbf{A}\mathbf{X}}{\mathbf{P}'\mathbf{X}} = \bar{\kappa} = \text{const.}$$

for all $\mathbf{P}$. But if $\mathbf{A}$ and therefore $\mathbf{P}(r)$ are restricted only by productivity and indecomposability assumptions, then this equation can hold only if

$$\mathbf{A}\mathbf{X} = \bar{\kappa}\mathbf{X}.$$

But this means $\mathbf{X}$ must be a characteristic vector of $\mathbf{A}$, and just as $\mathbf{A}$ has only one characteristic row vector $\mathbf{P}'_\lambda$, so does $\mathbf{A}$ have only one characteristic column vector $\mathbf{X}_\lambda$. Moreover, once the normalizing condition

$$\mathbf{a}'_0\mathbf{X}_\lambda = 1$$

is appended, the characteristic column vector is unique as to scale as well as proportions. We have immediately from the fact that λ is the unique, positive, characteristic root of $\mathbf{A}$,

$$\bar{\kappa} = \lambda = \frac{1}{1 + r_{max}} = \frac{1}{1 + g_{max}}.$$

Sraffa gives the name "standard commodity" to $\mathbf{X}_\lambda$. The symmetry between the standard commodity vector $\mathbf{X}_\lambda$ and the equal-organic-composition price vector $\mathbf{P}'_\lambda$ should be obvious: both are characteristic vectors of the matrix $\mathbf{A}$. There is, however, an essential difference that originates in the difference between the production and price equations

$$\mathbf{X} = \mathbf{C} + (1 + g)\mathbf{A}\mathbf{X},$$
$$\mathbf{P}' = \mathbf{a}'_0 + (1 + r)\mathbf{P}'\mathbf{A}.$$

In Sraffa's model, $\mathbf{C}$ is (implicitly) up for grabs; it can be made to share the proportions of the standard commodity $\mathbf{X}_\lambda$. Hence a standard commodity for which κ is invariant can be found for any productive, indecomposable $\mathbf{A}$. By contrast, there is no such freedom with respect to $\mathbf{a}'_0$. This vector is exogenous, and hence $\mathbf{P}'_\lambda$ cannot arbitrarily be forced to $\mathbf{a}'_0$ in the way $\mathbf{C}$ can be forced to $\mathbf{X}_\lambda$. This is precisely where the assumption of equal organic composition enters: for any given $\mathbf{A}$, $\mathbf{a}'_0$ must have just that composition that makes it a characteristic row vector.

The greater generality of Sraffa's solution is, however, at the same time its drawback, at least from the perspective of this book: Sraffa's solution requires consumption to be determined by output; both must fit the proportions of the standard commodity. In *all* our models, by contrast, output is determined by consumption, by means of the sub-system

$$\mathbf{X} = [\mathbf{I} - (1 + g)\mathbf{A}]^{-1}\mathbf{C},$$

$$\mathbf{a}_0'\mathbf{X} = 1.$$

It would only be by the sheerest coincidence that equilibrium consumption happened to have standard-commodity proportions, and it is only under this fortuitous circumstance that the output vector will be in standard proportions. Moreover, in neoclassical, neo-Marxian, and neo-Keynesian models, $\mathbf{C}$ and r are interdependent, so that $\mathbf{X}$ cannot be determined independently of r.

In short, Sraffa's standard commodity provides a logically consistent method of eliminating the influence of variations in the capital : output ratio on changes in the distribution of income: for any profit rate, we determine the distribution of income that would take place were production organized to provide the standard commodity. But clever as Sraffa's solution undoubtedly is, it accomplishes its purpose by obliging us to shift our focus from a model in which consumption proportions are variable — unknowns of the problem — to a model in which consumption is determined exogenously, by technology. For our purposes, therefore, the Sraffian solution is ultimately no more satisfactory than the Marxian.

The search for an invariant capital : output ratio well may be the economists' version of alchemy. In the absence of equal organic composition of capital across commodities, the value of capital per unit of output necessarily varies with the composition of output and the rate of profit. Neither is there any output vector but the standard commodity for which the capital : output ratio is invariant with respect to the rate of profit independently of the production structure.

Like alchemy, however, the exercise may prove useful even if its goal remains unrealized. We shall have occasion to return to the Marx-Sraffa results more than once as we explore the problems of closing the m-good production model along alternative lines.

But the significance of variations in the capital : output ratio should not be exaggerated. Even in a one-good model, the capital : output ratio depends on the profit rate once the assumption of fixed proportions is abandoned, *or* the assumption that wages are paid only after the completion of the harvest is dropped. The dependence of κ on $\mathbf{X}$ and r only makes matters more complicated; it impedes, but does not prevent us, from inquiring into price formation, growth, and distribution. It is perhaps time, therefore, to be done with alchemy and get on with the real tasks of this book.

The Neoclassical Model

In analyzing the neoclassical model, it is natural to turn to the utility-maximization hypothesis for m of the $m + 1$ equations required to close the model. The system

$$U(\mathbf{C}^1, \mathbf{C}^2) = \max \tag{11.16}$$

subject to

$$\mathbf{P}'\mathbf{C}^1 + \frac{\mathbf{P}'\mathbf{C}^2}{1 + r} = 1 \tag{11.17}$$

generates, for any $\langle \mathbf{P}, r \rangle$, corresponding vectors $\mathbf{C}^1$ and $\mathbf{C}^2$. And, as in the one-good model, we can express $\mathbf{C}^1$ and $\mathbf{C}^2$ as functions of r alone by taking note of the interdependence of $\mathbf{P}$ and r summarized in the price equation (11.5). Equation (11.17) becomes

$$\mathbf{P}'(r)\mathbf{C}^1 + \frac{\mathbf{P}'(r)\mathbf{C}^2}{1 + r} = 1, \tag{11.18}$$

and lifetime utility maximization yields vectors $\mathbf{C}^1(r)$ and $\mathbf{C}^2(r)$. As in the one-good case, consumption demand for the economy as a whole is found by adding the demand of the working generation $\mathbf{C}^1(r)$ to the demand of the retired generation $\mathbf{C}^2(r)/(1 + g)$:

$$\mathbf{C}(r, g) = \mathbf{C}^1(r) + \frac{\mathbf{C}^2(r)}{1 + g}. \tag{11.19}$$

Thus for any profit rate and any growth rate, we can calculate the required outputs according to the production equation

$$\mathbf{X} = \mathbf{C}(r, g) + (1 + g)\mathbf{A}\mathbf{X}, \tag{11.20}$$

or, using the notation $\mathbf{X}(r, g)$ to express the dependence of $\mathbf{X}$ on r and g implied by Eq. (11.20),

$$\mathbf{X}(r, g) = [\mathbf{I} - (1 + g)\mathbf{A}]^{-1}\mathbf{C}(r, g). \tag{11.21}$$

Observe that $\mathbf{C}(r, g)$ is defined for all r and for g in the interval $(-1, g_{max})$. Hence so is $\mathbf{X}(r, g)$. This might appear to suggest that all growth rates in this interval are compatible with any given profit rate. This is not the case, however. For Eq. (11.21) only constrains the output vector $\mathbf{X}(r, g)$ to be "utility-feasible," that is, to be compatible with the given demand vector $\mathbf{C}(r, g)$; whereas $\mathbf{C}(r, g)$ represents aggregate demand per worker, Eq. (11.20) has nothing to say about "production feasibility," the requirement embodied in Eq. (11.6) that the output will be producible by a single worker. Thus along with (11.20) we have the additional constraint

$$\mathbf{a}_0'\mathbf{X}(r, g) = 1. \tag{11.22}$$

For each r in $(-1, g_{\max})$, the set of growth rates for which $\mathbf{X}(r, g)$ is both utility- and production-feasible will be denoted $\{g(r)\}$.

How is $\{g(r)\}$ determined? Indeed, how can we be sure $\{g(r)\}$ is nonempty for any given r?

A False Start

One way to proceed would be to define g equal to r in (11.19) and (11.20). Thus we would have

$$\mathbf{X}(r, r) = \mathbf{C}(r, r) + (1 + r)\mathbf{A}\mathbf{X}(r, r)$$

and

$$\mathbf{C}(r, r) = \mathbf{C}^1(r) + \frac{\mathbf{C}^2(r)}{1 + r}.$$

Now multiply both equations through by $\mathbf{P}'$, to obtain

$$\mathbf{P}'\mathbf{X}(r, r) = \mathbf{P}'\mathbf{C}(r, r) + (1 + r)\mathbf{P}'\mathbf{A}\mathbf{X}(r, r),$$

$$\mathbf{P}'\mathbf{C}(r, r) = \mathbf{P}'\mathbf{C}^1(r) + \frac{\mathbf{P}'\mathbf{C}^2(r)}{1 + r} = 1.$$

If we substitute from the second of these equations into the first, we have

$$\mathbf{P}'\mathbf{X}(r, r) = 1 + (1 + r)\mathbf{P}'\mathbf{A}\mathbf{X}(r, r). \tag{11.23}$$

Multiply (11.5) through by $\mathbf{X}(r, r)$, and we get

$$\mathbf{P}'\mathbf{X}(r, r) = \mathbf{a}_0'\mathbf{X}(r, r) + (1 + r)\mathbf{P}'\mathbf{A}\mathbf{X}(r, r). \tag{11.24}$$

Finally, subtract (11.24) from (11.23), and we have

$$\mathbf{a}_0'\mathbf{X}(r, r) = 1,$$

which suggests that for all r,

$$r \in \{g(r)\}.$$

Were this to be true, our examination of the neoclassical model would be at an end, for by setting r equal to n, we would have

$$n \in \{g(n)\},$$

and the full-employment condition would be satisfied by an output that is both production- and utility-feasible. Existence of equilibrium would require us to assume only that $n < g_{max}$.

Alas, the one-good case has already shown the problem with this solution: it omits the economically relevant "ownership" condition, the requirement that capital goods must be held from one period to the next by the households that make up the economy. In the one-good case, this requirement becomes tantamount to requiring that the saving of the present working generation be equal to the seed-corn requirement for the next period, because this year's workers are the only households both motivated and able to hold capital goods.

The same requirement holds in the m-good model, at least up to a point. As in the one-good case, only this year's workers have an effective supply of saving. But it is obviously unreasonable to insist that the typical working household be willing to hold for future consumption as much of *each* good as is required for production to grow at the rate g: even though coal and steel might be required for future production, households need *never* wish to consume steel or coal directly.

Nor is it necessary for the household's between-period holdings of each good to match its future consumption desires; markets permit each household to trade the goods it holds for the goods it wishes to consume. From the household's point of view, as well as from the economy's, it is only necessary that the market value of household saving be equal to the present value of the basket it intends to consume next period. The *physical composition* of household saving can be whatever the economy requires for expansion. Specifically, for any given rate of growth g, the value of the household's desired saving,

$$\frac{\mathbf{P'C}^2(r)}{1+r},$$

must be equal to the market value of the requisite capital goods,

$$(1+g)\mathbf{P'AX}(r, g).$$

That is, workers' saving must equal gross capital formation in value terms:

$$\frac{\mathbf{P'C}^2(r)}{1+r} = (1+g)\mathbf{P'AX}(r, g). \tag{11.25}$$

Utility Feasibility, Production Feasibility, and Saving Feasibility

There are two problems with Eq. (11.25). First, how do we know that a solution exists? Evidently if $\mathbf{X}$ were arbitrary, a g could be found for any

r that would satisfy (11.25). But $\mathbf{X}$, far from being arbitrary, is constrained, indeed defined by (11.21); it is not obvious that for a given r, there is any g that satisfies (11.25) and (11.21) simultaneously.

Second, assuming that there is such a g—that is to say, assuming there exists a mapping $s : r \to g$ such that (11.25) and (11.21) are satisfied—how do we know that $s(r)$ satisfies the requirement of production feasibility, Eq. (11.22)? That is, how do we know $s(r)$ is a member of the set $\{g(r)\}$ defined by Eqs. (11.21) and (11.22)? The problem here is that (11.25) adds an equation to the system formed by Eqs. (11.21) and (11.22), giving us $m + 2$ in all—to determine $m + 1$ unknowns, the m components of $\mathbf{X}(r, g)$ and g. Thus there well may be no $\mathbf{X}(r, g)$ that is at once utility-feasible (11.21), production-feasible (11.22), and saving-feasible (11.25).

Both issues can be resolved. I first show that the mapping $s : r \to g$ exists and moreover that it is single-valued. Second, I shall show that $g = s(r)$ satisfies (11.22), so that $s(r) \in \{g(r)\}$.

The left-hand side of Eq. (11.25), saving per working household, is a function of r alone. With the wage rate fixed at unity it is also the average propensity to save, which in analogy with the one-good case, we can write as

$$\beta(r) = \frac{\mathbf{P}'\mathbf{C}^2(r)}{1 + r}. \tag{11.26}$$

(If $U(\mathbf{C}^1, \mathbf{C}^2)$ is Cobb-Douglas, then $\beta(r)$ is constant for all r, but in any case β is completely determined by r, at least in equilibrium.) Substitution from (11.26) into (11.25) gives

$$g = \beta(r) \frac{1}{\mathbf{P}'\mathbf{A}\mathbf{X}(r, g)} - 1. \tag{11.27}$$

If we multiply and divide the first term on the right through by $\cdot \mathbf{P}'\mathbf{X}(r, g)$, we have

$$g = \beta(r) \frac{1}{\mathbf{P}'\mathbf{X}(r, g)} \frac{1}{\kappa(r, \mathbf{X}(r, g))} - 1. \tag{11.28}$$

But from the wage-profit equation we have

$$\frac{1}{\mathbf{P}'\mathbf{X}} = 1 - (1 + r)\kappa(r, \mathbf{X})$$

so that

$$g = \beta(r) \left[\frac{1}{\kappa(r, \mathbf{X}(r, g))} - (1 + r) \right] - 1. \tag{11.29}$$

Evidently, apart from the dependence of β on r and the dependence of κ on r and g, Eq. (11.29) is identical to the one-good formula

$$g = s(r) = \beta \left[\frac{1}{a_1} - (1 + r) \right] - 1. \tag{2.17}$$

Indeed, if the capital: output ratio is independent of $\mathbf{X}$, and therefore of g, we are quite done, at least with the first part of the assignment: we can solve (11.29) explicitly for g as the required function $s(r)$. But this would oblige us, as we have seen, to adopt unacceptable restrictions either on the technology or on the composition of output.

However, in the absence of a constant capital: output ratio, the proof of the existence of the function $g = s(r)$—that is, g for which (11.29) holds good—is only slightly more complicated. Starting from (11.27), we form the "excess-demand" function

$$\psi(r, g) = (1 + g)\mathbf{P}'\mathbf{A}\mathbf{X}(r, g) - \beta(r) \tag{11.30}$$

and then proceed, by means of the intermediate value theorem, to prove the existence of a g for which $\psi(r, g)$ vanishes. We show first $\psi(r, -1) \leq 0$ and $\psi(r, g_{max}) > 0$. Then by virtue of the continuity of $\psi(r, g)$, an intermediate value of g exists for which $\psi(r, g) = 0$.

From (11.30) we have directly

$$\psi(r, -1) = -\beta(r) \leq 0.$$

At the other end of the g-interval, every element of $\mathbf{X}(r, g)$ increases without bound since

$$\mathbf{X}(r, g) = [\mathbf{I} - (1 + g)\mathbf{A}]^{-1}\mathbf{C}(r, g),$$

and the matrix $[\mathbf{I} - (1 + g)\mathbf{A}]$ approaches the singular matrix $[\mathbf{I} - \lambda^{-1}\mathbf{A}]$. Hence

$$\lim_{g \to g_{max}} \psi(r, g) = +\infty.$$

Thus for every r, there is at least one g for which workers' desired saving is just adequate to purchase the capital goods required to maintain accumulation at that rate of growth. To show there is only one such g, we need merely note that the derivative $\partial\psi/\partial g$ is positive everywhere in the interval $(-1, g_{max})$. Differentiating (11.30) gives

$$\frac{\partial\psi}{\partial g} = \mathbf{P}'\mathbf{A} \{[\mathbf{I} - (1 + g)\mathbf{A}]^{-1}\mathbf{C}^1(r)$$

$$+ (1 + g)[\mathbf{A} + 2(1 + g)\mathbf{A}^2 + 3(1 + g)^2\mathbf{A}^3 + \cdot \cdot \cdot]\mathbf{C}(r, g)\},$$

which is necessarily positive.

Thus the equation

$$\psi(r, g) = 0$$

defines a functional relationship $g = s(r)$ that satisfies (11.25) as well as (11.21); $g = s(r)$ is both saving-feasible and utility-feasible. The function s is, by the way, continuous and differentiable by virtue of the continuity and differentiability of ψ.

It remains to show that s defines a production-feasible g, so that the condition of production feasibility is satisfied whenever the growth rate is saving-feasible. In other words, we have still to verify that $s(r) \in \{g(r)\}$.

Suppose Eq. (11.25) holds. Then

$$1 - \mathbf{P}'\mathbf{C}^1(r) = [1 + s(r)]\mathbf{P}'\mathbf{A}\mathbf{X}(r, s(r))$$

and

$$-\frac{\mathbf{P}'\mathbf{C}^2(r)}{1 + s(r)} = -(1 + r)\mathbf{P}'\mathbf{A}\mathbf{X}(r, s(r)).$$

Adding these two equations together gives

$$1 - \mathbf{P}'\mathbf{C}(r, s(r)) = [s(r) - r]\mathbf{P}'\mathbf{A}\mathbf{X}(r, s(r)). \qquad (11.31)$$

Now recall the production and price equations, according to which

$$\mathbf{X}(r, s(r)) = \mathbf{C}(r, s(r)) + [1 + s(r)]\mathbf{A}\mathbf{X}(r, s(r)),$$

$$\mathbf{P}' = \mathbf{a}_0' + (1 + r)\mathbf{P}'\mathbf{A}.$$

Multiplying through respectively by $\mathbf{P}'$ and $\mathbf{X}(r, s(r))$, we have

$$\mathbf{P}'\mathbf{X}(r, s(r)) = \mathbf{P}'\mathbf{C}(r, s(r)) + [1 + s(r)]\mathbf{P}'\mathbf{A}\mathbf{X}(r, s(r)),$$

$$\mathbf{P}'\mathbf{X}(r, s(r)) = \mathbf{a}_0'\mathbf{X}(r, s(r)) + (1 + r)\mathbf{P}'\mathbf{A}\mathbf{X}(r, s(r)).$$

Subtracting the second equation from the first gives

$$\mathbf{a}_0'\mathbf{X}(r, s(r)) - \mathbf{P}'\mathbf{C}(r, s(r)) = [s(r) - r]\mathbf{P}'\mathbf{A}\mathbf{X}(r, s(r)). \qquad (11.32)$$

The right-hand sides of (11.31) and (11.32) are identical. Consequently so are the left-hand sides, from which it follows that

$$\mathbf{a}_0'\mathbf{X}(r, s(r)) = 1.$$

This shows that $s(r)$ is production-feasible as well as savings- (and utility-) feasible: in short, $s(r) \in \{g(r)\}$.

Figure 11.4 illustrates the saving function

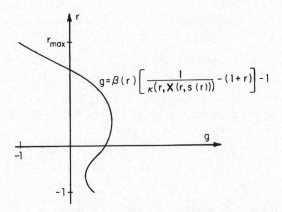

Figure 11.4 Neoclassical saving function with multiple goods

$$g = s(r) = \beta(r) \left[\frac{1}{\kappa(r, \mathbf{X}(r, s(r)))} - (1 + r) \right] - 1$$

in the $r \times g$ plane. The saving function slopes generally from the "northwest" to the "southeast" of the diagram: the expression within brackets vanishes at $r = r_{max}$ and is positive everywhere else, whereas $\beta(r)$ is constrained to lie within $[0, 1]$; thus

$$s(r_{max}) = -1$$

and

$$s(-1) > -1,$$

provided only that workers' propensity to save $\beta(r)$ remains positive at the lower end of the profit interval.

There is an important change from the one-good story, however: a Cobb-Douglas utility function, for which the propensity to save $\beta(r)$ is constant, no longer is sufficient to ensure a linear saving function or even a saving function that is *everywhere* downward-sloping. For whether or not $\beta(r)$ is independent of r, variation in the capital:output ratio $\kappa(r, \mathbf{X}(r, s(r)))$ can lead to nonlinearity and even changes in sign of the slope, either because of changes in relative prices or because of changes in the composition of output. We have

$$s'(r) = -\frac{\partial \psi / \partial g}{\partial \psi / \partial r}, \qquad (11.33)$$

and whereas $\partial \psi / \partial g$ is necessarily positive, there is no such guarantee with respect to $\partial \psi / \partial r$.

Nevertheless, the one-good sufficiency condition for the existence of neoclassical equilibrium generalizes quite straightforwardly to the m-good case. If

$$s(-1) \geq n, \qquad (11.34)$$

then the continuity of $s(r)$ guarantees the existence of an equilibrium, that is, a $(3m + 3)$-dimensional point $\langle g^*, r^*, W^*, \mathbf{C}^*, \mathbf{P}^*, \mathbf{X}^* \rangle$ for which

$$g^* = n$$

$$g^* = s(r^*)$$

$$W^* = 1$$

$$\mathbf{P}'^* = \mathbf{a}_0'[\mathbf{I} - (1 + r)\mathbf{A}]^{-1}$$

$$\mathbf{X}^* = [\mathbf{I} - (1 + g^*)\mathbf{A}]^{-1}\mathbf{C}(r^*, g^*)$$

$$\mathbf{a}_0'\mathbf{X}^* = 1.$$

Thus, it seems fair to say that the complexity introduced into the fixed-proportions neoclassical model by expanding the number of goods is mathematical rather than economic in nature. The simplicity of the one-good analysis, which rests on the constancy of the capital : output ratio, survives only under special, restrictive assumptions. But the key result—the existence of equilibrium—survives under conditions that are neither more nor less general than in the one-good case.

The Neo-Marxian Model

Extending the neo-Marxian model to the m-good case presents more serious difficulties than extending the neoclassical model. In the first place, the labor theory of value breaks down as a theory of price: just as in the one-good case an excessive elasticity of substitution causes the mapping from ε to W to degenerate, so does, in the m-good case, the variability of the capital : output ratio—even with fixed proportions governing production in each industry. This is, however, not a fatal defect in the neo-Marxian theory; it remains possible to go directly from the subsistence wage to equilibrium steady growth, bypassing the labor theory of value altogether.

More serious is the problem of interpreting the subsistence wage in the multiple-good context. Having abandoned the idea of a biological subsistence, we are obliged to take seriously the possibility of substitution between consumption goods according to relative prices. And having abandoned the idea that saving can take place only out of profits, we must take account of the difference between the composition of subsistence and the composition of the basket actually consumed by working-class households.

In the interests of orderly discussion, we shall first examine the difficulties of the labor theory of value, simplifying matters by making the classical assumptions that all wages are consumed and all profits saved, and ignoring for the moment the possibility of substitution in the consumption basket. In this case we can identify the equilibrium consumption bundle C^* with the exogenously given subsistence $\mathbf{C}^N$ of a single worker (and his family):

$$\mathbf{C}^N = \begin{bmatrix} C_1^N \\ \cdot \\ \cdot \\ \cdot \\ C_m^N \end{bmatrix},$$

the superscript N standing for "necessities."

The Marxian theory assigns values to the m commodities according to the total labor time, direct and indirect, required in their production. Direct labor requirements are $\mathbf{a}_0'$, the requirements of labor for "seed" are $\mathbf{a}_0'\mathbf{A}$, the requirements two years back are $\mathbf{a}_0'\mathbf{A}^2$, and so forth. Hence, analogously with the one-good case, total labor requirements are given by the infinite sum

$$\mathbf{a}_0'[\mathbf{I} + \mathbf{A} + \mathbf{A}^2 + \cdots] = \mathbf{a}_0'[\mathbf{I} - \mathbf{A}]^{-1}.$$

But this is a special case of the price equation. Denoting the price vector associated with $r = 0$ by $\mathbf{P}_0$, the price equation gives

$$\mathbf{P}_0' = \mathbf{a}_0'[\mathbf{I} - \mathbf{A}]^{-1},$$

which is to say that labor values are simply the prices associated with a zero rate of profit.

The labor-time value of one man-year of effort v is the total time that must be expended to provide subsistence for one worker and his family over a year:

$$v = \mathbf{P}_0'\mathbf{C}^N. \tag{11.35}$$

Similarly, the total surplus value generated by a worker is the labor value of the gross product of a man-year of effort, after deducting the value of subsistence and the value of material inputs:

$$\mathscr{s} = \mathbf{P}_0'\mathbf{X} - \mathbf{P}_0'\mathbf{C}^N - \mathbf{P}_0'\mathbf{AX}. \tag{11.36}$$

If we take account of the assumed relationship between subsistence and total consumption,

$$\mathbf{C}^* = \mathbf{C}^N,$$

as well as the relationship between production and consumption summarized in the production and normalization equations

$$\mathbf{X} = \mathbf{C} + (1 + g)\mathbf{AX} \tag{11.4}$$

and

$$\mathbf{a}_0'\mathbf{X} = 1, \tag{11.6}$$

we can write equilibrium output $\mathbf{X}^*$ and the (as yet unknown) rate of growth g^* as functions of $\mathbf{C}^* = \mathbf{C}^N$ alone:

$$\mathbf{X}^* = [\mathbf{I} - (1 + g^*)\mathbf{A}]^{-1}\mathbf{C}^*,$$

$$\mathbf{a}_0'\mathbf{X}^* = 1.$$

Now premultiply Eq. (11.4) by $\mathbf{P}_0'$, and rearrange terms, to obtain

$$\mathbf{P}_0'\mathbf{X} - \mathbf{P}_0'\mathbf{C} - \mathbf{P}_0'\mathbf{AX} = g\mathbf{P}_0'\mathbf{AX},$$

whereby Eq. (11.36) becomes

$$\mathscr{s}^* = g^*\mathbf{P}_0'\mathbf{AX}^*.$$

Thus the equilibrium rate of exploitation can be written

$$\mathscr{e}^* = \frac{\mathscr{s}^*}{\mathscr{v}^*} = g^* \frac{\mathbf{P}_0'\mathbf{AX}^*}{\mathbf{P}_0'\mathbf{C}^N}. \tag{11.37}$$

Alternatively, we may write

$$\mathscr{e}^* = r^* \frac{\mathbf{P}_0'\mathbf{AX}^*}{\mathbf{P}_0'\mathbf{C}^N}, \tag{11.38}$$

since under classical saving assumptions the equation

$$g = r \tag{11.39}$$

holds in the m-good as well as in the one-good context.[3]

---

3. Equation (11.39) is obtained by postmultiplying the price equation
$$\mathbf{P}' = W\mathbf{a}_0' + (1 + r)\mathbf{P}'\mathbf{A} \tag{11.5}$$
by $\mathbf{X}$, rearranging terms, and subtracting the result,
$$\mathbf{P}'\mathbf{X} = W\mathbf{a}_0' + (1 + r)\mathbf{P}'\mathbf{AX},$$
from the corresponding transformation of the production equation

The result of this argument is that we can determine the rate of exploitation from subsistence consumption, along with the equilibrium composition of output and equilibrium rates of profit and growth. But the labor theory of value has been supposed, at least in the past, to assert much more; in particular it has been supposed to determine the equilibrium profit rate, and hence equilibrium prices, *from* a given rate of exploitation, without reference to the composition of demand, that is, without reference to the structure of $\mathbf{C}^N$.

However, Eqs. (11.37) and (11.38) cannot in general serve as the basis for determining r^* from a given ε^* because a given rate of exploitation does not in general map to a unique rate of profit independently of $\mathbf{C}^N$. The problem turns out — hardly surprisingly — to be the variability of the capital: output ratio. For the mapping from ε to r and g to be single-valued, we must restrict the technology *à la* Marx so that $\mathbf{a}_0'$ and hence $\mathbf{P}_0'$ is a characteristic vector of $\mathbf{A}$, or fix the subsistence vector $\mathbf{C}^N$ in advance.

In the first solution, because $\mathbf{P}_0'$ is a characteristic vector of $\mathbf{A}$, we have $\mathbf{P}_0' = \mu(0)\mathbf{a}_0'$ and thus $\mathbf{P}' = \mu(r)\mathbf{a}_0'$. This gives two equations:

$$\mu(0)\mathbf{a}_0' = \mathbf{a}_0' + \mu(0)\mathbf{a}_0'\mathbf{A},$$

$$\mu(r)\mathbf{a}_0' = \mathbf{a}_0' + (1 + r)\mu(r)\mathbf{a}_0'\mathbf{A}.$$

By multiplying the first of these through by $(1 + r)\mu(r)$ and the second by $\mu(0)$, we obtain a common term $\mu(0)(1 + r)\mu(0)\mathbf{a}_0'\mathbf{A}$ that can be eliminated by subtraction, leaving us with

$$\mu(r) = \frac{\mu(0)}{1 + r - r\mu(0)}. \tag{11.41}$$

Now substitute from the equations

$$\mathbf{P}_0'\mathbf{A} = (\mu(0) - 1)\mathbf{a}_0'$$

and

$$\mathbf{P}'\mathbf{X} = \mathbf{P}'\mathbf{C} + (1 + g)\mathbf{P}'\mathbf{A}\mathbf{X}$$

given by premultiplying Eq. (11.4) by $\mathbf{P}'$. This gives

$$\mathbf{P}'\mathbf{C} - W\mathbf{a}_0'\mathbf{X} = (r - g)\mathbf{P}'\mathbf{A}\mathbf{X}.$$

The left-hand side of the equation vanishes by virtue of the classical saving assumption which says that wages ($W = 1$) must just cover the cost of subsistence

$$\mathbf{P}'\mathbf{C}^N = 1, \tag{11.40}$$

and the assumption of production feasibility which says that the direct labor requirements must total one man-year:

$$\mathbf{a}_0'\mathbf{X} = 1. \tag{11.6}$$

The consequence is that the rate of profit and the rate of growth, on the right-hand side of the equation, must be equal.

$$\mathbf{P}_0' = \frac{\mu(0)}{\mu(r)} \mathbf{P}'$$

into the equation

$$\varepsilon^* = r^* \frac{\mathbf{P}_0' \mathbf{A} \mathbf{X}^*}{\mathbf{P}_0' \mathbf{C}^N}.$$

We obtain

$$\varepsilon^* = r^* \frac{[\mu(0) - 1]\mathbf{a}_0' \mathbf{X}^*}{\dfrac{\mu(0)}{\mu(r^*)} \mathbf{P}' \mathbf{C}^N} = r^* \frac{\mu(0) - 1}{\dfrac{\mu(0)}{\mu(r^*)}}$$

or, by virtue of (11.41),

$$\varepsilon^* = r^* \frac{\mu(0) - 1}{1 + r^* - r^* \mu(0)}. \tag{11.42}$$

Thus, with equal organic composition of capital the rate of exploitation uniquely determines rates of profit and growth: if we solve Eq. (11.42) for r, we obtain

$$r^* = \frac{\varepsilon^*}{[\mu(0) - 1](1 + \varepsilon^*)}. \tag{11.43}$$

Alternatively, if output is restricted by a fixed $\mathbf{C}^N$ the mapping between r^* and ε^* is one-to-one, even though in general a closed-form solution for r^* in terms of ε^* is not available.[4]

Without one of these two restrictions, we cannot take the rate of exploitation as the starting point of the analysis, not if the aim is to

---

4. If output is restricted to standard-commodity proportions, we get a simple expression for r^* (and g^*) in terms of ε^*. In this case $\mathbf{X}^*$ is a characteristic vector of $\mathbf{A}$, and we have

$$\mathbf{C}^N = [\mathbf{I} - (1 + g^*)\mathbf{A}]\mathbf{X}^*$$

with

$$\mathbf{X}^* = (1 + g_{max})\mathbf{A}\mathbf{X}^*.$$

Combining these two equations gives

$$\mathbf{C}^N = (g_{max} - g^*)\mathbf{A}\mathbf{X}^*$$

and

$$\varepsilon^* = g^* \frac{\mathbf{P}_0' \mathbf{A} \mathbf{X}^*}{(g_{max} - g^*)\mathbf{P}_0' \mathbf{A} \mathbf{X}^*} = \frac{g^*}{g_{max} - g^*} = \frac{r^*}{r_{max} - r^*}.$$

Again, a unique relationship exists between the rate of exploitation and rates of growth and profit. Solving for r^* and g^*, we have

$$r^* = g^* = \frac{\varepsilon^* g_{max}}{1 + \varepsilon^*} = \frac{\varepsilon^* r_{max}}{1 + \varepsilon^*} \tag{11.44}$$

independent of the technology.

provide a determinate theory of the rate of profit and growth. Nor are labor values very useful in determining relative prices. We can certainly "transform" labor values into prices by means of the equations

$$\mathbf{P}_0' = \mathbf{a}_0'[\mathbf{I} - \mathbf{A}]^{-1}$$

and

$$\mathbf{P}' = \mathbf{a}_0'[\mathbf{I} - (1 + r)\mathbf{A}]^{-1}. \tag{11.9}$$

By substituting from the first into the second and solving for $\mathbf{P}$ we obtain

$$\mathbf{P}' = \mathbf{P}_0'[\mathbf{I} - \mathbf{A}][\mathbf{I} - (1 + r)\mathbf{A}]^{-1},$$

but nothing is gained by this transformation: as Paul Samuelson (1971) has emphasized, the technology $\begin{bmatrix} \mathbf{a}_0' \\ \mathbf{A} \end{bmatrix}$ and the profit rate r remain necessary and sufficient to determine prices after we reformulate the price equation as a transformation of labor values. There is no advantage of taking the indirect route of the transformation equation, which goes by way of the labor-values vector $\mathbf{P}_0$, when we can just as well take the direct route of Eq. (11.9).

However, as in the one-good case, a subsistence wage plus the classical saving equation $g = r$ suffice to close the neo-Marxian model, without reference to labor values or the rate of exploitation. But in the multiple-good case, the *composition* of subsistence must be specified in physical terms, a complication that does not exist when corn is the only commodity.

With no saving out of wages and no consumption out of profits, the subsistence wage gives us the equations

$$\mathbf{C}^* = \mathbf{C}^N, \tag{11.45}$$

$$\mathbf{P}'\mathbf{C}^N = 1. \tag{11.40}$$

These equations, along with the production and price equations

$$\mathbf{X} = \mathbf{C} + (1 + g)\mathbf{A}\mathbf{X}, \tag{11.4}$$

$$\mathbf{a}_0'\mathbf{X} = 1, \tag{11.6}$$

$$\mathbf{P}' = \mathbf{a}_0' + (1 + r)\mathbf{P}'\mathbf{A}, \tag{11.5}$$

provide adequate information to determine rates of profit and growth, as well as the output composition and distributive shares.

Moreover, the model is separable. Equations (11.5) and (11.40) form a determinate subsystem of $m + 1$ independent equations that permit us to solve for r^* and $\mathbf{P}^*$ without knowing the equilibrium composition of output.

On the other hand, the *shares* of income going to wages and profits depend not only on $\mathbf{P}^*$ and r^* but on the equilibrium $\mathbf{X}^*$. Specifically, profit and wage shares are

$$\frac{(1 + r^*)\mathbf{P}'^*\mathbf{A}\mathbf{X}^*}{\mathbf{P}'^*\mathbf{X}^*}, \qquad \frac{1}{\mathbf{P}'^*\mathbf{X}^*},$$

which are not independent of $\mathbf{X}^*$ unless the capital : output ratio is independent of $\mathbf{X}^*$. Thus, once again only special assumptions about technology or output proportions make the distribution of income — in terms of profit and wage *shares,* as distinct from profit and wage *rates* — independent of the composition of output.

The Cambridge Saving Equation

In the main, these results carry over even if we relax the saving assumptions. Take, for instance, Pasinetti's version of the Cambridge equation, which has capitalists saving a proper fraction s_C rather than all of their income, and workers saving a fraction s_W of their income, and assumes that workers effectively control the disposition of profits that accrue to the share of capital they own. In the one-good case, these assumptions led to the short-run saving equation

$$g = s(r, \delta) = s_W \frac{1 - a_1}{a_1} + (s_C - s_W)\delta r, \qquad (6.4)$$

and when ownership proportions δ and $1 - \delta$ have adjusted to steady-growth proportions $\hat{\delta}$ and $(1 - \hat{\delta})$,

$$g = s(r) = \max\left(s_W \frac{1 - a_1}{a_1}, s_C r\right). \qquad (6.5)$$

To apply this argument to the m-good case requires us to specify a mechanism for determining the structure of consumption as well as its level. In the neo-Marxian model, we continue to define a subsistence-consumption vector $\mathbf{C}^N$ that determines the profit rate and price level by adding the equation

$$\mathbf{P}'\mathbf{C}^N = 1 \qquad (11.40)$$

to the m-dimensional price equation (11.5). But $\mathbf{C}^N$ becomes a nominal, unobservable subsistence, since workers' consumption differs from $\mathbf{C}^N$ for two reasons: first, workers are now assumed to share in profit income to the extent of their past saving, and, second, workers save a fraction s_W of their total income. In addition to necessities, workers consume "luxuries,"

$$\mathbf{C}^L = \begin{bmatrix} C_1^L \\ \cdot \\ \cdot \\ \cdot \\ C_m^L \end{bmatrix},$$

with the value of workers' luxury consumption equal to the difference between their income from capital and their saving:

$$\mathbf{P}'\mathbf{C}^L = (1 - \delta)r\mathbf{P}'\mathbf{A}\mathbf{X} - s_W[1 + (1 - \delta)r\mathbf{P}'\mathbf{A}\mathbf{X}].$$

The total consumption of a single worker is

$$\mathbf{C}^W = \mathbf{C}^N + \mathbf{C}^L = \begin{bmatrix} C_1^N + C_1^L \\ \cdot \\ \cdot \\ \cdot \\ C_m^N + C_m^L \end{bmatrix},$$

which must satisfy the budget constraint

$$\mathbf{P}'\mathbf{C}^W = (1 - s_W)[1 + (1 - \delta)r\mathbf{P}'\mathbf{A}\mathbf{X}]. \tag{11.46}$$

Now, also, capitalists are assumed to consume as well as to save. Capitalists' consumption,

$$\mathbf{C}^C = \begin{bmatrix} C_1^C \\ \cdot \\ \cdot \\ \cdot \\ C_m^C \end{bmatrix},$$

satisfies the budget constraint

$$\mathbf{P}'\mathbf{C}^C = (1 - s_C)\delta r\mathbf{P}'\mathbf{A}\mathbf{X}, \tag{11.47}$$

and the market value of aggregate consumption is

$$\mathbf{P}'(\mathbf{C}^W + \mathbf{C}^C) = (1 - s_W)[1 + r\mathbf{P}'\mathbf{A}\mathbf{X}] + (s_W - s_C)\delta r\mathbf{P}'\mathbf{A}\mathbf{X}. \tag{11.48}$$

Now suppose $\mathbf{C}^N$ is given, and $\mathbf{C}^L$ and $\mathbf{C}^C$ are any consumption vectors satisfying (11.46) and (11.47) respectively, with $\mathbf{X}$ also satisfying

$$X = C + (1 + g)AX, \tag{11.49}$$

$$C = C^N + C^L + C^C = C^W + C^C.$$

Such an X exists for any g, but there is no guarantee that the solution X satisfies the condition of production feasibility. If it does, that is, if

$$a'_0 X = 1, \tag{11.6}$$

then we can postmultiply the price equation through by X to obtain

$$P'X = 1 + (1 + r)P'AX. \tag{11.50}$$

Next we premultiply (11.49) through by P' and substitute from (11.50) and (11.48). After rearranging terms, we have

$$g = s(r, \delta, X) = s_W \frac{P'X - P'AX}{P'AX} + (s_C - s_W)\delta r$$

or

$$g = s(r, \delta, X) = s_W \frac{1 - \kappa(r, X)}{\kappa(r, X)} + (s_C - s_W)\delta r. \tag{11.51}$$

In other words, satisfying the saving equation (11.51) is necessary for production feasibility. Observe that before specifying subsistence, that is, in the absence of (11.40), Eq. (11.51) is defined for all r between -1 and r_{max}.

Equation (11.51) is identical to the one-good, quasi-Kaldorian saving equation, except for the replacement of the fixed capital:output ratio a_1 by the variable ratio $\kappa(r, X)$. This has important implications. In the first place, the structure of the one-good, long-run (Pasinetti) equation carries over to the m-good case: with $\delta = \hat{\delta}(r)$, we have

$$g = s(r, X) = \max \left(s_W \frac{1 - \kappa(r, X)}{\kappa(r, X)}, s_C r \right). \tag{11.52}$$

Equation (11.52) is shown in Figure 11.5, along with the profit rate determined by subsistence consumption C^N. Observe that the $\hat{\delta} = 0$ portion of the saving function is no longer a vertical line, nor does it necessarily have a positive slope: its slope depends on the relationship of the output bundle X to r.

The equilibrium growth rate is determined by the intersection of the two curves. Formally, the determination of equilibrium is described by the two subsystems

$$\left. \begin{array}{c} P'C^N = 1 \\ P' = a'_0[I - (1 + r)A]^{-1} \end{array} \right\} \tag{11.53}$$

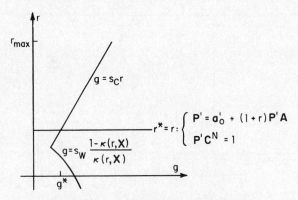

Figure 11.5 Neo-Marxian equilibrium

$$
\left.\begin{aligned}
g = s(r, \mathbf{X}) = s_W \frac{1 - \kappa(r, \mathbf{X})}{\kappa(r, \mathbf{X})} + (s_C - s_W)\delta r \\
= \max\left(s_W \frac{1 - \kappa(r, \mathbf{X})}{\kappa(r, \mathbf{X})}, s_C r\right). \\
\mathbf{X} = [\mathbf{I} - (1 + g)\mathbf{A}]^{-1}(\mathbf{C}^W + \mathbf{C}^C) \\
\mathbf{P}'\mathbf{C}^W = (1 - s_W)[1 + (1 - \delta)r\mathbf{P}'\mathbf{A}\mathbf{X}] \\
\mathbf{P}'\mathbf{C}^C = (1 - s_C)\delta r\mathbf{P}'\mathbf{A}\mathbf{X}.
\end{aligned}\right\} \quad (11.54)
$$

Once again the model is separable. The subsystem (11.53) determines $r*$ and $\mathbf{P}*$ independently of $g*$, $\mathbf{X}*$, and $\mathbf{C}*$. The equilibrium growth rate $g*$ is also independent of the composition of output and consumption,

$$g* = s_C r*,$$

except when equilibrium occurs in the $\hat{\delta} = 0$ region.

So once r is determined by a particular $\mathbf{C}^N$, substitution of another $\mathbf{C}^N$ compatible with the same r, like substitution of one $\mathbf{C}^L$ or $\mathbf{C}^C$ for another compatible with the budget constraints (11.46) and (11.47), affects the rate of growth only if r and $\kappa(r, \mathbf{X})$ are sufficiently small to make $s_W[1 - \kappa(r, \mathbf{X})]/\kappa(r, \mathbf{X})$ greater than $s_C r$, and in consequence to drive $\hat{\delta}$ to zero. For the composition of consumption to influence the growth rate, workers must end up owning all but a vanishing share of the capital stock.

One final point about Figure 11.5: as the saving function is drawn, its two branches intersect only once, as in the one-good case. There is no compelling reason to draw it this way, however. If the capital:output

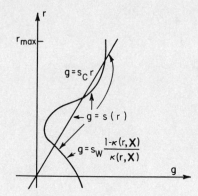

Figure 11.6 Saving function with disconnected intervals of peoples' capitalism

ratio varies sufficiently, there can be multiple intersections, and correspondingly, the $\hat{\delta} > 0$ and $\hat{\delta} = 0$ regions will each be composed of disconnected intervals, as in Figure 11.6. At the upper end of the saving function, however, in the neighborhood of r_{max}, we can be sure that the $\hat{\delta} > 0$ region obtains. For in the limit as r approaches r_{max}, $\kappa(r, \mathbf{X})$ approaches $1/(1 + r_{max})$ so that

$$s_W \frac{1 - \kappa(r, \mathbf{X})}{\kappa(r, \mathbf{X})} \leq s_W r_{max} < s_C r_{max},$$

which is to say that the $\hat{\delta} > 0$ region must obtain in the neighborhood of r_{max}.

If we shift the focus from rates of growth and profit to distributive shares, then there is no escaping the influence of consumption proportions on the outcome. As was the case even with the classical saving function $g = r$, the composition of consumption affects the composition of output and hence the capital:output ratio, on which the shares of profits and wages depend as well as on the profit rate itself.

A Role for Utility Maximization

One loose end of the neo-Marxian theory should be tied up. When it came to specifying workers' luxury consumption and capitalists' consumption, I argued that any vector $\mathbf{C}^L$ and any vector $\mathbf{C}^C$ would do so long as they satisfied the budget constraints (11.46) and (11.47). In particular, there is no reason why the specific consumption vector $\mathbf{C}^L$ might not emerge from a utility-maximization process on the part of workers

$$U^W(\mathbf{C}^W) = \max$$

subject to

$$\mathbf{P}'\mathbf{C}^W = (1 - s_W)[1 + (1 - \delta)r\mathbf{P}'\mathbf{AX}],$$

which gives $\mathbf{C}^L$ as the difference

$$\mathbf{C}^L = \mathbf{C}^W - \mathbf{C}^N.$$

By the same token $\mathbf{C}^C$ may be taken to emerge from the utility maximization of capitalists,

$$U^C(\mathbf{C}^C) = \max$$

subject to

$$\mathbf{P}'\mathbf{C}^C = (1 - s_C)\delta r\mathbf{P}'\mathbf{AX}.$$

But doesn't the introduction of utility maximization transform the neo-Marxian model into a neoclassical one? After all, doesn't the equilibrium now depend on consumers' preferences?

There are two separate issues. To be sure, consumer preferences affect equilibrium, but this hardly makes the model neoclassical. There remains a crucial difference between the role of preferences in the neo-Marxian model (or in the neo-Keynesian model, in which household preferences enter rather similarly) and their role in the neoclassical model: here consumption preferences determine the composition of output — if tonsorial styles change and workers and capitalists want more hair dryers and fewer razor blades, they will get them. $\mathbf{C}^W$ and $\mathbf{C}^C$ determine the composition of $\mathbf{X}^*$, but (provided $\hat{\delta} > 0$) not the rate of profit, the rate of growth, the real wage, or the structure of relative prices. By contrast, in the neoclassical model, not only the composition of output but also rates of growth and profit, the real wage, and the price structure respond to household utility maximization. A key difference is that in the neo-Marxian model, unlike the neoclassical model, s_W and s_C are not determined by life-cycle utility maximization.

What makes a model neo-Marxian (or neo-Keynesian) on the one hand or neoclassical on the other is not whether preferences enter into the model, but the role they play. What matters is the domain over which preferences are defined. In the neoclassical model, preferences are defined over future as well as present consumption, and the trade-off between the two, along with the assumption of full employment, determines the equilibrium configuration — r^*, g^*, and $\mathbf{P}^*$, as well as $\mathbf{X}^*$ and $\mathbf{C}^*$. In the neo-Marxian model, it is subsistence consumption and the saving propensities s_W and s_C that determine r^*, g^*, and $\mathbf{P}^*$;

barring $\hat{\delta} = 0$, the influence of household preferences is limited to $\mathbf{X}^*$ and $\mathbf{C}^*$. It is only when s_W and s_C are assumed to reflect a life-cycle utility-maximization process that the neo-Marxian (and neo-Keynesian) models and the neoclassical model might reasonably be said to begin to converge. But even were utility maximization assumed to underlie s_W and s_C, the convergence would only be partial: the three approaches still differ with respect to the role of the distribution of income in the saving function, not to mention differences with respect to full employment, the subsistence wage, and capitalists' animal spirits.

The Existence of Equilibrium

We have yet to establish that a neo-Marxian equilibrium actually exists. Provided $\mathbf{C}^N$ is producible, the existence of an equilibrium r^* and $\mathbf{P}^*$ that satisfies equation system (11.53) is obvious, but the same cannot be said for the remaining elements, comprising the vector $\langle g^*, \mathbf{X}^*, \mathbf{C}^* \rangle$, that must satisfy equation system (11.54). All we have established so far is that production feasibility, Eq. (11.6), is the key to generalizing the Pasinetti saving function to the m-good form of Eq. (11.51). But this does not tell us whether for a given r^*, there exists a corresponding vector $\langle g^*, \mathbf{X}^*, \mathbf{C}^* \rangle$. Conceivably equation system (11.54) may define an empty set. We must show the existence of the requisite vector $\langle g^*, \mathbf{X}^*, \mathbf{C}^* \rangle$.

The proof of the existence of equilibrium is a straightforward application of Brouwer's fixed-point theorem. A mapping of $\mathbf{X} \rightarrow \mathbf{X}^\circ$ is constructed in two steps. First we use the saving function to assign to each production-feasible $\mathbf{X}$ a growth rate g and a capital-stock distribution $\hat{\delta}$. Utility maximization in turn gives a consumption vector $\mathbf{C}^\circ$. Then the consumption vector $\mathbf{C}^\circ$ defines a growth rate g° and an output vector $\mathbf{X}^\circ$ via the production equation. By construction, this mapping satisfies the conditions of Brouwer's theorem. Its construction also ensures that a fixed point satisfies all the equilibrium conditions. The only difficulty in the argument is the step from $\mathbf{C}^\circ$ to $\mathbf{X}^\circ$: the mapping does not necessarily define a production-feasible vector when the growth rate g° is equal to -1. At $g^\circ = -1$, therefore, the definition of the step $\mathbf{C}^\circ \rightarrow \mathbf{X}^\circ$ must be revised to permit the production equation to be bypassed if necessary. This does not, however, invalidate the proof because it will be shown that at the fixed point of the mapping, the production equation is indeed satisfied.

Now to the proof itself. Define

$$\Lambda = \{\mathbf{X} \geq 0 : \mathbf{a}_0' \mathbf{X} = 1\}.$$

That is, let Λ be the set of all production-feasible vectors $\mathbf{X}$. Then begin by choosing any $\mathbf{X} \in \Lambda$. Define the corresponding $\hat{\delta}$ and g from the saving function

$$g = s_W \frac{1 - \kappa(r^*, \mathbf{X})}{\kappa(r^*, \mathbf{X})} + (s_C - s_W)\delta r^*$$

$$= \max\left(s_W \frac{1 - \kappa(r^*, \mathbf{X})}{\kappa(r^*, \mathbf{X})}, s_C r^*\right).$$

Next, define $\mathbf{C}^W$ and $\mathbf{C}^C$ from the constrained utility-maximization systems

$$U^W(\mathbf{C}^W) = \max$$

subject to

$$\mathbf{P}'*\mathbf{C}^W = (1 - s_W)[1 + (1 - \hat{\delta})r^*\mathbf{P}'*\mathbf{A}\mathbf{X}]$$

and

$$U^C(\mathbf{C}^C) = \max$$

subject to

$$\mathbf{P}'*\mathbf{C}^C = (1 - s_C)\hat{\delta}r^*\mathbf{P}'*\mathbf{A}\mathbf{X}.$$

Assume that the utility functions are both strictly quasi-concave so that the solutions to these maximization problems are unique. (These assumptions could be relaxed, but the point is not to establish the most general result possible.) Now set

$$\mathbf{C}^\circ = \mathbf{C}^W + \mathbf{C}^C$$

and—provided a solution exists—define $\mathbf{X}^\circ$, the image of $\mathbf{X}$, by the system

$$\left.\begin{aligned} \mathbf{X}^\circ &= [\mathbf{I} - (1 + g^\circ)\mathbf{A}]^{-1}\mathbf{C}^\circ \\ \mathbf{a}_0'\mathbf{X}^\circ &= 1 \\ g^\circ &\geq -1 \end{aligned}\right\} \tag{11.55}$$

There is, it should be observed, no guarantee that a solution exists to (11.55).[5] In the event that the system (11.55) defines an empty set, let

5. We can in fact construct a matrix $\mathbf{A}$ and utility functions U^W and U^C for which no solution exists. Let $\mathbf{C}^\circ$ and $\mathbf{A}$ be such that $\mathbf{P}'*\mathbf{A}\mathbf{C}^\circ$ is very small—this is where the appropriate choice of utility functions and technology comes in. Then since in general

$$\mathbf{P}'*\mathbf{C}^\circ = 1 + (r^* - g)\mathbf{P}'*\mathbf{A}\mathbf{X}$$

for any $\mathbf{X} \in \Lambda$, and

$$g° = -1$$

and define $\mathbf{X}°$ by the system

$$\left.\begin{array}{c} \mathbf{X}° = \theta°\mathbf{C}° \\ \mathbf{a}_0'\mathbf{X}° = 1 \\ 0 < \theta° < 1 \end{array}\right\} \qquad (11.56)$$

How do we know equation system (11.56) has a solution? We can show that it does if the solution set to (11.55) is empty. Define

$$\mathbf{X}° = \theta\mathbf{C}°,$$

from which we have directly

$$\mathbf{a}_0'\mathbf{X}° = \theta\mathbf{a}_0'\mathbf{C}°.$$

Now $\mathbf{a}_0'\mathbf{C}° > 1.$[6] Hence we can choose $\theta = \theta°$ in the interval $(0, 1)$ so that

$$\mathbf{a}_0'\mathbf{X}° = \theta°\mathbf{a}_0'\mathbf{C}° = 1. \qquad (11.57)$$

Thus the solution sets to (11.55) and (11.56) cannot both be empty, and the mapping $\mathbf{X} \rightarrow \mathbf{X}°$ is well defined. This mapping is continuous if we assume the utility functions are well behaved (that is, smooth). By construction, it carries the set Λ — which is a simplex and therefore closed, bounded, and convex — into itself. The mapping consequently satisfies the assumptions of Brouwer's fixed-point theorem; there exists an $\mathbf{X} \in \Lambda$ for which $\mathbf{X}° = \mathbf{X}$. To show that a fixed point of the mapping is indeed an equilibrium, it remains only to verify that such an $\mathbf{X}$ satisfies (11.55) rather than (11.56).

$$\mathbf{P}'{*}\mathbf{C}° = \mathbf{a}_0'\mathbf{C}° + (1 + r{*})\mathbf{P}'{*}\mathbf{A}\mathbf{C}°$$

for any $\mathbf{C}°$, we have

$$\mathbf{a}_0'\mathbf{C}° = 1 + (r{*} - g)\mathbf{P}'{*}\mathbf{A}\mathbf{X} - (1 + r{*})\mathbf{P}'{*}\mathbf{A}\mathbf{C}°.$$

Now, by assumption $\mathbf{P}'{*}\mathbf{A}\mathbf{C}°$ is vanishingly small, so the last term on the right-hand side can be ignored. And $r{*}$ can be chosen to be large enough to make the second term positive. Thus the right-hand side can be made to exceed unity. But $\mathbf{a}_0'\mathbf{X} \geq \mathbf{a}_0'\mathbf{C}°$, so that the condition $\mathbf{a}_0'\mathbf{X} = 1$ is violated.

6. To prove this, assume the opposite: $\mathbf{a}_0'\mathbf{C}° \leq 1$. By virtue of the indecomposability and productivity of $\mathbf{A}$, the matrix

$$[\mathbf{I} - (1 + g°)\mathbf{A}]^{-1}$$

increases monotonically with $g°$ and becomes unbounded as $g°$ approaches $g_{\max}$. This implies the existence of $g° \geq -1$ such that the equation

$$\mathbf{a}_0'[\mathbf{I} - (1 + g°)\mathbf{A}]^{-1}\mathbf{C}° = 1$$

holds. But the left-hand side of this equation is equal to $\mathbf{a}_0'\mathbf{X}°$, contrary to the assumption that the solution set to (11.55) is empty. This contradiction establishes the proposition.

Suppose the contrary. Then we have $\theta^\circ \in (0, 1)$ and

$$\mathbf{P}'*\mathbf{X} = \theta^\circ \mathbf{P}'*\mathbf{C}^\circ. \tag{11.58}$$

Substitute from the saving equation into Eq. (11.58) and we obtain

$$\mathbf{P}'*\mathbf{X} = \theta^\circ(-g\mathbf{P}'*\mathbf{AX} + 1 + r*\mathbf{P}'*\mathbf{AX})$$
$$= \theta^\circ[\mathbf{P}'*\mathbf{X} - (1 + g)\mathbf{P}'*\mathbf{AX}]$$

or

$$(1 - \theta^\circ)\mathbf{P}'*\mathbf{X} = -\theta^\circ(1 + g)\mathbf{P}'*\mathbf{AX}.$$

But the left-hand side of the last equation is necessarily positive, whereas the right-hand side is equal to zero—a contradiction establishing that a fixed point of the mapping $\mathbf{X} \to \mathbf{X}^\circ$ satisfies (11.55) rather than (11.56). Such an $\mathbf{X}$, along with its associated g and $\mathbf{C}$, defines an equilibrium $\langle g^*, \mathbf{X}^*, \mathbf{C}^* \rangle$ that satisfies (11.54): $\mathbf{C}^\circ$ is production- and utility-feasible by its very construction, and $g^\circ = g$ since $\mathbf{a}_0'\mathbf{X} = 1$ is sufficient for Eqs. (11.49) and (11.51)—which respectively define g° and g—to hold simultaneously for the same growth rate.

The Subsistence Wage

The labor theory of value apart, the formal apparatus of the neo-Marxian model thus extends straightforwardly to the multiple-commodity case. But the very ease of extending the model obscures a real problem: the interpretation of the fixed real wage. In the one-commodity model, subsistence is a fixed amount of corn per worker. But the extension of a fixed amount of corn to a fixed *vector* of goods raises substantive problems once subsistence is defined in social and historical terms rather than in biological terms. We shall analyze these problems first in the context of the classical saving equation

$$g = r, \tag{11.39}$$

and then we shall turn to a model characterized by the Cambridge equation

$$g = s(r, \delta, \mathbf{X}) = s_W \frac{1 - \kappa(r, \mathbf{X})}{\kappa(r, \mathbf{X})} + (s_C - s_W)\delta r. \tag{11.51}$$

In the first case, workers neither save nor enjoy non-wage income. The problem here is that a fixed consumption vector rules out the possibility of substituting one good for another within the worker's consumption basket. One does not have to be very neoclassically inclined to believe in the possibility of substitution, indeed to believe in substitution responsive to the relative prices of the various goods. But substitution poses a dilemma for the neo-Marxian model in specifying the real wage: in what terms is the wage fixed?

One way out is to consider subsistence consumption as a nominal basket of goods that workers struggle about but do not necessarily consume. That is, workers and capitalists may be assumed to bargain over a real wage that reflects a conventional consumption bundle in a given historical situation. The real wage emerges as a consequence of this struggle. Commodity prices must allow workers to purchase the "conventional" consumption bundle, the product of history and class struggle, with their nominal wages whether or not any particular worker wants to consume the conventional bundle. In nineteenth-century England, for example, workers as a class struggled for the social acceptance of white bread in the conventional bundle, whatever the tastes of individual workers between white and rye bread. In twentieth-century America the struggle shifted to automobiles and television sets, once again independent of the specific tastes of particular workers. In effect, conventional consumption serves as a vector of relative weights on commodity prices:

$$\mathbf{P}'\mathbf{C}^N = 1. \tag{11.40}$$

Adding this condition to the price equation

$$\mathbf{P}' = \mathbf{a}_0' + (1 + r)\mathbf{P}'\mathbf{A}$$

determines the rate of profit r^* as well as the structure of prices $\mathbf{P}(r^*)$.

Actual choice of consumption proportions can be determined in a separate process since any consumption vector that satisfies the budget constraint $\mathbf{P}'(r^*)\mathbf{C} = 1$ is consistent with $\mathbf{P}(r^*)$. (Needless to say, the choice of $\mathbf{C}$ will affect $\mathbf{X}$ and distributive shares.) In fact we can even allow $\mathbf{C}$ to be determined by utility maximization without sacrificing anything that is essential to the neo-Marxian model:

$$U(\mathbf{C}) = \max$$

subject to

$$\mathbf{P}'*\mathbf{C} = 1.$$

An alternative to this two-stage process is to fix the real wage in utility terms (Johansen 1963, p. 309). In other words, the consumption bundle would have to be adequate to keep the worker on or above a specified indifference curve. Formally the real wage would be fixed by limiting consumption to vectors such that

$$U(\mathbf{C}) \geq \overline{U}, \qquad (11.59)$$

with $\overline{U}$ presumably determined by class struggle and history. There are problems with this solution, however, that in my mind makes it less appropriate for a neo-Marxian model than the solution suggested in the previous paragraphs. First there is the problem of interpersonal utility comparisons that would arise were we to relax the assumption of identical workers. A second difficulty is that, even if all workers are assumed to be identical, constraining $U(\mathbf{C}) \geq \overline{U}$ does not determine a unique consumption vector. In fact, it merely defines an $(m - 1)$ dimensional subspace of "subsistence" consumption bundles. It might appear natural to resolve the remaining indeterminacy by *maximizing* the profit rate (or, equivalently, the growth rate) subject to (11.59). But maximization of profit and growth rates would appear to require conspiratorial, or at least concerted, behavior on the part of capitalists in order to achieve the consumption vector $\mathbf{C}$ satisfying (11.55) that is most conducive to their own interest. The problem is that a necessity for concerted action seems to me quite alien to Marx.

Examination of the Cambridge equation case strongly reinforces the notion of subsistence as a conventional consumption bundle, linked to actual consumption only indirectly. That is, the subsystem

$$\mathbf{P}'\mathbf{C}^N = 1,$$

$$\mathbf{P}' = \mathbf{a}_0' + (1 + r)\mathbf{P}'\mathbf{A}$$

determines r^* and $\mathbf{P}(r^*)$, and the subsystem

$$g = s(r^*) = s_W \frac{1 - \kappa(r^*, \mathbf{X})}{\kappa(r^*, \mathbf{X})} + (s_C - s_W)\delta r^*$$

$$= \max \left(s_W \frac{1 - \kappa(r^*, \mathbf{X})}{\kappa(r^*, \mathbf{X})}, \, s_C r^* \right),$$

$$U^W(\mathbf{C}^W) = \max$$

subject to

$$\mathbf{P}'\mathbf{C}^W = (1 - s_W)[1 + (1 - \delta)r\mathbf{P}'\mathbf{A}\mathbf{X}],$$

$$U^C(\mathbf{C}^C) = \max$$

subject to

$$\mathbf{P}'\mathbf{C}^C = (1 - s_C)\delta r^*\mathbf{P}'\mathbf{A}\mathbf{X},$$

$$\mathbf{X} = [\mathbf{I} - (1 + g)\mathbf{A}]^{-1}(\mathbf{C}^W + \mathbf{C}^C)$$

determines $\mathbf{X}^*$ and $\mathbf{C}^* = \mathbf{C}^W + \mathbf{C}^C$, as well as $\hat{\delta}$ and g^*. The growth rate g^* continues to be independent of $\mathbf{X}^*$,

$$g^* = s_C r^*,$$

except at a $\hat{\delta} = 0$ equilibrium.

If necessities were defined in biological terms, it might make sense to conceive of the worker as employing utility maximization only to determine luxury consumption, for we could determine $\mathbf{C}^L$ by subtraction:

$$\mathbf{C}^L = \mathbf{C}^W - \mathbf{C}^N.$$

Unfortunately, a biological definition of subsistence, as we saw early on, is both alien to the spirit of Marx's own writings and patently unrealistic. In any case, we cannot infer $\mathbf{C}^N$ from actual behavior. Nor can we infer $\mathbf{C}^N$ from equilibrium prices since $\mathbf{P}^*$ is compatible with *any* consumption vector that satisfies

$$\mathbf{P}'^*\mathbf{C} = 1.$$

Allowing utility maximization to guide the allocation of the worker's budget evidently blurs the distinction between "necessities" and "luxuries."

Thus whatever one assumes about the saving function, one is led to stress the moral component of subsistence (Marx 1867, p. 171). If workers and a significant proportion of the rest of society believe that laboring men and women are entitled to white bread as against rye, or to ride in their own cars rather than on public transportation, the subsistence basket will include these items, whether or not an individual worker opts for rye bread and the Transport Authority. Thus subsistence seems an ideological variable, or at the very least a variable with a strong ideological component! This interpretation is perhaps better regarded as suggesting a line of inquiry rather than as a fully developed idea. It seems fair to regard the problem of extending the definition of subsistence to the multiple-commodity case as an unresolved issue.

However, it seems even at this stage appropriate to relabel the subsistence wage to make the terminology more consistent with the thrust of the argument. I propose, therefore, except when my pen catches me unawares, to refer to the neo-Marxian wage as a "conventional wage."

The Neo-Keynesian Model

Mercifully, the neo-Keynesian model presents no new problems. The investment-demand function generalizes directly, provided capitalists

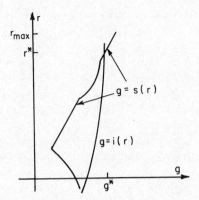

Figure 11.7 Neo-Keynesian equilibrium

are indifferent as to which branch of production they invest in—a natural corollary of perfect competition. With this assumption, equilibrium profit and growth rates are determined jointly by the investment-demand function

$$g = i(r) \tag{11.60}$$

and the saving function, which we shall take to have the Cambridge properties

$$g = s(r, \delta, \mathbf{X}) = s_W \frac{1 - \kappa(r, \mathbf{X})}{\kappa(r, \mathbf{X})} + (s_C - s_W)\delta r \tag{11.51}$$

and

$$g = s(r, \mathbf{X}) = \max \left(s_W \frac{1 - \kappa(r, \mathbf{X})}{\kappa(r, \mathbf{X})}, s_C r \right). \tag{11.52}$$

The graphs of the two functions (11.60) and (11.52) are illustrated in Figure 11.7 for the case where the $\hat{\delta} = 0$ and $\hat{\delta} > 0$ regions of (11.52) are interspersed. In Figure 11.7, equilibrium $\langle r^*, g^* \rangle$ is unique. But nothing in the structure of the model precludes multiple equilibria or speaks to the issue of stability.

Existence of Equilibrium

Needless to say, a diagram like Figure 11.7 does not prove the existence of equilibrium. A key assumption has been smuggled in: Eq. (11.52) must be *shown* to exist more or less as drawn. The formal argument for the existence of a continuous saving function simply extends the neo-Marxian proof of the existence of equilibrium $\langle g^*, \mathbf{X}^*, \mathbf{C}^* \rangle$ for a given

r^*. Instead of beginning with r^*, we vary r parametrically, showing that the saving function is defined for each r. Continuity follows from the fact that $\mathbf{P}$ varies continuously with r; this along with the assumption of well-behaved utility functions (positing, as in the neo-Marxian model, that current consumption is determined by household utility maximization) is sufficient to guarantee continuity of the mapping $r \rightarrow \mathbf{X}$, and therefore the mapping $r \rightarrow g$ defined by Eq. (11.51). If the investment-demand function is assumed to be continuous, the existence of neo-Keynesian equilibrium is guaranteed, although somewhat stronger restrictions on $i(r)$ are required to ensure an interior $(-1 < r < r_{max})$ equilibrium.

The Separability of $\hat{\delta} > 0$ Equilibrium

The same separability that characterizes the neo-Marxian model obtains here also. In the $\hat{\delta} > 0$ range of the saving function, equilibrium profit and growth rates, as well as the price vector $\mathbf{P}^*$, are independent of consumption demand. With $\hat{\delta} > 0$, we have

$$g = s_C r,$$

which together with Eq. (11.60) determines $\langle r^*, g^* \rangle$. The price equation allows us to solve directly for $\mathbf{P}^*$:

$$\mathbf{P}'^* = \mathbf{a}_0'[\mathbf{I} - (1 + r^*)\mathbf{A}]^{-1}.$$

As observed in connection with the neo-Marxian model, no difficulty is caused by letting household utility maximization dictate consumption proportions. If consumers want hair dryers rather than razor blades, they can have them without necessarily affecting profit and growth rates. Distributive shares are another matter. The neo-Keynesian model, like the neo-Marxian model, allows final demand to influence distributive shares through its effect on the capital:output ratio.

People's Capitalism

Equilibrium on the $\hat{\delta} = 0$ branch of the saving function presents different problems. Here equilibrium profit and growth rates, prices, and distributive shares depend on consumption preferences, for the $\hat{\delta} = 0$ relationship between g and r,

$$g = s_W \frac{1 - \kappa(r, \mathbf{X})}{\kappa(r, \mathbf{X})},$$

depends on $\mathbf{X}$.

Some care must be taken with the interpretation of Figure 11.7. We cannot determine whether or not equilibrium is found in its $\hat{\delta} = 0$ branch without knowledge of consumer preferences. For the saving function as a whole depends on $\mathbf{X}$ and thus on $\mathbf{C}^W$ and $\mathbf{C}^C$. With sufficiently large changes in $\kappa(r, \mathbf{X})$ as a function of $\mathbf{C}$, we could have equilibria on different branches of the saving function, each corresponding to the particular $\mathbf{X}$ appropriate to a given $\mathbf{C}$. Figure 11.8 illustrates this theoretical possibility. Figure 11.8(a) shows an equilibrium on the $\hat{\delta} > 0$ branch of the saving function. For sufficiently different household preferences, however, it is conceivable that the capital:output ratio might change enough to displace the equilibrium to the $\hat{\delta} = 0$ branch of the saving function, as in Figure 11.8(b).

Thus the invariance of r^*, g^*, and $\mathbf{P}(r^*)$ in the neo-Keynesian model with respect to consumption demand must be qualified in two respects. First, invariance is limited to the $\hat{\delta} > 0$ branch of the saving function. Second, by virtue of the existence of the $\hat{\delta} = 0$ branch, the invariance is marginal even along the $\hat{\delta} > 0$ branch; that is, only small changes in consumption demand are guaranteed to leave r^*, g^*, and $\mathbf{P}(r^*)$ intact.

Most readers would consider it anomalous for consumption demand not only to influence the capital:output ratio and through it, the distribution of income and wealth, but also to have such a powerful effect that workers come to own the entire capital stock. Indeed, many who are already predisposed to Keynesian (or Marxian) views of the world will find it difficult to take the $\hat{\delta} = 0$ branch of the saving function very seriously. I have said my piece on the subject in Chapter 6; but perhaps the conclusion of that chapter bears repeating, namely

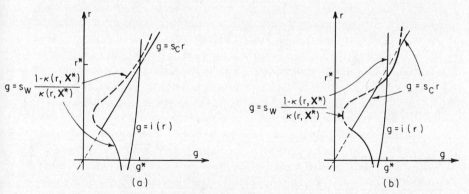

Figure 11.8 Two neo-Keynesian equilibria for different consumption demands. (a) $\hat{\delta} > 0$; (b) $\hat{\delta} = 0$

that the possibility of a long-run equilibrium from which capitalists are absent as a class, which the $\hat{\delta} = 0$ equilibrium is supposed to represent, hardly hinges on a mechanical calculation of saving propensities, capital : output ratios, and the like, but on issues of control and power.

Summary

The principal results of the one-good fixed-coefficient model *do* carry over to the multiple-good case. Neoclassical, neo-Marxian, and neo-Keynesian theories each add a sufficient number of independent relationships to the basic production model to make possible, if not certain, a just-determined equilibrium.

But none of the results that depend on a constant output : capital ratio survive, except under special assumptions about output proportions (equivalent to Sraffa's standard commodity) or the structure of production (Marx's equal organic composition of capital). This complicates the argument throughout, but it is in the neo-Marxian model that the economic significance of multiple commodities is greatest. On the one hand, the labor theory of value fails to determine equilibrium in the absence of equal organic composition of capital. On the other hand, and far more important, the existence of multiple goods undermines the meaning of the subsistence wage, so much so that it seems at the very least appropriate to reincarnate the Marxian wage as a "conventional wage," a standard of living around which class struggle revolves but which nobody need actually consume.

Finally, the multiple-good model permits an important clarification of the role of the utility function in general-equilibrium theory. Far from being the exclusive property of the neoclassical model, consumer sovereignty finds a place in all three models, neo-Marxian and neo-Keynesian as well as neoclassical. The difference between neoclassical and nonneoclassical models nevertheless remains important: in neo-Marxian and neo-Keynesian models the role of household utility maximization is limited to determining the composition of consumption and hence of output; in the neoclassical model, not only the composition of output but equilibrium profits and wages, growth rates, and relative prices also respond to household preferences.

It is fair to say that thus far the existence of a multiplicity of goods extends as well as complicates the analysis, but hardly contradicts intuition based on the one-good model. This felicitous state of affairs does not, however, survive the introduction of a multiplicity of technologies.

12 Multiple Technologies: The Reswitching Debate

It is not difficult conceptually to extend the models to allow for a multiplicity of techniques for producing each good. A specific technique h_i for the ith good is represented by an $(m + 1)$-vector which details labor and material inputs for a unit of output:

$$\begin{bmatrix} a_{0i}^{h_i} \\ a_{1i}^{h_i} \\ \cdot \\ \cdot \\ \cdot \\ a_{mi}^{h_i} \end{bmatrix}$$

With H_i techniques available for good i, the index h_i takes on integral values $1, \ldots, H_i$.

I shall reserve the term *technology* for a matrix of m techniques, one for each industry; $\mathbf{a}_0^h$ will denote a specific vector of labor coefficients and $\mathbf{A}^h$ an associated matrix of capital coefficients; a technology as a whole $\begin{bmatrix} \mathbf{a'}_0^h \\ \mathbf{A}^h \end{bmatrix}$ is described by a list $\mathbf{h}$ of the industry-specific techniques comprising the overall technology:

$$\begin{bmatrix} \mathbf{a'}_0^h \\ \mathbf{A}^h \end{bmatrix} = \begin{bmatrix} a_{01}^{h_1} & \cdot & \cdot & \cdot & a_{0m}^{h_m} \\ a_{11}^{h_1} & \cdot & \cdot & \cdot & a_{1m}^{h_m} \\ \cdot & & & & \cdot \\ \cdot & & & & \cdot \\ \cdot & & & & \cdot \\ a_{m1}^{h_1} & \cdot & \cdot & \cdot & a_{mm}^{h_m} \end{bmatrix}$$

with $\mathbf{h} = \langle h_1, \ldots, h_m \rangle$. There are in all ΠH_i technologies to consider.

At one level of discourse, all that remains to complete the story is to formulate a satisfactory rule assigning technologies to profit rates, for nowhere in the previous chapter does the argument require technological coefficients to be constant. The essential assumptions of the mathematics of Chapter 11—the boundedness of the profit domain $(-1, r_{\max})$ and the continuity of the price and output vectors as functions of the rate of profit—are met as well with ΠH_i as with one technology, provided we can find a rule for assigning technologies to profit rates that preserves the continuity of the price vector.

It is natural to insist that at each rate of profit, least-cost technologies prevail. That is, we define a price system for each profit rate and each technology by the equation

$$\mathbf{P}'_\mathbf{h} = \mathbf{a}_0'^\mathbf{h} + (1 + r)\mathbf{P}'_\mathbf{h}\mathbf{A}^\mathbf{h} \qquad (12.1)$$

and assign a particular technology and price vector to the profit rate r if and only if there is no alternative technology that produces any good at lower cost, given the price system $\mathbf{P_h}$. In other words, a specific technology $\mathbf{h}°$ is assigned to r if and only if for all technologies

$$\mathbf{P}'_{\mathbf{h}°} \leq \mathbf{a}_0'^\mathbf{h} + (1 + r)\mathbf{P}'_{\mathbf{h}°}\mathbf{A}^\mathbf{h}. \qquad (12.2)$$

Several questions come to mind: (1) Does a least-cost technology exist for every r? (2) More than one? (3) Does the least-cost assignment rule satisfy the requirement of continuity of prices as functions of r?

The answer to the first question is yes: proofs are given by Michio Morishima (1964), David Levhari (1965), and James Mirrlees (1969), building on Paul Samuelson's (1951) nonsubstitution theorem for Leontief matrices (which in effect treats the particular profit rate $r = 0$).

The answer to the second question is yes and no: there can be a number of points in the profit domain $(-1, r_{\max})$ at which two (or more) technologies tie for cost-minimization honors, but the number of such points is necessarily finite and the open intervals between these points are characterized by a single cost-minimizing technology. The points at which ties occur are called "switch" points; they are boundary points for the technologies that dominate on each side, and the two technologies yield identical (cost-minimizing) price vectors at these points.

The answer to the third question is also yes: this follows directly from the continuity of each of the technology-specific price equations (12.1) and the fact that prices associated with alternative cost-minimizing technologies are equal at switch points.

Indeed, the relationship between choice of technology and the rate of profit is simplified by another consequence of the nonsubstitution theorem (Levhari 1965, p. 101), namely, that the prices associated with a cost-minimizing technology are uniformly lower than the prices associated with any other technology. Thus the cost-minimizing technology for any rate of profit is the technology that *maximizes* the reciprocal $1/P_i$, where the particular choice of i is immaterial: for a given rate of profit, cost minimization amounts to maximization of the real wage!

In the one-good case examined in Chapter 9, we arrived at this result by a different route. There we ranked techniques directly by their profit rate at varying wage levels. The result was a wage-profit frontier of the form represented in Figure 9.1 and reproduced here as Figure 12.1. Observe that in line with the multiple-good convention fixing wages in money terms, the wage-axis is relabeled $1/P$. Evidently the wage-profit relationship is symmetric: cost-minimizing technologies both maximize the real wage for a given profit rate and maximize the profit rate for a given real wage.

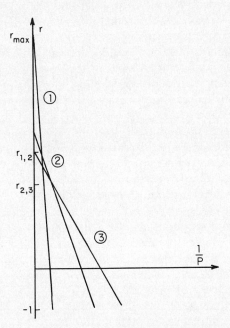

Figure 12.1 Wage-profit frontier with multiple technologies

Novelties of the Multiple-Good Case

Even though the effects of a multiplicity of technologies on the existence of long-run equilibrium are essentially similar in one-good and m-good models, long-run comparative statics and certain short-run results are quite different. It was observed in Chapter 9 that

1. In the neoclassical model, a higher rate of population growth is associated not only with a higher equilibrium rate of profit (assuming equilibrium to be stable), but also with a lower capital : output ratio.
2. In the neo-Marxian model, a higher conventional wage is associated with a higher capital : output ratio, as well as with a lower rate of profit.
3. In the neo-Keynesian model, more expansive animal spirits are associated with a lower capital : output ratio, as well as with a higher rate of profit.

As far as the rate of profit is concerned, these comparative statics carry over into the multiple-good versions of the models. But in the one-good model, the effect on the capital : output ratio depends on a negative relationship between the rate of profit r and the capital intensity of production. As we shall see, this relationship can no longer be assumed once we allow for a multiplicity of goods.

In the short run, the one-good model suggests even stronger results. Evidently no combination of biology and technology can determine the distribution of income in a one-technology model, since there are no technical margins to vary as the pie is sliced differently. But with a multiplicity of technologies the rate of capital accumulation is arguably the *cause* of changes in the rate of profit. If as time unfolds, accumulation leads to an increase in a_1, then one will observe a fall in r. Thus at any moment of time, prior capital accumulation appears to determine the distribution of income between wages and profits, without any need for the equations that distinguish neoclassical, neo-Marxian, and neo-Keynesian approaches; wage and profit rates are determined solely from production considerations. Of course, in a model with a finite number of technologies, the mapping from technology to profit rate is not a function: a technology determines an *interval* of profit rates with which it is compatible, rather than a single profit rate as in the continuous-substitution case. In Figure 12.1, technology 1 (represented by the circled number) maps to the interval $[r_{1,2}, r_{max}]$, technology 2 to $[r_{2,3}, r_{1,2}]$, and technology 3 to $[-1, r_{2,3}]$.

Observe first that the interpretation that cause and effect run from the size of the capital stock to the profit rate is misleading, quite apart from the minor difference between a mapping and a function. Accumulation alone does not determine the path of a_1 without some specific assumption about the short-run determination of employment, and neoclassical, neo-Marxian, and neo-Keynesian stories with respect to employment differ in the short run as well as the long.

In any case, the argument of the one-good model does not automatically carry over to the m-good case: there may or may not be a way of aggregating inputs of capital and output over m sectors that preserves the one-to-one correspondence between intervals of the profit domain and the capital : output ratio, and the inverse relationship characteristic of the one-good model may not survive in the m-good model.

We can quickly rule out the price vector $\mathbf{P}$ as a possible measure of capital values; it is evident that any measure of value that attempts to generalize the one-dimensional concept of a quantity of corn must, for a given technology, be invariant with respect to the rate of profit, and we already saw in the last chapter that the value of capital $\mathbf{P'AX}$ and the capital : output ratio $\kappa(r, \mathbf{X})$ can vary all over the lot as r varies — even with only one technology. But this variation is clearly due to price changes: $\mathbf{P}$ is a function of r. Variation in $\mathbf{P'AX}$ and $\kappa(r, \mathbf{X})$ does not in itself preclude the existence of a different measure of aggregate capital that preserves the remarkable feature of the one-good case of an inverse relationship between r and a_1.

Indeed, a long tradition, going back to Stanley Jevons, Eugen von Böhm-Bawerk, and Knut Wicksell, and argued most vigorously in our times by Paul Samuelson, held not only that, for a given set of technologies, the competitive profit rate and wage rate could be determined (at least up to an interval) from the capital : output ratio, but also that the inverse relationship between the competitive return to capital and the capital : output ratio was a general property with a physical basis in technological relationships, one that would survive in a multiple-good model. Hence it was thought legitimate to incorporate these properties in an "aggregate production function" relating three scalars — "output," "capital," and "labor" — each representing an aggregate of physical units. In the case of continuous substitution, the marginal productivity of "capital" becomes the derivative of the value of output with respect to the aggregate value of material inputs to production. In the case of discrete technologies, an analogous relationship might be assumed to hold; in place of a derivative relating a single rate of profit to a particular "capital : output" ratio, an interval of the profit domain would naturally correspond to each "capital : output" ratio. In both cases, of course, the aggregate production function would preserve the inverse relationship between the profit rate and the capital:output ratio.

Such biotechnological determinism, as I observed in Chapter 10, has obvious appeal for defenders of the capitalist faith: it emphasizes past accumulation in the explanation of income distribution. Its appeal, it was also observed, is more limited for neo-Marxians, who emphasize capitalists' present power vis-à-vis workers, and neo-Keynesians, who emphasize capitalists' investment propensities. It is not surprising therefore that it fell to heretics rather than to the orthodox to challenge the biotechnological explanation of distribution. As part of their critique Joan Robinson (1953–54, 1956), Piero Sraffa (1960), and others argued that, in the context of discrete alternatives, nothing prevented what came to be called "reswitching," that is, the phenomenon of a technology that is cost-minimizing in one interval of the profit domain coming back in a second, disjoint, interval. The Robinson-Sraffa conjecture is represented in Figure 12.2: after dictating a switch from technology 1 to technology 2 at $r_{1,2}$, cost minimization dictates reswitching to technology 1 at $r_{2,1}$.

Evidently, if reswitching occurs, then at least the discrete version of

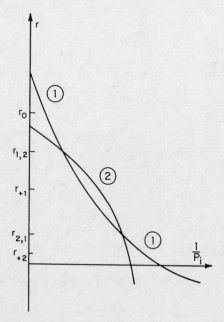

Figure 12.2   Reswitching along the wage-profit frontier

the aggregate production function cannot have the properties ascribed to it, and the various conjectures that rely on a one-to-one correspondence between points or intervals of the profit domain and capital intensity would have to be abandoned, not to mention those that rely on an inverse relationship between the rate of profit and capital intensity. In particular, prior accumulation could account for neither the profit rate nor its path over time.

Figure 12.2 shows why immediately. If a particular technology, like technology 1, is compatible with disconnected profit-rate intervals, then L and $\langle X_{-1,1} - C_{-1,1}, \ldots, X_{-1,m} - C_{-1,m} \rangle$ cannot uniquely determine the interval in which the profit rate lies. Over time, the inverse relationship between the competitive return to capital and the capital intensity of production fares as badly. If *any* measure of capital intensity determined solely by technology implies that capital deepening accompanies the switch from technology 1 to technology 2 as the rate of profit falls from r_0 to r_{+1}, then the same values would necessarily imply a lower capital intensity in the switch back to technology 1 as the rate of profit falls further to r_{+2}.

The debate about reswitching and related controversies engaged many of the "brightest and the best" on both sides of the Atlantic in the early 1960s; a detailed account is provided by Geoffrey Harcourt (1972), and my own summary is provided in the Notes on the Literature at the end of this book. To shorten a long story, the American side in the person of Levhari (1965) offered a proof of the impossibility of reswitching of discrete technologies. The triumph was short-lived, however. Luigi Pasinetti (1966b) and others quickly provided both counterexamples and a dissection of the error in the Levhari proof.

The Significance of Reswitching

The possibility that reswitching might take place does *not*, as has been observed, affect the existence of equilibrium in *any* of the three models. (But the possibility of reswitching may alter the positive relationship between rates of profit and growth that characterizes stable equilibria in the one-good model.) Thus it has been observed that the conclusions drawn from the one-good model with respect to the rate of profit and the capital : output ratio remain partly valid in the m-good case: it is principally the part that hinges on a negative relationship between r and a_1 that is called into question.

Nevertheless, Jevons-Wicksell-Samuelson biotechnological determinism suffered real damage as a result of the reswitching debate. Once it is proved impossible to generalize the inverse relationship between a_1

and r to the m-good case, it can hardly be argued that the quantities of material and human resources available for production and the technology jointly determine short-run distribution, and that changes in profit and wage rates are the *result* of accumulation: technology 1 is compatible with two distinct profit intervals, and the move from one of these to the other can have nothing to do with accumulation. Thus the inadequacy of short-run biotechnological determinism is not unique to a one-technology model, and resolvable by expanding the array of available technologies, as the biotechnological determinist wing of the neoclassical camp may have supposed.

It would be difficult to exaggerate the psychological impact of the debate and its outcome. There is no doubt that the prestige of the heretics rose while the prestige of the orthodox high priests fell. But I would contend that this impact owed more to the stakes that had been implicitly wagered than to the intrinsic importance of the debate itself.

The problem is that the points scored against biotechnological determinism have been interpreted as points against neoclassical theory. But to tar neoclassical theory with the biotechnological brush is — in my judgment — an error: despite its espousal by some neoclassical economists, biotechnological determinism is part of the short-run neoclassical story only in its Chicago version, not in the more general version of neoclassical theory. It seems a bit unreasonable to condemn a theory because of the excesses of some who have espoused it.

In any case, the more telling criticisms against short-run biotechnological determinism seem to me to lie in another area altogether, in the labor-market assumptions which the Chicago story requires to support the notion that prior accumulation determines the choice of technology: even in a one-good model, prior accumulation determines the capital: output ratio only in conjunction with the assumption that the market mechanism brings about full employment in each period, not just in the long run. A conventional wage, animal spirits, or gradual adjustment of the demand and supply of labor lead to very different theories of distribution even with the capital stock given. And the time path of capital accumulation can be said to "determine" the paths of profit and wage rates only if one begs the question of what determines accumulation. Again neoclassical, neo-Marxian, and neo-Keynesian models have very different stories to tell.

Reswitching is even less relevant to long-run models of steady growth. In the long run, as we have seen in Chapter 10, the rate of population growth can by itself determine *at most* the rate of growth: even in the one-good model, the steady-state capital: output ratio is endogenously determined in neoclassical, as well as in neo-Marxian and neo-Keynesian theory. Thus reswitching could at most affect the uniqueness and stability of equilibrium, not its existence. The existence of equilibrium in the long-run neoclassical model, contrary to the claims of Piero Garegnani (1966, p. 565) and others, is no more affected by the possibility of reswitching than it is in the neo-Marxian or neo-Keynesian model. As for the stability of equilibrium, it would take an explicit formulation of disequilibrium dynamics in the three models — beyond the scope of both the reswitching critique and this book — to demonstrate that the heterogeneity of capital adds more instability to the neoclassical model than to the neo-Marxian and neo-Keynesian models.

In short, the real issue lies in the differences between the three approaches, not in the esoterica of reswitching. If God himself were to appear in a whirlwind and offer to limit the set of feasible technologies to those for which reswitching was impossible, or even to guarantee that feasible technologies would meet the stringent requirements for the existence of a suitable capital aggregate (Solow 1955–56), it would hardly make the neoclassical model more compelling in the long run or biotechnological determinism more convincing in the short. But if the absence of reswitching or the possibility of aggregating capital would not strengthen inherently weak arguments, neither does the possibility of reswitching and the problems of aggregating capital detract much from those arguments.

13 Continuous Substitution

The results of introducing continuous substitution into the m-good model parallel the one-good case. Continuous substitution makes a real difference only in the neoclassical model: as before, high substitution elasticities ensure the existence of neoclassical equilibrium, whereas modest substitution elasticities give results akin to the fixed proportions model.

Formally, the only departure from the fixed proportions case is that the elements of $\begin{bmatrix} \mathbf{a}_0' \\ \mathbf{A} \end{bmatrix}$ become variables linked together by a set of m constant-returns-to-scale production functions of the general form

$$\frac{1}{a_{0i}} = f^i\left(\frac{a_{1i}}{a_{0i}}, \ldots, \frac{a_{mi}}{a_{0i}}\right), \qquad i = 1, \ldots, m, \qquad (13.1)$$

and by the marginal-productivity relationships $MP_K = (1 + r)$ and $MP_L = W \equiv 1$, which become, respectively,

$$P_i f_j^i \begin{Bmatrix} = \\ > \\ \leq \end{Bmatrix} P_j(1 + r) \quad \text{as} \quad a_{ji} \begin{Bmatrix} > \\ = \end{Bmatrix} 0, \qquad i, j = 1, \ldots, m, \quad (13.2)$$

$$P_i\left(f^i - \sum_h f_h^i \frac{a_{hi}}{a_{0i}}\right) \begin{Bmatrix} = \\ > \\ \leq \end{Bmatrix} 1 \quad \text{as} \quad a_{0i} \begin{Bmatrix} > \\ = \end{Bmatrix} 0, \qquad i = 1, \ldots, m, \quad (13.3)$$

with f_j^i representing the derivative of f^i with respect to a_{ji}/a_{0i}. As in the one-good case, the marginal-productivity relationships jointly imply the price equation

$$P_i = a_{0i} + (1 + r) \sum_h P_h a_{hi}, \qquad i = 1, \ldots, m, \qquad (13.4)$$

284

so m of the marginal-productivity relationships can be suppressed without losing any information. It turns out to be convenient to suppress the labor equation, (13.3), so we are left with (13.1), (13.2), and (13.4) to determine $\mathbf{P}$, $\mathbf{a}_0$, and $\mathbf{A}$ as functions of r.

The Impossibility of Reswitching

One important point of difference with the preceding chapter might be noted at once: the impossibility of reswitching in the continuous-substitution case. This is easily shown by the following argument. Let r_1 and r_2 be two profit rates assumed to map to the same $\begin{bmatrix} \mathbf{a}_0' \\ \mathbf{A} \end{bmatrix}$. Now suppose that there are two goods i and j that are used as inputs in each other's production. Then, denoting the prices associated with r_1 by P_i^1 and P_j^1 and the prices associated with r_2 by P_i^2 and P_j^2, we have

$$P_i^1 f_j^i = P_j^1(1 + r_1),$$
$$P_i^2 f_j^i = P_j^2(1 + r_2).$$

But since r_1 and r_2 are assumed to map to the same $\begin{bmatrix} \mathbf{a}_0' \\ \mathbf{A} \end{bmatrix}$, f_j^i is necessarily identical in the two equations. So we can combine the two equations into one:

$$\frac{P_i^1}{P_i^2} = \frac{P_j^1(1 + r_1)}{P_j^2(1 + r_2)}. \tag{13.5}$$

Similarly, we may write

$$\frac{P_j^1}{P_j^2} = \frac{P_i^1(1 + r_1)}{P_i^2(1 + r_2)}. \tag{13.6}$$

Now substitute from (13.6) into (13.5) and cancel out the common factor P_i^1/P_i^2. We have

$$(1 + r_1)^2 = (1 + r_2)^2, \tag{13.7}$$

which in view of the nonnegativity constraint

$$1 + r \geq 0$$

leads directly to the result

$$r_1 = r_2.$$

The argument is somewhat more complicated if goods i and j are not directly utilized in each other's production, but by virtue of the assumption of indecomposability (every good requires something of every other good, directly or indirectly, in its production), we can always construct chains of marginal-productivity equations linking any two goods and reach an equation similar to (13.7), with both sides of the equation raised to a power reflecting the lengths of the chains connecting goods i and j.

This result does not imply that "capital" can be aggregated. The absence of reswitching removes one obstacle to the construction of a value aggregate which maintains both (1) a one-to-one relationship with $\begin{bmatrix} \mathbf{a}_0' \\ \mathbf{A} \end{bmatrix}$ and (2) a monotonic relationship with the profit rate. But the absence of this particular obstacle does not establish the existence of such an aggregate, and the other obstacles are indeed formidable, as Robert Solow has long ago (1955–56) shown.

In any case "aggregate capital" is irrelevant to the present formulation of the problem. The production relations (13.1) are defined in purely physical terms, and "capital" enters each production function as a vector of commodity inputs, not a value aggregate. There is thus no circularity in the present characterization of capital and production, as distinct from the aggregate production function in which "capital" appears with labor as one of two arguments, a concept criticized with telling effect by Joan Robinson and her followers in Cambridge, England, during the 1950s and 1960s. (See the Notes on the Literature at the end of the book for further discussion.)

The Neoclassical Model

With this as background, we can turn our attention directly to the neoclassical model. Its structure carries over intact from the fixed-proportions case. For any r, we start with Eqs. (13.1)–(13.4). By virtue of utility maximization,

$$U(\mathbf{C}^1, \mathbf{C}^2) = \max \tag{11.16}$$

subject to

$$\mathbf{P}'\mathbf{C}^1 + \frac{\mathbf{P}'\mathbf{C}^2}{1+r} = 1, \tag{11.17}$$

we have demand functions $\mathbf{C}^1(r)$ and $\mathbf{C}^2(r)$. For a given rate of growth g, aggregate demand is

$$\mathbf{C}(r, g) = \mathbf{C}^1(r) + \frac{\mathbf{C}^2(r)}{1+g}. \tag{11.19}$$

But g is not arbitrary, for r and g are related by requirements of production and ownership feasibility, as reflected in the production equation

$$\mathbf{X}(r, g) = [\mathbf{I} - (1 + g)\mathbf{A}]^{-1}\mathbf{C}(r, g), \tag{11.21}$$

the output-normalizing equation

$$\mathbf{a}_0'\mathbf{X}(r, g) = 1, \tag{11.22}$$

and the saving equation

$$g = \beta(r)\left[\frac{1}{\kappa(r, \mathbf{X}(r, g))} - (1 + r)\right] - 1, \tag{11.29}$$

with $\beta(r)$ the average propensity to save

$$\beta(r) = \frac{\mathbf{P}'\mathbf{C}^2(r)}{1 + r} = 1 - \mathbf{P}'\mathbf{C}^1(r).$$

As in the fixed-proportions case, the saving function $g = s(r)$ defined by (11.29) and (11.21) also satisfies (11.22) for any r and associated $\begin{bmatrix} \mathbf{a}_0' \\ \mathbf{A} \end{bmatrix}$.

In formal terms, the issue is what a positive elasticity of substitution in production does to the range of $s(r)$. In particular, what must be assumed to make its range equal to $(-1, +\infty)$, and thereby assure the existence of equilibrium for any exogenously given rate of population growth?

We shall cast our answer in terms of what seems the most natural extension of the constant-elasticity-of-substitution production function, namely the class of production functions

$$\frac{1}{a_{0i}} = \gamma_i \left[\eta_{1i}\left(\frac{a_{1i}}{a_{0i}}\right)^{-\rho_i} + \cdots + \eta_{mi}\left(\frac{a_{mi}}{a_{0i}}\right)^{-\rho_i} + 1 - \sum_h \eta_{hi} \right]^{-1/\rho_i},$$

$$\gamma_i, \eta_{1i}, \ldots, \eta_{mi} > 0, \qquad \sum_h \eta_{hi} < 1,$$

or in more symmetric form,

$$1 = \gamma_i^{-\rho_i}\left[\sum_h \eta_{hi}a_{hi}^{-\rho_i} + \left(1 - \sum_h \eta_{hi}\right)a_{0i}^{-\rho_i} \right]. \tag{13.8}$$

Observe that the elasticity of substitution σ_{hj}^i between any two inputs h and j is constant not only over the domain of those inputs, but also across pairs of inputs; thus we can write

$$\sigma^i = \frac{1}{1 + \rho_i}$$

uniquely for each production function, suppressing the input indices.

The results, as was suggested at the outset of this chapter, parallel the one-good case. If $\sigma^i \geq 1$ for all i ($0 \geq \rho_i \geq -1$), then the range of $s(r)$ becomes equal to $(-1, +\infty)$ and the existence of equilibrium is guaranteed. However, the existence of only one good whose production function exhibits less than unitary elasticity is sufficient to put the existence of equilibrium in doubt: $\sigma^i < 1$ for some good i ($\rho_i > 0$) puts a finite limit on the growth rate, and the range $(-1, g_{max})$ may or may not include the exogenously given population growth rate n.

These assertions will be proved successively. First we consider the case in which all σ^i are greater than or equal to unity. It will be shown that as the rate of profit falls toward its minimum r_{min}, the capital : output ratio $\kappa(r, \mathbf{X})$ approaches $(1 + r_{min})^{-1}$, with the result that the saving function $s(r)$ defined by (11.29) and (11.21) approaches -1. It will then be shown that as r increases without bound, the value of output $\mathbf{P}'\mathbf{X}$ remains finite, so that $s(r)$ goes to $+\infty$. Thus the range of $s(r)$ is the interval $(-1, +\infty)$. The introduction of one good i for which $\sigma^i < 1$ changes the argument in one critical way: r has a finite maximum, and as r approaches r_{max}, $\kappa(r, \mathbf{X})$ approaches $(1 + r_{max})^{-1}$ and $s(r)$ approaches -1. Hence

$$\lim_{r \to r_{max}} s(r) = \lim_{r \to r_{min}} s(r) = -1,$$

so $s(r)$, a continuous function, has a finite maximum. Thus it is possible that its range does not include $g = n$.

Now for the proofs of these assertions.

The Behavior of $s(r)$ at r_{min}

With production defined by (13.8), the mapping from r to $\mathbf{P}$, $\mathbf{a}_0$, and $\mathbf{A}$ is governed by the relationships

$$P_i \gamma_i^{-\rho_i} \eta_{ji} a_{ji}^{-(1+\rho_i)} \begin{Bmatrix} = \\ \leq \end{Bmatrix} P_j(1 + r) \quad \text{as} \quad a_{ji} \begin{Bmatrix} > \\ = \end{Bmatrix} 0, \qquad i, j = 1, \ldots, m,$$

$$(13.9)$$

$$P_i = a_{0i} + (1 + r) \sum_h P_h a_{hi}, \qquad i = 1, \ldots, m, \qquad (13.4)$$

$$1 = \gamma_i^{-\rho_i} \left[\sum_h \eta_{hi} a_{hi}^{-\rho_i} + \left(1 - \sum_h \eta_{hi}\right) a_{0i}^{-\rho_i} \right], \qquad i = 1, \ldots, m. \quad (13.8)$$

Multiplying (13.9) through by a_{ji} and summing over j gives

$$P_i \gamma_i^{-\rho_i} \sum_j \eta_{ji} a_{ji}^{-\rho_i} = (1 + r) \sum_j P_j a_{ji},$$

and substituting the left-hand side for the right in (13.4) gives

$$P_i = a_{0i} + P_i \gamma_i^{-\rho_i} \sum_h \eta_{hi} a_{hi}^{-\rho_i}.$$

Now solve for a_{0i}/P_i to obtain

$$\frac{a_{0i}}{P_i} = 1 - \gamma_i^{-\rho_i} \sum_h \eta_{hi} a_{hi}^{-\rho_i},$$

which in combination with (13.8) yields

$$\frac{a_{0i}}{P_i} = \gamma_i^{-\rho_i} \left(1 - \sum_h \eta_{hi} \right) a_{0i}^{-\rho_i} \tag{13.10}$$

and

$$P_i = \gamma_i^{\rho_i} \left(1 - \sum_h \eta_{hi} \right)^{-1} a_{0i}^{1+\rho_i}. \tag{13.11}$$

At this point observe that as the rate of profit falls, the profit-maximizing own-intensity of each commodity, a_{ii}, rises. If $\sigma^i > 1$, a_{ii} is bounded from above by $\gamma_i^{-1} \eta_{ii}^{1/\rho_i}$ for $0 > \rho_i > -1$, so $(1 + r)$ is bounded by $\gamma_i \eta_{ii}^{-1/\rho_i}$ from below.[1] Thus the greatest lower bound to the gross profit rate is defined by

$$1 + r_{min} = \max_i \gamma_i \eta_{ii}^{-1/\rho_i}.$$

Now consider what happens to $s(r)$ as $(1 + r)$ falls to $(1 + r_{min})$, which for definiteness we shall associate with good i. From (13.8), a_{0i} approaches 0 as a_{ii} approaches its maximum value. Hence from (13.10) and (13.11) both a_{0i}/P_i and P_i approach 0. But as P_i approaches 0, it pays to use good i to the exclusion of other inputs in the production of *every* good, unless the prices of other produced goods fall to 0 as fast. In any case, a glance at (13.4) and (13.8) will verify that as $(1 + r)$ approaches $(1 + r_{min})$, it becomes progressively less profitable to utilize labor in the production of any good, not just good i. Thus, a_{0j} approaches 0 for all goods, and consequently, by virtue of (13.11), *every* P_j goes to 0. But then too,

---

1. In the Cobb-Douglas case ($\sigma^i = 1$) the production function becomes defined by the limit of (13.8) as ρ_i approaches 0,

$$1 = \gamma_i \prod_h a_{hi}^{\eta_{hi}} a_{0i}^{1 - \sum_h \eta_{hi}},$$

and the gross rate of profit is bounded from below by -1. The argument goes through with hardly any modification even if *all* goods are produced by means of Cobb-Douglas production functions.

according to (13.10), so does every a_{0j}/P_j approach 0. However, by assumption, $\mathbf{a}_0'\mathbf{X} = 1$. Consequently, the value of gross output $\mathbf{P}'\mathbf{X}$ approaches infinity as r goes to $r_{\min}$:

$$\mathbf{P}'\mathbf{X} = \sum_h \frac{P_h}{a_{0h}} a_{0h}X_h > \min_h \frac{P_h}{a_{0h}} \sum a_{0h}X_h = \min_h \frac{P_h}{a_{0h}} \longrightarrow +\infty.$$

So, as r approaches $r_{\min}$, the output : capital ratio

$$\frac{1}{\kappa(r, \mathbf{X})} = \frac{\mathbf{P}'\mathbf{X}}{\mathbf{P}'\mathbf{A}\mathbf{X}} = (1 + r)\frac{\mathbf{P}'\mathbf{X}}{\mathbf{P}'\mathbf{X} - \mathbf{a}_0'\mathbf{X}} \tag{13.12}$$

approaches $(1 + r_{\min})$, and desired saving approaches -1:

$$\beta(r)\left[\frac{1}{\kappa(r, \mathbf{X})} - (1 + r)\right] - 1 = \beta(r)[(1 + r_{\min}) - (1 + r_{\min})] - 1 = -1.$$
$$\tag{13.13}$$

The Behavior of $s(r)$ as r Approaches ∞

At the opposite end of the profit interval, I have asserted that desired saving increases without bound. The proof of this proposition lies in the contradiction implicit in assuming the contrary. Desired saving,

$$\beta(r)\left[\frac{1}{\kappa(r, \mathbf{X})} - (1 + r)\right] - 1 = \beta(r)\frac{\mathbf{a}_0'\mathbf{X} \cdot}{\mathbf{P}'\mathbf{X} - \mathbf{a}_0'\mathbf{X}}(1 + r) - 1, \quad (13.14)$$

evidently approaches $+\infty$ with r, unless (1) $\beta(r)$ approaches 0 or (2) $\mathbf{P}'\mathbf{X}$ approaches ∞. As a relatively modest assumption about the utility function, we shall simply assume the average saving propensity $\beta(r)$ is bounded away from 0. It remains to demonstrate that $\mathbf{P}'\mathbf{X}$ is bounded.

Recall the basic equilibrium conditions

$$P_i\gamma_i^{-\rho_i}\eta_{ji}a_{ji}^{-(1+\rho_i)}\begin{Bmatrix}=\\\leq\end{Bmatrix} P_j(1 + r) \quad \text{as} \quad a_{ji}\begin{Bmatrix}>\\=\end{Bmatrix} 0, \quad i, j = 1, \ldots, m,$$
$$\tag{13.9}$$

$$P_i = a_{0i} + (1 + r)\sum_h P_h a_{hi}, \quad i = 1, \ldots, m, \tag{13.4}$$

$$1 = \gamma_i^{-\rho_i}\left[\sum_h \eta_{hi}a_{hi}^{-\rho_i} + \left(1 - \sum_h \eta_{hi}\right)a_{0i}^{-\rho_i}\right] \quad i = 1, \ldots, m, \tag{13.8}$$

and the consequence derived from these three sets of relationships:

$$P_i = \gamma_i^{\rho_i}\left(1 - \sum_h \eta_{hi}\right)^{-1}a_{0i}^{1+\rho_i}. \tag{13.11}$$

From (13.11) we have

$$\mathbf{P}'\mathbf{X} = \sum_i a_{0i}^{p_i}\gamma_i^{p_i}\left(1 - \sum_h \eta_{hi}\right)^{-1}a_{0i}X_i,$$

with $a_{0i}X_i < 1$ for all i by virtue of the normalization $\mathbf{a}_0'\mathbf{X} = 1$. Hence for $\mathbf{P}'\mathbf{X}$ to remain finite, it suffices that no a_{0i} approach 0 as r goes to ∞. Now suppose the contrary. Then taking (13.8) and (13.9) together, there must be some input a_{ji}, $j \neq i$, which continues to enter into the production of i at a nonvanishing rate as r goes to ∞. Moreover, from (13.11) we have P_i approaching 0 as r approaches ∞, and from (13.4) we have

$$\frac{P_i}{P_j} \geq a_{ji}(1 + r).$$

Therefore,

$$\frac{P_i}{P_j} \to \infty \quad \text{as} \quad r \to \infty$$

and

$$P_j \to 0 \quad \text{as} \quad r \to \infty.$$

But, invoking (13.11) again, if P_j goes to 0, so does a_{0j}, which implies the existence of an input a_{hj}, $h \neq j$ that remains finite as r goes to ∞. Thus, as before,

$$\frac{P_j}{P_h} \to \infty \quad \text{and} \quad P_h \to 0.$$

By repeating the argument, we can extend the chain indefinitely. But the number of goods is finite. So before we have gone $m + 1$ "rounds," we must have a cycle in which some good i appears twice as a material input in the production of other goods. Consider the product chain of price ratios between these two appearances:

$$\frac{P_i}{P_j}\frac{P_j}{P_h}\cdots\frac{P_m}{P_i}.$$

Each of the factors of this expression approaches ∞, but by cancelling denominators with successive numerators, we can see that the product must be unity! This is the contradiction that proves that no a_{0i} can go to 0 and hence that $\mathbf{P}'\mathbf{X}$ must remain finite, so that $s(r)$ increases without bound.

Thus, if all goods are produced with an elasticity of substitution at least equal to unity, the range of the neoclassical saving function $s(r)$ is equal to the interval $(-1, +\infty)$; and an equilibrium must exist. But—

and this brings us to the final part of the argument — the existence of one good for which σ^i is less than unity changes this result dramatically. The range of the saving function becomes finite, and the existence of neoclassical equilibrium is no longer guaranteed.

Inelastic Substitution

If $\sigma^i < 1$, then ρ_i is positive. Consequently, as r increases, a_{ii} must fall in order for the marginal-productivity equation

$$\gamma_i^{-\rho_i}\eta_{ii}a_{ii}^{-(1+\rho_i)} = 1 + r$$

to hold. Finally, a_{ii} approaches a lower limit $\gamma_i^{-1}\eta_{ii}^{1/\rho_i}$ dictated by (13.8), as $(1 + r)$ approaches its upper limit, $\gamma_i\eta_{ii}^{-1/\rho_i}$. But as a_{ii} approaches this lower limit, a_{0i} must increase without bound, or else (13.8) would be violated. As a result, P_i increases without bound as $(1 + r)$ approaches $\gamma_i\eta_{ii}^{-1/\rho_i}$. Now as P_i approaches infinity, other industries can react in one of two ways: either industry j reduces its utilization of good i per unit of output to the vanishing point, $a_{ij} \to 0$, or the price of good j increases without bound, $P_j \to \infty$. (The price equation (13.4) confirms that these are the only two possibilities.) Now if P_j increases without bound, other industries face the same choice, either $a_{jh} \to 0$ or $P_h \to \infty$.

Thus, overall, the production system behaves in one of two ways as $(1 + r)$ approaches $\gamma_i\eta_{ii}^{-1/\rho_i}$. Either *all* prices increase without bound, in which case we have

$$\mathbf{P'X} = \sum a_{0i}^{\rho_i}\gamma_i^{\rho_i}\left(1 - \sum_h \eta_{hi}\right)^{-1} a_{0i}X_i$$

$$\geq \min_i a_{0i}^{\rho_i}\gamma_i^{\rho_i}\left(1 - \sum_h \eta_{hi}\right)^{-1} \sum_i a_{0i}X_i$$

$$= \min_i a_{0i}^{\rho_i}\gamma_i^{\rho_i}\left(1 - \sum_h \eta_{hi}\right)^{-1} \to \infty$$

and

$$\beta(r)\,\frac{\mathbf{a_0'X}}{\mathbf{P'X} - \mathbf{a_0'X}}\,(1 + r) - 1 \to -1.$$

Or, there exists a subset of goods whose prices become infinite that are eliminated from production (and consumption) as $(1 + r)$ becomes greater than or equal to $\gamma_i\eta_{ii}^{-1/\rho_i}$. But the second possibility violates an assumption made early on about the production system, namely that it be indecomposable, with each good utilizing, directly or indirectly, something of every other good in its production. Hence we may conclude—as long as we insist on indecomposability—that $\gamma_i \eta_{ii}^{-1/\rho_i}$ represents the maximum feasible (gross) rate of profit, and that $s(r)$ approaches a finite value, -1, at r_{max}. Finally, since we have already observed that $s(r)$ approaches a limiting value of -1 at r_{min} (and this result is unchanged by introducing one or more goods produced under conditions of less-than-unitary substitution elasticity), and since $s(r)$ is continuous, this function necessarily has a finite maximum in the interval (r_{min}, r_{max}).

Indeed, indecomposability leads to an even stronger and somewhat surprising result. Indecomposability in effect rules out the possibility of a substitution elasticity in excess of unity, since an obvious property of the production function (13.8) with $\rho_i < 0$ is the possibility of production with as few as one input. But the existence of equilibrium for an arbitrarily chosen population growth rate requires a substitution elasticity *at least* equal to unity everywhere. Thus, in the class of production functions for which the elasticity of substitution is constant and uniform, the only one that simultaneously satisfies the indecomposability assumption and guarantees the existence of neoclassical equilibrium is one for which the elasticity of substitution is *exactly* unity. In other words, to guarantee the existence of neoclassical equilibrium under the assumption of indecomposability, we must assume that all industries operate according to Cobb-Douglas production functions!

The Neo-Marxian Model

The neo-Marxian (and neo-Keynesian) models are changed relatively little by the introduction of continuous substitution. In the neo-Marxian model equilibrium prices and factor proportions are determined by the conventional wage

$$P_1 C_1^N + \cdots + P_m C_m^N = 1 \tag{13.15}$$

in combination with the m production functions

$$\frac{1}{a_{0i}} = f^i\left(\frac{a_{1i}}{a_{0i}}, \ldots, \frac{a_{mi}}{a_{0i}}\right) \tag{13.1}$$

and the $m^2 + m$ marginal productivity relationships

$$P_i f_j^i \begin{Bmatrix} = \\ \leq \end{Bmatrix} P_j(1 + r) \quad \text{as} \quad a_{ji} \begin{Bmatrix} > \\ = \end{Bmatrix} 0, \tag{13.2}$$

$$P_i \left(f^i - \sum_h f_h^i \frac{a_{hi}}{a_{0i}}\right) \begin{Bmatrix} = \\ \leq \end{Bmatrix} 1 \quad \text{as} \quad a_{0i} \begin{Bmatrix} > \\ = \end{Bmatrix} 0. \tag{13.3}$$

As in the neoclassical case, we can suppress (13.3)—or any other m relations in the set defined by (13.1) and (13.2)—and substitute for these relationships the price-equation system

$$P_i = a_{0i} + (1 + r) \sum_h P_h a_{hi}. \tag{13.4}$$

The growth rate is determined jointly by the saving function

$$g = s(r, \mathbf{X}) = s_W \frac{1 - \kappa(r, \mathbf{X})}{\kappa(r, \mathbf{X})} + (s_C - s_W)\delta r$$

$$= \max\left(s_W \frac{1 - \kappa(r, \mathbf{X})}{\kappa(r, \mathbf{X})}, s_C r \right),$$

the production equation

$$\mathbf{X} = [\mathbf{I} - (1 + g)\mathbf{A}]^{-1} (\mathbf{C}^W + \mathbf{C}^C), \tag{13.16}$$

and the consumption-demand equations given by

$$U^W(\mathbf{C}^W) = \max$$

subject to

$$\mathbf{P}'\mathbf{C}^W = (1 - s_W)[1 + (1 - \delta)r\mathbf{P}'\mathbf{A}\mathbf{X}]$$

and

$$U^C(\mathbf{C}^C) = \max$$

subject to

$$\mathbf{P}'\mathbf{C}^C = (1 - s_C)\delta r\mathbf{P}'\mathbf{A}\mathbf{X}.$$

Observe that the marginal-productivity relationships continue to hold in the neo-Marxian model. But as in the one-good case, with the wage determined by convention rather than by full employment, marginal-productivity theory reduces simply to competitive profit maximization.

Observe also that the existence of neo-Marxian equilibrium is hardly sensitive at all to the change from fixed proportions to continuous substitution—again a contrast with the neoclassical model. To be sure, a substitution elasticity greater than or equal to unity allows productivity per worker to increase without bound and hence allows an equilibrium to exist for an arbitrarily high real wage. But the additional generality is highly artificial: the increase in output per head takes place at the *lower* end of the profit interval, and there is no guarantee that a high real wage is compatible with positive growth. (Capital requirements increase with the real wage, and the surplus may be insufficient to maintain—not to mention expand—the capital stock, an argument familiar to *aficionados* of the Golden Rule formulated by Edmund Phelps (1961) and others.) Thus, even a high degree of substitution does not enrich the neo-Marxian model. And a modest degree of substitution, $\sigma^i < 1$, leaves the fixed-proportions story virtually unchanged.

The Neo-Keynesian Model

The neo-Keynesian model substitutes an investment-demand function

$$g = i(r)$$

for the conventional wage (13.15). Otherwise equilibrium is defined by the same set of relationships that define the neo-Marxian equilibrium. As in the fixed-proportions case, the system of equations and inequalities is separable into two subsystems provided $\hat{\delta} > 0$. If this condition is met, we have investment-demand, saving, the production function, and marginal-productivity relationships

$$g = i(r)$$

$$g = s_C r$$

$$\frac{1}{a_{0i}} = f^i \left(\frac{a_{1i}}{a_{0i}}, \ldots, \frac{a_{mi}}{a_{0i}} \right) \tag{13.1}$$

$$P_i f^i_j \begin{Bmatrix} = \\ \leq \end{Bmatrix} P_j (1 + r) \quad \text{as} \quad a_{ji} \begin{Bmatrix} > \\ = \end{Bmatrix} 0 \tag{13.2}$$

$$P_i \left(f^i - \sum_h f^i_h \frac{a_{hi}}{a_{0i}} \right) \begin{Bmatrix} = \\ \leq \end{Bmatrix} 1 \quad \text{as} \quad a_{0i} \begin{Bmatrix} > \\ = \end{Bmatrix} 0. \tag{13.3}$$

to determine g^*, r^*, $\mathbf{P}^*$, and $\begin{bmatrix} \mathbf{a}'_0 \\ \mathbf{A} \end{bmatrix}^*$. And we have the production equation

$$\mathbf{X} = [\mathbf{I} - (1 + g)\mathbf{A}]^{-1}(\mathbf{C}^W + \mathbf{C}^C)$$

and consumption-demand equations

$$U^W(\mathbf{C}^W) = \max$$

subject to

$$\mathbf{P}'\mathbf{C}^W = (1 - s_W)[1 + (1 - \delta)r\mathbf{P}'\mathbf{A}\mathbf{X}],$$

and

$$U^C(\mathbf{C}^C) = \max$$

subject to

$$\mathbf{P}'\mathbf{C}^C = (1 - s_C)\hat{\delta}r\mathbf{P}'\mathbf{A}\mathbf{X}$$

to determine $\mathbf{C}^*$, $\mathbf{X}^*$, and distributive shares.

In the people's-capitalism range, in which $\hat{\delta} = 0$, the system is not separable. In this case we have

$$g = s_W \frac{1 - \kappa(r, \mathbf{X})}{\kappa(r, \mathbf{X})}$$

in place of

$$g = s_C r,$$

and $\mathbf{C}^*$ and $\mathbf{X}^*$ must be determined simultaneously with g^*, r^*, $\mathbf{P}^*$, and $\begin{bmatrix} \mathbf{a}_0' \\ \mathbf{A} \end{bmatrix}^*$. But all this is familiar from Chapter 11, with the exception of the marginal-productivity relationships and the inclusion of $\begin{bmatrix} \mathbf{a}_0' \\ \mathbf{A} \end{bmatrix}$ among the unknowns of the problem.[2]

It is fair to say that, as in the one-good case, the shift to variable proportions is hardly earth-shattering in the two nonneoclassical models. For this reason, nonneoclassical theorists have not had the same need to "enrich" their models by introducing continuous substitution into the story that neoclassicals have had, and have therefore been content with much simpler models of production. Necessity is indeed the mother of invention!

---

2. The only real novelty of continuous substitution is that it changes the sufficiency conditions for equilibrium in the model outlined in Chapter 4. There we had to assume that a zero wage was permissible in order for continuity of the investment-demand function and the assumption $i(-1) > s(-1)$ to ensure the existence of equilibrium. With a substitution elasticity greater than or equal to unity, however, we can eliminate the possibility of a corner solution with a zero real wage. Sufficient to guarantee the existence of equilibrium are (1) an investment function that is continuous everywhere, (2) $i(-1) > s(-1)$, and—the new feature—(3) $i(r)$ is bounded from above. The reason why a high degree of substitution allows us to eliminate the possibility of a corner solution is that the range of the saving function becomes infinite; with a bounded continuous investment-demand function that exceeds desired saving at $r = -1$, we are guaranteed that saving and investment functions will intersect for some r.

14 Monopoly and Degree-of-Monopoly Theory

At the end of Chapter 10 we examined the role of product-market structure in the analysis of equilibrium. There it was argued that the assumption of competitive product markets was a common feature of all the models, not a peculiarly neoclassical assumption. It followed that replacing competition with monopoly, oligopoly, or monopolistic competition would not provide a theory of equilibrium alternative to the three elaborated in this book, but simply a set of conditions alternative to the marginal-productivity conditions appropriate to a competitive market structure. In particular, the so-called "degree-of-monopoly" theory formulated by Michal Kalecki (1938, 1943) was argued to be compatible with neoclassical as well as with neo-Keynesian and neo-Marxian models, a complement to any of the three rather than a separate theory of growth and distribution.

The present chapter elaborates this theme. Since the structure of product markets turns on demand-curve slopes, the argument is clearer in the context of many goods than in the context of a single good, where it makes little sense to argue in terms of product — or firm — demand curves. With many goods, by contrast, there is no difficulty in expressing the degree of monopoly in each industry in terms of elasticities of demand faced by producers.

A good starting point, perhaps, is to assume that each industry is a pure monopoly: each industrial monopolist acts independently of the others. In this case product demands jointly determine the degree of monopoly in each industry: marginal revenue is related to industry demand by the equations

$$MR_i = \frac{1 + e_i}{e_i} P_i, \qquad i = 1, \ldots, m, \qquad (14.1)$$

where e_i is the elasticity of demand for good i. Profit maximization ensures that e_i will in general be negative and exceed unity in absolute value. Moreover, e_i will in general depend on all the P's, not just P_i. With constant returns to scale in production and a wage fixed at unity, marginal cost à la Kalecki, exclusive of "normal" profit, is given by the marginal productivities of capital and labor:

$$MC_i = \frac{P_j}{f_j^i}, \qquad i, j = 1, \ldots, m, \tag{14.2}$$

$$MC_i = \left(f^i - \sum_h f_h^i \frac{a_{hi}}{a_{0i}} \right)^{-1}, \qquad i = 1, \ldots, m.$$

Profit maximization implies equality between marginal revenue and marginal cost for inputs used at positive levels,

$$\frac{1 + e_i}{e_i} P_i = \frac{P_j}{f_j^i}, \qquad i, j = 1, \ldots, m, \tag{14.3}$$

$$\frac{1 + e_i}{e_i} P_i = \left(f^i - \sum_h f_h^i \frac{a_{hi}}{a_{0i}} \right)^{-1}, \qquad i = 1, \ldots, m,$$

with corresponding inequalities for zero-level inputs. Multiplying through each of the labor equations by the appropriate $a_{0i} = f^i(\cdot)^{-1}$ and substituting from the capital equations, we have

$$P_i = \frac{e_i}{1 + e_i} \left(a_{0i} + \sum_j P_j a_{ji} \right).$$

Defining the degree of monopoly by the equation

$$\mu_i = \frac{e_i}{1 + e_i},$$

we arrive at the result

$$P_i = \mu_i \left(a_{0i} + \sum_j P_j a_{ji} \right), \qquad i = 1, \ldots, m. \tag{14.4}$$

Observe that Eq. (14.4) *replaces the competitive price equation*

$$P_i = a_{0i} + (1 + r) \sum_h P_h a_{hi}, \tag{13.4}$$

in contrast with the one-good case where both equations can hold simultaneously. The difference between the two cases is the requirement implicit in the m-good version of the competitive price equation of a uniform profit rate across industries, which is in general inconsistent with an arbitrary degree-of-monopoly vector $\mu = \langle \mu_1, \ldots, \mu_m \rangle$. Observe also that Eq. (14.4) holds with fixed as well as with variable proportions: in the fixed proportions case we have directly

$$MC_i = a_{0i} + \sum_j P_j a_{ji}.$$

The argument leading to (14.4) is otherwise unchanged.

Equation (14.4) generalizes its one-good analog (10.10) in providing for each μ an equilibrium set of prices, as well as real wage and profit rates. Given a fixed degree of monopoly for each industry and fixed technological coefficients, we can solve (14.4) directly for $\mathbf{P}$, and calculate the overall rate of profit by the formula

$$r = \frac{\sum_i (1 - \mu_i^{-1}) P_i X_i}{\sum_i \sum_j P_j a_{ji} X_i}, \qquad (14.5)$$

with the numerator representing aggregate profits and the denominator aggregate capital. The X's in Eq. (14.5) are given by a demand function

$$\mathbf{X} = \mathbf{X}(\mathbf{P}).$$

With μ a variable function of $\mathbf{P}$ or with factor proportions variable, the solution becomes mathematically more complex even though the economics remains the same in principle. In the case of continuous substitution, for example, we must solve m price equations of (14.4) together with the $m^2 + m$ profit-maximization relationships represented by (14.3) for the $m^2 + m$ technological coefficients $\begin{bmatrix} \mathbf{a}_0' \\ \mathbf{A} \end{bmatrix}$ and the m prices. Once again the demand function $\mathbf{X}(\mathbf{P})$ completes the structure of the degree-of-monopoly theory, allowing us to solve (14.5) for r.

Closing the Model

It must be recognized that the degree-of-monopoly vector μ provides at best half a theory; it lacks a theory of accumulation from which we can determine the rate of growth. To complete the theory in the one-good case we turned to an investment-demand function as the most Kaleckian of alternatives. Here we begin with two simpler alternatives.

First, we might determine the rate of economic growth from the rate of population growth, as in the neoclassical model:

$$g = n. \qquad (2.18)$$

Or we might determine the rate of growth from the Cambridge saving function common to both neo-Marxian and neo-Keynesian approaches,

$$g = s(\mu, \mathbf{X}) = s_W \frac{1 - \kappa}{\kappa} + (s_C - s_W)\delta r = \max\left(s_W \frac{1 - \kappa}{\kappa}, s_C r\right), \quad (14.6)$$

with r equal to the overall profit rate defined by Eq. (14.5), and the capital : output ratio κ defined, as before, by the equation

$$\kappa = \frac{\sum_i \sum_j P_j a_{ji} X_i}{\sum_i P_i X_i}. \quad (14.7)$$

Neither of these approaches presents serious difficulties. By contrast, the specifically neo-Keynesian closure

$$g = i(r) \quad (4.6)$$

presents a problem in its assumption of a uniform rate of growth across industries, which implicitly assumes investor indifference with respect to the sectoral composition of investment. This assumption makes sense in the context of perfect competition, but it is hardly appropriate in the monopoly context. In the first place, particular capitalists are associated with particular branches of business activity, so that even if the sectoral rate of profit

$$r_i = \frac{(1 - \mu_i^{-1})P_i}{\sum_j P_j a_{ji}} \quad (14.8)$$

were the same across industries, there would be no reason to expect uniform responses with respect to investment and growth. That is, the sectoral analog of (4.6),

$$g_j = i_j(r_j), \quad (14.9)$$

need not be identical across sectors. Second, the rate of profit would be equal across industries only by chance, so that even with uniform animal spirits — that is, with identical investment-demand functions (14.9) — the pattern of investment demand for the equilibrium vector of profit rates $\langle r_1, \ldots, r_m \rangle$ need hardly produce uniform growth across sectors.

At this point one might think to introduce a stock market whose function it would be both to equalize profit rates by divorcing share prices from the value of physical capital, and to homogenize animal spirits by giving capitalists access to all sectors of the economy. In addition to the m "real" rates of profit defined by Eq. (14.8), we would have, in equilibrium, a uniform "financial" rate of profit

$$r^f = \frac{(1 - \mu_i^{-1})P_i X_i}{X_i \sum_j P_j a_{ji} + Q_i}, \qquad i = 1, \ldots, m, \qquad (14.10)$$

with Q_i representing the "good will" of firm i, the capitalized value of its monopoly power over the ith good. Correspondingly, we would have two concepts of capital, "real" capital

$$K = \sum_i \sum_j P_j a_{ji} X_i \qquad (14.11)$$

and "financial" capital

$$K^f = \sum_i \left(\sum_j P_j a_{ji} X_i + Q_i \right). \qquad (14.12)$$

In place of (4.6) or (14.9), we would now have growth determined in each sector by a single function

$$g = i(r^f). \qquad (14.13)$$

A stock market is not, however, in itself a solution to the problem of extending the concept of an investment-demand function to the monopoly case. Indeed, it raises a problem as difficult as the one it resolves: the system (14.10) guarantees only that the Q's be such as to produce a uniform r^f. It says nothing about the level of the Q's and the *magnitude* of r^f. Unless we can answer the question of what determines share prices on the stock exchange and the level of the financial rate of profit, we are back to square one, since a principal goal of the theory is precisely to determine the rate of profit!

Instead of investment demand we could turn to the life-cycle theory of saving to complete the model, but this approach presents a similar problem. The rate of profit that enters into household utility calculations is neither the average rate of profit determined by Eq. (14.5) nor sectoral rates of profit determined by Eq. (14.8), but an intertemporal rate of discount reflecting the marginal rate of substitution between present and future consumption. Once again, all these rates coincide under competitive conditions but not under monopoly.

A stock market that equalized rates of profit and made it possible for households to exchange future for present goods at this rate would bring each household's discount rate into line with the financial rate of profit. But once again we open up the question of what determines the financial rate of profit.

Evidently, monopoly requires us to supplement neoclassical as well as neo-Keynesian theories with a theory of asset pricing, at least if we use the life-cycle hypothesis or animal spirits (rather than full employment or a classical saving function) to close the model. One possibility is to close the model in neo-Keynesian fashion by introducing both the classical saving function and the animal-spirits function simultaneously, with r^f and $\mathbf{Q} = \langle Q_1, \ldots, Q_m \rangle$ new unknowns linked together by the m equations of (14.10). The complete system starts with the $MR = MC$ equations (14.3), the price equations (14.4), and the demand function $\mathbf{X} = \mathbf{X}(\mathbf{P})$, and adds the equations

$$r^f = \frac{(1 - \mu_i^{-1}) P_i X_i}{X_i \sum_j P_j a_{ji} + Q_i}, \qquad i = 1, \ldots, m \qquad (14.10)$$

$$K = \sum_i \sum_j P_j a_{ji} X_i \qquad (14.11)$$

$$K^f = \sum_i \left(\sum_j P_j a_{ji} X_i + Q_i \right) \qquad (14.12)$$

$$g = i(r^f) \qquad (14.13)$$

$$g = s(r^f, \boldsymbol{\mu}, \mathbf{X}) = s_W \frac{1 - \kappa}{\kappa} + (s_C - s_W) \delta r^f \frac{K^f}{K}$$

$$= \max \left(s_W \frac{1 - \kappa}{\kappa}, s_C r^f \frac{K^f}{K} \right). \qquad (14.14)$$

The unknowns of this system are $\mathbf{P}$, $\mathbf{Q}$, $\mathbf{X}$, r^f, K^f, K, g, and $\begin{bmatrix} \mathbf{a}_0' \\ \mathbf{A} \end{bmatrix}$.

The alternative, neoclassical, closure requires both the full-employment assumption and the life-cycle hypothesis. All that changes in the descriptions of equilibrium is that in place of (14.13) and (14.14) we have

$$g = n \qquad (2.18)$$

and (with a Cobb-Douglas utility function)

$$g = \beta \left[\frac{1}{\kappa} - \left(1 + r^f \frac{K^f}{K} \right) \right] - 1. \qquad (14.15)$$

Observe that if we take this tack, degree-of-monopoly theory hardly modifies the conceptual structure of neoclassical or neo-Keynesian theory. This structure, whose distinctive features are expressed respectively in (2.18) and (14.15) for the neoclassical model and (14.13) and

(14.14) for the neo-Keynesian, carries over with very little change from the competitive case; degree-of-monopoly theory in fact changes only the part common to both theories, the marginal conditions and the price equation. By contrast, the conceptual structure of neo-Marxian theory—which consists of adding Eqs. (14.5) and (14.6) to the $MR = MC$ equations, the price equations, and the demand equations — is more seriously affected: class power may still be said to determine the conventional wage, but it does so through the degree of monopoly (Kalecki 1971).

Two Problems

However the growth side of the model might be closed, there remain two problems with the present interpretation of degree-of-monopoly theory. The first is that the argument as stated involves a substantial amount of implicit theorizing. We started with demand curves for the m outputs $\langle X_1, \ldots, X_m \rangle$, derived equilibrium prices and quantities, and then added elements of neoclassical, neo-Keynesian, or neo-Marxian theories to determine the rate of growth. Given g^*, we can then determine the equilibrium consumption pattern by the production equation

$$\mathbf{C}^* = [\mathbf{I} - (1 + g^*)\mathbf{A}]\mathbf{X}^*. \tag{14.16}$$

The implicit element in the theory lies in the reasoning behind Eq. (14.16), which derives $\mathbf{C}^*$ from $\mathbf{X}^*$. By contrast, the arguments advanced in Chapter 11 for all the theories—neoclassical, neo-Keynesian, and neo-Marxian—started with household demands for consumption $\langle C_1, \ldots, C_m \rangle$ and derived the composition of aggregate output from the solution to (14.16), that is, by means of the inverse relationship

$$\mathbf{X}^* = [\mathbf{I} - (1 + g^*)\mathbf{A}]^{-1}\mathbf{C}^*,$$

$$\mathbf{a}_0'\mathbf{X}^* = 1.$$

In principle, nothing prevents us from starting from consumer demand here as in the competitive case. The only loss is one of mathematical simplicity; the separable structure in which $\mathbf{X}^*$ and $\mathbf{P}^*$ are independent of g^* and logically prior to $\mathbf{C}^*$ gives way to an inseparable structure requiring simultaneous solution of the equilibrium values of all the variables. (Takashi Negishi [1961] provides a formal proof of the existence of equilibrium in a similar context.)

The discussion in Chapter 10 elided a more serious difficulty. By making the rate of profit depend on the elasticity of demand, the theory in its present form precludes the possibility of a positive rate of profit under conditions of perfect competition, taking perfect competition as a limiting case in which the elasticity of firm demand becomes infinite in absolute value and the degree of monopoly passes to unity. This is symptomatic of an even more serious problem: the identification of firm with industry demand.

We have blurred the distinction between firm and industry demands by restricting attention to "pure" monopoly, defined as a structure in which the firm is identical with the industry and independent of other producers, which has the effect of eliminating interaction *à la* Cournot, Stackelberg, Chamberlin, or Robinson. But if industry i is not a pure monopoly in this sense, the industry and firm demand curves are no longer the same. In the limit, the demand curve *perceived* by each producer in a perfectly competitive industry is infinitely elastic. As a result, $e_i = -\infty$ and $\mu_i = 1$. And in this case r_i, according to (14.8), is equal to 0. Thus the theory as it now stands has no room for a "normal" competitive return to the owners of capital.

A Revised Theory

This problem can be solved by redefining cost to include a normal rate of profit, and redefining elasticity of demand in terms of the perceptions of the firm. As before we have

$$MR_i = \frac{1 + e_i}{e_i} P_i = \mu_i^{-1} P_i,$$

but now e_i represents the elasticity perceived in industry i. Once the assumption of a single seller is relaxed, industries can run the gamut from pure monopoly through oligopoly and monopolistic competition to perfect competition, but nothing is lost for our purposes — except additional algebra — by stipulating that firms in the same industry all perceive, or misperceive, e_i identically. The marginal-cost equations become

$$MC_i = \frac{P_j(1 + r)}{f_j^i} = \left(f^i - \sum_h f_h^i \frac{a_{hi}}{a_{0i}} \right)^{-1}, \qquad (14.17)$$

where r is the (unknown) normal rate of profit. In equilibrium we have $MR_i = MC_i$ in all industries, whether competitive or monopolistic, which is to say that the equations

$$\mu_i^{-1} P_i = \frac{P_j(1+r)}{f_j^i} = \left(f^i - \sum_h f_h^i \frac{a_{hi}}{a_{0i}} \right)^{-1} \tag{14.18}$$

hold exactly for each input that appears at a positive level, and the appropriate inequality holds for each zero-level input. Multiplying through by a_{0i} in the labor equations and substituting from the capital equations, we end up with

$$P_i = \mu_i \left[a_{0i} + (1+r) \sum_j P_j a_{ji} \right] \tag{14.19}$$

as a replacement both to (14.4) and to the competitive price equation.

In this form, degree-of-monopoly theory is compatible with each of the approaches to growth and distribution elaborated in this book. The basic structure of the problem remains unchanged, including the need to add $m + 1$ additional relationships to close the model. Only the marginal conditions, and hence the price equation, distinguish the monopoly case from the competitive case.

In this model, the financial rate of return can be identified with the normal rate of profit, since that is the rate of profit generally available to owners of capital without special access to monopoly profits. Thus Eq. (14.10) becomes

$$r = \frac{(1 - \mu_i^{-1}) P_i X_i + r X_i \sum_j P_j a_{ji}}{X_i \sum_j P_j a_{ji} + Q_i}, \qquad i = 1, \ldots, m.$$

We can solve for "good will" as a function of a given degree of monopoly μ_i and the rate of profit r:

$$Q_i = \frac{(1 - \mu_i^{-1}) P_i X_i}{r}, \qquad i = 1, \ldots, m.$$

Specifically, Q_i is the present value of an infinite stream of monopoly superprofits discounted at the rate r. For the aggregate value of financial capital we have the equation

$$K^f = \sum_i \left(\sum_j P_j a_{ji} X_i + \frac{(1 - \mu_i^{-1}) P_i X_i}{r} \right),$$

and for the aggregate value of physical capital the equation

$$K = \sum_i \sum_j P_j a_{ji} X_i.$$

With these modifications, we can continue to write the neoclassical saving equation as

$$g = \beta \left[\frac{1}{\kappa} - \left(1 + r \frac{K^f}{K} \right) \right] - 1. \tag{14.20}$$

Everything else in the neoclassical theory goes through as in the competitive case. Specifically, the model is closed by the union of (1) the neoclassical saving function (14.20) with (2) demand functions obtained by maximization of the utility function

$$U(\mathbf{C}^1, \mathbf{C}^2)$$

subject to

$$\mathbf{P}'\mathbf{C}^1 + \frac{\mathbf{P}'\mathbf{C}^2}{1 + r} = 1;$$

(3) the production and normalization equations

$$\mathbf{X} = [\mathbf{I} - (1 + g)\mathbf{A}]^{-1}\mathbf{C} \tag{14.21}$$

and

$$\mathbf{a}_0'\mathbf{X} = 1; \tag{14.22}$$

(4) the full employment condition

$$g = n;$$

and (5) the marginal conditions summarized in Eqs. (14.18) and (14.19).

The neo-Marxian model is closed by (1) a given conventional wage

$$P_i C_i^N + \cdots + P_m C_m^N = 1 \tag{13.15}$$

in combination with (2) the classical saving equation

$$g = s(r, \mu, \mathbf{X}) = s_W \frac{1 - \kappa}{\kappa} + (s_C - s_W)\delta r \frac{K^f}{K}$$

$$= \max \left(s_W \frac{1 - \kappa}{\kappa}, s_C r \frac{K^f}{K} \right); \tag{14.23}$$

(3) the demand function emerging from maximization of workers' and capitalists' *one-period* utility functions $U(\mathbf{C}^W)$ and $U(\mathbf{C}^C)$ subject respectively to the budget constraints

$$\mathbf{P}'\mathbf{C}^W = (1 - s_W)[1 + (1 - \delta)rK^f]$$

and

$$\mathbf{P}'\mathbf{C}^C = (1 - s_C)\delta r K^f;$$

(4) the production and normalization equations (14.21) and (14.22); and (5) the marginal conditions of Eqs. (14.18) and (14.19).

Finally, the neo-Keynesian model substitutes

$$g = i(r)$$

for the conventional-wage equation, but is otherwise identical in its formal structure to the neo-Marxian model.

Summary

The main results of substituting monopoly for competition can now be summarized. Unlike the one-good case, we cannot reconcile an exogenously given degree of monopoly with an endogenously determined profit rate merely by varying the capital:output ratio. For in the context of m goods, there is no reason to expect a uniform real rate of return across industries under monopoly conditions. Nevertheless, there is a sense in which profit rates are equal in equilibrium: a stock market can be posited that equalizes *financial* rates of return by assigning appropriate amounts of "good will" to each firm's book value of capital.

The m-good story changes in one other respect from the one-good case. Here we have allowed for two different interpretations of cost, one following Kalecki (1943) rather closely in defining cost *exclusive* of normal profit, the other including a normal rate of profit as a constituent of cost. The first definition requires us to treat the financial rate of profit as an unknown of the problem since nothing ties it to any real rate in the system, although both neoclassical and neo-Keynesian models require—albeit in different ways—a uniform rate of profit. The second definition solves this difficulty by tying the financial rate of profit to the normal rate of profit, the rate of return accessible to capitalists enjoying no special privileges. But in return for solving the problem of determining the financial rate of profit, we encounter another: determining the normal rate of profit.

Thus the structure of the problem is similar in both interpretations: in both we have to determine a rate of profit to close the model. The degree of monopoly thus modifies the competitive case more by offering a different theory with respect to the distribution of profit across industries than by offering a fundamentally different theory of profit. In this crucial respect, the monopoly case offers nothing new. The three theories—neoclassical, neo-Marxian, and neo-Keynesian—are each compatible with monopoly as well as with competition, and each offers a theory of distribution and growth, as well as of relative prices, that is basically invariant with respect to the structure of markets.

However, the relative ease with which the theories are modified to take account of monopoly should not lull us into believing that there are no important differences between monopoly and competition. Perhaps that most important of these is the role of the firm. Under competitive conditions, with constant returns to scale, the neoclassical firm plays no real role at all. For the competitive neoclassical firm does nothing that each household cannot do for itself. Even its very size is indeterminate. It is, in short, simply an abstraction of the household in its productive capacity.

Under imperfect competition, however, industrial structure becomes of crucial importance to the determination of equilibrium r^*, g^*, $\mathbf{P}^*$, $\mathbf{X}^*$, and $\mathbf{C}^*$ even in the neoclassical model. For the degree of monopoly vector μ plays a central role in determining the equilibrium configuration, and — except in the polar case of pure monopoly — the degree of monopoly is determined by the demands perceived by the several producers, not by the industry demand as a whole. Hence the individual firm and its interaction with other firms necessarily become a central focus of study.

By contrast, in the neo-Marxian model the firm already plays a critical role in the analysis under conditions of perfect competition, for it is an important, if not the only, locus of the class struggle that determines the real wage and the input coefficients, not to mention the corporate retention ratios that enter into the more sophisticated versions of Cambridge saving theory presented in Chapter 6. And in the competitive as well as monopolistic versions of the neo-Keynesian model, the firm plays a role in the determination of investment demand, a very different role from the one that it plays in the neo-Marxian model, but hardly less important.

Thus, like the issue of variable versus fixed coefficients, monopoly versus competition is not really an issue between the theories. Nevertheless, it is once again easy to see why neoclassicals have been disproportionately concerned with the microeconomics of monopoly. For in the absence of monopoly, a central institution of capitalism — the firm — disappears altogether from their theory.

PART THREE

Toward an Understanding of Capitalism

15 An Overall Summary

Over the quarter-century 1953–1977 real gross national product per head increased more than fourfold in Japan, an annual rate in excess of 7 percent. During the same period British per-capita GNP increased by only 60 percent, a rate of about 2 percent per year. Neoclassical, neo-Marxian, and neo-Keynesian theories agree on some of the factors responsible for this difference. For instance, they all ascribe a large measure of the difference between Japan and the United Kingdom to differences in the rate of capital accumulation. And indeed, whereas Japan on average devoted 30 percent of her gross national product to fixed-capital formation during the twenty-five years in question, the United Kingdom devoted only 20 percent of GNP to this end. But if the three theories agree on according a central role to accumulation, they emphasize fundamentally different reasons in explaining accumulation itself.

In neoclassical theory, the long-run rate of growth is determined — technological change apart — by the rate of population growth. But in neoclassical terms a quarter-century is not necessarily so long a period that short-run theory is inapplicable, and, in the short run, neoclassical theory appeals to the psychology of households: Japan saves more and grows faster because Japanese households are more future-oriented than British households.

Neo-Keynesian theory also emphasizes psychology, but it is the psychology of businessmen rather than the psychology of households that matters. Japan has had a higher rate of capital accumulation and growth than Britain because her capitalists have been more optimistic about the future, more willing to take risks, more adventurous — in short, Japanese animal spirits have been more expansive than British

311

animal spirits. According to neo-Keynesian theory, a higher profit rate also results from the difference in investor optimism; capitalists are assumed to save a higher proportion of their incomes than workers, and the profit rate therefore responds positively to investment propensities. In the neo-Keynesian view, paradoxically, a tendency on the part of the Japanese to save a higher proportion of their incomes than the British would partially or even totally offset the impact of higher Japanese investment demand on the rate of profit.

Neo-Marxian theory, in contrast with both neoclassical and neo-Keynesian approaches, starts neither from the psychology of the household nor the psychology of the businessman. Rather, it takes conflict between workers and capitalists as the point of departure and explains the difference in accumulation and growth rates by ascribing greater power to Japanese capitalists and British workers than to their counterparts in the other country. This translates into a higher profit rate in Japan, and since property owners are assumed to save a higher fraction of their incomes than workers, the result is a higher rate of saving and a higher rate of growth. In contrast with the neo-Keynesian case, a higher propensity to save can only reinforce the effect of a higher rate of profit on the rate of growth.

The three theories obviously suggest fundamentally different approaches to the study of capitalism. But the differences between neoclassical and nonneoclassical approaches are not, as is often contended, differences in the degree of logical consistency. To be sure, neo-Marxians and, even more emphatically, neo-Keynesians have frequently attacked neoclassical theory for its presumed logical shortcomings. Nor are neoclassical critics of neo-Keynesian and neo-Marxian approaches any less quick to point out logical defects in these theories. By contrast, a principal conclusion of this book is that the mutual attacks directed against logical error are in general misplaced. This is not to say that the mutual criticism has not added to the logical cohesion of the models. But in my judgment, critics who have taken the tack of logical criticism might have at the same time listened more closely to the other side to find out what was being said. They would have discovered theories which, properly formulated and understood, are roughly equal in logical consistency and completeness to their own.

This is not intended to suggest that these theories are equally valid; the point is rather to shift the ground of the argument from logic to empirical relevance. But there is a prior problem, the problem that lies at the heart of this book: how do we properly formulate and understand the three theories?

Neoclassical Theory

Neoclassical theory means different things to different people. For some, neoclassical theory means "supply and demand," so any model that utilizes supply and demand relationships is *ipso facto* neoclassical. For others, neoclassical economics is tantamount to smoothness in production: indeed, a production function that exhibits continuous substitution and constant returns to scale is commonly described as "neoclassical." For others still, neoclassical theory is a set of marginal-productivity relationships. In this view "neoclassical" investment theory, for example, is distinguished from other theories by the assumption of competitive profit maximization and the corresponding first-order conditions according to which equating the marginal productivity of capital to the cost of capital determines the optimal capital stock (Jorgenson and Siebert, 1968). Finally, there are some who regard neoclassical economics as simply the toolbox of marginal analysis; its logic therefore is simply the logic of constrained maximization.

None of these positions is taken here. *All* the models, neo-Marxian and neo-Keynesian as well as neoclassical, incorporate supply and demand relationships; *all* are compatible with continuous substitution in production; *all* are compatible with some form of marginal-productivity theory; and *all* utilize marginal analysis wherever there are margins to vary. The distinguishing features of the neoclassical model are not the presence of these elements but the way they combine to determine equilibrium. Supply and demand, for instance, become *exclusive* determinants of equilibrium in the neoclassical model because the Invisible Hand is assumed to clear *every* market in the system, including the market for labor. This is tantamount to assuming full employment, or at least an equilibrium rate of unemployment—a big step from simply assuming that supply and demand are central features of the economy.

Along with full employment, household preferences play a central role in the determination of equilibrium profit and wage rates, and this central role is a second distinguishing feature of the neoclassical model. Household preferences enter the neoclassical model in two ways: first, leisure:goods preferences determine the supply curve for labor; second, intertemporal consumption preferences determine the supply curve of new capital. Of these, the second is more critical, at least in determining long-run equilibrium. For if leisure:goods trade-offs are separable from intertemporal consumption trade-offs, the capital:labor ratio is in the long run independent of leisure:goods trade-offs. Leisure: goods trade-offs determine the number of man-hours worked in a year, but not capital per man-hour, or the distribution of income between capital and labor. By contrast, household saving propensities are crucial both to the long-run capital: labor ratio and to long-run distribution, whether or not preferences are separable.

In the neoclassical model, household saving propensities are assumed to be determined by the maximization of utility derived from both present and future consumption, subject to a budget constraint imposed by lifetime resources — in short, the model assumes the saving theory formulated originally by Irving Fisher and now associated with Franco Modigliani, and in a somewhat different form (and a very different name) with Milton Friedman. With household preferences given, wage and profit rates determine desired saving, which determines the rate of growth, at least in the short run. But growth in turn affects wage and profit rates: wage and profit rates are assumed to adjust gradually according to the degree of excess demand or excess supply in the labor market.

If factor proportions can vary, employment is determined in each period by profit maximization at the (momentarily) given wage; in the presence of continuous substitution, profit maximization dictates equality between the marginal productivity of labor and the wage rate. By contrast, if factor proportions are fixed, then growth in the capital stock uniquely determines growth in employment: the two rates must be equal.

The long-run capital: labor ratio and long-run profit and wage rates and shares are determined jointly by (1) technology, (2) household consumption preferences over time, and (3) the rate of growth of population. Profit and wage rates are in long-run equilibrium at the level where the ratio of households' desired saving to the capital stock is just equal to the growth rate of population.

The rate of growth of capital and output, however, is determined by population growth alone, at least if we abstract, as we do almost everywhere in this book, from technological progress. So the neoclassical model is separable, with growth determined independently of preferences and technology, and distribution depending on both.

It should be emphasized that neither the existence nor uniqueness of long-run equilibrium is guaranteed. With fixed coefficients, the existence of equilibrium depends, for a given rate of population growth, solely on the utility function. So does uniqueness. Moreover, for quite plausible utility functions (like the Cobb-Douglas, for which desired saving is proportional to wages), long-run equilibrium — if it exists — will be unstable.

Variability of factor proportions does not necessarily guarantee existence, uniqueness, or stability either. But if factors are continuously substitutable, *and* if the elasticity of substitution is greater than or equal to unity, which is to say that substitution possibilities must be at least as great as those afforded by a Cobb-Douglas production function, *then* one can guarantee the existence of equilibrium and (local) stability, at least if the problem of "overshooting" peculiar to discrete-time models is elided. If the household propensity to save is independent of the rate of profit (Cobb-Douglas utility), then equilibrium is unique and globally stable. Moreover, at a stable equilibrium, conventional comparative statics hold: the higher the rate of population growth, the higher is the equilibrium rate of profit; and the higher the propensity to save, the lower is the rate of profit. And if factor proportions vary, the capital: output ratio is inversely related to the rate of profit, so higher profit rates go with less capital-intensive methods of production.

Observe that the long-run equilibrium is not in general an "efficient" or Pareto-"optimal" growth path. Each generation can achieve a higher level of utility if the market is subordinated to a government-imposed rate of profit equal to the rate of population growth.

Finally, attention should be paid to the fact that besides the theory outlined in the preceding paragraphs, there is a more extreme "Chicago" version of the neoclassical model in which the real wage is determined by the marginal productivity of labor at full employment, *in the short run as well as the long.* In the main, this theory does not differ in its dynamics from the version in which full employment obtains only in the long run. In particular, the paths of short-run equilibrium will necessarily converge to the same long-run equilibrium when the utility function is Cobb-Douglas and the elasticity of substitution in production is greater than or equal to one.

But the version of the theory in which full employment exists at every moment of time requires special attention because it has been a source of serious misunderstanding: it creates the appearance that distribution depends only on an exogenously given technology and labor force.

There are several difficulties in accepting the "biotechnological determinism" implicit in this view. First, the marginal productivity of labor at full employment depends on the accumulation of capital, and accumulation depends on household preferences. Thus technology and population alone can never explain long-run distribution. Second, even in the short run, where capital is fixed, the full-employment marginal productivity of labor depends on prior accumulation, and thus on household preferences. Third, full employment is not a number so much as it is a concept — a job for every willing worker — and willingness to work may depend on the preferences of households with respect to leisure and goods. So the wage rate is not determined even in the short run by the size of the labor force and technology alone.

It is difficult in any case to argue convincingly that the second of the two versions of short-run equilibrium is any more neoclassical than the first. They differ only with respect to the speed of adjustment, and neoclassical theorists, except for an extreme contingent whose center of gravity is at the University of Chicago, are generally quite silent on how quickly demand and supply in the labor market (or in any other market) are supposed to adjust. Short-run disequilibrium — in particular, short-run unemployment — in my judgment does no violence to the basic tenets of neoclassical theory. But without short-run full employment, there is little room for biotechnological determinism in the neoclassical model. In the long run, preferences play a central role in the neoclassical determination of the distribution of income between profits and wages, even if the growth rate is determined solely by population dynamics.

Neo-Marxian Theory

The neo-Marxian model starts from altogether different premises. The building blocks are not individuals or households, but classes — capitalists and workers — each bound together by a common interest born of a common relationship to the production process. It is not goods : leisure choices made by the household, but conflict between capitalists and workers — conflict not only over the wage rate but also over the duration, intensity, and organization of work (conflict, that is to say, not only over the distribution but also over the size of the economic pie) — that, along with technology and the stock of capital goods, determines labor-market equilibrium. It is not intertemporal consumption preferences but institutional characteristics of capital and labor that determine the rate of accumulation.

At the heart of the neo-Marxian analysis is a subsistence wage. But subsistence is a misleading terminology, and a modest step toward the *aggiornamento* of Marxian economics might be to rename the wage rate. The term "conventional" wage rate is proposed.

The problem with the notion of subsistence goes back at least to Marx's own times. Whatever the case previously, in mid-nineteenth-century England a "subsistence" wage could not be identified with a biologically determined level of living. Marx went out of his way to emphasize the social, historical, and even moral determinants of subsistence. This creates as many problems as it resolves, especially when we relax the assumption of a single commodity. But the idea that workers are on the borderline of starvation or malnutrition is no part of the subsistence-wage theory employed here, and criticism along those lines is given short shrift.

Neo-Marxian equilibrium is derived from the conventional wage, the (distinct) saving propensities of capitalists and workers, and a technology that is determined both by physical production relationships and the social relations of production. Formally, at least in the context of a single good produced under conditions of fixed proportions, we can start from the rate of exploitation (or surplus value) rather than from the conventional wage, but the second concept is more general than the first since it continues to provide a basis for a consistent theory even where the simplifying assumptions do not hold. In any case exploitation and subsistence are only formally alternatives since the rate of exploitation depends directly on the level of the conventional wage, as well as on the physical productivity of the system and the social relations of production, which jointly determine the amount of surplus compatible with a given wage.

If, nevertheless, for sentimental reasons we start from a given rate of exploitation, distributive shares are easily calculated: with wages paid at the end of the production period, the ratio of aggregate profits to aggregate wages is equal to the rate of surplus value. With fixed technical coefficients, wage and profit shares translate directly into wage and profit rates.

With variable proportions, by contrast, a given rate of exploitation may or may not close the model. But given the wage, the distribution side of the model can be closed by a technically determined relationship between the capital : output ratio and the profit rate, which along with the production function provides enough additional information to determine capital : output and labor : output ratios.

In the case of continuous substitution, the relationship between the capital : output ratio and the profit rate that closes the model is a marginal-productivity relationship, an aspect of the model that will undoubtedly surprise many: how does a marginal-productivity equation find its way into a neo-Marxian framework of analysis? The answer is that the marginal-productivity equation itself implies nothing more than competitive profit maximization, and hence is as appropriate to the neo-Marxian (or the neo-Keynesian) model as to the neoclassical, once continuous substitution is assumed. It is only in conjunction with full employment that the marginal productivity equation takes on a special, neoclassical, meaning.

Given the relative power of capitalists and workers and the technology, equilibrium growth is determined by the saving equation. In this respect, the neo-Marxian model is quite different from the neoclassical. In the neoclassical model, growth is affected by accumulation only in the short run, when the system is out of long-run equilibrium: in the long run, growth is determined by population dynamics, and the accumulation equation determines the equilibrium profit rate *from* the exogenously given growth rate. In the neo-Marxian model, the causality runs the other way, from the rate of profit to the rate of growth.

Hence another surprise, at least for those whose view of reality is formed by neoclassical theory: there is no necessity for the equilibrium rate of growth of employment to conform to the rate of growth of population! But how can that be? What happens when the economy runs out of people, or (if employment growth lags behind population growth) when mass unemployment appears?

The answer to this question requires two conceptual changes from the neoclassical model. First, neo-Marxian theory shifts the focus from the economy as a whole to the capitalist mode of production, viewed as one among many modes that complement as well as compete with each other: petty commodity production (in which, unlike capitalism, wage labor plays a relatively minor role); household production (in which not only is wage labor absent, but production takes place for the direct use of the producers rather than for the market); government production (in which the state replaces the capitalist as proprietor).

If resources can move between sectors, mass unemployment is hardly a necessary consequence of insufficient growth within the capitalist sector; the capitalist mode may simply fade away, at least relatively. Neither does the rate of growth of population impose a limit on the growth of the capitalist sector until it has absorbed the resources of other modes of production. And, since the capitalist sector in one country can draw human resources from outside its national boundaries, domestic population growth is even less of a constraint.

Nevertheless, it may be argued that sooner or later, population growth—in the world at large if not in any particular country—will limit the growth of any specific capitalist system. And this would be an inescapable conclusion if long-run equilibrium is understood, as in neoclassical theory, to be a configuration that, random shocks apart, will endure forever once it is achieved, which in the absence of technological progress makes it impossible for the equilibrium growth rate of output and employment to differ from the long-run rate of population growth. But a period much shorter than the indefinite future of neo-classical equilibrium is appropriate to neo-Marxian (and neo-Keynesian) theory, a period more like a generation, or at most a century.

The neo-Marxian/neo-Keynesian conception of the long run stems from the purpose of the theory. All models of growth and distribution — neoclassical, neo-Marxian, and neo-Keynesian — abstract from economic fluctuations, from the business "cycle," rightly or wrongly assuming that fluctuations can be grafted onto the model once its basic, long-run mechanisms are understood. (The exception to this methodological position is Michal Kalecki [1968], who argued that the long run can only be understood as a series of short runs, which is to say that fluctuations are integral to the model rather than a second-order overlay.) So much is the common property of all three approaches. But economic reality is, as we have just seen, very different in neoclassical and nonneoclassical theories. For the first, the object of study is the "economy," conceived as immortal. So it is perfectly appropriate for neoclassical theorists to define equilibrium in terms of an indefinite future. For the neo-Marxians and neo-Keynesians, by contrast, the focus is a particular form of economy, capitalism, viewed as eminently mortal. Thus it would be highly inappropriate to conceive of equilibrium as lasting for an infinite period. On the contrary: the long-run equilibrium need endure only as long as it takes to smooth out fluctuations, perhaps a generation, or — for believers in long waves — a century.

The consequence of this very different definition of equilibrium is that full employment disappears as a long-run constraint. "Reserve armies" recruited from other sectors of the economy or from across the nation's borders fill the gap between labor requirements and the labor force already engaged in capitalist production. By the same token, the labor force in the capitalist sector itself becomes a "reserve army" for the rest of the economy when the growth of employment within the capitalist sector falls short of workers' net reproduction rate. In short, the neo-Marxian model makes labor-force growth endogenous, determined by demand, rather than — as in the neoclassical model — exogenous.

Thus the neo-Marxian model posits competitive labor markets without wage competition — a contradiction only superficially. Unlimited supplies of labor at the conventional wage (over the long run of a generation or so) prevent wages from rising in response to demand. However, the conventional wage itself may rise over time, if working-class power increases or technological progress enlarges the pie over which capitalists and workers struggle. By the same token, the availability of a livelihood outside the capitalist sector[1] is assumed to prevent long-run overt unemployment and wage cutting in the event that growth of capitalist production is insufficient to absorb the net reproduction of the capitalist sector labor force. In both cases, supply is adapted to demand by mechanisms other than the wage rate.

One final point. In the neo-Marxian model, as in the neoclassical, the existence of long-run equilibrium is not guaranteed. But the issue here is only whether or not the conventional wage is less than productivity. No utility function complicates the existence question as it does in neoclassical theory. By the same token, the neoclassical problem of multiple equilibria has no counterpart in the neo-Marxian model. Neither is there a problem of stability. Departures of the real wage from equilibrium—as a result, for example, of price inflation—are assumed to be temporary: unless there are shifts in class power, class struggle is equilibrating, restoring conventional wages.

As a consequence, the variability of factor proportions makes much less difference to the neo-Marxian model than to the neoclassical. The neo-Marxian story, as we have seen, is quite consistent with variable proportions, even with continuous substitution. But substitution elasticities greater than or equal to unity paradoxically limit the domain of feasible rates of exploitation and thereby limit the applicability of the labor theory of value, even while guaranteeing the existence of neo-Marxian equilibrium for any given wage. (However, very high wage rates imply low and even negative rates of growth!) Finally, the guarantee of stability of equilibrium, which is the chief contribution of continuous substitution (at an elasticity of unity or more) in the neoclassical model, has no counterpart in the neo-Marxian model, since equilibrium is stable whatever might be assumed about factor proportions.

Neo-Keynesian Theory

The distinguishing feature of neo-Keynesian theory is the role played by investment demand. In neoclassical theory, investment demand is determined by population growth. In neo-Marxian theory, investment demand is determined by saving.[2] By contrast, the psychology of the

1. Over time small business and the household are supplemented and even replaced by the government as a locus of production.

2. The only counterpart in Marx of the Keynesian emphasis on investment demand is the "realization problem," the problem of translating desired saving into investment. In pre-Keynesian Marxism—Rosa Luxemburg (1913) apart—this is a secondary problem, and one that enters only in the context of economic fluctuations, not in the context of steady growth.

businessman is a primary determinant of investment demand in neo-Keynesian theory, and the equilibrium requirement that investment demand equal the supply of saving is thus neither a matter of adjusting desired saving to a rate determined by population dynamics, as in the neoclassical model, nor a tautology, as in the neo-Marxian. Neo-Keynesian causality presents a sharp contrast to both the neoclassical model and the neo-Marxian model: investment and saving determine the rate of profit and the rate of growth simultaneously.

The determination of wages is also in sharp contrast with the neo-Marxian model, as well as with the neoclassical model. In the neo-Keynesian analysis, wages are determined residually: the output left over after capitalists' appetites are satisfied is available to workers as wage goods. If factor proportions are continuously variable, then the capital:labor ratio adjusts so that the marginal productivity of labor equals the real wage. Once again, "marginal productivity" theory in this context is nothing more than competitive profit maximization coupled with constant returns to scale.

The customary rationalization of the neo-Keynesian view of distribution relies on the argument that wages are fixed in money terms and the price level adjusts to clear the market for goods; in particular the price level adjusts the *real* wage to clear the market for wage goods. Thus capitalists' and workers' demands play asymmetrical roles in the model: the greater is capitalists' demand for investment, the greater must be their share of the economic pie in order to cover their demand. By contrast, the working class has no such leverage: their consumption must adjust to the resources available after capitalists' demands are met.

This rationalization is incomplete. It is not enough to assume that the wage bargain is made in terms of money rather than goods to reach the result that the price level adjusts the real wage to the supply of wage goods available after capitalists' appetites for expansion have been met. It must be assumed as well either that workers suffer from money illusion or that workers anticipate price changes but are powerless to change money wages in response. Now money illusion may be a reasonable assumption for the very short period with which Keynes himself was concerned, but it is hardly acceptable for the longer period appropriate to the neo-Keynesian analysis. So the neo-Keynesian argument must fall back on the assumption of powerlessness: workers are unable to resist any erosion of purchasing power that might be entailed by the process of carrying through capitalists' investment plans.

The powerlessness of workers in the neo-Keynesian model does not lie solely in the nature of the wage bargain, but also in the institutional structure of capital markets. A central neo-Keynesian assumption, albeit more implicit than explicit, is that capitalists have special access to bank credit. The point is not only that capitalists have disproportionate control of assets suitable for collateral and consequently that workers can borrow comparatively little relative to their incomes; equally — perhaps more — important, capitalists can borrow on the basis of prospective returns while workers need collateral. In consequence, capitalists' effective demand in goods markets depends on their animal spirits, whereas workers' demand depends on their income and assets. This asymmetry, as much as the nature of the wage bargain, is the key to the neo-Keynesian aphorism: capitalists get what they spend, workers spend what they get.

Two factors mitigate, even if they do not eliminate, the resulting distributional conflict between capitalists and workers. First, higher investment means higher growth of employment and aggregate wages as well as of output. Indeed, the pragmatic trickle-down defense of capitalism, exemplified by Keynes's (non-Keynesian) introduction to *The Economic Consequences of the Peace* (1920), has always emphasized its ability to deliver the goods, to workers as well as to capitalists — in the long run if not the short.

Even in the short run, the conflict is muted by the existence of variable proportions, which allow output and employment to vary in response to changes in investment demand, and therefore take some of the adjustment burden off the wage rate. This is of course the basis of the multiplier, perhaps the most enduring contribution of Keynesian theory to contemporary economic analysis.

The neo-Keynesian multiplier differs in crucial respects from its Keynesian forebear, at least in the textbook form that has reached two generations of students. In assuming a uniform propensity to save across the entire population, the textbook Keynesian multiplier obscures the role of supply-side parameters — specifically the profit share and the elasticity of substitution in production. The resulting distortion rivals the distortion caused by ignoring variability of factor proportions, in which case the multiplier goes to zero and the entire burden of adjusting demand and supply falls, *à la* Kaldor (1956), on the demand side, with the price level adjusting the real wage to the available supply of goods.

There is no little irony in the emergence of the supply side in the one model distinguished by the central role afforded the demand side. The essential lesson is a simple one: the role of supply-side considerations can only be assessed in counterpoint to the role of demand. If the conventional Keynesian multiplier analysis hardly brings out the supply side, it is likely because of the economic conditions that prevailed at the time the Keynesian model was developed; the multiplier analysis does not inherently exclude supply considerations.

By contrast, approaches that ignore demand, be they neoclassical or neo-Marxian, are conceptually limited. Incapable of analyzing the impact of demand changes on output, they are equally incapable of addressing the constraints imposed from the supply side: there is no multiplier whatsoever in either of the two non-Keynesian models.

Neo-Keynesian theory, like neo-Marxian theory, has neither need nor place for full employment. In Joan Robinson's exposition (1956, 1962), full-employment growth is a fortuitous coincidence of the population growth rate with the growth rate at which capitalists' investment demand and the supply of saving are in equilibrium. Nicholas Kaldor (1956, 1957, 1961), it is true, assumed full employment, but for this very reason Kaldor's models are treated in this book as "hybrid" rather than as neo-Keynesian.

Although the absence of full employment is a common feature uniting neo-Keynesian and neo-Marxian models, there are important differences in the labor-market theories implicitly underlying the two approaches. The neo-Marxian theory, we have observed, is basically a long-run theory of unlimited supplies of labor at a conventional wage determined independently of the marginal productivity of labor in the capitalist sector. The neo-Keynesian theory, by contrast, suppresses the labor-supply function altogether. It assumes that wages in the capitalist sector include a hefty element of economic rent, so that they can be varied substantially without affecting supply. At the same time, there is an implicit notion that standards of fairness prevent wage competition even in the face of substantial unemployment.

Evidently the neo-Keynesian labor-market theory owes much to the origins of Keynes's *General Theory* (1936) in the Great Depression, as much as neo-Marxian theory owes to its origins in the generally buoyant conditions of the mid-nineteenth century. These genetics are betrayed by a peculiar asymmetry of the neo-Keynesian model. The Marxian emphasis on the creation and re-creation of "reserve armies" finds no echo in the neo-Keynesian model, and in fact there is no apparent neo-Keynesian mechanism for accommodating an equilibrium growth rate in excess of the internal resources of the capitalist sector. Hence full employment appears as a constraint in the neo-Keynesian model, but — unlike the neoclassical model — one that need not be binding.

As is the case for neoclassical and neo-Marxian models, the existence of long-run neo-Keynesian equilibrium is not guaranteed. Neither is uniqueness or stability. Stability depends on the relative responsiveness of investment and saving to changes in the rate of profit.

The contrast with the neoclassical model is noteworthy. The introduction of variable factor proportions, even with continuous substitution at an elasticity greater than unity, does not greatly affect the stability of neo-Keynesian equilibrium (or its existence for that matter), for equilibrium profit and growth rates depend essentially on capitalists' psychological makeup. Thus, it becomes easier to understand both the neoclassical preoccupation with continuous substitution and elasticities, and the indifference — if not hostility — to this concern among nonneoclassicals (neo-Marxians as well as neo-Keynesians). Even if it is not integral to the neoclassical argument, continuous substitution makes a substantial difference to its outcome, a difference that finds hardly an echo in the nonneoclassical camp.

The Cambridge Saving Equation

The saving function that has dominated neo-Keynesian theory differs in an important respect from what is conventionally regarded as "Keynesian." In the conventional representation of the Keynesian saving function, the propensity to save is constant and independent of class, whether class be defined in terms of income or in terms of the Marxian opposition between capitalists and workers. By contrast, neo-Keynesian saving theory is essentially classical; at its core is the class-based difference in propensities to save that characterizes the neo-Marxian approach. Indeed, the two saving theories, neo-Marxian and neo-Keynesian, are presented as identical throughout this book. The difference between neo-Keynesians and neo-Marxians lies not in the saving function but in the choice between investment demand and a conventional wage as the second of the relationships that close the model.

Refinements of the classical saving function are discussed in Chapter 6. The stark version, in which capitalists save everything and workers nothing, is replaced by Kaldor's more plausible version (1956) in which a fraction of wages are saved and a fraction of profits consumed. With a Kaldorian saving function, the relationship between growth and profit rates depends on both propensities to save, the propensity to save out of wages as well as the propensity to save out of profits — a hardly surprising result even if it dilutes the simplicity of the classical growth and profit relationship, in which growth and profit rates are always equal. But the essence of the classical approach—a positive relationship between growth and profit rates—is preserved by the assumption that the propensity to save out of profits is greater than the propensity to save out of wages.

The refinement of the classical saving function took a more controversial turn with the publication of Luigi Pasinetti's famous 1962 article. The essence of Pasinetti's position is, first, that the logical consequence of saving out of wages is the accumulation of capital and concomitant claims on profits on the part of workers, and second, that workers' propensity to save out of their share of profits is the same as their propensity to save out of wages, not the (higher) propensity to save that Kaldor imputes to all profits regardless of the class of the profit recipient. In Pasinetti's saving function, saving propensities are associated with specific classes (workers and capitalists) not with specific forms of income (wages and profits).

This seemingly small change in assumptions turns out to make a substantial difference to the results. If capitalists end up owning *any* positive share of capital, only their saving propensity matters for the existence of long-run equilibrium: the steady-growth configuration of profits and wages, investment and consumption, is altogether independent of workers' propensity to save. Thus by correcting what he termed a logical slip in Kaldor's formulation, Pasinetti claimed to have restored the elegance of the simple classical saving theory, in which not only is there a positive relationship between growth and profits, but the relationship depends only on capitalists' saving propensities—and this without having to assume that workers save nothing.

Pasinetti's restoration of the classical proportions between profit and growth into the saving function, it should be pointed out, is more successful in characterizing neo-Keynesian equilibrium than in analyzing its stability. For stability analysis, provided the short-run responsiveness of saving to changes in the profit rate exceeds the long-run, the relevant saving function is the short-run "quasi-Kaldorian" function that takes the workers' share of capital as fixed.

Two difficulties have been noted with Pasinetti's result. First, Kaldor (1966) insisted that he meant what he said when contrasting profits with wages rather than capitalists' income with workers', and thus that no logical error had been committed. For Kaldor the important determinant of the propensity to save is not whether capitalists or workers get the income but whether the income is in the hands of corporations or individuals. In Kaldor's view, capital is identified with the corporation and profits are identified with corporate income. The corporate propensity to save replaces the entrepreneurial capitalists' propensity to save, and is independent of nominal ownership of capital.

There is much truth in this view, but it cannot answer Pasinetti's objection to Kaldor's formulation unless the corporate propensity to save is unity, that is, unless all profits are retained and plowed back into capital formation by the corporation. But this is patently untrue. Dividend payouts remain a substantial fraction of corporate income. So, whereas Kaldor's rejoinder leads to a more complex model than Pasinetti offered, the basic Pasinetti result — that workers' saving propensities are irrelevant to the determination of equilibrium if capitalists end up with any positive share of capital — survives intact.

A second objection to the Pasinetti result, voiced by Paul Samuelson and Franco Modigliani (1966a), is the possibility of a "people's capitalism" in which workers end up owning *all* the capital; in this case only the saving propensity of workers matters in determining the equilibrium configuration of distribution and growth. Moreover, the long-run tendency of a capitalist mode of production, according to Samuelson and Modigliani, is toward a people's capitalism equilibrium (what they term an "anti-Pasinetti" regime), so that we are faced not just with a theoretical possibility but with a prospect that is empirically likely.

However, the Samuelson-Modigliani calculations are hardly compelling, both because the calculations utilize current, disequilibrium values of the output:capital ratio and propensities to save as estimates of equilibrium values and because they are based on measures of profit and workers' saving propensities that are biased in favor of the people's capitalism equilibrium. This is not to say that the Samuelson-Modigliani result is incorrect; rather, repeating their calculations for a plausible range of parameter values leaves the long-run tendency of capitalism in doubt.

A more basic problem with the Samuelson-Modigliani argument is that, like Pasinetti's, it does not address the distinctions between claims on profit, ownership of capital, and control of capitalist production. To the extent that workers might own capital but fail to control production, the significance of people's capitalism as a genuine alternative to capitalists' capitalism is as problematic as socialism in which the people own the means of production but a bureaucratic party exercises actual control over the production process. Even with ownership as concentrated as it is in contemporary America, a significant body of opinion holds that effective control has long since passed to top management (Berle and Means 1932) or to the technostructure (Galbraith 1967).

Greater diffusion of ownership would only strengthen the Berle-Means-Galbraith case.

Moreover, even if control is identified with ownership, there is no reason to assume that claims on profit necessarily convey ownership. To the extent that workers' saving takes the form of pension funds, saving deposits, or bonds, even an asymptotically vanishing share of total capital in the hands of capitalists may constitute legal ownership — as well as effective control — of means of production.

Pension funds are a particularly interesting case of divergence between claims on profits and direct ownership of capital for two reasons. First, pension funds constitute an important fraction of savings treated as "personal" in the national income accounts, even though pension-fund accumulation is at best an indirect form of personal saving. Second, the dynamics of pension-fund accumulation lead, in the spirit of Pasinetti's argument, to the result that *neither* capitalists' nor workers' direct saving matters in determining the configuration of long-run equilibrium, at least not if pension funds end up with a positive share of the capital stock. By virtue of a higher propensity to save, pensions end up crowding capitalists out altogether.

To be sure, the crowding out of capitalists by pension funds depends critically on the assumption of a uniform rate of profit on all categories of capital. It does not hold if capitalists enjoy a differential sufficient to offset their lower propensity to save.

Neither would crowding out necessarily lead to a new or radically different mode of production. Despite the alarm raised by Peter Drucker (1976) about the imminent arrival of "pension-fund socialism," the real issue once again is control rather than ownership. Even allowing that pension funds would be in a stronger position than ordinary shareholders to work their will upon top management and the technostructure, fiduciary responsibility would have to be interpreted by pension-fund trustees in a boldly innovative way to bring about any real change. To the traditional trustee concern to provide for the retirement of workers would have to be added a concern for the quality of the work life of those on whose behalf the pension fund owns capital. Initiative and support for a variety of stockholder resolutions — for example, to change the structure of control in the enterprise in the direction of greater shop-floor democracy — would then become not only feasible but, conceivably at least, mandatory!

The more plausible scenario, however, is that the fiduciary ownership vested in pension-fund trustees would be so constrained by law, custom, and the class interest of the trustees that pension-fund socialism would deliver very little to the ordinary worker on the promise of control over the production process that is implicit in the concept of socialism—perhaps no more than in the Soviet Union, where the transfer of title to "the people" (by a more violent form of crowding out) was accompanied by concentration of effective control in party and state bureaucracies; perhaps no more than would a people's capitalism in the United States, unless management and technostructure were radically transformed in the bargain.

This is not to write off pension funds as a possible avenue of change, but to put matters in perspective: pension-fund socialism is not, as Drucker would have it, a matter of relative growth rates of capital ownership. The growth of pension funds creates a potential for changes in the mode of production, but hardly the certainty of such change.

To summarize, nonneoclassical saving theory differs from neoclassical theory in two respects. First, it assumes that capitalists save a higher fraction of their incomes than do workers. Indeed in the two-period version of the life-cycle model, capitalists, being nothing but retired workers, consume principal as well as interest: their saving propensity is negative. Second, the microeconomic foundations of the two theories differ. In place of the rationalistic utility maximization assumed to underlie household saving behavior in the neoclassical model, Chapter 7 proposes a microeconomic basis for nonneoclassical theory in which household saving is but the consequence of lags in adjustment of spending to income, a "disequilibrium" phenomenon that persists as long as income grows.

Marginal-Productivity Theory

One of the novelties of this exposition is the assertion that marginal productivity is not the exclusive property of neoclassical theory. In all the theories, variable proportions transform two exogenous parameters, the capital : output and the labor : output ratios, into unknowns, and constant returns to scale together with a marginal-productivity equation provide the two relationships that offset the greater number of unknowns.

The proposition that the wage rate equals the marginal productivity of labor, or the equivalent that the profit rate equals the marginal productivity of capital, requires only (1) continuous factor substitution, (2) constant returns to scale, and (3) competitive profit maximization. Acceptance or rejection of any or all of these three assumptions is quite independent of the choice between neoclassical theory and the neo-Marxian or neo-Keynesian alternatives.

Continuous factor substitution is of course as much an abstraction as fixed proportions. To be sure, short-run variability in factor proportions exists when the capital-utilization rate varies in response to fluctuations in demand. But "Okun's Law" (Okun 1962) suggests a short-run employment elasticity of output of about 3.0, which is consistent with the assumptions of long-run constant returns to scale and diminishing marginal productivity only because the employment mix (for example, the mix of production and maintenance workers) is assumed to change with the level of employment, and this in turn because of expectations that changes in demand are to some extent transitory. Hence short-run variability of factor proportions does not provide a very convincing illustration of the relevance of the continuous-substitution model to the long-run case.

But some production activities, like corn growing, evidently fit the continuous-substitution characterization reasonably well in the long run as well as in the short; others, like copper smelting and refining, come closer to the fixed-proportions pole, apart from short-run variability in capacity-utilization rates. In any case the issue of how to characterize production is not one that involves different world views. It is really quite secondary to the issues that divide neoclassicals, neo-Marxians, and neo-Keynesians. That neither Karl Marx nor Joan Robinson ever characterized production in terms of continuous substitution is quite beside the point. Neither did Léon Walras—at least not until the third edition of the *Elements of Pure Economics* (first edition, 1874 and 1877; third edition, 1896).

Nor should constant returns to scale be very divisive. The absence of increasing returns is assumed simply to facilitate the argument for competition. The absence of decreasing returns merely supposes divisibility of the production process and inclusion of all relevant inputs in the arguments of the production function. The effect of constant returns to scale is the well-known product-exhaustion theorem, factor payments at rates equal to factor marginal productivities just equaling, in the aggregate, the total product.

Neither is profit maximization inherently controversial. To be sure, alternatives to profit maximization have been proposed and are the subject of continuing debate. But for better or for worse, profit maximization is not an issue that divides neoclassical, neo-Marxian, and neo-Keynesian theorists. The only controversial issue is perfect competition. Doubtless no neo-Keynesian or neo-Marxian would today characterize product markets as perfectly competitive, despite the fact that Keynes and Marx themselves did so. Marx, to be sure, wrote at a time when the characterization may have been plausible. Keynes's excuse is less obvious. The most sympathetic explanation imputes a desire to be as faithful to his mentor Alfred Marshall as the novelty of his theory would permit. On the other hand, it is plausible that *both* Keynes and Marx conducted their analysis in terms of perfect competition only to impress upon their readers that their respective diagnoses of the ills of capitalism did not hinge on "special" assumptions, like the assumption of monopoly.

But if neo-Marxians and neo-Keynesians would deny the competitiveness of contemporary capitalism, so would neoclassicists, except perhaps at the University of Chicago and its outposts. Monopolistic competition or oligopoly is then not an alternative to neoclassical theory, but an alternative to marginal-productivity relations. In particular, Michal Kalecki's "degree of monopoly" (1938, 1943) is presented here not as an alternative theory of the rate of profit, but as a substitute for competitive marginal conditions in determining the capital : output ratio. (In Nicholas Kaldor's later models, investors' "animal spirits" substitute for the degree of monopoly or the marginal productivity equation in determining the capital : output ratio. Thus the degree of monopoly is determined implicitly.) The essential point is that an exogenously given degree of monopoly or some equivalent relationship can substitute for the marginal productivity relationship of perfect competition in any of the models — neoclassical, neo-Marxian, neo-Keynesian, or hybrid.

All this notwithstanding, there is a sense in which marginal-productivity relationships become a theory in themselves. When linked with the assumption of full employment and a given capital stock, the marginal-productivity relationship takes on a much stronger meaning than simply competitive profit maximization in a world of continuous substitution and constant returns to scale. With the capital stock and employment given, as it is in the extreme version of short-run neoclassical theory I have labeled the "Chicago Story," the marginal productivity of labor at full employment *determines* the real wage, and the full-employment marginal productivity of capital *determines* the profit rate. By contrast, in the neo-Marxian and neo-Keynesian models, causality runs in the opposite direction, factor prices determining marginal productivities. In the neo-Marxian model, the real wage determines the marginal productivity of both labor and capital; in the neo-Keynesian model, the rate of profit determines the two marginal productivities.

Observe that even in neoclassical theory full employment alone is not enough to transform marginal-productivity relationships into a long-run theory of distribution. In long-run neoclassical theory, the capital : labor ratio is endogenously determined, so that the wage rate cannot be determined solely by the marginal productivity of labor at full employment—not even in Chicago. Instead, distribution must reflect household preferences with respect to present and future consumption.

Thus, it is fair to conclude that there are two marginal-productivity theories. The first is a relatively innocuous, general theory that involves nothing more controversial than competitive profit maximization—and provides correspondingly little contribution to the theory of growth and distribution under capitalism. The second is more powerful, and very special, providing by itself a theory of distribution, for the short run at least, whose "only" defects are (1) that it assumes full employment and (2) that it begs the question of accumulation. The wonder is that it is precisely this theory that so many students come away with from their study of economics. Only slightly more wondrous is that by and large they believe it!

Multiple Goods

The objective of the theories necessarily becomes much more ambitious in the context of a multiplicity of commodities: each must explain relative prices of various goods as well as aggregate growth and distribution. Willy-nilly, the models become exercises in general equilibrium. Observe that this is true of *all* the models, notwithstanding the identification of general-equilibrium theory with neoclassical theory in graduate schools throughout the land. The models become more complex not only because more commodities mean more equations and more unknowns, but because qualitatively new features enter the picture. The consequence of these new features is that certain propositions of the one-good case do not generalize to the many-good case.

The first novelty is that even with fixed coefficients the capital : output ratio becomes a variable that depends on (1) the relative prices of the various commodities that make up the economy's capital stock, these prices in turn varying with the rate of profit, and (2) the composition of output. Of course, the capital : output ratio can vary even with only one good, and therefore with no variation in relative prices or output composition. The novelty of the multiple-good case is that variability exists even when all input coefficients are assumed to be fixed.

The direct consequence of the variability of the capital : output ratio is to make the distribution of income, defined in terms of the *shares* of wages and profits, and for a given output composition, vary nonlinearly with the rate of profit. The ultimate consequence is to impeach *any* proposition of the one-good case that depends explicitly or implicitly on the determination of the capital:output ratio uniquely by the profit rate. In the multiple-good, fixed-proportions situation, such propositions remain valid only in two special cases. First, the capital:output ratio is both independent of the composition of output and invariant with respect to the profit rate if the vector of labor coefficients bears a particular relationship to the matrix of commodity inputs. Specifically, the labor-coefficient vector must be a *row* characteristic vector of the commodity-input matrix, a condition essentially equivalent to Marx's condition of equal organic composition of capital in all industries. Second, the capital:output ratio is always invariant with respect to the profit rate for one particular output composition, independently of the relationship of labor coefficients to commodity coefficients. Specifically, the composition of output must be a *column* characteristic vector of the commodity-input matrix, a condition that makes this particular output mix equal to Piero Sraffa's standard commodity (1960).

These results are more telling for the neo-Marxian and neo-Keynesian models than for the neoclassical, which may explain why nonneoclassicals have paid more attention to the special cases than have partisans of orthodoxy. Indeed, the complexity added to the neoclassical model by abandoning the restrictive assumptions that maintain the simplicity of a constant output:capital ratio is technical rather than conceptual in nature: the proof of the existence of equilibrium becomes more complicated, but nothing else changes.

By contrast, the conceptual basis of the one-good neo-Marxian model is seriously threatened by the introduction of additional commodities. First, even in conjunction with the simplest classical saving theory, the labor theory of value fails as a basis for growth and consumption rates, or profit and wage rates. Only with technology constrained by equal organic composition of capital or consumption stipulated in advance does a given rate of exploitation map to a determinate equilibrium configuration.

This failure, however, is more significant for ultramontanists than for partisans of the approach to Marx favored in this book, in which the starting point is a conventional wage rather than a rate of exploitation. But, as has been noted, the conventional wage is not without its problems too. Were subsistence viewed in biological terms, extending the set of commodities from one to many would pose only minor difficulties. In place of a wage of, say, 20 bushels of corn (or grain in American usage) per year, we would specify a vector of 20 bushels of corn, 1 blanket of wool, 2 cords of fire wood, and so forth. (Even here there are potential problems: within the category of food grains, there are wheat, rye, barley, oats, and the food values of the grains differ; then too, there are heavier and lighter wools; and the heating value of poplar is not the same as the heating value of maple. But these are comparatively minor difficulties.) When, however, subsistence is recognized to be a social rather than a biological notion, and the existence of a multiplicity of commodities is recognized, important conceptual problems arise: how is subsistence defined in physical terms in the light of substitution possibilities? How is the price sensitivity of the consumption mix to be reflected?

This book hardly does more than recognize the seriousness of these questions. It sketches a line of attack, rather than providing a complete answer. The essential feature of the proposed approach is to emphasize the moral element of the original Marxian formulation of the subsistence wage, to see the subsistence wage as a conventional bundle of commodities that forms the basis of wage demands even though no worker may consume precisely that bundle. Hence the proposal to abandon the terminology of subsistence in favor of the terminology of convention.

The precise bundles that individual workers consume may reflect substitution possibilities and be more or less sensitive to relative prices without affecting the rigidity—at any given time and place—of the conventional bundle. Of course, time and place are of the essence: the issue in nineteenth-century England was whether subsistence included wheat bread or rye bread; in twentieth-century America the commodities at issue have become beefsteak and automobiles; vacation homes may become an issue in the twenty-first century. The wage becomes even more problematic when the saving function is modified to allow workers to save and, consequently, to receive part of aggregate profits. In this case, subsistence must become purely notional, for it becomes impossible to separate workers' consumption out of wages from their consumption out of profits. None of these difficulties need be fatal to the neo-Marxian approach. But to ignore them is surely to remove the possibility of developing the neo-Marxian approach into a convincing explanation of the workings of modern capitalism.

A multiplicity of commodities introduces one other problem in the neo-Marxian model, one that is shared by the neo-Keynesian approach: determining equilibrium growth and profit rates by a conventional wage or by animal spirits leaves the composition of output indeterminate. This not only (apart from special cases) leaves distributive shares indeterminate, it also leaves the equilibrium itself incomplete, at least relative to the neoclassical model in which consumer demand determines the composition of output at the same time as it determines the profit rate and relative prices.

The obvious solution is to introduce household preferences into the neo-Marxian and neo-Keynesian approaches, to assume that the composition of consumption, and hence output, is determined by households maximizing utilities at given prices. It will be objected that the introduction of household preferences into these models robs them of their distinctive quality, making them indistinguishable from the neoclassical approach. But the objection is misplaced. In the neoclassical model, consumers' preferences play a crucial role in determining the rate of profit and relative prices as well as the composition of output. In neo-Marxian and neo-Keynesian approaches, household preferences determine *only* the composition of output; rates of profit and growth and relative prices are determined by the interaction of a nonneoclassical saving function with a conventional wage rate or with an investment-demand function. The issue is thus not the presence or absence of household preferences in the model, but the role preferences play.

The assertion that preferences determine only the composition of output in the neo-Marxian and neo-Keynesian models must be qualified in the case of a people's-capitalism equilibrium. If workers end up with all the capital, then the growth rate in the neo-Marxian model and the profit rate as well as the growth rate in the neo-Keynesian become sensitive to the composition of output and hence to utility maximization. But even in this special case, household preferences affect equilibrium profit and growth rates differently than in the neoclassical model. Here preferences enter only to the extent that they influence the capital : output ratio. In the neoclassical model, preferences determine the shape of the saving function, even with a constant capital : output ratio.

A new problem shows up when the assumption of fixed proportions is modified to allow an array of linear technologies, each of which involves different input proportions. In this situation it is possible for a particular technology to be cost-minimizing over two distinct intervals of the rate of profit, separated by an interval of profit rates over which a second technology minimizes costs. In the language of the famous controversy of the sixties, nothing precludes reswitching.

So what? At one level, reswitching matters very little: in particular, the existence of equilibrium, in many ways *the* issue from the perspective of this book, is unaffected. But at another level, reswitching matters quite a lot: propositions that depend on a negative relationship between the rate of profit and the capital : output ratio, a relationship that holds quite generally in the one-good case, fail in the presence of reswitching. The reason is clear: whatever the measure of the capital : output ratio, it must, for a given technology, be invariant with respect to the rate of profit — or else we may be unable to order technologies unambiguously according to their capital : output ratios. But let the technology vary with the rate of profit, and *no* measure of capital values can meet this test *and* change monotonically with the rate of profit under conditions of reswitching. If the cost-minimizing technology, and hence the composition of capital, that obtain for rates of profit between, say, 0.20 and 0.25 also obtain between 0.05 and 0.10, but a different technology and composition of capital obtain between 0.10 and 0.20, then the value of capital must be the same over the two intervals [0.05, 0.10] and [0.20, 0.25], and higher or lower in between.

The most notorious of the propositions invalidated by the presence of reswitching has been associated with neoclassical theory, not because it is intrinsically neoclassical but because its ideological implications accord so well with the ideological thrust of the neoclassical model. An inverse relationship between the rate of profit and the capital : output ratio has lent itself to the idea that the profit rate is determined by the level of accumulation, and falls over time *because* accumulation takes place.

There are, to be sure, problems with this argument quite apart from its failure in the presence of reswitching. First, there is a bit of sleight of hand involved in going from a static relationship between the rate of profit and the capital : output ratio to an argument about causality, particularly a dynamic argument about the path of the rate of profit. The existence of a particular relationship between the profit rate and the stock of capital says nothing about how the capital stock has come to be what it is; moreover, without a theory of employment, the capital stock does not determine a capital : output *ratio*. Both these issues — accumulation and employment — are, as we have seen, resolved very differently by the three theories analyzed in this book.

Finally, although the neoclassical tradition emphasizes a particular interpretation of the supposed negative relationship between profit rate and capital : output ratio, the relationship itself is not the peculiar property of the neoclassical tradition. The connection between the falling rate of profit and the rising organic composition of capital in the Marxian tradition is an alternative expression of the same idea.

In any case, it has already been indicated that from the perspective of this book, reswitching is something of a storm in a teacup. Not only is reswitching irrelevant to questions of existence of equilibrium, its very presence is limited to the case where the array of techniques is discrete:

in conditions of continuous substitution, the possibility of reswitching disappears. (This, to be sure, does *not* restore the inverse relationship between the rate of profit and the capital : output ratio, for the absence of reswitching is necessary for this relationship but hardly sufficient.)

Even the question of whether or not a negative relationship between the profit rate and the capital : output ratio holds good, though surely more significant than the question of reswitching, is hardly at the core of what divides economists and economic theories. Were such a negative relationship to hold, because God in her infinite wisdom had seen fit to disqualify technologies inconsistent with it, the case for neoclassical theory would hardly be strengthened. The issues that divide neoclassical from neo-Marxian and neo-Keynesian theories would remain. Similarly, the presence of reswitching hardly weakens the case for the neoclassical model expounded in this book, whatever it might do to the more extravagant claims of the extremists of the neoclassical camp.

There remains one result of the multiple-goods case worthy of note. With continuous substitution, neoclassical equilibrium can, as in the one-good case, be guaranteed to exist by assuming a sufficiently high elasticity of substitution. There is a difficulty with this assumption: elasticities of substitution in excess of unity conflict with the assumption of "indecomposability," the assumption that something of every good is required directly or indirectly in the production of every other good. The *only* constant-elasticity production function that simultaneously guarantees the existence of neoclassical equilibrium and meets the indecomposability condition is the Cobb-Douglas production function. Thus if indecomposability is considered a reasonable representation of the technological integration characteristic of contemporary capitalism, the neoclassical economist is faced with a real dilemma: to avoid the possibility that population growth is incompatible with saving propensities and technology, he must commit himself to characterizing production by Cobb-Douglas production functions! (To be sure, the dilemma is not peculiar to the multiple-good case: in the one-good case, a substitution elasticity greater than unity also implies that goods can be produced with labor or capital alone, so that the guarantee of the existence of equilibrium hinges on technological assumptions that are, to say the least, restrictive.)

No such dilemma exists for the neo-Marxian or neo-Keynesian economist, for the existence of neo-Marxian or neo-Keynesian equilibrium is hardly sensitive to the elasticity of substitution in production. Once again, the difference between neoclassical and classical saving functions makes for important differences in the role of production conditions.

16 Testing the Models: Energy and Employment

An eminent economist sat quietly through one of the seminars I gave as this book was taking shape. At the end, he asked a question as simple to phrase as it was difficult to answer: "How might you," he asked, "empirically distinguish the various theories you have developed today?"

A profound question. Empirical tests are easy to formulate: the models differ in important ways in their implications for real-world behavior. But these tests are difficult to implement and interpret without making unrealistic demands on the models and imposing unrealistic assumptions on the data.

Take the comparative-statics exercise sketched at the beginning of Chapter 6. There we observed that neo-Marxian and neo-Keynesian models make opposite predictions with respect to the effect of capitalists' propensity to save on the equilibrium growth rate. The neo-Marxian model leads to a straightforward, positive relationship between s_C and g^*: the higher the fraction of profits plowed back into investment, the higher is the rate of steady growth. The paradoxical neo-Keynesian result, an *inverse* relationship between s_C and g^*, is a consequence of the role of investment demand in that model: when s_C increases, it takes a lower profit *rate* to provide the amount of saving necessary to satisfy the *existing* investment demand, and investment demand itself responds adversely to the fall in the rate of profit, thus leading to a lower equilibrium rate of growth. This opposition suggests a straightforward cross-sectional test: evidence indicating a positive association between s_C and g would support the neo-Marxian view, evidence of a negative association the neo-Keynesian.

The problems with such a test are many. In the first place, it assumes that the data sample consists of observations of long-run equilibria. Furthermore, the theoretical contrast in the behavior of $dg*/ds_C$ is based on models more suited to exposition than to prediction, abstracting as both do from technological change, government, foreign trade, and natural resources.

But even if we wave these difficulties aside, another equally formidable one appears, Hydra-like, in their place. For cross-sectional comparisons of this kind to yield meaningful results, the second determinant of equilibrium — the conventional wage or the investment-demand function — must be identical across the sample. Or, at least, variations in the wage rate or investment demand must be uncorrelated with changes in the propensity to save. But while the second version of the requirement — orthogonality of error terms — appears more plausible, it is only superficially less stringent, and impossible to verify in practice. Without orthogonality, however, a cross-sectional scatter of equilibrium $\langle r*, g* \rangle$ pairs permits us to identify neither an investment-demand function nor a "subsistence"-determined profit rate. The scatter would remain nothing but a scatter; the test would be inconclusive.

The Comparative Statics of an Energy Shock

Analyzing the effect on equilibrium of a change on the production side of the model adds another dimension to the problems of empirically distinguishing one model from another, and has the additional virtue of shedding considerable light on the models themselves. The real-world phenomenon that underlies this exercise is the abrupt increase in the relative cost of energy since 1973, but the exercise is reasonably far removed from that reality.

To model an energy shock, we must modify the production relation of Chapter 9 to allow for a nonproduced material input. The simplest way to do this is to write corn production X as a function of energy E as well as of seed corn K and labor L:

$$X = F(K, E, L).$$

With constant returns to scale, output per worker X/L can be expressed as a function of seed corn per worker, $k \equiv K/L$, and energy per worker, $e \equiv E/L$:

$$\frac{X}{L} = F(k, e, 1) \equiv f(k, e).$$

Now assume all energy to be imported at a price ω that is independent of E, and paid for by exports of corn. We can then express net output per worker (that is, output net of energy costs) as a function $h(k, \omega)$ which generalizes the production function $f(k)$ of Chapter 9:

$$h(k, \omega) = \max_{e} [f(k, e) - \omega e]. \tag{16.1}$$

An interior solution to this maximization problem is characterized by the marginal-productivity equation

$$MP_E \equiv f_e = \omega. \tag{16.2}$$

In addition, we have under conditions of competitive profit maximization the marginal-productivity equations

$$MP_K \equiv f_k = (1 + r), \tag{16.3}$$

$$MP_L \equiv f(k, e) - f_e e - f_k k = \frac{W}{P}. \tag{16.4}$$

Now $f_k \equiv h_k$, so substituting from (16.1) and (16.2) into (16.4), we obtain a modified marginal-productivity equation for labor, namely

$$MP_L \equiv h(k, \omega) - h_k k = \frac{W}{P}. \tag{16.5}$$

If we also substitute from (16.3), we obtain the price equation

$$h(k, \omega) = \frac{W}{P} + (1 + r)k. \tag{16.6}$$

The modeling of an energy shock focuses on the signs of three derivatives—$dr^*/d\omega$, $d(W/P)^*/d\omega$, and $dg^*/d\omega$—in each of the three models. We start with the neo-Marxian and neo-Keynesian models, in which the key results are unambiguous, and then move to the neoclassical model, in which the behavior of r^* and $(W/P)^*$ depend on assumptions about the technological relationship between energy and capital.

In the neo-Marxian model, with a given wage rate, the impact of an increase in the price of energy is determined by differentiating the price equation (16.6) and the marginal-productivity equation (16.5) with respect to ω, while W/P is held fixed. The results are

$$\frac{dr^*}{d\omega} = \frac{h_\omega}{k}, \tag{16.7}$$

$$\frac{dk^*}{d\omega} = \frac{h_\omega - h_{k\omega}k}{h_{kk}k}. \tag{16.8}$$

From (16.1) and (16.2) we have

$$h_\omega = -e, \tag{16.9}$$

so $dr^*/d\omega$ is unambiguously negative.

The sign of $dk^*/d\omega$ depends on special assumptions about technology. From (16.9) we have

$$h_{k\omega} \equiv h_{\omega k} = -\frac{de}{dk},$$

which is to say that the sign of $h_{k\omega}$ is the opposite of the change in energy that optimally accompanies a change in the capital : labor ratio for a fixed energy price. "Optimality" is defined by Eq. (16.1), that is, in terms of maximum net output. From (16.2) we have

$$\frac{de}{dk} = -\frac{f_{ek}}{f_{ee}} \equiv -\frac{f_{ke}}{f_{ee}}.$$

No one should, at this point, choke on the assumption of diminishing marginal productivity: $f_{ee} < 0$.[1] Thus the sign of de/dk is the same as the sign of $f_{ek} \equiv f_{ke}$: energy changes positively with capital if additional energy makes capital more productive at the margin, negatively if additional energy makes capital less productive marginally. In the first case ($f_{ke} > 0$), capital and energy are *complements,* in the second case ($f_{ke} < 0$), *substitutes.*

Neither case can be ruled out of court. For example, energy and capital are clearly substitutes in the production of shelter — witness the increase in the utilization of insulating materials that has resulted from higher heating (and cooling) costs. But energy and capital are just as clearly complements in activities like agricultural mechanization — increases in the utilization of machinery per man-year of farm labor necessitate more fuel to run the machines. I do not know enough to hazard a guess for the sign of f_{ke} overall.

Observe that the sign of $h_{k\omega}$ is opposite to the sign of f_{ke}. If capital and energy are complements, then

$$h_{k\omega} < 0, \tag{16.10}$$

which is to say that the net (after energy cost) marginal productivity of capital decreases with a rise in the price of energy: more of each increment in output that results from increases in the capital : labor ratio must be paid over for energy. If capital and energy are substitutes, then the net marginal productivity of capital increases with the price of energy.

1. See the appendix to Chapter 9 for a discussion of the assumptions that underlie diminishing marginal productivity.

In the neo-Marxian model, a sufficient condition for $dk^*/d\omega > 0$ is that energy and capital be substitutes:

$$h_{k\omega} > 0 \quad \Rightarrow \quad h_\omega - h_{k\omega}k < 0,$$

so that the numerator of (16.8) is negative, and diminishing marginal productivity of capital ($f_{kk} \equiv h_{kk} < 0$) makes the denominator negative too. But $h_{k\omega} > 0$ is stronger than necessary. The expression $h_\omega - h_{k\omega}k$ can still be negative if capital and energy are complements, provided the complementarity is moderate. Specifically, "moderate complementarity" means that whenever $h_{k\omega} < 0$, the elasticity of energy with respect to capital is less than unity:

$$h_\omega - h_{k\omega}k < 0 \quad \Leftrightarrow \quad \frac{de}{dk}\frac{k}{e} < 1.$$

In economic terms, to assume

$$h_\omega - h_{k\omega}k < 0 \tag{16.11}$$

is to assume that the net marginal productivity of *labor* falls with increases in the price of energy. Thus a sufficient condition for $dk^*/d\omega > 0$ in the neo-Marxian model is that an increase in the price of energy decreases the net marginal productivity of labor.

The effect on growth is determined by the saving function. With $\hat{\delta} > 0$, we have

$$g = s_C r$$

and

$$\frac{dg^*}{d\omega} = s_C \frac{dr^*}{d\omega} = s_C \frac{h_\omega}{k} < 0.$$

The growth rate moves in the same direction as the profit rate. The $\hat{\delta} = 0$ case is more complicated. Here it is possible for the growth rate to move in the opposite direction to the profit rate. We have

$$g = s_W \frac{h(k,\omega) - k}{k}$$

and

$$\frac{dg^*}{d\omega} = s_W \frac{\sigma}{(1+r)a_1} \frac{h_\omega - h_{k\omega}k}{k} + s_W \frac{h_\omega}{k},$$

where σ is the elasticity of substitution between labor and capital in the production function $h(k,\omega)$,

$$\sigma = \frac{dk}{d\left(\dfrac{W/P}{1+r}\right)} \frac{(W/P)/(1+r)}{k} = -\frac{(W/P)/(1+r)}{h(k,\,\omega)k\,h_{kk}}$$

(σ is assumed to be less than unity in all the geometric representations of an energy shock), and a_1 is the capital : output ratio,

$$a_1 = \frac{k}{h(k,\,\omega)}.$$

In the $\hat{\delta} = 0$ range it is theoretically possible that an increase in the price of energy would stimulate saving through its effect on the equilibrium capital : output ratio. Sufficient to rule this out, however, is the assumption that energy and seed corn are no more than moderately complementary: the assumption

$$h_\omega - h_{k\omega}k < 0 \qquad\qquad (16.11)$$

guarantees $dk*/d\omega > 0$ and $dg*/d\omega < 0$.

Figure 16.1 is drawn for the case in which $\hat{\delta}$ is positive and energy and capital are moderately complementary; that is, both (16.10) and (16.11) hold:

$$h_{k\omega} < 0, \qquad\qquad (16.10)$$

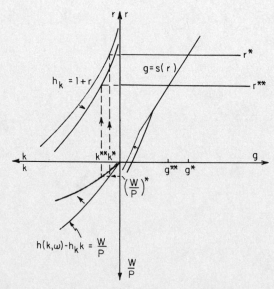

Figure 16.1 Neo-Marxian response to an energy shock

$$h_\omega - h_{k\omega} k < 0. \tag{16.11}$$

As ω increases, the equilibrium growth rate as well as the profit rate falls, from $\langle r^*, g^* \rangle$ to $\langle r^{**}, g^{**} \rangle$, and the equilibrium capital:labor ratio rises from k^* to k^{**}.

The economic logic of the neo-Marxian case is straightforward, the possibility of exceptional behavior of the saving function with $\hat\delta = 0$ aside. With wages fixed, the adjustment falls on profits and growth. In the absence of excessive complementarity between energy and capital, the net marginal productivity of labor falls, and the capital:labor ratio increases.

The neo-Keynesian model essentially reverses this logic. The investment demand *function* is by assumption insensitive to the price of energy and productivity considerations, and so is saving, once again excepting the $\hat\delta = 0$ case. The real wage rate varies to accommodate the entire burden of the energy shock. Assuming $\hat\delta > 0$, we have

$$i(r) = s_C r$$

at equilibrium, so

$$i' \frac{dr^*}{d\omega} = s_C \frac{dr^*}{d\omega},$$

which evidently requires $dr^*/d\omega = 0$. Differentiating (16.6) with r^* held constant and substituting from the marginal-productivity equation (16.3), we have

$$\frac{d(W/P)^*}{d\omega} = h_\omega < 0.$$

Differentiating (16.3), we obtain

$$\frac{dk^*}{d\omega} = -\frac{h_{k\omega}}{h_{kk}}.$$

The effect on the capital:labor ratio of a change in the price of energy depends on whether energy and capital are substitutes, in which case $dk^*/d\omega > 0$, or complements, in which case $dk^*/d\omega < 0$.

In the $\hat\delta > 0$ case, the growth rate too is invariant with respect to the price of energy:

$$\frac{dg^*}{d\omega} = s_C \frac{dr^*}{d\omega} = 0.$$

Figure 16.2 summarizes these results. Observe that on the assumption that capital and energy are moderately complementary, the effect

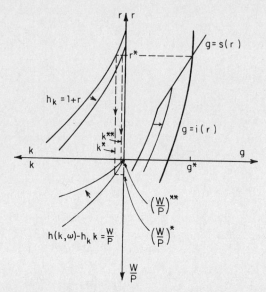

Figure 16.2   Neo-Keynesian response to an energy shock

of an energy shock on the capital: labor ratio is diametrically opposed to the effect in the neo-Marxian model.

In the $\hat{\delta} = 0$ region of the saving function, the neo-Keynesian logic becomes more complicated and the results more ambiguous. With saving determined by the equation

$$g = s_W \frac{h(k, \omega) - k}{k},$$

differentiating the investment = saving equilibrium condition gives

$$\frac{dr^*}{d\omega} = \frac{-s_W \dfrac{\sigma}{(1 + r)a_1} h_{k\omega} + s_W \dfrac{h_\omega}{k}}{i' - s_W \dfrac{\sigma}{(1 + r)a_1}}.$$

The denominator is sign-definite:

$$s' \equiv \frac{ds(r)}{dr} = s_W \frac{\sigma}{(1 + r)a_1},$$

and $i' - s' < 0$ is the condition for stability of equilibrium. But the numerator is sign-definite only if we assume that the elasticity of energy with respect to capital $(de/dk)(k/e) \equiv (h_{k\omega}k/h_\omega)$ does not exceed $(1 + r)a_1/\sigma$, in which case we have not only

$$\frac{dr^*}{d\omega} > 0$$

but also

$$\frac{dk^*}{d\omega} = \frac{s_W \dfrac{h_\omega}{k} - i'h_{k\omega}}{(i' - s')h_{kk}} < 0.$$

Where $h_{k\omega}k/h_\omega > (1 + r)a_1/\sigma$, the equilibrium profit rate will fall. It is even possible that the wage rate will rise. However, all this would presumably be of limited interest to a working class that found itself the owners of all but a vanishing share of the capital stock.

Neoclassical comparative statics are more complicated than the conventional $(\hat{\delta} > 0)$ neo-Marxian and neo-Keynesian case. The mathematics, indeed, closely parallels the mathematics of a neo-Keynesian people's capitalism. Assume for simplicity a Cobb-Douglas utility function, so that the neoclassical saving function is

$$g = \beta\left[\frac{1}{a_1} - (1 + r)\right] - 1.$$

With full employment, we have

$$g = n.$$

Combining these two equations gives

$$n = \beta\left[\frac{1}{a_1} - (1 + r)\right] - 1. \tag{16.12}$$

Now differentiate the output : capital ratio with respect to ω. The result is

$$\frac{d(1/a_1)}{d\omega} \equiv \frac{d(h(k, \omega)/k)}{d\omega} = \frac{\left(h_k \dfrac{dk^*}{d\omega} + h_\omega\right)k - h(k, \omega)\dfrac{dk^*}{d\omega}}{k^2}.$$

Thus, differentiating (16.12) yields

$$\frac{dr^*}{d\omega} = \frac{\left(h_k \dfrac{dk^*}{d\omega} + h_\omega\right)k - h(k, \omega)\dfrac{dk^*}{d\omega}}{k^2}.$$

Differentiating the marginal-productivity equation (16.3) gives a second equation relating $dr*/d\omega$ and $dk*/d\omega$:

$$h_{kk}\frac{dk*}{d\omega} + h_{k\omega} = \frac{dr*}{d\omega}.$$

If we solve these two equations jointly for $dr*/d\omega$ and $dk*/d\omega$, we have

$$\frac{dr*}{d\omega} = \frac{h_\omega - h_{k\omega}k}{k\left[1 - \dfrac{\sigma}{(1+r)a_1}\right]} + h_{k\omega}, \tag{16.13}$$

$$\frac{dk*}{d\omega} = \frac{h_\omega - h_{k\omega}k}{h_{kk}k\left[1 - \dfrac{\sigma}{(1+r)a_1}\right]}. \tag{16.14}$$

If we differentiate the price equation and substitute these results, we obtain

$$\frac{d(W/P)*}{d\omega} = \frac{-\dfrac{\sigma}{(1+r)a_1}(h_\omega - h_{k\omega}k)}{1 - \dfrac{\sigma}{(1+r)a_1}}. \tag{16.15}$$

Now the second and third of these results are sign-definite only on the assumption that energy and capital are substitutes or moderate complements. The expression

$$1 - \frac{\sigma}{(1+r)a_1}$$

is negative at a stable equilibrium. Consequently, with

$$h_\omega - h_{k\omega}k < 0, \tag{16.11}$$

the effect of an increase in the price of energy on both the capital : labor ratio and the real wage is negative:

$$\frac{dk*}{d\omega} < 0,$$

$$\frac{d(W/P)*}{d\omega} < 0.$$

An even stronger assumption is necessary to resolve the issue of the

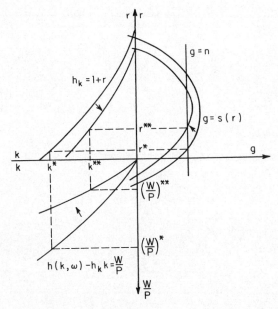

Figure 16.3 Neoclassical response to an energy shock

rate of profit; "moderate complementarity" is compatible with a positive or negative change in the profit rate. If energy and capital are substitutes, however (or indeed if $h_{k\omega}k/h_\omega < (1 + r)a_1/\sigma$), the sign of $dr^*/d\omega$ is unambiguously positive. These results are illustrated in Figure 16.3.

The neoclassical results stand in sharp contrast to the neo-Marxian and neo-Keynesian models. Except for the case of people's capitalism, results in these models with respect to profit, wage, and growth rates do not require precise assumptions about technology. By contrast, the effects on profits and wages in the neoclassical model depend critically on the technical relationship between energy and capital.

Table 16.1 summarizes the comparative statics of the three models. The conventional, $\hat{\delta} > 0$, region of the saving function is assumed for the neo-Marxian and neo-Keynesian models. No assumption is made as to whether energy and capital are substitutes or complements.

The table suggests major difficulties in comparisons across theories. To begin with, the important structural differences between neoclassical and neo-Keynesian theories are not reflected in Table 16.1. Indeed, the neoclassical indeterminateness of the signs of $dr^*/d\omega$ and $d(W/P)^*/d\omega$ means that there is no pattern of responses that would

TOWARD AN UNDERSTANDING OF CAPITALISM

Table 16.1. Comparative summary of responses to an energy shock

Model	$\dfrac{dr^*}{d\omega}$	$\dfrac{dg^*}{d\omega}$	$\dfrac{d(W/P)^*}{d\omega}$
Neo-Marxian	−	−	0
Neo-Keynesian	0	0	−
Neoclassical	?	0	?

? = indeterminate.

better fit the neo-Keynesian model than the neoclassical. In a two-way contest, the neo-Keynesian model is licked before the match fairly begins.

Worse, the data may well speak in contradictory terms. If the growth rate is adversely affected by a change in the price of energy, that is a point for the neo-Marxian theory, and a point against the neoclassical and neo-Keynesian. A fall in real wages, by contrast, is a point against the neo-Marxian approach, and a point for the other two models.

But what if we take a casual backward glance at the seventies, which suggests — once we abstract from technological progress — something that all three models preclude: namely, a fall in both growth and real wage rates? Are we to conclude that our casual empiricism is defective? Does the problem lie in the simplifications built into all the models: abstraction from government, natural resources, imperfect competition and the like? Or is the difficulty more fundamental: do the models each miss important aspects of the real world that no amount of relaxation of simplifying assumptions will set right?

Problems may lie with data interpretation, with simplifying assumptions common to all three models, *and* with the postulates peculiar to each. None of these difficulties excludes the others. My own inclination is to suspect the postulates: Chapter 20 presents a model that attempts to integrate Marxian and Keynesian insights, to incorporate important aspects of reality missed by each model taken alone. One of the appealing features of this model is precisely that it provides a framework in which an energy shock can have an adverse effect on wages, profits, *and* growth — all at the same time. By contrast, such results are consistent with the three models examined so far only if we are willing to back off to some extent from the postulates that distinguish each from the others.

Indeed, some retreating might well be in order. Neo-Marxians will point out that a given conventional wage can hardly be expected to persist across situations in which productivity is very different. In the original formulation of Chapter 3, productivity was identified as one of the background parameters that influence the level of wages. The distinguishing feature of the neo-Marxian model is not the independence of the wage rate from productivity, but its independence from the marginal productivity of labor at "full employment," a concept that has no meaning in neo-Marxian terms. Thus neo-Marxians might well reject the analysis that underlies the "neo-Marxian" results summarized in Figure 16.1.

By the same token, neo-Keynesians need hardly accept the idea that capitalists' animal spirits will be unaffected by a change in natural-resource prices severe enough to shift the production function $h(k, \omega)$ markedly. It might well be argued that investment demand will fall, which would evidently reduce equilibrium profit and growth rates, contrary to Figure 16.2.

Nor is there anything to prevent the neoclassically inclined from joining the ranks of revisionists. It need hardly be construed as a rejection of the notion of a natural rate of growth to argue that labor-force growth, n in our notation, is sensitive to economic conditions; one may argue that an energy shock might induce a change in n and still be a long way both from the neo-Marxian idea of an endogenous labor force and from the Malthusian idea that the rate of population growth plays an equilibrating role in the economy.

The upshot of these modifications would clearly be to move all three theories closer together in their predictions. This hardly makes any of them right — it only makes it harder to distinguish among them.

Alternative Employment Theories

Another area in which we might search for an empirical basis for choosing one model over the others is in the employment theories associated with the different approaches. At first blush, this would seem to be promising ground. Neoclassical theory is firmly wedded to the idea of full employment, or at least a natural rate of unemployment, whereas the two nonneoclassical theories reject the idea of $g^* = n$ as the normal tendency of the capitalist economy. Thus the historical record on employment and unemployment might be a reasonable basis on which to compare the explanatory power of the theories.

The difficulty here is that neo-Marxian theory rejects the idea of a persistent and growing unemployment on the one hand, or a growing excess demand for labor on the other, as firmly as it rejects the idea of full employment. For neo-Marxians, we have observed, the labor force is endogenous to the model rather than a given of the problem. Thus variations in growth rates are likely in the long run to be reflected in labor-force participation rates, average age of retirement, immigration, and relative rates of growth of noncapitalist sectors of the economy, rather than in unemployment or in a chronic excess demand for labor.

The neo-Keynesian view of these matters is more ambiguous. An important asymmetry was noted in Chapter 5 whereby full employment acts as a constraint in the neo-Keynesian model, but one that need not be binding. This assumption could conceivably be refuted by employment data: there is in the neo-Keynesian model at least the possibility that visible unemployment is widespread and growing. But the possibility need never materialize, even on neo-Keynesian assumptions. Although n is in principle exogenous, Joan Robinson qualifies the neo-Keynesian position with respect to the possibility of a rising rate of overt unemployment by suggesting that "opportunities for self-employment [may be] sufficiently favorable" to forestall the lengthening of the bread line (1962, p. 54). In other words, we may observe $g^* = n$ because, as on neo-Marxian assumptions, n adjusts to g^* rather than because, as on neoclassical assumptions, g^* adjusts to n. Attempts to distinguish these models from each other or from the neoclassical model on the basis of the statistical record on unemployment would likely prove as frustrating as the other tests we have examined.

There remains an important difference between neoclassical and nonneoclassical theories of employment: it is an exclusively neoclassical view that the wage rate responds to excess demand or excess supply in the labor market. But in the nonneoclassical model developed in Chapter 20, there is still the possibility of a positive relationship between changes in wages and changes in employment. Dynamics, to be sure, are very different in this synthetic model, running not from employment to wages as in the neoclassical view but from aggregate demand to *both* wages and employment. However, this structural difference can show up statistically only in the pattern of lags and leads. And this is hardly a reliable test: the statistical record might well exhibit a simultaneity that is compatible with *both* neoclassical and nonneoclassical views.

A strong suggestion emerges from all this: the existence of important conceptual differences between the theories does not guarantee that it will be possible to discover these differences empirically. The next two chapters are in effect an extended test of this preliminary conclusion. Chapters 17 and 18 attempt to compare the explanatory power of neoclassical and classical approaches to the theory of saving.

17 Alternative Theories of Saving

The opposition between classical and neoclassical theories of saving has been noted at various points in this book. Perhaps the most striking difference between the theories is the contrast between the negative slope of the neoclassical saving function elaborated in Chapter 2 and the positive slope of the classical saving function developed in later chapters. In principle, cross-country comparisons should permit us to discover which of the two views of the relationship between saving and the distribution of income is correct. The temptation to fit a saving function to international data is, however, to be resisted for at least two reasons. First, the theoretical opposition between classical and neoclassical saving functions exists in stark form only in the case of fixed production coefficients. Second, statistical estimation by means of cross-country comparisons would quickly run up against the identification problem that we encountered in the last chapter, where we tried to compare the responses of neo-Marxian and neo-Keynesian equilibria to changes in s_C. Indeed, it is quite possible that we would end up merging distinct saving functions for different countries into a single saving function of dubious significance.

But even without cross-country comparisons, we can still examine differences between the theories that might lead us to a conclusion about their relative plausibility. One such test is quite straightforward: the two theories differ markedly with respect to their implications for the relative concentration of labor and property incomes, or what amounts to the same thing, the relative concentration of labor income and wealth. To the extent that neoclassical life-cycle considerations, specifically, provision for retirement, are *quantitatively* important reasons for saving (quantitatively important in terms of saving, not in terms of numbers of savers), the distribution of assets should be roughly similar to the distribution of labor income. By contrast, nonneoclassical theory is consistent with a much higher concentration of wealth than of labor income.

To a first approximation at least, data for the United States support the nonneoclassical view in this regard: as Table 17.1 shows, in 1962 approximately 5 percent of the U.S. population received 20 percent of the pretax income while owning half of the income-producing assets (businesses, farms, stocks and bonds, bank deposits, real estate, patents, and so forth). The distribution of total wealth (income-producing assets plus owner-occupied housing and automobiles) was only moderately less skewed. Nor, as Table 17.2 shows, was the situation very different for the 55- to 64-year-old population, the group one might think most likely to reflect retirement considerations in its saving behavior.[1]

These results are hardly conclusive. One can surely construct income profiles and utility functions that would make the life-cycle hypothesis consistent with the data. And one can appeal to the existence of social security to explain the undersaving of the lower-income groups. Or one might attribute the disproportionate saving of upper-income groups to a bequest motive or to monument building. But at some point in the path of ad hoc corrections, neoclassical theory risks losing much of its distinctive flavor, differing from nonneoclassical theory only in its basis in utility maximization.

But the word "only" is misplaced here, for we have observed that assigning a key role to utility maximization in the determination of equilibrium growth and distribution as well as equilibrium prices gives to household preferences an enormously greater role in the neoclassical model than they play in the neo-Keynesian and neo-Marxian models.

The issue, let me be clear, is not whether households maximize utility, but over what domain of choices and with what effect. Neo-Marxian and neo-Keynesian models, at least as developed here, have room for utility maximization at the level of determining the composition of output. But neoclassical theory alone applies the same logic to the determination of desired saving and thereby to the determination of the rate of profit and the level of wages.

1. For our purposes, distributional data on *labor* income would be more to the point than the data on total personal pretax income that Tables 17.1 and 17.2 utilize. However, the distribution of labor income is evidently less concentrated than the distribution of property income, which only strengthens the argument that the concentration of wealth is greater than neoclassical life-cycle considerations suggest.

Table 17.1. Household distribution of pretax income and wealth in the United States, all households (1962)

Income class	Households		Pretax income		All assets		Income-producing assets	
	Number of units (millions)	Percentage	Aggregate (billions of dollars)	Percentage	Aggregate (billions of dollars)	Percentage	Aggregate (billions of dollars)	Percentage
Less than $5000	27.7	47.8	70.9	19.2	238.3	19.6	140.4	16.5
$5000–7499	12.2	21.1	75.9	20.6	161.1	13.3	98.6	11.6
$7500–9999	9.0	15.5	77.7	21.0	172.2	14.2	100.8	11.9
$10000–14999	6.2	10.7	74.1	20.1	173.7	14.3	106.0	12.5
More than $15000	2.7	4.7	70.6	19.1	462.6	38.1	399.3	47.0
Totals[a]	57.9	—	369.2	—	1214.9	—	850.3	—

Source: Projector and Weiss (1966).

a. Totals do not add, presumably because of rounding errors at the source.

Table 17.2. Household distribution of pretax income and wealth in the United States, head aged 55–64 (1962)

Income class	Households		Pretax income		All assets		Income-producing assets	
	Number of units (millions)	Percentage	Aggregate (billions of dollars)	Percentage	Aggregate (billions of dollars)	Percentage	Aggregate (billions of dollars)	Percentage
Less than $5000	5.2	50.0	12.2	17.8	68.0	20.1	42.5	17.3
$5000–7499	2.0	19.2	12.9	18.6	41.4	12.2	25.9	10.5
$7500–9999	1.3	12.5	11.3	16.5	51.9	15.3	34.3	14.0
$10000–14999	1.2	11.5	14.3	20.9	43.9	13.0	26.3	10.7
More than $15000	0.7	6.7	19.8	28.9	140.5	41.5	122.8	50.0
Totals[a]	10.4	—	68.4	—	338.3	—	245.7	—

Source: Projector and Weiss (1966).
a. Totals do not add, presumably because of rounding errors at the source.

Two Neoclassical Theories of Household Saving

Up to now neoclassical saving theory has meant the life-cycle hypothesis of Franco Modigliani and his collaborators. Milton Friedman's version, the other principal variant of neoclassical saving theory, has been mentioned only in passing because it emphasizes a distinction that is irrelevant in the perfect-certainty mold in which this discussion has been cast, namely the distinction between "permanent" and "transitory" income. The essence of Friedman's permanent-income hypothesis is that consumption is independent of random shocks to income, which are buffered by the households' stock of productive assets. By contrast, the life-cycle hypothesis, while not ignoring the random component of income, deemphasizes the distinction between permanent and transitory. It concentrates instead on the relationship of consumption and income to the economic life cycle that includes on the expenditure side periods of family formation, child rearing, and old age, and on the income side periods of training (on and off the job), peak productivity and income, and retirement.

Although both theories emphasize the adaptation of consumption to resources available over a long period of time rather than to income received in a short period of time, they differ with respect to the period over which consumption is smoothed. The life-cycle hypothesis focuses on the proverbial threescore and ten years allotted for our earthly sojourn. The permanent-income hypothesis is more ambiguous. In its pure form it appears to assume an infinite life span, but at one point in the conclusion to *A Theory of the Consumption Function*, Friedman suggests that the permanent-income hypothesis is confirmed by the absence of orgies on paydays and deprivation and want in between, clearly a much shorter time horizon. Indeed, the very vagueness of the time horizon is at once an intellectual weakness and a polemical strength: in its "no orgies on payday" form, the argument appeals even to the most nonneoclassical among us, whereas a lifetime or multigeneration horizon requires a more willing suspension of disbelief than many can muster.

But for present purposes, what the two versions of neoclassical theory share—an emphasis on household rationality, specifically on deliberate smoothing of consumption according to a utility-maximizing plan—is more important than what divides them. In this chapter, therefore, we shall consider the two together, not ignoring their differences but considering them as alternative expressions of the idea that rational planning is the basis of household saving decisions.

The unity of the two views emerges clearly in the derivation of

TOWARD AN UNDERSTANDING OF CAPITALISM

estimating equations from the underlying neoclassical theory. Both the life-cycle and the permanent-income hypotheses start from a consumption function that recalls the analysis of Chapter 2,

$$C = \alpha W,$$

where C represents consumption, W here represents wealth (including "human" capital — W reduces to wages in the model of Chapter 2), and α is a propensity to consume which in principle depends on wealth and the profit (or interest) rate as well as on the utility function but in practice is generally treated as a constant. The two theories diverge principally in their procedures for estimating wealth or the permanent income that wealth produces.

The Life-Cycle Hypothesis

In Modigliani's original formulation of the life-cycle hypothesis (Modigliani and Blumberg 1954; Ando and Modigliani 1963), wealth was broken down into two major constituents, physical and human capital, the first estimated by the stock of assets Z and the second by extrapolation of the current rate of labor income YL into the future. This gave the consumption function

$$C = \alpha Z + \beta YL.$$

A more recent generalization of the theory (Modigliani 1975; Modigliani and Steindel 1977) added an additional term to make explicit allowance for the effects on consumption of the rate of return on assets:[2]

$$C = (\alpha + \alpha'r)Z + \beta YL.$$

The new term rZ is measured by current levels of property income YP. So the consumption equation becomes

$$C = \alpha Z + \beta_1 YL + \beta_2 YP,$$

with $\beta_2 = \alpha'$.

This would suffice in a purely private economy and was perhaps empirically adequate up to the early post – World War II period, when the life-cycle hypothesis was originally formulated. In the early 1950s social security and other transfer payments were hardly 5 percent of

2. A similar term in rYL is omitted on the grounds that it is "supposed to be small" (Modigliani and Steindel 1977, p. 189).

disposable income in the United States. But in recent years, transfer payments have become 15 percent of disposable income and can no longer be ignored in the study of consumption and saving behavior. One solution consistent with the life-cycle hypothesis would be to incorporate social-security "wealth" *à la* Feldstein (1974) into the analysis. The alternative, in fact the approach adopted by Modigliani and Steindel, is to include transfer payments directly as a variable separate from both labor income and property income. The resulting equation is

$$C = \alpha Z + \beta_1 YL + \beta_2 YP + \beta_3 YT,$$

where YT represents transfer payments.

If we recognize that, capital gains apart, ΔZ is simply S_{-1}, we can eliminate the level of assets from the equation altogether by writing it in first-difference form. Making use of the identity

$$Y \equiv YL + YP + YT,$$

where Y represents disposable income, we have the short-run saving function

$$S = (1 - \alpha)S_{-1} + (1 - \beta_1)\Delta YL + (1 - \beta_2)\Delta YP + (1 - \beta_3)\Delta YT \quad (17.1)$$

to represent the life-cycle hypothesis.

The Permanent-Income Hypothesis

The permanent-income hypothesis elides the difference between human and nonhuman assets and converts (17.1) into a relationship between consumption and permanent income Y^P,

$$C = \mu Y^P, \tag{17.2}$$

where, in principle at least, $Y^P = rW$. Permanent income, however, is not estimated *à la* Modigliani from current wealth and current levels of measured income. Rather, households are assumed to revise their estimates of permanent income in the light of two factors, departures of actual income from the current estimate of permanent income and the trend rate of growth of permanent income. In difference-equation form, the adjustment mechanism is

$$\Delta Y^P = \eta(Y - Y^P_{-1}) + \psi Y^P_{-1}. \tag{17.3}$$

The difficulty with Eq. (17.3) is well known: it includes the unobservable variable Y^P on the right-hand side. Friedman's own way out of this difficulty was tantamount to solving Eq. (17.3) for Y^P in terms of past Y's,

$$Y_t^P = \eta \sum_{\tau=0}^{\infty} (1 + \psi - \eta)^\tau Y_{t-\tau},$$

and substituting the resulting expression into Eq. (17.2):

$$C = \mu\eta \sum_{\tau=0}^{\infty} (1 + \psi - \eta)^\tau Y_{t-\tau}. \tag{17.4}$$

But for our purposes an alternative procedure is more illuminating. Taking the first difference of Eq. (17.2), we have

$$\Delta C = \mu \Delta Y^P.$$

If we substitute from Eq. (17.3) into this equation, we obtain

$$\Delta C = \mu\eta(Y - Y_{-1}^P) + \mu\psi Y_{-1}^P.$$

Substituting back into Eq. (17.2) gives

$$C = (1 + \psi - \eta)C_{-1} + \mu\eta Y, \tag{17.5}$$

or, since $Y \equiv C + S$,

$$S = (\eta - \psi - 1)C_{-1} + (1 - \mu\eta)Y. \tag{17.6}$$

An important property of Eqs. (17.5) and (17.6) is that all past information or permanent income available at time -1 is summarized in C_{-1}. In Friedman's formulation, this is the result of the particular adjustment equation posited for permanent income. If instead of Eq. (17.3) we were to assume

$$\Delta Y^P = \eta_1(Y - Y_{-1}^P) + \eta_0(Y_{-1} - Y_{-1}^P) + \psi Y_{-1}^P, \tag{17.7}$$

we would now have

$$C = (1 + \psi - \eta_1 - \eta_0)C_{-1} + \mu\eta_1 Y + \mu\eta_0 Y_{-1} \tag{17.8}$$

and

$$S = (\eta_1 + \eta_0 - 1 - \psi)C_{-1} + (1 - \mu\eta_1)Y - \mu\eta_0 Y_{-1} \tag{17.9}$$

in place of Eqs. (17.5) and (17.6). Lagged income figures in both of these equations.

To be sure, the permanent-income hypothesis does not rest on any precise form of the permanent-income adjustment equation. As Robert Hall (1978) has shown, a forward-looking rational-expectations definition of permanent income leads to equations similar to Eqs. (17.5) and

(17.6), which in particular share the property that C_{-1} summarizes all prior information about permanent income.

In Hall's formulation this result rests squarely on the assumption of rational expectations. By contrast, in Friedman's approach Eqs. (17.5) and (17.6) imply no specific expectations hypothesis beyond the functional form of Eq. (17.3). But rational expectations can be invoked to resolve an ambiguity in these two equations. Since there are two independent variables in each, only two of the three parameters μ, η, and ψ can be estimated. One of these three must be fixed in advance. A way to do this is to assume rational expectations govern Eq. (17.3) so that, using E to denote mathematical expectation,

$$EY^P = EY_{+1},$$

from which it follows that ψ is equal to the trend rate of growth of Y—provided that the growth process is a stationary one.[3] Indeed, this is precisely the assumption that Friedman made, albeit without benefit of rational-expectations terminology—*A Theory of the Consumption Function* having been published in the year -4 of the Muthian era.[4]

It should be observed that the specific form of Eq. (17.6) makes the permanent-income hypothesis look rather more different from the life-cycle hypothesis than it really is. If we rewrite C_{-1} in (17.6) as $Y_{-1} - S_{-1}$, we obtain

$$S = (1 + \psi - \eta)S_{-1} + (1 - \mu\eta)\Delta Y + [(1 - \mu)\eta - \psi]Y_{-1}. \quad (17.10)$$

3. From the equation of permanent income as a distributed lag on observed income,

$$Y_t^P = \eta \sum_{\tau=0}^{\infty} (1 + \psi + \eta)^\tau Y_{t-\tau},$$

we have

$$EY_t^P = \eta \sum_{\tau=0}^{\infty} (1 + \psi - \eta)^\tau EY_{t-\tau}.$$

Now if the growth process has a stationary trend g, $EY_{t-\tau} = (1 + g)^{-\tau}EY_t$, and

$$EY_t^P = (EY_t)\eta \sum_{\tau=0}^{\infty} \left(\frac{1 + \psi - \eta}{1 + g}\right)^\tau,$$

so that in general, at least for $|1 + \psi - \eta| < 1 + g$,

$$EY_t^P = \frac{\eta(1 + g)}{g - \psi + \eta} EY_t.$$

Since $EY_{+1} = (1 + g)EY$, $EY^P = EY_{+1}$ implies $g = \psi$.

4. The concept of a trend rate of growth may be ambiguous when the "trend" is generally perceived to have changed, as has been the case since the end of the postwar boom in the early 1970s: quite apart from temporary difficulties, the conventional wisdom is that future growth will not measure up to past growth. Nevertheless, apart from tests of the stability of regression coefficients over time, there is little we can do about this problem—without abandoning the rational-expectations postulate. (If we are willing to forsake rational expectations, we can vary ψ parametrically and interpret η and μ accordingly.)

Equation (17.10) differs from the life-cycle specification of Eq. (17.1) in only two respects: first, income differences enter into (17.10) in aggregate form, but into (17.1) in terms of the components ΔYL, ΔYP, and ΔYT; second, lagged income enters into the permanent-income specification but not into the life-cycle specification.

The first of these differences is of no great moment. Friedman has insisted more than Modigliani and his collaborators on the uniformity of the saving propensity across classes. But in the life-cycle view different coefficients for different components of income do not necessarily establish differences in marginal propensities to save: it is possible to interpret differences in coefficients as differences in the relationship between changes in the observed income variables and changes in the anticipated future streams of income. So the choice between the aggregated and disaggregated specification of income is not one that cuts to the heart of neoclassical theory.

The second difference between the life-cycle and permanent-income specifications is the presence of lagged income in Eq. (17.6) but not in Eq. (17.1). This is more consequential but hardly crucial, originating in part in differences between the two hypotheses with respect to the household's marginal propensity to save over the very long run, and in part in the specifics of the permanent-income adjustment equation. Rewrite Eq. (17.9) as

$$S = (1 + \psi - \eta_1 - \eta_0)S_{-1} + (1 - \mu\eta_1)Y - [1 + \psi - \eta_1 - (1 - \mu)\eta_0]Y_{-1},$$
$$(17.11)$$

and it is clear that for the single variable ΔY to replace the two variables Y and Y_{-1}, the coefficients of the last two terms must add to zero. In other words,

$$1 - \mu\eta_1 = 1 + \psi - \eta_1 - (1 - \mu)\eta_0$$

or

$$(1 - \mu)(\eta_1 + \eta_0) = \psi.$$

For instance, let $\mu = 1$, which corresponds to the life-cycle idea that income is spent completely over one's lifetime. In addition, let $\psi = 0$, which assumes away any trend in permanent income. Then Eq. (17.11) becomes

$$S = (1 - \eta_1 - \eta_0)S_{-1} + (1 - \eta_1)\Delta Y,$$

indistinguishable in form, except for aggregation of income, from the life-cycle specification.

We come finally to the question of the relationship of the life-cycle and permanent-income specifications to the neoclassical theory from which they ostensibly derive. The most striking thing here is how little is left of the theory once it is translated into a form suitable for testing against empirical data. All that Eqs. (17.1) and (17.10) say is that current household saving depends on the household's past saving and changes in its income, or on these variables and lagged income. This, to be sure, represents a difference from textbook versions of Keynesian theory that disregard the strictures and qualifications of the master (Keynes 1936, p. 97), not to mention common sense, in making consumption and saving depend *only* on current income. But Eqs. (17.1) and (17.10) hardly require the calculating, rational household that maximizes the utility of a stream of consumption subject to a constraint on lifetime wealth, for in point of fact, the importance of previous levels of saving and first differences in income in determining current saving is not the exclusive property of neoclassical theory.

A Nonneoclassical Alternative: The Disequilibrium Hypothesis

Quite the contrary. Theories that begin from very different premises about household behavior lead to very similar reduced forms. Cases in point are the "habit-persistence" theory of Tillman Brown (1952) and Hendrik Houthakker and Lester Taylor (1966) and a near cousin, the "disequilibrium hypothesis" presented in summary form in Chapter 7 of this book and in more detail in an earlier article (Marglin 1975). The common feature of the two theories is that the consumer is a creature of habit who requires time to adjust his consumption to changes in income: the household saves only by virtue of incomplete adjustment of spending to income. Formally, the consumption function discussed in Chapter 7 was

$$\Delta C = \theta(Y - C_{-1}) + \zeta \Delta Y. \tag{7.1}$$

It might well be asked here why it is that spending adjusts to income rather than to assets. If households are as inclined to spending as the disequilibrium hypothesis assumes, why do households not spend until their wealth is exhausted?

A fair question indeed, and one that deserves a careful response. In my view, household behavior with respect to saving and spending is the resultant of *two* forces: a cultural pressure to spend partially balanced by a contradictory cultural pressure to save. The result is to make wealth relatively inviolate, to limit the appetite to what can be spent without eroding assets (except as a temporary measure when income is falling).

Let me amplify. The cultural pressure to spend stems from the fact that in our society, consumption is a sovereign remedy for the problems of life. Whether what ails one is a physical, emotional, spiritual, or even a sexual lack, some commodity or other will cure the problem. It is a commonplace by now that an automobile provides not only transportation but power and identity, the power and identity that are too frequently lacking in the workplace, in the community, and even in the home. This accounts in part at least for the emphasis on growth in Western and Westernized societies: even in the richest of the societies pleased to identify themselves as part of Western Civilization, most individuals do not have "enough"—there can be no such thing as "enough" once commodities begin to serve the needs of prestige and esteem. Thus "delivering the goods" becomes a literal necessity in our society: social stability requires an ever-increasing material abundance.

The skepticism about the efficacy of consumption as a cure-all that is implicit in this account does not mean that I hold consumption to be irrelevant to human well-being. Large parts of the world need as well as want more consumption, and need it urgently. But it is, I think, fair to say that we in the West, socialist as well as capitalist, have taken one aspect of human existence and elevated it to the central focus of activity.

Advertising is not the villain, but the tip of the iceberg that shows above the surface. Long before Madison Avenue became synonymous with the manipulation of consumer wants, sumptuary laws were enacted in an attempt to prevent sartorial display from undoing the symbolic order of society. Robert Owen (remembered for his contribution to the theory and practice of utopian socialism) wrote in his autobiography (1857) of a youthful experience that indicates how deeply embedded conspicuous consumption had become by the end of the eighteenth century:

[A] widow, shortly after she became so, was desirous of buying at Mr. McGuffog's establishment [McGuffog was a dry-goods merchant to whom Owen was apprenticed] a piece of the finest Irish linen for chemises that he had for sale. Now Mr. McGuffog was in the habit of buying the finest articles of every description that he could meet with, going frequently to London to make these purchases to supply his regular customers among the high nobility; and he had at this time the finest that could then be made by any manufacturer. The price was eight shillings the yard, allowing him his usual moderate profit. The lady looked and looked again at this fabric, and said, "have you no finer than this piece, which is not fine enough for my purpose?" Mr. McGuffog was surprised at this speech, for he knew it was fine enough to satisfy the wants of the finest duchess in the land. But with his usual knowledge of character, he said, "Upon recollection I may have in my upper warehouse a finer piece — I will go and see." He went, and brought the fellow piece to the one he had previously shown at eight shillings and he said, "I have found one, but the price is ten shillings per yard, and is perhaps higher in price than you would wish to give." The widow examined this new piece and said no, it was not too high in price and was the very fabric she wished for. Mr. McGuffog smiled within himself when he discovered, as he suspected, that the fabric was in this instance valued by its cost, and not for its intrinsic worth, as he knew was often the case (p. 21).[5]

This much of the story may be familiar, if not these particular details. But it is easy to overemphasize conspicuous consumption and commodity fetishism. In fact, there is much validity in the Western belief in consumption as a means of solving the problems of life, at least of Western life. Consumption may not be a particularly good solution, but within our society it is frequently the *only* solution available: however developed we may be materially, we are singularly poor in providing solutions that do not center around commodities. One example will suffice to illustrate the point. It is generally recognized that American cities have become increasingly unattractive and undesirable places for living, not to mention for raising a family. Whereas in the nineteenth century the amenities of urban life improved markedly, in the twentieth cities have become increasingly dangerous, unhealthy, and dirty — and show no signs of getting better. The solution, for some at least, is escape — to suburbs or to a vacation home in the country. The relevant point is that homes in the suburbs or in the country are not primarily fetishes; "exit," in Albert Hirschman's dichotomy (1970), is the only solution that works.

To be sure, there are drawbacks to this solution. In the first place the requisite command over resources is not available to everybody, perhaps not to a majority, even though availability of such commodities as living space may not be as inherently restricted as commodities that serve primarily as vehicles to prestige, esteem, and power. In any case, the situation may be tolerable as long as most people believe that with the passage of time, they too will share in the good life. Provided people generally compare their current consumption levels not with each

5. As a commentary on Benjamin Franklin's dictum that honesty is the best policy, consider the sequel: "In making out the bill he charged this so-called ten-shillings-a-yard piece, at the rate of eight shillings only, saying he would not charge her more, because at that price it afforded him a fair profit. The widow said nothing, but never again was a customer."

other, but with their own past, growth in consumption can increase satisfaction all around; most people, if not everybody, can see themselves as winners. And failure may be redeemable, in one's own lifetime if one is young enough, otherwise in one's children's. Even the perception of failure in the consumption race may be socially tolerable — if those who end up losers blame themselves rather than society for their failure.

However, commodity-based solutions to problems of social life would leave something to be desired even if they were generalizable. They are not without costs, both material and psychic, even for the fortunate minority for whom they are feasible. But "voice," the second of Hirschman's alternatives, requires a very different institutional environment, one that does *not* take the individualistic framework of our society for granted and puts the emphasis on changing the institutions rather than on individual problem solving within those institutions. Thus the emphasis on consumption that characterizes the West is not a problem of false consciousness, as is sometimes suggested. Far from being false, belief in the power of consumption is distinctly appropriate to individual survival in our society as it exists — however inappropriate this belief might be once social institutions become variables of the problem rather than fixed parameters.

But pressures to spend are only one side of the coin. Even as our social institutions encourage spending, our society places a high cultural value on saving to protect oneself and one's family from economic consequences of illness or accident — the proverbial rainy day — as well as to provide for one's old age. That the failures of individual provision for contingencies like catastrophic illness or retirement have led to private and public insurance schemes virtually all over the West has undermined but hardly eradicated the cultural belief in the virtue of saving. For some the saving ethic is so strong that they willingly lock themselves into saving programs through life insurance or through payroll-deduction plans. Others, perhaps most of us, are better able to resist the power of the saving ethic. But most of us at least try to hold on to what we have by accident or willpower managed to accumulate.

Thus it seems to me appropriate to strike a trial balance of the opposing pressures to spend in the manner of Eq. (7.1), which in terms of saving may be written

$$S = (1 - \theta)S_{-1} + (1 - \theta - \zeta)\Delta Y. \qquad (17.12)$$

In the disequilibrium view, the household will, with constant income, just maintain its assets. However, as income varies from one period to the next, the household will find itself with more or less income than it is accustomed to. Saving takes place when income rises on average and households are on balance facing the relatively easier and more pleasant task of learning to spend income rather than the harder task of pulling in their horns.

Chapter 7 posited lower adjustment rates, that is, lower values of θ and ζ, for capitalists than for workers. On the upside, capitalist's needs press less urgently against increases in income, by virtue of their higher relative income.[6] On the downside, capitalists' assets provide a more ample buffer. Taken together, these arguments provide a rationale for the inequality $s_C > s_W$, critical to nonneoclassical saving theory, a rationale that does not depend on utility maximization.

But it is one thing to posit differences between θ_C and θ_W or between ζ_C and ζ_W and another thing to establish these differences empirically, especially when the data base consists of aggregate time series. One approach to distinguishing these parameters empirically lies in the fact that labor income, YL, and transfer payments, YT, typically form a higher proportion of disposable income for working-class households than for capitalists; conversely, property income, YP, typically forms a higher proportion of capitalists' income. For this reason, if we consider income and saving as aggregates in Eq. (17.12) and we rewrite this equation as

$$S = (1 - \theta_0)S_{-1} + (1 - \theta_1 - \zeta_1)\Delta YL + (1 - \theta_2 - \zeta_2)\Delta YP \\ + (1 - \theta_3 - \zeta_3)\Delta YT, \tag{17.13}$$

then differences between $\theta_W + \zeta_W$ and $\theta_C + \zeta_C$ may show up in differences between the coefficients of the three components of income. In the disequilibrium view, the coefficients $1 - \theta_i - \zeta_i (i = 1, 2, 3)$ are each weighted averages of $1 - \theta_W - \zeta_W$ and $1 - \theta_C - \zeta_C$, with the weights reflecting workers' and capitalists' shares of the aggregates ΔYL, ΔYP, and ΔYT. Similarly, $1 - \theta_0$ is a weighted average of $1 - \theta_W$ and $1 - \theta_C$, with the weights reflecting shares of saving.

Observe that despite the similarity between the coefficient of S_{-1} and the coefficients of ΔYL, ΔYP, and ΔYT, the most we can hope to do with aggregate data is to distinguish the *sums* $\theta_W + \zeta_W$ and $\theta_C + \zeta_C$. In order to distinguish the individual parameters θ_W and ζ_W from θ_C and ζ_C, we would need data on the class composition of saving. Even with respect to the sums, there are of course no guarantees: both random error and multicollinearity among ΔYL, ΔYP, and ΔYT may obscure real differences in capitalists' and workers' short-run adjustment speeds.

6. James Duesenberry (1949) emphasized the importance of relative income more than three decades ago, but this insight, having proved difficult to integrate into neoclassical theory, has hardly been exploited in the development of saving theory.

Testing Differences between the Theories

In view of the potential for multicollinearity, the disequilibrium hypothesis will be tested with income expressed as an aggregate, as in Eq. (17.12), and with income expressed in terms of its components, as in Eq. (17.13). Indeed, a natural division suggests itself. The permanent-income hypothesis is generally formulated without distinguishing types of income, despite the possibility that the ratios of transitory to permanent income may be higher on average for one type of income than another. It is reasonable therefore to test the permanent-income specification (17.6) against the aggregative version of the disequilibrium hypothesis, Eq. (17.12). By contrast, decomposition of income is built into current versions of the life-cycle hypothesis, so it is reasonable to test the life-cycle specification of neoclassical theory, Eq. (17.1), against the corresponding specification of the disequilibrium hypothesis, Eq. (17.13).

The tests, needless to say, can hardly revolve about goodness of fit; the alternative specifications are all too similar, when they are not identical, to put much stock in differences between R^2's. But if the theories cannot be distinguished on the basis of goodness of fit, they do differ in their implications for coefficient values. Consider, for instance, the equation

$$S = b_0 S_{-1} + b_1 \Delta YL + b_2 \Delta YP + b_3 \Delta YT, \qquad (17.14)$$

which is consistent with both the life-cycle and the disequilibrium hypotheses. In the life-cycle model, $1 - b_0$ is the propensity to consume out of wealth, held by Modigliani to be of the order of 0.08 to 0.13 on an annual basis (Ando and Modigliani 1963) or 0.02 to 0.033 on the quarterly basis on which we shall analyze the data. Thus the life-cycle model would lead one to expect b_0 to be of the order of 0.967 to 0.98 in a quarterly model, and this hypothesis can be tested directly by the confidence interval around $\hat{b}_0$. The parameter $1 - b_1$ on the life-cycle view is the response of consumption to expected labor income. Its anticipated magnitude (Ando and Modigliani 1963) is of the order of 0.60 to 0.75, which translates into b_1 of the order of 0.25 to 0.40, a prediction which once again can be tested by the point estimate and the estimated standard error of b_1.

The life-cycle hypothesis has much less to say about the coefficients of property income and transfer payments. For Modigliani and Steindel, the parameter b_2 depends on the relative importance of income and substitution effects: theoretical considerations place only very wide bounds on b_2, limiting it to the unit interval (Modigliani and Steindel

1977). A priori bounds on the parameter b_3 are not quite as wide: "In the spirit of the life-cycle hypothesis, we expect that the propensities to consume out of these payments—certainly the early impact—would be appreciably higher than that out of labor income" (Modigliani and Steindel 1977, p. 190). In other words, we would expect $b_3 < b_1$.

The disequilibrium hypothesis also leads to a set of predictions about the coefficients of Eq. (17.14), some of them similar to and some of them different from the predictions that follow from the life-cycle interpretation. At the outset we might as well defer to the constraint posed by the data and assume $\theta_W = \theta_C$, interpreting coefficient differences in Eq. (17.14) in terms of differences between ζ_W and ζ_C. If in particular we assume $\zeta_W > \zeta_C$, and add to this the plausible assumption that capitalists' share of property income exceeds their share of labor income, then the disequilibrium hypothesis predicts $b_2 > b_1$. Similar reasoning produces the prediction $b_2 > b_3$. If we assume also that capitalists' share of labor income exceeds their share of transfer payments (though both may be small), then we have $b_1 > b_3$. In principle, these predictions may be tested separately against the hypotheses $b_1 = b_2, b_2 = b_3, b_1 = b_3$ and jointly against the hypothesis $b_1 = b_2 = b_3$. But whatever the outcome of these tests, they hardly permit us to distinguish between it and the life-cycle hypothesis; none of these predictions need contradict the life-cycle hypothesis as Modigliani and his collaborators have defined it. In any case, transfer payments turn out to be much too complicated an issue to permit a simple test of this kind. But I get ahead of the story.

Chapter 7 suggested that a key difference between neoclassical and nonneoclassical saving theories lies in their predictions for the relative magnitudes of the average saving propensities s_W and s_C, which depend, respectively, on b_1 and b_2. In emphasizing the relationship between saving and provision for retirement, neoclassical theory leads to the conclusion $s_W > s_C$, if not to the stronger conclusion $s_C < 0$: workers preparing for retirement save a higher fraction of their incomes than "capitalists," who in the neoclassical conception of the world are for the most part retired workers. By contrast, the nonneoclassical theory hinges critically on the assumption $s_C > s_W$. If we neglect the property income and transfer payments received by working households, workers' saving, S_W, is given by the equation

$$S_W = b_0 S_{W,-1} + b_1 \Delta YL$$

or

$$\frac{S_W}{YL} \frac{YL}{YL_{-1}} = b_0 \frac{S_{W,-1}}{YL_{-1}} + b_1 \frac{\Delta YL}{YL_{-1}}.$$

On a steady-growth path, $YL/YL_{-1} = (1 + g)$, $\Delta YL/YL_{-1} = g$, and $S_W/YL = S_{W,-1}/YL_{-1} = s_W$. In consequence,

$$s_W(1 + g) = b_0 s_W + b_1 g$$

or

$$s_W = \frac{b_1 g}{1 + g - b_0}.$$

Taking $g = 0.006$ (the approximate quarterly growth rate of real per-capita income over the interval 1952–1979), we can estimate s_W by the equation

$$\hat{s}_W = \frac{0.006\hat{b}_1}{1.006 - \hat{b}_0}.$$

A similar argument applies to s_C, so that

$$\hat{s}_C = \frac{0.006\hat{b}_2}{1.006 - \hat{b}_0}.$$

Combining the two equations, we have

$$\hat{s}_C - \hat{s}_W = \frac{0.006(\hat{b}_2 - \hat{b}_1)}{1.006 - \hat{b}_0}.$$

It will be observed that in view of the relative magnitudes of different types of income, we are on much more tenuous ground in neglecting transfers and labor income received by property owners than in neglecting property income and transfers received by wage earners. Some solace may be found in the realization that time-series data leave us little choice in the matter. In any case the bias involved in neglecting the multiplicity of income sources is in the direction of underestimating the difference $|s_C - s_W|$, which is to say that it increases the probability of rejecting the hypothesis $s_C - s_W > 0$ when this hypothesis is true; the bias does not increase the probability of incorrectly rejecting the hypothesis $s_C - s_W = 0$.

So far, the disequilibrium hypothesis has suggested only qualitative restrictions on the parameters. In order to derive quantitative restrictions, we must form an idea of what constitutes a reasonable adjustment speed under this view of spending behavior. A thought experiment with respect to the cumulative adjustment of spending to income might be useful to this end. Suppose we start from a situation in which spending has initially adapted to income, then add one dollar to income and maintain income at its new level indefinitely. For a household whose adjustment is governed by the equation

$$\Delta C = \theta(Y - C_{-1}) + \zeta \Delta Y, \tag{7.1}$$

the change in consumption after t quarters is

$$\Sigma \Delta C = \theta + \zeta + \theta(1 - \theta - \zeta) + \cdots + \theta(1 - \theta - \zeta)(1 - \theta)^{t-2}.$$

Now we may ask what constitutes a plausible value of $\Sigma \Delta C$ on the assumption that saving is a disequilibrium response to income changes. There must be an element of arbitrariness in the answer, but it seems to me that for workers at least, it is reasonable to expect that the adjustment $\Sigma \Delta C$ be 50 percent complete after four quarters. Otherwise the notion of household saving as a disequilibrium phenomenon loses a great deal of its force. If we ignore capitalists' share of labor income, we can estimate the adjustment of consumption to labor income

$$\Sigma \Delta C = \theta_W + \zeta_W + \theta_W(1 - \theta_W - \zeta_W) + \theta_W(1 - \theta_W - \zeta_W)(1 - \theta_W)$$
$$+ \theta_W(1 - \theta_W - \zeta_W)(1 - \theta_W)^2$$

by the expression $1 - \hat{b}_0^3 \hat{b}_1$.[7] A reasonably strong test of the disequilibrium hypothesis is thus provided by whether or not the confidence interval around $1 - \hat{b}_0^3 \hat{b}_1$ lies wholly above 0.5. For the case where the point estimate $1 - \hat{b}_0^3 \hat{b}_1$ lies below 0.5, a weaker test is provided by whether or not the upper end of the confidence interval includes 0.5.

Testing of the disequilibrium hypothesis against the permanent-income hypothesis proceeds in an analogous manner. Consider the equation

$$S = c_0 S_{-1} + c_1 \Delta Y + c_2 Y_{-1}, \tag{17.15}$$

which is consistent with both hypotheses, albeit with different restrictions on the coefficients. Under the strict version of the permanent-income hypothesis reflected in Eqs. (17.6) and (17.10), the coefficients c_0, c_1, and c_2 are constrained by the equation

$$c_0 - c_1 + c_2 = 0,$$

which is equivalent to the constraint $d_2 = 0$ in the equation

$$S = d_0 C_{-1} + d_1 Y + d_2 Y_{-1}. \tag{17.16}$$

---

7. In principle we can perform a similar thought experiment with transfer payments and estimate $\Sigma \Delta C$ by $1 - \hat{b}_0^3 \hat{b}_3$. But, even though capitalists' share of transfer payments is undoubtedly smaller than their share of labor income, there are difficulties with transfer payments that make it less suitable for this test than labor income. These problems will be examined in the next chapter.

TOWARD AN UNDERSTANDING OF CAPITALISM

Thus the notion that all previous information is reflected in C_{-1} is tested by whether the confidence interval of $\hat{c}_0 - \hat{c}_1 + \hat{c}_2$ includes zero. By contrast, the disequilibrium model hypothesizes

$$c_2 = 0,$$

which can be tested directly by whether the confidence interval around $\hat{c}_2$ includes zero.

This is not, however, a very interesting test of the permanent-income hypothesis. As we have seen, it addresses the form of the permanent-income adjustment equation more than the substance of the underlying theory. First, if the adjustment of the permanent income is assumed to depend on lagged measured income as well as current measured income, that is, if Eq. (17.3) is replaced by Eq. (17.7), then the coefficient of Y_{-1} becomes $-\mu\eta_0$, as in Eq. (17.9), rather than 0. Thus, $E\hat{d}_2$ in Eq. (17.16) becomes $-\mu\eta_0$, and $E(\hat{c}_0 - \hat{c}_1 + \hat{c}_2)$ is no longer equal to zero. Second, if $(1 - \mu)(\eta_1 + \eta_0) = \psi$, then the equation $c_2 = 0$ holds in the permanent-income hypothesis as well as in the disequilibrium hypothesis.

More meaningful tests of the two hypotheses require us to determine what are plausible parameter values under the two views of spending behavior. For the permanent-income hypothesis to be substantively meaningful, the adjustment of permanent income to measured income must be relatively slow. To be sure, one can always maintain the permanent-income formalism, no matter how rapid the adjustment of permanent income to measured income appears to be, even if it is near-instantaneous. But for high values of η, the idea of permanent income would become devoid of empirical as well as theoretical content.

This said, what constitutes slow or fast adjustment? It might fix our ideas to examine the consequences of different speeds of adjustment to a one-dollar increase in measured income—a thought experiment analogous to the examination of the adjustment of spending to income under the disequilibrium hypothesis. Assume that before this addition to measured income, permanent income has fully adjusted to observed income, and that apart from the extra dollar, observed income has been and continues to grow at a constant trend rate ψ. Then we have after t quarters

$$Y_t = Y_0^P(1 + \psi)^{t-1} + 1.$$

The difference between permanent income with and without the one-dollar injection is

$$Y_t^P - Y_0^P(1 + \psi)^t = \eta \sum_{\tau=0}^{t-1} (1 + \psi - \eta)^\tau.$$

Evidently, as t tends to infinity, the reflection of the extra dollar of measured income is complete (indeed, more than complete, since the injection of income sets up unfulfilled expectations of further increases). To be precise,

$$Y_t^P - Y_0^P(1 + \psi)^t \rightarrow \frac{\eta}{\eta - \psi} \quad \text{as} \quad t \rightarrow \infty.$$

But this is of little interest. What matters is how rapid the adjustment is in the *short* run, for instance, after four quarters. Once again there is an element of arbitrariness involved in fixing a numerical benchmark, but if the adjustment of permanent income to changes in measured income is more than 50 percent complete in a year, it seems to me difficult to preserve the substance of the permanent-income hypothesis. Thus if we specify the permanent-income hypothesis as

$$S = (\eta - \psi - 1)C_{-1} + (1 - \mu\eta)Y, \tag{17.17}$$

then we can interpret the inequality

$$Y_4^P - Y_0^P(1 + \psi)^4 = \eta \sum_{\tau=0}^{3} (1 + \psi - \eta)^\tau < 0.5$$

as favorable to the permanent-income hypothesis. This can be tested (strongly) by whether the confidence interval for

$$(\hat{d}_0 + 1 + \psi)(1 - \hat{d}_0 + \hat{d}_0^2 - \hat{d}_0^3) = \hat{\eta} \sum_{\tau=0}^{3} (1 + \psi - \hat{\eta})^\tau$$

lies below 0.5 and (weakly) by whether this confidence interval includes 0.5. The coefficient $\hat{d}_0$ is estimated from the equation

$$S = d_0 C_{-1} + d_1 Y. \tag{17.18}$$

That is, d_2 in Eq. (17.16) is constrained to be equal to zero.

We can also test the hypothesis that the long-run marginal propensity to save is positive, as the permanent-income hypothesis asserts. We have

$$1 - \hat{\mu} = \frac{\hat{d}_0 + \hat{d}_1 + \psi}{\hat{d}_0 + 1 + \psi}$$

and can test the alternatives $1 - \mu > 0$ and $1 - \mu = 0$ by the confidence interval around $1 - \hat{\mu}$.[8]

Finally, we can test the speed of adjustment of spending to income on the disequilibrium interpretation of Eq. (17.15) just as we tested the speed of adjustment by the coefficients of Eq. (17.14). With c_2 constrained to equal zero, we have

$$S = c_0 S_{-1} + c_1 \Delta Y,$$

and four quarters after the commencement of a one-dollar injection of income, the change in spending is

$$\Sigma \Delta C = \theta + \zeta + \theta(1 - \theta - \zeta) + \theta(1 - \theta - \zeta)(1 - \theta)$$
$$+ \theta(1 - \theta - \zeta)(1 - \theta)^2 = 1 - c_0^3 c_1.$$

For the hypothesis $\Sigma \Delta C \leq 0.5$ to be rejected, the confidence interval around $1 - \hat{c}_0^3 \hat{c}_1$ must lie wholly above 0.5. For the hypothesis $\Sigma \Delta C \geq 0.5$ to be rejected, this confidence interval must lie wholly below 0.5.

The Meaning and Measurement of "Household" Saving

My intention is to use these tests to compare alternative views of saving with one another, but beforehand we face a preliminary issue, or rather a set of issues, that surround the very definition of saving. The appropriate definition might appear straightforward: saving is addition to the stock of capital goods. But *which* capital goods? The means of production, plant and equipment and goods in process, of course. But do we include or exclude consumer durables like television sets and automobiles? What about owner-occupied housing? Do we include or exclude corporate retention of earnings and pension-fund saving?

Neither neoclassical theory nor national-income accounting conven-

---

8. The propensity to save out of permanent income, $1 - \mu$, is slightly different conceptually from the long-run steady-growth saving ratio s. From (17.18) we have

$$\frac{S}{Y} \frac{Y}{Y_{-1}} = d_0 \frac{C_{-1}}{Y_{-1}} + d_1 \frac{Y}{Y_{-1}}$$

or

$$s(1 + g) = d_0(1 - s) + d_1(1 + g).$$

So

$$s = \frac{d_0 + (1 + g)d_1}{d_0 + 1 + g}.$$

With $-d_0 \simeq d_1$ and $\psi = g$, we have

$$\frac{s}{1 - \mu} \simeq d_1.$$

tions necessarily provide appropriate definitions for household saving. This section will examine arguments for and against the inclusion of consumer durables and additions to the stock of housing in household saving, as well as arguments for and against the inclusion of organizational saving carried on by pension funds and corporations. The point is not so much to arrive at *the* correct definition of saving as to explore the relationship between differences in definition and differences in approaches to the study of a capitalist economy.

Consumer Durables and Owner-occupied Housing

The rationale for the inclusion of consumer durables in saving is that automobiles, television sets, and houses are, like productive capital and financial assets, purchased in order to provide a flow of services and utilities. Hence, according to the neoclassical view, these goods should be lumped with the accumulation of the means of production rather than with consumption.

In the case of the permanent-income hypothesis, this practice makes sense, at least if we limit the time horizon to a short enough period. The more plausible interpretation of the permanent-income argument is that transitory income is used to smooth consumption over a period in which ups and downs in income effectively cancel each other out. What better way, over a decade or even half a decade, to smooth consumption than to use transitory income to purchase durables? With this interpretation of the permanent-income hypothesis, it doubtless makes sense to include durables in saving.

But in the case of the life-cycle hypothesis, the average time horizon is much longer, and the inclusion of durables is more questionable. The essence of saving over the life cycle is provision for retirement, and it is scarcely plausible that a middle-aged wage earner at the peak of his earning power saves for his retirement by buying a television set, an automobile, or a boat.

The inclusion of housing in saving is perhaps more defensible because houses are not acquired solely for the flow of services they provide. Houses are also a store of value more or less easily converted into other forms of consumption later on. Some houses are undoubtedly bought with the expectation of selling them to supplement pension income once retirement age is reached.

In any case, none of these arguments is very compelling outside the neoclassical framework. The goal that over the last forty years has motivated the study of household consumption and saving is rather different from the one implicit in the neoclassical enterprise in either of its variants. Neoclassical saving theory came into its own in response to the challenge of Keynesian theory, whose concern was not with the determination of the flow of household consumption *services,* but with the determination of the flow of household *expenditures.* For stabilization purposes, the essence of "consumption" is not the durability of goods but the regularity of spending and its impact on the national economy. Let feasts and potlatches play an important role in our economy, and they should be counted with investment for stabilization purposes—as long as their occurrence is determined by "animal spirits" rather than by income. Similarly, for stabilization purposes, imports are customarily counted with saving as leakages from spending; their composition with respect to durables and nondurables is not an issue.

Even though the focus of the present study is hardly stabilization policy *à la* Keynes, neoclassical definitions of saving are no more satisfactory from a nonneoclassical point of view. In the nonneoclassical perspective on growth and distribution, saving is important because of its impact on profits and wages. The theoretical mechanisms differ between the neo-Keynesian and neo-Marxian models, but in both the only saving that matters is the saving that adds to producers' goods; the accumulation of consumers' durables and even owner-occupied housing is equivalent to consumption of nondurables and services in its effects on profits and wages.

The mode of production is crucial here. Consumer durables and owner-occupied housing are certainly capital goods, but they are capital goods in a "subsistence" sector in which production takes place within the household, directly for the use of the producer, unmediated by market transactions. Indeed, if all production took place in a subsistence mode or even in a petty-commodity mode, the saving decisions of a household would be far less significant than they are in an economy in which the capitalist sector dominates. In subsistence or petty-commodity sectors, saving, whether it takes the form of a durable consumption good or the form of the tools of one's trade, is a personal matter of no more general concern than the household's decisions with respect to the mix of apples and nuts it consumes. In these sectors the household as producer merges with the household as consumer, and the benefits of the household's accumulation of capital go directly and solely to the household itself.

In a capitalist mode of production, by contrast, accumulation (more accurately, accumulation of producers' goods) acquires an important new characteristic: the sowing and reaping of the fruits of accumulation become separated; those who work for wages but do not save acquire a stake in the saving behavior of others. In consequence, there are what economists are wont to call "pecuniary externalities" in the relationship between accumulation and growth.[9] Even in the neoclassical model, savers do not, even in a regime of perfect competition, garner all the returns to saving—except in the limit as the quantity of saving goes to zero; a portion of the returns goes to workers, whose productivity and real wages are increased by accumulation. At a stable long-run equilibrium, the wage rate responds positively to the saving propensity.

The pecuniary externalities associated with accumulation even have a name, the "Wicksell effect," after the Swedish economist who first discussed the phenomenon early in this century. But its specificity to the capitalist mode of production,[10] in which capital and labor are separate, has gone unremarked, in keeping with the orthodox tendency to lump capitalism together with other economic forms and to treat wage labor as just another commodity.

The role of accumulation under capitalism becomes even more critical when the externalities of saving are linked to the importance of accumulation in promoting social stability. I have suggested that because of the importance of consumption in our society, capitalism must deliver the goods in increasing volume in order to maintain the legitimacy of the existing social order. Once the role of saving in political acquiescence is understood, it is no wonder that the Invisible Hand is found insufficient—that in a society in which the capitalist mode of production is preeminent, other people's saving matters, so the rate of accumulation becomes a political issue of the first magnitude.

For the limited purposes of this chapter, the importance of placing saving in a social context is to emphasize the distinction between accumulation that expands the means of production and accumulation that adds to the stock of consumer durables and owner-occupied housing. For durables and housing, however important they may be to social stability, are accumulated within the subsistence mode of production, not the capitalist. Externalities do not link the wage earner to another purchaser of an automobile or a television set as they link him to the purchaser of new machinery that enhances productivity and increases wages.

Roughly speaking, leaving durables and housing out of the picture defines household saving in terms of what used to be called "loanable

9. The terminology is misleading: "pecuniary" suggests an opposition to real, an opposition that does not hold here.

10. Not quite: there is also potential for a Wicksell effect under "state socialism," in which control over production and accumulation are concentrated in relatively few hands despite the nominal abolition of private property.

funds." In the loanable-funds view, saving is limited to the accumulation of financial assets, as a measure of the resources that households make available to the rest of the economy for accumulation. Restricting the meaning of saving to the accumulation of financial assets makes the average household propensity to save in the American economy over the past three decades about 4 percent of disposable income, a reduction of almost one-half from the 7.5 percent figure that results from including investment in owner-occupied housing in saving, and a reduction of more than one-half from the 9 + percent that results from using a more extensive concept that includes durables.

Pension-Fund Saving

Another problem with the conventional measure of household saving is the treatment of pension-fund accumulation. In the national income accounts as well as in most studies of consumption and saving behavior, private pension funds are treated more or less as an extension of the household: private pension-fund saving is counted both in disposable income and in personal saving. This makes sense in terms of neoclassical theory: a rational household *ought* to integrate the saving done in its name by a pension fund with its direct saving out of disposable income. But it will hardly do to *assume* that households integrate their direct saving with the saving carried out on their behalf by pension funds in a test of alternative theories, when it is precisely the rationality of households that is at issue.

For the record, an early empirical examination of the actual degree of integration of the two kinds of saving, a study by Philip Cagan (1965), painted a picture that was highly critical of the neoclassical view of household rationality. However, more recent work by Alicia Munnell (1976) gives at least partial support to the neoclassical view. She interprets the data for men in the age group 45–59 as indicating that for each dollar of pension-fund saving, direct saving on the part of the household is reduced by 60 cents, neither the full dollar that neoclassical theory would predict nor the zero dollars that nonneoclassical theory would predict. In a sense Munnell has chosen the most favorable ground for her case: middle-aged men can be expected to be more sensitive to retirement than the average wage earner. So no matter how solid her case might be on its own ground, it may be impossible to draw any meaningful inferences for the population as a whole.

Pensions financed out of social security taxes raise similar issues. Martin Feldstein (1974) has created a veritable industry by arguing, with impeccable neoclassical logic, that households will regard the discounted present value of future pensions as part of their wealth and adjust their direct saving accordingly. By contrast, the view embodied in the disequilibrium hypothesis is that social security taxes and payments will affect consumption and saving only to the extent that they show up as a reduction in disposable income.

I should probably add that I have always thought that the message of social security, particularly the message of its well-nigh universality in the capitalist world, is exactly the opposite of the lesson that neoclassical economists appear to draw. The very emergence of social security programs during the past half-century seems to me strong evidence of the *failure* of individuals to provide for their retirement or disability along lines congenial to the life-cycle hypothesis. The absence of private institutional structures to deal adequately with these problems is only with the greatest difficulty explained by neoclassical theory.

It is extremely difficult to test the neoclassical and nonneoclassical views of the role of social security in saving behavior. Time-series evidence on the role of social security "wealth" is largely beside the point, since this variable acts like a time trend and could be a proxy for any number of other influences. Cross-country data might be more useful, but dramatic cross-country comparisons are often cross-cultural as well. When we briefly turn our attention to Japan at the end of the next chapter, we shall see the significance of this point. For the present, we shall therefore ignore social security "wealth" and "saving." We shall, however, examine similar issues that emerge in the context of transfer *payments,* a large fraction of which are social security benefits. And we shall also address similar theoretical issues when we compare results with and without private pension-fund saving included in household saving. (Evidently pension-fund saving makes a considerable quantitative difference all by itself. Over the years, more than one-third of household financial saving has in fact been the work of pension funds: the financial saving rate falls from 4 percent to 2.5 percent when additions to private—including state and local government—pension-fund reserves are excluded from household loanable funds.)

Corporate saving is conceptually similar to pension-fund saving even though it is treated quite differently in the national income accounts. It is, of course, even more important quantitatively. If undistributed profits as well as additions to public and private pension-fund reserves are included in household saving,[11] the net saving rate increases to the

11. Public pension funds are state and local government retirement funds, which—to complicate matters—are excluded from personal saving in the national income accounts.

order of 9 percent or 16 percent, depending on whether or not housing and durables are also included.

Integration of Corporate and Personal Saving Decisions

In the neoclassical perspective, there is no more reason to separate corporate saving from personal saving than there is to separate pension funds from households. Either the corporation is the agent of the stockholders, as the truest believers would have it; or even if corporate managers pursue retention policies adverse to an individual's perceived interest, the individual can adjust his direct saving in the light of the saving carried out by the corporations whose shares he owns.[12]

In the nonneoclassical view, corporate saving is determined quite separately from, and to a large extent independently of, the interest of the households who are the nominal owners of the corporation. The denizens of the executive suite who dispose, as well as the technostructure which proposes, have their own axes to grind in determining the rate of corporate saving, and these interests—first in preserving their tenure of office, then in extending their power and prestige—may be better served than the interests of the stockholders that the corporation is supposed in legal theory to serve. To some extent, of course, tax laws harmonize the interests of owners and managers; for example, the double taxation of dividends (first as corporate profit, then as personal income) that characterizes U.S. tax law is avoided by retention of earnings within the corporate coffers. Corporate retention of earnings is thus to some extent in the interest of owners as well as managers. But the harmonization of interests remains imperfect, and corporate saving is, along with risk taking, the area in which the interests of owners and managers most glaringly diverge: left to its own devices, the managerial class would never find it desirable to pay out any dividends, instead plowing back all earnings into expansion. Dividends reflect a compromise with the interests of the stockholders, who as a class if not as individuals constrain the retention policies of corporate managers.

But if owners at least influence the rate of corporate saving, corpor-

12. The point at issue is *not* the role of corporate saving in the neoclassical consumption function as an indicator of future wealth or permanent income. Two decades ago Modigliani warned against using profit as a predictor of wealth: short-run variations in profit "are dominated by transitory phenomena and hence are a poor measure of change in the relevant long run, or permanent, property income" (Ando and Modigliani 1963, pp. 76–77). And these strictures apply with equal or greater force to retained earnings, which are more volatile than total profits and include an even larger transitory component than do profits. Rather, the neoclassical point is that corporate retentions enter the consumption equation as part and parcel of the current *saving* of households.

ate saving in turn influences household saving only to the extent that it affects the flow of disposable income. For the householder, the bird in the hand is not just worth two in the bush, the bird in the hand is the *only* bird. Hence the appropriate measure of household accumulation of the means of production is one that excludes corporate saving.

This at least seems to me the logic of the nonneoclassical position. But the matter is not quite so simple, for there are divisions within the nonneoclassical camp just as there are divisions among neoclassicals. The debate between Luigi Pasinetti and Nicholas Kaldor that we examined in Chapter 6 turned in part on whether or not the ultimate claimants on profit, the capitalists and workers who own corporate shares, actually determine saving propensities out of profits. Pasinetti's saving function in its pure form implicitly assumes that ownership conveys control of the accumulation process, whereas Kaldor's spirited defense of his own saving function stresses the difference between organizational saving, typified by corporate retention of earnings, and the personal saving of the household.

Even if the simplest form of Pasinetti's saving function depends on owners and workers exercising ultimate control over the saving rate, the underlying argument remains relevant in a world in which corporations play an independent role. Pasinetti's essential insight requires only that some part of profits be paid out to shareholders: it really does not matter for Pasinetti's purposes whether shareholders take account of corporate saving in their personal saving decisions. But for our purposes it matters quite a lot. The meaningfulness of household saving as a separate category of private saving makes sense only if corporate and personal saving propensities are relatively independent. If one accepts the notion that households treat all income homogeneously — income they actually lay hands on and income that stays in corporate (or pension-fund) coffers — then one is led to integrate organizational saving into household saving, whether one is otherwise neoclassically or nonneoclassically inclined.

Corporate Saving: The Evidence

The empirical case that corporate and personal saving are in fact integrated into a single decision process by the household rests on two studies. First is Edward Denison's finding (1958), amplified by Paul David and John Scadding (1974), that overall private saving — the sum of personal and corporate saving — has remained roughly constant as a fraction of gross national product over this century. This is supposed to reflect an adjustment of personal saving to the corporate saving rate.

Second is Martin Feldstein's finding (1973; see also Feldstein and Fane 1973) that corporate retentions affect consumption in aggregate time series in the direction and magnitude that the neoclassical view of an integrated decision process would predict. This is supposed to demonstrate, as Feldstein puts it, that "households see through the corporate veil."

The Denison-David-Scadding evidence turns out to establish nothing of relevance. Joaquim de Andrade has argued (1981) that if gross private income replaces gross national product as the denominator, the "constancy" of the private saving ratio depends critically on the subperiods into which one divides the twentieth century. More damaging to the inference that personal and corporate saving are substitutes is Andrade's suggestion that corporate saving is at least as constant relative to gross private income over the century as is the overall saving ratio, in which case there is in reality no substitution to be accounted for!

Feldstein's argument rests on the coefficient of retained earnings in the annual time-series regression (1973, p. 166):

$$C = 41 + 0.57\, Y^d + 0.19\, Y^d_{-1} + 0.024\, (W_{-1} + G)$$
$$(0.06) \qquad (0.03) \qquad\quad (0.008)$$

$$+\ 0.49\, RN + 3.00\, RU$$
$$(0.09) \qquad (0.86)$$

$$DW = 2.03 \qquad R^2 = 0.99 \qquad \text{INTERVAL} = 1929-1941,$$
$$1948-1966$$

C = consumption (NIA basis)
Y^d = disposable income (NIA basis)
W = wealth
G = capital gains
RN = retained earnings
RU = rate of unemployment

At first blush, the result is indeed impressive. For every dollar of increased retained earnings, households appear to increase their consumption by half a dollar, just what one might expect in equilibrium, at least if households (1) pay income tax at approximately the same rate as corporations, (2) adjust their direct saving to corporate saving, and (3) always bear in mind the double taxation on dividends that retained earnings escape under present tax laws.

Feldstein's interpretation can hardly be sustained, however. Feldstein argues that causality runs *from* retained earnings *to* personal saving: households note a change in the retentions of the corporations of which they are shareholders and adjust their direct saving accordingly. The implicit assumption with respect to the availability of time and resources, not to mention inclination, for the requisite calculations stretches one's power of imagination. The Rockefellers, with a Chase Manhattan Bank at their disposal, may fit Feldstein's model, but even allowing for the high concentration of share ownership, the Rockefellers are hardly the norm, even for the 1 percent of the population that accounts for the ownership of 50 percent of the publicly traded stock.

It will be objected that the implausibility of the assumptions is irrelevant. In positivist fashion (Friedman 1953), many defenders of the neoclassical faith will insist that it is prediction that counts. Without granting this point, it can be observed that Feldstein's argument fails on predictive grounds too. The problem is that consumption and retained earnings enter into Feldstein's equation simultaneously, and though Feldstein makes retained earnings the cause and consumption the effect, it is equally consistent with the data and much more plausible to reverse the causal ordering. When consumption demand is extraordinarily high (relative to what past income would predict), output responds positively, and—especially in oligopolies that follow mark-up pricing rules—so do corporate profits. Dividends adjust slowly to corporate profits, especially to "transitory" profits, and the bottom line (so to speak) is that retained earnings adjust to consumption. This is quite the opposite from Feldstein's logic, but equally consistent with his results.

One might try to test the two views of causality by lags and leads in the relationship between consumption and retained earnings, according to procedures developed by Clive Granger (1969) and Christopher Sims (1972). But the exercise would necessarily lead to ambiguous results. In the first place, current levels of consumption and retained earnings will be correlated no matter which of the two competing causal mechanisms we posit, or for that matter, if we posit a third mechanism, the dependence of both consumption and retained earnings on one or more excluded variables. And indeed, preliminary tests along Granger-Sims lines by de Andrade as well as by Thomas Brush (1979) indicate simultaneity rather than a pattern in which one of the two variables clearly leads the other.

But even if subsequent analysis were to show that consumption leads retained earnings, Feldstein's view could still be rescued by appeal to the rational-expectations hypothesis, according to which households correctly anticipate future retained earnings (up to a random error) and adjust consumption in advance. In view of the complexity of the structure that determines retained earnings, it would be difficult indeed to distinguish spurious from true causality in a rational-expectations model. With rational expectations, the argument that households see through the corporate veil becomes equivalent to the proposition that prayer uttered with a pure heart is always answered. Both are incontrovertible by evidence, with data to the effect that consumption leads retained earnings becoming evidence for rational expectations as data to the effect that prayers are not always answered become evidence for the impurity of heart.

It must be admitted that we lack an adequate test of the hypothesis of household integration of corporate saving into personal saving decisions. One thing is clear: such a test will require us to turn from aggregate time series to cross-section data.[13] De Andrade has performed one indirect test using cross-section data that hinges on the high concentration of stock ownership. He begins by asking us to adopt the permanent-income hypothesis, at least for the sake of argument. Assume in particular that saving is a constant proportion of permanent income. But follow neoclassical logic and include indirect (corporate) as well as direct (personal) saving in both household saving and household income. Then the proportionality postulate and the concentration of stock ownership together lead to a simple prediction: since indirect saving rises more than proportionately with permanent income, the ratio of direct saving to direct permanent income — saving and income exclusive of retained earnings — ought to fall sufficiently as permanent income rises to offset the increase in indirect saving. But supporters of the permanent-income hypothesis, including Friedman himself, have insisted that the data support the proportionality of *direct* saving to *direct* permanent income: corporate saving has generally been excluded from household income in empirical work on the permanent-income hypothesis, including tests of the proportionality hypothesis. If proportionality holds for the narrow definition of income and saving, one must evidently abandon either the broader definition of saving and income *or* the proportionality assumption itself. The data cannot support the proportionality assumption on both the narrow and the broad definition of income and saving.

De Andrade's test is defective in one crucial respect: it is a test of the integration of corporate and saving decisions only if one accepts the

13. Perhaps not. After reading a draft of this chapter, Mark Watson suggested using instrumental variables to test the exogeneity of retained earnings in the Feldstein equation. An instrumental-variables test would appear to be immune to at least some of the criticisms of the Granger-Sims procedure.

permanent-income hypothesis lock, stock, and barrel. Unfortunately the proportionality assumption is the weakest link of the permanent-income hypothesis, not really derivable from its underlying neoclassical premises. Friedman's preoccupation with proportionality stemmed from the role of a constant propensity to save out of permanent income in developing a neoclassical argument that resolved the paradoxical relationship between time-series and cross-sectional saving ratios. But from our perspective the constancy of the saving ratio across income classes is only one issue. The other issue is the rationality and deliberation of the decision process, and one can easily give up the proportionality assumption without sacrificing the neoclassical insistence on rational behavior.

A more satisfactory test of whether organizational saving is reflected in household saving behavior would examine the direct saving behavior of households at similar levels of permanent and transitory disposable income, age, and family size but with very different proportions of corporate stock in their asset portfolios. If "integrationist" logic obtains, then the tax-corrected overall (personal plus corporate) saving of all households in this group should be the same except for a random error, with differences in direct saving just balancing differences in the retained earnings of the corporations in the households' portfolios. I should expect, rather, that—random error apart—*direct* household saving will be equal across this group of households.

Summary: Alternative Saving Measures

Evidently there is no absolutely compelling way of measuring household saving. Neoclassical logic leads to an expansive measure that includes consumer durables and corporate retentions along with personal saving as it is measured in the national income accounts. Nonneoclassical logic would exclude not only durables, but also investment in owner-occupied housing. Nonneoclassical views are more divided on retained earnings. The thrust of Pasinetti's argument is toward the ultrarationalist position that households "see through the corporate [and pension-fund] veil." My own position, by contrast, is that household saving is independent of organizational saving except insofar as organizational saving affects disposable income.

These conceptual differences suggest three alternative saving measures: *PRISAV*, which includes all private saving; *PGSAV*, which includes the "productive" saving of households and organizations, that is, the loanable funds made available directly by households along with the additions to pension-fund reserves and the retained earnings of

Table 17.3. Relationship among alternative measures of household saving

	Housing and durables excluded from saving	Housing and durables included in saving
Organizational saving excluded from saving	*LFSAV*	*HHSAV*
Organizational saving included in saving	*PGSAV*	*PRISAV*

corporations; and *LFSAV*, which includes only the direct financial saving of households. For completeness, we might include a fourth measure, *HHSAV*, defined to include durables and investment in owner-occupied housing but to exclude indirect (that is, organizational) financial saving. Table 17.3 shows the relationship among these different measures schematically. Observe that none of these measures corresponds exactly to the definition of personal saving in the national income accounts, *NIASAV*, which conceptually falls between the four stools. There is first of all a statistical discrepancy that arises from the difference in technique used to measure saving in the national income accounts and that used to measure saving by the Flow of Funds data that form the basis of our measures: the first treats saving as a residual, the second measures saving directly. There are also important conceptual differences: *NIASAV* includes private pension-fund saving but excludes public (state and local government employee) pension-fund saving as well as corporate retentions; *NIASAV* includes investment in owner-occupied housing but excludes consumer durables; *NIASAV* also includes investment in plant and equipment by nonprofit institutions, which is excluded from all of our saving measures.

Table 17.4 shows the relationships among the alternative measures of saving. Tables 17.5 and 17.6 give a quantitative picture of saving over most of the postwar period, both in per capita dollars of constant purchasing power and as a percentage of disposable income. Figure 17.1(a)–(c) shows the ratio of *LFSAV* to each of the other measures. Particularly noteworthy, as we shall see when we examine the regression results, is the contracyclical pattern of these graphs. *LFSAV* increases both relatively and absolutely during periods of high unemployment, such as the recessions of 1958, 1961, and 1975. We turn in the next chapter to these regression results.

Table 17.4. Relationships among alternative measures of saving

$$PRISAV = NIASAV - STATDISC + CDURA + RNA + CGIA - NONPROF$$
$$PGSAV = PRISAV - CDURA - NETRCON$$
$$LFSAV = PGSAV - RNA - PFRA$$
$$HHSAV = LFSAV + CDURA + NETRCON$$

$PRISAV$ = total private saving, including financial saving of households and pension funds, corporate retentions, and investment in consumer durables and owner-occupied housing

$NIASAV$ = personal saving, as measured in the national income accounts

$STATDISC$ = statistical discrepancy between national income accounts and Flow of Funds measures of the sum of financial saving by households and private pension funds and investment in owner-occupied housing

$CDURA$ = investment in consumer durables, net of depreciation

RNA = corporate retained earnings net of capital-consumption adjustment and inventory-valuation adjustment'

$CGIA$ = net additions to reserves of state and local government employee retirement funds (not included in personal saving in the national income accounts)

$NONPROF$ = investment in plant and equipment by nonprofit institutions, net of depreciation

$PGSAV$ = "productive" saving of households and organizations, resources made available by households, pension funds, and businesses to nonhousehold sectors

$NETRCON$ = investment in owner-occupied housing, net of depreciation

$LFSAV$ = household financial saving in the form of funds made available to nonhousehold sectors

$PFRA$ = addition to pension-fund reserves, including private funds and retirement funds of state and local government employees. (Private pension-fund saving, which is the difference between total and public pension-fund saving, $PFRA - CGIA$, is included in personal saving in the national income accounts)

$HHSAV$ = household saving including consumer durables and investment in owner-occupied housing along with financial saving

Table 17.5. Saving and its components in constant (1972) dollars per capita

	1952	1953	1954	1955	1956	1957	1958	1959	1960	1961
NIASAV	177	183	163	152	192	192	194	168	151	172
−*STATDISC*	−34	−18	−24	−34	−42	−35	−32	−50	−50	−35
+*CGIA*	21	19	15	17	22	19	23	23	24	25
+*CDURA*	88	100	68	114	77	66	30	58	54	32
+*RNA*	85	71	81	125	96	87	67	110	93	93
−*NONPROF*	7	7	10	10	11	11	12	12	12	13
=**PRISAV**	398	384	342	432	419	388	334	398	360	345
−*NETRCON*	115	121	122	156	141	113	101	130	114	95
−*CDURA*	88	100	68	114	77	66	30	58	54	32
=**PGSAV**	194	163	151	162	202	209	203	210	192	218
−*RNA*	85	71	81	125	96	87	67	110	93	93
−*PFRA*	49	48	49	53	54	58	60	67	64	65
=**LFSAV**	60	43	21	−15	51	63	76	33	35	61
+*TOTDUR*	204	221	190	270	218	179	131	188	168	127
=**HHSAV**	264	265	211	255	268	242	207	221	204	187
DPINIA	2,430	2,489	2,471	2,570	2,640	2,646	2,632	2,695	2,707	2,740

(*continued*)

Table 17.5 continued

	1962	1963	1964	1965	1966	1967	1968	1969	1970	1971
NIASAV	169	154	203	224	230	274	247	226	294	303
−*STATDISC*	−46	−62	−50	−36	−44	−27	−18	28	−5	8
+*CGIA*	25	27	30	32	36	34	36	39	47	47
+*CDURA*	62	83	103	134	148	131	159	147	106	132
+*RNA*	132	144	164	200	205	184	164	129	78	113
−*NONPROF*	15	14	15	16	16	14	13	13	12	11
=**PRISAV**	420	457	535	609	646	635	611	500	517	576
−*NETRCON*	98	101	103	97	87	72	92	91	72	103
−*CDURA*	62	83	103	134	148	131	159	147	106	132
=**PGSAV**	260	272	329	378	411	432	361	263	340	341
−*RNA*	132	144	164	200	205	184	164	129	78	113
−*PFRA*	65	68	80	81	93	84	89	92	97	105
=**LFSAV**	63	61	85	98	114	165	107	42	165	122
+*TOTDUR*	160	184	206	231	235	203	251	237	177	236
=**HHSAV**	223	245	291	329	348	367	358	279	342	358
DPINIA	2,811	2,863	3,024	3,169	3,288	3,387	3,492	3,562	3,662	3,750

(*continued*)

Table 17.5 continued

	1972	1973	1974	1975	1976	1977	1978	1979	AVG
NIASAV	251	351	342	348	288	253	270	265	230
−*STATDISC*	−43	3	−6	−63	−86	−55	−78	−90	−37
+*CGIA*	55	53	51	56	62	73	84	67	38
+*CDURA*	165	181	115	97	139	161	171	144	109
+*RNA*	145	144	55	107	129	175	187	149	125
−*NONPROF*	12	10	6	3	4	3	4	3	10
=**PRISAV**	647	717	562	668	698	715	785	713	529
−*NETRCON*	133	138	101	87	125	170	193	186	116
−*CDURA*	165	181	115	97	139	161	171	144	109
=**PGSAV**	349	398	346	484	434	383	422	383	303
−*RNA*	145	144	55	107	129	175	187	149	125
−*PFRA*	107	113	118	129	154	182	186	152	92
=**LFSAV**	96	141	173	248	152	26	49	82	86
+*TOTDUR*	298	319	216	184	264	332	363	330	226
=**HHSAV**	394	460	389	433	416	358	412	411	312
DPINIA	3,858	4,078	4,008	4,049	4,156	4,278	4,439	4,510	3,300

TOTDUR = *NETRCON* + *CDURA*; *DPINIA* = disposable personal income, national-income-accounts basis. Other variables are defined in Table 17.4.

Sources: National Income and Product Accounts, Flow of Funds Accounts.

Table 17.6. Saving and its components as percentages of disposable income

	1952	1953	1954	1955	1956	1957	1958	1959	1960	1961
NIASAV	7.3	7.4	6.6	5.9	7.3	7.3	7.4	6.3	5.6	6.3
−STATDISC	−1.4	−0.7	−1.0	−1.3	−1.6	−1.3	−1.2	−1.8	−1.8	−1.3
+CGIA	0.9	0.8	0.6	0.7	0.8	0.7	0.9	0.9	0.9	0.9
+CDURA	3.6	4.0	2.8	4.4	2.9	2.5	1.1	2.2	2.0	1.2
+RNA	3.5	2.9	3.3	4.8	3.6	3.3	2.6	4.1	3.4	3.4
−NONPROF	0.3	0.3	0.4	0.4	0.4	0.4	0.5	0.4	0.5	0.5
=PRISAV	16.4	15.4	13.8	16.8	15.9	14.6	12.7	14.8	13.3	12.6
−NETRCON	4.7	4.9	4.9	6.1	5.3	4.3	3.8	4.8	4.2	3.5
−CDURA	3.6	4.0	2.8	4.4	2.9	2.5	1.1	2.2	2.0	1.2
=PGSAV	8.0	6.5	6.1	6.3	7.6	7.9	7.7	7.8	7.1	8.0
−RNA	3.5	2.9	3.3	4.8	3.6	3.3	2.6	4.1	3.4	3.4
−PFRA	2.0	1.9	2.0	2.0	2.1	2.2	2.3	2.5	2.4	2.4
=LFSAV	2.5	1.7	0.9	−0.6	1.9	2.4	2.9	1.2	1.3	2.2
+TOTDUR	8.4	8.9	7.7	10.5	8.2	6.8	5.0	7.0	6.2	4.6
=HHSAV	10.9	10.6	8.5	9.9	10.2	9.2	7.9	8.2	7.5	6.8
DPINIA	100.0	100.0	100.0	100.0	100.0	100.0	100.0	100.0	100.0	100.0

(*continued*)

Table 17.6 continued

	1962	1963	1964	1965	1966	1967	1968	1969	1970	1971
NIASAV	6.0	5.4	6.7	7.1	7.0	8.1	7.1	6.3	8.0	8.1
−*STATDISC*	−1.6	−2.2	−1.7	−1.1	−1.3	−0.8	−0.5	0.8	−0.1	0.2
+*CGIA*	0.9	0.9	1.0	1.0	1.1	1.0	1.0	1.1	1.3	1.3
+*CDURA*	2.2	2.9	3.4	4.2	4.5	3.9	4.5	4.1	2.9	3.5
+*RNA*	4.7	5.0	5.4	6.3	6.2	5.4	4.7	3.6	2.1	3.0
−*NONPROF*	0.5	0.5	0.5	0.5	0.5	0.4	0.4	0.4	0.3	0.3
=**PRISAV**	14.9	15.9	17.7	19.2	19.6	18.7	17.5	14.0	14.1	15.4
−*NETRCON*	3.5	3.5	3.4	3.1	2.6	2.1	2.6	2.5	2.0	2.7
−*CDURA*	2.2	2.9	3.4	4.2	4.5	3.9	4.5	4.1	2.9	3.5
=**PGSAV**	9.2	9.5	10.9	11.9	12.5	12.8	10.3	7.4	9.3	9.1
−*RNA*	4.7	5.0	5.4	6.3	6.2	5.4	4.7	3.6	2.1	3.0
−*PFRA*	2.3	2.4	2.7	2.5	2.8	2.5	2.5	2.6	2.6	2.8
=**LFSAV**	2.2	2.1	2.8	3.1	3.5	4.9	3.1	1.2	4.5	3.3
+*TOTDUR*	5.7	6.4	6.8	7.3	7.1	6.0	7.2	6.7	4.8	6.3
=**HHSAV**	7.9	8.6	9.6	10.4	10.6	10.8	10.3	7.8	9.3	9.5
DPINIA	100.0	100.0	100.0	100.0	100.0	100.0	100.0	100.0	100.0	100.0

(*continued*)

Table 17.6 continued

	1972	1973	1974	1975	1976	1977	1978	1979	AVG
NIASAV	6.5	8.6	8.5	8.6	6.9	5.9	6.1	5.9	6.9
−STATDISC	−1.1	0.1	−0.2	−1.5	−2.1	−1.3	−1.8	−2.0	−1.1
+CGIA	1.4	1.3	1.3	1.4	1.5	1.7	1.9	1.5	1.1
+CDURA	4.3	4.4	2.9	2.4	3.3	3.8	3.8	3.2	3.3
+RNA	3.8	3.5	1.4	2.6	3.1	4.1	4.2	3.3	3.8
−NONPROF	0.3	0.2	0.2	0.1	0.1	0.1	0.1	0.1	0.3
=PRISAV	16.8	17.6	14.0	16.5	16.8	16.7	17.7	15.8	15.9
−NETRCON	3.5	3.4	2.5	2.1	3.0	4.0	4.3	4.1	3.6
−CDURA	4.3	4.4	2.9	2.4	3.3	3.8	3.8	3.2	3.3
=PGSAV	9.0	9.8	8.6	12.0	10.4	9.0	9.5	8.5	9.0
−RNA	3.8	3.5	1.4	2.6	3.1	4.1	4.2	3.3	3.8
−PFRA	2.8	2.8	3.0	3.2	3.7	4.3	4.2	3.4	2.7
=LFSAV	2.5	3.4	4.3	6.1	3.6	0.6	1.1	1.8	2.5
+TOTDUR	7.7	7.8	5.4	4.5	6.4	7.7	8.2	7.3	6.9
=HHSAV	10.2	11.3	9.7	10.7	10.0	8.4	9.3	9.1	9.4
DPINIA	100.0	100.0	100.0	100.0	100.0	100.0	100.0	100.0	100.0

TOTDUR = NETRCON + CDURA; DPINIA = disposable personal income, national-income-accounts basis. Other variables are defined in Table 17.4.

Sources: National Income and Product Accounts, Flow of Funds Accounts.

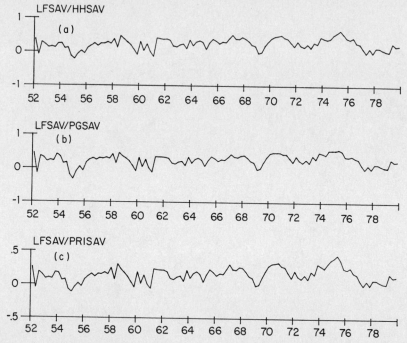

Figure 17.1 Ratio of *LFSAV* to alternative saving measures, (a) *LFSAV/ HHSAV*; (b) *LFSAV/PGSAV*; (c) *LFSAV/PRISAV*

18 Distinguishing Saving Theories Empirically

It is probably clear by now that tests for distinguishing the appropriateness of alternative saving theories are difficult to conceptualize and even more difficult to carry through in practice. The similarity of the estimating equations suggests that results consistent with one theory will frequently be consistent with another, whether the structures of the two theories are as similar as those of the life-cycle and the permanent-income hypothesis or as different as both of these are from the disequilibrium hypothesis. The problem is altogether different from the usual econometric ritual of bolstering one or the other version of neoclassical theory against the textbook Keynesianism that holds consumption to be a linear function of income, a theory hardly better than a straw man in the context of this book no matter how seriously it might have been held a generation ago.

It is not difficult to give examples of tests that superficially appear to support neoclassical saving theory, but that on closer examination turn out to support a nonneoclassical view equally well. The life-cycle hypothesis, for example, emphasizes that in preparation for retirement, younger people will tend to save more than old folks at the same level of income. The disequilibrium hypothesis leads to a similar prediction for a different reason: younger people will tend to save more than the elderly only because they will generally be on the steepest part of the age-earnings gradient and thus will find their incomes continually advancing ahead of their habitual standard of living. Similar results for very different reasons. Another example: the permanent-income hypothesis predicts a rising propensity to save out of measured income across households on the grounds that transitory income, which tends to be saved, is correlated with measured income. The disequilibrium hypothesis predicts a rising propensity to save on different grounds: increases in income, whether transitory or not, tend to be saved in the short run. Once again, the same results but different reasoning.

This is not to say that there are no real differences between neoclassical and nonneoclassical views. As has been observed, a critical point of contention between the permanent-income and the disequilibrium hypothesis is the speed of adjustment of spending to measured income. One useful test, therefore, is provided by the reaction of households to "windfalls" that might come their way from time to time. According to the permanent-income hypothesis, households should treat windfalls as additions to capital rather than to income, whereas the disequilibrium hypothesis would lump at least small windfalls together with other changes in income. Unfortunately, as is often the case, a proper test along those lines is more easily described than executed. As Thomas Mayer (1972, pp. 93–106) pointed out after a careful review of the existing literature, "this set of tests has not been very successful as a whole," both because of the ambiguity of results and because of problems with the data and even with the test methodology. We shall shortly examine social security windfalls as part of a larger attempt to sort out the life-cycle hypothesis and the disequilibrium hypothesis. Suffice it to say that Mayer's conclusion is not seriously attacked. Although the results give little aid or comfort to the life-cycle view, they are not sufficiently strong to compel a believer to renounce the faith.

Another potential test hinges on the contrast between the life-cycle emphasis on age as a determinant of saving propensity and the disequilibrium emphasis on lags in adjustment. This test hinges on the saving behavior of different groups of similarly aged individuals who, by virtue of occupational differences, have different rates of change of income. Take lawyers and laborers. According to the life-cycle model, lawyers aged 25 to 30 should save a smaller fraction of their income than laborers of similar age (indeed, the lawyers might be expected to dissave) because the lawyers are as a group much further below the peak of their age-earnings profile than laborers; on life-cycle assumptions both groups would strive equally hard to maintain a reasonably constant age-consumption profile. By contrast, the disequilibrium hypothesis leads to the prediction that the lawyers will save more, since their incomes are rising faster than their ability to adjust, whereas laborers are on a relatively flat income trajectory and have had ample opportunity to adjust their spending to their income. In the absence of the relevant data, however, this test must be on the agenda of future research rather than an accomplished fact.

Time-Series Analysis

Because of problems with cross-section and panel data, this chapter relies on time-series data to test alternative saving theories.[1] The raw material of the analysis is quarterly Flow of Funds data over the period 1952:1 to 1979:4. Where disaggregation of income is required, I have followed the procedure developed by Charles Steindel (1977) and reported in Modigliani and Steindel (1977) for allocating personal taxes between labor and property income.

These data will be analyzed by means of the equations derived in the previous chapter,

$$S = b_0 S_{-1} + b_1 \Delta YL + b_2 \Delta YP + b_3 \Delta YT \qquad (17.14)$$

and

$$S = c_0 S_{-1} + c_1 \Delta Y + c_2 Y_{-1}, \qquad (17.15)$$

as well as variants of these equations suggested in the course of the analysis itself. Observe that important simplifying assumptions are implicit in estimating saving equations separately from overall systems of equations derived from the theoretical models that were elaborated in the first part of this book. Specifically, it must be assumed that the observations consist of a set of short-run equilibria, in which saving intentions are realized up to a random error and across which the saving function is stable. Since these assumptions conform to the dynamics posited for each of the models, they should not be particularly difficult to digest — especially if the complications of estimating entire equation systems are actively contemplated.

The saving equations are estimated by two-stage least squares with correction for first-order autocorrelation, using the technique outlined in Fair (1970). In the equations below, hats are used to designate variables whose values are estimated by instruments, and the variable U_{-1} represents the lagged error. (However, R^2's — which are "constant adjusted" throughout the chapter — are calculated for the original values of the variables, not the values estimated in the first stage.) In all cases, the interval is 1952:3 to 1979:4, one observation of the original

---

1. Working with time series has problems of its own, since much information is lost in the process of aggregation. For example, on reading a draft of this chapter, Zvi Griliches suggested that aggregation may cancel out such a large part of transitory income as to obscure a very real difference at the household level between the influence of transitory and permanent income. A similar argument could be made with respect to the disequilibrium hypothesis, especially if allowance is made for nonlinearities in the process of adjusting spending to income.

set $1952:1-1979:4$ being lost because the present formulation relies on first differences, a second observation being lost because of autocorrelation of error terms. When preliminary results indicated heteroskedasticity of error terms, the variables have been transformed to eliminate the heteroskedasticity, generally by dividing through by an adjustment factor that reduces the time trend in the variables; the precise adjustment factor is indicated separately for each equation as a variable of the form

$$ADJ = 1 + A*TIME,$$

where $TIME = 1, \ldots, 110$ and $A = 0.006$ or $A = 0.003$. (The appendix to this chapter gives detail on the regressions, including a discussion of the data and data sources and a description of estimation procedures. Particular attention is paid to the procedures used to test conformity to the assumptions of least-squares estimation. Except as noted, the equations reported in this chapter "passed" both heteroskedasticity and Chow tests.)

Saving as PRISAV

Consider first what might well be called the ultraneoclassical definition of saving, *PRISAV*. The regression results for Eq. (17.14) are as follows:

PRISAV.1

$$S = \underset{(0.008)}{0.968\ S_{-1}} + \underset{(0.17)}{1.11\ \widehat{\Delta YL}} + \underset{(0.10)}{0.15\ \widehat{\Delta YP}} + \underset{(0.53)}{1.03\ \widehat{\Delta YT}} - \underset{(0.09)}{0.40\ \Delta U_{-1}}.$$

$$DW = 2.07 \qquad R^2 = 0.75 \qquad ADJ = 1 + 0.006*TIME$$

These results are consistent with the life-cycle view of saving behavior. In particular, the coefficient of S_{-1}, 0.968, is within the range predicted by the life-cycle hypothesis, corresponding to a quarterly propensity to consume out of wealth of 0.032, or an annual consumption propensity of 0.128. Given the standard error of b_0, 0.008, an (approximate) 95-percent confidence interval around the annual consumption propensity is defined by (0.064, 0.192). The coefficient of ΔYP, 0.15, is also within the (relatively wide) range suggested by Modigliani; the imprecision of the estimate reflected in the standard error of 0.10 is not really a problem from the life-cycle point of view.

The other two coefficients are more problematic from the life-cycle perspective. The coefficient on ΔYL, 1.11, is improbably high from a life-cycle perspective, and the 95-percent confidence interval (0.77, 1.45) fails altogether to intersect the predicted range (0.25, 0.40). The coefficient on ΔYT, 1.03, is equally improbable, but the high standard error is here reassuring: it tells us not to take the estimate too seriously.

A high propensity to save out of transfer payments has been observed by others using somewhat different specifications of the life-cycle hypothesis. Modigliani and Steindel (1977) themselves explain the result as a consequence of the windfall payments made on various occasions to receivers of old-age and survivors' benefits before the system was indexed to inflation in 1975. As has been observed, life-cycle/permanent-income logic suggests that windfalls will be treated differently from regular receipts, as an addition to the stock of wealth rather than as a constant flow. The implication is that the coefficient on windfalls should be of the order of unity, a sharp contrast with the coefficient of near zero expected for regular transfer payments.

But my own experiments with alternative specifications suggest that the problem lies elsewhere. To be sure, if we follow Modigliani-Steindel and not only separate the three windfall payments of 1965:3, 1970:2, and 1971:2 but also separate the pension and disability component of transfers (old-age and survivors' disability, medical-care, and government-retirement benefits) from the rest, we no longer obtain an implausibly high coefficient on "regular" (nonwindfall) pension benefits. Indeed, the regular pension and disability variable, ΔSS, has a *negative* coefficient:

PRISAV.2

$$S = 0.982\, S_{-1} + 1.11\, \Delta\widehat{YL} + 0.20\, \Delta\widehat{YP} - 1.09\, \Delta\widehat{SS}$$
$$\quad (0.011) \qquad (0.18) \qquad\quad (0.10) \qquad\quad (1.33)$$

$$\quad + 3.27\, WF + 1.62\, \Delta\widehat{YOT} - 0.43\, U_{-1}.$$
$$\quad (2.25) \qquad (0.66) \qquad\quad (0.09)$$

$$DW = 2.07 \qquad R^2 = 0.83 \qquad ADJ = 1 + 0.003*TIME$$

YT = total transfer payments in personal income
$OASI$ = old-age and survivors' and disability benefits
$GRET$ = government-retirement benefits
WF = $DUM_{-1}*\Delta OASI - DUM*\Delta OASI_{+1}$
$$DUM \begin{cases} = 1,\ 65:3,\ 70:2,\ 71:2 \\ = 0,\ \text{otherwise} \end{cases}$$
ΔSS = $\Delta OASI + \Delta GRET - WF$
ΔYOT = $\Delta YT - \Delta SS - WF$

Paradoxically, the results are too good to sustain the Modigliani-Steindel interpretation: taken literally, the coefficient on windfalls, 3.27, suggests that for every dollar of windfall payments, saving increases by over three dollars. The high standard error on the coefficient of WF might appear to be a *deus ex machina* for the life-cycle hypothesis: an approximate 95-percent confidence interval is $(-1.23, 7.77)$, which evidently includes the predicted value of the coefficient, 1.0. But the size of this confidence interval creates a problem as big as the one it resolves: it is in fact too large to sustain the belief that windfalls are the main source of the high coefficient on transfer payments in the previous equation.

Consider the difference between the coefficients on windfalls and regular pension benefits: $3.27 + 1.09 = 4.36$. If we take account of the standard error of the coefficients of ΔSS and WF as well as the estimated covariance of the two coefficients, we arrive at a standard error of the difference equal to 3.10. There is no evidence that behavior with respect to regular payments and behavior with respect to windfalls differ from one another!

Additional experiments reinforce skepticism about the life-cycle interpretation of transfer payments. The three windfall payments isolated by Modigliani and Steindel were perhaps the most dramatic because they included a large retroactive component. But they were by no means the only extraordinary payments of pension and disability benefits. Before indexing of social security payments took effect in 1975, Congress was well on its way to a habit of voting benefit increases in election years. Apart from 1970, already included in the Modigliani-Steindel windfall variable, there were sharp increases in benefits in 1968, 1972, and 1974. In view of the lag between enactment and effect of these increases, it is arguable on neoclassical logic that spending should anticipate the actual receipt of benefits, and that the actual increase should not occasion higher spending. A higher coefficient is thus to be expected for a variable reflecting the increase (EY) than for regular social security payments.

The same argument applies to the Modigliani-Steindel data points. In addition to the windfall component, there were substantial permanent increases reflected in the extraordinarily large increases for $65:3$, $70:2$, and $71:2$. Although according to neoclassical logic, the coefficient for the permanent component might not be as large as the coefficient on windfalls, it should—since the payments were anticipated for some time—be higher than the coefficient on ordinary pension benefits. Hence a new variable, CU, to reflect the catch-up or permanent part of these special payments. A similar argument might be made for the increase that acompanied the introduction of Medicaid in 1966–1967. To be sure, the argument is somewhat less compelling here because of the in-kind nature of Medicaid payments, but consistency favors including a variable MC that reflects the introduction of Medicaid payments. Finally, and perhaps the best test case for the life-cycle/permanent-income view, is the post-1975 experience with indexing.

Indexing works like this: if the rate of inflation (as measured by the annual increases in the consumer price index from the first quarter of the previous year) exceeds 3 percent, benefit payments increase to offset the erosion of purchasing power over the previous year; the increase takes effect at the beginning of the third quarter. Needless to say, indexing was operative in every year between the time that the law went into effect and the end of the time series in 1979. Thus we have five observations of indexing at work: $75:3$, $76:3$, $77:3$, $78:3$, and $79:3$. Since indexing is institutionalized and its extent fully known in advance, neoclassical logic once again suggests that a variable which reflects these increases, IN, should have a higher coefficient than changes in real per capita social security benefits that reflect the expansion of the number of pensioners and the erosion of purchasing power. This logic is reinforced by the neoclassical assumption of foresight: in an inflationary context, some part of the annual increase in benefits should be set aside to maintain an even flow in consumption as purchasing power erodes over the course of the year.

However, an experiment with social security benefits decomposed into ordinary benefits and the several types of extraordinary payments lends no support to the neoclassical view. The results are reported below:

PRISAV.3

$$S = \underset{(0.012)}{0.962\ S_{-1}} + \underset{(0.18)}{1.07\ \Delta \widehat{YL}} + \underset{(0.10)}{0.17\ \Delta \widehat{YP}} + \underset{(2.45)}{4.03\ \widehat{\Delta SS}}$$

$$+ \underset{(2.51)}{3.01\ WF} - \underset{(1.81)}{0.30\ CU} - \underset{(1.08)}{0.02\ EY} + \underset{(2.17)}{0.06\ MC}$$

$$+ \underset{(1.47)}{0.36\ IN} + \underset{(0.69)}{1.52\ \Delta \widehat{YOT}} - \underset{(0.09)}{0.42\ U_{-1}}.$$

$$DW = 2.08 \qquad R^2 = 0.76 \qquad ADJ = 1 + 0.006 * TIME$$

$$WF = DUM_{-1} * \Delta OASI - DUM * \Delta OASI_{+1}$$

$$DUM \begin{cases} = 1,\ 65:3,\ 70:2,\ 71:2 \\ = 0,\ \text{otherwise} \end{cases}$$

$$CU = DUM * (\Delta OASI + \Delta OASI_{+1})$$

$$DUM \begin{cases} = 1,\ 65:3,\ 70:2,\ 71:2 \\ = 0,\ \text{otherwise} \end{cases}$$

$$EY = DUM*\Delta OASI$$
$$DUM \begin{cases} = 1,\ 68:2,\ 72:4,\ 74:2,\ 74:3 \\ = 0,\ \text{otherwise} \end{cases}$$
$$MC = DUM*\Delta OASI$$
$$DUM \begin{cases} = 1,\ 66:3 - 67:2 \\ = 0,\ \text{otherwise} \end{cases}$$
$$IN = DUM*\Delta OASI$$
$$DUM \begin{cases} = 1,\ 75:3,\ 76:3,\ 77:3,\ 78:3,\ 79:3 \\ = 0,\ \text{otherwise} \end{cases}$$

$$\Delta SS = \Delta OASI + \Delta GRET - WF - CU - EY - MC - IN$$
$$\Delta YOT = \Delta YT - \Delta OASI - \Delta GRET$$
$$YT = \text{total transfer payments in personal income}$$
$$OASI = \text{old age and survivors' benefits}$$
$$GRET = \text{government-retirement benefits}$$

Taken separately, the coefficients of extraordinary-benefit variables differ insignificantly from the coefficient of ΔSS. Using a procedure outlined in the appendix to this chapter for testing constraints on coefficients (Theil 1971, chap. 6), the hypothesis

$$b_{\Delta SS} = b_{WF} = b_{CU} = b_{EY} = b_{MC} = b_{IN}$$

was also found to be consistent with the regression data. The only ray of light for the neoclassical view is that all the standard errors are sufficiently large that no plausible hypothesis, including the hypothesis

$$b_{WF} = b_{CU} = b_{EY} = b_{MC} = b_{IN} = 1,$$

is likely to be rejected.

If we rerun the regression on the assumption

$$b_{\Delta SS} = b_{WF} = b_{CU} = b_{EY} = b_{MC} = b_{IN},$$

we obtain the results:

PRISAV.4

$$S = \underset{(0.012)}{0.973\ S_{-1}} + \underset{(0.19)}{1.13\ \widehat{\Delta YL}} + \underset{(0.10)}{0.17\ \widehat{\Delta YP}} + \underset{(1.54)}{0.13\ \widehat{\Delta YPEN}}$$

$$+ \underset{(0.72)}{1.43\ \widehat{\Delta YOT}} - \underset{(0.09)}{0.41\ U_{-1}}.$$

$$DW = 2.08 \qquad R^2 = 0.75 \qquad ADJ = 1 + 0.006*TIME$$
$$\Delta YPEN = \Delta OASI + \Delta GRET$$
$$\Delta YOT = \Delta YT - \Delta YPEN$$

The coefficient on pension/disability benefits, 0.13, is now quite reasonable, that is, consistent with what both neoclassical and nonneoclassical theory would predict. This suggests that what is critical is not separating extraordinary from ordinary pension benefits, but separating pensions from other transfer payments.

Of course, we still have to explain the relatively high coefficient on ΔYOT: it is hardly plausible that recipients of these transfer payments themselves save \$1.43 for each \$1.00 of benefits they receive. An examination of the makeup of YOT proves useful here. This category is composed of four separate elements: unemployment insurance, veterans' benefits, aid to families with dependent children, and "other." Unfortunately the largest single category is "other," which makes it difficult to get a handle on the subject of composition. But if not the largest element, unemployment benefits are evidently the most volatile, and might conceivably, particularly since the equations are all expressed in first-difference form, account for the magnitude of the coefficient of ΔYOT. The idea is that ΔYOT is a proxy for consumer anxiety: when unemployment and unemployment benefits are increasing (that is, when ΔYOT is high), the typical consumer gets frightened and reduces consumption; thus the saving rate rises.

Two points might be made about this story. First, however plausible, it is hardly consistent with life-cycle/permanent-income rationality, according to which the individual takes a sufficiently long view that the ups and downs of the business cycle should not affect consumption, but rather saving. Indeed, in the neoclassical view saving should behave procyclically rather than anticyclically. Second, it should be pointed out that the interpretation of ΔYOT as a proxy for anxiety does not completely square with the further evidence that a direct consideration of an unemployment variable introduces. If we add the variable ΔRUA, defined as the change in the unemployment rate normalized by multiplication by real per capita disposable income, we obtain a *negative* coefficient for ΔRUA and an even higher (and more highly significant) coefficient on ΔYOT:

PRISAV.5

$$S = \underset{(0.014)}{0.983}\, S_{-1} + \underset{(0.26)}{0.76}\, \Delta \widehat{YL} + \underset{(0.11)}{0.17}\, \Delta \widehat{YP} - \underset{(1.74)}{0.78}\, \Delta \widehat{YPEN}$$

$$+ \underset{(1.84)}{4.86}\, \Delta \widehat{YOT} - \underset{(0.009)}{0.019}\, \Delta \widehat{RUA} - \underset{(0.09)}{0.42}\, U_{-1}.$$

$$DW = 2.07 \qquad R^2 = 0.70 \qquad ADJ = 1 + 0.006 * TIME$$

ΔRUA = change (measured in percentage points) of unemployment rate multiplied by real per-capita disposable income

It is still possible that ΔYOT is a proxy for consumer anxiety, and that anxiety is in turn positively correlated with saving: such factors as the duration and composition of unemployment and the existence of discouraged workers may be better reflected in the change in transfer payments, particularly in ΔYOT, than in the change in the unemployment rate. "Anxiety" may be a more complicated idea than can be reflected in the change in the unemployment rate alone.

The econometric evidence supports the view that the change in the unemployment rate, ΔRUA, does not pick up the entire contribution of ΔYOT to the explanation of saving: if we impose constraints on transfer payments in order to assimilate them to other forms of income, the coefficient of ΔRUA becomes insignificant. For instance, set the coefficient of transfer payments equal to zero, and we have the following equation:

PRISAV.6

$$S = 0.976\ S_{-1} + 1.16\ \Delta\widehat{YL} + 0.16\ \Delta\widehat{YP} + 0.002\ \Delta\widehat{RUA} - 0.37\ U_{-1}.$$
$$(0.007) \qquad (0.21) \qquad (0.10) \qquad (0.003) \qquad (0.09)$$

$$DW = 2.03 \qquad R^2 = 0.75 \qquad ADJ = 1 + 0.006*TIME$$

The coefficient of ΔRUA has the wrong sign from the life-cycle perspective but in any case is only two-thirds of its standard error.

Observe that the overall results remain generally favorable to the life-cycle interpretation of saving behavior—indeed even more so than when we began. The propensity to consume out of wealth implied by PRISAV.5 is 0.068 on an annual basis; PRISAV.6 implies a consumption propensity of 0.096. The coefficient on labor income in PRISAV.5 is more congenial than before, and the 95-percent confidence interval stretches well into Modigliani's predicted range of 0.25 to 0.40. Indeed, in PRISAV.5 only the transfer-payment coefficients continue to be troublesome, but the coefficients of $\Delta YPEN$ and ΔYOT will prove a puzzle from the nonneoclassical point of view as well as from the neoclassical. And, as noted, the coefficient of ΔRUA in PRISAV.5 has the correct sign from the neoclassical point of view.

There is a problem that has been suppressed up to now: introducing a constant term into any of these regressions gives results not easily reconciled with life-cycle logic. Typical is the following:

PRISAV.7

$$S = 61.04 + 0.829\, S_{-1} + 0.55\, \Delta\widehat{YL} + 0.18\, \Delta\widehat{YP} + 0.12\, \Delta\widehat{YPEN}$$
$$\quad (16.17) \quad (0.043) \qquad (0.26) \qquad\quad (0.11) \qquad\qquad (1.72)$$

$$\quad + 5.09\, \Delta\widehat{YOT} - 0.026\, \Delta\widehat{RUA} - 0.41\, U_{-1}.$$
$$\quad\;\; (1.81) \qquad\qquad (0.009) \qquad\quad (0.09)$$

$$DW = 2.04 \qquad R^2 = 0.73 \qquad ADJ = 1 + 0.006*TIME$$

The problem is not the magnitude of the constant term or its t-statistic: 61.04 is small enough relative to average *PRISAV* (more than 500) and *PRISAV/ADJ* (just under 400) to be unproblematic in itself. Moreover, it is of the same order of magnitude as the statistical discrepancy between national income and Flow of Funds measures of saving (reported in Table 17.5), so that the relatively high t-statistic (3.8) is equally unproblematic.

The problem, from the point of view of the life-cycle hypothesis, lies rather in the implications of the constant term for the coefficient of lagged saving. No longer is this coefficient in the neighborhood of 0.97. Instead we find a coefficient of approximately 0.83, a result hardly compatible with life-cycle logic since it implies an annual propensity to consume out of wealth of the order of 0.68.

Whatever the problems of these regression results from a neoclassical point of view, they are in any case minor compared to the problems of interpretation in a nonneoclassical perspective. If we take *PRISAV.4* and *PRISAV.6* as the basis of our calculations, the estimated speed of adjustment of spending to income and standard error are

$$\textit{PRISAV.4} \qquad \Delta C = 1 - \hat{b}_0^3 \hat{b}_1 = -0.04$$
$$(0.17)$$

$$\textit{PRISAV.6} \qquad \Delta C = 1 - \hat{b}_0^3 \hat{b}_1 = -0.08,$$
$$(0.18)$$

hardly supportive of the notion of rapid adjustment of spending to income. For property income we have more congenial results:

$$\textit{PRISAV.4} \qquad \Delta C = 1 - \hat{b}_0^3 \hat{b}_2 = 0.84$$
$$(0.10)$$

$$\textit{PRISAV.6} \qquad \Delta C = 1 - \hat{b}_0^3 \hat{b}_2 = 0.85,$$
$$(0.10)$$

but the relative magnitudes of the coefficients of labor and property income are exactly the opposite of what the disequilibrium hypothesis predicts.

Indeed the data lead us to reject a key hypothesis of the disequilibrium view, namely $b_2 > b_1$. We have instead

$$PRISAV.4 \qquad \hat{b}_2 - \hat{b}_1 = -0.95$$
$$(0.24)$$

$$PRISAV.6 \qquad \hat{b}_2 - \hat{b}_1 = -1.00.$$
$$(0.26)$$

In both cases we have t-statistics of about 4, which should disturb even the most nonneoclassical among us.

The consequences for steady-growth average propensities to save are equally disturbing. As reported in Table 18.1, the propensity to save out of labor income far exceeds the propensity to save out of property income. The difference is, moreover, statistically significant.

Table 18.1 Long-run saving ratios

Equation	$\hat{s}_W$	$\hat{s}_C$	$\hat{s}_C - \hat{s}_W$
PRISAV.4	0.21	0.03	−0.17
	(0.08)	(0.02)	(0.07)
PRISAV.6	0.23	0.03	−0.20
	(0.05)	(0.02)	(0.05)

The relative performance of the nonneoclassical approach improves when the aggregate version of the disequilibrium hypothesis is compared with the permanent-income hypothesis. Consider Eq. (17.15):

$$S = c_0 S_{-1} + c_1 \Delta Y + c_2 Y_{-1}. \qquad (17.15)$$

The estimated equation[2] is

PRISAV.8

$$S = \; 0.78\, S_{-1} + \; 0.36\, \Delta\hat{Y} + \; 0.032\, Y_{-1} - \; 0.36\, U_{-1}.$$
$$(0.056) \qquad (0.08) \qquad (0.008) \qquad (0.09)$$

$$DW = 2.02 \qquad R^2 = 0.70 \qquad ADJ = 1 + 0.006*TIME$$

Contrary to the prediction of the disequilibrium hypothesis, the coefficient of Y_{-1} is significantly different from zero. But the permanent-income hypothesis fares no better. The expression

$$\hat{c}_0 - \hat{c}_1 + \hat{c}_2 = \; 0.45$$
$$(0.10)$$

2. A Chow test, described in the appendix to this chapter, suggests that the coefficients are unstable over time.

also differs significantly from zero. Lagged income enters into the explanation of saving in ways that neither hypothesis predicts.

But the significance of Y_{-1}, I have suggested, is a secondary issue. More important tests lie in the speed with which spending adjusts to income. Taking each theory as a separate null hypothesis, the results of these tests are somewhat more in line with disequilibrium thinking than with a permanent-income approach. When we constrain c_2 to be equal to zero, we obtain

PRISAV.9

$$S = 0.984\,S_{-1} + 0.48\,\Delta\hat{Y} - 0.43\,U_{-1}.$$
$$\quad\ (0.007)\qquad (0.08)\qquad (0.09)$$

$$DW = 2.15 \qquad R^2 = 0.77 \qquad ADJ = 1 + 0.003*TIME$$

In consequence we have, after four quarters,

PRISAV.9 $\qquad \Delta C = 1 - \hat{c}_0^3 \hat{c}_1 = 0.54.$
$$\qquad\qquad\qquad\qquad\qquad (0.08)$$

This result is evidently consistent with a rapid adjustment ($\Delta C > 0.5$); but given the standard error, we are hardly in a position to reject the hypothesis of slow adjustment ($\Delta C < 0.5$) either.

For future reference we may note the steady-growth average propensity to save. Analogous to $\hat{s}_C$ and $\hat{s}_W$, we have

PRISAV.9 $\qquad \hat{s} = \dfrac{0.006\,\hat{b}_1}{1.006 - \hat{b}_0} = 0.13.$
$$\qquad\qquad\qquad\qquad\qquad (0.04)$$

Finally, it is worth observing that in the aggregate formulation, the variable ΔRUA is insignificant:

PRISAV.10

$$S = 0.985\,S_{-1} + 0.45\,\Delta\hat{Y} - 0.005\,\Delta\widehat{RUA} - 0.43\,U_{-1}.$$
$$\quad\ (0.007)\qquad (0.08)\qquad (0.003)\qquad\qquad (0.09)$$

$$DW = 2.13 \qquad R^2 = 0.78 \qquad ADJ = 1 + 0.003*TIME$$

And the coefficients of other variables are virtually insensitive to the presence of ΔRUA in the equation.

To test the permanent-income hypothesis, we constrain $c_0 - c_1 + c_2$ to be equal to zero, which, as we have seen, is equivalent to estimating the unconstrained equation

$$S = d_0 C_{-1} + d_1 Y.$$

The results are

PRISAV.11

$$S = 0.033\ C_{-1} + 0.123\ \hat{Y} + 0.66\ U_{-1}.$$
$$(0.056) \qquad (0.048) \qquad (0.07)$$

$$DW = 2.14 \qquad R^2 = 0.66 \qquad ADJ = 1 + 0.006*TIME$$

The coefficients suggest a much more rapid adjustment of permanent income to measured income than is compatible with the spirit of the neoclassical position: with $\psi = 0.006$, we have

PRISAV.11 $\qquad Y_4^p - Y_0^p(1 + \psi)^4 = (\hat{d}_0 + 1 + \psi)(1 - \hat{d}_0 - \hat{d}_0^2 - \hat{d}_0^3)$
$$= 1.006.$$
$$(0.0003)$$

According to this result, adjustment is more than complete after four quarters, and the standard error of the adjustment speed is negligible. The estimated long-run propensity to save is

PRISAV.11 $\qquad 1 - \hat{\mu} = \dfrac{\hat{d}_0 + \hat{d}_1 + \psi}{\hat{d}_0 + 1 + \psi} = 0.16.$
$$\qquad\qquad\qquad\qquad\qquad\qquad (0.004)$$

These results are not changed markedly by the addition of a constant term, an unemployment variable, or both—even though, contrary to permanent-income logic, both are significantly different from zero. With both a constant term and ΔRUA present, the regression equation is

PRISAV.12

$$S = -223.32 + 0.015\ C_{-1} + 0.22\ \hat{Y} - 0.029\ \Delta\widehat{RUA} + 0.50\ U_{-1}.$$
$$(102.26) \quad (0.062) \qquad (0.056) \qquad (0.007) \qquad\quad (0.08)$$

$$DW = 2.05 \qquad R^2 = 0.67 \qquad ADJ = 1 + 0.006*TIME$$

All in all, although the aggregate results are less favorable to the neoclassical view than to the nonneoclassical view, a fair reading of the evidence is that the aggregate results hide what from the nonneoclassical viewpoint must be considered a multitude of sins. In particular the relatively rapid adjustment of spending to aggregate income obscures the slow adjustment of spending to labor income.

Regression Results with LFSAV

If we take a narrow view of saving, however, the data tell a very different story, one much more supportive of the nonneoclassical position. First, look at the life-cycle hypothesis. The original formulation,

$$S = b_0 S_{-1} + b_1 \Delta YL + b_2 \Delta YP + b_3 \Delta YT, \qquad (17.14)$$

presents, in more extreme form, the same paradox with respect to transfer payments that we encountered in the preceding section—an inordinately high, and highly significant, coefficient:

LFSAV.1

$$S = 0.79\, S_{-1} + 0.26\, \Delta \widehat{YL} + 0.35\, \Delta \widehat{YP} + 2.47\, \Delta \widehat{YT} - 0.35\, U_{-1}.$$
$$\quad\ (0.04) \qquad (0.15) \qquad\ \ (0.33) \qquad\ \ (0.57) \qquad\ \ (0.09)$$

$$DW = 1.97 \qquad R^2 = 0.55 \qquad ADJ = 1 + 0.003*TIME$$

The source of the paradox also appears to be the same as before. Once again windfalls are not the problem: separating out windfalls and other extraordinary payments leads to coefficients statistically indistinguishable from one another. By contrast, separating pension and disability benefits from other transfers suggests that it is these other transfers that are responsible for the high t-statistic on transfer payments. Here are the results of separating all three components—ordinary pension and disability payments, extraordinary pension and disability payments, and other transfers:

LFSAV.2

$$S = 0.87\, S_{-1} + 0.31\, \Delta \widehat{YL} + 0.71\, \Delta \widehat{YP} + 0.78\, \Delta \widehat{SS}$$
$$\quad\ (0.05) \qquad\ (0.15) \qquad\ \ (0.26) \qquad\ \ (2.05)$$

$$+\ 3.33\, WF - 0.24\, CU - 0.51\, EY + 2.93\, MC$$
$$\ \ (2.25) \qquad\ (1.64) \qquad\ (0.94) \qquad\ (1.99)$$

$$-\ 0.35\, IN + 2.59\, \Delta \widehat{YOT} - 0.43\, U_{-1}.$$
$$\ (1.23) \qquad\ (0.61) \qquad\quad\ (0.09)$$

$$DW = 2.02 \qquad R^2 = 0.60 \qquad ADJ = 1 + 0.003*TIME$$

A test of the hypothesis

$$b_{\Delta SS} = b_{WF} = b_{CU} = b_{EY} = b_{MC} = b_{IN}$$

produced no evidence to reject it.

The lesson of this experiment is that the appropriate disaggregation of transfer payments continues to be a separation not of regular from extraordinary pension and disability payments, but of pension and disability benefits from other transfer payments. When we do so, we obtain the following results:

LFSAV.3

$$S = 0.80\ S_{-1} + 0.27\ \Delta\widehat{YL} + 0.40\ \Delta\widehat{YP} + 2.27\ \Delta\widehat{YPEN}$$
$$(0.06)(0.18)(0.38)(1.54)$$

$$+ 2.59\ \Delta\widehat{YOT} - 0.36\ U_{-1}.$$
$$(0.65)(0.09)$$

$$DW = 1.97 \qquad R^2 = 0.56 \qquad ADJ = 1 + 0.003*TIME$$

The coefficient of pension and disability benefits, 2.27, continues to exceed the plausible range. But the high standard error makes this result less worrisome than the corresponding result in LFSAV.1 when $\Delta YPEN$ and ΔYOT were replaced by $\Delta YT = \Delta YPEN + \Delta YOT$.

The neoclassically inclined may take comfort from the coefficients of ΔYL and ΔYP, which are well within the range predicted by the life-cycle hypothesis. But this is small consolation: the major conclusion from LFSAV.3 is that the coefficient of S_{-1} is far too small to be consistent with life-cycle logic: $\hat{b}_0 = 0.80$ suggests a quarterly propensity to consume out of wealth equal to 0.20, or an annual consumption propensity equal to 0.80!

Alternative formulations do not change this result. Under the LFSAV definition, the constant term is always statistically insignificant, and its magnitude is economically trivial, invariably less than 10 percent of the average rate of saving. By contrast, when ΔYOT is present in the equation, introducing ΔRUA does not produce a significant coefficient, and in any case *reduces* the goodness of fit (which is disturbing but hardly unheard-of with two-stage least squares).

Suppose, however, we impose the constraint that the coefficient of all transfer payments equal zero. Then the coefficient of ΔRUA becomes significant, albeit with a positive sign. We have

LFSAV.4

$$S = 0.89\ S_{-1} + 0.59\ \Delta\widehat{YL} + 0.74\ \Delta\widehat{YP}$$
$$(0.03)(0.17)(0.33)$$

$$+ 0.009\ \Delta\widehat{RUA} - 0.36\ U_{-1}.$$
$$(0.003)(0.09)$$

$$DW = 1.96 \qquad R^2 = 0.55 \qquad ADJ = 1 + 0.006*TIME$$

Whatever we do with respect to transfer payments and unemployment, the coefficient of lagged saving remains less than 0.90, a result difficult to integrate into the life-cycle view.

One man's poison is another man's meat: regressions LFSAV.1 –

Table 18.2. Four-quarter adjustment of
spending to labor and property income

Equation	Labor income $1 - \hat{b}_0^3 \hat{b}_1$	Property income $1 - \hat{b}_0^3 \hat{b}_2$
LFSAV.3	0.86 (0.11)	0.80 (0.22)
LFSAV.4	0.59 (0.11)	0.49 (0.23)

LFSAV.4 are for the most part consistent with the disequilibrium hypothesis. Consider the implicit speeds of adjustment of spending to different sources of income reported in Table 18.2. *LFSAV*.3 is evidently more congenial to the disequilibrium view than is *LFSAV*.4. But even where the results do not give strong support to the disequilibrium hypothesis, in the sense that they are compatible with a four-quarter adjustment far below 0.50, they hardly provide grounds for rejecting the hypothesis of rapid adjustment of spending to income. At worst, the evidence is inconclusive.

Similarly inconclusive results hold with respect both to differences in short-run marginal propensities to save out of different forms of income and to differences in long-run average saving ratios. Table 18.3 presents the short-run estimates from *LFSAV*.3 and *LFSAV*.4. Despite the relatively large differences in the estimates of the coefficients of ΔYL and ΔYP between the two equations, the estimated coefficient *differences*, as well as the estimated standard error, are remarkably close to one another. Unfortunately for the nonneoclassical view, the coefficient difference, though of the right sign, is small relative to its standard error.

Table 18.4 shows a similar state of affairs for long-run saving ratios. Once again, the differences $\hat{s}_C - \hat{s}_W$ have the right sign but in both cases

Table 18.3. Short-run propensities to save

Equation	$MPS_{YL} = \hat{b}_1$	$MPS_{YP} = \hat{b}_2$	$\hat{b}_2 - \hat{b}_1$
LFSAV.3	0.27 (0.18)	0.40 (0.38)	0.13 (0.40)
LFSAV.4	0.59 (0.17)	0.74 (0.33)	0.14 (0.38)

Table 18.4. Long-run saving ratios

Equation	$\hat{s}_W$	$\hat{s}_C$	$\hat{s}_C - \hat{s}_W$
LFSAV.3	0.008	0.012	0.004
	(0.006)	(0.013)	(0.012)
LFSAV.4	0.030	0.037	0.007
	(0.009)	(0.018)	(0.019)

are small, not only in absolute terms but relative to the coefficient standard error.

A partisan of the nonneoclassical point of view can find reinforcement at two points in the analysis. In the first place, the small absolute values of both $\hat{s}_W$ and $\hat{s}_C$ recall an observation made in Chapter 7, namely that the disequilibrium hypothesis is more an explanation of why households do *not* save than why they do. That chapter, indeed, argued that necessary conditions for positive self-sustaining household saving by either workers or capitalists are

$$MPS_W \frac{1 - a_1}{a_1} > \theta_W \quad \text{and} \quad MPS_C r > \theta_C. \tag{7.13}$$

Since on present assumptions $MPS_W = \hat{b}_1$, $MPS_C = \hat{b}_2$, and $\hat{\theta}_W = \hat{\theta}_C = 1 - \hat{b}_0$, we can estimate the minimum values of the output : capital ratio, $(1 - a_1)/a_1$, and the rate of profit, r, that are compatible with positive saving by means of the ratios $(1 - \hat{b}_0)/\hat{b}_1$ and $(1 - \hat{b}_0)/\hat{b}_2$. Table 18.5 presents the results of these calculations. None of these results is conclusive: in the *LFSAV*.3 estimates, the standard errors are high enough to include zero in a 95-percent confidence interval, and these estimates therefore provide no useful information. By contrast, the *LFSAV*.4 estimates appear to suggest that self-sustaining saving is

Table 18.5. Minimum values of output : capital ratio and profit rate for positive saving

Equation	Output : capital ratio $(1 - \hat{b}_0)/\hat{b}_1$	Profit rate $(1 - \hat{b}_0)/\hat{b}_2$
LFSAV.3	0.76	0.50
	(0.62)	(0.55)
LFSAV.4	0.19	0.15
	(0.06)	(0.07)

feasible. The minimum necessary values of the output : capital ratio and the profit rate appear to be less than what — borrowing terminology from Nicholas Kaldor — we might call the "stylized magnitudes" of contemporary capitalism: if we take (0.33, 0.66) as a plausible range for the output : capital ratio and (0.10, 0.20) as a plausible range for the profit rate, the point estimates on the second line of Table 18.5 would appear to be quite reasonable. The problem with this line of reasoning is that the plausible ranges are expressed in annual terms, while the estimates in Table 18.5 are quarterly. The quarterly figures corresponding to the two ranges are, respectively, (0.08, 0.16) and (0.025, 0.05); both are well below the point estimates 0.19 and 0.15. In view of the relatively large standard errors, however, the results remain inconclusive: the 95-percent confidence intervals for these estimates extend well into the plausible ranges for the output : capital ratio and the profit rate.

The second line of defense to which the nonneoclassical argument might retreat is to appeal to the nature of the data that form the basis of the present analysis. The attempt to infer class propensities to save or class saving ratios ignores the fact that both workers and capitalists receive labor income *and* property income. The result, it was observed, is to bias the estimate of class differences downward. This problem is in principle remediable, but not in the context of aggregate time-series data.

We turn now to a comparison of the disequilibrium hypothesis and the permanent-income hypothesis. As before, we start from the equation

$$S = c_0 S_{-1} + c_1 \Delta Y + c_2 Y_{-1}, \tag{17.15}$$

which gives the following regression results:

LFSAV.5

$$S = 0.82\, S_{-1} + 0.40\, \Delta \hat{Y} + 0.0026\, Y_{-1} - 0.27\, U_{-1}.$$
$$(0.06) \qquad (0.15) \qquad (0.0021) \qquad (0.09)$$

$$DW = 1.85 \qquad R^2 = 0.53 \qquad ADJ = 1 + 0.006*TIME$$

As the disequilibrium hypothesis predicts, the coefficient of Y_{-1} is insignificant. By contrast, the permanent-income prediction with respect to the "total" coefficient for lagged income is $c_0 - c_1 + c_2 = 0$, which is not supported by the estimate

$$LFSAV.5 \qquad \hat{c}_0 - \hat{c}_1 + \hat{c}_2 = 0.43.$$
$$\phantom{LFSAV.5 \qquad \hat{c}_0 - \hat{c}_1 + \hat{c}_2 = }(0.15)$$

These results must, however, be taken with a grain of salt. Not only does this test fail—as has been noted—to go to the core of the two theories, it is less decisive than it appears even on its own terms. The problem begins from the fact that the (negative of the) sum of squared residuals is not a single-peaked function of the regression coefficients. This is not in itself so serious; the same is true for most of the *LFSAV* regressions and for many of the others too. The problem is that in the present case the two peaks are very close together in height: as an alternative to *LFSAV*.5 we have

LFSAV.6

$$S = -0.22\,S_{-1} + 0.21\,\Delta\hat{Y} + 0.033\,Y_{-1} + 0.79\,U_{-1}.$$
$$(0.09) \qquad (0.12) \qquad (0.006) \qquad (0.06)$$

$$DW = 1.98 \qquad R^2 = 0.52 \qquad ADJ = 1 + 0.006*TIME$$

The sum of squared residuals of the two regressions differ by less than 2.5 percent, hardly grounds for extreme confidence in *LFSAV*.5. *LFSAV*.6 is not, it should be observed, any more favorable to the permanent-income hypothesis: we have

$$LFSAV.6 \qquad \hat{c}_0 - \hat{c}_1 + \hat{c}_2 = -0.40.$$
$$(0.12)$$

But it is evidently far less congenial to the disequilibrium hypothesis: the t-statistic on the simple coefficient of Y_{-1} exceeds 5. One can favor *LFSAV*.5 over *LFSAV*.6 on the grounds that its coefficients look more "reasonable" (especially the coefficient of S_{-1}), but that is hardly the way of classical statistics.[3]

If we drop Y_{-1} from the equation to conform to the disequilibrium hypothesis, the ambiguity disappears. The estimate

---

3. Mark Watson has pointed out to me that the coefficients of lagged saving in *LFSAV*.5 and *LFSAV*.6 look more different than in fact they are. From *LFSAV*.5 we have
$$S = 0.82\,S_{-1} + 0.40\,\Delta Y + 0.0026\,Y_{-1} + U$$
or, lagging all variables one period,
$$U_{-1} = S_{-1} - 0.82\,S_{-2} - 0.40\,\Delta Y_{-1} - 0.0026\,Y_{-2}.$$
Substituting the right-hand sides into *LFSAV*.5, we obtain
LFSAV.5
$$S = 0.55\,S_{-1} + 0.22\,S_{-2} + 0.40\,Y - 0.29\,Y_{-1} - 0.11\,Y_{-2}.$$
A corresponding transformation of *LFSAV*.6 produces the result
LFSAV.6
$$S = 0.57\,S_{-1} + 0.17\,S_{-2} + 0.21\,Y - 0.35\,Y_{-1} + 0.19\,Y_{-2}.$$
The coefficients on lagged saving are nearly identical in the two transformed equations.

*LFSAV.*7

$$S = 0.88\ S_{-1} + 0.48\ \Delta\hat{Y} - 0.30\ U_{-1}$$
$$\quad (0.03) \qquad (0.12) \qquad\quad (0.09)$$

$$DW = 1.86 \qquad R^2 = 0.52 \qquad ADJ = 1 + 0.006*TIME$$

clearly dominates, in terms of R^2, the alternative regression at the other peak of the sum-of-squared-residuals function. The implicit four-quarter adjustment speed is in line with disequilibrium thinking. We have

$$\text{\textit{LFSAV.}}7 \qquad 1 - \hat{c}_0^3\hat{c}_1 = 0.67,$$
$$(0.08)$$

a result whose occurrence has less than 5-percent probability if the true adjustment speed is less than 0.5 and the standard error is 0.08. The estimated long-run equilibrium saving ratio

$$\text{\textit{LFSAV.}}7 \qquad \hat{s} = 0.024$$
$$(0.007)$$

is, it should be observed, close to the average *LFSAV* saving rate of 0.025.

A constant term is insignificant, but including ΔRUA in the regression suggests that *LFSAV* is strongly influenced by the business cycle. Neither $1 - \hat{c}_0^3\hat{c}_1$ nor $\hat{s}$ changes much, nor do their standard errors, but the coefficient on ΔRUA is highly significant:

*LFSAV.*8

$$S = 0.87\ S_{-1} + 0.55\ \Delta\hat{Y} + 0.0075\ \Delta\widehat{RUA} - 0.35\ U_{-1}.$$
$$\quad (0.03) \qquad (0.12) \qquad\quad (0.0027) \qquad\qquad (0.09)$$

$$DW = 1.96 \qquad R^2 = 0.60 \qquad ADJ = 1 + 0.003*TIME$$

According to *LFSAV.*8, a one-percentage-point increase in the unemployment rate triggers a change of 0.75 percentage points in the saving rate. (Remember that ΔRUA is normalized by multiplying the change in the unemployment rate by real per capita disposable income.) This represents a considerable impact, considering that the average saving rate is 2.5 percent for S defined by *LFSAV.* A plausible hypothesis, it has been suggested, is that a rise in the unemployment rate makes people generally fearful, which leads them to defer spending to better, or at least more certain, times.[4]

This hypothesis implies much less mechanical behavior than did the original formulation of the disequilibrium hypothesis, but behavior nevertheless much closer to the disequilibrium hypothesis in spirit than to the permanent-income hypothesis. For one thing, the coefficient of ΔRUA has the wrong sign from the permanent-income point of view: according to the permanent-income hypothesis, transitory phenomena like the business cycle should depress saving rather than consumption.

One might well object to drawing inferences about the permanent-income hypothesis from an equation whose form is derived from the competing hypothesis. Fair enough. But the permanent-income form

$$S = d_0 C_{-1} + d_1 Y$$

leads to the same result. First, if we estimate this equation without an unemployment term, we once again obtain two very different estimates with approximately equal explanatory power. We have

LFSAV.9

$$S = -0.751\ C_{-1} + 0.754\ \hat{Y} - 0.15\ U_{-1},$$
$$(0.064) \qquad (0.062) \qquad (0.10)$$

$$DW = 1.84 \qquad R^2 = 0.46 \qquad ADJ = 1 + 0.006*TIME$$

LFSAV.10

$$S = 0.035\ C_{-1} - 0.007\ \hat{Y} + 0.69\ U_{-1}.$$
$$(0.085) \qquad (0.083) \qquad (0.07)$$

$$DW = 2.13 \qquad R^2 = 0.48 \qquad ADJ = 1 + 0.006*TIME$$

In this case, the estimate with higher R^2 is the one in which the autocorrelation of error terms is strongly positive — LFSAV.10 — but once again the difference in sums of squared residuals is so small — less

---

4. This interpretation is supported by the regression results for the same equation, with HHSAV — which includes net investment in durables and housing as part of saving:
HHSAV

$$S = 0.985\ S_{-1} + 0.26\ \Delta\hat{Y} - 0.0043\ \Delta\widehat{RUA} - 0.41\ U_{-1}.$$
$$(0.010) \qquad (0.08) \qquad (0.0027) \qquad (0.09)$$

$$DW = 2.10 \qquad R^2 = 0.61 \qquad ADJ = 1 + 0.003*TIME$$

The coefficient of ΔRUA has the opposite sign from LFSAV.8. But more important, it is insignificantly different from zero. The two equations together suggest that the increase in financial saving that takes place as unemployment increases represents postponement of expenditure on durables and housing.

than 2.5 percent—that it would be foolish to invest much in the statistical superiority of $LFSAV.10$.

Neither equation offers much support for the permanent-income view. $LFSAV.10$ suggests that the four-quarter adjustment of permanent income to measured income equals 100 percent:

$$LFSAV.10 \qquad (\hat{d_0} + 1 + \psi)(1 - \hat{d_0} - \hat{d_0^2} - \hat{d_0^3}) = 1.006,$$
$$(0.0005)$$

identical (by coincidence) to the estimate for the $PRISAV$ definition of saving. The $LFSAV.9$ estimate is much smaller, but still excessive from a permanent-income point of view:

$$LFSAV.9 \qquad (\hat{d_0} + 1 + \psi)(1 - \hat{d_0} - \hat{d_0^2} - \hat{d_0^3}) = 0.70.$$
$$(0.11)$$

The 95-percent confidence interval barely reaches the cutoff of 0.5.

By contrast, the two estimates of the long-run saving propensity are quite close together. From $LFSAV.10$ we obtain the estimate

$$LFSAV.10 \qquad 1 - \hat{\mu} = 0.033,$$
$$(0.004)$$

and from $LFSAV.9$ the estimate

$$LFSAV.9 \qquad 1 - \hat{\mu} = 0.034.$$
$$(0.004)$$

Once again, a constant term is insignificant, but the addition of ΔRUA tips the balance in favor of the regression with the more "reasonable" coefficients:

$LFSAV.11$

$$S = -0.791\, C_{-1} + 0.792\, \hat{Y} + 0.0095\, \Delta\widehat{RUA} - 0.31\, U_{-1}.$$
$$(0.054) \qquad (0.052) \qquad (0.0027) \qquad (0.09)$$

$$DW = 1.92 \qquad R^2 = 0.54 \qquad ADJ = 1 + 0.006*TIME$$

The four-quarter adjustment becomes more consistent with the permanent-income spirit,

$$LFSAV.11 \qquad (\hat{d_0} + 1 + \psi)(1 - \hat{d_0} - \hat{d_0^2} - \hat{d_0^3}) = 0.63,$$
$$(0.10)$$

but it is not clear what importance should be attached to this estimate since the equation is misspecified from a permanent-income point of view. In any case, the long-run saving propensity is virtually unchanged. Finally, observe that—from the point of view of the permanent-income hypothesis—the significant, positive coefficient of ΔRUA is a distinct embarrassment, especially in view of the magnitude of the coefficient.[5]

All in all, the permanent-income hypothesis fares as badly as the life-cycle hypothesis under a narrow definition of saving. Lagged income is significant when it should not be; the adjustment of permanent income to measured income is implausibly rapid; and, most disturbing, a change in the unemployment rate has a significant positive impact (both statistically and economically) on saving. Other than to drop the LFSAV definition of saving, there appears to be little one can do to rescue the neoclassical view of household saving behavior.

Nonneoclassical theory fares markedly better. To be sure, the evidence for a key assumption, namely $s_C > s_W$, is weak at best, but there is nothing in the data that runs sharply counter to the spirit of nonneoclassical theory. These results are in sharp contrast with those that emerged from what I have labeled the ultraneoclassical definition of saving, PRISAV. Perhaps surprisingly, the question of definition turns out to be far from academic: nothing less than the plausibility of alternative views of household saving behavior is at stake.

Intermediate Definitions of Saving: HHSAV and PGSAV

The inclusion of durables and housing or pension-fund and retained earnings gives results more supportive of neoclassical than of nonneoclassical theory. Although the argument is necessarily repetitious, these regressions do bring out some worthwhile points. First, conclusions reached with respect to transfer payments are unaffected by the definition of saving. Regular pension and disability payments have an insignificant impact on saving, and the regression results are in both cases consistent with the hypothesis that the coefficients on extraordinary payments are equal to the coefficient on regular payments. When saving is defined to include durables and housing, we have[6]

HHSAV.1

$$S = 0.977\,S_{-1} + 0.69\,\Delta\widehat{YL} + 0.10\,\Delta\widehat{YP} + 0.10\,\Delta\widehat{SS}$$
$$\quad\;(0.016)\qquad\;(0.15)\qquad\quad(0.09)\qquad\quad(2.09)$$

$$+ 3.42\,WF - 0.47\,CU + 0.31\,EY - 0.03\,MC$$
$$\;\;(2.12)\qquad\;\;(1.49)\qquad\;\;(0.88)\qquad\;\;(1.82)$$

5. As with the disequilibrium hypothesis, the coefficient of ΔRUA is both negative and insignificant when durables and housing are included in saving.

6. A Glejser test indicated heteroskedasticity of error terms.

$$- 1.34\,IN + 1.12\,\widehat{\Delta YOT} - 0.47\,U_{-1}.$$
$$(1.14)(0.56)\phantom{\widehat{\Delta YOT} -}(0.08)$$

$$DW = 2.11 \qquad R^2 = 0.69 \qquad ADJ = 1 + 0.003*TIME$$

The hypothesis

$$b_{\Delta SS} = b_{WF} = b_{CU} = b_{EY} = b_{MC} = b_{IN}$$

turned out to be consistent with the data.

The same regression with $PGSAV$ produces similar results with respect to the relationships among the various components of transfer payments:

$PGSAV.1$

$$S = 0.967\,S_{-1} + 0.55\,\widehat{\Delta YL} + 0.80\,\widehat{\Delta YP} + 0.06\,\widehat{\Delta SS}$$
$$(0.019)\phantom{S_{-1} +}(0.16)\phantom{\widehat{\Delta YL} +}(0.20)\phantom{\widehat{\Delta YP} +}(2.18)$$

$$+ 3.81\,WF - 1.35\,CU - 0.88\,EY + 1.88\,MC$$
$$(2.36)(1.65)(0.99)(2.02)$$

$$- 1.44\,IN + 2.60\,\widehat{\Delta YOT} - 0.49\,U_{-1}.$$
$$(1.40)(0.63)\phantom{\widehat{\Delta YOT} -}(0.08)$$

$$DW = 2.09 \qquad R^2 = 0.71 \qquad ADJ = 1 + 0.006*TIME$$

In this case also the hypothesis of equal coefficients for regular and extraordinary benefit payments cannot be rejected.

When this regression is run with coefficients on regular and extraordinary pension and disability payments constrained to be equal, we obtain the following results:

$HHSAV.2$

$$S = 0.966\,S_{-1} + 0.73\,\widehat{\Delta YL} + 0.08\,\widehat{\Delta YP} + 0.46\,\widehat{\Delta YPEN}$$
$$(0.017)\phantom{S_{-1} +}(0.17)\phantom{\widehat{\Delta YL} +}(0.10)\phantom{\widehat{\Delta YP} +}(1.31)$$

$$+ 1.11\,\widehat{\Delta YOT} - 0.45\,U_{-1},$$
$$(0.59)\phantom{\widehat{\Delta YOT} -}(0.09)$$

$$DW = 2.12 \qquad R^2 = 0.68 \qquad ADJ = 1 + 0.003*TIME$$

$PGSAV.2$

$$S = 0.973\,S_{-1} + 0.71\,\widehat{\Delta YL} + 0.73\,\widehat{\Delta YP} - 1.26\,\widehat{\Delta YPEN}$$
$$(0.019)\phantom{S_{-1} +}(0.17)\phantom{\widehat{\Delta YL} +}(0.23)\phantom{\widehat{\Delta YP} -}(1.39)$$

$$+ 2.90\,\widehat{\Delta YOT} - 0.46\,U_{-1}.$$
$$(0.66)\phantom{\widehat{\Delta YOT} -}(0.09)$$

$$DW = 2.08 \qquad R^2 = 0.69 \qquad ADJ = 1 + 0.006*TIME$$

In both cases, the coefficient on saving is in line with life-cycle reasoning. In contrast, by disequilibrium standards, the adjustment of spending to labor income is quite slow:

$$HHSAV.2 \qquad 1 - \hat{b}_0^3 \hat{b}_1 = 0.34,$$
$$(0.16)$$

$$PGSAV.2 \qquad 1 - \hat{b}_0^3 \hat{b}_1 = 0.35.$$
$$(0.16)$$

From a disequilibrium point of view, the only solace in these results is the high standard error.

A bigger problem for nonneoclassical theory is the relative coefficients of property income and labor income, which reflect adversely on the assumption $s_C > s_W$. Indeed, in the $HHSAV$ regressions, the coefficient of ΔYP essentially vanishes. A plausible explanation comes easily, however. There are two differences between the $LFSAV$ and the $HHSAV$ regressions. On the one hand, investment in consumer durables and owner-occupied housing is added to saving. On the other, the imputed value of services of durables and housing is added to property income, which has the effect of increasing property income relative to its $LFSAV$ magnitude by about 50 percent. But investment in durables and housing is relatively insensitive to this component of property income; coupled with the higher level of ΔYP, this insensitivity tends to depress the property income coefficient. By contrast, in the post–World War II period, as automobiles, television sets, washing machines, and the like became the norm rather than the exception for the American working class, investment in durables became accordingly sensitive to labor income. For these reasons the coefficient of ΔYL increases moderately and the coefficient of ΔYP decreases substantially as we move from the $LFSAV$ to the $HHSAV$ definition of saving.

The $PGSAV$ story is different. $PGSAV$ adds pension-fund saving and retained earnings to $LFSAV$, at the same time including the first in labor income and the second in property income. The effect is necessarily to increase the coefficients of both kinds of income in relationship to saving. The result reported in $PGSAV.2 — \hat{b}_1 = 0.71$, $\hat{b}_2 = 0.73 —$ might be taken as confirmation of a uniform propensity to save from the neoclassical perspective, but it is merely a coincidence from the nonneoclassical point of view.

As has been observed in earlier footnotes, the unemployment variable has virtually no impact on saving in the $HHSAV$ measure of saving:[7]

---

7. A Lagrange multiplier test indicated heteroskedasticity of error terms.

HHSAV.3

$$S = 0.976 \ S_{-1} + 0.72 \ \Delta\widehat{YL} + 0.07 \ \Delta\widehat{YP} + 0.0007 \ \Delta\widehat{RUA} - 0.41 \ U_{-1}.$$
$$\quad (0.010) \qquad (0.18) \qquad (0.10) \qquad (0.0029) \qquad (0.09)$$

$$DW = 2.08 \qquad R^2 = 0.67 \qquad ADJ = 1 + 0.003*TIME$$

It has been proposed that this difference from the corresponding *LFSAV* equation reflects substitution between financial saving and investment in durables and housing over the cycle.

With saving defined to include pension-fund and corporate saving, the unemployment variable continues to be statistically significant:

PGSAV.3

$$S = 0.959 \ S_{-1} + 0.87 \ \Delta\widehat{YL} + 0.70 \ \Delta\widehat{YP} + 0.010 \ \Delta\widehat{RUA} - 0.41 \ U_{-1}.$$
$$\quad (0.011) \qquad (0.18) \qquad (0.22) \qquad (0.003) \qquad (0.09)$$

$$DW = 2.01 \qquad R^2 = 0.71 \qquad ADJ = 1 + 0.006*TIME$$

This equation suggests that a one-percentage-point increase in the unemployment rate will increase the *PGSAV* rate of saving by one percentage point. The direction and even the magnitude of the changes are the same as with the *LFSAV* measure. But the economic significance of a one-percentage-point increase in saving is obviously much smaller when the average saving rate is 9 percent, as in the *PGSAV* case, than when the average saving rate is 2.5 percent, as in the *LFSAV* case.

The saving ratios reported in Table 18.6 may appear to be destructive to nonneoclassical theory. But these results are more a consequence of the definition of saving than of shortcomings in the theory.

Table 18.6. Long-run saving ratios

Equation	$\hat{s}_W$	$\hat{s}_C$	$\hat{s}_C - \hat{s}_W$
HHSAV.2	0.11	0.01	−0.10
	(0.06)	(0.02)	(0.05)
HHSAV.3	0.15	0.01	−0.13
	(0.04)	(0.02)	(0.05)
PGSAV.2	0.13	0.13	0.004
	(0.08)	(0.10)	(0.06)
PGSAV.3	0.11	0.09	−0.02
	(0.02)	(0.03)	(0.04)

One final point. As was the case with *PRISAV*, experiments with a constant term are disturbing to the life-cycle view. Once again, it is not so much the size of the constant term but the effect on the coefficient of S_{-1} that is important. The following results are representative:

HHSAV.4

$$S = 25.7 + 0.89 \, S_{-1} + 0.61 \, \widehat{\Delta YL} + 0.10 \, \widehat{\Delta YP}$$
$$\quad (11.5) \quad (0.04) \qquad (0.18) \qquad\quad (0.10)$$

$$\quad - \, 0.0007 \, \widehat{\Delta RUA} - 0.38 \, U_{-1},$$
$$\quad\;\; (0.0029) \qquad\quad (0.09)$$

$$DW = 2.03 \qquad R^2 = 0.68 \qquad ADJ = 1 + 0.003*TIME$$

PGSAV.4

$$S = 20.5 + 0.88 \, S_{-1} + 0.80 \, \widehat{\Delta YL} + 0.66 \, \widehat{\Delta YP}$$
$$\quad (9.2) \quad (0.04) \qquad (0.18) \qquad\quad (0.22)$$

$$\quad + \, 0.008 \, \widehat{\Delta RUA} - 0.38 \, U_{-1}.$$
$$\quad\;\; (0.003) \qquad\quad (0.09)$$

$$DW = 1.97 \qquad R^2 = 0.73 \qquad ADJ = 1 + 0.006*TIME$$

Clearly it is stretching the confidence interval to make it compatible with the life-cycle prediction about the propensity to consume out of wealth.

The two intermediate definitions of saving add little that is new to the comparison of the permanent-income and the disequilibrium hypothesis. The basic equation continues to be

$$S = c_0 S_{-1} + c_1 \Delta Y + c_2 Y_{-1}. \tag{17.15}$$

The coefficient $\hat{c}_2$ is significant in both *HHSAV.5* and *PGSAV.5*, contrary to the prediction of the disequilibrium hypothesis. The permanent-income hypothesis fares somewhat better: $\hat{c}_0 - \hat{c}_1 + \hat{c}_2$ is significant in the *HHSAV* regression but not in the corresponding *PGSAV* regression. We have

HHSAV.5

$$S = 0.71 \, S_{-1} + 0.17 \, \Delta \hat{Y} + 0.027 \, Y_{-1} - 0.30 \, U_{-1},$$
$$\quad (0.07) \qquad (0.07) \qquad (0.006) \qquad (0.09)$$

$$DW = 1.98 \qquad R^2 = 0.66 \qquad ADJ = 1 + 0.003*TIME$$

PGSAV.5

$$S = 0.81\, S_{-1} + 0.68\, \Delta\hat{Y} + 0.014\, Y_{-1} - 0.32\, U_{-1}.$$
$$\quad (0.05) \qquad (0.11) \qquad (0.004) \qquad (0.09)$$

$$DW = 1.89 \qquad R^2 = 0.71 \qquad ADJ = 1 + 0.006*TIME$$

The implicit overall coefficient for Y_{-1} is given by

$$HHSAV.5 \qquad \hat{c}_0 - \hat{c}_1 + \hat{c}_2 = 0.57,$$
$$(0.10)$$

$$PGSAV.5 \qquad \hat{c}_0 - \hat{c}_1 + \hat{c}_2 = 0.14.$$
$$(0.12)$$

If we drop Y_{-1} from Eq. (17.15), we have the following results by which to test the disequilibrium hypothesis:[8]

HHSAV.6

$$S = 0.981\, S_{-1} + 0.30\, \Delta\hat{Y} - 0.42\, U_{-1},$$
$$\quad (0.010) \qquad (0.08) \qquad (0.09)$$

$$DW = 2.13 \qquad R^2 = 0.59 \qquad ADJ = 1 + 0.003*TIME$$

PGSAV.6

$$S = 0.957\, S_{-1} + 0.65\, \Delta\hat{Y} - 0.39\, U_{-1}.$$
$$\quad (0.012) \qquad (0.11) \qquad (0.09)$$

$$DW = 1.93 \qquad R^2 = 0.69 \qquad ADJ = 1 + 0.006*TIME$$

The two equations lead to different estimates of the speed at which spending adjusts to income:

$$HHSAV.6 \qquad 1 - \hat{c}_0^3\hat{c}_1 = 0.71$$
$$(0.07)$$

$$PGSAV.6 \qquad 1 - \hat{c}_0^3\hat{c}_1 = 0.43,$$
$$(0.09)$$

but each is reasonable from a disequilibrium point of view. Not surprisingly, the estimates of the long-run saving ratio are closer together:

$$HHSAV.6 \qquad \hat{s} = 0.07.$$
$$(0.03)$$

$$PGSAV.6 \qquad \hat{s} = 0.08.$$
$$(0.02)$$

8. A Glejser test indicated heteroskedasticity of error terms.

Imposing the constraint $c_0 - c_1 + c_2 = 0$ gives the permanent-income equations

HHSAV.7

$$S = \underset{(0.046)}{0.024} \, C_{-1} + \underset{(0.041)}{0.073} \, \hat{Y} + \underset{(0.08)}{0.57} \, U_{-1},$$

$$DW = 2.07 \qquad R^2 = 0.53 \qquad ADJ = 1 + 0.006*TIME$$

PGSAV.7

$$S = \underset{(0.045)}{-0.771} \, C_{-1} + \underset{(0.041)}{0.787} \, \hat{Y} - \underset{(0.09)}{0.26} \, U_{-1}.$$

$$DW = 1.87 \qquad R^2 = 0.70 \qquad ADJ = 1 + 0.006*TIME$$

Here the results differ from the previous exercise with LFSAV: neither for HHSAV nor for PGSAV do the two peaks of the sum-of-squared-residuals function give similar results in terms of goodness of fit. In each case the reported results clearly dominate the regression in which the coefficient of U_{-1} has the opposite sign.

Observe that autocorrelation is positive in the HHSAV regression and negative in the PGSAV regression. The consequence is widely different values for $\hat{d}_0$ and correspondingly different results for the speed of adjustment of permanent income. By contrast, the estimates of the long-run propensity to save out of permanent income are very similar. The implied four-quarter adjustments are as follows:

HHSAV.7 $\qquad (\hat{d}_0 + 1 + \psi)(1 - \hat{d}_0 - \hat{d}_0^2 - \hat{d}_0^3) = \underset{(0.0003)}{1.006,}$

PGSAV.7 $\qquad (\hat{d}_0 + 1 + \psi)(1 - \hat{d}_0 - \hat{d}_0^2 - \hat{d}_0^3) = \underset{(0.08)}{0.66.}$

The estimates of the long-run marginal propensity to save are

HHSAV.7 $\qquad 1 - \hat{\mu} = \underset{(0.003)}{0.10,}$

PGSAV.7 $\qquad 1 - \hat{\mu} = \underset{(0.004)}{0.095.}$

Introduction of a constant term or an unemployment variable affects the disequilibrium and the permanent-income specifications almost the same way under the HHSAV definition of saving:

HHSAV.8

$$S = 33.1 + 0.86\,S_{-1} + 0.26\,\Delta\hat{Y} - 0.0048\,\Delta\widehat{RUA} - 0.38\,U_{-1},$$
$$\quad (11.8) \quad (0.04) \qquad (0.08) \qquad (0.0026) \qquad\qquad (0.09)$$

$$DW = 2.04 \qquad R^2 = 0.63 \qquad ADJ = 1 + 0.003*TIME$$

HHSAV.9

$$S = -188.4 + 0.05\,C_{-1} + 0.12\,\hat{Y} - 0.016\,\Delta\widehat{RUA} + 0.57\,U_{-1}.$$
$$\quad (95.0) \quad (0.05) \qquad (0.05) \qquad (0.006) \qquad\qquad (0.08)$$

$$DW = 2.02 \qquad R^2 = 0.52 \qquad ADJ = 1 + 0.006*TIME$$

In both these equations the constant term is significant and has a sizable effect on the coefficient of lagged saving or lagged consumption. The coefficient of ΔRUA, as in the disaggregated versions of the saving equation, has a negative sign, though it is significantly different from zero only in the permanent-income specification.

The same exercises with *PGSAV* produce different results. The constant term is significant in the disequilibrium equation but insignificant in the permanent-income equation. The unemployment variable has a positive coefficient, as in the *LFSAV* regressions, but it is both statistically insignificant and small relative to the average saving ratio:

PGSAV.8

$$S = 22.5 + 0.86\,S_{-1} + 0.69\,\Delta\hat{Y} + 0.0043\cdot\Delta\widehat{RUA} - 0.39\,U_{-1},$$
$$\quad (9.09) \quad (0.04) \qquad (0.11) \qquad (0.0027) \qquad\qquad (0.09)$$

$$DW = 1.97 \qquad R^2 = 0.73 \qquad ADJ = 1 + 0.006*TIME$$

PGSAV.9

$$S = -20.3 - 0.80\,C_{-1} + 0.82\,\hat{Y} + 0.0051\,\Delta\widehat{RUA} - 0.33\,U_{-1}.$$
$$\quad (33.3) \quad (0.05) \qquad (0.04) \qquad (0.0028) \qquad\qquad (0.09)$$

$$DW = 1.93 \qquad R^2 = 0.72 \qquad ADJ = 1 + 0.006*TIME$$

Taken together, tests on *HHSAV*.5–*HHSAV*.9 and *PGSAV*.5–*PGSAV*.9 once again give mixed results. The significance of Y_{-1} and the constant term are problematic for the disequilibrium hypothesis in the *HHSAV* regressions. By contrast, the speed of adjustment of spending to income implicit in *HHSAV*.6 is consistent with the disequilibrium hypothesis. The permanent-income specification fares no better in the *HHSAV* regressions. The overall coefficient on Y_{-1} is significant in *HHSAV*.5, as is the constant term in *HHSAV*.9; the high adjustment speed implicit in *HHSAV*.7 is an additional problem. The significant

TOWARD AN UNDERSTANDING OF CAPITALISM

negative coefficient of ΔRUA in $HHSAV.9$ is not a problem only if ΔRUA is interpreted as correcting a procyclical bias in the measurement of permanent income.

The permanent-income hypothesis does markedly better than the disequilibrium hypothesis in the $PGSAV$ regressions. Whereas the constant term and Y_{-1} are both significant in the disequilibrium specification, neither is significant in the permanent-income specification. Moreover, the adjustment speeds are each plausible, but the adjustment speed implicit in $PGSAV.6$ is on the low side from the disequilibrium point of view and the adjustment speed implicit in $PGSAV.7$ is on the high side from the permanent-income point of view. Finally, the insignificance of the employment variable is a plus for the permanent-income hypothesis.

Summary of Results

Tables 18.7–18.9 summarize the parameter estimates for alternative specifications and alternative definitions of saving. Taken together with the tests of significance of constant terms, unemployment, and lagged income, the overwhelming impression is one of inconclusiveness. There is, indeed, something for everybody.

The neoclassically inclined will find support for their position in the $PGSAV$ regressions and to a lesser extent in the $PRISAV$ and $HHSAV$ results. The estimates of b_0 for these definitions of saving are consistent

Table 18.7. Life-cycle and disequilibrium parameter estimates[a]

Parameter	Predicted interval	$PRISAV$	$LFSAV$	$HHSAV$	$PGSAV$
$\hat{b}_0$	0.967–0.98	0.973	0.80	0.966	0.973
		(0.012)	(0.06)	(0.017)	(0.019)
$1 - \hat{b}_0^3 \hat{b}_1$	>0.5	−0.04	0.86	0.34	0.35
		(0.17)	(0.11)	(0.16)	(0.16)
$\hat{s}_W$	>0	0.21	0.008	0.11	0.13
		(0.08)	(0.006)	(0.06)	(0.08)
$\hat{s}_C$	>0	0.03	0.012	0.01	0.13
		(0.02)	(0.013)	(0.02)	(0.10)
$\hat{s}_C - \hat{s}_W$	>0	−0.17	0.004	−0.10	0.004
		(0.07)	(0.012)	(0.05)	(0.06)

a. All estimates are from the following equation: $S = b_0 S_{-1} + b_1 \Delta YL + b_2 \Delta YP + b_3 \Delta YPEN + b_4 \Delta YOT + \rho U_{-1}$.

Table 18.8. Life-cycle and disequilibrium hypotheses: Alternative parameter estimates[a]

Parameter	Predicted interval	PRISAV	LFSAV	HHSAV	PGSAV
$\hat{b}_0$	0.967–0.98	0.976 (0.007)	0.89 (0.03)	0.976 (0.010)	0.959 (0.011)
$1 - \hat{b}_0^3\hat{b}_1$	>0.5	−0.08 (0.18)	0.59 (0.11)	0.33 (0.16)	0.23 (0.15)
$\hat{s}_W$	>0	0.23 (0.05)	0.030 (0.009)	0.15 (0.04)	0.11 (0.02)
$\hat{s}_C$	>0	0.03 (0.02)	0.037 (0.018)	0.01 (0.02)	0.09 (0.03)
$\hat{s}_C - \hat{s}_W$	>0	−0.20 (0.05)	0.007 (0.019)	−0.13 (0.05)	−0.02 (0.04)

a. All estimates are from the following equation: $S = b_0 S_{-1} + b_1 \Delta YL + b_2 \Delta YP + b_3 \Delta RUA + \rho U_{-1}$.

Table 18.9. Permanent-income and disequilibrium parameter estimates[a]

Equation	Parameter	Predicted value	PRISAV	LFSAV[b]	HHSAV	PGSA
(1)	$\hat{c}_0 - \hat{c}_1 - \hat{c}_2$	0	0.45 (0.10)	0.43[1] (0.15)	0.57 (0.10)	0.14 (0.12)
(1)	$\hat{c}_2$	0	0.032 (0.008)	0.0026[2] (0.0021)	0.027 (0.006)	0.01 (0.00
(2)	$(\hat{d}_0 + 1.006)(1 - \hat{d}_0 - \hat{d}_0^2 - \hat{d}_0^3)$	<0.5	1.006 (0.0003)	0.70[3] (0.11)	1.006 (0.0003)	0.66 (0.08)
(3)	$1 - \hat{c}_0^3\hat{c}_1$	>0.5	0.54 (0.08)	0.67 (0.08)	0.71 (0.07)	0.43 (0.09)
(2)	$1 - \hat{\mu}$	>0	0.16 (0.004)	0.033 (0.004)	0.10 (0.003)	0.09 (0.00
(3)	$\hat{s}$	>0	0.13 (0.04)	0.024 (0.007)	0.07 (0.03)	0.08 (0.02

a. Estimates are from the following equations:

    (1) $S = c_0 S_{-1} + c_1 \Delta Y + c_2 Y_{-1} + \rho U_{-1}$

    (2) $S = d_0 C_{-1} + d_1 Y + \rho U_{-1}$

    (3) $S = c_0 S_{-1} + c_1 \Delta Y + \rho U_{-1}$

b. Alternative estimates (see text): [1] −0.40 , [2] 0.033 , [3] 1.006.

                (0.12)   (0.006) (0.0005)

with the life-cycle hypothesis, as are the corresponding estimates of $s_C - s_W$. The effect of the constant term on b_0 and the significance of the unemployment variable are problems for the life-cycle hypothesis, as is the failure of the data to distinguish behavior with respect to extraordinary pension and disability benefits from behavior with respect to ordinary benefits. But these are relatively minor problems.

The $PGSAV$ regressions also give reasonably strong support to the permanent-income hypothesis. In the first place, the speed of adjustment of permanent income to measured income is in line with the spirit of Friedman's theory. Moreover, neither lagged income nor a constant term nor an unemployment variable is significant — all as the permanent-income hypothesis predicts.

By contrast, the disequilibrium hypothesis does relatively badly when saving is defined to include organizational saving, durables and housing, or both. The adjustment speed for aggregate income is consistent with the disequilibrium view, but this result is not supported by the disaggregated data: the estimated speed of adjustment of spending to *labor* income is invariably below what the disequilibrium idea suggests. Neither do the estimates of $s_C - s_W$ accord with nonneoclassical theory. In the $HHSAV$ and the $PRISAV$ regressions $\hat{s}_C - \hat{s}_W$ is negative, and in the $PGSAV$ regression $\hat{s}_C - \hat{s}_W$ vanishes for all intents and purposes.

All in all, defining "household" saving to include corporate and pension-fund saving puts neoclassical saving theory in a very favorable light relative to nonneoclassical theory. And including investment in durables and housing changes the picture only marginally. These definitions of saving are by and large consistent with the neoclassical view of the household as deliberate and rational, allocating resources to maximize utility over the long term.

A very different picture emerges when saving is restricted to accumulation of financial assets and organizational saving is excluded. Neither the life-cycle hypothesis nor the permanent-income hypothesis is supported by the $LFSAV$ regression results: the life-cycle hypothesis is inconsistent with the estimated propensity to consume out of wealth, and the permanent-income hypothesis, for its part, is inconsistent with the estimated speed of adjustment of permanent to measured income. Moreover, the unemployment variable has the wrong sign from the point of view of both varieties of neoclassical theory.

By contrast, the $LFSAV$ regression results by and large support the disequilibrium hypothesis. Adjustment speeds are sufficiently high to sustain the idea of saving as a disequilibrium phenomenon, and $\hat{s}_C - \hat{s}_W$ has the sign predicted by nonneoclassical theory. (The high standard error of $\hat{s}_C - \hat{s}_W$ is bothersome, but hardly fatal.) Moreover, the presence of a significant, positive coefficient for ΔRUA is relatively easy to reconcile with the disequilibrium view of household behavior, even if it makes the theory a little less neat and simple.

All in all, the *LFSAV* regressions support the notion of households that react rather than act, whose saving habits are determined more by reflex than by deliberation. Nor do households, when all is said and done, generate much saving. The steady-growth *LFSAV* saving rates are, like the historical averages, of the order of 2.5 percent or less of disposable income. It was clear by the end of the last chapter that if a distinction is made between households and organizations, the household becomes a relatively unimportant source of saving: its 2.5-percent saving rate has represented on average little more than a quarter of "productive" private saving (that is, private saving exclusive of durables and housing). According to disequilibrium theory even this modest contribution is in a sense an overstatement: household saving emerges from the *LFSAV* regressions as a consequence of growth rather than a cause, the household sector's own contribution being insufficient for self-sustaining growth at capital:output ratios and profit rates generally reckoned to prevail in the American economy. The overall thrust of the *LFSAV* regressions is clearly to deemphasize the household, to direct attention to the pension fund and the corporation as determinants of saving in the modern capitalist economy. In the disequilibrium view, organizations—not people—save.

Taken together, these results differ markedly from the results of the typical econometric exercise, which customarily give strong support to the researcher's hypothesis. Not that there is usually very much at stake. Sometimes the alternative to the null hypothesis is not even clearly specified. More often the alternative is a straw man. All that such exercises demonstrate is that a particular model is compatible with one or another data set. The unsuspecting reader is not reminded that there are one, ten, perhaps a hundred plausible alternatives that might be equally compatible with the given observations. Real alternatives, as we have seen, may be extremely difficult to distinguish on the basis of econometric tests.

Nevertheless, it is surprising how frequently the data support the researcher's preferred hypothesis, which—since preferences usually run to one variety or another of neoclassical theory—must be disturbing to the nonneoclassically inclined. A hypothetical example of the research process may shed some light on the problem. Imagine a specialist in saving behavior who confronts his particular version of truth with data on a panel of households. As might be anticipated, his first encounter is disappointing. Several coefficients are of the wrong magnitude, some are of doubtful significance, and one has the wrong sign. He ponders the results, until finally it comes to him: the sample includes a group of middle-aged Hungarians, and he realizes that he never intended his theory to apply to *them*. Solution: excise the middle-aged Hungarians from the panel. At the same time, further reflection —into which the researcher is driven by the frustrations of his first round of unsatisfactory results—leads him to modify the original theory, dropping one term, adding another. So with revised theory as well as revised data, the fray is rejoined. To shorten a possibly lengthy story, the iterative process of revision of both data and theory continues until satisfactory results—as measured by R^2, t-statistics, and so forth —appear. At which point the "new theory," along with its supporting evidence, is ready for presentation in the learned journals of the profession.

It is far from my intention in relating this tale to accuse anybody of hypocrisy, not to mention dishonesty. On the contrary: my own econometric procedures with respect to the treatment of transfer payments hardly differ in principle from deleting middle-aged Hungarians. Nor do I feel particularly apologetic about these procedures: in my judgment the iterative interaction of theory and data is hardly to be condemned—indeed, it is difficult to think of a more sensible way of structuring research. Unfortunately, however sensible, such procedures violate all the canons of classical statistics. Classical statistical procedure requires in effect that bets be made once and for all *before* consulting the data, that no more thinking be done once results start coming from the computer. But this seems a high price to pay for the sake of the purity of statistical measures that are of doubtful usefulness in any case.

The moral then is not that social scientists who manipulate data and theory to fit each other are cynical, hypocritical, or dishonest. Rather, the point is to demystify the statistical results that emerge from the exercise.

Cross-Country Comparisons as an Alternative Test

This is not to argue for theoretical nihilism, certainly not for a theoretical relativism of the genus, "You pay your money and you take your choice." But if time series (as well as cross sections of families or individuals) are indecisive, and if panel data are difficult to assemble and even then often speak in confused and ambiguous terms, we must look to other data sources. Cross-country comparisons may appear to

429

be a natural way of avoiding the problems of time series, individual and family cross sections, and panel data.

The difficulty with cross-country data was noted at the beginning of the previous chapter: an identification problem arises from the structure of the theories that have been considered in this book. In each case the saving function is but one of the two determinants of equilibrium, and there is no good reason to assume that the saving function will be stable across national boundaries while the other determinants of equilibrium vary. Quite the contrary: cultural differences between countries may be a major source of variation in saving behavior.

Comparisons of household saving rates between the United States and Japan indicate the nature of the problem. Over the period 1965–1981, household saving (as measured in the national income accounts) has averaged 19 percent of disposable income in Japan against 7 percent in the United States. Is it the relative absence of collective provision for retirement that spurs individual foresight in Japan? Or, perhaps, do cause and effect go the other way: are Japanese householders simply more future-oriented, which obviates the need for collectively financed and administered old-age pensions? Either of these explanations would be compatible with neoclassical theory, the second emphasizing a distinctive psychology of Japanese households, the first the absence of social security "wealth" in Japanese households' assets.

However, the explanation of the Japanese personal saving rate might be sought along very different lines, in which behavior can be derived not from individual preferences but from the distinctive structure of employee compensation. Consider, in particular, the semiannual bonus that forms a comparatively large part of Japanese workers' income. Does the bonus play an important role in elevating the saving rate by virtue of its variability with the fortunes of the employer? Variable income, would, according to the disequilibrium hypothesis, be inherently more difficult to incorporate into the household's spending habits than regular pay. Consequently, it may be much easier for the Japanese family to hear the stern voice of conscience with respect to the bonus than with respect to ordinary pay, and to devote it to provision for a rainy day or to retirement rather than spend it on goods that afford immediate gratification.

It will be recognized how squarely in the realm of conjecture we now are. Moreover, investigating the Japanese experience in particular, and undertaking cross-cultural comparisons in general, may or may not teach us anything useful about the determinants of saving in our own society. But if it does, it will not be because Japanese data can be made to fit one or another reduced form tolerably well; it will be because it makes us reflect more intelligently on the institutional and cultural foundations of Western saving behavior.

Once again, such research lies in the future. For the present we must either back off from purely empirical means of distinguishing between theories, or despair of sorting out the competing claims. Consistent positivists should prefer agnosticism. The rest of us will prefer to look more closely at the premises of the theories, not to find logical inconsistencies or omissions (which would prove a frustrating search), but to examine the extent to which these theories correspond to a plausible conception of the world. In short, if we are to choose between theories of saving at this stage of our knowledge, it must be on the basis of their inherent plausibility.

Testing Neoclassical Theory by Its Premises

On this ground, I submit, the neoclassical view, rooted in utility maximization, is woefully lacking as a theoretical basis of saving behavior. As we have seen, all the theories analyzed in preceding chapters of this book — neo-Marxian and neo-Keynesian as well as neoclassical — have room for utility maximization. But only neoclassical theory applies the same logic to the determination of saving that is used to determine the composition of current consumption.

Neoclassical theorists are on relatively safe ground in conceptualizing the demand for canned peaches and canned pears as an aggregate of individual choices between alternative combinations of the two fruits, individual choices made in terms of an indifference-curve framework. But significant sleight of hand is involved in extending the indifference-curve framework to intertemporal choice. If the discussion is to go beyond formal mathematics, neoclassical economists must answer a fundamental question: where do preferences come from? The question is easy to answer in the context of the peaches-pears paradigm, where the custom is to argue that indifference curves emerge from a prehistory of trial and error: purchases of different mixes of the fruits (perhaps at random in the beginning) are followed closely by consumption, and preferences are formed in consequence of the relative satisfaction generated by consuming different commodity bundles. The essential point is that the results of choice are immediate, and the entire process can be repeated until preferences are honed to a fine edge, at which point the history of rational consumer choice can be imagined to begin.

Even as a "just-so" story, however, the trial-and-error development of preferences makes little sense in the context of long-term planning of consumption, especially in the life-cycle version of the model. In this case, the consequences of one's choices are played out only over one's lifetime, and even believers in reincarnation would for the most part grant that there is little opportunity to apply the lessons of a previous life to the present. It is difficult to imagine individuals or households having meaningful preferences between consumption today and consumption a decade or two hence, in the way one can imagine preferences between peaches today and pears today.

But even if we sweep the problems of the preference map under the rug, there remain real difficulties in moving from the timeless peaches-pears framework to the intertemporal context. In the first, the budget constraint can be plausibly argued to be known with reasonable certainty: the shopper goes to the supermarket with, say, twenty dollars in his jeans. But in the intertemporal context, the budget is lifetime wealth, which for most of us consists primarily of our "human capital," the discounted present value of our lifetime earnings. The inescapable fact, however, is that the variance around projections of earnings is in general so enormous as to make a mockery of the exercise: neither the prospects of interruptions in employment over one's lifetime, whether due to the vagaries of the business cycle or to the vagaries of one's own health, nor the prospects for occupational advancement are meaningfully quantifiable for most people. In short, uncertainty makes "lifetime" earnings necessarily a subjective and unmeasurable magnitude subject to continual revision, so that consistency between saving decisions and the axioms of utility theory is in principle unverifiable.

An Attempt at Synthesis

This is not to say that no one at all uses the utility-maximization schema, or a reasonable facsimile, in saving decisions. People whose employment prospects are reasonably certain, who follow a reasonably predictable career path, and whose lives are otherwise sufficiently ordered that long-term planning makes intellectual and emotional sense might conceivably make decisions according to the life-cycle hypothesis. Middle-aged professionals come immediately to mind as a case in point. (A colleague of mine once observed that the life-cycle hypothesis is just what one would expect of a tenured college professor!) But this group is hardly representative of the population as a whole — neither of the top 1 or 2 percent of the income distribution who account for a disproportionate amount of the total saving and for whom other motives than provision for retirement appear to be significant, nor of the bottom 80 to 90 percent of the distribution who account for most savers, if not for most saving.

Indeed, it is perhaps chimerical to look for a single theory that explains all household consumption and saving behavior. The disequilibrium hypothesis may explain the behavior of the bottom 80 to 90 percent of the income distribution, whose prospects are so uncertain that deliberate choice and planning are beside the point. In this group, habit may explain most of the consumption but relatively little of the saving, since their average propensity to save is apparently quite low. The life-cycle hypothesis may adequately account for most of the remainder of the population distribution—the professionals and executives whose futures are sufficiently secure to make deliberate provision for the future a reasonable notion and whose relative means make the pressure to spend less imperative. If this is the case, then the life-cycle hypothesis may account for a larger fraction of household saving than it does of consumption, but both fractions may nevertheless still be small.

This leaves us with the upper end of the income distribution, not just the super-rich but the top 1 to 2 percent, some two to four million individuals in the United States. I am tempted to argue that the disequilibrium hypothesis applies to this group too, but the theory necessarily loses a good deal of its punch: large assets make it possible for these households to maintain consumption for a relatively long time in the face of declines in income, and the pressures to consume weigh with markedly less urgency against increases in income for the rich than for the rest of us. Indeed, candor compels the admission that we know very little about the saving behavior of the people who do the most saving.

From a nonneoclassical point of view, neoclassical theory is limited in two respects. First, it is relevant at best to a comparatively small subset of households. Second, household saving is at best a small part of the story of accumulation in the capitalist sector of the economy. Over the period 1952–1979, productive private saving, as measured by *PGSAV*, averaged 9 percent of disposable income. Productive saving by households, as measured by *LFSAV*, was 2.5 percent of disposable income, hardly one-quarter of the total. Evidently corporate saving (equal to 3.8 percent of disposable income) and pension-fund saving (2.7 percent) are the major part of the story. As for the first, the state of the art has hardly progressed beyond John Lintner's explanation (1956) of the determination of corporate dividends. As for the second, we have no theory at all, unless we count Peter Drucker's tract (1976) as a theory.

Our ignorance is presumably remediable, but not until we free ourselves from the straitjacket of neoclassical theory, which concentrates our attention on the less important, if not the trivial, while failing absolutely to come to grips with the essence of the problem.

Appendix: Sources and Methods

Four alternative definitions of saving—*PRISAV, LFSAV, HHSAV,* and *PGSAV*—have been utilized in the regression analysis of this chapter. Each concept of saving requires, for consistency's sake, a different definition of income and its components. After a preliminary discussion of the problems of using the national income accounts, I will turn to the definition appropriate to the narrowest conception of saving, *LFSAV.* Then I will expand the definition to take account of durables, housing, and organizational saving.

Alternative Definitions of Saving and Income

There are two problems with the national income accounts. First, income is divided into four categories rather than the three that I have used: in addition to labor income, property income, and transfer payments, there is a category called "proprietors' income." [9] Second, in the national income accounts "personal tax and nontax payments" are not allocated among the various types of income.

To solve these problems, I use procedures developed by Charles Steindel for his dissertation (1977) and incorporated in Modigliani and Steindel (1977). First, labor income (*LYG*) is defined as the sum of "wage and salary disbursements" (*SWX*) and "other labor income" (*OLIX*), plus a fraction (*ASW*) of *SWX* that reflects an imputed labor share of proprietors' income,

$$LYG = (1 + ASW) \cdot SWX + OLIX.$$

Then, to determine disposable labor income from *LYG,* personal taxes must be allocated between labor and nonlabor incomes. Again I follow Steindel, who devised a set of effective tax rates for each kind of income. Denoting the tax rate on labor income by *LTR,* we have taxes on labor income (*TAXL*) as

$$TAXL = LTR \cdot (1 + ASW) \cdot SWX + CSIX.$$

CSIX is equal to "personal contributions for social insurance." Disposable labor income is the difference between gross labor income and labor-income taxes,

$$LYDZ = LYG - TAXL.$$

Because of revisions subsequent to Steindel's estimates that changed property-income data, his more or less symmetric procedure for estimating dispos-

---

9. Quotation marks will be used throughout this appendix to indicate the names of series in the *National Income and Product Accounts of the United States, 1929–1976* (1981).

able property income was not followed. Instead, disposable property income is determined by the residual that is left after subtracting disposable labor income and "transfer payments" ($TRANSX$) from an adjusted disposable income ($DPIADJ$), the adjustment being the addition of user fees ($OTAX$) to disposable income as it is defined in the national income accounts ($DPINIA$).[10] Property income (PYD) is

$$PYD = DPIADJ - LYDZ - TRANSX,$$

$$DPIADJ = DPINIA + OTAX.$$

We turn now to the definitions of income and its components specific to each of the four definitions of saving.

LFSAV   Both LYD and PYD are defined to be compatible with Steindel's extended definition of disposable income ($DPINIA + OTAX$), and consequently with personal saving as defined in the national income accounts. Therefore these definitions must be modified to reflect the absence in $LFSAV$ of the two components of NIA personal saving, namely, private pension-fund saving and investment in owner-occupied housing. The first adjustment is straightforward. Labor income (YL^{LF}) is defined by the difference between $LYDZ$ and private pension-fund saving, $NETPEN = PFRA - CGIA$:

$$YL^{LF} = LYDZ - NETPEN.$$

The second adjustment is more complicated: since $LFSAV$ excludes net additions to the *stock* of owner-occupied housing, the corresponding adjustment to income is the exclusion of the *flow* of housing services. Property income is correspondingly reduced by the imputed rents in the national income accounts, $RENTIMPX = GHP - HCCA - HINT$, where (from Table 8.8, "Imputations . . . ," of *National Income Accounts*) GHP represents the "gross housing product" of owner-occupied housing, $HCCA$ represents a "capital consumption allowance," and $HINT$ represents "net interest." Thus property income is given by

$$YP^{LF} = PYD - RENTIMPX.$$

Transfer payments are given by $TRANSX$:

$$YT^{LF} = TRANSX.$$

In those regressions in which transfer payments are disaggregated, $YPEN$ is

10. User fees were calculated by Steindel from the categories "other taxes" and "nontaxes" in tables 3.2 and 3.4 of the *National Income and Product Accounts*. These categories include such like items as "tuition and related educational charges" and "hospital and health charges." Although the division between user fees and taxes may approach an arbitrary distinction, it appears reasonable to follow Steindel in including these categories with disposable income rather than with taxes.

defined as the sum of "old-age, survivors, disability and health insurance benefits" and "government employees retirement benefits"; YOT is the sum of "government unemployment insurance benefits," "veterans benefits," and "other transfer payments." Thus

$$TRANSX = YPEN + YOT.$$

Transfer payments and its two subcomponents, alone among the components of income, are invariant with respect to the definition of saving.

Finally, income (Y^{LF}) is defined as the sum of the three components, disposable labor income, disposable property income, and transfer payments:

$$Y^{LF} = YL^{LF} + YP^{LF} + YT^{LF}.$$

In the permanent-income regressions, consumption (C^{LF}) is the difference between income and saving:

$$C^{LF} = Y^{LF} - LFSAV.$$

HHSAV When saving is redefined to include investment in durables as well as housing, the definition of property income changes accordingly. In addition to the services of owner-occupied housing, the services of consumer durables are appropriately included in YP^{HH}:

$$YP^{HH} = YP^{LF} + CDY.$$

The measurement of CDY, simple in principle, is hardly unproblematic in practice. Nor are the problems mere technical details: *experiments with alternative measures indicate that the coefficient of property income is extremely sensitive to how CDY is measured.* The problem lies in specifying a rate of return on the stock of consumer durables. Following what he took to be conventional practice, Steindel originally formulated the gross rate of return as the yield on high-grade corporate bonds. Interest on consumer debt was subtracted to arrive at the net return.

Implicit in this procedure is a model of behavior in which households adjust their investment in durables until the net return at the margin is equal to the return in the financial sector. The relevance of this model is questionable, to say the least. But it *is* a natural neoclassical way of modeling income from durables. And since the very inclusion of durables in saving puts us squarely on neoclassical turf, we should not object too strongly to this procedure, however dubious it may seem in terms of common sense.

But even within the neoclassical framework, the procedure Steindel followed is flawed. The rate of return to which households adjust, according to neoclassical theory, is evidently a real rate of return. But the corporate bond yield is a *nominal* interest rate whose steady increase over the postwar period is the result of accelerating inflation, not of an increasing real rate of return. By the same token, the *real* burden of interest payments on consumer durables is reduced by the inflationary erosion of the real value of household debt.[11] These considerations are reflected in the equation for CDY that follows:

$$CDY = \{RCB - 4*[\ln(PCD) - \ln(PCD_{-1})]\}*(KNCD72_{-1} + ECD/8)$$
$$- INTX + \frac{INTX}{RCB}*4*[\ln(PC) - \ln(PC_{-1})] + RENTIMPX.$$

The first element on the right-hand side,

$$RCB - 4*[\ln(PCD) - \ln(PCD_{-1})],$$

is a real rate of return measured by the difference between Moody's AAA corporate bond yield (RCB) and the current rate of increase of the implicit price deflator for durables (PCD). The second element is a measure of the real stock of consumer durables, taken to be the (beginning-of-quarter) value of consumer durables in constant dollars ($KNCD72_{-1}$) plus one-eighth of the current quarter's constant-dollar expenditure at an annual rate ($ECD/8$). The next term is the nominal "interest paid by consumers to business" ($INTX$). Finally, this interest is capitalized at the nominal rate RCB, and the erosion of debt by inflation is calculated as the percentage change in the implicit price deflator for consumption (PC),

$$\frac{INTX}{RCB}*4*[\ln(PC) - \ln(PC_{-1})].$$

I should hardly defend this procedure for calculating income from consumer durables. It can be challenged at many points. But it does, I believe, fairly represent the neoclassical spirit and is probably no less satisfactory than alternatives that might be proposed.

Labor income and transfer payments are unchanged from their $LFSAV$ definitions:

$$YL^{HH} = YL^{LF}, \qquad YT^{HH} = YT^{LF}.$$

As before, income is the sum of the components:

$$Y^{HH} = YL^{HH} + YP^{HH} + YT^{HH},$$

and consumption is the difference between income and saving

$$C^{HH} = Y^{HH} - HHSAV.$$

PGSAV The modifications in the definition of income to accommodate the integration of organizational saving with household saving are straightforward: labor income is redefined to include pension-fund saving,

$$YL^{PG} = YL^{LF} + PFRA,$$

11. Steindel has subsequently revised his procedures to take account of inflation. In addition he models the adjustment between returns from consumer durables and returns from financial saving to reflect the fact that imputed income from durables escapes the tax collector's net, a consideration omitted in my formulation (personal communication, 1982).

and property income is redefined to include "undistributed profits," RNA,

$$YP^{PG} = YP^{LF} + RNA.$$

As measured by RNA, corporate saving is defined to reflect the "inventory-valuation adjustment" and "capital consumption allowance" in the national income accounts.

Income, as before, is the sum of labor income, property income, and transfer $(YT^{PG} = YT^{LF})$:

$$Y^{PG} = YL^{PG} + YP^{PG} + YT^{PG}.$$

And consumption is the difference between income and saving:

$$C^{PG} = Y^{PG} - PGSAV.$$

PRISAV The final definition of saving combines households' financial saving both with investment in durables and housing and with organizational saving. Correspondingly, the definition of income includes both the adjustments to income made under the $HHSAV$ definition of saving and the adjustments made under the $PGSAV$ definition. We have:

$$YL^{PRI} = YL^{LF} + PFRA$$

$$YP^{PRI} = YP^{LF} + CDY + RNA$$

$$YT^{PRI} = YT^{LF}$$

$$Y^{PRI} = YL^{PRI} + YP^{PRI} + YT^{PRI}$$

$$C^{PRI} = Y^{PRI} - PRISAV.$$

Table 18.10 summarizes the data for alternative definitions of income and saving. The purpose of this table is not to permit verification of the regressions reported in this chapter — that would require quarterly data — but to convey the magnitudes and trends of the various components of income and saving.

Data Sources

The data for this chapter's regressions came from five sources: Flow of Funds data originating with the Board of Governors of the Federal Reserve System; the National Income and Product Accounts of the Department of Commerce; the Federal Reserve Bank of St. Louis; the Bureau of Labor Statistics of the Department of Labor; and Charles Steindel.

Saving data came, for the most part, from the household sector of the Flow of Funds Accounts. The only exceptions were the data on corporate saving, the source of which was the National Income and Product Accounts. Income series were constructed, as has been indicated, from national income data, supplemented by Flow of Funds data, utilizing procedures developed by Steindel. Table 18.11 gives complete quarterly listings of the series borrowed from Steindel, ASW, LTR, and $OTAX$. Finally, the Bureau of Labor Statistics was the source for the unemployment rate, represented by the rate of unemployment

Table 18.10. Alternative measures of income and saving in constant (1972) dollars per capita

Variable	1952	1953	1954	1955	1956	1957	1958	1959	1960	1961	1962	1963	1964
$LYDZ$	2,016	2,073	2,027	2,103	2,174	2,154	2,092	2,150	2,164	2,157	2,219	2,241	2,370
PYD	290	289	301	317	313	323	344	347	338	355	368	391	422
$TRANSX$	134	139	156	163	168	185	214	215	223	246	245	253	257
$DPIADJ$	2,441	2,501	2,483	2,583	2,655	2,663	2,650	2,712	2,724	2,758	2,832	2,885	3,048
$DPINIA$	2,430	2,489	2,471	2,570	2,640	2,646	2,632	2,695	2,707	2,740	2,811	2,863	3,024
$OTAX$	11	12	13	14	15	17	17	17	17	19	21	22	24
$NETPEN$	28	29	34	36	32	39	37	44	40	39	39	41	50
$RENTIMPX$	60	71	81	85	87	88	92	96	102	108	113	116	119
YL^{LF}	1,988	2,044	1,993	2,067	2,141	2,115	2,054	2,106	2,124	2,118	2,179	2,200	2,319
YP^{LF}	230	218	220	232	226	235	252	250	236	247	255	275	302
YT^{LF}	134	139	156	163	168	185	214	215	223	246	245	253	257
$YPEN$	35	43	49	62	68	81	90	103	109	120	131	137	142
YOT	99	96	106	102	100	104	124	112	113	126	114	116	114
Y^{LF}	2,353	2,401	2,369	2,463	2,535	2,536	2,521	2,571	2,582	2,611	2,680	2,728	2,879
$LFSAV$	60	43	21	-15	51	63	76	33	35	61	63	61	85
CDY	71	116	106	65	52	107	101	93	126	93	122	111	123
YP^{HH}	301	334	326	297	277	342	353	344	362	341	377	386	425
Y^{HH}	2,423	2,517	2,475	2,528	2,587	2,643	2,622	2,665	2,709	2,704	2,802	2,839	3,002
$HHSAV$	264	265	211	255	268	242	207	221	204	187	223	245	291
$PFRA$	49	48	49	53	54	58	60	67	64	65	65	68	80
RNA	85	71	81	125	96	87	67	110	93	93	132	144	164
YL^{PG}	2,037	2,092	2,042	2,120	2,196	2,173	2,114	2,173	2,188	2,183	2,244	2,268	2,400
YP^{PG}	315	289	301	357	322	322	319	360	328	340	387	418	466
Y^{PG}	2,487	2,520	2,499	2,640	2,686	2,681	2,648	2,748	2,739	2,769	2,877	2,939	3,123
$PGSAV$	194	163	151	162	202	209	203	210	192	218	260	272	329
$CDY+RNA$	156	188	187	189	148	195	168	203	219	186	255	255	287
YP^{PRI}	386	405	407	422	374	429	421	454	455	434	510	530	589
Y^{PRI}	2,557	2,637	2,606	2,705	2,738	2,788	2,749	2,842	2,865	2,862	2,999	3,051	3,246
$PRISAV$	398	384	342	432	419	388	334	398	360	345	420	457	535

Variable	1965	1966	1967	1968	1969	1970	1971	1972	1973	1974	1975	1976	1977	1978	1979
LYDZ	2,489	2,583	2,643	2,728	2,799	2,837	2,864	2,970	3,043	2,961	2,916	3,011	3,113	3,224	3,194
PYD	437	448	452	448	430	447	463	442	556	535	531	529	550	606	699
TRANSX	269	286	325	352	371	422	471	498	533	566	658	676	677	674	684
DPIADJ	3,195	3,318	3,420	3,528	3,601	3,706	3,798	3,911	4,132	4,062	4,105	4,217	4,341	4,505	4,576
DPINIA	3,169	3,288	3,387	3,492	3,562	3,662	3,750	3,858	4,078	4,008	4,049	4,156	4,278	4,439	4,510
OTAX	26	29	33	36	39	43	48	53	54	54	56	60	63	66	66
NETPEN	49	57	50	53	53	50	58	52	61	68	73	92	109	102	85
RENTIMPX	124	127	132	131	132	133	133	130	128	119	118	117	108	101	90
YL^{LF}	2,440	2,526	2,593	2,675	2,747	2,787	2,806	2,918	2,983	2,893	2,843	2,919	3,005	3,122	3,109
YP^{LF}	313	322	319	318	298	314	330	313	427	416	413	413	442	506	609
YT^{LF}	269	286	325	352	371	422	471	498	533	566	658	676	677	674	684
YPEN	155	172	200	222	232	256	281	301	340	357	385	414	436	448	461
YOT	115	114	125	130	139	165	190	197	193	209	274	262	241	226	223
Y^{LF}	3,022	3,134	3,238	3,345	3,416	3,523	3,607	3,730	3,943	3,875	3,915	4,008	4,124	4,302	4,401
LFSAV	98	114	165	107	42	165	122	96	141	173	248	152	26	49	82
CDY	159	153	138	160	185	182	205	197	228	109	167	142	189	146	184
YP^{HH}	472	474	457	477	483	496	535	510	656	525	580	555	631	651	793
Y^{HH}	3,181	3,287	3,375	3,504	3,602	3,705	3,812	3,927	4,171	3,984	4,081	4,150	4,312	4,447	4,585
HHSAV	329	348	367	358	279	342	358	394	460	389	433	416	358	412	411
PFRA	81	93	84	89	92	97	105	107	113	118	129	154	182	186	152
RNA	200	205	184	164	129	78	113	145	144	55	107	129	175	187	149
YL^{PG}	2,521	2,619	2,677	2,764	2,839	2,884	2,912	3,026	3,096	3,011	2,972	3,073	3,187	3,308	3,260
YP^{PG}	513	526	503	482	427	392	443	458	572	471	520	541	617	693	758
Y^{PG}	3,302	3,431	3,505	3,598	3,637	3,698	3,826	3,982	4,201	4,048	4,150	4,291	4,480	4,675	4,702
PGSAV	378	411	432	361	263	340	341	349	398	346	484	434	383	422	383
CDY + RNA	359	357	321	324	314	260	318	342	373	164	274	271	364	333	333
YP^{PRI}	672	679	641	642	612	574	648	655	800	580	687	683	806	838	942
Y^{PRI}	3,461	3,584	3,643	3,758	3,823	3,880	4,031	4,179	4,429	4,158	4,317	4,433	4,669	4,821	4,887
PRISAV	609	646	635	611	500	517	576	647	717	562	668	698	715	785	713

Sources: National Income and Product Accounts, Flow of Funds Accounts.

Table 18.11. Data for regressions

Year and quarter	ASW	LTR	OTAX	FHFR	FHEX
1952:1	0.186	0.110	11.177	65.600	66.500
1952:2	0.186	0.110	11.328	66.300	70.400
1952:3	0.186	0.110	11.326	67.000	74.700
1952:4	0.186	0.110	11.552	67.700	74.000
1953:1	0.181	0.112	12.324	68.300	76.800
1953:2	0.181	0.112	12.332	69.100	78.700
1953:3	0.181	0.112	12.244	69.800	77.100
1953:4	0.181	0.112	12.158	70.200	77.500
1954:1	0.184	0.101	12.587	67.800	73.000
1954:2	0.184	0.101	12.628	67.700	68.900
1954:3	0.184	0.101	12.760	67.900	67.900
1954:4	0.184	0.101	12.931	69.200	67.000
1955:1	0.178	0.105	13.573	70.900	67.600
1955:2	0.178	0.105	13.763	71.500	66.600
1955:3	0.178	0.105	13.846	72.600	68.900
1955:4	0.178	0.105	13.995	73.900	68.900
1956:1	0.174	0.109	15.155	75.800	69.400
1956:2	0.174	0.109	15.120	77.300	71.700
1956:3	0.174	0.109	15.091	78.700	72.300
1956:4	0.174	0.109	15.173	80.400	74.200
1957:1	0.171	0.111	16.645	83.600	78.100
1957:2	0.171	0.111	16.601	85.000	79.800
1957:3	0.171	0.111	16.640	86.400	79.700
1957:4	0.171	0.111	16.599	86.800	80.500
1958:1	0.173	0.111	16.338	87.900	82.300
1958:2	0.173	0.111	17.614	89.300	85.700
1958:3	0.173	0.111	17.794	90.400	89.400
1958:4	0.173	0.111	17.911	91.700	91.600
1959:1	0.168	0.116	18.200	94.800	89.600
1959:2	0.168	0.116	16.382	96.700	89.400
1959:3	0.168	0.116	16.443	97.900	90.900
1959:4	0.168	0.116	16.416	99.300	91.100
1960:1	0.162	0.116	16.989	103.200	89.700
1960:2	0.162	0.116	17.150	104.700	91.700
1960:3	0.162	0.116	17.019	105.500	93.400
1960:4	0.162	0.116	16.962	107.000	94.500
1961:1	0.161	0.119	18.416	108.100	97.100
1961:2	0.161	0.119	18.587	110.100	99.700
1961:3	0.161	0.119	18.564	111.100	101.200
1961:4	0.161	0.119	18.843	112.700	103.200
1962:1	0.156	0.122	20.481	115.800	108.100

(continued)

Table 18.11   continued

Year and quarter	ASW	LTD	OTAX	FHFR	FHEX
1962:2	0.156	0.122	20.641	117.300	108.500
1962:3	0.156	0.122	20.725	118.600	110.000
1962:4	0.156	0.122	20.908	118.100	112.100
1963:1	0.150	0.125	21.760	121.600	112.600
1963:2	0.150	0.125	21.881	123.000	111.400
1963:3	0.150	0.125	22.079	124.100	113.500
1963:4	0.150	0.125	22.154	126.200	116.100
1964:1	0.148	0.114	23.561	125.100	117.700
1964:2	0.148	0.114	23.894	118.200	118.300
1964:3	0.148	0.114	24.194	119.700	117.300
1964:4	0.148	0.114	24.157	121.100	117.700
1965:1	0.145	0.109	25.422	123.600	118.000
1965:2	0.145	0.109	25.568	124.500	120.300
1965:3	0.145	0.109	25.868	122.500	126.100
1965:4	0.145	0.109	26.465	123.900	130.700
1966:1	0.138	0.114	29.109	133.200	136.100
1966:2	0.138	0.114	29.085	137.700	140.300
1966:3	0.138	0.114	29.303	140.500	147.300
1966:4	0.138	0.114	29.305	143.200	152.200
1967:1	0.135	0.120	32.753	146.600	160.200
1967:2	0.135	0.120	33.100	147.300	161.300
1967:3	0.135	0.120	33.163	151.600	165.400
1967:4	0.135	0.120	33.237	154.400	169.200
1968:1	0.133	0.125	35.685	159.400	174.200
1968:2	0.133	0.125	36.014	162.100	181.600
1968:3	0.133	0.141	36.645	179.600	183.200
1968:4	0.133	0.141	36.733	184.900	185.500
1969:1	0.130	0.142	38.925	192.100	185.000
1969:2	0.130	0.142	39.018	196.300	187.900
1969:3	0.130	0.142	39.132	196.600	190.000
1969:4	0.130	0.142	39.322	200.300	193.600
1970:1	0.127	0.139	43.341	203.600	194.600
1970:2	0.127	0.139	43.420	207.300	207.500
1970:3	0.127	0.133	43.587	203.900	204.900
1970:4	0.127	0.133	43.077	208.700	208.600
1971:1	0.127	0.132	47.496	207.500	212.400
1971:2	0.127	0.132	47.859	211.900	219.800
1971:3	0.127	0.132	47.992	211.700	221.000
1971:4	0.127	0.132	48.449	212.800	224.700
1972:1	0.120	0.136	51.510	222.200	234.900
1972:2	0.120	0.136	52.423	224.600	243.400

(continued)

Table 18.11. continued

Year and quarter	ASW	LTR	OTAX	FHFR	FHEX
1972:3	0.120	0.136	52.960	229.100	237.900
1972:4	0.120	0.136	53.919	233.300	259.800
1973:1	0.120	0.141	54.144	248.100	261.700
1973:2	0.120	0.141	53.958	256.000	262.200
1973:3	0.120	0.141	54.073	260.900	264.700
1973:4	0.120	0.141	53.632	268.500	271.700
1974:1	0.119	0.148	54.294	279.700	281.000
1974:2	0.119	0.148	54.182	290.000	293.500
1974:3	0.119	0.148	54.387	300.800	305.300
1974:4	0.119	0.148	53.283	311.900	314.400
1975:1	0.116	0.154	54.889	322.600	329.500
1975:2	0.116	0.116	55.689	291.300	346.500
1975:3	0.116	0.143	56.210	326.500	356.300
1975:4	0.116	0.143	56.889	334.900	367.200
1976:1	0.114	0.147	57.933	342.100	370.700
1976:2	0.114	0.147	58.323	349.700	370.700
1976:3	0.114	0.147	58.847	355.400	382.400
1976:4	0.114	0.147	66.701	364.600	395.500
1977:1	0.113	0.152	61.898	372.900	399.300
1977:2	0.113	0.152	62.030	380.300	408.000
1977:3	0.113	0.152	62.620	386.300	426.400
1977:4	0.113	0.152	63.690	397.100	439.300
1978:1	0.116	0.159	64.470	411.700	445.400
1978:2	0.116	0.159	65.185	427.400	448.000
1978:3	0.116	0.159	65.752	444.500	461.300
1978:4	0.116	0.159	66.652	457.700	478.700
1979:1	0.116	0.178	66.593	472.400	485.800
1979:2	0.116	0.178	65.927	491.700	491.900
1979:3	0.116	0.178	66.505	511.000	514.900
1979:4	0.116	0.178	66.969	528.700	539.100

Note: ASW and LTR are adjustment factors calculated by Steindel to determine disposable labor income. OTAX represents user fees added to disposable income, expressed in constant (1972) dollars per capita, seasonally adjusted at an annual rate. FHFR and FHEX are Federal High Employment Budget Receipts and Expenditures, as calculated by the Federal Reserve Bank of St. Louis in billions of current dollars, SAAR.

for all workers. The Federal Reserve Bank of St. Louis was the source for the series used to measure the high-employment deficit in the federal government budget (*FED*), defined as the difference between high employment expenditures (*FHEX*) and high employment receipts (*FHFR*):

$$FED = FHEX - FHFR.$$

The basic series *FHEX* and *FHFR* are also listed in Table 18.11. With this table anyone with access to Flow of Funds Accounts, National Income and Product Accounts, and Bureau of Labor Statistics data should be able to reproduce the regressions reported in this chapter.

All data, it should be added, were seasonally adjusted at the source. Current-dollar aggregates were deflated twice, first by dividing through by population, then by dividing through by the price level. With three exceptions, the price level was measured by the "implicit price deflator for personal consumption expenditures," with 1972 as the base year. (The exceptions were as follows: first, the measurement of the services of durables, for which the consumer-durable deflator was used; second, the GNP deflator was used for the high-employment government deficit; third, exports (*EX*), another instrument, were deflated by the export deflator.)

All data were available on a quarterly basis except for two series, the unemployment rate and rent imputations. For the unemployment rate, monthly data were averaged to obtain quarterly observations. For rent imputations, annual series were converted to a quarterly basis by linear interpolation.

Finally, the data utilized included all revisions through October, 1982. In principle Flow of Funds and national income data are compatible.

Estimation Procedures

The possibility of simultaneity bias led to a decision to use two-stage least squares to estimate all the equations. Preliminary experiments having indicated first-order autocorrelation of error terms, all equations were estimated with the lagged error term as an independent variable. Accordingly, the estimation technique used was that proposed by Fair (1970) for dealing with first-order autocorrelation in the presence of a lagged dependent variable. In the general case we start from an equation of the form

$$S = b_0 S_{-1} + \mathbf{X}'\mathbf{b} + U. \tag{18.1}$$

In the version of the Fair method employed for the regressions reported in this chapter,[12] the instrument list consisted of excluded exogenous variables $\mathbf{Z}'$ (that is, variables not included in the original equation, Eq. (18.1)), plus the lagged values of dependent and independent variables S_{-1}, S_{-2}, and $\mathbf{X}'_{-1}$. Each component of $\mathbf{X}'$, each X_i, is replaced by the $\hat{X}_i$ estimated from the first-stage equation

$$X_i = a_{i0} S_{-1} + a_{i1} S_{-2} + \mathbf{Z}'\mathbf{c}_i + \mathbf{X}'_{-1}\mathbf{d}_i + \epsilon.$$

Thus the second-stage regression becomes

$$S - \rho S_{-1} = b_0 (S_{-1} - \rho S_{-2}) + (\hat{\mathbf{X}}' - \rho \mathbf{X}'_{-1})\mathbf{b} + \epsilon. \tag{18.2}$$

---

12. Experiments with an alternative method involving the transformed variables gave similar results.

For the first iteration, the parameter ρ in Eq. (18.2) is estimated from the ordinary-least-squares version of Eq. (18.1), namely

$$S = b_0 S_{-1} + \mathbf{X'b} + \rho U_{-1} + \epsilon.$$

Each iteration of Eq. (18.2) gives new values of b_0 and $\mathbf{b}$, which generates a new value of ρ from Eq. (18.1), rewritten as

$$U = S - b_0 S_{-1} - \mathbf{X'b}.$$

Specifically, we have

$$\hat{\rho} = \frac{\Sigma UU_{-1}}{(n-1)(SEE)^2}$$

where n is the number of observations and SEE is the equation standard error. The new value $\hat{\rho}$ is used in Eq. (18.2) for the next iteration. The algorithm terminates when successive values of $\hat{\rho}$ differ by 0.005 or less.

The instrument list was chosen with a view to having as little variation as possible of the instruments as the definitions of income and saving change from one set of regressions to another: the "excluded exogenous" instruments were current and lagged high-employment deficits (FED and FED_{-1}) and current and lagged exports (EX and EX_{-1}), as well as the components of income and saving required to ensure a uniform instrument list. The instruments common to all regressions were FED, FED_{-1}, EX, EX_{-1}, YL^{LF}_{-1}, YP^{LF}_{-1}, YT^{LF}_{-1}, $REN\text{-}TIMPX_{-1}$, CDY_{-1}, $PFRA_{-1}$, RNA_{-1}, $NETRCON_{-1}$, $CDURA_{-1}$. As noted, each regression adds the lagged dependent and independent variables from the first stage to the instrument list. Thus for $LFSAV.3$, for example, the additional instruments were $LFSAV_{-1}$, $LFSAV_{-2}$, ΔYL^{LF}_{-1}, ΔYP^{LF}_{-1}, ΔYT^{LF}_{-1}, $\Delta YPEN_{-1}$, ΔYOT_{-1}. As the next section indicates, heteroskedasticity required that the data be rescaled to remove or reduce the time trend.[13]

PARAMETER ESTIMATION Many of the parameters of interest were functions of the estimated coefficients, frequently nonlinear functions. For instance, the four-quarter cumulative adjustment of spending to labor income in the equation

$$S = \hat{b}_0 S_{-1} + \hat{b}_1 \Delta YL + \hat{b}_2 \Delta YP + \hat{b}_3 \Delta YPEN + \hat{b}_4 \Delta YOT + \hat{\rho} U_{-1}$$

is given by $1 - \hat{b}_0^3 \hat{b}_1$. The conventional procedure for estimating standard errors of linear combinations of coefficients was applied to nonlinear functions, which involved an approximation inherent in replacing the linear weights of

13. As will be explained later in this appendix, the adjustment took the form of dividing through all variables, in both the first- and second-stage regressions, by a variable ADJ defined as $ADJ = 1 + 0.006 \cdot TIME$ or $ADJ = 1 + 0.003 \cdot TIME$, with $TIME = 1, \ldots, 110$. Experiments were carried out with other definitions of ADJ to test the robustness of the estimates. This adjustment transformed the constant term in the first-stage regression into a term of the form $CONSTANT/ADJ$. A constant term was therefore added to the first-stage regression once the data were rescaled.

the conventional procedure with first derivatives.[14] In the general case where the coefficient vector is $\hat{\mathbf{b}} = \langle \hat{b}_0, \ldots, \hat{b}_n \rangle$ and the parameter in question is defined by $F(\mathbf{b})$, the standard error of $F(\mathbf{b})$ is given by the square root of the variance

$$\langle F_0, \ldots, F_n \rangle \; \mathbf{VCOV}(\hat{\mathbf{b}}) \begin{bmatrix} F_0 \\ \cdot \\ \cdot \\ \cdot \\ F_n \end{bmatrix},$$

where $F_i \equiv \partial F / \partial b_i$ and $\mathbf{VCOV}(\hat{\mathbf{b}})$ is the variance-covariance matrix associated with $\hat{\mathbf{b}}$.

As an example, consider the equation

LFSAV.3

$$S = 0.80 \, S_{-1} + 0.27 \, \widehat{\Delta YL} + 0.40 \, \widehat{\Delta YP} + 2.27 \, \widehat{\Delta YPEN}$$
$$+ 2.59 \, \widehat{\Delta YOT} - 0.36 \, U_{-1}.$$

The variance-covariance matrix is

	S_{-1}	ΔYL	ΔYP	$\Delta YPEN$	ΔYOT
S_{-1}	0.0035				
ΔYL	0.0032	0.033			
ΔYP	0.0091	0.010	0.15		
$\Delta YPEN$	−0.076	−0.15	−0.32	2.39	
ΔYOT	−0.0035	0.03	0.033	−0.16	0.42

In *LFSAV*.3, the cumulative adjustment of spending to labor income is

$$F(\hat{\mathbf{b}}) = 1 - \hat{b}_0^3 \hat{b}_1 = 0.86,$$

and the vector of first derivatives is

$$\langle F_0, \ldots, F_n \rangle = \langle -3\hat{b}_0^2 \hat{b}_1, -\hat{b}_0^3, 0, 0, 0 \rangle$$
$$= \langle -0.51, -0.51, 0, 0, 0 \rangle.$$

Using the relevant elements of the variance-covariance matrix, we have the variance of $1 - \hat{b}_0^3 \hat{b}_1$ as the quadratic form

$$\langle -0.51, -0.51 \rangle \begin{bmatrix} 0.0035 & 0.0032 \\ 0.0032 & 0.033 \end{bmatrix} \begin{bmatrix} -0.51 \\ -0.51 \end{bmatrix} = 0.011.$$

Finally, we have $\sqrt{0.011} = 0.11$, which is the standard error of $1 - \hat{b}_0^3 \hat{b}_1$ reported in the discussion of *LFSAV*.3 in the main body of this chapter.

It should be observed that in all cases estimates of standard errors are contingent on the estimated value of $\hat{\rho}$, the coefficient of the lagged error term.

14. The conventional procedure is described in Theil (1971, p. 131).

Neither the program utilized for these regressions nor other regression programs of which I am aware include a procedure for estimating the covariance of $\hat{\rho}$ and $\hat{b}$. As Cooper (1972) has shown, the consequence is to underestimate the standard errors of the regression coefficients.

Tests of Least-Squares Assumptions

This section first takes up two aspects of error structure, autocorrelation and heteroskedasticity. Attention is then turned to stability of the regression coefficients over time and a test for the uniformity of the coefficients of various subcategories of pension/disability benefits.

AUTOCORRELATION Virtually all the regressions revealed first-order autocorrelation of error terms; almost invariably, the coefficients on the lagged error terms proved highly significant. Two problems remain, the problem of higher-order correlation and the problem of interpreting autocorrelation in the context of the models of household saving behavior with which this and the last chapter have been concerned.

The problem of higher-order correlation was addressed in two ways: first, an examination of the Durbin-Watson statistic, and, second, direct analysis of the higher-order autocorrelations. None of the Durbin-Watson statistics was very far from the null-hypothesis value of 2.0. However, this test is no more than suggestive because the regression equations include the lagged dependent variable on the right-hand side. Consequently, the Durbin-Watson test was supplemented by an experimental comparison of actual patterns of higher-order correlation with the predictions of the first-order model.

Consider the equation

LFSAV.3

$$S = \underset{(0.06)}{0.80}\, S_{-1} + \underset{(0.18)}{0.27}\, \Delta \widehat{YL} + \underset{(0.38)}{0.40}\, \Delta \widehat{YP} + \underset{(1.54)}{2.27}\, \Delta \widehat{YPEN}$$

$$+ \underset{(0.65)}{2.59}\, \Delta \widehat{YOT} - \underset{(0.09)}{0.36}\, U_{-1}.$$

$$DW = 1.97 \qquad R^2 = 0.56 \qquad ADJ = 1 + 0.003 * TIME$$

The patterns of actual and predicted higher-order correlation are given in Table 18.12. For the first three lags, the sample sign patterns alternate between negative and positive, as predicted. After the first three lags, both predicted and sample autocorrelations essentially vanish. Moreover, except for the third-order lag, the actual pattern approximates the pattern of geometric decay that a first-order process predicts. These impressionistic results are supported by an analysis of the residuals in the least-squares regression

$$U = \rho U_{-1} + \epsilon.$$

Table 18.12. *LFSAV*.3: Sample and predicted autocorrelations

Lag	Sample autocorrelation $\Sigma UU_{-1}/(n-1)(SEE)^2$	Estimated standard error	Predicted autocorrelation ρ^t	Predicted standard error $t\rho^{t-1} SE_\rho$
$t = 1$	-0.33[a]	0.10	-0.36[a]	0.09
2	0.085	0.10	0.13	0.06
3	-0.13	0.11	-0.045	0.03
4	-0.013	0.11	0.016	0.016
5	0.026	0.11	-0.006	0.007

a. The sample and predicted first-order correlations differ because of a difference in the technique used to estimate autocorrelation in the analysis of residuals and the technique used to estimate ρ.

A Box-Pierce test (Harvey 1981, chap. 6) was performed for five lags. The resulting Q-statistic, 2.9, was well below the mean of the distribution of χ_4^2.

Similar tests were carried out for the other definitions of saving, but I will report only the *PRISAV* results, since the autocorrelation patterns for *HHSAV* and *PGSAV* were similar, respectively, to *PRISAV* and *LFSAV*. The *PRISAV* equation corresponding to *LFSAV*.3 is

PRISAV.4

$$S = 0.973\, S_{-1} + 1.13\, \widehat{\Delta YL} + 0.17\, \widehat{\Delta YP} + 0.13\, \widehat{\Delta YPEN}$$
$$\quad (0.012) \qquad (0.19) \qquad (0.10) \qquad (1.54)$$

$$+\ 1.43\, \widehat{\Delta YOT} - 0.41\, U_{-1}.$$
$$\quad (0.72) \qquad\quad (0.09)$$

$$DW = 2.08 \qquad R^2 = 0.75 \qquad ADJ = 1 + 0.006*TIME$$

The autocorrelation patterns are presented in Table 18.13. Again, except for

Table 18.13. *PRISAV*.4: Sample and predicted autocorrelations

Lag	Sample autocorrelation $\Sigma UU_{-1}/(n-1)(SEE)^2$	Estimated standard error	Predicted autocorrelation ρ^t	Predicted standard error $t\rho^{t-1} SE_\rho$
$t = 1$	-0.40[a]	0.10	-0.41[a]	0.09
2	0.061	0.11	0.17	0.07
3	-0.066	0.11	-0.070	0.04
4	0.045	0.11	0.029	0.02
5	0.028	0.11	-0.012	0.01

a. The sample and predicted first-order correlations differ because of a difference in the technique used to estimate autocorrelation in the analysis of residuals and the technique used to estimate ρ.

one lag — in this case, the second — the predicted and sample autocorrelations follow the same pattern until both series essentially vanish at $t = 5$. Further analysis of residuals leaves matters up in the air; a Box-Pierce test on the residuals of $U = \rho U_{-1} + \epsilon$ gave a Q-statistic of 3.3 for five lags, a result consistent with the absence of higher-order correlation.

Turning now to the question of interpretation, it should be noted first that negative values of ρ preclude the usual interpretation of autocorrelation as the consequence of omitted variables which themselves move slowly over time (Theil 1971, pp. 250–251). A possible explanation of negative autocorrelation is that households partially compensate in one period for mistakes made in the previous period: if, for example, they overshoot the saving mark in one quarter, they will save less than they otherwise would in the next. But, it must be admitted, such an explanation makes more sense for neoclassical theory, with its emphasis on deliberation and rationality, than for nonneoclassical theory, with its emphasis on habit and learning.

Even with respect to neoclassical theory, this interpretation is hardly the only possible one. Zvi Griliches suggested to me that the error structure might be more reasonably interpreted in terms of an errors-in-variables approach. If saving is viewed as the change in wealth, with both current and lagged wealth subject to error, then intended saving and desired wealth are related by the identity $S^* \equiv W^* - W^*_{-1}$. Actual saving is related to intended saving by the equation $S = S^* + \zeta - \zeta_{-1}$, where ζ represents the error in measurement of wealth. Suppose now that in terms of intended saving, the regression equation in general has the form

$$S^* = b_0 S^*_{-1} + \cdots + \epsilon,$$

where ϵ obeys the usual restrictions that justify least squares — it is normally distributed with identical mean and variance in each period and serially uncorrelated over time. With measured saving in place of desired saving, we will have

$$S = b_0(S_{-1} - \zeta_{-1} + \zeta_{-2}) + \cdots + \epsilon + \zeta - \zeta_{-1}.$$

This equation suggests that if the errors-in-variables approach is assumed to be true, *all* our equations are misspecified. S_{-1} is by definition correlated with the error term ζ_{-1} and thus is endogenous rather than predetermined; treating S_{-1} as exogenous, as was done throughout this chapter, will lead to a downward bias in the estimate b_0. The assumed error structure also has implications for the choice of instruments. S_{-2} cannot be used as an instrument — as our version of the Fair technique prescribed — because the error in S_{-2} is correlated with the error in S_{-1}. Finally, observe that the autocorrelation pattern suggested by the errors-in-variables approach is very different from the pattern when the true structure is given by the equation $U = \rho U_{-1} + \epsilon$. With $U = \epsilon + \zeta - (1 + b_0)\zeta_{-1} + b_0\zeta_{-2}$ and $U_{-1} = \epsilon_{-1} + \zeta_{-1} - (1 + b_0)\zeta_{-2} + b_0\zeta_{-3}$, an equation of the form $U = \rho U_{-1} + \epsilon$ can still be estimated — the estimate $\hat{\rho}$ will reflect the relative size of the errors ϵ and ζ as well as the coefficient b_0 — but the pattern of autocorrelation will not follow the geometric-decay model. Rather, the higher-order autocorrelations, beginning with $E(UU_{-3})$, will all be zero.

It is a plausible hypothesis, especially on neoclassical assumptions, that the errors-in-variables approach captures some, if not all, of the error structure. This hypothesis was tested by experimenting with the equation

$$S = b_0 S_{-1} + b_1 \Delta YL + b_2 \Delta YP + b_3 \Delta YPEN + b_4 \Delta YOT + \rho U_{-1}.$$

The equation was estimated with S_{-1} treated as an endogenous variable; S_{-1} is then omitted from the instruments, and S_{-2} is replaced by S_{-3} in the list of instruments. For *LFSAV* and *PRISAV* the results were as follows:

LFSAV

$$S = 0.82\ \hat{S}_{-1} + 0.07\ \widehat{\Delta YL} + 0.46\ \widehat{\Delta YP} + 2.53\ \widehat{\Delta YPEN}$$
$$(0.06) \qquad (0.20) \qquad (0.37) \qquad (1.58)$$

$$+ 2.40\ \widehat{\Delta YOT} - 0.34\ U_{-1},$$
$$(0.70) \qquad\quad (0.09)$$

$$DW = 2.03 \qquad R^2 = 0.54 \qquad ADJ = 1 + 0.003 * TIME$$

PRISAV

$$S = 0.982\ \hat{S}_{-1} + 0.71\ \widehat{\Delta YL} + 0.22\ \widehat{\Delta YP} + 0.37\ \widehat{\Delta YPEN}$$
$$(0.013) \qquad (0.21) \qquad (0.11) \qquad (1.64)$$

$$+ 1.05\ \widehat{\Delta YOT} - 0.38\ U_{-1}.$$
$$(0.77) \qquad\quad (0.09)$$

$$DW = 2.14 \qquad R^2 = 0.74 \qquad ADJ = 1 + 0.006 * TIME$$

Evidently, these results are not very different from those reported for *LFSAV*.3 and *PRISAV*.4, except that in the *PRISAV* equation the coefficient on labor income does not exceed unity (in contrast with the corresponding coefficient in *PRISAV*.4). To be sure, the estimates of the coefficients of $\hat{S}_{-1}$ are higher than the corresponding estimates of S_{-1} in the earlier regressions, but the differences are not large.

Examination of the autocorrelation patterns reveals a difference between the *PRISAV* and the *LFSAV* regressions. A comparison of Table 18.14 with

Table 18.14. Sample autocorrelations for errors-in-variables specification

Lag	*LFSAV*		*PRISAV*	
	Autocorrelation	Standard error	Autocorrelation	Standard error
$t = 1$	-0.35	0.10	-0.40	0.10
2	0.094	0.11	0.013	0.11
3	-0.17	0.11	-0.038	0.11
4	-0.008	0.12	-0.020	0.11
5	0.007	0.11	0.062	0.11

Table 18.13 suggests that the *PRISAV* pattern conforms more closely to the errors-in-variables specification than it does to the first-order autocorrelation model. By contrast, for the *LFSAV* case, a comparison of Table 18.14 with Table 18.12 suggests little difference between the two specifications. Box-Pierce tests for the residuals of the first-order autocorrelation equation $U = \rho U_{-1} + \epsilon$ gave Q-statistics of 5.2 and 4.8 for five lags, results which do not suggest higher-order autocorrelation.

Overall, these results suggest two conclusions. First, the errors-in-variables approach appears empirically as well as conceptually to fit the neoclassical model better than the nonneoclassical, but even in the neoclassical case the evidence is far from conclusive. Second, and perhaps more important, the regression coefficients, particularly the coefficient of S_{-1}, do not appear to be sensitive to the choice between the two specifications. But this conclusion must be qualified by the limited nature of the experiment.

HETEROSKEDASTICITY TESTS Three different tests were performed on the unadjusted data: the Goldfeld-Quandt test (1965), the Glejser test (1969), and Lagrange multiplier tests (Breusch and Pagan 1979). In all but the *HHSAV* regressions, one or another of these tests suggested heteroskedasticity: in the *PRISAV* regressions, the Goldfeld-Quandt test; in the *LFSAV* regressions, a Lagrange multiplier test; and in the *PGSAV* regressions, both Goldfeld-Quandt and Lagrange multiplier tests.

However, adjusting the data as suggested by one test sometimes introduced heteroskedasticity according to a different test. For instance, in the *LFSAV* regressions (where the problem was most acute), Lagrange multiplier tests generally indicated heteroskedasticity: regressing the squared residuals ϵ^2 of a regression of the form

$$S - \hat{\rho}S_{-1} = b_0(S_{-1} - \hat{\rho}S_{-2}) + \ldots + \epsilon \tag{18.3}$$

against the squared sum of a constant and $TIME$ ($= 1, \ldots, 110$),

$$\epsilon^2 = (e_0 + e_1 TIME)^2,$$

regularly produced R^2 and corresponding χ^2 values that suggested (at the 5-percent level) a statistically significant increase in the size of the error over time. This result was hardly surprising in itself, given the trend in income and saving.

The Lagrange multiplier test has the virtue of suggesting a cure for the problem of heteroskedasticity: rescale the data by dividing through the equation by a variable *ADJ*,

$$ADJ = \left| \frac{\hat{e}_0 + \hat{e}_1 TIME}{\hat{e}_0} \right|.$$

In the *LFSAV* regressions, the ratio e_1/e_0 turned out generally to be of the order of 0.007, approximately equal to the time trend in disposable income per capita.

By construction, rerunning the regression with rescaled data made the errors homoskedastic—at least as far as the Lagrange multiplier test could determine. But the Glejser test, which did not suggest heteroskedasticity when performed on the original data, suggested heteroskedasticity on the rescaled data. Specifically, a regression of the form

$$|\epsilon| = f_0 + f_1(S_{-1} - \hat{\rho}S_{-2}),$$

where ϵ is the residual from the rescaled version of Eq. (18.3), produced an estimate $\hat{f}_1$ that was significant at the 5-percent level.

The coefficient $\hat{f}_1$ was in general negative, suggesting that higher weight should be given to observations with higher values of $S_{-1} - \hat{\rho}S_{-2}$. (Recall that $\hat{\rho}$ is in general negative, so that $S_{-1} - \hat{\rho}S_{-2}$ is a quasi-sum of saving lagged once and saving lagged twice.) It turns out that the 1975 recession, which produced particularly high values of *LFSAV* along with unusually low residuals, was chiefly responsible for this result: experiments indicated that, with the three observations 1975 : 2 – 1975 : 4 omitted, the *t*-statistic on $\hat{f}_1$ drops from values well above 2.0 to values well below. But the recession of 1975 cannot be willed away: the solution to the heteroskedasticity problem must deal with cycles as well as with the trend.

One approach, the one reported in the main body of this chapter, lies in adjusting the scaling factor to strike a balance between the two measures of heteroskedasticity. In general, regressions run on data rescaled by dividing through by

$$ADJ = 1 + 0.003*TIME$$

(or, with other definitions of saving, $ADJ = 1 + 0.006*TIME$) managed to pass all the heteroskedasticity tests, including a second Lagrange multiplier test of the form

$$\epsilon^2 = e_0 + e_1 TIME + e_2(TIME)^2.$$

A second solution was to reformulate the Lagrange multiplier test on the original (unadjusted) data. The equation

$$\epsilon^2 = [g_0 + g_1 TIME + g_2(S_{-1} - \hat{\rho}S_{-2})]^2, \tag{18.4}$$

with ϵ taken from Eq. (18.3), includes the key variable of the Glejser test, $S_{-1} - \hat{\rho}S_{-2}$, along with *TIME*. This regression was in general highly significant; a 1-percent significance level was typical. When, for example, ϵ^2 was taken from *LFSAV*.3 run with the original, unadjusted data, the fitted equation for (18.4) was

$$\epsilon^2 = 34.3 + 0.30\ TIME - 0.075\ (S_{-1} + 0.35\ S_{-2}).$$
$$\quad\ (7.3)\quad\ (0.10)\qquad\ (0.040)$$

$$DW = 2.12 \qquad R^2 = 0.08$$

The χ^2 statistic, equal to the product of R^2 (constant-adjusted) and the number of observations, is equal to 8.81, which with 2 degrees of freedom is significant at the 1-percent level.

When the variables were rescaled by dividing through by

$$ADJ = \left| \frac{\hat{g}_0 + \hat{g}_1 TIME + \hat{g}_2(S_{-1} - \hat{\rho}S_{-2})}{\hat{g}_0} \right|,$$

the resulting regression generally exhibited homoskedastic errors as measured by all the tests. Nevertheless, this procedure appeared to me deficient in its lack of an underlying rationale. The simpler adjustments that are linear functions of time can be understood as removing or reducing the time trend in the unscaled variables. In contrast, the compound adjustment $|[\hat{g}_0 + \hat{g}_1 TIME + \hat{g}_2(S_{-1} - \hat{\rho}S_{-2})]/\hat{g}_0|$ appears arbitrary.

The saving grace, perhaps, is that alternative procedures appear to give similar results. Consider the $LFSAV$ regression in which the dependent variables are S_{-1}, ΔYL^{LF}, ΔYP^{LF}, $\Delta YPEN$, and ΔYOT. Scaling the variables by

$$ADJ = 1 + 0.003 \cdot TIME$$

produced the results reported in the main text:

LFSAV.3

$$S = \underset{(0.06)}{0.80}\, S_{-1} + \underset{(0.18)}{0.27}\, \widehat{\Delta YL} + \underset{(0.38)}{0.40}\, \widehat{\Delta YP} + \underset{(1.54)}{2.27}\, \widehat{\Delta YPEN}$$

$$+ \underset{(0.65)}{2.59}\, \widehat{\Delta YOT} - \underset{(0.09)}{0.36}\, U_{-1}.$$

$$DW = 1.97 \qquad R^2 = 0.56 \qquad ADJ = 1 + 0.003 \cdot TIME$$

Consider, for comparative purposes, the results with the original data,

$$S = \underset{(0.06)}{0.80}\, S_{-1} + \underset{(0.18)}{0.16}\, \widehat{\Delta YL} + \underset{(0.36)}{0.54}\, \widehat{\Delta YP} + \underset{(1.42)}{2.36}\, \widehat{\Delta YPEN}$$

$$+ \underset{(0.63)}{2.76}\, \widehat{\Delta YOT} - \underset{(0.09)}{0.35}\, U_{-1}.$$

$$DW = 1.99 \qquad R^2 = 0.59 \qquad ADJ = 1$$

Consider also the results of scaling the data by dividing through by the compound adjustment that emerges from the residuals of the original equation. In this case we have

$$S = \underset{(0.06)}{0.76}\, S_{-1} + \underset{(0.16)}{0.22}\, \widehat{\Delta YL} + \underset{(0.44)}{0.30}\, \widehat{\Delta YP} + \underset{(1.59)}{3.00}\, \widehat{\Delta YPEN}$$

$$+ \underset{(0.56)}{2.62}\, \widehat{\Delta YOT} - \underset{(0.09)}{0.34}\, U_{-1}.$$

$$DW = 1.96 \qquad R^2 = 0.67$$

$$ADJ = \frac{34.3 + 0.30\, TIME - 0.075\, (S_{-1} + 0.35\, S_{-2})}{34.3}$$

For the purposes to which we have put these saving regressions, the results seem reasonably robust to the scaling of the variables.

STABILITY OF REGRESSION COEFFICIENTS The standard Chow test for ordinary least squares cannot be directly applied to the two-stage case. But the same principle can be applied in a test that requires the introduction of dummy variables that are defined to equal zero for one subinterval and to equal the original variables in the remaining periods. The test is adapted from Theil (1971, chap. 6).

In general, to test n restrictions on a vector of coefficients $\hat{\mathbf{b}}$ given by the equation $\mathbf{M}\hat{\mathbf{b}} = \mathbf{m}$, we exploit the fact that

$$(\mathbf{M}\hat{\mathbf{b}} - \mathbf{m})'\mathbf{VCOV}(\hat{\mathbf{b}})(\mathbf{M}\hat{\mathbf{b}} - \mathbf{m})$$

is asymptotically χ_n^2. In the present case, we start from a model of the general form

$$S = a_0 S_{-1} + \mathbf{X}'\mathbf{a} + U.$$

This model is replaced by the augmented model

$$S = a_0 S_{-1} + \mathbf{X}'\mathbf{a} + \tilde{\mathbf{X}}'\mathbf{b} + U, \tag{18.5}$$

where $\tilde{\mathbf{X}}'$ is a vector of semi-dummy variables $\langle \tilde{X}_1, \ldots, \tilde{X}_n \rangle$, each of which is defined by an equation of the form

$$\tilde{X}_{it} = \begin{cases} 0, & 1 \le t < t_0 \\ X_{it}, & t_0 \le t \le 110 \end{cases}.$$

Time t_0 is the breakpoint between the two subintervals.

The first stage of the estimation procedure also must change to accommodate the presence of $\tilde{\mathbf{X}}'$. If each of the X_i is estimated by an equation of the form

$$X_i = c_{i0} S_{-1} + c_{i1} S_{-2} + \mathbf{Z}'\mathbf{d}_i + \mathbf{X}'_{-1}\mathbf{e}_i + \epsilon,$$

INTERVAL: 1–110

then the semi-dummy variables are estimated by an equation of the same form over the second subinterval:

$$\tilde{X}_i = c_{i0} S_{-1} + c_{i1} S_{-2} + \mathbf{Z}'\mathbf{d}_i + \mathbf{X}'_{-1}\mathbf{e}_i + \epsilon.$$

INTERVAL: t_0–110

Stability of the regression coefficients in Eq. (18.1) is tantamount to the coefficient vector $\mathbf{b}$ in Eq. (18.5) being insignificantly different from zero.

In place of the general formulation $M\hat{b} = m$, we have the constraint

$$[\ \mathbf{0}_n\ ,\ \ \mathbf{I}_n\ ] \begin{pmatrix} \hat{\mathbf{a}} \\ \hat{\mathbf{b}} \end{pmatrix} = \ \mathbf{0}\ .$$

$$n \times n \quad n \times n \quad 2n \times 1 \qquad n \times 1$$

Writing $\mathbf{q} = [\mathbf{0}_n, \mathbf{I}_n] \begin{pmatrix} \hat{\mathbf{a}} \\ \hat{\mathbf{b}} \end{pmatrix}$, the quadratic form

$$\mathbf{q}'\mathbf{VCOV}(\hat{\mathbf{a}},\ \hat{\mathbf{b}})\mathbf{q}$$

is, under the null hypothesis of coefficient stability, asymptotically χ_n^2.

I did not follow the customary practice of dividing the interval $1952:3-1979:4$ into two equal subintervals. Instead, $1971:3$, which marked the introduction of Richard Nixon's experiment with wage-price controls, was chosen as the breakpoint. Two factors dictated this choice. First, the generally prevalent notion that the great postwar boom came to an end in the 1970s suggested that the interval be divided somewhat later than at a breakpoint corresponding to a mechanical division into two equal periods. But some candidates for the breakpoint that were plausible from an economic point of view were problematic from a statistical point of view. For example, the emergence of OPEC as an effective cartel in the aftermath of the Yom Kippur War, or the inflation of 1974 and recession of 1975, left what seemed to be too few observations for the second period. Hence the compromise choice of $1971:3$.

This test did not indicate — except as noted — any instability of the regression coefficients in the reported regressions. More precisely, the χ^2 statistics on which this Chow test turns were, in all cases but *PRISAV*.8, insignificant at the 5-percent level.

A TEST OF THE UNIFORMITY OF COEFFICIENTS FOR PENSION/DISABILITY BENEFITS
Finally, it might be noted that the χ^2 test of the significance of extraordinary pension and disability benefits in equations *PRISAV*.3, *LFSAV*.2, *HHSAV*.1, and *PGSAV*.1 utilized the same basic quadratic form,

$$(M\hat{b} - m)'\mathbf{VCOV}(\hat{b})(M\hat{b} - m),$$

with $m = 0$ and

$$M\hat{b} = \begin{bmatrix} 0 & 0 & 0 & 1 & -1 & 0 & 0 & 0 & 0 & 0 \\ 0 & 0 & 0 & 1 & 0 & -1 & 0 & 0 & 0 & 0 \\ 0 & 0 & 0 & 1 & 0 & 0 & -1 & 0 & 0 & 0 \\ 0 & 0 & 0 & 1 & 0 & 0 & 0 & -1 & 0 & 0 \\ 0 & 0 & 0 & 1 & 0 & 0 & 0 & 0 & -1 & 0 \end{bmatrix} \begin{bmatrix} \hat{b}_{S-1} \\ \hat{b}_{\Delta YL} \\ \hat{b}_{\Delta YP} \\ \hat{b}_{\Delta SS} \\ \hat{b}_{WF} \\ \hat{b}_{CU} \\ \hat{b}_{EY} \\ \hat{b}_{MC} \\ \hat{b}_{IN} \\ \hat{b}_{\Delta YOT} \end{bmatrix}.$$

The results were as follows:

$$PRISAV.3 \quad \chi^2 = 3.92$$
$$LFSAV.2 \quad \chi^2 = 5.25$$
$$HHSAV.1 \quad \chi^2 = 4.53$$
$$PGSAV.1 \quad \chi^2 = 5.77$$

With 5 degrees of freedom, none of these results came near to significance at the 5-percent level.

19 Criticism and Evaluation

My first intention in this chapter is to gather up the threads of the critique that has been the leitmotif of this book. I begin more or less where I left off at the end of the last chapter, with the neoclassical model. The essence of my dissatisfaction with that model lies not only with the two aspects of neoclassical saving theory to which objections have been raised — the assumption of the universality of utility maximization and the abstraction from concentration of ownership and control under capitalism. In addition I would quarrel with a third assumption, that the labor market functions essentially like the horse market of Eugen Böhm-Bawerk or the fish market of Alfred Marshall.

Neoclassical Theory

Let me first round off my criticism of neoclassical saving theory. I have pretty much said my piece with respect to the universality of utility maximization, and by way of summary I shall only say that a plausible hypothesis for the limited context of static choice becomes patently unrealistic when transplanted to the realm of intertemporal choice.

I used to argue (Marglin 1975) that no society would, at the peril of its very survival, leave anything as important as capital accumulation to as haphazard a process as the market aggregation of individual choices. It appeared to me that the domain over which individual choice could be exercised was so circumscribed that neither the rate of capital accumulation nor any other socially important outcome hinged on the aggregate of the individual decisions. The central point of the argument was, I should emphasize, not to deny the reality of choice but to

456

assert the greater importance of the process of generating constraints to which choice is subject.

Such reasoning goes along well with the view of the household as constrained by social and economic pressure to spend virtually all the income it can get its hands on. By the same token, one is led to see the corporation as providing for its own accumulation almost in self-defense. As a business leader put it to a Congressional committee probing business policies in the period just after World War II (Sutton et al. 1956, p. 86), "If you give it [profits] all to the stockholders, by what rhyme or reason do we assume that they are going to save enough and have it ready for you when you want it?" For him the answer was obvious: "We have to take calculated risks in business, but as an administrator, I would not care to take that risk." In providing for its own future through the device of retained earnings, the corporation serves the social function of ensuring a rate of capital accumulation adequate to permit capitalism to continue to deliver the goods.

I am less happy with the implications of this argument now than I was a decade ago. The disequilibrium hypothesis stresses the independence of household saving from corporate saving. One side of the coin is that households adjust their saving to corporate retention policies only to the extent that corporate retentions affect disposable income. That part of the argument is quite consistent with an emphasis on self-defense in the explanation of corporate retention policy. The problem is rather the implications of self-defense with respect to how causality works in the *other* direction. To argue that corporations and other organizations, rather than households, control the overall rate of saving is in effect to argue *against* independence of the two components of private saving, and instead to argue for a Denison's Law in reverse. In this view any constancy of the overall saving rate in the long run is attributable not to adjustments of households' direct saving to changes in corporate saving, but the other way around; changes in household saving are offset by changes of roughly equal magnitude and opposite sign in corporate and other organizational saving.

I should be the first to admit that there is little empirical justification for taking a strong position one way or the other on this matter. Corporations may in fact control the rate of saving, but, on the other hand, we may — like it or not — have reached such a level of social disintegration that even outcomes crucial to the future of our society have got beyond social control, and are influenced, if not completely determined, by the results of haphazard aggregation! That is why the argument of the last chapter stressed disagreement on the rather narrow issue of the particular mechanism of choice, the universality of utility maximization and its applicability to the determination of patterns of intertemporal consumption, and downplayed the broader issue of whether or not households have any real say in the determination of intertemporal consumption patterns. And there is where I shall leave this issue, as a question (a fundamental one to my mind) about the nature of contemporary capitalism that still requires much thought and research.

In any case, we could dispense with utility maximization altogether and still preserve quite a bit of the distinctive quality of the neoclassical approach, at least as that approach has been characterized in this book. Utility maximization provides a basis for the saving function. But the formal structure of the neoclassical model does not require us to go behind the saving function at all. We could rather make it a primitive of the argument, taking the relationship between desired saving and the profit rate as a datum. It is, as we have observed, the denial of concentration of ownership and control of capital rather than utility maximization that gave the neoclassical saving function of Chapter 2 its peculiar shape.[1]

The abstraction from concentration of ownership and control has also been dealt with at sufficient length to require relatively little elaboration here. The essence of the neoclassical position was captured in the simple model of Chapter 2, that saving can be understood primarily in terms of the life-cycle needs of a relatively homogeneous body of households who accumulate capital during their working years to provide for their retirement. This not only poses problems for the neoclassical model of equilibrium (specifically, the problem of stability) that require extreme assumptions to resolve (the assumption of an excessive degree of factor substitution in production), but more important, flies in the face of the reality of the concentration of productive assets in a relatively few hands.

This failing of neoclassical theory is a more general one than the distortion of the saving function. Orthodox economists recognize concentration as an element of capitalist reality only when it shows up in the form of monopoly or oligopoly. Otherwise capitalism is generally

1. But if the descriptive theory would survive, the normative theory, which is largely absent from this book but is an equally important part of neoclassical theory taken as a whole, would be irreparably damaged: neoclassical welfare economics depends critically on the utility-maximization assumption. (Ironically, even on its own terms, the central normative proposition — the Pareto "optimality" of competitive equilibrium — fails in the context of open-ended growth models. As we saw in Chapter 2, governmental intervention is required to achieve even this highly restrictive notion of the Good.)

lumped together with petty commodity production under the general rubric of "market economy."

Milton Friedman's *Capitalism and Freedom* (1962) is a case in point. Friedman argues the link between economics and political arrangements in terms that recall the Jeffersonian insistence on an economy of small farmers, artisans, and mechanics as the only enduring basis for political democracy. But Friedman fails to press the Jeffersonian case for petty-commodity production, arguing instead for *capitalism* as the basis for political democracy. For Friedman, apparently, capitalism is indistinguishable from petty-commodity production: *Capitalism and Freedom*, at least, shows absolutely no awareness of the difference between the two modes of production, as if competition among capitalists canceled out the effects of concentration of control within a relatively small class of owners and managers. (It is important to stress the *relative* smallness of the capitalist class; a capitalist class composed of even just one percent of the U.S. population would number some two million souls.)

It will be objected that the assumption of a relatively uniform distribution of assets is an artifact of my interpretation rather than an essential of the neoclassical approach. And, to be sure, the neoclassical model in its fullest generality allows for different "endowments" among the households that comprise the model. Nevertheless, although endowments may indeed differ in the sophisticated formulations of Kenneth Arrow, Gerard Debreu, and Frank Hahn (Arrow and Debreu 1954; Debreu 1959; Arrow and Hahn 1971), there, as in the whole corpus of neoclassical theory, the systematic element in the pattern of "endowments"—the concentration of ownership and control of the means of production in a small fraction of the households—is totally ignored, as are the consequences of concentration for the nature of equilibrium.

The Labor Market in Neoclassical Theory

Finally, the neoclassical model founders on the assumption that the labor market functions like the textbook market of partial-equilibrium theory. Observe that the issue that divides neoclassical and nonneoclassical theories is put in terms of the competitiveness of the labor market only at the risk of greatly confusing the issue: neither neo-Marxian nor neo-Keynesian theory requires that monopoly or monopsony play a role in determining wages or employment. Rather the divisive issue is whether or not wage adjustment clears the labor market, real wages increasing in response to excess demand and falling in response to excess supply, so that equilibrium is characterized by full employment or — generalizing slightly to allow for the disutility of labor, costs of job search, and the like — by a natural rate of unemployment.

Among neoclassical economists two groups must be distinguished, those who take the postulates of the theory seriously and those who do not. The first group seems incapable of imagining the price mechanism breaking down in the absence of monopoly or like causes of market failure. By contrast, Chicago-oriented positivists do not see any need to examine the assumptions at all; for them, "cleared market is simply a principle, not verifiable by direct observation, which may or may not be useful in constructing successful hypotheses about the behavior of [time] series [on employment and wage rates]" (Lucas and Sargent 1978, p. 64).

Within the orthodox camp, however, those who specialize in the study of labor economics — and are presumably closest to this problem — are among the most skeptical of the relevance of neoclassical theory. Indeed, as a special branch of the general field, labor economics finds its basic reason for existence in the inapplicability of conventional theory as a description of labor markets and related institutions.

In point of fact, it is extremely difficult to test the neoclassical view. Short-run unemployment does not disprove the theory, for the version of the theory emphasized in this book does not require that markets clear in the short run. Only the Lucas-Sargent sect finds merit in the assumption that markets clear at every moment of time: for more sober neoclassicals, like Robert Solow, "it is plain as the nose on my face that the labor market . . . [does] not clear in any meaningful sense" (1978, p. 208). (At the same time, Solow was moved to confess, "Deep down I really wish I could believe that Lucas and Sargent are right, because the one thing I know how to do well is equilibrium economics.")

What about the long run? It was observed in Chapter 16 that the absence of an important trend in the unemployment rate might seem at first blush to support the neoclassical position, but that further consideration leads to the realization that the nonneoclassical alternative no more predicts a trend in the unemployment rate than does the neoclassical theory: if in the long run capitalist growth is inadequate to absorb increases in the labor force, other modes of production will grow at the expense of capitalism, and massive overt unemployment will not occur. Similarly, shifts from other modes of production to capitalism will prevent the appearance of "overfull" employment if the equilibrium growth rate tends to exceed the internal capacities of capitalism for growth. In short, the labor force is not a parameter but a variable.

Neither would a trend in the unemployment rate be especially damaging to neoclassical theory. Neoclassical economists have appealed to changes in both institutions and tastes in explaining the dismal employment record of the 1970s and early 1980s: both the welfare state and a decreased taste for work are supposed to have nudged the "natural rate" of unemployment upward. So whether we attribute the higher average unemployment of the recent past to trend or to cycle, we can hardly use unemployment rates to distinguish neoclassical and nonneoclassical views of the labor market.

It might also appear that, as a disequilibrium phenomenon, the Phillips curve supports the neoclassical contention that wage competition adjusts demand and supply in the labor market. The problem with this argument is that the neoclassical foundations provided by Richard Lipsey (1960) are hardly the only possible foundations. Even within the neoclassical camp, Lucas (1972, 1975) has offered a very different explanation of the Phillips curve, one based on producers' misperceptions of price changes. (Lucas's hypothesis has consistency with period-by-period labor-market clearing to be said for it, but this — as Solow's reaction to Lucas-Sargent (1978) indicates — is a dubious virtue outside of Chicago.) And, as we shall see in the next chapter, a positive correlation between changes in output and employment and changes in prices and wages is compatible with a very different view of the world from that projected by either variety of neoclassical theory. At an empirical level, the difficulty in using the Phillips curve to test the neoclassical theory of the labor market is similar to the problem of using the estimating equation for the life-cycle or permanent-income hypothesis to test neoclassical saving theory: nonneoclassical theory is consistent with the same empirical regularities.

Taken together, the central assumptions of the neoclassical approach paint a picture of a world that is responsive to the desires and preferences of households, the "sovereign consumers" who determine not only the mix of output but also the distribution of income and relative prices; a world in which classes play no role; a world in which the Invisible Hand guarantees to every willing worker a place on the assembly line, if not a place in the sun; a world in which anyone can realize the American Dream of progressing through hard work and abstinence from worker to capitalist; a world in which conflict may exist but is limited to the distribution of goods and services, the division of the pie being a separable issue from its size (apart from differences in taste between apple pie and blueberry pie). Suffice it to say that this is a fine fairy tale, a good story by which to put children to bed — but not a very serious basis for the study of a capitalist economy.

Neo-Marxian Theory

It is not only neoclassical theory that is defective; there are in fact plenty of criticisms to go around. In the case of the neo-Marxian model, difficulties are presented by (1) the labor theory of value — once the simplifying assumption of a single good produced with fixed coefficients is abandoned; (2) the subsistence wage — once the context shifts to a multiple-good model; and (3) the relationship between class interests and individual actions.

The Labor Theory of Value

For the relatively narrow purposes of this book, the labor theory of value has been seen to be at best superfluous and at worst insufficient: superfluous in the one-good, fixed-coefficient corn model and insufficient in the context of either a high elasticity of substitution in production or a multiplicity of commodities. Neither is the labor theory of value necessary to a neo-Marxian model of growth, distribution, and prices: the approach can be carried through directly, starting from the subsistence wage.

Marx's own position is often thought to be inconsistent and even incorrect. He is said to make labor values equal to equilibrium prices in volume I of *Capital* (1867), recognizing only belatedly in volume III (1894; edited by Friedrich Engels from manuscript after Marx's death) that — in the absence of an equal organic composition of capital across industries — competitive prices will systematically diverge from labor values.

From the internal evidence the most likely explanation is that the inconsistency is apparent rather than real: Marx all along intended labor values to directly determine competitive prices only in a petty-commodity mode of production, in which the category of profit is altogether absent (an idea developed more fully by Alexander Chayanov 1925) and the rate of profit can consequently be taken to be zero. In a capitalist mode of production, a commodity's relative price will in general differ from its labor value according to the capital intensity of its production. In this reading, there is no inconsistency whatsoever between the two volumes of *Capital*: prices are assumed to be equal to values in volume I only to argue the negative point that the essence of capitalist profit does not lie in exchange — a point of view that is now common to virtually all economic theory, certainly to the three theories examined in this book, even if Marx's own terminology remains controversial. (This does not, however, prevent the middleman's unscrupulous exactions on both the producer and the consumer from remaining a perpetual target of populist rhetoric.)

Nevertheless, Marx held to the labor theory of value as a basis of price theory, believing that in every case labor values could be transformed into prices by a procedure that would maintain equality between aggregate surplus value and aggregate profits. As is well known, Marx's own algorithm, illustrated by an arithmetic example, was flawed, but these errors have long since been set right: by Ladislaus von Bortkiewicz some three-quarters of a century ago (1906–07, 1907), and more recently and fully by Francis Seton (1957).

The Bortkiewicz-Seton solution fails, however, to meet a fundamental defect of the labor theory: to transform labor values into prices, one must know the rate of profit, and the rate of profit cannot in general be determined from the rate of exploitation alone. Moreover, once the rate of profit is known, prices can be determined directly, without recourse to labor values. Hence labor values are superfluous to the determination of prices even when they are sufficient to do so.

Wherein then lies the continuing appeal of the labor theory of value? This question can only be answered in terms of a fundamental controversy over the nature of capitalist production: against the dominant view that emphasized parity between the contribution of land, capital, and labor, and *hence* parity between the claims of landlords, capitalists, and workers, Marx argued the centrality—under capitalism as under previous modes of production—of the worker. Thus viewed, the labor theory of value is an attempt to isolate the important substantive features of capitalist relations of *production*, features that are obfuscated by the appearance of parity in capitalist relations of *exchange*. It is not at all, or is only secondarily, a basis for describing capitalist equilibrium.

Amartya Sen offers an apt analogy: according to Sen, the labor theory of value describes capitalist production in the same way the statement "Michelangelo made this statue of David" characterizes the relationship of the great Italian sculptor to his work (Sen 1978, p. 177). Sen goes on to observe:

> The description is remarkably selective on facts: it says nothing about the tools and instruments used in making the statue; it is silent on the ownership of the huge block of marble that Michelangelo used; it eschews the patronage that Michelangelo received. The description is not based on the assumption that Michelangelo would have been able to make the statue even without these other things but in the role of Michelangelo in the making of the statue and the role of these other things. In going from all possible factual statements about a phenomenon to a pithy description, there is, in

a sense, a loss of information, but there is also, in another sense, a *gain* of focus. (p. 177)

The same point is made by a steelworker whose story is the preface to Studs Terkel's *Working* (1972):

Pyramids, Empire State Building — these things just don't happen. There's hard work behind it. I would like to see a building, say the Empire State, I would like to see on one side of it a foot-wide strip from top to bottom with the name of every bricklayer, the name of every electrician, with all the names. So when a guy walked by, he could take his son and say, "See, that's me on the forty-fifth floor. I put the steel beam in." Picasso can point to a painting. What can I point to? A writer can point to a book. Everybody should have something to point to. (p. xxxii)

But perhaps Bertolt Brecht's spare poem "A Worker Reads History" puts the point best:

Who built the seven gates of Thebes?
The books are filled with names of kings.
Was it kings who hauled the craggy blocks of stone?
And Babylon, so many times destroyed,
Who built the city up each time? In which of Lima's houses,
That city glittering with gold, lived those who built it?
In the evening when the Chinese wall was finished
Where did the masons go? Imperial Rome
Is full of arcs of triumph. Who reared them up? Over whom
Did the Caesars triumph? Byzantium lives in song,
Were all her dwellings palaces? And even in Atlantis of the legend
The night the sea rushed in,
The drowning men still bellowed for their slaves.

Young Alexander conquered India.
He alone?
Caesar beat the Gauls.
Was there not even a cook in his army?
Philip of Spain wept as his fleet
Was sunk and destroyed. Were there no other tears?
Frederick the Great triumphed in the Seven Years War. Who
Triumphed with him?

Each page a victory,
At whose expense the victory ball?
Every ten years a great man,
Who paid the piper?

So many particulars.
So many questions.[2]

In these terms, the labor theory of value is a theory of class relationships, a theory of the *source* of value rather than a theory of growth, distribution, and relative prices. According to this theory, the source of value continues under capitalism as under previous modes of production to lie in the working class. Indeed, for Marx and his followers, the difference between capitalism and other modes of production in this respect is only the transparency of the proposition in the context of precapitalist modes of production and its relative opaqueness in the context of capitalism.

The labor theory of value does not deny that the amount and quality of land, natural resources, and capital goods contribute to the productivity of labor and thus affect the value of goods as well as the value of labor. Its point is rather that neither *landlords* nor *capitalists* contribute to the production process and the generation of value. It is to be emphasized that this assertion about landlords and capitalists, sometimes put (misleadingly, I think) in terms of the "unproductiveness of capital," is anything but tautological—even though the argument on both sides of the labor theory of value frequently takes the assertion as an axiom rather than a theorem.

The landlord, especially the absentee landlord who may never set foot on his estates, has had a bad press over the years, and few indeed are the singers of his praises as an agent of production. The capitalist has generally fared better—at least with the rise to preeminence of the capitalist mode of production. His contribution as an organizer of production, captain of industry, and catalyst of latent energy has been hailed not only by defenders of capitalism, but by its critics. Listen to Marx and Engels in the *Communist Manifesto* (1848) attribute to capitalists

> wonders far surpassing Egyptian pyramids, Roman aqueducts, and Gothic cathedrals . . .
> The bourgeoisie, during its rule of scarce one hundred years has created more massive and more colossal productive forces than have all preceding generations together. Subjection of nature's forces to man, machinery, application of chemistry to industry and

2. From Bertolt Brecht, *Selected Poems*, trans. H. R. Hays (New York: Harcourt Brace Jovanovich, 1947), p. 109. Copyright 1947 by Bertolt Brecht and H. R. Hays; renewed 1975 by Stefan S. Brecht and H. R. Hays. Reprinted by permission of Harcourt Brace Jovanovich, Inc.

agriculture, steam-navigation, railways, electric telegraphs, clearing of whole continents for cultivation [*sic*], canalization of rivers,
whole populations conjured out of the ground—what earlier
century had even a presentiment that such productive forces
slumbered in the lap of social labor? (pp. 12, 14)

This has long been the dominant view, even if few orthodox economists
would (or could) match the fervor of Marx and Engels.

The role of the division of labor epitomizes and focuses the issue of
the role of the capitalist in the production process. Adam Smith beheld
the increasing specialization of workers under the watchful eye of the
capitalist or his agent and saw only efficiency, perceiving no differences
save the size of the market between the "technical" division of labor
within the capitalist workshop and the "social" division of labor outside, between the division of labor at the subcommodity level and the
division of labor at the commodity level.

Marx's position, as he developed it in his later years, was anomalous.
On the one hand he expressed a keen awareness of the very different
relations of production implied by the two forms of division of labor,
the social division of labor corresponding to the rough equality of a
society of petty proprietors, the technical division of labor to the gross
inequality of a society in which workers are subordinated to capitalists.
Volume I of *Capital* put the crucial point thus: "Division of labor within
the workshop implies the undisputed authority of the capitalist over
men, that are but parts of a mechanism that belongs to him" (1867, p.
356). But in the main, Marx follows Adam Smith in attributing the
progress of the technical division of labor to its greater efficiency. The
same reasons—the greater dexterity and skill of the workmen whose
productive life is confined to performing "one and the same simple
operation" and the avoidance of "gaps in the working day" in moving
from one task to another—are to be found in volume I of *Capital* (pp.
339–340) as in *The Wealth of Nations*. (Marx's third reason, the development of specialized tools appropriate to each task, differs only slightly
from Smith's emphasis on the impetus to technical innovation that is
supposedly fostered by specialization.) In short, for Marx, the technical
division of labor facilitates, indeed necessitates, capitalist control of the
production process, but this is simply an unavoidable by-product of its
efficiency, a serendipitous (from the capitalist's point of view) consequence of the dialectic progress of the forces of production. Marx thus
undercuts his own theory of the source of value.

There is, however, a contrary view. "What Do Bosses Do?" (Marglin
1974) takes the position that the capitalist's role in production is

essentially artificial and parasitic. In my view the capitalist *creates* the technical division of labor in order to make for himself an essential role in the production process. Standing between the producers of subcommodities and the market, which by definition exists for commodities but not for parts of commodities — for pins but not for pin-heads — the capitalist makes workers depend on him to integrate the separate components they make into a marketable commodity. In effect, the capitalist arrogates the commodity market to himself and offers the workers a labor market in its place. It is not the technical division of labor that gives rise to the capitalist as coordinator and organizer of production, but the capitalist as organizer that gives rise to the technical division of labor. The capitalist joins together what he himself has put asunder!

But if the capitalist's role is as artificial as all that, what prevents the workers from circumventing his control, from organizing production directly themselves? As Paul Samuelson has put the question (1971, p. 406), recalling Smith's just-so story of beaver and deer, "What hold does the capitalist have on the worker . . . who hunts when he pleases on superabundant acres?" The capitalist's "hold" is precisely the organizing ability he brings to production, the vector of personal traits and talents, ranging from extraordinary greed to extraordinary intelligence, that sets him off from his fellow men.

But if this is so, have I not in my turn undercut *my* case, in tacitly admitting that entrepreneurship is a scarce factor that a competitive economy not only will but ought optimally — if only in the limited sense of Pareto — to reward? Nothing could be further from the truth. The Pareto optimality of competitive pricing depends not only on the scarcity of goods and factors, but also on the assumption that each is a pure private good having the property that more for one person means less for another. By contrast, entrepreneurial ability, at least in the limited sense of the ability to organize production, is quintessentially a "public" or "collective" good, in the sense that if I share my knowledge of the production process and insights into organization with you, this does not make them less available to me. To be sure, the widespread sharing of this information will reduce the rewards that I might claim for it, but that is altogether a different matter. It is in the nature of public goods that market allocation, even competitive market allocation, will in general lead to overpricing and underproduction.

Observe that the distinction between public and private goods that I focus on here is only one of the two distinctions conventionally made in the vast literature on public goods. The feature that makes a good collective rather than private in terms of the present discussion is the possibility of simultaneous enjoyment of the good, not the possibility of preventing others' enjoyment. The first issue deals with the efficiency of market allocation, the second with its feasibility. Market allocation of public goods may indeed be feasible, but that does not make it efficient. Thus the feasibility of "privatizing" entrepreneurial ability does not, for present purposes, make it into a private good.

In short, the value of entrepreneurship is limited to a particular social context, the "war of all against all" of Hobbesian individualism, that allows individuals to appropriate to themselves returns to a public good which by nature or nurture they happen to possess. It is no more optimal than it would be to organize a national militia or local police on the basis of market appropriation of the returns to protecting the public.

Thus, as a description of the source of value under capitalism, the labor theory hinges on a distinction between the "productive labor" of the working class and the "unproductive labor" of the capitalist class and its agents. Once again, these terms are to be understood as statements *about* the social context of production rather than as statements *within* a particular context. The capitalist's organizing function may be essential under capitalism, but his labor is nevertheless unproductive if a different mode of production, in which this function were collectively discharged and the ability to discharge it collectively transmitted from generation to generation, would do away with the need for the capitalist to embody these functions.

A reasonably exact parallel is provided by the role of the feudal lord in medieval society. The seigneurial provision of police and military power was productive or unproductive not according to whether it was necessary within the feudal order (which it surely was), but according to whether the feudal order was itself necessary for provision of these functions.

This discussion would not be complete without some mention of the normative purpose of the labor theory of value. Unacknowledged, even denied by Marx, a clear purpose of the labor theory of value was—in my judgment at least—to provide a "scientific" basis for the moral condemnation of capitalism as an exploitative system.

The parallel with the role of utility maximization in neoclassical economics is too striking to go unremarked. The two arguments are equally superfluous for purposes of characterizing equilibrium, but essential to the value judgments implicit in the two views of capitalism. That the one aims at establishing the virtue of capitalism and the other its vice in no way detracts from the symmetry of the ideological role of a fundamental component of the theory.

This is not to say that utility theory and the labor theory of value are exclusively ideological. Both serve also to direct research on the determinants of growth, distribution, and relative prices. If one takes the neoclassical model seriously, one will look to the psychology of households. By contrast, if one follows the neo-Marxian lead, one will look to the relations of production and focus on the balance of class power. It will come as no surprise that I find the second a more useful starting point.

The Subsistence Wage

The main difficulty with the subsistence wage begins, as we have seen, with the importance of social, historical, and cultural elements in the classical idea of subsistence, starting with Adam Smith. Recognition of the cultural determinants of subsistence immediately opens up the possibility of substitution within the consumption bundle, and transforms the subsistence wage into a notional, or even an ideological, concept. Of course, to label the subsistence wage "ideological" hardly solves the problems that surround it. Indeed, this book does no more than to suggest a line of attack, and to offer the new name "conventional wage" as more appropriate to the meaning of the concept.

The consequences for the neo-Marxian analysis of reorienting the meaning of subsistence are profound. In addition to moving moral and ideological considerations from the periphery to the center of the analysis, a significant change in emphasis in itself, this reorientation implies an important reinterpretation of the relationship between subsistence and surplus.

In classical Marxism, subsistence is taken as a given and surplus derived as a residual—by subtracting subsistence and depreciation from gross output. In the words of Maurice Cornforth, surplus comes into being only "when the productivity of labor has risen so that producers can produce . . . above what they need for themselves" (1962, pp. 42–43). This line of reasoning has not been followed in the exposition of the neo-Marxian models in this book, for it really fits a biological notion of subsistence better than it does the present notion. In any case, in Chapter 3 the derivation of surplus as a residual was qualified by the observation that the input coefficients cannot be viewed as primarily technological, whatever one might assume about subsistence.

If the determination of subsistence is not a biological process, but a social process that hinges on the relative power of contending classes, then it becomes hard to defend the logical primacy customarily accorded subsistence. The point is that surplus is not a fixed quantity given by biotechnological conditions, over which exploiters and exploited struggle. It is rather a variable, the magnitude of which is determined simultaneously with the magnitude of subsistence and the magnitude of input coefficients, in a process of struggle between workers and capitalists that takes place against the backdrop of culture, history, and technology. In other words, surplus does not exist as a biotechnological datum for contending classes to struggle over; it must be created as a social category before it can be appropriated. It presupposes rather than causes classes and class conflict.

Neither is the creation of surplus a once-and-for-all process. The rate of productivity growth may itself be affected by the institutional structures that divide product into surplus and subsistence. And the conventional wage is subject to continual redefinition as productive capacity or the balance of class power changes. Moreover, new institutions are deliberately created — by capitalists for enlarging the investable surplus at the expense of subsistence, and by workers for enlarging subsistence at the expense of profits and investment. Examples of institutional arrangements designed to enlarge surplus are the practice of retaining corporate earnings for investment and the development of pension funds. Examples of institutions created to enlarge subsistence are at one level the trade union and the practice of collective bargaining and at another the various programs of the "welfare state," ranging from unemployment compensation and old-age pensions to subsidization of medical care and family allowances.

In short, what might appear to be a relatively minor updating of the meaning of subsistence turns out to entail significant changes in the Marxian approach. "Subsistence" and "surplus," like "capital" and "commodity," become terms that signify social relationships as well as quantities.

Class Interests and Individual Actions

If the neoclassical model sees social outcomes as the aggregate of individual actions, the neo-Marxian model sees individual actions as derivative of class interests. But the issue of how class interests inform the actions of individuals is hardly analyzed. Indeed, it is usually raised by critics of the neo-Marxian approach rather than by its partisans.

To some extent the issue is a false one. The Marxian definition of classes in terms of production relations is based precisely on the assumption that production relations define groups whose members have common interests that will more or less spontaneously induce common actions requiring only minimal coordination. But common interests are not a sufficient condition for common action. Jean-Jacques Rousseau perceived long before Karl Marx appeared on the scene that there are instances where the separate interests of individuals add up to the common interest of the group only when there is a basis for each to believe that the group will act in concert. Indeed the "general will" (the common interest) is distinguished from the "will of all" (the sum of the separate interests of the group members) in part by the assurance on the part of each member that "others will act as he does" (Rousseau 1762, bk. IV, chap. 1, p. 102).

The problem is characterized by game theorists as an exercise in plea bargaining known as the "prisoners' dilemma": its essence is that the conflict between the class of cops and the class of robbers will lead predictably to poorer bargains for the robbers when each negotiates in isolation from the others than when the robbers coordinate their stories. In isolation each robber rationally succumbs to the temptation to rat on his fellow thieves — thus clinching the prosecution's case — in return for a lighter sentence for himself. By contrast, if each robber could be assured of the fidelity of the others, he would rationally resist temptation, thus depriving the cops of crucial testimony and successfully undermining the prosecution's case.

An economic analogy arises in Joan Robinson's analysis (1962) of a prolonged boom that might threaten to exhaust the economy's labor resources. In isolation, each capitalist is tempted to increase the wages he offers in order to attract labor to his enterprise. But this works against his class interest in maintaining low wages as the basis of high profits; indeed, each capitalist would presumably forswear wage competition on condition that all others do so.

Neoclassical critics of the assumption of tacit if not formal agreement to a unified course of action are presumably led to their position because the central mechanism of competitive markets requires precisely the assumption that the separate interests of individuals prevail. If one rejects the neoclassical argument where essential class interests are at stake, the problem remains of articulating a mechanism whereby in a competitive regime the class interest of "capital" as a whole and "labor" as a whole can be made to prevail against the separate interests of each atom of capital and labor.

One line of argument is that the capitalist class will act through the state, "the executive [of which] is but a committee for managing the common affairs of the whole bourgeoisie" (Marx and Engels 1848), to provide an institutional structure in which the general capitalist interest can prevail over the separate interests of each capitalist. In the context of Robinsonian "overfull" employment, the appropriate institutional structure might be one that facilitates foreign immigration to shore up the domestic reserve army, as virtually every capitalist country (with the important exceptions of Japan and the United States) did in the post–World War II boom that lasted until the 1970s.

There are obvious limitations with this theory, however. In the first place, as many neo-Marxians have recognized, the state in capitalist society is a much more complex phenomenon than simply a committee of the bourgeoisie. It is in one sense a battleground of contending classes, and in another sense a separate class itself, relating to the process of production and appropriation in a unique way by virtue of its power to tax and its dominant position, if not monopoly, with respect to the means of violence.

In the second place, state coordination of capitalist class interests is only one possible way of bringing the individual agent's actions into line with the interests of the class. Children are socialized to class behavioral norms, and a network of informal institutions exists to reinforce that socialization in day-to-day life, as does the severity of the social penalties for disobeying these norms. (It is, of course, not only capitalists who rely on socialization to ensure the prevalence of class interests. English workers ostracize deviants by "sending them to Coventry," and there *is* honor even among thieves, as the punishments reserved for "stool pigeons" attest.) This presumably is the basis for Joan Robinson's reliance on the "fellow-feeling" of capitalists to resolve the contradictions of overfull employment in the neo-Keynesian model: more than the Napoleonic Wars have been won on the playing fields of Eton.[3] The same ideas might equally well be invoked on the other side of class conflict in the context of the neo-Marxian model.

In short, the harmonization of the actions of individual agents to class interests is a real problem for neo-Marxian theory, and one can hardly pretend that this brief discussion resolves the outstanding issues. But it does indicate an approach and serves, I hope, to put the problem in perspective: the conflict between the individual interest and the class interest is not the fatal flaw that opponents of class-based theories contend.

3. Ironically, one of the reasons for the failure of British capitalism in the twentieth century appears to have been that British capitalists never did quite succeed in "getting it together" to the extent that German, Japanese, or even American capitalists did. This lack of cohesion prevented them from acting on the fellow-feeling that might have served as the basis for coherent actions that would have advanced their class interests. William Lazonick (1983) documents this failure in the context of the cotton-textile industry.

One word remains to be said about the role of classes in the neo-Marxian model. It is frequently objected that the division of a heterogeneous population into "capitalists" and "workers" is amazingly naive. And so it is — interpreted as anything but a first approximation to a complex reality. And like other first approximations (such as the neoclassical characterization of production in terms of three factors — land, labor, and capital), the two-class model obstructs rather than facilitates understanding when pressed to do anything more than frame the analytic methodology. I suspect that divisions within both the working class and the capitalist class are as essential to an understanding of capitalism as is the opposition between these two broad classes. And class relationships that cut across modes of production may be equally important, for example the alliance that has been put together from time to time in the United States between capitalists and petty commodity producers with respect to governmental policy.

The tendency among Marxists to speak of internal class divisions in terms of "strata" rather than in terms of a finer class structure suggests that the oppositions between groups of workers and the oppositions between groups of capitalists are less fundamental than the antagonism between the two broad classes. This may be true, or it may be wishful thinking. It seems in any case premature to let terminology unconsciously determine the issue.

One final word. The difference between the neoclassical and neo-Marxian models ought not to obscure the many fundamental assumptions that they share. Chief among these assumptions are profit maximization to guarantee equal profit rates across industries in the absence of monopoly, and utility maximization to determine the demands for individual commodities. The two models also share a common defect: the absence of a role for the psychology of businessmen in determining the equilibrium configuration.

Neo-Keynesian Theory

The neo-Keynesian model responds to precisely this lack: investment demand plays a central role in the determination of neo-Keynesian equilibrium. Such a central role, in fact, that Nicholas Kaldor was once moved to dichotomize models of capitalism solely in terms of whether they are driven by saving or by investment (Kaldor 1966, p. 312). There is both irony and error in Kaldor's characterization. The irony lies in the fact that in Kaldor's own models, at least the models of the 1950s and early 1960s for which he is most well known, full employment replaces investment demand in determining equilibrium growth and distribution. The error lies in the fact that a saving function — albeit a saving function different from the neoclassical one — plays fully as important a role in determining equilibrium as does the investment function. Only in the short run in which investment demand can be considered to be exogenous can the neo-Keynesian model accurately be said to be investment-driven. In the long run the appropriate distinction between models is whether an investment-demand function plays an autonomous role, as it does in the neo-Keynesian approach, not whether investment drives the model.

Neither is the presence or absence of an investment function necessarily *the* crucial distinguishing feature of the models. Neoclassical and neo-Marxian models are both savings-driven, but are hardly equivalent for that reason. In the one the saving function determines the distribution of income, in the other the rate of growth. There are of course other differences between the neoclassical and neo-Marxian saving functions, but these differences are manifestly less important than the fact that one assumes full employment and the other a subsistence wage.

The neo-Keynesian model too is not without its problems. I have laid great stress on the importance to neo-Keynesian theory of the concentration of assets and therefore of collateral that allows capitalists privileged access to credit. Mention has also been made of a fundamental asymmetry in capital markets that allows capitalists access on the basis of prospective returns, while others must borrow on the basis of existing assets. But the absence of serious discussion of the influence of the availability and cost of credit on investment demand must be counted a shortcoming of the analysis. An even more serious shortcoming is the neo-Keynesian treatment of wages.

The Money Wage

The problem begins with the assumption that the wage is fixed in money terms. The Keynesian pedigree of this assumption is indisputable, but the context to which the neo-Keynesians apply the assumption is quite different from the short-period context of Keynes's own theoretical apparatus. In the short run, fluctuations in investment demand are reflected in fluctuations in output; the rate of capacity utilization changes in accordance with aggregate demand. The distributional conflict between capitalists and workers is, as it were, a non-zero-sum game. Moreover, in the very short period, money illusion is at least a plausible argument, if hardly compelling even there. But in the long run, the period with which neo-Keynesian analysis concerns itself, there is no excess capacity to accommodate investment demand. Distribution must bear the brunt of adjusting aggregate demand to supply. In contrast with the short period, the long-run conflict is a zero-sum game—at least in the absence of technological substitution or technological change.

But how, in the long-period context, do the neo-Keynesians explain the independence of money wages and prices? Surely, money illusion won't do. Indeed, the only consistent rationale for this assumption appears to be the powerlessness of the working class to do anything about real wages no matter what the level.

Needless to say, this assumption is implicit rather than explicit in the neo-Keynesian model. The rhetoric is, after all, Marxian: capitalists' and workers' interests are firmly opposed to one another. But in the neo-Keynesian model, the essential Marxian notion of class *conflict* gives way to a kind of functionalism. Class interests may be opposed, but the class struggle is long since over. Victorious, the capitalist class works its will on a supine working class. Whatever the money wage might be, capitalists are free to utilize the central bank and the banking system to manipulate money, credit, and prices to their own ends while workers look on helplessly. It is as much the assumption of powerlessness as the assumption that capitalists save and workers consume that gives effect to the neo-Keynesian aphorism "workers spend what they get while capitalists get what they spend."

Unfortunately for the neo-Keynesian theory, the facts do not support the notion that the class struggle is long since over. Casual empiricism and econometric analysis reinforce each other in support of the view that if formally the wage *bargain* is executed in money terms (and even that is true less and less frequently as wages become indexed to the cost of living), wage *bargaining* is conducted in real terms. Recent behavior of the price level plays a powerful role in virtually every statistical explanation of how the wage rate is determined, a role hardly consistent with a supine working class.

Regression analyses formulated in terms of both the neoclassical and the neo-Marxian models accord with this general view. In both, the recent behavior of the price level is significant in explaining the behavior of wage rates over the post–World War II period in the United States. In these regressions, the dependent variable is the quarterly rate of change of money wages $\Delta(\ln W)$. In the neoclassical version the principal independent variables are the rates of change of output per man-hour $\Delta[\ln (X/L)]$ and the consumer price index $\Delta(\ln P)$ over the previous three years; $\Delta[\ln (X/L)]_{-1}$ and $\Delta(\ln P)_{-1}$ represent quarterly rates of change between quarter -5 and quarter -1, and subscripts -2

TOWARD AN UNDERSTANDING OF CAPITALISM

and -3 are to be understood analogously. Other variables are RUS, the deviation in the unemployment rate in the previous quarter from the average unemployment rate; and two dummy variables, DUM1 and DUM2, introduced to take account of Richard Nixon's brief flirtation with a wage-price freeze. The neoclassical results estimated by ordinary least squares are

$$\Delta(\ln W) = \underset{(0.10)}{0.39} \, \Delta[\ln (X/L)]_{-1} + \underset{(0.09)}{0.35} \, \Delta[\ln (X/L)]_{-2}$$

$$+ \underset{(0.09)}{0.28} \, \Delta[\ln (X/L)]_{-3} + \underset{(0.11)}{0.75} \, \Delta(\ln P)_{-1} + \underset{(0.12)}{0.014} \, \Delta(\ln P)_{-2}$$

$$+ \underset{(0.08)}{0.22} \, \Delta(\ln P)_{-3} - \underset{(0.00039)}{0.00064} \, RUS - \underset{(0.0045)}{0.0092} \, DUM1$$

$$+ \underset{(0.0045)}{0.0135} \, DUM2.$$

$$DW = 1.66 \qquad R^2 = 0.51 \qquad \text{INTERVAL} = 1952:1-1979:4$$

$$DUM1 = \begin{cases} 1, & 1971:4 \\ 0, & \text{otherwise} \end{cases}$$

$$DUM2 = \begin{cases} 1, & 1972:1 \\ 0, & \text{otherwise} \end{cases}$$

Observe first that the coefficients of the productivity-change variables sum approximately to unity, as do the coefficients of the price-change variables. This is hardly surprising in a neoclassical model, given that the wage share has not changed markedly since the end of World War II. In particular, it is noteworthy that the coefficients of the price-change variables over the preceding three years add up to 0.98+, a result duplicated in experiments with alternative lag structures. Such high coefficients support the view that changes in the price level strongly and quickly influence money wages.

I hardly wish to insist on this particular form of the wage equation. In particular, the coefficients of the price-change variables are sensitive to the measurement of inflation.[4] But the general idea — the importance

4. For instance, regressions using the implicit deflator for consumption expenditure give somewhat higher coefficients for the inflation rates $\Delta(\ln P)_{-1}$, $\Delta(\ln P)_{-2}$, $\Delta(\ln P)_{-3}$. Corresponding to the coefficients 0.75, 0.014, and 0.22 reported in the text are coefficients 0.86, 0.063, and 0.22. These results are not surprising since the consumption-expenditure deflator results in a substantially lower rate of inflation than does the consumer price index. The CPI seems, however, more appropriate for present purposes since it, rather than the consumption deflator, figures into wage bargaining.

of recent price-level changes in explaining wage behavior—is consistent with regression results not only from alternative neoclassical formulations, but with results from an equation based on the neo-Marxian model as well.

In the exposition of the neo-Marxian model in Chapter 3, wages were assumed to be driven by the difference between the current real wage and the conventional wage. Here we modify that assumption to reflect technological change: both the current wage and the conventional wage are expressed in ratio form, with output as the denominator. Moreover, the conventional wage is itself taken as a constant share of output, whose magnitude μ is estimated in the regression equation. With the addition of price-change terms, the model becomes

$$\frac{\Delta W}{W_{-1}} = -\theta \left[\left(\frac{W/P}{X/L} \right)_{-1} - \mu \right] + \sum \gamma_t \left(\frac{\Delta P}{P_{-1}} \right)_{-t},$$

where $\Delta W/W_{-1} \simeq \Delta(\ln W)$ is the one-quarter rate of change in hourly compensation; $[(W/P)/(X/L)]_{-1}$ is the actual wage share in quarter -1; and $(\Delta P/P_{-1})_{-t} \simeq \Delta(\ln P)_{-t}$ is the average rate of change in the CPI between quarter $-4t-1$ and quarter $-4(t-1)-1$, that is, between quarters -5 and -1 for $t = 1$, between quarters -9 and -5 for $t = 2$, and between quarters -13 and -9 for $t = 3$. The corresponding regression equation, estimated by ordinary least squares, is

$$\Delta(\ln W) = \underset{(0.0200)}{0.0495} - \underset{(0.0347)}{0.0704} \left(\frac{W/P}{X/L} \right)_{-1} + \underset{(0.08)}{0.61} \, \Delta(\ln P)_{-1}$$

$$- \underset{(0.10)}{0.15} \, \Delta(\ln P)_{-2} + \underset{(0.07)}{0.10} \, \Delta(\ln P)_{-3}$$

$$- \underset{(0.004)}{0.010} \, DUM1 + \underset{(0.004)}{0.013} \, DUM2.$$

$$DW = 1.65 \qquad R^2 = 0.56 \qquad INTERVAL = 1952{:}1 - 1979{:}4$$

We have $\hat{\theta} = 0.0704$ and $\hat{\theta}\hat{\mu} = 0.0495$, so $\hat{\mu} = 0.703$. Thus, on a steady-growth path on which $\Delta(\ln P)_{-1} = \Delta(\ln P)_{-2} = \Delta(\ln P)_{-3}$,

$$\frac{\Delta W}{W_{-1}} = -0.07 \left[\left(\frac{W/P}{X/L} \right)_{-1} - 0.70 \right] + 0.56 \frac{\Delta P}{P_{-1}}.$$

The neo-Marxian specification suggests a smaller coefficient on the price-change variable but a similar lag structure: the effect of inflation is concentrated in the first year, with price changes lagged more than one year being small in magnitude and statistically insignificant. The main point is that price changes still play a significant role — economically as well as statistically — in the explanation of wage behavior.

To be sure, the neo-Keynesian analysis can be modified to incorporate working-class resistance to monetary erosion of real wages. Joan Robinson's "inflation barrier" is a formalization of precisely this idea. The difficulty is that the model becomes overdetermined: one cannot insist on an independent investment-demand function, an independent saving function, and the inflation barrier — and still formulate growth and distribution in terms of a conventional equilibrium system. Neither Robinson nor any other of her generation of neo-Keynesians resolved this problem, and the inflation barrier thus has had all the earmarks of an afterthought rather than a core element of the analysis. Robinson's own solution was implicitly to throw out the specifically Keynesian element of the model, the investment-demand function. The "neo-Keynesian" model thus becomes Marxian in the determination of the real elements of equilibrium (real wages, profits, and growth) and Keynesian in its monetary elements (prices and money wages).

In the work of the subsequent generation of neo-Keynesians, the focus has shifted toward a shorter period in which fluctuations are central to the analysis. But the problem of working-class resistance to erosion of the real wage exists in the short period too, especially in an economy without huge resources of excess capacity, so it is instructive to see how the problem has been attacked. In the so-called New Cambridge models developed by the Cambridge (England) Economic Policy Group, the attempts of workers to protect themselves from inflation are only marginally successful. An inflation barrier takes the form of an equation described in one account of the model as reflecting "compensation for past price and tax changes and . . . *ex ante* changes in the disposable real wage" (Cripps and Godley 1976, p. 336) and described in another as saying that "all workers obtain settlements at the beginning of each year which provide (at the moment of settlement) full compensation for [changes] in prices and the tax rate" (Fetherston and Godley 1978, p. 44). But markup pricing determines the actual profit rate and hence, given the capital:output ratio, the *real* wage. Workers' efforts to protect themselves are largely frustrated, the inflation "barrier" becoming a Maginot Line that contributes mightily to determining the rate of inflation, but little to defending real wages.

It should be noted that demand plays a role in the New Cambridge model, but only with respect to inventories, government expenditures, and exports; fixed-investment demand is excluded on the grounds that over the private sector as a whole it is financed by income in essentially the same way as consumption: to posit a separate investment demand is to take "insufficient account of the budget constraint of the private sector as a whole" (Fetherston and Godley 1978, p. 34).

This is hardly the place to assess this model in its entirety. Suffice it to say that in the typology of this book, the absence of a role for investment demand in the determination of the profit rate makes the model less rather than more neo-Keynesian. Indeed, except for the absence of an explicit role for class power in the determination of markups, the New Cambridge model appears to be much more neo-Marxian in spirit than neo-Keynesian.[5]

The Hegemony of Neoclassical Theory

One fact that nothing in this book accounts for is the hegemony of neoclassical theory, particularly in the Anglo-American world. In some respects the hegemony is exaggerated both by the orthodox and the heretic. A mainstream economist like Dale Jorgenson labels his preferred theory of investment "neoclassical" simply because it employs a marginal-productivity relationship to determine the optimal capital stock (Jorgenson and Siebert 1968). Jorgenson's theory is in fact neither neoclassical nor a complete theory of investment: Jorgenson is content to show that the cost of capital plays a role in the determination of investment demand; he does not even attempt to explain the differences among firms in their responsiveness to the cost of capital or to other variables. To be fair, however, heretics too incline to label all marginal-productivity relationships as neoclassical, without making the crucial distinction of whether or not those relationships are assumed inside the context of full employment.

The analytic framework of utility maximization is generally regarded as "neoclassical." And so it is, when applied to intertemporal decisions. But in the multiple-good context we have utilized the same framework in the neo-Marxian and neo-Keynesian models. The plain fact is that, on the one hand, these models simply lack independent microeconomic theories of demand, and on the other hand, utility maximization is up to a point compatible with Marxian and Keynesian approaches. Provided its role is limited to determining the composition

5. Our long-run focus should not obscure the Keynesian pedigree of the New Cambridge models in the short-run policy framework for which these models were elaborated. These models are firmly Keynesian in their focus on the determination of aggregate output and employment as central questions, as well as in their emphasis on aggregate demand as a determinant of both.

of output, utility maximization need in no sense be the exclusive property of the neoclassical school, whatever its historical origins.

So one reason for the hegemony of neoclassical theory is the failure to isolate specifically neoclassical assumptions from the broader theoretical structure under which these assumptions are subsumed (dare I say "hidden"?) in the typical economics curriculum. But most will agree that this is only part of the story. The specifically neoclassical assumptions also dominate in the competition among alternative approaches to the study of capitalism.

One argument for the superiority of the neoclassical approach is its use in large-scale forecasting models: if there were a better theoretical basis, then the forecasters, for whom the proof of the pudding must surely lie in the eating rather than in the recipe, would eagerly embrace it. There is no question that model builders as a whole pay lip service to neoclassical theory. This is not surprising: economics, like other scholarly pursuits, affords much greater status to theory than to empirical application, and the model builders would jeopardize their intellectual standing altogether were they to present themselves as heretics or agnostics rather than as defenders of the faith.

But in reality, the connection of large-scale forecasting models to the distinctively neoclassical features of economic theory is quite tenuous. None, to the best of my knowledge, assumes full employment. Neither does any of the prominent forecasting models posit an inherent tendency to full employment, or even a tendency to a natural rate of unemployment that is independent of initial conditions. And while household saving behavior is invariably consistent with one version or another of the permanent-income or life-cycle hypothesis, the consistency is at the level of estimating equations which were shown in the previous chapter to be compatible as well with nonneoclassical theories.

In general it is fair to say that the hegemony of neoclassical theory does not stand on its superiority in practical application. The logic of constrained maximization has been a useful tool with a variety of applications, but this logic is *not* equivalent to economic theory, certainly not to neoclassical theory.

Neither does the hegemony of neoclassical theory rest on its superiority in confrontation with other theories at the level of empirical tests designed explicitly to distinguish the relative power of alternative theories. As the last chapter showed, it is extremely difficult to test alternative theories against one another, and in fact most of the "testing" that goes on is directed toward choosing among variations on a single theme. Testing in economics is akin to choosing among alternative specifications of epicycles in an earth-centered model of the solar system. The sun-centered model is not even considered, much less tested.

What, then, does account for the preeminence of neoclassical theory?

Theory and Ideology

The answer, I think, is ideology. The appeal of neoclassical theory lies not in its superior explanatory or predictive capacity, but in the aid and comfort, nay, the sanctification, it gives to the pursuit of self-interest as a principle for organizing interpersonal relationships. In the neoclassical view of a well-ordered society, economic outcomes are the consequences of the interactions of large numbers of households each pursuing its own conception of the Good while allowing others to pursue their notions in equal liberty. And, wonderfully, anarchy does not produce chaos. Quite the contrary: the Invisible Hand not only works, it works well.

Roughly speaking, the existence of competitive equilibrium and its Pareto optimality, the twin towers of the neoclassical church, guarantee that the actions of the various households that make up the economy are not only mutually consistent but also harmonious. A competitive equilibrium provides the largest pie that the society's resources are capable of producing. We have already observed that the Pareto optimality theorem fails in the context of an open-ended model, and to this objection we might add the standard ones of externalities, incomplete information, and incomplete markets, as well as a more fundamental criticism of the notion of society as a collection of Robinson Crusoes whose interaction is limited to the exchange of goods and services. But even if we waive all these objections, the significance of Pareto optimality is generally recognized to be quite limited; it takes no account of the distribution of the economic pie, not to mention the distribution of power or the relationship of economic to political power, or the implications of institutionalized competition in the economic sphere for the quality of human interaction in noneconomic matters.

Nevertheless, neoclassical theory serves an important ideological role. Even though few neoclassical economists outside of Chicago would deny the importance of these issues, neoclassical theory necessarily leads one to separate even the most economic of them, the distributional questions, from questions of the organization of production. Thus neoclassical theory has the effect of removing capitalism as an issue and replacing it by an issue that reduces to "my blood or thy blood," an issue in which the moral claims of the disputants are decidedly difficult to disentangle.

The specificity of the capitalist mode of production is, as it were, too trivial a detail for neoclassical theory to bother with. Indeed, orthodox theorists from Knut Wicksell ("We may assume either that the land-owner will hire laborers for a wage . . . or that the laborers will hire the land for a rent" [1901, p. 109]) to Paul Samuelson ("Remember that in a competitive market it really doesn't matter who hires whom; so have labor hire 'capital' " [1957, p. 894]) have seen great virtue in its generality. But in abdicating from the analysis of the capitalist mode of production in a world in which capitalism is, to say the least, controversial, neoclassical theory can hardly be read other than as a defense of capitalism. And the commitment of intellectual resources to the development of a theory is hardly neutral ideologically — when that theory is not only increasingly esoteric, uncritical, and irrelevant but also supports the status quo by ensuring that the embarrassing questions do not get asked.

It is of course not only neoclassical economics that has an ideological ax to grind. I have already remarked on the ideological role of the labor theory of value in the Marxian world view. To that observation I would add only that part of the attraction of the neo-Marxian approach is precisely this ideological content. It stands in sharp contrast to neoclassical theory in emphasizing the inequity inherent in capitalism as a mode of production which inevitably exploits the many to the benefit of the few.

The ideology of neo-Keynesian theory is more difficult to pinpoint. The coexistence of conservative and radical neo-Keynesians under the same tent is evidence of a breadth of appeal that suggests an amorphous if not inarticulate ideology. Probably the essence of the neo-Keynesian position is reformist. Since the class struggle is effectively over, revolution is beside the point, and reform becomes the order of the day.

The role afforded capitalists' fellow-feeling in resolving the problem of excess demand perhaps provides a clue to the larger neo-Keynesian ideology: if capitalists can be counted on to submerge their individual interests to the larger class interest in this respect, then, surely, reforms necessary for the survival of capitalism as a mode of production can be agreed on and enforced upon the capitalist class as a whole. No class struggle intrudes upon the neo-Keynesian world, as it does upon the neo-Marxian, to prevent reform from permanently solving the problems of capitalism. In the Keynesian world view, for instance, government spending is a solution to the problem of insufficient private investment demand. In the Marxian world view, by contrast, solving the problem of insufficient demand by means of government spending puts downward pressures on profits and growth, and upward pressure on prices; the solution to one problem creates or exacerbates another. (In the neoclassical view, the problem of insufficient demand is simply wished away!)

Thus the connection between neoclassical, neo-Keynesian, and neo-Marxian models of the economy with conservative, liberal, and radical political stances turns out to be more reasonable than one might at first imagine. Not because the models compel particular political views, but because the ambiguities of the reality these models are supposed to describe leave a wide latitude for ideology in the choice of models.

The infusion of ideological preconceptions is hardly unique to economic theory. In the sixteenth and seventeenth centuries, astronomy divided along ideological lines in much the same way that economics does today. The opposition between Ptolemaic and Copernican theories was as much an opposition of views of the relationship of the mundane to the divine as an opposition of views on the motion of the planets (Kuhn 1957). If today the role of ideology in the natural sciences is muted, it is not because these areas of inquiry are free of ideology. It is rather because there is a single ideology that unites men and women of science, at least in astronomy, physics, and the nonbehavioral sciences generally. By contrast, the credence currently given to the more extreme claims of sociobiology (for instance, Wilson 1975, 1978) is essentially ideological. Our abysmal ignorance of the relative importance of nature and nurture with respect to such issues as competitiveness, patriarchy, and the like maintains a vacuum into which sociobiology has rushed. Here the situation is more similar to economics, where ignorance about capital accumulation and labor markets makes it possible for ideological considerations to tilt the scales in favor of neoclassical theory.

It is not any part of my argument that theorists, be they economists, sociobiologists, or physicists, are necessarily conscious ideologues. Relatively few neoclassical economists would describe themselves as primarily ideologues or even defenders of capitalism; the leaders of the profession, or most of them in any case, are as ready to point out the limitations of competitive equilibrium as they are to point out its virtues. But, consciously or not, ideology conditions neoclassical theory —as it does neo-Marxian or neo-Keynesian theory.

It is to be expected that everyone denies the ideological component of his particular theory while affirming the foregoing, or its equivalent, for opposing theories. Indeed, it could hardly be otherwise. Evidently, a theory must be seen as at least a possible path to truth. And in general truth and ideology are seen as polar opposites, the one inconsistent with the other. Thus the denial of an ideological component becomes a necessary condition for the development of a theory.

In my judgment the opposition of truth and ideology is a methodological error. What is ideology, after all, but the unproved (though not necessarily unprovable) assumptions, beliefs, and values that must — at our current state of knowledge at any rate — underlie *any* intellectual inquiry, or for that matter, any form of contemplation or action? Ideology need not be immutable (though some ideologies are more robust to factual evidence than others). On the contrary, ideology, like its theoretical projections, should be ultimately testable. And one ideology may turn out to be more in accord with observation than another. It is in the very nature of ideology, however, that it be presently beyond the grasp of verification, and the subject therefore of the sharp disagreement that is born of the union of interest and ignorance. Only this seems certain: the ideological component of theory can be transcended not by stubborn denial but by frank recognition.

Appendix: Further Observations on Regression Data and Results

The data for all regressions in this chapter come from the Bureau of Labor Statistics, Department of Labor. The wage variable W is measured by the seasonally adjusted index of compensation per hour for the non-farm business sector. Output per man-hour X/L is measured by the seasonally adjusted index of non-farm business output per hour of all persons. The price level P is measured by the (revised) seasonally adjusted index of consumer prices (all items). The unemployment variable, $RUS = RU_{-1} - \overline{RU}$, is the difference between the previous quarter's unemployment rate for all persons, RU_{-1}, and the average unemployment rate, $\overline{RU}$, over the period 1952–1979.

The Neoclassical Equation

Several tests were run to examine the conformity of the reported results to the assumptions of least-squares estimation. Tests of the significance of the lagged error term bore out the Durbin-Watson statistic in indicating the absence of autocorrelation of errors. In any case, introduction of the lagged error term hardly changed the regression coefficients.

The stability of the coefficients of the inflation terms was tested by a regression that included three semi-dummy terms, $\Delta(\ln P)_{-1} * DUM3$, $\Delta(\ln P)_{-2} * DUM3$, and $\Delta(\ln P)_{-3} * DUM3$, with $DUM3$ defined by

$$DUM3 = \begin{cases} 1, & 1972:3-1979:4 \\ 0, & 1952:1-1972:2 \end{cases}$$

This test did not indicate that inflation affected wage change differently after the Nixon wage-price freeze than before: both the individual t-statistics and the overall F-statistic on the three terms taken together were insignificant.

Heteroskedasticity tests along lines proposed by Goldfeld and Quandt (1965), Glejser (1969), and Breusch and Pagan (1979) were carried out as well. Only the Lagrange multiplier test (due to Breusch and Pagan) suggested heteroskedasticity of error terms.

A regression with a constant term had the effect of substantially reducing the coefficients on the productivity variables, making them statistically insignificant. At the same time, the coefficients on the inflation variables were also reduced. The results of this regression are

$$\Delta(\ln W) = \underset{(0.0017)}{0.0063} + \underset{(0.12)}{0.12} \, \Delta[\ln (X/L)]_{-1} + \underset{(0.11)}{0.11} \, \Delta[\ln (X/L)]_{-2}$$

$$+ \underset{(0.11)}{0.047} \, \Delta[\ln (X/L)]_{-3} + \underset{(0.11)}{0.63} \, \Delta(\ln P)_{-1}$$

$$- \underset{(0.11)}{0.021} \, \Delta(\ln P)_{-2} + \underset{(0.08)}{0.15} \, \Delta(\ln P)_{-3}$$

$$- \underset{(0.00037)}{0.00066} \, RUS - \underset{(0.0043)}{0.010} \, DUM1 + \underset{(0.0043)}{0.012} \, DUM2.$$

$$DW = 1.76 \qquad R^2 = 0.57 \qquad \text{INTERVAL} = 1952:1-1979:4$$

The unemployment variable, although not the focus of this discussion, deserves comment. First, the t-statistic of RUS hardly supports the idea of a Phillips curve. More important, the influence of unemployment on the change in wages is relatively small. According to the results reported in the main body of this chapter, each *four* percentage points of unemployment reduce the growth in money wages by 0.0025 per quarter, or one percent per year.

The dummy variables $DUM1$ and $DUM2$ are also of some interest. Taken together, their coefficients support the idea that Nixon's ninety-day wage-price freeze at the end of 1971 was successful in holding down wages as long as it lasted, but that the loss was made up as soon as the freeze was lifted.

The Neo-Marxian Equation

Tests for autocorrelation and heteroskedasticity of error terms, as well as for stability of the inflation coefficients, were carried out for the neo-Marxian equation along the same lines as for the neoclassical equation. In this case, neither heteroskedasticity nor autocorrelation appeared to be a problem, and once again regression coefficients were hardly changed by the introduction of the lagged error term; neither did the stability test suggest that inflation affected wage changes differently in the post-freeze era than before.

It should be noted that the estimate $\hat{\mu} = 0.70$ is not directly an estimate of a conventional wage share defined as a share of the product — that is, as the ratio of the wage bill to the gross value of product. There are two reasons for this. First, the variable $(W/P)/(X/L)$ is constructed from indices rather than dollar values, so the scaling is arbitrary. Second, the price level is measured by the CPI rather than the GNP or nonfarm-business deflator, so the "wage share" is essentially the product-wage share multiplied by the ratio of the nonfarm-business deflator (P_{NFB}) to the CPI (P_{CPI}). In effect, $(W/P)/(X/L) = (P_{NFB}/P_{CPI})$ $(W/P_{NFB})/(X/L)$. The mean of the wage-share series defined by $(W/P)/(X/L)$ is approximately 0.57 and the mean of the product-wage share series for nonfinancial corporations is approximately 0.65; so the conventional product-wage share corresponding to $\hat{\mu} = 0.70$ is approximately 0.80. Since, over the period 1952–1979, the product-wage share actually fluctuated between 0.63 and 0.68, the gap between the conventional share and the actual share meant a continual pressure on wages that could be contained only so long as labor productivity was growing rapidly — as in the 1950s and 1960s but not in the 1970s. When output per worker stopped growing rapidly enough to permit simultaneous growth in the real wage rate and constancy of the wage share, this pressure either had to change factor shares or become inflationary. In the 1970s it did both: the U.S. economy experienced both a profit squeeze and a sharp acceleration of inflation, in part at least for this reason.

This neo-Marxian view of the inflation process is intuitively appealing, but it cannot be said to rely on strong statistical support. Most of the explanatory power of the neo-Marxian equation, like that of the neoclassical equation, lies in the inflation-rate variable. Moreover, although the coefficients of the specifically neo-Marxian terms, as well as their standard errors, are reasonably robust to the measurement of the price level, they are sensitive to the interval over which the regression is run.

Finally, it is worth reporting the results of an experiment designed to test for the existence of a Phillips curve. Adding the variable RUS to the neo-Marxian equation reduces the t-statistic on the coefficient of $(W/P)/(X/L)$ sharply but, as in the neoclassical case, the unemployment variable is neither statistically nor economically significant.

20 A Synthesis of Marx and Keynes

After a chapter devoted principally to nay-saying and fault-finding, it is fair to ask what I would put in the place of the theories I have criticized. Needless to say, my own analysis affords relatively little room for neoclassical theory; I should never have written this book were I still of that persuasion.

But this is again negative; there remain two theories — neo-Marxian and neo-Keynesian — from which to choose. In my judgment, each of these theories offers an important insight into the workings of a capitalist economy: real-wage struggle and investment demand both play important roles, along with saving behavior, in determining growth, distribution, and relative prices.

To be sure, the Keynesian analysis might profit by taking a page from the Marxian book and situating investor optimism or pessimism at least partly in the class relations of capitalists and workers, rather than making animal spirits a primitive of the system. One way of formalizing the relationship of animal spirits to class relations would be to consider investment demand a function of an entire (subjective) probability distribution of outcomes; to represent investment demand as a function of a single parameter, the expected rate of profit, is to project this function onto the $r \times g$ plane, with r representing the first moment of the probability distribution. The class power of capitalists, measured by the degree to which they are able to lay the risk associated with investment onto workers, would be hidden from view in the higher moments — particularly the variance — of the distribution. Thus capitalist power translates into a relatively tight distribution of outcomes around the mean, and for risk-averse capitalists the tighter the distribution, the greater is investment demand.

As an illustration, consider the effect of the Japanese bonus system on the animal spirits of Japanese capitalists. A consequence of the bonus system is to make real wages and profits move together in response to stochastic shocks to output, which in turn means that although Japanese capitalists may not be able to appropriate extraordinary profits to the same extent that (say) British capitalists can, neither need they fear that failure will be compounded by the intransigence of workers unwilling to absorb part of the blow. Thus, even if Japanese capitalists and British capitalists were to have the same underlying investment-demand function — in terms of a complete description of the probability distribution of outcomes — the projections of their respective investment demand onto the $r \times g$ plane would differ because of differences in probabilities based on the differing realities of class relationships in the two countries. In particular, suppose both groups to be equally risk-averse. Then Japanese investment demand will exceed British investment demand if both have access to the same set of projects. In this view, Japanese animal spirits are more expansive than British not simply because of differences in the way Japanese and British capitalists see the world, but also because the worlds they see are different.

Equilibrium in an Overdetermined Model

Even if this line of thought is followed, however, it does not suffice to reconcile the neo-Keynesian with the neo-Marxian world. Class power is at best part of the story of investment demand, and investment demand plays a role independent of the conventional wage in $r \times g$ space. Thus, as Figure 20.1 illustrates, there are too many equations for

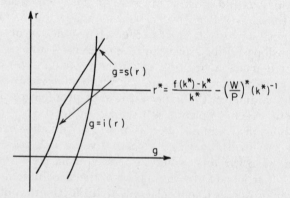

$$g = s(r)$$

$$r^* = \frac{f(k^*) - k^*}{k^*} - \left(\frac{W}{P}\right)^* (k^*)^{-1}$$

$$g = i(r)$$

Figure 20.1 Conventional wages and investment demand overdetermine the system

the number of unknowns. The model is overdetermined, and it would take the most fortuitous of coincidences to make the saving function and the investment function intersect at exactly the rate of profit determined by the conventional wage.

Joan Robinson's inflation barrier has been seen to be an unsatisfactory way out of the dilemma because it in effect transforms the neo-Keynesian model into a neo-Marxian one, suppressing the role of investment demand by making resistance to erosion of a conventional wage an absolute constraint upon accumulation. But to retain investment demand—along with the saving function and the conventional wage—as a determinant of equilibrium requires a drastic revision of the whole approach to growth and distribution.

This revision begins with the very meaning of equilibrium: saving, investment, and the conventional wage can all enter simultaneously into the determination of the steady-growth configuration only if we are prepared to reject the most basic of axioms, one that has united economists of persuasions dramatically different in almost every other respect. I measure my words, for no less than the sanctity of supply = demand as a characterization of equilibrium is at issue.

It will be objected that I exaggerate the unity of the economics profession in this regard, and consequently the novelty of my own position. Certainly the icon of supply = demand has already been dealt a severe blow by rationing theorists like Robert Barro and Herschel Grossman (1976) and Edmond Malinvaud (1977, 1980). But the focus of rationing theory is very different. In the Barro-Grossman model, demand and supply can diverge in the short run, but not in the long. The same is true for Malinvaud, who explicitly limits his analysis to "medium-term studies, those concerning spontaneous evolution during a small number of successive years" (1980, p. 58).[1] By contrast, in the long run on which this book focuses, the supply = demand characterization of equilibrium has not been seriously challenged.

There is another important difference between the tack taken by rationing theory and the course followed here. The rationing-theory alternative to supply = demand ("market clearing" or "Walrasian" equilibrium in rationing terminology) is a set of "regimes"; which one holds sway depends upon which of the model's constraints are binding. In this respect the characterization of equilibrium is reminiscent of Joan Robinson's typology of metallic ages (1962) or Nicholas Kaldor's

---

1. Nevertheless, Malinvaud's simulations (1980, chap. 4) cover a period of fifteen or more years, which approaches the long run as it is conceived in this book, if not the asymptotic long run of neoclassical theory.

succession of a "Marxian" regime by a "Keynesian" one (1957).[2] This too contrasts sharply with the present synthesis: here the various elements of the model — saving, investment, and the conventional wage — enter simultaneously rather than selectively; the equilibrium configuration is sensitive to each of these variables whatever the parameter values might happen to be. As in rationing theory, the price mechanism fails to balance demand and supply in the goods market as well as in the labor market, but here it fails to do so permanently rather than temporarily — without relying on rationing, at least not in any plausible sense of that term.

I am not sufficiently conversant with the history of economic method and doctrine to trace the development of the idea of the economy as a system where equilibrium is characterized by the equality of supply and demand.[3] Whatever its roots, however, there is nothing particularly compelling about this characterization of equilibrium in the dynamic context; and once the identification of equilibrium with demand = supply is abandoned, the investment function, the saving function, and the conventional wage can simultaneously influence long-run equilibrium without overdetermining the system. The rest of this chapter lays out a model in which instead of equality between supply and demand, it is equality between the rate of wage inflation and the rate of price inflation that characterizes long-run equilibrium. We begin by combining neo-Marxian wage adjustment with neo-Keynesian price adjustment.

2. The parallel can be taken a step further: the market-clearing equilibrium (in Barro-Grossman's terminology) or Walrasian equilibrium (in Malinvaud's) is the short-run analog of Robinson's golden age — a coincidence of parameter values that fortuitously resolves the overdetermination that results from superimposing an exogenously given labor-force growth rate (instead of an exogenously given conventional wage) on the saving and investment equations.

3. There is a larger issue, which it is even more subversive to raise: namely, the origin of the idea of the economy as an equilibrium system, a separate question from the characterization of equilibrium. I suspect that economics has been heavily influenced in this regard by the methodology of classical physics. In contrast with the mainstream, Marx explicitly took Darwin rather than Newton as his inspiration for a historical model of social development. Indeed, for Marx's purposes, Darwin did not go far enough in substituting evolution for equilibrium. Marx's social analog to natural selection was not adaptation to an environment that changes only because of exogenous shocks. Rather, in the Marxian view, society — the environment — is itself the product of the very process of struggle upon which natural selection operates. The model appropriate to this view is a *nonstationary* dynamic system. By contrast, the model outlined in this chapter is a stationary system; it differs from conventional models only in the economic characterization of equilibrium.

If the price level is endogenous to the model (as it must be in a model that seeks to reflect Keynes as well as Marx), the simplest extension of the neo-Marxian wage-adjustment equation is

$$w = -\theta\left[\left(\frac{W}{P}\right)_{-1} - \left(\frac{W}{P}\right)^*\right], \tag{20.1}$$

where w is the rate of change of money wages $\Delta W/W_{-1}$; $(W/P)^*$ is the conventional wage; and θ is the speed of adjustment. The neo-Keynesian price-adjustment model outlined in Chapters 4 and 6 was summarized in Eq. (6.18) as

$$Ps(r,\delta) = P_{-1}i(r_{-1}) \tag{6.18}$$

or

$$p = \frac{i(r_{-1}) - s(r, \delta)}{s(r, \delta)}, \tag{20.2}$$

where p is the rate of change of the price level $\Delta P/P_{-1}$. Observe that the money supply is passive in this model. Either the central bank adjusts the volume of money to accommodate the wage claims of workers and the investment demand of capitalists, or the velocity of money adjusts. The money supply is a thermometer, not a thermostat.

Prices, wages, and profits continue to be connected by the price equation

$$Pf(k) = W + (1 + r)Pk \tag{20.3}$$

and one of the marginal productivity relationships

$$\left.\begin{array}{l} f(k) - f'(k)k = \dfrac{W}{P} \\[2mm] f'(k) = 1 + r. \end{array}\right\} \tag{20.4}$$

Short-Run Equilibrium

The determination of short-run equilibrium is illustrated in Figure 20.2. Current investment demand is assumed to be fixed in money terms on the basis of last period's price and profit rate. Real investment demand is thus obtained by dividing the money demand by the current price level, $P_{-1}i(r_{-1})/P$. Taking account of the price equation and the marginal productivity relationships, we have real investment demand as a function of the current rate of profit (through the price equation) as well as of the previous rate of profit:

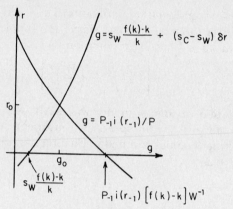

Figure 20.2 Short-run equilibrium

$$i^d(r, r_{-1}) = \frac{P_{-1}i(r_{-1})}{P}. \tag{20.5}$$

Similarly, for a given δ—that is, with a given distribution of owner-ship of capital between workers and capitalists—the desired saving rate is a quasi-Kaldorian function of r,

$$s(r, \delta) = s_W \frac{f(k) - k}{k} + (s_C - s_W)\delta r.$$

Equilibrium is determined by the intersection of investment and saving functions:

$$i^d(r, r_{-1}) = s(r, \delta).$$

A positive equilibrium profit rate, denoted r_0 in Figure 20.2, is guaranteed by assuming that saving out of wages is insufficient to finance desired investment, formally

$$s_W W k^{-1} < P_{-1}i(r_{-1}).$$

Once the equilibrium rate of profit is known, the equilibrium price P_0, real wage W_0/P_0, and capital:labor ratio k_0 follow from Eqs. (20.3) and (20.4). The growth rate is given by the saving function

$$g_0 = s(r_0, \delta_0).$$

So short-run equilibrium is completely determinate.

Despite the resemblance of Figure 20.2 to the familiar Marshallian "cross," the mechanism for achieving short-period equilibrium differs fundamentally from the neoclassical mechanism. In the neoclassical model r is a rate of interest, the *price* or *cost* of capital services, which adjusts both desired saving through income and substitution effects and investment demand by making capital cheaper or more expensive. In the present model, by contrast, r is a rate of profit or return to capital, which acts through the general price level on desired saving (*à la* Kaldor) to shift control over resources between capitalists and workers, that is, between high- and low-propensity savers, and acts on investment demand, also through the price level, to vary the amount of capital goods that can be purchased with the money available, namely $P_{-1}i(r_{-1})$.

Long-Run Equilibrium

In general, the successive short-period equilibria determined by Eqs. (20.1)–(20.4) will differ one from the other. A constant rate of profit over time is of course possible; for this to happen, the solution to Eqs. (20.1) and (20.2) must provide equal rates of wage and price inflation,

$$w = p, \tag{20.6}$$

and thereby a constant *real* wage rate and a constant profit rate. Substituting from Eqs. (20.1) and (20.2) into Eq. (20.6), the condition of a constant profit rate is

$$\theta\left[\left(\frac{W}{P}\right)^* - \left(\frac{W}{P}\right)\right] = \frac{i(r) - s(r, \delta)}{s(r, \delta)}.$$

But if $s(r, \delta)$ is to be constant over time, δ must be constant, which requires $\delta = \hat{\delta}(r)$ and $s(r, \delta) = s(r)$. That is, the saving function becomes the long-run function

$$s(r) = \max\left(s_W \frac{f(k) - k}{k}, s_C r\right), \qquad \delta = \hat{\delta}(r),$$

and we have

$$p = \frac{i(r) - s(r)}{s(r)} \tag{20.7}$$

in place of Eq. (20.2). By virtue of the price equation, Eq. (20.3), wage inflation can be expressed in terms of the rate of profit and the capital:labor ratio

$$w = -\theta\left[f(k_{-1}) - (1 + r_{-1})k_{-1} - \left(\frac{W}{P}\right)^*\right].$$

Substituting into Eq. (20.6) and taking account of the functional de-. pendence of k on r implicit in the marginal-productivity relationship $f'(k) = 1 + r$, we obtain an equation in r alone:

$$-\theta\left[f(k) - (1 + r)k - \left(\frac{W}{P}\right)^*\right] = \frac{i(r) - s(r)}{s(r)}. \tag{20.8}$$

We shall denote the solution to (20.8) by $\bar{r}$ and the associated capital : labor and output : labor ratios by $\bar{k}$ and $f(\bar{k})$. With saving intentions assumed to be realized, the rate of growth is given by the equation

$$\bar{g} = s(\bar{r}).$$

When $r = \bar{r}$, we can speak of *the* rate of inflation $\bar{w} = \bar{p}$, given by the common value of the left-hand and right-hand sides of Eq. (20.8).

Distribution and growth are illustrated in Figure 20.3. The first quadrant is taken directly from Figure 20.1. The second quadrant shows both price inflation and wage inflation as functions of the rate of profit; the growth-distribution configuration $\langle \bar{r}, \bar{g} \rangle$ is given by the intersection of these two functions. It should be clear from the diagram that sufficient conditions for a positive rate of inflation are (1) that investment demand exceed the supply of saving at the profit rate r^* associated with the conventional wage,

$$i(r^*) > s(r^*);$$

and (2) that investment demand equal saving for some rate of profit higher than r^*,

$$i(r) = s(r) \qquad \text{for } r > r^*.$$

As promised, the model sketched here is a just-determined system:

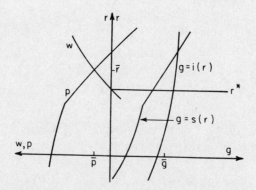

Figure 20.3 Growth, distribution, and inflation

$\langle \bar{r}, \bar{g} \rangle$ is an equilibrium, even though it is not an equilibrium in the customary, supply = demand, sense of that term. The inequality between *real* investment demand $i(r)$ and the supply of saving $s(r)$ is, like the departure of the real wage from the conventional wage, a permanent feature of the steady-growth path, not a transitory phenomenon. In the present model, a long-run equilibrium is a point at which the pressure that workers are able to put on wages just balances the pressure that aggregate demand places on aggregate supply. The result is a standoff: the attempts of workers to maintain the conventional wage and the investment intentions of capitalists are both frustrated in part.

Formally, we may characterize both the short-run adjustment process and long-run steady growth in terms of difference equations in r and δ, as in Chapters 6 and 9. The equations

$$Ps(r, \delta) = P_{-1}i(r_{-1}) \tag{6.18}$$

and

$$\delta = \delta_{-1} \frac{1 + s_C r_{-1}}{1 + s(r_{-1}, \delta_{-1})} \tag{6.6}$$

define two functions,

$$r = G(r_{-1}, \delta_{-1}) \quad \text{and} \quad \delta = H(r_{-1}, \delta_{-1}).$$

The novelty is that W is now a variable that depends on r_{-1} rather than a constant. Thus the current price level is no longer a function of r alone. Differentiating (20.3) no longer gives a single derivative

$$\frac{dP}{dr} = \frac{Pk}{\dfrac{W}{P}} = \frac{P^2 k}{W}$$

but two partial derivatives

$$\frac{\partial P}{\partial r} = \frac{Pk}{\dfrac{W}{P}} = \frac{P^2 k}{W}$$

and

$$\frac{\partial P}{\partial r_{-1}} = \frac{\dfrac{dW}{dr_{-1}} + Pk \dfrac{\partial G}{\partial r_{-1}}}{\dfrac{W}{P}}.$$

The term dW/dr_{-1} is found by differentiating the wage equation:

$$\frac{dW}{dr_{-1}} = \frac{\partial W}{\partial k_{-1}} \frac{dk_{-1}}{dr_{-1}} + \frac{\partial W}{\partial r_{-1}}$$

$$= -\theta \left[f'(k_{-1}) \frac{dk_{-1}}{dr_{-1}} - (1 + r_{-1}) \frac{dk_{-1}}{dr_{-1}} - k_{-1} \right] W_{-1}$$

$$= \theta k_{-1} W_{-1}.$$

Thus

$$\frac{\partial P}{\partial r_{-1}} = \frac{\theta k_{-1} W_{-1} + Pk \dfrac{\partial G}{\partial r_{-1}}}{\dfrac{W}{P}}.$$

Hence, when we differentiate (6.18) with respect to r_{-1}, we obtain

$$\frac{\partial P}{\partial r_{-1}} s(r, \delta) + P \left[\frac{\partial s}{\partial r} \frac{\partial G}{\partial r_{-1}} + \frac{\partial s}{\partial \delta} \frac{\partial H}{\partial r_{-1}} \right] = \frac{\partial P_{-1}}{\partial r_{-1}} i(r_{-1}) + P_{-1} i'(r_{-1})$$

or

$$\frac{\partial G}{\partial r_{-1}} = \frac{\dfrac{W}{P} \left[\dfrac{P^2_{-1} k_{-1}}{W_{-1}} i(r_{-1}) + P_{-1} i'(r_{-1}) \right] - W \dfrac{\partial s}{\partial \delta} \dfrac{\partial H}{\partial r_{-1}} - \theta k_{-1} W_{-1} s(r, \delta)}{Pks(r, \delta) + W \dfrac{\partial s}{\partial r}}$$

$$(20.9)$$

Observe that the right-hand side of Eq. (20.9) differs from the corresponding equation of Chapters 6 and 9 only in the coefficients of $i(r_{-1})$ and $i'(r_{-1})$ and in the presence of a new term, $-\theta k_{-1} W_{-1} s(r, \delta)$, in the numerator. Otherwise, the matrix of partial derivatives

$$\mathbf{J} = \begin{bmatrix} \dfrac{\partial G}{\partial r_{-1}} & \dfrac{\partial G}{\partial \delta_{-1}} \\ \dfrac{\partial H}{\partial r_{-1}} & \dfrac{\partial H}{\partial \delta_{-1}} \end{bmatrix}$$

parallels the matrices in Chapters 6 and 9.

Stability depends, as always, on satisfying the Routh-Hurwitz conditions

$$|\det \mathbf{J}| < 1,$$

$$|\text{tr } \mathbf{J}| < |1 + \det \mathbf{J}|.$$

The rate of profit continues to play a central role in the analysis, but as a result of Eq. (20.9), the crucial issue is not, as in Chapters 6 and 9, the relative responsiveness of saving and investment to the rate of profit; it is rather the relative responsiveness of wage and price inflation that matters.

For θ close enough to zero, a sufficient condition for

$$|\text{tr } \mathbf{J}| < |1 + \det \mathbf{J}|$$

at a stationary point $\langle \bar{r}, \bar{\delta} \rangle$ is[4]

$$\frac{i'(\bar{r})s(\bar{r}) - i(\bar{r})s'(\bar{r})}{[s(\bar{r})]^2} < \theta \bar{k}. \tag{20.10}$$

Now with $r = \bar{r}$ and δ adjusted to $\bar{r}$ (that is, with $\bar{\delta} = \hat{\delta}(\bar{r})$),

$$p = \frac{i(\bar{r}) - s(\bar{r})}{s(\bar{r})},$$

so in the long run

$$\frac{dp}{dr} = \frac{i'(\bar{r})s(\bar{r}) - i(\bar{r})s'(\bar{r})}{[s(\bar{r})]^2}.$$

With $r = \bar{r}$ we also have

$$w = -\theta \left[f(\bar{k}) - (1 + \bar{r})\bar{k} - f(k^*) + (1 + r^*)k^* \right],$$

so

$$\frac{dw}{dr} = \theta \bar{k}.$$

Hence the economic content of (20.10) is that price inflation must be algebraically less responsive than wage inflation to changes in the rate of profit:

$$\frac{dp}{dr} < \frac{dw}{dr}. \tag{20.11}$$

As Figure 20.3 is drawn, this condition is clearly met: price inflation responds negatively to the rate of profit at $\bar{r}$, whereas the response of wage inflation is always positive.

Note that (20.10) by itself is not sufficient for stability. For one thing,

4. The easiest way to reach this result is to exploit the similarities between the elements of $\mathbf{J}$ and the corresponding matrices of Chapters 6 and 9. Noting that, at $\langle \bar{r}, \bar{\delta} \rangle$, $P/P_{-1} = W/W_{-1} = i(\bar{r})/s(\bar{r})$, the only difference between $\mathbf{J}$ and the earlier two matrices is the new term $-\theta \bar{k} W_{-1} s(\bar{r})$ in the numerator of $\partial G / \partial r_{-1}$.

there is an upper limit that must be placed on the speed of adjustment of wages in order to avoid the problem of overshooting: there exists θ_0 such that for $\theta > \theta_0$, neither of the Routh-Hurwitz conditions will be satisfied. But this problem is specific to the discrete-time formulation of the model and disappears in a continuous-time version.

More serious is the condition on price inflation that emerges from the first of the Routh-Hurwitz conditions. As in Chapters 6 and 9 it is the *short-run* saving function rather than the long-run function that matters in the inequality

$$|\det \mathbf{J}| < 1.$$

In the short run with $r = \bar{r}$

$$\frac{\partial p}{\partial r} = \frac{i'(\bar{r})s(\bar{r}, \bar{\delta}) - i(\bar{r})\dfrac{\partial s}{\partial r}}{[s(\bar{r}, \bar{\delta})]^2}$$

with

$$\frac{\partial s}{\partial r} = s_W \frac{\sigma f(\bar{k})}{(1 + \bar{r})\bar{k}} + (s_C - s_W)\bar{\delta},$$

and the condition corresponding to (20.10) is

$$\frac{i'(\bar{r})s(\bar{r}, \bar{\delta}) - i(\bar{r})\dfrac{\partial s}{\partial r}}{[s(\bar{r}, \bar{\delta})]^2} < \theta\bar{k}. \tag{20.12}$$

As Figure 20.3 is drawn, substitution in production is assumed to be inelastic ($\sigma < 1$), so

$$\frac{\partial s}{\partial r} < s'(r).$$

Thus whereas (20.10) necessarily holds when (20.12) is satisfied, the opposite is not the case. Merely comparing the slopes of p and w is in general misleading; the equilibrium in Figure 20.3 need not be stable.

The Comparative Statics of an Energy Shock

We can gain considerable insight into this model, and just possibly some insight into a problem of contemporary capitalism, by examining the impact on equilibrium of a shift in the production function meant to reflect an increase in the price of energy. As in Chapter 16, we replace the function $f(k)$ by the function $h(k, \omega)$, in which ω is the price of energy. For simplicity energy is assumed to be wholly imported, a charge upon output that is met before wages, profits, and even depreciation. We continue to write

$$h(k, \omega) = \frac{W}{P} + (1 + r)k \qquad (16.6)$$

$$MP_K \equiv h_k = 1 + r$$

$$MP_L \equiv h(k, \omega) - h_k k = \frac{W}{P}. \qquad (16.5)$$

The derivative h_ω is negative:

$$h_\omega = -e,$$

where e is energy per worker.

The effects of a change in ω are found by differentiating the equilibrium condition

$$-\theta \left[h(\bar{k}, \omega) - (1 + \bar{r})\bar{k} - \left(\frac{W}{P} \right)^* \right] = \frac{i(\bar{r}) - s(\bar{r})}{s(\bar{r})}$$

with respect to ω. After eliminating

$$h_k \frac{d\bar{k}}{d\omega} - (1 + \bar{r}) \frac{d\bar{k}}{d\omega} = 0$$

we can solve for $d\bar{r}/d\omega$:

$$\frac{d\bar{r}}{d\omega} = \frac{\theta h_\omega}{\dfrac{dw}{dr} - \dfrac{dp}{dr}} = \frac{\theta h_\omega}{\theta \bar{k} - (i's - s'i)/s^2}, \qquad (20.13)$$

where dw/dr and dp/dr are the long-run relationships derived earlier in this chapter, i, s, i', and s' being shorthand expressions that omit reference to the functional dependence on r.

The derivative $d\bar{r}/d\omega$ is negative: if equilibrium is stable, then condition (20.10) must be satisfied, and the denominator of (20.13) will be positive; and the numerator is negative by virtue of the relationship $h_\omega = -e$. Thus as the price of energy increases, the profit rate will normally fall from $\bar{r}$ to $\bar{\bar{r}}$, as in Figure 20.4. In consequence, the rate of growth of output, employment, and capital will fall also:

$$\bar{\bar{g}} = s(\bar{\bar{r}}) < \bar{g} = s(\bar{r}).$$

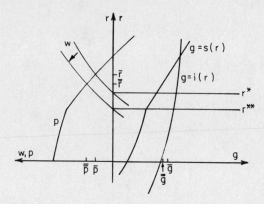

Figure 20.4 Steady-growth paths for alternative energy prices

By contrast, the wage rate can move either way. We differentiate the price equation (16.6) to obtain

$$\frac{d(\overline{W/P})}{d\omega} = \frac{\partial(\overline{W/P})}{\partial\omega} + \frac{\partial(\overline{W/P})}{\partial r}\frac{d\overline{r}}{d\omega}$$

$$= h_\omega - \overline{k}\frac{d\overline{r}}{d\omega} = h_\omega\left[1 - \frac{\theta k}{\theta\overline{k} - (i's - s'i)/s^2}\right].$$

Evidently the sign of $d(\overline{W/P})/d\omega$ hinges on the sign of $(i's - s'i)/s^2 = dp/dr$. As Figure 20.4 is drawn, the rate of price inflation responds negatively to a change in the rate of profit, so the real wage falls as the price of energy rises. But this is hardly an inevitable conclusion, since stable equilibrium is compatible with $dp/dr > 0$.

The equilibrium rate of inflation moves in the opposite direction to the real wage rate. At equilibrium

$$\overline{w} = \overline{p},\tag{20.6}$$

so

$$\frac{d\overline{w}}{d\omega} = \frac{\partial w}{\partial\omega} + \frac{dw}{dr}\frac{d\overline{r}}{d\omega} = -\theta h_\omega + \theta\overline{k}\frac{\theta h_\omega}{\theta\overline{k} - (i's - s'i)/s^2} = \frac{\partial p}{\partial r}\frac{d\overline{r}}{d\omega} = \frac{d\overline{p}}{d\omega}.$$

Thus with dp/dr negative, the steady-state rate of inflation increases with the price of energy: workers respond to erosion of conventional wages by driving up money wages, which increases $\overline{p}$ to $\overline{\overline{p}}$.

Finally, observe that the equilibrium capital:labor ratio responds ambiguously to the price of energy. From Eq. (16.5) we have

$$\frac{d\bar{k}}{d\omega} = -\frac{h_{k\omega}}{h_{kk}} + \frac{1}{h_{kk}}\frac{d\bar{r}}{d\omega}$$

$$= -\frac{1}{h_{kk}}\left[\frac{-\theta(h_\omega - h_{k\omega}\bar{k}) - h_{k\omega}(i's - s'i)/s^2}{\theta\bar{k} - (i's - s'i)/s^2}\right]. \qquad (20.14)$$

The numerator of this equation is of indefinite sign: both $(i's - s'i)/s^2$ and $h_{k\omega}$ can be either positive or negative. Of course, if an increase in the rate of profit reduces excess aggregate demand, in other words, if price inflation responds negatively to the rate of profit, and if capital and energy are substitutes ($h_{k\omega} > 0$), then the numerator is positive, and the capital : labor ratio responds positively to an increase in the price of energy. But a lot of "ifs" are required to reach this conclusion. It makes more sense to emphasize the ambiguity of the sign of $d\bar{k}/d\omega$.

It would hardly do to claim that the present model explains the consequences of the energy shock. The model is far too primitive to support any such pretension. But it is at least reassuring that the implications of Figure 20.4—a slowdown in growth, a reduction in profit *and* wage rates, as well as an increase in the rate of inflation—are consistent with the general experience of the last decade, at least if we correct wage data for technological change. None of the models examined in Chapter 16, by contrast, allows simultaneously for a fall in the growth rate, the profit rate, *and* the real wage. Consistency with recent experience is achievable with neoclassical, neo-Marxian, and neo-Keynesian models only by backing off from their distinguishing features—the exogeneity of labor growth, the real wage, and investment demand.

Thus we may now venture a partial answer to the question posed in Chapter 16—whether the failure of the neoclassical, neo-Marxian, and neo-Keynesian approaches to accord with recent experience is a failure of data interpretation, or of the simplifying assumptions common to all the models, 'or of the postulates peculiar to the models. Whatever the problems of data and simplifying assumptions, the model of this chapter draws unfavorable attention to the postulates of the other models. Neo-Marxian and neo-Keynesian as well as neoclassical models appear to provide a much weaker basis for understanding current economic phenomena than a model built on the insights of both Marx and Keynes.

The Trade-off between Real Growth and Wage-Price Stability

It may also be said on behalf of the present model that it offers a plausible explanation for a phenomenon that has forcefully intruded itself on the contemporary economist: "stagflation." The steady state of Figure 20.3 has room for both inflation—symptom of excess demand—*and* unemployment—symptom of excess capacity. Price inflation reflects excess demand, and wage inflation reflects the power of workers to resist erosion of real wages. But since the rate of growth of employment remains unrelated to the growth of population, excess demand can as well coexist with "unnatural" and even growing unemployment as with overfull employment. In the long run, growing unemployment is likely to be hidden in a slowdown in the rate of growth of the labor force, in line with a conception of a "reserve army" inspired by Marx.

The Phillips Curve

The structure of the model also suggests that variations in investment demand—over time or across steady states—will be reflected in the rate of inflation as well as in growth and distribution. Figure 20.5 shows the *short-run* response to an increase in investment demand: the profit rate increases from r_0 to r_0' and the growth rate from g_0 to g_0'. At the same time the price level increases from P_0 to P_0' and the real wage falls from W_0/P_0 to W_0/P_0'. Since in the short run the money wage is fixed, output responds to investment in the neo-Keynesian manner outlined in Chapter 9:

$$\frac{dX}{dI^G} = \frac{1}{s_W + (s_C - s_W)\delta \dfrac{(1+r)a_1}{\sigma}}. \qquad (9.36)$$

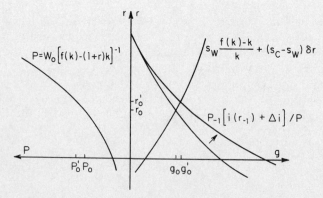

Figure 20.5 Short-run response to change in investment demand

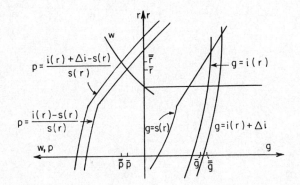

Figure 20.6 Steady-growth paths for alternative investment-demand functions

The comparison across steady-growth configurations associated with two investment-demand functions, as in Figure 20.6, reveals a similar pattern of results: higher profit, growth, and inflation rates, and a lower real wage. These results provide the alternative basis for the generalized Phillips curve promised in the last chapter.[5] In contrast with the neoclassical foundations articulated by Richard Lipsey (1960), it is not the level of unemployment that determines the path of wages, but the level of aggregate demand that determines both employment *and* wages. There is no need to assume that the same process operates in the labor market as in Böhm-Bawerk's horse market and Marshall's fish market.

The Paradox of Thrift

Apart from accommodating the coexistence of excess demand and unemployment, a major novelty of the present hybrid model is the twist it gives to the Keynesian and neo-Keynesian "paradox of thrift." In the short run, the pre-Keynesian conventional wisdom is restored. As Figure 20.7 indicates, an increase in capitalists' propensity to save from s_C to s'_C — similar results follow for a shift from s_W to s'_W — increases the

---

5. This model has no place for a Phillips curve, in the strict sense of the term, as a relationship between unemployment and wage inflation, at least not in the long run. For in the long run, the labor force is endogenous, and consequently unemployment is not a variable of the model. But in the *generalized* sense of the term, as a positive relationship between the rate of growth g and the rate of inflation ($p = w$), we can continue to speak of a Phillips curve or a "Phillips-curve relationship."

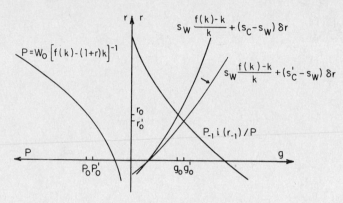

Figure 20.7 Short-run response to shift in capitalists' propensity to save

short-run rate of growth while depressing the profit rate and price level.

Over a longer period, a similar relationship holds between saving propensities and the rate of profit. However, the relationship between saving propensities and the rate of growth becomes indeterminate, which is perhaps not so surprising once it is recalled that the neo-Keynesian and neo-Marxian theories synthesized in the present model are diametrically opposed on this score.

The steady-state results follow directly from the equilibrium condition

$$w = p. \tag{20.6}$$

With $\hat{\delta} > 0$, we have

$$s(r) = s_C r.$$

As a result, differentiating Eq. (20.6) with respect to s_C determines the impact of capitalists' saving propensity on the equilibrium rate of profit. This gives

$$\frac{d\bar{r}}{ds_C} = \frac{\partial p / \partial s_C}{\dfrac{dw}{dr} - \dfrac{dp}{dr}} = - \frac{\bar{r}i/s^2}{\theta\bar{k} - (i's - s'i)/s^2}. \tag{20.15}$$

In Eq. (20.15), a positive denominator validates intuition based on the neo-Keynesian model: $d\bar{r}/ds_C < 0$. And as long as the profit rate falls, the effects on inflation are beneficial:

$$\frac{d\overline{w}}{ds_C} = \frac{dw}{dr}\frac{d\overline{r}}{ds_C} = \frac{d\overline{p}}{ds_C} = \theta\overline{k}\frac{d\overline{r}}{ds_C},$$

so the new equilibrium rate of inflation $\overline{\overline{p}}$ is lower than the old.

By contrast, the effect on the equilibrium growth rate are inherently ambiguous. As in Chapter 6, we have

$$\frac{d\overline{g}}{ds_C} = \overline{r} + s_C\frac{d\overline{r}}{ds_C}. \tag{20.16}$$

But unlike Chapter 6, in which both the neo-Marxian result

$$\frac{dg^*}{ds_C} = r^* > 0$$

and the neo-Keynesian result

$$\frac{dg^*}{ds_C} = r^*\frac{i'}{i' - s_C} < 0$$

are sign-definite, the sign of the right-hand side of Eq. (20.16) depends on the parameter values. Written out in full, Eq. (20.16) becomes

$$\frac{d\overline{g}}{ds_C} = \overline{r}\frac{\theta\overline{k} - \dfrac{i'}{s}}{\theta\overline{k} - (i's - s'i)/s^2}. \tag{20.17}$$

Even if the denominator of (20.17) is positive, we know nothing about the sign of the numerator, which depends both on the strength of real-wage resistance (as measured by θk) and on the relative responsiveness of the investment and saving functions to the rate of profit. If real-wage resistance is sufficiently strong, or if saving is sufficiently responsive to the rate of profit, that i'/s is small in comparison to θk, then $d\overline{g}/ds_C$ will be positive, in which case $\overline{\overline{g}} > \overline{g}$; otherwise $d\overline{g}/ds_C$ will be negative. The two cases are shown in Figure 20.8(a) and (b).[6]

The comparison with investment-demand variation is noteworthy. Figure 20.6 reflects a pattern of positive association between inflation and growth rates — the essence of the generalized Phillips-curve relationship. By contrast, the association between inflation and growth

---

6. In the $\hat{\delta} = 0$ region, orthodox results once again hold: $\dfrac{d\overline{r}}{ds_W}, \dfrac{d\overline{p}}{ds_W} < 0$ and $\dfrac{dw}{dr} < \dfrac{dp}{dr}$ together imply $\dfrac{d\overline{g}}{ds_W} > 0$.

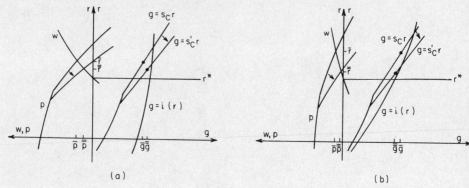

Figure 20.8 The ambiguous paradox of thrift. (a) $\bar{\bar{g}} > \bar{g}$; (b) $\bar{\bar{g}} < \bar{g}$

rates that accompanies variation in the propensity to save is inherently ambiguous. There is no reason whatsoever to expect a Phillips curve to emerge from changes in employment and money wages that result from changes in saving behavior!

Fiscal Policy in an Ambiguous World

The ambiguity of the paradox of thrift bears on policy choices between measures designed to increase the profitability of investment and measures to increase the propensity to save. The first are a more plausible tonic for stagnation than the second, but success in improving the growth rate will come at the cost of a higher inflation rate. Measures to increase the propensity to save may work better in controlling the rate of inflation—but with ambiguous results for the rate of growth.

In practice it is of course difficult to change the profitability of investment without changing the propensity to save in the same direction. Policy measures like reduction in corporate income tax rates, for instance, presumably increase both desired saving, as a function of pretax income, and investment, as a function of the pretax rate of profit.

Fiscal policy is thus inherently ambiguous. It is possible that measures ostensibly designed to operate on the rate of growth through their effect on desired saving will produce results—but by way of a very different mechanism, through their effect on investment demand rather than through their effect on saving propensities. Indeed, increases in the propensity to save may act as a drag, capable of dampening and even reversing the expansionary impact of a stimulus to investment demand.

Wage-Push Inflation

Finally, it should be observed that the present model makes sense of the distinction between "demand-pull" and "wage-push" inflation, a distinction difficult to integrate into models characterized by equilibrium of the standard demand = supply variety. Indeed, for a long time many economists were disposed to deny the distinction between the two kinds of inflation, correctly noting that *all* inflation is characterized by excess demand. Nevertheless the distinction is a useful one: the two kinds of inflation differ not only in terms of their source, but also in terms of their implications for the relationship between inflation and unemployment.

The origins of demand-pull inflation lie in the saving-investment nexus, the origins of wage-push inflation in attempts to defend the conventional wage. Excess demand accompanies wage-push inflation as it does demand-pull inflation, but the effects of variations in the conventional wage on growth, profits, and inflation differ significantly from the effects of variations in investment demand or saving propensities on these magnitudes. An increase in the conventional wage at $t = -1$ will drive up the current money wage from W_0 to W'_0, as well as the price level, but will *decrease* the rate of profit and the rate of growth. In the short run, as W_0 increases, the price level

$$P = \frac{Wa_0}{1 - (1 + r)a_1}$$

increases, and real saving falls in order to maintain the balance between (fixed) money investment and money saving,

$$P_{-1} i(r_{-1}) = Ps(r, \delta).$$

At the new short-run equilibrium, $s(r, \delta)$ and r are lower and P higher than at the equilibrium that would have taken place if the conventional wage had remained unchanged. Figure 20.9 illustrates these results.

The long-run effects of an increase in the conventional wage on growth and profit rates depend on the relative response of wage inflation and excess aggregate demand to the rate of profit. By contrast, the effects on the equilibrium rate of inflation depend on the response of excess aggregate demand alone. The relevant equations are

$$\frac{d\bar{r}}{d(W/P)^*} = - \frac{\theta}{\dfrac{dw}{dr} - \dfrac{dp}{dr}}$$

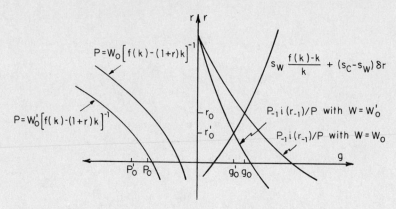

Figure 20.9 Short-run response to an increase in the conventional wage

and

$$\frac{d\overline{w}}{d(W/P)^*} = \frac{\partial w}{\partial(W/P)^*} + \frac{dw}{dr}\frac{d\overline{r}}{d(W/P)^*} = \frac{d\overline{p}}{dr}\frac{d\overline{r}}{d(W/P)^*}.$$

Figure 20.10 indicates the two possibilities. In Figure 20.10(a) the rate of inflation increases with a rise in the conventional wage, whereas in Figure 20.10(b) it decreases. In both cases the rates of profit and growth fall.

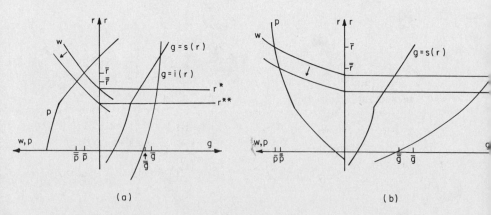

Figure 20.10 Steady-growth paths at two conventional wages.
(a) $\overline{\overline{p}} > \overline{p}$; (b) $\overline{\overline{p}} < \overline{p}$

Productivity Growth

A similar exercise leads to an analogous result for a change in the rate of productivity growth in a variant of the model that incorporates "technical" change. (The quotation marks serve as a reminder that the neo-Marxian strain in the model makes the rate of productivity growth as sensitive to changes in the social relations of production as to changes in technology.) Suppose for simplicity that changes in the production function are Harrod-neutral, or labor-augmenting. Then, with μ representing the rate of technical change and k representing the ratio of capital to "effective" labor $k = K/L(1 + \mu)^t$, the production function $f(k) = X/L(1 + \mu)^t$ is invariant over time. Now assume that the conventional wage is defined as a *share* of product instead of as a wage rate. Then, in place of Eq. (20.1), we have

$$w = -\theta \left[\left(\frac{WL}{PX} \right)_{-1} - \left(\frac{WL}{PX} \right)^* \right].$$

To every wage share v there is a corresponding profit rate r^7 and capital : (effective) labor ratio k, given jointly by the profit-share equation

$$\frac{(1 + r)k}{f(k)} = 1 - v$$

and the marginal-productivity equation

$$f'(k) = 1 + r.$$

Evidently a constant wage *share* implies a rising wage *rate:*

$$\frac{W}{P} = vf(k)(1 + \mu)^t.$$

Thus technical change leaves the model basically unchanged, except for the substitution of a wage share for a wage rate. Provided the elasticity of substitution in production σ is less than 1, the w-curve continues to have a positive slope since in general

$$\frac{dw}{dr} = \frac{\theta k}{f(k)} (1 - \sigma).$$

The only real difference is that the equilibrium condition is no longer

7. The correspondence between v and r is one-to-one for constant-elasticity-of-substitution production functions, except for the Cobb-Douglas case, in which v is constant and independent of r.

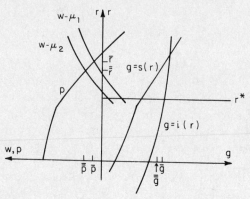

Figure 20.11 Growth, distribution, and inflation with technical change

$p = w$. Since a constant profit rate implies real wage growth at the rate μ, the equilibrium condition becomes $w - p = \mu$, or

$$p = w - \mu.$$

Equilibrium is represented in Figure 20.11. The w-curve, reflecting wage inflation as a function of the rate of profit, is now replaced by the curve labeled $w - \mu$. A fall in the rate of productivity growth evidently affects equilibrium like an increase in the conventional wage or the price of energy. For instance, if μ decreases from μ_1 to μ_2, the consequence is higher inflation, a lower profit rate, and lower growth.

Observe that productivity growth affects the equilibrium rate of output and capital growth differently in this model from the corresponding neoclassical model, in which a natural rate of growth, $n + \mu$, dictates equilibrium output and capital growth rates. Here the impact of productivity growth on $\bar{g}$ is only indirect. At a given rate of profit, employment growth adapts to the rate of productivity growth, so that the sum of the two equals the equilibrium $\bar{g}$ given by the balance of the pressure workers bring to bear on wages and the pressure of investment demand on the supply of saving. Productivity growth enters into the determination of $\bar{g}$ only because the profit rate responds to the rate of productivity growth, and because investment demand and saving supply respond to the rate of profit.

Some Comparative Statics

Evidently the consequences of disturbing a steady-growth path depend very much on which parameter is varied. An increase in investment

Table 20.1. Responses of profit, growth, and inflation rates to changes in investment demand, saving propensity, conventional wage, productivity growth, and energy price

		Source of disturbance				
		Δi	Δs_C	$\Delta(W/P)^*$	$\Delta\mu$	$\Delta\omega$
Consequences	$\Delta\bar{r}$	+	−	−	+	−
	$\Delta\bar{g}$	+	?	−	+	−
	$\Delta\bar{p}$	+	−	+[a]	−[a]	+[a]

a. Assumes $dp/dr < 0$.

? = indeterminate; + = increase; − = decrease.

demand does not affect the rate of growth in the same way as does a decrease in capitalists' propensity to save. Neither does an increase in the conventional wage or the price of energy or a decrease in the rate of productivity growth lead to the same consequences for inflation as does a fall in investment demand. The results are summarized in Table 20.1. *Observe in particular that only a shift in the investment-demand function produces the standard Phillips-curve result of a positive association between $\Delta\bar{g}$ and $\Delta\bar{p}$.* The association is of ambiguous sign in the event that it is capitalists' propensity to save that changes, and is likely to be negative when the conventional wage, the rate of productivity growth, or the price of energy changes.

Expectations, Naive and Rational

Even those who are not addicted to perfect foresight might criticize the price-adjustment mechanism

$$p = \frac{i(r_{-1}) - s(r, \delta)}{s(r, \delta)} \tag{20.2}$$

for the naiveté of the expectations it implies: according to Eq. (20.2), capitalists either never learn to anticipate price changes or they are powerless to incorporate the lessons of the past into their investment planning. This assumption did little harm in the pure neo-Keynesian model, where inflation (or deflation) was but a transitory phenomenon; the system described in Chapters 4 and 6 converged to a steady-state growth path with a constant price level P^* *despite* the myopia of the capitalist class. In the present model, by contrast, a changing price level is a permanent feature of a steady-growth path, rather than purely a disequilibrium phenomenon. The impact of *persistent* inflation on price expectations can hardly be disregarded.

In the appendix to this chapter it is shown, however, that even with so-called rational expectations — perfect foresight up to a random error — the main results hold. The proposed synthesis of Marxian and Keynesian insights is not bound up with the assumption of naive or impotent capitalists unable to anticipate inflation effectively. To be more precise, it will be shown that under plausible assumptions, the certainty equivalent P^{ce} of the distribution of the future price level can be approximated by a weighted average of the mean of the distribution EP and the current price level P_{-1}:

$$P^{ce} = \lambda EP + (1 - \lambda)P_{-1}.$$

The deterministic short-run equilibrium condition

$$i^d(r, r_{-1}) \equiv \frac{P_{-1}i(r_{-1})}{P} = s(r, \delta)$$

becomes a stochastic equation in P and r,

$$i^d \equiv \frac{P^{ce}i(r_{-1})}{P} = s(r, \delta).$$

The long-run equilibrium condition

$$P_{-1}i(r) = Ps(r)$$

becomes

$$P^{ce}i(r) = EPs(r).$$

The characterization of equilibrium turns out to depend critically on capitalists' risk aversion with respect to investment commitments. In the limit as risk aversion goes to zero, λ approaches unity, and in the neighborhood of $p = 0$, $P^{ce} \to EP$. The model becomes neo-Keynesian in its real parts, and the neo-Marxian influence is felt only in the determination of the rate of inflation. With what might be called absolute risk aversion, $\lambda \to 0$ and the results approach the naive-expectations case we have implicitly been assuming up to now. For intermediate degrees of risk aversion, the results are intermediate between the two extremes. Figure 20.12 gathers these results together for the basic model without productivity growth.

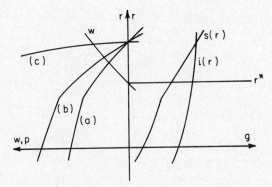

Figure 20.12 Steady growth with rational expectations: p-curves reflect (a) absolute risk aversion ($\lambda = 0$); (b) intermediate risk aversion ($0 < \lambda < 1$); (c) no risk aversion ($\lambda = 1$)

The Wage Equation

Workers' expectations, as well as capitalists', should be modeled more sensitively than the naive adjustment functions

$$w = -\theta\left[\left(\frac{W}{P}\right)_{-1} - \left(\frac{W}{P}\right)^*\right],$$

or

$$w = -\theta\left[\left(\frac{WL}{PX}\right)_{-1} - \left(\frac{WL}{PX}\right)^*\right]$$

allow. It is reasonable that wage claims will reflect persistent price inflation in addition to the departure of the actual wage from the conventional wage, as in the following modification of the wage equations:

$$w = -\theta\left[\left(\frac{W}{P}\right)_{-1} - \left(\frac{W}{P}\right)^*\right] + \gamma p_{-1},$$

and

$$w = -\theta\left[\left(\frac{WL}{PX}\right)_{-1} - \left(\frac{WL}{PX}\right)^*\right] + \gamma p_{-1}.$$

The parameter γ reflects the degree to which price inflation is incorporated into current wage claims. Figure 20.13 indicates the effect on

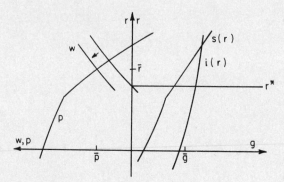

Figure 20.13 Steady growth with anticipation of price inflation in wage bargaining

steady-growth equilibrium of introducing price inflation into the determination of wages. The response of equilibrium is similar to the response to a change in the conventional wage: profit and growth rates normally respond negatively, whereas the response of the inflation rate itself depends on the slope of the price-inflation function, dp/dr, at equilibrium. When price inflation responds negatively to the rate of profit, as in Figure 20.13, introducing price expectations into the analysis of wage behavior increases the rate of inflation.

Observe that as $\gamma \to 1$, the equilibrium configuration approaches the neo-Marxian in its real parts: the only possible steady state is one at which the actual wage is equal to the conventional wage. Joan Robinson's inflation barrier here operates as an absolute constraint.

The parameter γ reflects the degree to which workers effectively anticipate price inflation. Should we not, therefore, suppose that at the very least γ equals 1? If we adapt the notion of risk aversion from the analysis of capitalists' behavior to workers' behavior, γ might easily exceed unity!

Here, I think, the analogy between capitalists and workers breaks down: capitalists' investment behavior depends essentially on expectations, whereas workers' wage behavior is only partially determined by expectations. Equally, perhaps more, important is the power of the working class to translate their inflationary expectations into wage claims. The adverb is the operative word in the phrase "effectively anticipate" of the previous paragraph. Thus even though workers might reasonably be supposed to anticipate inflation fully, at least in long-run equilibrium, it is by no means inconsistent to assume $\gamma < 1$. Indeed, in the neo-Marxian wage equation analyzed in Chapter 19, the estimated coefficient of p was of the order of 0.6. If this is, despite the defects of the estimation procedure, the right order of magnitude for the United States, then the inflation barrier operates but not with complete effectiveness.

Caveat Lector

Expectations are only one area in which the model developed in this chapter is highly simplified. Like the other models of this book, it is in its present form at best a vehicle for organizing one's thoughts. If it is to do any more, it must be elaborated to take account of government spending and taxation, international economic relations, natural-resource limitations — to mention only some of the most glaring omissions. Neither will it do, quite apart from technological change, to analyze production in the simplified manner of a relationship $f(k)$; to ignore the influence of the cost of capital on investment demand; or to treat the money supply in a purely passive manner. But all this is rightly the subject of another book, not an appropriate coda for this one.

Appendix: Rational Price Expectations

In what follows we replace the assumption that P_{-1} is used to formulate capital-expenditure plans by the assumption that, up to a random error, perfect foresight obtains: the actual future price is correctly anticipated in the manner of the rational-expectations model of John Muth (1961) and his legions of disciples. The point is not to suggest that prices are in fact forecast in this manner, but rather to show that rational expectations do not in themselves undermine the principal result of the model of this chapter — the simultaneous dependence of equilibrium on investment demand, the supply of saving, *and* the conventional wage.

To be sure, there are formulations of the rational-expectations hypothesis that do undermine the model; however, the damage is caused not by rational expectations per se, but by a particular choice either of the probability distribution of the price level or of the utility function capitalists are assumed to maximize.

To show this requires us to model expectations explicitly. We begin with the notion of certainty equivalence: P^{ce} will denote the certainty equivalent of a probability distribution of the price level $v(P, P_{-1})$ that is assumed to be conditional on P_{-1}. That is, P^{ce} represents the particular price level which — were it anticipated with perfect certainty — would lead to the same investment expenditure as the probability distribution v induces. If desired investment in real terms continues to be a function of the last period's rate of profit,[8] then investment expenditure can be written $P^{ce}i(r_{-1})$. Short-run equilibrium requires that investment expenditure equal money saving:

$$P^{ce}i(r_{-1}) = Ps(r, \delta).$$

Equivalently, short-run equilibrium may be characterized by equality between *real* investment demand and *real* saving:

$$i^d \equiv \frac{P^{ce}i(r_{-1})}{P} = s(r, \delta).$$

Both sides of this equation are now functions of a random variable, real investment demand by virtue of P in the denominator, real saving by virtue of r — which continues to be linked to P by the price equation

$$Pf(k) = W + (1 + r)Pk \qquad (20.3)$$

and (ignoring productivity growth) the marginal-productivity equations

$$\left. \begin{array}{l} f(k) - f'(k)k = \dfrac{W}{P}, \\[2mm] f'(k) = 1 + r. \end{array} \right\} \qquad (20.4)$$

In the long run we have

$$P = EP \qquad (20.18)$$

on average, where EP is the conditional expectation of P over the *ex ante* probability distribution $v(P, P_{-1})$. A stochastic long-run equilibrium is characterized by the equation

$$r = r_{-1} + \epsilon, \qquad (20.19)$$

where ϵ is a stationary random variable with zero mean. Taking Eqs. (20.18) and (20.19) into account, the condition for a long-run equilibrium becomes

$$P^{ce}i(r) = EPs(r). \qquad (20.20)$$

Equation (20.20) is the counterpart of Eq. (20.7) for the stochastic case.

It is commonly thought to be a property of rational expectations that the equation

$$P^{ce} = EP \qquad (20.21)$$

8. It might be objected that rational expectations require that $i(r_{-1})$ be replaced by a function whose argument is the certainty equivalent of the anticipated profit rate, for the same reason that P_{-1} is replaced by P^{ce}. This objection seems to me, however, to be misplaced. The argument against naive price expectations hinges on the persistence of inflation (or deflation), even under equilibrium conditions. By contrast, r, unlike P, has no trend in the steady state, so that naive expectations with respect to the profit rate are fulfilled on the steady-growth path. There is no need to gild the lily by insisting that profit-rate expectations be realized out of equilibrium as well.

holds. Were this the case, rational expectations would strike a heavy blow to the model of this chapter. For when Eq. (20.21) holds, Eq. (20.20) reduces to

$$i(r) = s(r),$$

and we are back to the neo-Keynesian model, at least as far as the real elements of the system are concerned. All that is left for the wage-adjustment equation (20.1) to do is to determine the rate of inflation.

But the belief that rational expectations imply Eq. (20.21) is a mistaken one. It is, as has been said, the "right" choice of probability distribution or utility function that produces Eq. (20.21). For instance, if the price level is correctly anticipated with perfect certainty, the probability distribution $v(P, P_{-1})$ is concentrated into a single point, and we have directly

$$P^{ce} = EP = P.$$

Equation (20.21) can be reached with less extreme assumptions about the probability distribution, by making suitable restrictions about the utility function that capitalists are assumed to use to assess investment plans. (An example will be offered presently.) In general, however, rational expectations are compatible with the result $P^{ce} \neq EP$, indeed with the result

$$P^{ce} < EP, \tag{20.22}$$

which, as we shall see, is the crucial step in the argument for the continued dependence of long-run equilibrium on $(W/P)^*$ as well as on $i(r)$ and $s(r)$ in the probabilistic, rational-expectations setting.

We turn now to the problem of establishing (20.22), beginning with a model of investment behavior. Assume that capitalists choose a level of expenditure M to maximize $\Omega(M)$, defined as the expected value of utility $U(\cdot)$ over the probability distribution $v(P, P_{-1})$:

$$\Omega(M) = \int_0^\infty U(\cdot)v(P, P_{-1}) \, dP. \tag{20.23}$$

The argument of this utility function will be taken to be the difference between realized investment *ex post* (that is, once the price level is known) and desired investment *ex ante*, with both realized and desired investment measured in real terms. Realized investment is M/P and desired investment is $i(r_{-1})$, so the difference is

$$\frac{M}{P} - i(r_{-1}).$$

Figure 20.14 depicts realized investment as a function of the price level for three different levels of expenditure, $M = 200$, $M = 300$, and $M = 400$. Desired investment is shown in the same figure as a constant, $i(r_{-1}) = 2$. The diagram presupposes that $v(P, P_{-1})$ is positive only over the finite interval $[P_{-1}, P_{max}] = [100, 200]$.

As the figure is drawn, the lowest of the three levels of commitment,

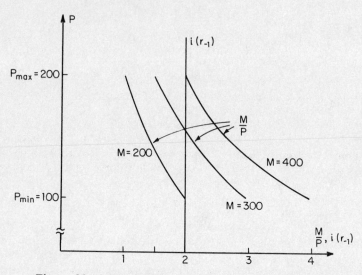

Figure 20.14 Desired and realized investment demand

$M = 200$, represents the extreme in conservative behavior: capitalists exhibiting such extreme conservatism would invariably end up with less investment than desired, achieving the desired level of investment at the lower end of the probability distribution, $P = P_{-1} = 100$. The highest of the three levels, $M = 400$, corresponds to the extreme of aggressive behavior: capitalists making such a heavy commitment would end up with more investment than they really want unless the price level reaches the upper end of the distribution, $P = P_{max} = 200$. $M = 300$ represents intermediate behavior, with the distribution between undercommitment and overcommitment depending on the precise shape of $v(P, P_{-1})$.

The next step in the argument is to assume an asymmetry in the utility function: let capitalists' behavior reflect a relative aversion to overcommitment. In other words, capitalists, by assumption, prefer to end up with too little investment than to end up with too much, "too little" and "too much" both being measured against the level of desired investment.

The simplest utility function to reflect this form of risk aversion is

$$U\left(\frac{M}{P} - i(r_{-1})\right) = \begin{cases} \alpha\left(\frac{M}{P} - i(r_{-1})\right), & \frac{M}{P} \leq i(r_{-1}) \\ -\beta\left(\frac{M}{P} - i(r_{-1})\right), & \frac{M}{P} \geq i(r_{-1}) \end{cases} \quad 0 < \alpha < \beta.$$

(20.24)

This utility function is illustrated in Figure 20.15.

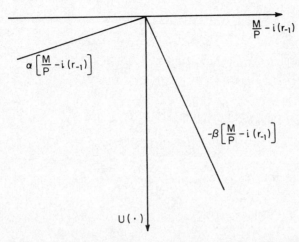

Figure 20.15 Utility as a piecewise linear function of the difference between realized and desired investment

Finally, we assume for simplicity that $v(P, P_{-1})$ is uniformly distributed over the interval $[P_{-1}, P_{max}]$:

$$v(P, P_{-1}) = \begin{cases} (P_{max} - P_{-1})^{-1}, & P_{-1} \leq P \leq P_{max}. \\ 0 & \text{otherwise} \end{cases} \quad (20.25)$$

With these simplifications, Eq. (20.23) becomes

$$\Omega(M) = (P_{max} - P_{-1})^{-1} \left[\int_{P_{-1}}^{\frac{M}{i(r_{-1})}} -\beta \left(\frac{M}{P} - i(r_{-1}) \right) dP + \int_{\frac{M}{i(r_{-1})}}^{P_{max}} \alpha \left(\frac{M}{P} - i(r_{-1}) \right) dP \right]. \quad (20.26)$$

Differentiating $\Omega(M)$ with respect to M and setting the derivative equal to zero, we obtain

$$M = (P_{max})^{\frac{\alpha}{\alpha+\beta}} (P_{-1})^{\frac{\beta}{\alpha+\beta}} i(r_{-1}). \quad (20.27)$$

Now actual and expected rates of inflation are related by the formula

$$p = \frac{EP - P_{-1}}{P_{-1}} (\epsilon + 1),$$

where, according to the probability distribution defined by (20.25), ϵ is drawn from the uniform distribution on the interval $[-1, 1]$. Hence on average $\epsilon = 0$, so

$$Ep = \frac{EP - P_{-1}}{P_{-1}}$$

and

$$EP = (1 + Ep)P_{-1}.\tag{20.28}$$

It also follows from the assumption of a uniform distribution for P that EP, $P_{\max}$, and P_{-1} are related by the formula

$$P_{\max} = 2EP - P_{-1}.\tag{20.29}$$

Thus substituting from Eqs. (20.28) and (20.29) into Eq. (20.27), we have

$$M = (1 + 2Ep)^{\frac{\alpha}{\alpha+\beta}}P_{-1}i(r_{-1}),$$

which differs from the naive-expectations model by the presence of the expression $(1 + 2Ep)^{\frac{\alpha}{\alpha+\beta}}$.

Thus, with $U(\,\cdot\,)$ defined by Eq. (20.24), the certainty equivalent of $v(P, P_{-1})$ is

$$P^{ce} = (1 + 2Ep)^{\frac{\alpha}{\alpha+\beta}}P_{-1},\tag{20.30}$$

for which, in the neighborhood of $Ep = 0$, the linear Taylor-series approximation is

$$P^{ce} = \frac{2\alpha}{\alpha+\beta}EP + \frac{\beta-\alpha}{\alpha+\beta}P_{-1}.\tag{20.31}$$

Equation (20.31) expresses P^{ce} as a weighted average of EP and P_{-1}, the expected future price and the current price. Writing $\lambda = 2\alpha/(\alpha + \beta)$, we have $1 - \lambda = (\beta - \alpha)/(\alpha + \beta)$. Rational expectations are clearly compatible with behavior that leads to expression (20.22). The relationship $P^{ce} < EP$ involves no implication of consistent underestimation of future inflation.

The short-run equilibrium condition

$$P^{ce}i(r_{-1}) = Ps(r, \delta)$$

becomes

$$(1 + 2Ep)^{\frac{\alpha}{\alpha+\beta}}P_{-1}i(r_{-1}) = Ps(r, \delta).$$

In the long run, the equilibrium condition

$$P^{ce}i(r) = EPs(r)\tag{20.20}$$

becomes

$$(1 + 2Ep)^{\frac{\alpha}{\alpha+\beta}}P_{-1}i(r) = EPs(r)$$

or

$$\frac{P^{ce}}{EP} \equiv \frac{(1 + 2Ep)^{\frac{\alpha}{\alpha+\beta}}}{1 + Ep} = \frac{s(r)}{i(r)}.\tag{20.32}$$

By contrast, in the deterministic naive-expectations model, we have

$$p = \frac{i(r) - s(r)}{s(r)} \tag{20.7}$$

or

$$\frac{1}{1 + p} = \frac{s(r)}{i(r)}.$$

The stochastic characterization of equilibrium differs in three ways from the deterministic characterization. First, there is the obvious difference that the expected inflation rate Ep replaces the actual inflation rate p. Second, the expression $(1 + 2Ep)^{\frac{\alpha}{\alpha+\beta}}$ has, as has been observed, no counterpart in the deterministic model. Third, Eq. (20.32) does not have a closed-form solution in Ep analogous to (20.7), except in the limiting case as α/β approaches 0.

The first of these differences requires no extensive comment: Ep is the natural analog of p in the stochastic context. The second difference is the basis of the assertion that rational expectations alone do not significantly modify the deterministic results: the value of $(1 + 2Ep)^{\frac{\alpha}{\alpha+\beta}}$ depends critically on the parameters α and β, that is, on the degree of risk aversion. The third difference obliges us to display the consequences of different choices of α and β numerically.

Table 20.2 gives the values of P^{ce}/EP and hence, from Eq. (20.32), corresponding values of $s(r)/i(r)$ for three different values of Ep, $Ep = 0.05, 0.10$, and 0.20. Table 20.3, by contrast, gives the values of Ep that correspond to three different values of $P^{ce}/EP = s(r)/i(r)$,

$$\frac{P^{ce}}{EP} = \frac{s(r)}{i(r)} = 0.952, 0.909, 0.830.$$

These values correspond to inflation rates of 0.05, 0.10, and 0.20 in the deterministic case. The columns of Table 20.2 provide, as it were, a vertical cross section of Ep-curves constructed for alternative values of α and β; the

Table 20.2. P^{ce}/EP for alternative values of Ep, α, and β

			Ep	
α	β	0.05	0.10	0.20
0.0	1.0	0.952	0.909	0.833
0.1	0.9	0.962	0.926	0.862
0.25	0.75	0.975	0.951	0.906
0.5	0.5	0.999	0.996	0.986

Table 20.3. Ep for alternative values of P^{ce}/EP, α, and β

α	β	$\dfrac{P^{ce}}{EP} = \dfrac{s(r)}{i(r)}$		
		0.952	0.909	0.833
0.0	1.0	0.05	0.10	0.20
0.1	0.9	0.06	0.12	0.25
0.25	0.75	0.10	0.19	0.38
0.5	0.5	0.44	0.71	1.24

columns of Table 20.3 provide a horizontal cross section. (Since α and β enter in ratio form, no generality is lost by assuming $\alpha + \beta = 1$.)

These tables are more or less self-explanatory, but two remarks may be in order. First, observe that the first row of each table reproduces the naive-expectations case exactly, a result that also follows directly from substituting $\alpha = 0$ into Eq. (20.32). That is, the consequences of extreme conservatism are equivalent to those of naive forecasting, even though the mechanisms differ markedly. Second, observe that with moderate risk aversion ($\alpha = 0.1$ or $\alpha = 0.25$), the results are qualitatively similar to the naive-expectations case. Only in the absence of risk aversion (row 4 of Table 20.2), does the ratio P^{ce}/EP approach unity for modest rates of expected inflation, which is to say that only in the absence of risk aversion does the Ep-curve become (for small Ep) a horizontal line. (A similar result is represented in row 4 of Table 20.3: in the absence of risk aversion the expected rate of inflation for modest levels of excess demand becomes inordinately high relative to the naive-expectations

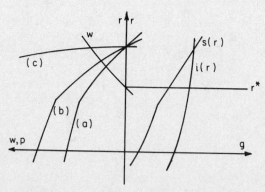

Figure 20.16 Steady growth with rational expectations: Ep-curves reflect (a) $\alpha = 0$, equivalent to naive-expectations case; (b) $0 < \alpha < 0.5$, rational expectations with risk aversion; (c) $\alpha = 0.5$, no risk aversion

case, not to mention the postwar experience of western Europe and North America.)

The key result, however, can be obtained without recourse to these tables. We have in general

$$\frac{P^{ce}}{EP} = \frac{(1 + 2Ep)^{\frac{\alpha}{\alpha+\beta}}}{1 + Ep} < 1$$

for $\alpha \leq 0.5$. Nevertheless, the degree of risk aversion is an important determinant of the magnitude by which P^{ce}/EP differs from unity. For small Ep, the Taylor-series expansion (20.31) produces the result

$$P^{ce} \rightarrow EP$$

as $\alpha/(\alpha + \beta)$ approaches 0.5. This explains why the Ep-curve becomes horizontal at low rates of expected inflation in the absence of risk aversion. As in the pure neo-Keynesian case, the equilibrium condition becomes

$$1 = \frac{s(r)}{i(r)}$$

or $i(r) = s(r)$.

Figure 20.16, a reproduction of Figure 20.12, gathers these results together. Steady-growth equilibria are illustrated for Ep-curves drawn for two different degrees of risk aversion, each being predicated on rational expectations. For comparison, the naive-expectations p-curve of Figure 20.3 is also shown in Figure 20.16.

21 Final Words

I have tried in Chapters 15 and 19 to summarize and criticize alternative approaches to understanding capitalism, and it would be out of place to attempt to recapitulate either the summary or the criticism in any detail. But it might not be amiss to set down in succinct form the major propositions that emerge from this study.

1. It is not differences in logical consistency or completeness that distinguish neoclassical, neo-Marxian, and neo-Keynesian theories from one another. For all intents and purposes, the theories are equal in this domain: each provides a logically coherent explanation of how a capitalist economy *might* function.

2. Neither is the characterization of production — specifically the issue of fixed production coefficients versus continuous substitution — a divisive issue. Each theoretical approach can be cast in fixed-coefficient or continuous-substitution terms; the differences between the theories are independent of how production is characterized. The elasticity of substitution, to be sure, has some bearing on stability, particularly the stability of neoclassical equilibrium; however, the dividing line is not a zero substitution elasticity, but a unitary elasticity.

3. Nor is the characterization of product markets especially controversial. All three theories are compatible with competitive product markets, but all three can be recast in monopolistic terms as well.

4. It follows (with the additional assumption of profit maximization) that a version of marginal-productivity theory is compatible with all three approaches: equality between marginal productivities and input prices are simply the first-order conditions of competitive profit maximization. But if "general" marginal-productivity theory is, when wedded to competitive product markets and profit maximization, the

common property of neo-Keynesians, neo-Marxians, and neoclassicals alike, a "special" version of the theory is exclusively neoclassical: neoclassical theory alone interprets the marginal-productivity equations in terms of a causality that runs from the labor force and the capital stock to the distribution of income. (On its own terms, it should be noted, the neoclassical attempt is more successful for the short run than for the long, and even for the short run the success is only partial.)

5. The results of the one-good model carry over, in the main, to a general-equilibrium setting in which a multiplicity of goods and markets is taken into account: general equilibrium is in no way the exclusive domain of neoclassical theory.

6. One important consequence of taking a general-equilibrium approach is that it permits a comparison of the role of consumer sovereignty in the three models. In the neoclassical model, household utility functions, defined over present and future consumption, affect the distribution of income and the structure of relative prices as well as the composition of output. In the neo-Marxian and neo-Keynesian models, the domain of utility functions—if they exist at all—is restricted to present consumption; accordingly households' tastes at most influence the output mix.

I have concentrated up to now on what does *not* distinguish the theories: logical coherence, the characterization of production and markets, the number of goods and markets—all these are non-issues from the point of view of this book. What does, then, divide the theories?

7. Different assumptions about labor and capital markets—about the determinants of employment and accumulation—are the distinguishing features of neoclassical, neo-Marxian, and neo-Keynesian approaches to capitalism.

8. Since the three theories meet the criteria of logical coherence equally well, they must be judged on the empirical relevance and realism of their assumptions, as well as on the fruitfulness of the lines of inquiry they suggest. But it is in fact extremely difficult to test the assumptions of the models, a result amply demonstrated by the inconclusive confrontation of neoclassical and nonneoclassical saving theories in the arena of the time-series data.

9. The empirical difficulties of testing theories against one another must be counted as a major reason, along with the very real stakes that are bound up with different approaches to capitalism, why theoretical controversy about the choice of models continues to be so heated fifty years after Keynes's *General Theory* and one hundred years after both

Marx's *Capital* and Walras's *Elements of Pure Economics.* The marriage of ignorance and interest has proved a fertile union for theoretical dispute.

10. It goes without saying that I find neoclassical theory wanting in its view of the nature of labor and capital markets in a capitalist economy. But neo-Marxian and neo-Keynesian models are not without their problems too. Chief among these difficulties is that each ignores the insights of the other, providing therefore a partial picture of the capitalist economy. These insights can be integrated into a single model, but at the cost of a substantial revision of the characterization of equilibrium. The synthetic model that integrates Keynesian and Marxian assumptions appears to be more promising than either model taken singly as a framework for organizing one's thinking about the determination of growth, distribution, and prices under capitalism; it is also more promising for analyzing the responsiveness of a capitalist economy to external shocks, as well as for coming to grips with the interplay between inflation and growth.

A Modest Plea

The critical tone of much of the argument notwithstanding, the point of this book has not been to condemn theory. Far from it. It is not only that facts without theory are meaningless; in a very real sense there are no facts without theory. Rather there is a welter of impressions that can lead only to confusion and bewilderment until theory distinguishes the important — the "facts" — from the unimportant. Nor is my intention to indict all of conventional economic theory. Much of it, as we have seen, is shared by neo-Marxians and neo-Keynesians. By the same token, future theory will not simply negate conventional theory; doubtless it will preserve as it supersedes. Georg Friedrich Hegel had a word for the process of simultaneously preserving and superseding — *aufheben* — but we lack an equally succinct English equivalent to characterize the dialectic of intellectual development (where it makes more obvious sense than as a method of historical explanation).

My personal conviction, however, is that while aspects of conventional economic theory will prove enduring, the specifically neoclassical assumptions — that full employment and consumers' intertemporal preferences determine the equilibrium configuration of growth, distribution, and prices — will not. So although this book does not argue for suppression of conventional theory, it does argue, at the very least, for parity in research and teaching for alternatives to the neoclassical approach.

A full and fair presentation of neo-Marxian and neo-Keynesian theories will accomplish three ends. First, it will permit even the most devout of the faithful to distinguish the essentially neoclassical elements of their theory from the assumptions shared by other theories, for the distinguishing features of one theory can emerge only in comparison with others. Second, it will permit the true believer and the heretic alike to see neoclassical theory as one approach rather than *the* approach. Third, and most important, it hastens the day of constructing a theory that adequately explains the capitalist mode of production.

None of this may have anything to do with the necessity of changing capitalism. But it just may have something to do with our freedom to change it for the better.

Notes on the Literature

1. Introduction

First a word on labels. Alternatives to "neoclassical" are "neo-Walrasian" or "marginalist," but the first seems a bit too narrow and the second downright misleading. Neo-Walrasian would have preserved a nice symmetry with neo-Marxian and neo-Keynesian, but it does not reflect the breadth of sources as well as the term "neoclassical" does. "Marginalist" has become identified with smoothness in production, a secondary issue from my point of view. The label "neo-Marxian" is less problematic, even though important features of the model are anticipated by Ricardo. For the purposes of this book, one might almost say that Marx is Ricardo plus the reserve army, a concept that requires situating capitalism in a larger network of economic relations. "Neo-Keynesian" is a concession of accuracy to common usage, not to mention phonic sensibility. A more accurate terminology, like "neo-Keynes-Kaleckian," would place altogether too high a premium on truth-in-labeling. Observe that the term "neo-Keynesian" has come more and more, especially in the United States, to mean "fixprice" models of the kind elaborated by Robert Barro and Herschel Grossman (1971, 1976) and Edmond Malinvaud (1977, 1980), rather than the Harrod-Kaldor-Robinson type models elaborated in this book.

Many books overlap the purposes of this one. Those that provide an overview are decidedly neoclassical in orientation; moreover, they tend to concentrate on growth and to concern themselves with distribution only tangentially. Subject to these qualifications, Avinash Dixit (1976) provides a useful introduction. At higher levels of sophistication are Edwin Burmeister and A. Rodney Dobell (1970) and Burmeister (1980). More advanced still is Christopher Bliss (1975). Bliss is as neoclassical in his approach as the others, but his book is easily the most thoughtful and penetrating of these texts. Harry Johnson (1973) is distinctive in coming at the problem from the point of view of distribution theory rather than growth theory. Lance Taylor (1983) is exceptional in three ways: first, his focus is on Third World countries and their relationship to the advanced capitalist nations, with equal attention to the short run and the long; second, although Taylor's book is essentially a theoretical text, the hand of the applied model builder is readily discernible; third, neo-Marxian and neo-Keynesian ideas play a prominent role in Taylor's analysis. Joseph Stiglitz and Hirofumi Uzawa (1969) have assembled a collection of papers that is still a good starting point a decade and a half later. Their bibliography is also useful. Amartya Sen (1970) also provides an excellent collection, with an introduction that gives an integrative overview. Some of the most important nonneoclassical articles written in the 1960s and early 1970s, including six cited in this book, are reprinted in E. K. Hunt and Jesse Schwarz (1972).

Sen (1963) was the first, to my knowledge, to locate the difference between theories in differences in the equations used to close a common model—the first, that is, to use the approach that I have taken in this book. Sen, however, confines his analysis to the short period and limits the comparison to neoclassical and neo-Keynesian models. Donald Harris (1978) comes closest to the scope, if not the method, of this book, but important analytic differences give his work a very different thrust. First, Harris (like many others) identifies neoclassical theory with smoothness in production; second, he interprets the neo-Marxian view of the labor market differently, treating the labor supply as exogenous rather than endogenous. Barro and Grossman (1971, 1976) and Malinvaud (1977, 1980) also compare alternative theories, but their approaches differ from mine in two respects. First, their emphasis is on the short run, and second, they see price inflexibility (as well as money-wage inflexibility) as the big difference between neoclassical equilibrium (market-clearing or Walrasian equilibrium in their terminology) and Keynesian equilibrium. (Neither considers a specifically Marxian approach.) Finally, Frank Hahn recently published (1982) a revised version of lectures on the post-Sraffian critique of neoclassical theory which he gave at Harvard University in 1975 as the present book was taking initial shape. I was struck then as now with the large measure of agreement between Hahn and myself on specific points, particularly on the logical coherence of neoclassical theory. Important differences remain, however. Hahn apparently has a much more catholic notion of neoclassical theory: what are for me major conceptual differences between theories seem for him to be minor variations on the same theme.

2. The Neoclassical Approach

The neoclassical model outlined in this chapter makes three key assumptions: first, that prices clear all markets; second, that households maximize utility over all goods; and third, that the class structure, such as it is, is recreated anew in each generation by the life-cycle process of work and retirement. The first two assumptions are explicit both in the model of this chapter and in the canonical statements of the neoclassical model by Kenneth Arrow and Gerard Debreu (1954) and Debreu (1959). The third assumption is explicit here but is necessarily implicit rather than explicit in Arrow-Debreu type models: the

Arrow-Debreu argument is cast in terms of given endowments and a finite number of actors; an Arrow-Debreu equilibrium corresponds neither to a steady-growth equilibrium nor to a sequence of temporary, period-by-period equilibria, such as was introduced in the discussion of stability at the end of this chapter. Since it is nowhere assumed in Arrow-Debreu type economies that endowments are equal, one might be tempted to argue that these models are compatible with the assumption of permanent classes of capitalists and workers. However, although households are not necessarily homogeneous in Arrow-Debreu type models, the absence of any discussion whatsoever of the consequences of systematic, class-based differences among households suggests that differences among households are purely random.

The concept of overlapping generations was developed by Paul Samuelson (1958) in order to dramatize the Pareto inoptimality of competitive equilibrium in the context of an infinite-period model, a point that had previously been made by Tjalling Koopmans (1957, pp. 111–112), drawing on the work of Edmond Malinvaud (1953). Peter Diamond (1965) expanded the overlapping-generations model to include production, his main purpose being an examination of the consequences of public debt for the efficient allocation of resources over time. The present model is virtually identical to Diamond's except for the assumption here of fixed coefficients, which is not relaxed until Chapter 9. Diamond simply assumes the existence of stable competitive equilibrium, which this chapter demonstrates is problematic. (The problems do not disappear with the introduction of continuous substitution in production.)

The application of utility maximization to intertemporal consumption decisions—the "life-cycle hypothesis"—goes back to Irving Fisher (1930). Its modern form is the work of Franco Modigliani and his collaborators. Modigliani and Blumberg (1954), Ando and Modigliani (1963), Modigliani (1975), and Modigliani and Steindel (1977) are representative works in a vast literature. Milton Friedman has developed Fisher's ideas along lines that stress uncertainty. His "permanent-income" hypothesis, originally presented in 1957, has spawned an equally vast literature. These two variants of neoclassical saving theory are examined in more detail and contrasted with nonneoclassical theory in Chapters 17 and 18.

3. The Neo-Marxian Approach

Karl Marx's writings, chiefly *Capital* (in three volumes, published respectively in 1867, 1893, and 1894), are the original source for the model set out in this chapter. There are, of course, tremendous problems of interpretation: despite his claim to having provided a scientific understanding of capitalism, and therewith a scientific basis for socialism, what Marx "really meant" is frequently as opaque as what Jesus or Buddha really meant. An example will suffice: the basis for treating the labor force as endogenous in the neo-Marxian model is Marx's assumption "that the portion of the newly created money-capital capable of being converted into variable capital will always find at hand the labor-power into which it transforms itself" (1893, p. 501). But this hardly fits with his assumption that "the general movement of wages are exclusively regulated by the expansion and contraction of the industrial reserve army" (1867, p. 637). The two statements can be reconciled—the first can be interpreted as an assumption about the long run, the second as an assumption about the short run—but so can the contradictory statements of great religious leaders. It is the need to reconcile the two statements that creates the problem of interpretation; how successful one might be in this endeavor is another matter altogether.

Among classical Marxian texts, Rosa Luxemburg's *Accumulation of Capital* (1913) was probably the closest in spirit to the model presented here. Luxemburg's distinctive contribution was her insistence on embedding capitalism in a larger socioeconomic framework. Luxemburg emphasized the larger framework as a solution to the problem of matching capitalists' saving with investment demand (the realization problem); but she also considered supply-side aspects of the relationship of capitalist to noncapitalist modes of production.

The most comprehensive contemporary statement of Marx's economics in terms of a formal model is Michio Morishima (1973). Leif Johansen (1963) presents a basically similar but less complete model. Johansen was concerned with the question of the compatibility of utility theory with the labor theory of value and, consequently, did not address the question of the rate of growth or its relationship to distribution. (The role of utility maximization in the neo-Marxian model is discussed in Chapter 11 of this book.) John Roemer (1978; 1981, chap. 9) outlines a model similar to Johansen's, but Roemer adds a degree of freedom to the model by assuming that unemployed workers are supported out of profits. He resolves the resulting indeterminacy by introducing an investment-demand function, an idea which—despite its considerable merit (see Chapter 4)—appears to me to be un-Marxian in the extreme. David Laibman (1977) presents what he calls a "Marxian model of economic growth," but it also includes a decidedly un-Marxian element, namely, the natural rate of growth $g = n$. Laibman can accommodate this essentially neo-classical assumption without overdetermining the model by means of a variable output: capital ratio. Harris's model (1978) makes the wage rate a function of demand and supply conditions in the labor market; again investment demand plays an autonomous role. I would regard this model as a synthesis of Marxian, Keynesian, and neoclassical elements, closer in spirit if not mechanics to the model developed in Chapter 20 than to a pure Marxian model. Despite the differences, there is a common element in all these models, namely, the key role attached to the rate of exploitation or the subsistence wage and (except for Johansen) a "classical" saving function, the crucial property of which (as is shown in Chapter 6) is that capitalists' saving propensity exceeds workers' saving propensity.

Paul Sweezy (1942) provides an elementary introduction to the labor theory of value and related matters, but there is little discussion in Sweezy's text of the social relations of production as a determinant of productivity and profitability —in my opinion a distinctive feature of the Marxian approach, even if for the most part one that lies outside the scope of this book. In addition to the references cited at the end of this chapter, Herbert Gintis (1976), Richard Edwards (1979), David Montgomery (1979), and David Noble (1977, 1979) are recommended. These works share a common emphasis on class struggle as a determinant of the relations of capitalist production. Harry Braverman (1974) argues from a different implicit presupposition, namely, that class struggle is a thing of the past: the evolution of capitalist relations of production reflects the strategy of a victorious capitalist class rather than an active, continuing struggle between capitalists and workers.

4. The Neo-Keynesian Approach

John Maynard Keynes's *General Theory* (1936) is the starting point. However, the *Treatise on Money* (1930) not only anticipates much of the argument of the *General Theory*, but in its emphasis on the relationship between the balance of (desired) investment and (desired) saving and profits, anticipates more explicitly the neo-Keynesian position. The metaphor of the widow's cruse, for instance, comes from the *Treatise*, not the *General Theory*. Michal Kalecki is rightly regarded as a founding father of equal standing. His earliest contributions were published in 1933, 1934, and 1935. His relative obscurity (relative, that is, to Keynes) is the result of three causes: first, he originally wrote in Polish, hardly a language of international communication in economics; second, he was—unlike Keynes—young and unestablished when his work appeared; third, the three articles to which I have alluded are—again in contrast to Keynes—terse in the extreme, covering together 34 pages in the 1971 volume of his collected essays.

Roy Harrod's original paper on the dynamic implications of the Keynesian system appeared in 1939; it was later expanded into a series of lectures in which investment demand figures more prominently (1948). Harrod revised the 1948 volume much later (1973), but in my judgment the revised version is less effective than the 1948 statement, which is the basis of the argument in this chapter. Evsey Domar (1946) is often lumped together with Harrod as the coauthor of the "Harrod-Domar" model. It puzzles me that anybody who has read both Harrod and Domar can join them together. Harrod, in true Keynesian spirit, makes capitalists' "animal spirits," along with society's saving propensity, the driving force behind the warranted rate of growth. The opposition between warranted and natural rates of growth is the linchpin of Harrod's model. Domar concentrates exclusively on the relationship between growth, on the one hand, and the saving rate and the output : capital ratio, on the other.

Robinson (1956, 1962) is the immediate source for the model developed in this chapter. Nicholas Kaldor (1956, 1957, 1961) uses Keynesian ideas in his analysis—particularly in emphasizing the relationship between the distribution of income and the rate of growth. (As observed, however, these ideas come as much from the *Treatise* as from the *General Theory*.) However, Kaldor's assumption of full employment seems to me (and, I gather through personal communication, to him also in retrospect) as more neoclassical than neo-Keynesian. Kaldor's models are discussed in Chapters 8 and 10.

As noted in the text of this chapter, the investment-demand function is the long-run counterpart of Keynes's marginal-efficiency-of-capital schedule, with one important difference: the rate of interest — the cost of capital services — is held constant, and the prospective rate of profit is varied. The role accorded investment demand in shaping equilibrium is the most distinctive feature of the neo-Keynesian model. Orthodox economics approaches the neo-Keynesian view in James Tobin's q-theory (1969, Tobin and Brainard 1977). But q-theory makes investment hinge on differences between prospective profitability and the cost of capital services only in the short run; for the long run, the theory reduces to the neoclassical view that investment is determined by full-employment growth. Malinvaud's investment theory (1980) is even closer in spirit to the neo-Keynesian position because prospective profitability enters directly rather than through the proxy of stock-market valuations.

5. Neo-Marxian and Neo-Keynesian Conceptions of the Labor Market

The basic Marxian account of the reserve army is in *Capital* (1867, chap. 25). Keynes's *General Theory* (1936) devotes chapters 2 and 19 to the labor market. Although Keynes does not rule out money illusion, he explains the failure of the wage rate to clear the labor market in terms of the relativistic orientation of the working class. For Keynes, the typical worker's struggle is with other workers, not with capitalists: workers are concerned with relative real wages rather than with the real wage itself. Hence the focus on money wages. It is natural that neoclassical economists like John Hicks (1974) and Robert Solow (1980) have been more concerned than nonneoclassical economists to rationalize the failure of the wage rate to clear the labor market: the more central to one's theory is the clearing of markets by the price mechanism and the shaping of behavior by individual utility maximization, the greater is the puzzle of a labor market in which the wage rate does not adjust demand and supply.

The conception of the reserve army elaborated here has much in common with W. Arthur Lewis's ideas (1954) on growth in labor-surplus economies. The difference is that Lewis, like most development economists, sees surplus labor as a condition specific to poor, densely populated countries like India. Here "surplus labor" is seen as a general characteristic of capitalist development. A theory of value for the labor-surplus economy is constructed in Marglin (1976b), but this theory is neoclassical rather than Marxian in conception.

Michael Piore (1979) never uses the term "reserve army" but provides both thoughtful description and analysis of the role of international migration in making up deficiencies in domestic labor supply. Piore's emphasis is chiefly on the United States, but he includes some comparative material on western Europe.

6. Generalizing the Classics: The Cambridge Saving Equation

The classical economists — Adam Smith (1776) and David Ricardo (1817) as well as Marx — took it as self-evident that no saving comes out of wages. Today they would presumably exclude the components of personal saving that make working-class saving appear sizable, namely pension-fund saving and investment in owner-occupied housing. (Alternative definitions and measures of saving are discussed in Chapter 17.) The important contributions to the development of the Cambridge saving equation have been cited in the text of this chapter. Additional references are Meade (1963), Pasinetti (1966a), Robinson (1966), and Samuelson and Modigliani (1966b).

The debate over ownership and control actually antedates Adolph Berle and Gardiner Means (1932). Thorstein Veblen (1921) contrasted financial and industrial interests, and William Ripley (1927) argued what was to become Berle's and Means's central theme. James Burnham (1941) and Robert Brady (1943) are transitional figures who anticipated some of John Kenneth Galbraith's argument (1967) on the power of the technostructure. David Kotz (1978) suggests that effective control lies not with technostructure or top management or shareholders, but with bankers, whose influence rests on their power both as trustees of large blocks of voting stock and as corporate creditors. To balance Peter Drucker's apocalyptic vision of pension funds (1976), there is a more sympathetic account by Jeremy Rifkin and Randy Barber (1978).

7. Foundations for the Cambridge Saving Equation

Neoclassicals have to their credit the attempt to provide microeconomic underpinnings to macroeconomic theory. But they get lower marks for their insistence on formulating these underpinnings in terms of atomistic individual maximizing behavior. This chapter attempts to provide alternative, nonneoclassical underpinnings for one set of macroeconomic relationships, namely, saving behavior. The theory of household behavior sketched in this chapter appeals more to Herbert Simons's theory of "satisficing" (1955, 1956) than to the traditional neoclassical theory of maximizing behavior. Francis Green (1980) criticizes neoclassical consumption theory specifically and defends the disequilibrium approach.

8. Some Hybrid Models

The identification of full employment with neoclassical theory may require some explanation when nonneoclassical economists as eminent as Kaldor and Luigi Pasinetti have closed their models by assuming $g = n$. Kaldor evidently incorporated full employment into his models because it seemed appropriate in the long-run context, as distinct from the short-run context in which a Keynesian framework that allowed for an equilibrium with unemployment was more suitable. Kaldor presumably felt this assumption to be all the more reasonable since right from the beginning (1956), his model allowed for special cases in which either a real wage floor (Joan Robinson's inflation barrier) or a failure of investment demand might prevent the achievement of full employment.

Meeting Kaldor in 1974, as this book was taking shape, I asked him how he justified the assumption of full employment. His response bordered on the unique, at least in my experience of leaders of the economics profession: "I was wrong," he began. Others have admitted to error and then gone on to explain how they themselves discovered and corrected their error. Uniqueness lay not so much in Kaldor's confessing error, but in crediting someone else (in this case Joan Robinson) with convincing him that an important assumption of his model was mistaken.

Pasinetti was noncommittal with respect to his intention in assuming full employment (1962). He claimed only to offer a theory of "consistency with full employment" (p. 279).

Other hybrids besides those described here may exist, but the only one that I have come across is Johansen's (1960, chap. 2). Johansen makes investment demand exogenous and marries this assumption to a neoclassical natural rate of growth. The saving function is suppressed on the grounds that fiscal and monetary policy can adjust saving to the requirements of investment demand and full employment.

In his treatment of the saving function, Johansen has much in common with Tobin (1955, 1965), who transforms the saving function into an instrument of government policy by (1) introducing a money supply controlled by the government and (2) assuming asset preferences that make desired holdings of physical capital and money a function of the respective yields of the two assets. Rudiger Dornbusch and Jacob Frankel (1973) provide a clear summary of the development of the Tobin model through the early 1970s. Miguel Sidrauski's alternative formulations of household saving behavior (1967a and 1967b) focused attention on the question of the influence of financial variables (in particular, the rate of growth of the money supply) on steady-growth levels of capital and consumption per person. Duncan Foley collaborated with Sidrauski (1970, 1971) in extending the Tobin framework to analyze fiscal and monetary policy in a two-sector model à la Hirofumi Uzawa (1961, 1963).

In my taxonomy, the basic Tobin model fits under the hybrid rubric since, like Solow's 1956 model, it combines the neoclassical assumption that equilibrium growth is given by population dynamics with the textbook Keynesian assumption that saving is a constant fraction of income. In this framework, the steady-state capital:labor ratio and steady-state consumption generally depend on the rate of growth of the money supply. In contrast, Sidrauski (1967a) introduced intertemporal utility maximization in place of the Keynesian saving assumption to argue the "superneutrality" of money, that is, the independence of the steady-state capital:labor ratio and steady-state consumption per capita from the rate of growth of the money supply. Sidrauski recognized—and Stanley Fischer has recently emphasized (1979)—that this result holds only in comparisons of steady-growth configurations, not on transitional paths between steady states. In none of these models however, including Sidrauski's and Fischer's, are saving decisions situated in a life-cycle framework; consequently none addresses the problem raised at the end of this chapter of simultaneously satisfying the ownership condition and food-grain market equilibrium in the context of overlapping generations.

9. Variable Proportions

The contemporary theory of growth with continuous substitution begins with Solow's contribution (1956), a landmark even though in my judgment it is defective on two counts: first, it is not, despite its title, "neoclassical"; second, it fails in its objective of resolving the tension between warranted and natural rates of growth. (An incidental contribution of Solow's paper is the introduction of the constant elasticity of substitution production function, a concept imposed on the economics profession's consciousness later by Arrow, Chenery, Minhas, and Solow 1961.) With continuous substitution, the neoclassical model of this book is essentially the same as Diamond's (1965), although the present focus on existence and stability of equilibrium is different from Diamond's emphasis on the effect of public debt on the rate of growth; Diamond takes both existence and stability for granted.

For many economists, both neoclassical and nonneoclassical, the nature of the production function is the central point of theoretical controversy. Indeed, as has been noted, continuous substitution often identifies not only a production function but an entire model as "neoclassical." Solow's article is a case in point. Bliss (1975) and Hahn (1982) are — at least on this issue — closer to the position of this book in rejecting the characterization of production as a distinguishing feature of alternative theories. On the nonneoclassical side, Edward Nell (1967) takes a position similar to mine.

The 1950s and 1960s were a period of extensive debate about the production function. A main point of contention in the debate was the usefulness of the one-good model: at issue was the possibility of meaningfully aggregating heterogeneous capital goods into a scalar "value of capital" that preserves the negative, one-to-one relationship between capital and the competitive rate of profit. This debate figures in subsequent chapters, particularly in Chapter 12.

Neo-Marxian and neo-Keynesian models have not, to the best of my knowledge, been developed elsewhere in the context of continuous substitution. (Laibman's model [1977] is set in a continuous-substitution framework, but I have already suggested why I would not characterize Laibman's model as Marxian.) In particular, there is, as far as I know, no analysis of the labor theory of value under the assumption of continuous substitution. The same is true for the short-run neo-Keynesian multiplier; however, Sargent (1979, p. 52) provides a general formula for the multiplier that includes supply-side considerations.

10. Marginal Productivity and Marginal-Productivity Theory

Marginal productivity theory has an ancient if not altogether honorable pedigree. In the hands of John Bates Clark (1891, 1899) it achieved the status of natural law, a status that even the most devout neoclassical would be reluctant to accord it today. Neoclassical and nonneoclassical economists have agreed, erroneously in my judgment, in identifying neoclassical theory and marginal-productivity theory with one another. As indicated in this chapter, the cutting edge of neoclassical theory is sharpened by uniting marginal-productivity equations based on continuous substitution and competitive profit maximization with the assumption of full employment, or more precisely, with the application to the labor market of the price-clearing hypothesis. But the essence of the theory lies in price clearing, not in the marginal-productivity equations, that is, in the characterization of the labor market, not in the characterization of the production function.

This position is at odds with the criticism of marginal-productivity theory that underlay the capital controversy of the 1950s and 1960s and that hinged upon the problems of capital aggregation. The subject can be treated in full only in the many-good context of Chapters 11–14 (see especially Chapter 12 and the accompanying discussion in these notes), but a few words may be in order here. A line of criticism begun by Robinson (1953–54) and Piero Sraffa (1960), the capital-theoretic attack on marginal-productivity theory was developed by a younger generation of economists under Sraffa's titular leadership, a group often referred to as the Anglo-Italian school not only because of Sraffa but because of the prominence of Italians—such as Pasinetti (1966b, 1977) and Pierangelo Garegnani (1966, 1970)—who had sojourned at the University of Cambridge. My interpretation of the Anglo-Italian indictment of marginal-productivity theory is that in the many-good context, factor-demand functions need not be "well-behaved," that is, downward-sloping. As a counterexample to the usual stability conditions, the possibility of "perversely" sloped factor-demand functions can be taken as a criticism of the assumption of the price-clearing hypothesis: price clearing is, after all, as much an assumption about the stability of equilibrium as about existence. But many goods are hardly necessary for instability of neoclassical equilibrium. The models of Chapters 2 and 9 may exhibit instability even with only one good. In any case, my own sense is that criticism of labor-market price clearing based on the endogeneity of the labor supply is more telling, but that is a matter of judgment. Notwithstanding Pasinetti's role in developing the Anglo-Italian criticism of marginal-productivity theory, I have recently had called to my attention a paragraph in his latest book (1981, p. 204) that makes a distinction between marginal-productivity theories similar to the one suggested in this chapter.

It was remarked in this chapter that neoclassical theorists are hardly unanimous as to how rapidly markets clear, particularly the labor market. Most neoclassicals would, I think, accept double-digit unemployment rates prevailing throughout North America and western Europe as this book goes to press as evidence that the labor market is not clearing at the moment. However, a sect of true believers has long maintained that *all* markets *always* clear; if the toothpaste market—or the labor market—is not clearing as you read this, it is simply because these markets have closed for the day. This sect has adherents throughout the world, but its traditional center has been the University of Chicago. The current high priest is Robert Lucas, whose "Equilibrium Model of the Business Cycle" (1975) is essentially a stochastic version of Tobin's growth model (1965) with unanticipated fiscal-monetary shocks that are misperceived by producers.

11. The Basic Models in the Multiple-Good Context

It was observed that a constant overall capital : output ratio reduces the multiple-good case to the one-good models elaborated in the first part of this book. I thought myself quite clever for identifying Marx's equal organic composition of capital as symmetric to Sraffa's standard commodity, each being a way of ensuring a constant output : capital ratio, and each reducible to a characteristic vector of the capital matrix **A**. Peter Newman's review (1962) of Sraffa's *Production of Commodities* explained the standard commodity as a characteristic vector, but I thought the corresponding analysis of the Marxian case to be an original discovery—until I chanced upon Burmeister's exposition of growth theory (1980), in which he proves the proposition on the organic composition of capital that is advanced in this chapter and notes its symmetric relationship to Sraffa's standard commodity.

Despite the common identification of general-equilibrium models with neo-classical theory, all the models of this chapter are, willy-nilly, exercises in general equilibrium. They differ from more conventional general-equilibrium models not only because of the introduction of the neo-Marxian and neo-Keynesian elements that are the principal subject matter of this book, but because the composition of the capital stock is treated as endogenous. As noted, this assumption facilitates the discussion of the existence of equilibrium by allowing us to ignore the stability problem. The seminal discussion of stability in the multiple-good context is Hahn (1966). Drawing on Hahn and others, particularly Kyoshi Kuga (1977), Burmeister (1980, chap. 6) analyzes the stability issue for a hybrid model in which the neoclassical assumption of full employment $(g = n)$ is coupled with a classical saving assumption $(s_C = 1, s_W = 0)$.

For background on the models of this chapter, the reader should refer to the notes for Chapters 2, 3, and 4. Indeed, in the case of the neoclassical and neo-Marxian models, the usual formulation is in terms of general equilibrium (that is, multiple-good) models. By contrast, the neo-Keynesian model has generally been set out in aggregative terms.

Two specifics of the neo-Marxian model deserve bibliographic attention: the first is the transformation problem; the second is the conventional wage. On the transformation problem, there is now considerable agreement between critics and defenders of the Marxian approach. In contrast with the older view typified by Sweezy (1942), Marxians such as Alfredo Medio (1972) and Roemer (1981) appear to have no quarrel with Samuelson's argument (1971) that the labor theory of value is an inadequate theory of relative prices. Their arguments suggest a view with which I heartily agree—as the discussion of the labor theory of value in Chapter 19 indicates—namely, that the labor theory of value is better understood as a theory of profit than as a theory of price. There is an extensive literature on the relationship between the rate of exploitation and the rate of profit; see Nobuo Okishio (1963), Michio Morishima (1973, 1974), Ian Steedman (1977), and John Roemer (1981).

The conventional (or subsistence) wage merits more consideration than neo-Marxians have heretofore given it. Roemer (1981, pp. 150–153) clearly outlines the problems caused by divorcing the conventional wage from biological subsistence, but this seems to be as far as neo-Marxians have taken the argument.

An important difference between the role of consumer sovereignty in neoclassical and nonneoclassical theories emerged from the comparison of neoclassical with neo-Marxian theories and neo-Keynesian models in this chapter: in the first, household utility functions affect relative prices, as well as output; in the second, only the mix of outputs is affected. This difference was noted by Johansen in his comparison of neoclassical and Marxian theories (1963) and by Nell in his comparison of Walrasian and Ricardian theories (1967).

12. Multiple Technologies: The Reswitching Debate

Reswitching was held to be important because it is a sufficient—but not necessary—condition for the failure of monotonicity in the correspondence between the capital intensity of production and the rate of profit. Hence the reswitching debate must be understood as part of a larger debate about the existence of a "well-behaved" capital aggregate in a multiple-good world.

The opening salvo in the debate on the aggregation of capital was fired by Robinson (1953–54). David Champernowne (1953–54) proposed an alternative method of aggregating capital, and Solow (1955–56) demonstrated the stringency of the assumptions required for aggregation. Both Robinson, who attributed the recognition of the possibility of reswitching to Ruth Cohen (a Cambridge colleague), and Champernowne considered reswitching to be an anomaly. Sraffa (1960) was apparently the first to regard reswitching as other than anomalous or perverse.

David Levhari's attempt (1965) to prove the impossibility of reswitching of an entire technology in a model characterized by indecomposability was shown to be faulty by several individuals whose disproofs and counterexamples were published together in November 1966 in the *Quarterly Journal of Economics* under the title "Paradoxes in Capital Theory: A Symposium." (The title is interesting: for the nonneoclassical contributors to the symposium—Pasinetti (1966b), Morishima (1966), and Garegnani (1966)—the essence of the critique was that reswitching was no more paradoxical than the absence of reswitching.) A preliminary version of Pasinetti's paper was presented to the World Congress of the Econometric Society held in Rome in 1965. I understand that this version contained the essential elements of a counterexample to Levhari's conjecture even though it did not quite fit Levhari's assumptions; but I have not myself seen the 1965 version.

By this time, the debate had become so technical that outsiders could easily lose sight of the original issues. The participants were not terribly helpful. Garegnani's contribution to the *QJE* symposium was the only one to link the question of the functional relationship between capital intensity of production and the rate of profit to the broader question of the validity of neoclassical theory, and this paper did so only in a paragraph at the end. (See also Garegnani 1970 and Pasinetti 1977.) To this day the link is hardly clear. The point seems to be that reswitching makes impossible a one-to-one correspondence between the value of capital per worker and the rate of profit, and that consequently factor-demand curves may have the wrong shape. (The demand for labor per unit of capital is subject to the same difficulties as the demand for capital per worker.) "Wrong" presumably means upward-sloping, but upward-sloping demand curves hardly put the *existence* of neoclassical equilibrium in doubt: the slope of factor-demand curves has no bearing on the question of existence. It seems that the issue must be one either of uniqueness or of stability of long-run equilibrium, in other words, one of period-to-period transition outside a regime of steady growth. But if this is the case, the criticism is at best incomplete: it does not come to grips with the fallback neoclassical position that the appropriate models for analyzing heterogeneous capital are disaggregated general-equilibrium models (like the models of this chapter) in which the behavior of the value of aggregate capital is — for purposes of existence of equilibrium at least — beside the point. This, it should be emphasized, is the position that prominent neoclassicals like Solow (1955–56) and Samuelson (1962) consistently defended even when exploring the possibilities of capital aggregation. It would have to be demonstrated that with respect to uniqueness and stability, the neoclassical model is peculiarly vulnerable to the complications of heterogeneous capital. This may indeed be so, but to the best of my knowledge the argument is yet to be made. It has been observed, in any case, that a multiplicity of commodities is hardly necessary for neoclassical instability.

Robinson (1975) has dismissed the reswitching controversy on other grounds: the irrelevance of comparative statics. For Robinson the only possible usefulness of production functions is in comparative-statics exercises, which she judges irrelevant to a world in which comparisons across space or over time always involve comparisons between different production sets rather than comparisons within a single, given production set. (Pasinetti 1977 takes a similar view.)

Recent history may provide a test of Robinson's dictum: casual empiricism suggests that the increase in the relative price of energy after 1973 has reduced the energy intensity of production (and consumption). To be sure, the technological environment has not remained unchanged during this period, but it seems to me that the changes in production technique induced by the rise in energy prices have for the most part involved shifts to techniques already known, in broad outline if not in all details, before 1973 — that is, shifts within a given production set — rather than shifts to a new production set. In short, although I have my doubts, I am persuaded neither of the futility of comparative statics nor of the exclusively apologetic character of the continuous-substitution production function.

13. Continuous Substitution

The literature on growth models with many goods and technologies has focused on problems different from the ones addressed here. From von Neumann (1945–46) through Dorfman, Samuelson, and Solow (1958) and Morishima (1964), the focus was on the existence and efficiency of a balanced-growth path. These are problems of significantly greater technical difficulty in the context of models with durable capital goods than in the context of models, like those of this book, with circulating capital only. (It should be noted that, starting with von Neumann, production was characterized in these models by a finite array of linear technologies rather than by continuous substitution.)

The 1960s saw the elaboration of two-sector models reflecting Marx's division of the economy into capital-good and consumption-good departments. The seminal contributions were made by Uzawa (1961, 1962). The subsequent literature is summarized in Burmeister and Dobell (1970) and more briefly in Burmeister (1980). It is fair to say that the main novelty relative to the one-sector model lies in the additional complexity of the stability conditions. Hahn (1966) shifted attention to the analysis of stability in more general models, and the two-sector model appears now to have more of a past than a future.

Once again, a result I thought to be original turned out not to have been. Reviewing the literature for these notes, I found a proof of the impossibility of reswitching in a continuous-substitution framework in Burmeister and Dobell (1970).

14. Monopoly and Degree-of-Monopoly Theory

My view that degree-of-monopoly or mark-up theory is compatible with all of the theoretical approaches investigated in this book is hardly the dominant one. In particular, Kalecki's mark-up theory is generally viewed as a distinct theory of distribution, if not of growth. Ironically, however, there is little agreement as to where the mark-up theory belongs in the theoretical spectrum. At least one prominent nonneoclassical (Kaldor 1956) has categorized the mark-up theory as a subspecies of neoclassical economics. The more usual nonneoclassical view is that perfect competition is a hallmark of neoclassical theory and that the assumption of pervasive market imperfections stamps a theory as nonneoclassical. The American "post-Keynesians" centered at Rutgers University, who see themselves as the inheritors of Keynes and Kalecki, are typical of this second view (see, for example, Alfred Eichner and Jan Kregel 1975). For the record, there is a vast literature on general equilibrium with monopoly that could hardly be called anything but neoclassical. A recent paper by Oliver Hart (1983) provides an overview.

But the neoclassicals hardly have a monopoly on monopoly theory. Masahiko

Aoki (1977) has developed the neo-Marxian growth model for a regime of monopolies, and Tsuneo Ishikawa (1977) has elaborated the neo-Keynesian model in the monopoly context. (Unfortunately, at this writing, Ishikawa's work is available only in Japanese.)

15. Overall Summary

Since this chapter is a summary, there is little to add by way of bibliographic references to the notes relating to previous chapters. Of special interest is D. Mario Nuti's short critique (1970) which focuses on neoclassical theory but also addresses neo-Marxian and neo-Keynesian theory. The paper derives its interest from the difference between two versions published two years apart: the original version is Anglo-Italian to the core, whereas a postscript added in 1972 is much more in harmony with my own position. Robinson's (1971) book is the only comprehensive statement of her position after the dust had settled on the debate of the 1950s and 1960s.

16. Testing the Models: Energy and Employment

Malinvaud's simulation of an energy shock (1980, pp. 85–86) gave me the idea of testing the three models by examining the comparative statics of a shift in the production function resulting from a change in the price of energy. However, none of the models is here developed to the point where a test could be anything more than an exercise in casual empiricism.

17. Alternative Theories of Saving

The original source for both the permanent-income and life-cycle hypotheses is Fisher (1930), who provided the spirit as well as much of the technical apparatus for the neoclassical theory of intertemporal choice; indeed, the Fisherian apparatus is the basis of the indifference-curve approach that is now standard in presentations of the neoclassical theory of the household. In the best tradition of "normal science" (the term is Thomas Kuhn's 1962), the life-cycle and permanent-income hypotheses arose in response to an anomaly in the empirical data gathered to estimate simple Keynesian consumption functions: time-series evidence suggested a linear, homogeneous consumption function, whereas household budget studies suggested a positive intercept and a declining average propensity to consume. In my judgment the life-cycle and permanent-income approaches gained favor more because they provided a link between (Keynesian) macroeconomics and (neoclassical) microeconomics than because of their success in explaining the empirical evidence on consumption and saving. The relative obscurity of James Duesenberry's relative-income hypothesis (1949) or Tillman Brown's habit-persistence hypothesis (1952), reincarnated here as the disequilibrium hypothesis, or Richard Ball and Pamela Drake's precautionary-saving hypothesis (1964) seems to me to owe more to the dissonant note they strike with neoclassical theory than to a failure to explain the data. Thomas Mayer's (1972) thorough summary of empirical tests through the early 1970s, though hardly sympathetic to these theories, finds relatively little hard evidence that is necessarily inconsistent with them, and I suspect these theories are even more robust if household saving is defined in financial terms, as I have suggested is appropriate for purposes of analyzing a capitalist economy. As Mayer recognizes (p. 21), the failure of most tests to discriminate among theories is largely because the estimating equations for all these theories, as distinct from the interpretation of these equations, are quite similar.

In the 1970s empirical research on saving has tested the effect of private pension plans and social security on private saving. The first results of Martin Feldstein (1974) assigned an important role to social security "wealth" as a depressant of private saving. Subsequent work both from an ultraneoclassical position (for example, Barro 1974) and from a more eclectic standpoint (for example, Buiter and Tobin 1979; Tobin and Buiter 1980) suggests that Feldstein's conclusions may have been premature, to say the least. Empirical research reported in a recent book edited by George von Furstenberg (1979) gives relatively little comfort to the notion that social security *wealth* depresses saving, despite the evident sympathy of the editor for this view. (Some of the contributors do argue that social security *taxes* have a negative impact.)

Neoclassical saving theory received theoretical stimulus from the work of Robert Hall (1978) that recast it along rational-expectations lines. It remains to be seen what new insights the mini-industry spawned by Hall's contribution will produce.

It is surprising that so little has been written on the relationship between corporate and personal saving since — Feldstein (1973) and related work apart — the standard econometric practice of ignoring corporate saving in measuring household income and consumption is so at odds with neoclassical theory. Mayer calls attention to this point in an appendix (1972, pp. 365 – 370) but does little more than lament standard practice. Indeed, given the importance of retained earnings and pension-fund saving (not to mention capital-consumption allowances) relative to household financial saving in productive capital formulation — see Table 17.6 — the attention economists (present company included) have lavished on household saving seems disproportionate.

18. Distinguishing Saving Theories Empirically

The theory of saving suggested at the end of this chapter is evidently a variation on the classical theme, though it stresses the Marxian notion that how one relates to the production process (rather than income per se) is the determinant of saving behavior. An important section of the sociological literature — for instance, Edward Banfield (1968) — also stresses class determinants of saving behavior, but this literature is more disposed to take class as a consequence of individual psychology than to see individual psychology as an outcome of class experience.

19. Criticism and Evaluation

Neoclassical economists may be said to be divided into pragmatists and true believers. Prominent members of the first group are Arrow, Hahn, Samuelson, Solow, and Tobin. The guru-emeritus of the true believers is Friedman, present leadership having passed to the "rational expectations, equilibrium business cycle" school, led by Lucas. Representative works of the first group have been cited at various points in this book; to that list might be added recent overviews by Arrow (1980) and Hahn (1980). It is my sense that the pragmatic neoclassicals will be more in sympathy with criticism of neoclassical labor-market clearing than with criticism of neoclassical saving theory. The true believers, on the other hand, will have no sympathy with *either* criticism; their commitment to price as the mechanism of market clearing is as total as their commitment to household utility maximization as the mainspring of saving behavior. Apart from the papers of Lucas and Sargent already cited, reference might also be made to an influential collection of papers edited by Edmund Phelps (1970), the first half of which consists of articles that emphasize job search as an explanation of short-run unemployment consistent with the labor market being cleared by wage adjustment.

The literature on the labor theory of value was briefly summarized in connection with Chapter 11 and need not be reviewed again. By contrast, the criticism of the Marxian notions of subsistence and surplus can do with amplification. As noted in connection with Chapter 11, the idea of a subsistence wage based on class struggle, class compromise, and community standards—the so-called conventional wage—is yet to be fully integrated into the Marxian analysis. The closest the mainstream literature comes to this idea is J. Dennis Sargan's model of wage dynamics (1964).

Outside the context of capitalism, however, particularly among anthropologists, there has been extensive discussion of subsistence and surplus. There is now considerable evidence against the idea of a biologically determined subsistence, even in so-called "primitive" societies. Harry Pearson (1957) and Martin Orans (1966) made important contributions to developing the idea of subsistence as a cultural concept, and Marshall Sahlins (1972) has provided an excellent summary of the evidence that justifies his labeling hunting-gathering as the "original affluent society." The corollary of this view is that surplus is also a cultural concept—rather than the residual remaining after subtracting a biologically determined subsistence from a technologically determined output. This perspective is to be compared with the view expressed in orthodox Marxist texts, such as Maurice Cornforth (1962) and Ernest Mandel (1968), which take biology as the original basis of subsistence and argue that surplus emerges as a consequence of the increase in productivity that accompanies the shift to settled agriculture.

Jon Elster has argued forcefully and persuasively (1982) against functionalism as a method of explaining the relationship between class interests and individual actions within a Marxian framework. He has argued with equal force but less persuasively that functionalist explanations of social behavior should be replaced by explanations built on foundations of individual utility maximization, with social interaction modeled on game-theoretic lines. The issue of *Theory and Society* in which Elster's article appears also contains responses by Marxians both critical and supportive of Elster's position.

On wage bargaining, Keynes (1936) is the starting point of error. Keynes justified the hypothesis that bargaining takes place in money terms on the basis of both money illusion and workers' supposed relativistic orientation of keeping up with other working-class Joneses. For the short run, the justification is at least plausible, if not entirely persuasive. For the long run, it makes no sense at all.

20. A Synthesis of Marx and Keynes

Many nonneoclassical economists have attempted to synthesize Marxian and Keynesian ideas into a single model of growth and distribution. Reference has already been made to Harris (1978) and Roemer (1981), as well as to Robinson's inflation barrier (1956, 1962). Perhaps the closest to the present model in spirit, particularly in its emphasis on the simultaneous determination of the inflation rate and real magnitudes, is Bob Rowthorn (1980). Rowthorn, however, assumes that the steady state is characterized by a constant rate of unemployment—that is, by the equality $g = n$—an assumption I think misplaced.

The exercise in rational expectations at the end of the chapter is designed to demonstrate the robustness of the model to assumptions about expectations, not to endorse the rational-expectations view. Aficionados of rational expectations do have a point, and the point goes back to John Muth's observations (1961) with respect to the cobweb theorem long supposed by agricultural economists to govern price fluctuations in hog and cattle markets. For me the lesson of Muth's paper is not that expectations are necessarily "rational" (correct up to a stochastic error with zero mean); it is rather that if a particular result, like the cobweb theorem, depends on nonrational expectations, the burden of the proof is on the model builder to justify the specific expectations hypothesis. Muth's followers have cleverly used this argument to criticize rival (Keynesian) macroeconomic models that rely on nonrational expectations. But if sauce for the goose is sauce for the gander, rational-expectations models should be subject to the same standard: to the extent that the results of neoclassical macroeconomic models depend on rational expectations, it behooves the neoclassical model builder to justify this particular expectations hypothesis.

Muth chose the most favorable ground for rational expectations, a single agricultural market with repetitive trade for a relatively homogeneous good in an environment that can be taken as stable over time. Perhaps a case can be made for giving privilege to rational expectations in this setting, but the same case can hardly be made in the context of the economy as a whole. The usual justification, namely, consistency with other neoclassical assumptions, is convincing only to the believer.

In the analysis of an economy in steady-state equilibrium—as distinct from the analysis of stability of such an equilibrium—the rational-expectations assumption is more compelling. In any case, all the models—neo-Marxian and neo-Keynesian as well as neoclassical—assume rational expectations on the steady-growth path. In particular, neo-Keynesians justify the identity between expected and actual profit rates by the argument that on an equilibrium path the future will resemble the past, and therefore perfect foresight is not much of a trick. The distinguishing feature of expectations in the neo-Keynesian view is their causal role: expectations do not merely reflect an objectively given growth rate, they help to shape the growth rate. Keynes (1931, preface) himself put the matter thus: "There is a subtle reason drawn from economic analysis why, in this case, faith may work. For if we act consistently on the optimistic hypothesis, this hypothesis will tend to be realized; whilst by acting on the pessimistic hypothesis, we can keep ourselves for ever in the pit of want."

References

Akerlof, George. 1970. The market for lemons: Qualitative uncertainty and the market mechanism. *Quarterly Journal of Economics* 84:488–500.

Ando, Albert, and Franco Modigliani. 1963. The "life cycle" hypothesis of saving: Aggregate implications and tests. *American Economic Review* 53:55–86.

Aoki, Masahiko. 1977. Dual stability in a Cambridge-type model. *Review of Economic Studies* 44:143–151.

Arrow, Kenneth J. 1962. The economic implications of learning by doing. *Review of Economic Studies* 29:155–173.

——— 1980. Real and nominal values in economics. In *The Public Interest* (special edition). New York: National Affairs.

Arrow, Kenneth J., Hollis Chenery, Bagicha Singh Minhas, and Robert Solow. 1961. Capital-labor substitution and economic efficiency. *Review of Economics and Statistics* 43:225–250.

Arrow, Kenneth J., and Gerard Debreu. 1954. Existence of an equilibrium for a competitive economy. *Econometrica* 22:265–290.

Arrow, Kenneth J., and Frank Hahn. 1971. *General competitive analysis*. San Francisco: Holden Day.

Ball, Richard, and Pamela Drake. 1964. The relationship between aggregate consumption and wealth. *International Economic Review* 5:63–81.

Banfield, Edward C. 1968. *The unheavenly city: The nature and future of our urban crisis*. Boston: Little, Brown.

Baran, Paul A., and Paul M. Sweezy. 1966. *Monopoly capital: An essay on the American economic and social order*. New York: Monthly Review Press.

Barro, Robert. 1974. Are government bonds net wealth? *Journal of Political Economy* 82:1095–1117.

Barro, Robert, and Herschel Grossman. 1971. A general disequilibrium model of income and employment. *American Economic Review* 61:82–93.

548

———— 1976. *Money, employment and inflation.* Cambridge: Cambridge University Press.

Berle, Adolf A., and Gardiner C. Means. 1932. *The modern corporation and private property.* Revised. New York: Harcourt, Brace & World, 1967.

Bliss, Christopher J. 1975. *Capital theory and the distribution of income.* Amsterdam: North-Holland.

Board of Governors of the Federal Reserve System. 1976. *Flow of Funds accounts, 1946–1976: Annual total flows & year-end assets and liabilities.* Washington, D.C.: Board of Governors of the Federal Reserve System.

Brady, Robert. 1943. *Business as a system of power.* New York: Columbia University Press.

Braverman, Harry. 1974. *Labor and monopoly capital: The degradation of work in the twentieth century.* New York: Monthly Review Press.

Breusch, T. S., and A. R. Pagan. 1979. A simple test for heteroskedasticity and random coefficient variations. *Econometrica* 47:1287–94.

Brown, T. M. 1952. Habit persistence and lags in consumer behavior. *Econometrica* 20:355–371.

Brush, Thomas. 1979. Responsive substitution between corporate and personal saving: A critique. Senior honors thesis, Harvard College.

Buiter, Willem H., and James Tobin. 1979. Debt neutrality: A brief review of doctrine and evidence. In *Social security versus private saving,* ed. George M. von Furstenberg. Cambridge, Mass.: Ballinger.

Burmeister, Edwin. 1980. *Capital theory and dynamics.* Cambridge: Cambridge University Press.

Burmeister, Edwin, and A. Rodney Dobell. 1970. *Mathematical theories of economic growth.* New York: Macmillan.

Burnham, James. 1941. *The managerial revolution: What is happening in the world.* New York: John Day.

Cagan, Philip. 1965. *The effect of pension plans on aggregate saving: Evidence from a sample survey.* New York: Columbia University Press.

Champernowne, D. G. 1953–1954. The production function and the theory of capital: A comment. *Review of Economic Studies* 21:112–135.

Chayanov, A. V. 1925. *The theory of peasant economy,* ed. Daniel Thorner, Basile Kerblay, and R. E. F. Smith. Homewood, Ill.: Richard D. Irwin, 1966.

Clark, John Bates. 1891. Distribution as determined by a law of rent. *Quarterly Journal of Economics* 5:289–318.

———— 1899. *Distribution of wealth: A theory of wages, investment and profits.* New York: Macmillan.

Cooper, J. Philip. 1972. Asymptotic covariance matrix of procedures for linear regression in the presence of first-order autoregressive disturbances. *Econometrica* 40:305–310.

Cornforth, Maurice. 1962. *Historical materialism* (2nd ed.). New York: International Publishers.

Cripps, Francis, and Wynne Godley. 1976. A formal analysis of the Cambridge Economic Policy Group model. *Economica* 43:335–348.

David, Paul A., and John L. Scadding. 1974. Private savings: Ultrarationality, aggregation, and "Denison's law." *Journal of Political Economy* 82:225–249.

de Andrade, Joaquim. 1981. How do corporate savings affect households savings? Ph.D. diss., Harvard University.

Debreu, Gerard. 1959. *Theory of value.* New York: Wiley.

Debreu, Gerard, and I. N. Herstein. 1953. Nonnegative square matrices. *Econometrica* 21:597–607.

Denison, Edward. 1958. A note on private saving. *Review of Economics and Statistics* 40:261–267.

Diamond, Peter A. 1965. National debt in a neoclassical growth model. *American Economic Review* 55:1126–50.

Dixit, Avinash. 1976. *The theory of equilibrium growth.* Oxford: Oxford University Press.

Dobb, Maurice. 1970. The Sraffa system and critique of the neo-classical theory of distribution. *De Economist* 118:347–362.

—— 1973. *Theories of value and distribution.* Cambridge: Cambridge University Press.

Domar, Evsey D. 1946. Capital expansion, rate of growth, and employment. *Econometrica* 14:137–147.

Dorfman, Robert, Paul A. Samuelson, and Robert M. Solow. 1958. *Linear programming and economic analysis.* New York: McGraw-Hill.

Dornbusch, Rudger, and Jacob A. Frenkel. 1973. Inflation and growth: Alternative approaches. *Journal of Money, Credit and Banking* 5:141–156.

Drucker, Peter F. 1976. *The unseen revolution: How pension fund socialism came to America.* New York: Harper and Row.

Duesenberry, James S. 1949. *Income, saving, and the theory of consumer behavior.* Cambridge, Mass.: Harvard University Press.

Edwards, Richard. 1979. *Contested terrain.* New York: Basic Books.

Eichner, Alfred S., and J. A. Kregel. 1975. An essay on post-Keynesian theory: A new paradigm in economics. *Journal of Economic Literature* 13:1293–1314.

Elster, Jon. 1982. Marxism, functionalism and game theory. *Theory and Society* 11:453–482.

Fair, Ray C. 1970. The estimation of simultaneous equation models with lagged endogenous variables and first-order serially correlated errors. *Econometrica* 38:507–516.

Feldstein, Martin. 1973. Tax incentives, corporate saving, and capital accumulation in the United States. *Journal of Public Economics* 2:159–171.

—— 1974. Social security, induced retirement, and aggregate capital accumulation. *Journal of Political Economy.* 82:905–926.

Feldstein, Martin, and George Fane. 1973. Taxes, corporate dividend policy and personal savings: The British postwar experience. *Review of Economics and Statistics* 55:399–411.

Fetherston, Martin J., and Wynne Godley. 1978. "New Cambridge" macroeconomics and global monetarism: Some issues in the conduct of U.K.

economic policy. In *Public policies in open economies,* ed. Karl Brunner and Allan H. Meltzer. Amsterdam: North-Holland.

Fischer, Stanley. 1979. Capital accumulation on the transition path in a monetary optimizing model. *Econometrica* 47:1433–1439.

Fisher, Irving. 1930. *The theory of interest: As determined by impatience to spend income and opportunity to invest it.* Reprint. New York: Augustus M. Kelley, 1967.

Foley, Duncan K., and Miguel Sidrauski. 1970. Portfolio choice, investment, and growth. *American Economic Review* 60:44–63.

——— 1971. *Monetary and fiscal policy in a growing economy.* London: Macmillan.

Friedman, Milton. 1953. *Essays in positive economics.* Chicago: University of Chicago Press.

——— 1957. *A theory of the consumption function.* Princeton: Princeton University Press.

——— 1962. *Capitalism and freedom.* Chicago: University of Chicago Press.

Galbraith, John Kenneth. 1967. *The new industrial state.* Boston: Houghton Mifflin.

Garegnani, Pierangelo. 1966. Switching of techniques. *Quarterly Journal of Economics* 80:554–567.

——— 1970. Heterogeneous capital, the production function, and the theory of distribution. *Review of Economic Studies* 37:407–436.

Gintis, Herbert, 1976. The nature of the labor exchange and the theory of capitalist production. *Review of Radical Political Economics* 8:36–54.

Glejser, H. 1969. A new test for heteroscedasticity. *Journal of the American Statistical Association* 64:316–323.

Goldfeld, S. M., and R. E. Quandt. 1965. Some tests for homoscedasticity. *Journal of the American Statistical Association* 60:539–547.

Granger, C. W. J. 1969. Investigating causal relations by econometric models and cross-spectral methods. *Econometrica* 37:424–438.

Green, Francis. 1980. The consumption function: A study of a failure in positive economics. In *Issues in political economy: A critical approach,* ed. F. Green and P. Nore. New York: Humanities Press.

Hahn, Frank H. 1960. The stability of growth equilibrium. *Quarterly Journal of Economics* 74:206–226.

——— 1966. Equilibrium dynamics with heterogeneous capital goods. *Quarterly Journal of Economics* 80:633–646.

——— 1980. General equilibrium theory. In *The Public Interest* (special edition). New York: National Affairs.

——— 1982. The neo-Ricardians. *Cambridge Journal of Economics* 6:353–374.

Hall, Robert E. 1978. Stochastic implications of the life cycle–permanent income hypothesis: Theory and evidence. *Journal of Political Economy* 86:971–987.

Hansen, Alvin. 1938. *Full recovery or stagnation?* New York: Norton.

——— 1941. *Fiscal policy and business cycles.* New York: Norton.

——— 1951. *Business cycles and national income.* New York: Norton.

Harcourt, Geoffrey. 1972. *Some Cambridge controversies in the theory of capital.* Cambridge: Cambridge University Press.

Harris, Donald. 1978. *Capital accumulation and income distribution.* Stanford: Stanford University Press.

Harrod, Roy F. 1939. An essay in dynamic theory. *Economic Journal* 49:14–33.

———— 1948. *Towards a dynamic economics.* London: Macmillan.

———— 1973. *Economic dynamics.* London: Macmillan.

Hart, Oliver D. 1983. Imperfect competition in general equilibrium: An overview of recent work. Discussion paper of the Workshop in Theoretical Economics at the International Center for Economics and Related Disciplines, London School of Economics, London.

Harvey, A. C. 1981. *Time series models.* New York: Wiley.

Hicks, John. 1939. *Value and capital: An inquiry into some fundamental principles of economic theory.* London: Oxford University Press.

———— 1974. *The crisis in Keynesian economics.* Yrjö Jahnsson Lectures. Oxford: Basil Blackwell.

Hirschman, Albert O. 1970. *Exit, voice, and loyalty: Responses to decline in firms, organizations, and states.* Cambridge, Mass.: Harvard University Press.

Houthakker, Hendrik S., and Lester D. Taylor. 1966. *Consumer demand in the United States 1929–1970: Analyses and projections.* Cambridge, Mass: Harvard University Press.

Hunt, E. K., and Jesse G. Schwartz, eds. 1972. *A critique of economic theory.* Harmondsworth: Penguin Books.

Ishikawa, Tsuneo. 1977. Basic dynamic patterns of a modern capitalist economy (in Japanese). *Keizaigaku Ronshu* 43:2–23.

Johansen, Leif. 1959. Substitution versus fixed production coefficients in the theory of economic growth: A synthesis. *Econometrica* 27:157–176.

———— 1960. *A multi-sectoral study of economic growth,* 2nd ed. Amsterdam: North-Holland, 1974.

———— 1963. Labour theory of value and marginal utilities. *Economics of Planning* 3:89–103.

Johnson, Harry G. 1973. *The theory of income distribution.* London: Gray-Mills.

Jorgenson, Dale W., and Calvin D. Siebert. 1968. Optimal capital accumulation and corporate investment behavior. *Journal of Political Economy* 76:1123–51.

Kaldor, Nicholas. 1956. Alternative theories of distribution. *Review of Economic Studies* 23:83–100.

———— 1957. A model of economic growth. *Economic Journal* 67:591–624.

———— 1961. Capital accumulation and economic growth. In *The theory of capital,* Proceedings of a conference held by the International Economic Association, ed. F. A. Lutz and D. C. Hague. New York: St. Martin's Press.

———— 1966. Marginal productivity and the macro-economic theories of distribution. *Review of Economic Studies* 33:309–319.

Kaldor, Nicholas, and James A. Mirrlees. 1962. A new model of economic growth. *Review of Economic Studies* 29:174–192.

Kalecki, Michal. 1933. Outline of a theory of the business cycle. In Michal

Kalecki, *Selected essays on the dynamics of the capitalist economy.* Cambridge: Cambridge University Press, 1971.

——— 1934. On foreign trade and "domestic exports." In Michal Kalecki, *Selected essays on the dynamics of the capitalist economy.* Cambridge: Cambridge University Press, 1971.

——— 1935. The mechanism of the business upswing. In Michal Kalecki, *Selected essays on the dynamics of the capitalist economy.* Cambridge: Cambridge University Press, 1971.

——— 1938. Distribution of national income. In Michal Kalecki, *Selected essays on the dynamics of the capitalist economy.* Cambridge: Cambridge University Press, 1971.

——— 1943. Costs and prices. In Michal Kalecki, *Selected essays on the dynamics of the capitalist economy.* Cambridge: Cambridge University Press, 1971.

——— 1968. Trend and the business cycle. In Michal Kalecki, *Selected essays on the dynamics of the capitalist economy.* Cambridge: Cambridge University Press, 1971.

——— 1971. Class struggle and distribution of national income. *Selected essays on the dynamics of the capitalist economy.* Cambridge: Cambridge University Press, 1971.

Kalman, R. E., and J. E. Bertram. 1960. Control system analysis and design via the "second method" of Lyapounov: II Discrete time systems. *Journal of Basic Engineering: Transactions of the ASME* 83: 394–400.

Keynes, John Maynard. 1920. *The economic consequences of the peace.* New York: Harcourt, Brace and Howe.

——— 1930. *A treatise on money.* Vol. 1, *The pure theory of money.* London: Macmillan.

——— 1931. *Essays in persuasion.* London: Macmillan.

——— 1936. *The general theory of employment, interest, and money.* London: Macmillan.

Koopmans, Tjalling C. 1957. *Three essays on the state of economic science.* New York: McGraw-Hill.

Kotz, David M. 1978. *Bank control of large corporations in the United States.* Berkeley: University of California Press.

Kuga, Kiyoshi. 1977. General saddlepoint property of the steady state of a growth model with heterogeneous capital goods. *International Economic Review* 18:22–58.

Kuhn, Thomas S. 1957. *The Copernican revolution: Planetary astronomy in the development of Western thought.* Cambridge, Mass.: Harvard University Press.

——— 1962. *The structure of scientific revolutions.* Vol. 2, no. 2 of *International encyclopedia of unified science.* Chicago: University of Chicago Press.

Laibman, David. 1977. Toward a Marxian model of economic growth. *American Economic Review* 67:387–392.

Lazonick, William H. 1979. Industrial relations and technical change: The case of the self-acting mule. *Cambridge Journal of Economics* 3:231–262.

——— 1981. Production relations, labor productivity, and choice of technique: British and U.S. cotton spinning. *Journal of Economic History* 41:491–516.

―――― 1983. Industrial organization and technological change: The decline of the British cotton industry. *Business History Review* 57:195–236.

Levhari, David. 1965. A nonsubstitution theorem and switching of technique. *Quarterly Journal of Economics* 79:98–105.

Lewis, W. Arthur. 1954. Economic development with unlimited supplies of labour. *Manchester School* 22:139–191.

Lintner, John. 1956. Distribution of incomes of corporations among dividends, retained earnings, and taxes. *American Economic Review* 46:97–113.

Lipsey, Richard. 1960. The relation between unemployment and the rate of change of money wage rates in the United Kingdom, 1862–1957: A further analysis. *Economica,* n.s. 27:1–31.

Lucas, Robert E., Jr. 1972. Expectations and the neutrality of money. *Journal of Economic Theory* 4:103–124.

―――― 1975. An equilibrium model of the business cycle. *Journal of Political Economy* 83:1113–1144.

Lucas, Robert E., Jr., and Thomas J. Sargent. 1978. After Keynesian macroeconomics. In *After the Phillips curve: Persistence of high inflation and high unemployment.* Proceedings of a conference held in June 1978, Federal Reserve Bank of Boston.

Luxemburg, Rosa. 1913. *The accumulation of capital,* trans. Agnes Schwartzschild. London: Routledge and Kegan Paul, 1951.

Malinvaud, Edmond. 1953. Capital accumulation and efficient allocation of resources. *Econometrica* 21:233–268.

―――― 1977. *The theory of unemployment reconsidered.* Oxford: Basil Blackwell.

―――― 1980. *Profitability and unemployment.* Cambridge: Cambridge University Press.

Mandel, Ernest. 1968. *Marxist economic theory,* vol. 1. New York: Monthly Review Press.

Marglin, Stephen. 1974. What do bosses do? The origins and functions of hierarchy in capitalist production. Part 1. *Review of Radical Political Economics* 6:60–112.

―――― 1975. What do bosses do? The origins and functions of hierarchy in capitalist production. Part 2. *Review of Radical Political Economics* 7:20–37.

―――― 1976a. Growth, distribution, and prices. Harvard Institute for Economic Research Discussion Paper no. 470.

―――― 1976b. *Value and price in the labour-surplus economy.* Oxford: Clarendon Press.

Marglin, Stephen, and Masahiko Aoki. 1973. Three models of the capitalist economy (in Japanese). In *Radical economics: Economics of hierarchies,* ed. Masahiko Aoki. Tokyo: Chuokoron-sha.

Marx, Karl. 1865. *Value, price and profit.* Reprint. New York: International Publishers, 1935.

―――― 1867. *Capital: A critique of political economy.* Vol. 1, *The process of produc-*

tion of capital, ed. Frederick Engels, trans. Samuel Moore and Edward Aveling. Reprint. Moscow: Foreign Languages Publishing House, 1957.

——— 1893. *Capital: A critique of political economy.* Vol. 2, *The process of circulation of capital*, ed. F. Engels. Reprint. Moscow: Foreign Languages Publishing House, 1957.

——— 1894. *Capital: A critique of political economy.* Vol. 3, *The process of capitalist production as a whole*, ed. F. Engels. Reprint. Moscow: Foreign Languages Publishing House, 1959.

Marx, Karl, and Friedrich Engels. 1848. *The Communist manifesto*, ed. Samuel H. Beer, trans. Samuel Moore. Arlington Heights, Ill.: AHM Publishing Corp., 1955.

Mayer, Thomas. 1972. *Permanent income, wealth, and consumption: A critique of the permanent income theory, the life-cycle hypothesis, and related theories.* Berkeley: University of California Press.

McKenzie, Lionel. 1960. Matrices with dominant diagonals and economic theory. In *Mathematical methods in the social sciences, 1959*, Proceedings of the First Stanford Symposium, ed. Kenneth J. Arrow, Samuel Karlin, and Patrick Suppes. Stanford: Stanford University Press.

Meade, James. 1963. The rate of profit in a growing economy. *Economic Journal* 73:665–674.

Medio, Alfredo. 1972. Profits and surplus-value: Appearance and reality in capitalist production. In *A critique of economic theory*, ed. E. K. Hunt and Jesse G. Schwartz. Harmondsworth: Penguin Books.

Meek, Ronald L. 1967. *Economics and ideology and other essays: Studies in the development of economic thought.* London: Chapman and Hall.

——— 1977. *Smith, Marx, and after: Ten essays in the development of economic thought.* London: Chapman and Hall.

Mirrlees, James. 1969. The dynamic nonsubstitution theorem. *Review of Economic Studies* 36:67–76.

Modigliani, Franco. 1975. The life cycle hypothesis of saving twenty years later. In *Contemporary issues in economics*, Proceedings of the Conference of the Association of University Teachers of Economics, ed. Michael Parkin and A. R. Nobay. Manchester: Manchester University Press.

Modigliani, Franco, and Richard Blumberg. 1954. Utility analysis and the consumption function: An interpretation of cross-section data. In *Post Keynesian economics*, ed. Kenneth K. Kurihara. New Brunswick, N.J.: Rutgers University Press.

Modigliani, Franco, and Charles Steindel. 1977. Is a tax rebate an effective tool for stabilization policy? *Brookings Papers on Economic Activity*, 175–209.

Montgomery, David. 1979. *Workers' control in America: Studies in the history of work, technology, and labor struggles.* Cambridge: Cambridge University Press.

Morishima, Michio. 1964. *Equilibrium stability and growth: A multi-sectoral analysis.* London: Oxford University Press.

——— 1966. Refutation of the nonswitching theorem. *Quarterly Journal of Economics* 80:520–525.

———— 1973. *Marx's economics: A dual theory of value and growth.* Cambridge: Cambridge University Press.

———— 1974. Marx in the light of modern economic theory. *Econometrica* 42:611–632.

Munnell, Alicia. 1976. Private pensions and saving: New evidence. *Journal of Political Economy* 84:1013–32.

Muth, John. 1961. Rational expectations and the theory of price movements. *Econometrica* 29:315–335.

Negishi, Takashi. 1961. Monopolistic competition and general equilibrium. *Review of Economic Studies* 28:196–201.

Nell, E. J. 1967. Theories of growth and theories of value. *Economic Development and Cultural Change* 16:15–26.

Newman, Peter. 1962. Production of commodities by means of commodities. *Schweizerische Zeitschift für Sozial Wissenschaft und Statistik* 98:58–75.

Noble, David F. 1977. *America by design: Science, technology, and the rise of corporate capitalism.* New York: Alfred A. Knopf.

———— 1979. Social choice in machine design. In *Case studies in the labor process,* ed. Andrew Zimbalist. New York: Monthly Review Press.

Nuti, D. M. 1970. "Vulgar economy" in the theory of income distribution. *De Economist* 118:363–369. Reprinted with a postscript in *A critique of economic theory,* ed. E. K. Hunt and Jesse Schwartz. Harmondsworth: Penguin Books, 1972.

Okishio, Nobuo. 1963. A mathematical note on marxian theorems. *Weltwirtschaftliches Archiv* 91:287–298.

Okun, Arthur. 1962. Potential GNP: Its measurement and significance. *Proceedings of the Business and Economic Statistics Sections of the American Statistical Association* 1962:98–104.

Orans, Martin. 1966. Surplus. *Human Organization* 25:24–32.

Owen, Robert. 1857. *The life of Robert Owen.* London: Effingham Wilson.

Pasinetti, Luigi L. 1962. Rate of profit and income distribution in relation to the rate of economic growth. *Review of Economic Studies* 29:267–279.

———— 1966a. New results in an old framework: Comment on Samuelson and Modigliani. *Review of Economic Studies* 33:303–306.

———— 1966b. Changes in the rate of profit and switches of techniques. *Quarterly Journal of Economics* 80:503–517.

———— 1977. On "non-substitution" in production models. *Cambridge Journal of Economics* 4:389–394.

———— 1981. *Structural change and economic growth: A theoretical essay on the dynamics of the wealth of nations.* Cambridge: Cambridge University Press.

Pearson, Harry W. 1957. The economy has no surplus: Critique of a theory of development. In *Trade and market in the early empires: Economies in history and theory,* ed. Karl Polanyi, Conrad M. Arensberg, and Harry W. Pearson. New York: The Free Press.

Phelps, Edmund S. 1961. The golden rule of accumulation: A fable for growthmen. *American Economic Review* 51:638–642.

————, ed. 1970. *Microeconomic foundations of inflation policy and unemployment theory.* New York: Norton.

Pigou, A. C. 1933. *The theory of unemployment.* London: Macmillan.

———— 1945. *Lapses from full employment.* London: Macmillan.

Piore, Michael. 1979. *Birds of passage.* Cambridge: Cambridge University Press.

Projector, Dorothy S., and Gertrude S. Weiss. 1966. *Survey of financial characteristics of consumers.* Washington, D.C.: Board of Governors of the Federal Reserve System.

Ricardo, David. 1817. *On the principles of political economy and taxation.* Vol. 1 of *The works and correspondence of David Ricardo,* ed. Piero Sraffa. Cambridge: Cambridge University Press, 1962.

Rifkin, Jeremy, and Randy Barber. 1978. *The North will rise again: Pensions, politics and power in the 1980s.* Boston: Beacon Press.

Ripley, William Z. 1927. *Main Street and Wall Street.* Boston: Little, Brown.

Robinson, Joan. 1953–54. The production function and the theory of capital. *Review of Economic Studies* 21:81–106.

———— 1956. *The accumulation of capital,* 2nd ed. London: Macmillan, 1965.

———— 1961. Prelude to a critique of economic theory. *Oxford Economic Papers* 13:53–58.

———— 1962. *Essays in the theory of economic growth.* London: Macmillan.

———— 1965. A reconsideration of the theory of value. *New Left Review* 173–181.

———— 1966. Comment on Samuelson and Modigliani. *Review of Economic Studies* 33:307–308.

———— 1971. *Economic heresies: Some old-fashioned questions in economic theory.* London: Macmillan.

———— 1975. The unimportance of reswitching. *Quarterly Journal of Economics* 89:32–39.

———— 1978. *Contributions to modern economics.* Oxford: Basil Blackwell.

Roemer, John E. 1978. Marxian models of reproduction and accumulation. *Cambridge Journal of Economics* 2:37–53.

———— 1981. *Analytical foundations of Marxian economic theory.* Cambridge: Cambridge University Press.

Rousseau, Jean-Jacques. 1762. The social contract. In J.-J. Rousseau, *The social contract and discourses,* trans. G. D. H. Cole. New York: Dutton, 1950.

Rowthorn, Bob. 1980. *Capitalism, conflict, and inflation: Essays in political economy.* London: Lawrence and Wishart.

Sahlins, Marshall. 1972. *Stone-age economics.* New York: Aldine-Atherton.

Samuelson, Paul. 1951. Abstract of a theorem concerning substitutability in open Leontief models. In *Activity analysis of production and allocation,* ed. T. C. Koopmans. New York: Wiley.

———— 1957. Wages and interest: A modern dissection of Marxian economic models. *American Economic Review* 47:884–912.

———— 1958. An exact consumption-loan model of interest with or without the social contrivance of money. *Journal of Political Economy* 66:467–489.

———— 1962. Parable and realism in capital theory: The surrogate production function. *Review of Economic Studies* 29:193–206.

———— 1971. Understanding the Marxian notion of exploitation: A summary of the so-called transformation problem between Marxian values and competitive prices. *Journal of Economic Literature* 9:399–431.

Samuelson, Paul, and Franco Modigliani. 1966a. The Pasinetti paradox in neoclassical and more general models. *Review of Economic Studies* 33:269–301.

———— 1966b. Reply to Pasinetti and Robinson. *Review of Economic Studies* 33:321–330.

Sargan, J. D. 1964. Wages and prices in the UK. In *Econometric analysis for national economics planning*, ed. P. E. Hart, G. Mills, and J. K. Whittaker. London: Butterworth.

Sargent, Thomas. 1979. *Macroeconomic theory.* New York: Academic Press.

Sen, Amartya. 1963. Neo-classical and neo-Keynesian theories of distribution. *Economic Record* 39:53–64.

———— 1965. The money rate of interest in the pure theory of growth. In *The theory of interest rates,* ed. F. H. Hahn and F. P. R. Brechling. Proceedings of a conference held by the International Economic Association in Royaumont, France, 1962. London: Macmillan.

————, ed. 1970. *Growth economics.* Harmondsworth: Penguin Books.

———— 1978. On the labour theory of value: Some methodological issues. *Cambridge Journal of Economics* 2:175–190.

Seton, F. 1957. The "Transformation Problem." *Review of Economic Studies* 25:149–160.

Shell, Karl. 1971. Notes on the economics of infinity. *Journal of Political Economy* 79:1002–1011.

Sidrauski, Miguel. 1967a. Rational choice and patterns of growth in a monetary economy. *American Economic Review* 57:534–544.

———— 1967b. Inflation and economic growth. *Journal of Political Economy* 75:796–810.

Simon, Herbert. 1955. A behavioral model of rational choice. *Quarterly Journal of Economics* 69:99–118.

———— 1956. Rational choice and the structure of the environment. *Psychological Review* 63:129–138.

Sims, Christopher A. 1972. Money, income, and causality. *American Economic Review* 62:540–552.

Smith, Adam. 1776. *An inquiry into the nature and causes of the wealth of nations,* ed. Edwin Cannan. New York: Random House, Modern Library, 1937.

Solow, Robert M. 1955–56. The production function and the theory of capital. *Review of Economic Studies* 23:101–108.

———— 1956. A contribution to the theory of growth. *Quarterly Journal of Economics* 70:65–94.

———— 1960. Investment and technical progress. In *Mathematical methods in the social sciences, 1959*, Proceedings of the First Stanford Symposium, ed. Kenneth J. Arrow, Samuel Karlin, and Patrick Suppes. Stanford: Stanford University Press.

———— 1962. Substitution and fixed proportions in the theory of capital. *Review of Economic Studies* 29:207–218.

———— 1978. Summary and evaluation. In *After the Phillips curve: Persistence of high inflation and high unemployment.* Proceedings of a conference held in June 1978, Federal Reserve Bank of Boston.

———— 1980. On theories of unemployment. *American Economic Review* 70:1–11.

Sraffa, Piero. 1960. *Production of commodities by means of commodities: Prelude to a critique of economic theory.* Cambridge: Cambridge University Press.

Steedman, Ian. 1977. *Marx after Sraffa.* London: NLB.

Steindel, Charles. 1977. Personal consumption, property income, and corporate saving. Ph.D. diss., Massachusetts Institute of Technology.

Stiglitz, Joseph E. and Hirofumi Uzawa, eds. 1969. *Readings in the modern theory of economic growth.* Cambridge, Mass.: MIT Press.

Sutton, Francis, et al. 1956. *The American business creed.* Cambridge, Mass.: Harvard University Press.

Sweezy, Paul M. 1942. *The theory of capitalist development.* New York: Monthly Review Press.

Taylor, Lance. 1983. *Structuralist macroeconomics: Applicable models for the Third World.* New York: Basic Books.

Terkel, Studs. 1972. *Working.* New York: Pantheon Books.

Theil, Henri. 1971. *Principles of econometrics.* New York: Wiley.

Tobin, James. 1955. A dynamic aggregative model. *Journal of Political Economy* 63:103–115.

———— 1965. Money and economic growth. *Econometrica* 33:671–684.

———— 1969. A general equilibrium approach to monetary theory. *Journal of Money, Credit, and Banking* 1:15–29.

Tobin, James, and William Brainard. 1977. Asset markets and the cost of capital. In *Economic progress, private values, and public policy: Essays in honor of William Fellner,* ed. Bela Balassa and Richard Nelson. Amsterdam: North Holland.

Tobin, James, and Willem Buiter. 1980. Fiscal and monetary policies, capital formation, and economic activity. In *The government and capital formation,* ed. George M. von Furstenberg. Cambridge, Mass.: Ballinger.

Ure, Andrew. 1835. *The philosophy of manufactures.* London: Charles Knight.

U.S. Department of Commerce, Bureau of Economic Analysis. 1981. *The national income and product accounts of the United States, 1929–1976: Statistical tables.* Washington, D.C.: U.S. Department of Commerce.

Uzawa, Hirofumi. 1961. On a two-sector model of economic growth: I. *Review of Economic Studies* 29:40–47.

———— 1963. On a two-sector model of economic growth: II. *Review of Economic Studies* 30:105–118.

Veblen, Thorstein. 1921. *The engineers and the price system.* New York: Huebsch.

Velupillai, Kumaraswamy. 1980. Review of Luigi Pasinetti, *Lectures on the theory of production. Journal of Economic Studies,* n.s. 7:64–65.

———— 1982. Methodological morality in the Cambridge controversies: Some notes. Unpublished.

von Bortkiewicz, Ladislaus. 1906–1907. Value and price in the Marxian system (in German). *Archiv für Sozialwissenschaft und Sozialpolitik* 23:1–50; 25:10–51; 25:445–488.

———— 1907. On the correction of Marx's fundamental theoretical construction in the third volume of "Capital" (in German). *Jahrbücher für Nationalökonomie und Statistik* 34:319–335.

von Furstenberg, George M., ed. 1979. *Social security versus private saving.* Cambridge, Mass.: Ballinger.

von Neumann, John. 1945–46. A model of general economic equilibrium. *Review of Economic Studies* 13:1–9.

Walras, Léon. 1874. *Elements of pure economics or the theory of social wealth,* trans. William Jaffe. Homewood, Ill.: Richard D. Irwin, 1954.

Wicksell, Knut. 1901. *Lectures on political economy.* Vol. 1, *General Theory,* trans. E. Classen. London: Routledge and Kegan Paul, 1934.

Wilson, Edward. 1975. *Sociobiology: The new synthesis.* Cambridge, Mass.: Harvard University Press.

———— 1978. *On human nature.* Cambridge, Mass.: Harvard University Press.

Index